Dear Papa, Dear Charley

Dear Papa, Dear Charley

THE PEREGRINATIONS OF A REVOLUTIONARY

ARISTOCRAT, AS TOLD BY CHARLES CARROLL OF

CARROLLTON AND HIS FATHER, CHARLES CARROLL

OF ANNAPOLIS, WITH SUNDRY OBSERVATIONS ON

BASTARDY, CHILD-REARING, ROMANCE, MATRIMONY,

COMMERCE, TOBACCO, SLAVERY, AND THE POLITICS

OF REVOLUTIONARY AMERICA

RONALD HOFFMAN, Editor

SALLY D. MASON, Associate Editor

ELEANOR S. DARCY, Assistant Editor

VOLUME I

Published for the
Omohundro Institute of Early American History and Culture,
Williamsburg, Virginia,
the Maryland Historical Society, *Baltimore,*
and the Maryland State Archives, *Annapolis,*
by the University of North Carolina Press,
Chapel Hill and London

The Omohundro Institute of
Early American History and Culture
is sponsored jointly by the College of William and Mary
and the Colonial Williamsburg Foundation.
On November 15, 1996, the Institute adopted the present name
in honor of a bequest from Malvern H. Omohundro, Jr.

Publication of this work was assisted by a grant from the
National Historical Publications and Records Commission.

Library of Congress Cataloging-in-Publication Data
Carroll, Charles, 1737-1832.
Dear Papa, dear Charley : the peregrinations of a revolutionary aristocrat, as told by
Charles Carroll of Carrollton and his father, Charles Carroll of Annapolis, with sundry observations
on bastardy, child-rearing, romance, matrimony, commerce, tobacco, slavery, and the politics of
revolutionary America / Ronald Hoffman, editor, Sally D. Mason, associate editor,
Eleanor S. Darcy, assistant editor.
p. cm.
ISBN 978-1-4696-2843-1
1. Carroll, Charles, 1737-1832 — Correspondence.   2. United States. Declaration of Independence —
Signers — Correspondence.   3. Statesmen — United States — Correspondence.   4. Upper class —
Maryland — Correspondence.   5. Carroll, Charles, 1702-1782 — Correspondence.   6. Carroll family.
7. United States — Social life and customs — To 1775.   8. Maryland — Social life and customs — To
1775.   9. United States — History — Revolution, 1775-1783.   10. Maryland — History — Revolution,
1775-1783.   I. Carroll, Charles, 1702-1782.   II. Hoffman, Ronald, 1941-   III. Mason, Sally D.
IV. Darcy, Eleanor S.   V. Omohundro Institute of Early American History & Culture.
VI. Maryland Historical Society.   VII. Maryland State Archives.   VIII. Title.
E302.6.C3 A4   2001
973.3'092 — dc21
[B]   00-068314

∞
The paper in this book meets the guidelines for permanence and durability
of the Committee on Production Guidelines for Book Longevity of the Council on
Library Resources.

05   04   03   02   01   5   4   3   2   1

THIS BOOK WAS DIGITALLY PRINTED.

To the memory of

Dr. Joshua I. Cohen,

whose timely action saved the

Carrolls' papers for posterity,

and to Philip Carroll,

who has graciously permitted

their publication

PREFACE

· · ·
· ·
·

Descended from the O'Carrolls, a Gaelic Irish sept whose ancestral territory lay principally in what is today the Republic of Ireland's County Offaly, Charles Carroll of Carrollton's grandfather, a man historians have designated Charles Carroll the Settler, was the first Carroll to leave Europe for North America. Arriving in Maryland on October 1, 1688, he brought with him an appointment as attorney general in the colony's proprietary government and a determination to reverse the fate that English rule had imposed upon his Catholic kin. By the time of the Settler's birth in 1661, his father and other close relatives had already lost their lands and much of their wealth to confiscation as a consequence of their participation in the 1641 rebellion. The bitter memory of this and other similar injustices found expression in the Settler's defiant personality and fueled his ambition to prosper and prevail in Maryland, a province known for its official hospitality to Roman Catholics. Indicative both of his remembrance of the past and his designs for the future, the Settler changed the motto on his family's crest from *"In fide et in bello forte"* ("Strong in faith and war") to *"Ubicumque cum libertate"* ("Anywhere so long as there be freedom").

The optimism suggested by that alteration proved to be short-lived. Scarcely had Charles Carroll the Settler reached Maryland when the changes wrought by England's Glorious Revolution crossed the Atlantic to cause major problems for Catholics in Lord Baltimore's supposedly tolerant colony. Using the ouster of James II and the subsequent elevation of William and Mary to the English throne as a pretext, Maryland Protestants vented their long-standing jealousy of the proprietor's practice of awarding the most lucrative government posts to Catholics through a "risinge in arms" that transferred the right to govern the province from the proprietary family to the crown. In consolidating their victory, the Associators, as the Protestant rebels were known, began to put in place in the colony the same kinds of legal restrictions that circumscribed the lives of Catholics in England and Ireland, with the result that by 1704 Maryland law forbade Catholics to worship publicly, to give their children a Catholic education, and to hold public office without swearing oaths inimical to the Catholic religion.[1]

---

1. The definitive study of this period of Maryland history is Lois Green Carr and David William Jordan, *Maryland's Revolution of Government, 1689–1692* (Ithaca, N.Y., 1974).

Deprived by his allegiance to his faith of his post as attorney general with its promising implications of access to political power, the Settler found other means of acquiring wealth and influence. Twice wed, he advanced himself measurably through both unions, especially the second, which made him the son-in-law of Colonel Henry Darnall I, Maryland's most powerful Catholic and protector of Lord Baltimore's extensive propertied interests.[2] Quickly becoming Darnall's protégé and then his confidante, the Settler made himself so valuable that, upon Darnall's death in 1711, Lord Baltimore transferred to him all that gentleman's offices and responsibilities. Similarly, the Settler began his steady acquisition of land with the 1,381 acres Darnall bestowed upon him as a wedding gift, and at his death in 1720, the 47,777 acres he had accumulated made him the largest landowner in the province.

In addition to his activities as Lord Baltimore's representative and as a planter, the Settler developed extensive mercantile interests, practiced law in those courts that did not require the swearing of the noxious oaths, and began about 1700 to lend money on bonds and mortgages, an undertaking he pursued tenaciously and with such skill that by 1714 he had become the colony's largest lender. The value of the legacy he bequeathed to his heirs attests the full measure of his success: the total worth of his assets, excluding land, amounted to £7,535 and constituted the largest personal estate that had ever been probated in Maryland to that time.[3]

Unfortunately for his co-religionists and his descendants, Charles Carroll the Settler's political ambitions failed to reap similar rewards. Following the return of Maryland's government to the newly Protestant proprietary family in 1715, the Settler made a bold attempt to reclaim for Roman Catholics the privileges of office-holding they had enjoyed under the Lords Baltimore prior to 1690. Instead he succeeded only in goading the Protestant power structure into enacting further restrictions, the most onerous being a law depriving Catholics of the right to vote. They would not regain the franchise until the American Revolution.

On July 1, 1720, Charles Carroll the Settler died. Eighteen-year-old Charles, his eldest son and heir, was called home from school in France to assume responsibility for his family's affairs in behalf of his mother, his younger brother Daniel, and his two younger sisters, Mary and Eleanor. By 1742, Charles, then known as Charles Carroll of Annapolis, had buried them all and assumed sole responsibility for the estate the Settler had built. Along with this considerable material inheri-

---

2. Lord Baltimore still retained ownership of the colony's land and rights to specific revenues from it. To protect these interests, he maintained an active organization in Maryland during the period of royal rule, 1690–1715.

3. For a detailed analysis of the process by which the Settler built his fortune, see Ronald Hoffman, *Princes of Ireland, Planters of Maryland: A Carroll Saga, 1500–1782* (Chapel Hill, N.C., 2000), chap. 2.

tance, Charles Carroll of Annapolis also received an important intangible legacy—the memory of the experiences in Ireland and Maryland that spurred his father's quest to establish and make secure his Catholic family and their fortune. As their correspondence reveals, this heritage shaped Charles Carroll of Annapolis and his son, Charles Carroll of Carrollton, in remarkable ways.

ACKNOWLEDGMENTS

. . .
. .
.

Inevitably a project of this scope requires the good will, trust, and considerate efforts of scores of institutions and scholars. When I think back over how many individuals and organizations have helped in this publication, I am deeply honored. The project began with an initial two-year award from the National Endowment for the Humanities. Subsequently, the National Historical Publications and Records Commission granted the further support that sustained both the comprehensive microfilm edition of *The Charles Carroll of Carrollton Family Papers* and these three documentary volumes through publication. The Commission's record, given its limited resources, is truly remarkable. Rarely has any organization managed to do so much with so little. The Maryland State Archives has similarly provided vital assistance, and I am sincerely grateful for all that it has done under the leadership of Edward C. Papenfuse, a fine scholar who skillfully combines the roles of archivist and historian. The principal holder of the Carroll manuscripts, the Maryland Historical Society, paid me a great tribute by designating me as editor of the collection. The Society has provided office space, a host of necessary services, and contributed generously to the publication of these volumes. It says something about the tenure of this endeavor that I have transited five directors, all of whom have stood by the society's commitment: P. William Filby, Romaine S. Somerville, J. Jefferson Miller II, Charles T. Lyle, and Dennis A. Fiori. I owe a special debt of appreciation to Barbara Wells Sarudy, who, as acting director of the Society, enhanced the institution's involvement in the intellectual life of the project. The Department of History at the University of Maryland, where I was privileged to teach for twenty-three years, also constituted a source of important support, both financially and in the form of graduate student assistance. By a stroke of immense good fortune, I served during the period of this work under three highly sympathetic chairs. The late Walter Rundell, Jr., and my good friends Emory G. Evans and Richard Price never sent me packing when I made my many appeals. When I came to the Institute, its two sponsors, the College of William and Mary and the Colonial Williamsburg Foundation, agreed to my continuing the project and provided ongoing assistance. In this regard, I am especially indebted to former William and Mary Provost, Melvyn D. Schiavelli, the present Provost, Gillian T. Cell, and former Senior Vice President of the Colonial Williamsburg Foundation, Dennis A. O'Toole.

In the late 1980s the Carroll Foundation of London made a series of generous grants that enabled the editors to deepen their understanding of the Irish background of the Carroll family for this edition and its accompanying monograph on the family's experience in Ireland and Maryland, *Princes of Ireland, Planters of Maryland: A Carroll Saga, 1500–1782* (Chapel Hill, N.C., 2000). Gerald Carroll, who chaired the Carroll Foundation, shared my passion for this story. Our conversations form a sequence of vivid memories. Three other contemporary Carrolls have also been remarkably kind. Philip Carroll, who embodies many of the Carroll traits that I have found so alluring—keen intelligence, strength of character, and unrelenting purpose—graciously shared his knowledge of his forebears on Doohoragen Manor with me and Associate Editor Sally D. Mason. James Carroll, an officer in the Irish foreign service, sought me out when he was posted in Washington, D.C., and later smoothed the way for my research in Ireland. We had a fine time in the Irish midlands tracking the people of Ely O'Carroll. And, finally, I am grateful to Charles Carroll Carter, a former director of the Carroll House in Annapolis, for his enthusiastic support and many kind offers of assistance.

During the darkest days of the Carroll Papers, when I confronted the harsh reality of closing the project down, one individual proved truly indispensable—the Honorable Benjamin L. Cardin. Then Speaker of the Maryland House of Delegates, Mr. Cardin patiently heard my case, agreed that the Carroll Papers constituted a unique and precious legacy for the state of Maryland, and conferred with the general assembly's legislative leadership to see if the project could be pulled back from the brink of oblivion. He succeeded, and, were it not for his efforts, these acknowledgments would never have been written. Subsequently, Governors Harry Hughes, William Donald Schaefer, and Parris N. Glendening, along with Senators John C. Astle and Gerald W. Winegrad, and Senate Presidents Melvin A. Steinberg and Thomas V. Mike Miller, Jr., took their measure of the work and lent their support. I thank them all.

From the moment a historian crosses the threshold of a repository the meter on his record of debts starts running. At the Maryland Historical Society my work depended on the good will of the manuscripts and library personnel: Jennifer A. Bryan, Penny Catzen, Richard J. Cox, Donna Ellis, William B. Keller, Joseph C. Maguire, Mary K. Meyer, Francis P. O'Neill, Cynthia H. Requardt, Hester Rich, Karen A. Stuart, and Larry E. Sullivan. All of them were grand. My fare at the Maryland State Archives is equally substantial. The field of early Maryland history has its own special endowment—we are all enriched by the masterful quality of Lois Green Carr's research and writing and the warmth of her personality. Few can match Lois in human kindness and generosity, but her former colleague and friend, the late Phebe R. Jacobsen, was of the identical mold. The administrative efficiency and attention given the Carroll grants by the archives' administrator Christopher N. Allan were vital to our ability to continue.

The scholars that I have called on for help are numerous. During the many years John J. McCusker and I spent together at the University of Maryland, he never failed to answer my many queries with grace and thoroughness. Emory G. Evans similarly shared with me his extensive and intimate knowledge of the colonial Chesapeake. The late John Duffy patiently clarified many points regarding eighteenth-century medical practices and pharmacology. When the Carrolls wrote in Latin, French, and Greek, I turned to my Maryland colleagues J. Benedict Warren and Philip J. Benedict, now at Brown University, to Donna Evergates of Western Maryland College, and to my William and Mary associate Lu Ann Homza. The late John M. Hemphill II and Jacob M. Price shed light on the intersections of Maryland politics, commerce, and finance; Lorena S. Walsh opened up her research files for my benefit and guided me through the murky domains of the court, land, and probate materials that she has mastered; Rolf Loeber of the University of Pittsburgh elucidated the meanings of critical references to Ireland, and Elizabeth FitzPatrick, now at the National University of Ireland, Galway, offered invaluable insights on the Gaelic past as well as genealogical intricacies; my friend and occasional co-author Carville V. Earle helped me make sense of agricultural customs; Father John Lynch of the Catholic University of America's Department of Canon Law provided me with a pivotal legal opinion on Catholic marriage practices; Philip Gleason of the University of Notre Dame offered insights into early modern Jesuit pedagogy, Gary Myer of the Johns Hopkins University's Peabody Library courteously located holdings in that facility that were important for annotation, and former Institute fellow David Steinberg generously shared with me the Carroll material he uncovered in his research on Charles Willson Peale. Whenever I required help in disentangling Charles Carroll of Carrollton's career at the Continental Congress, Paul H. Smith was never too busy. Jonathan R. Dull of the Franklin Papers and other members of that project similarly helped to clear up aspects of Charles Carroll of Carrollton's dealings with Benjamin Franklin. Victoria Allan undertook analyses that delineated dimensions of the Carroll family's wealth, and Shirley V. Baltz brought to my attention materials bearing on the Carrolls from the papers of other families. In England, Father Geoffrey Holt, S.J., Leo Gooch, the Reverend F. J. Turner, and Maurice Whitehead of the University of Wales, Swansea, generously provided information on the religious and educational dimensions of England's eighteenth-century Catholic community. Maurice's assistance both in this aspect of the work and in many others has simply been invaluable.

I owe special thanks to the graduate students who worked on the Carroll Papers — they never failed to make life interesting and to move the work along: Jennifer A. Bryan, Daniel B. Deans, Mary C. Jeske, Gladys Kremen, Michael T. Parker, Daniel Preston, and James D. Rice. My ever demanding and perennially surprising advisee, Beatriz Betancourt Hardy, not only wrote an excellent dissertation on the Catholic gentry of colonial Maryland from which I learned much but also explicated dimensions of the Carrolls that I had failed to perceive. Her husband, Stephen G. Hardy, brought the Carroll Papers into the electronic age with indulgent understanding.

As the Carroll Papers evolved and expanded, a good friend, the late Alice C. Cole, provided editorial assistance and a sensitive reading. Andrew J. Darcy also pitched in when Assistant Editor Eleanor S. Darcy — his mom — had to be away, and his reflections on the Carrolls were invariably engaging. In a period of great uncertainty my late aunt, the incomparable Naomi Shapiro, agreed to lend a helping hand. A grand lady with a very big heart, she immediately fell in love with Charley and Papa and, in the project's pre-computer era, patiently typed and retyped with amazing stamina. Her untimely death left a large gap both in the project and in our lives. At the Institute, Thad W. Tate and David L. Ammerman first grasped what the Carroll Papers contained for enriching the field of early American studies. Norman S. Fiering, Joy Dickinson Barnes, and Cynthia Carter Ayres shared their enthusiasm and provided essential guidance. Their worthy successors — Fredrika J. Teute and Gil Kelly — continued the Institute's tradition of providing expert advice. Peter J. Albert — my first Ph.D. student and later co-editor of the multivolume United States Capitol Historical Society series Perspectives on the American Revolution brought his remarkable editorial skills, honed to near perfection during his editorship of the Samuel Gompers Papers, to copyediting the text for publication. In this massive task his colleague Diane Koch proved of enormous assistance, and, although my editorial staff and I sometimes — in the contemporary parlance — contested Peter's and Diane's suggestions, we never doubted the wisdom and experience upon which their recommendations were founded. Finally, Carroll Papers assistant editor Mary C. Jeske, research assistant Samuel T. Brainerd, and editorial assistant Rebecca L. Wrenn joined the Institute's senior editor of publications Virginia L. Montijo, editorial associate Peter M. Schweighofer, and editorial assistant Ginger Hawkins in giving the manuscript a last thorough reading, and for their sharp eyes and perceptive comments I am enormously grateful.

This long list of debts attests that documentary editions are labor intensive. They are also expensive to produce and publish. Hence, as publication drew near, the Carroll Papers was especially fortunate to have a very good and generous friend in Hays T. Watkins. Although Hays, the former chief executive officer of the CSX Corporation and a member of the Institute's Executive Board, firmly insisted that he receive only modest recognition, perhaps he will allow me to note that, in the discourse of Virginia's eighteenth-century gentry, his contribution would be most accurately described as "liberal."

During all these many years Sally D. Mason and Eleanor S. Darcy, the members of the Carroll Papers editorial staff, provided the dedication, the energy, and the enthusiasm needed to move the work ahead. They persevered, despite the departures and disruptions that simultaneously advanced and impeded our progress, never doubting for a moment the importance of the story the Carroll manuscripts tell. It is thus to Sally and Eleanor that the major portion of the credit for the completion and the quality of these volumes belongs. The adventures the three of us shared in the course of our work continually amazed and delighted us and brought us a host of valued friends both in this country and abroad. Knowing that they will celebrate with us this long-awaited publication measurably increases the pleasure we take in the achievement.

CONTENTS

. . .
. .
.

VOLUME I

VOLUME II

VOLUME III

ILLUSTRATIONS

. . .
. .
.

ABBREVIATIONS & SHORT TITLES

. . .
. .
.

ABBREVIATIONS

AD	autograph document
ADS	autograph document signed
AL	autograph letter
ALbDr	autograph letterbook draft
ALbDrS	autograph letterbook draft signed
ALS	autograph letter signed
CC	Charles Carroll
CCA	Charles Carroll of Annapolis
CCC	Charles Carroll of Carrollton
CSmH	The Huntington Library, San Marino, Calif.
D	document
d.	pence, deniers
DGU	Georgetown University, Washington, D.C.
DLC	Library of Congress, Washington, D.C.
DNA	National Archives, Washington, D.C.
DS	document signed
L	letter
LbC	letterbook copy
LS	letter signed
lt.	livres tournois
MdAA	Maryland State Archives, Annapolis
MdAAB	Archives, Archdiocese of Baltimore, Baltimore
MdBJ	Johns Hopkins University, Baltimore
MdBP	Peabody Library, Baltimore
MdHi	Maryland Historical Society, Baltimore
MH	Harvard University, Cambridge, Mass.
MWA	American Antiquarian Society, Worcester, Mass.
NjP	Princeton University Libraries, Princeton, N.J.
NN	The New York Public Library, Astor, Lenox and Tilden Foundations
PHi	Historical Society of Pennsylvania, Philadelphia

PPAmP	American Philosophical Society, Philadelphia
PT	printed transcript
s.	shillings, sols
ViHi	Virginia Historical Society, Richmond
ViU	University of Virginia Library, Charlottesville

SHORT TITLES

Abbot, *Washington: Colonial Series*
Abbot, W. W., et al., eds. *The Papers of George Washington: Colonial Series.* Charlottesville, Va., 1983–.

Abbot, *Washington: Confederation Series*
Abbot, W. W., et al., eds. *The Papers of George Washington: Confederation Series.* Charlottesville, Va, 1992–.

Abbot, *Washington: Revolutionary War Series*
Abbot, W. W., et al., eds. *The Papers of George Washington: Revolutionary War Series.* Charlottesville, Va., 1985–.

Arch. of Md.
Browne, William Hand, et al., eds. *Archives of Maryland.* 72 vols. Baltimore, 1883–1972.

Barnes, *Marriages and Deaths*
Barnes, Robert, comp. *Marriages and Deaths from the Maryland Gazette, 1727–1839.* Baltimore, 1973.

Bio. Dic. Md. Legis.
Papenfuse, Edward C., et al., eds. *A Biographical Dictionary of the Maryland Legislature, 1635–1789.* 2 vols. Baltimore, 1979–1985.

Bowie, *Prince George's*
Bowie, Effie Gwynn. *Across the Years in Prince George's County: A Genealogical and Biographical History of Some Prince George's County, Maryland, and Allied Families.* Richmond, Va., 1947.

Brigham, *American Newspapers*
Brigham, Clarence S. *History and Bibliography of American Newspapers, 1690–1820.* Worcester, Mass., 1947.

Burke and Burke, *Landed Gentry of Great Britain*
Burke, Bernard, and Ashworth P. Burke. *A Genealogical and Heraldic History of the Landed Gentry of Great Britain.* 11th ed. London, 1906.

Burke and Burke, *Peerage, 71st ed.*
Burke, Bernard, and Ashworth P. Burke. *A Genealogical and Heraldic History of the Peerage and Baronetage, the Privy Council, Knightage and Companionage.* 71st ed. London, 1909.

Burke and Burke, *Landed Gentry of Great Britain and Ireland*

Burke, John, and John Bernard Burke. *A Genealogical and Heraldic Dictionary of the Landed Gentry of Great Britain and Ireland*. London, 1846.

Burke, *Peerage*, 15th ed.
  Burke, John Bernard. *A Genealogical and Heraldic Dictionary of the Peerage and Baronetage of the British Empire*. 15th ed. London, 1853.

Cat. Lib.
  Catalogue of the Library of Charles Carroll of Carrollton . . . to Be Sold at Auction, Commencing on Monday Evening, December 5, 1864. . . . Maryland Room, McKeldin Library, University of Maryland, College Park.

Dielman
  Dielman-Hayward File. Library, Maryland Historical Society, Baltimore.

Dunlap's Md. Gaz.
  Dunlap's Maryland Gazette; or, The Baltimore General Advertiser.

Dunlap's Pa. Packet
  Dunlap's Pennsylvania Packet; or, The General Advertiser. Philadelphia.

Field, *Carroll*
  Field, Thomas Meagher, ed. *Unpublished Letters of Charles Carroll of Carrollton, and His Father, Charles Carroll of Doughoregan*. New York, 1902.

Fitzpatrick, *Writings of Washington*
  Fitzpatrick, John C., ed. *The Writings of George Washington from the Original Manuscript Sources, 1745–1799*. 39 vols. Washington, D.C., 1931–1944.

Freeman, *Washington*
  Freeman, Douglas Southall. *George Washington: A Biography*. 7 vols. New York, 1948–1957.

Heitman, *Historical Register*
  Heitman, F[rancis] B. *Historical Register of Officers of the Continental Army during the War of the Revolution, April, 1775 to December, 1783*. Washington, D.C., 1914.

Holt, *St. Omers*
  Holt, Geoffrey. *St. Omers and Bruges Colleges, 1593–1773: A Biographical Dictionary*. Catholic Record Society. Vol. LXIX. [London], 1979.

Jackson, *Diaries of Washington*
  Jackson, Donald, and Dorothy Twohig, eds. *The Diaries of George Washington*. 6 vols. Charlottesville, Va., 1976–1979.

JCC
  Ford, Worthington Chauncey, et al., eds. *Journals of the Continental Congress, 1774–1789*. 34 vols. Washington, D.C., 1904–1937.

Laws of Md. [month, year, chapter]
  Laws of Maryland Made and Passed at a Session of Assembly Begun and Held at the City of Annapolis, on. . . . [Annapolis], 1777, 1778, 1780. Also *Laws of Maryland, Made and Passed at a Session of Assembly, Convened by the Council of Safety, and Begun and Held at the City of Annapolis, on Wednesday the Fifth*

of February, in the Year of Our Lord One Thousand Seven Hundred and Seventy-seven.

Md. Gaz.

Maryland Gazette. Annapolis.

Md. Gen.

Maryland Genealogies: A Consolidation of Articles from the Maryland Historical Magazine. 2 vols. Baltimore, 1980.

Md. Hist. Mag.

Maryland Historical Magazine.

Md. Jour.

Maryland Journal, and the Baltimore Advertiser.

Newman, *Early Families*

Newman, Harry Wright. *Anne Arundel Gentry: A Genealogical History of Some Early Families of Anne Arundel County, Maryland.* 3 vols. Annapolis, Md., 1970–1979.

Newman, *Twenty-Two Pioneers*

Newman, Harry Wright. *Anne Arundel Gentry: A Genealogical History of Twenty-two Pioneers of Anne Arundel County, Maryland, and Their Descendants.* Baltimore, 1933.

Pa. Gaz.

Pennsylvania Gazette. Philadelphia.

Pa. Jour.

Pennsylvania Journal and the Weekly Advertiser. Philadelphia.

Peckham, *Toll*

Peckham, Howard H. *The Toll of Independence: Engagements and Battle Casualties of the American Revolution.* Chicago, 1974.

PMHB

Pennsylvania Magazine of History and Biography.

Price, *Johnson's Letterbook*

Price, Jacob M., ed. *Joshua Johnson's Letterbook, 1771–1774: Letters from a Merchant in London to His Partners in Maryland.* London, 1979.

Procs. Conv. [month, year]

Proceedings of the Convention of the Province of Maryland, Held at the City of Annapolis, on Friday the Twenty-first of June, 1776. Annapolis, n.d.; *Proceedings of the Convention of the Province of Maryland, Held at the City of Annapolis, on Thursday the Seventh of December, 1775.* Annapolis, n.d.; *Proceedings of the Convention of the Province of Maryland, Held at the City of Annapolis, on Wednesday the Eighth of May, 1776.* Annapolis, n.d.; *Proceedings of the Convention of the Province of Maryland, Held at the City of Annapolis, on Wednesday the Fourteenth of August, 1776.* Annapolis, n.d.; *Proceedings of the Conventions of the Province of Maryland, Held at the City of Annapolis, on the Twenty-second Day of June, 1774; on the Twenty-first Day of November, 1774;*

on the Eighth Day of December, 1774; on the Twenty-fourth day of April, 1775; and on the Twenty-sixth Day of July, 1775. Annapolis, n.d.

Rowland, *Carroll*
Rowland, Kate Mason. *The Life of Charles Carroll of Carrollton, 1737–1832, with His Correspondence and Public Papers.* 2 vols. New York, 1898.

Rutland, *Mason*
Rutland, Robert A., ed. *The Papers of George Mason, 1725–1792.* 3 vols. Chapel Hill, N.C., 1970.

Scharf, *Chronicles of Baltimore*
Scharf, J. Thomas. *Chronicles of Baltimore: Being a Complete History of "Baltimore Town" and Baltimore City from the Earliest Period to the Present Time.* Baltimore, 1874.

Scharf, *History of Baltimore*
Scharf, J. Thomas. *History of Baltimore City and County.* . . . Philadelphia, 1881. Reprint, ed. Edward G. Howard. Baltimore, 1971.

Scharf, *Maryland*
Scharf, J. Thomas. *History of Maryland from the Earliest Period to the Present Day.* 3 vols. Baltimore, 1879.

Scharf, *Western Maryland*
Scharf, J. Thomas. *History of Western Maryland.* 2 vols. Philadelphia, 1882. Reprint, Baltimore, 1968.

Smith, *Letters*
Smith, Paul H., et al., eds. *Letters of Delegates to Congress, 1774–1789.* Washington, D.C., 1976–.

Van Devanter, *"Anywhere"*
Van Devanter, Ann C., ed., *"Anywhere So Long as There Be Freedom": Charles Carroll of Carrollton, His Family, and His Maryland.* Baltimore, 1975.

VMHB
Virginia Magazine of History and Biography.

VPHD [session, year]
Votes and Proceedings of the House of Delegates of the State of Maryland. Annapolis.

VPS [session, year]
Votes and Proceedings of the Senate of the State of Maryland. Annapolis.

Warfield, *Founders*
Warfield, J. D. *The Founders of Anne Arundel and Howard Counties, Maryland.* Baltimore, 1905.

Weis, *Clergy*
Weis, Frederick Lewis. *The Colonial Clergy of Maryland, Delaware, and Georgia.* Lancaster, Mass., 1950. Reprint, Baltimore, 1978.

WMQ
William and Mary Quarterly.

CARROLL CHRONOLOGY

. . .
. .
.

1737

Sept. 19. CC is born in Annapolis, Md.

1748

August. CC departs from Annapolis for the College of the English Jesuits at St. Omer, French Flanders.

1753

Mar. 10. Horatio Sharpe becomes governor of Maryland.

November. CC begins his studies at the College of the French Jesuits in Rheims.

1755

Fall. CC matriculates at the French Jesuits' College of Louis le Grand, Paris.

1756

May 15. Great Britain formally declares war on France, officially beginning the Seven Years' War.

Nov. 7. CCA and Elizabeth Brooke sign their marriage settlement.

1757

Feb. 15. CCA and Elizabeth Brooke marry.

June 2. CCA leaves Annapolis for England.

July 8. CC receives his degree from the College of Louis le Grand.

July 17. CCA arrives in Portsmouth, England.

August–c. Dec. 1. CCA visits CC in Paris.

by Dec. 8. CC begins his study of civil law at Bourges.

by Dec. 14. CCA returns to London.

1758

June 11. CCA arrives in Annapolis.

1759

by Jan. 17. CC returns to Paris to complete his study of the civil law at the College of Louis le Grand.

by Mar. 4. Rachel Brooke Darnall moves in with the Carrolls.

Sept. 11. CC leaves Paris for London, where he is to study the common law.

Sept. 24. CC arrives in London.

1761

Mar. 12. Elizabeth Brooke Carroll, CC's mother, dies in Annapolis.

1763

Feb. 10. The Treaty of Paris ends the Seven Years' War.

July 17. CC embarks on a continental tour.

October. CC begins his courtship of Louisa (Martha) Baker.

Nov. 6. CC returns to London.

by Nov. 7. Mary Darnall joins her mother, Rachel, in CCA's household.

Dec. 20–22. CC meets Louisa's father, John Baker, in Bath, England.

1764

Jan. 9–24. CC visits John Baker at his estate in Southhampton.

Mar. 22–23. Parliament passes the Revenue, or Sugar, Act.

April. CC's courtship of Louisa Baker ends unsuccessfully.

Sept. 19. CC sails from Gravesend for America.

Dec. 8. CC arrives at Hampton, Va.

Dec. 26. CC leaves Old Point Comfort for Annapolis.

1765

Jan. 9. CC lands on Maryland's Eastern Shore.

Feb. 14. CC arrives in Annapolis.

Feb. 27, Mar. 8. Parliament passes the Stamp Act.

Sept. 15. CC signs his name Charles Carroll of Carrollton in a letter to his
English friend William Graves.

Nov. 1. The Stamp Act takes effect.

1766

Mar. 18. Parliament repeals the Stamp Act and passes the Declaratory Act
reaffirming its authority to enact binding legislation for the American
colonies.

May 27. CCC announces that he will shortly marry Rachel Cooke.

July 8. CCC falls ill and postpones his wedding to November.

Nov. 25. CCC's fiancée, Rachel Cooke, dies.

1767

June 29. Parliament passes the Townshend Acts.

Aug. 13. CCC announces his plans to marry his cousin Mary Darnall (Molly).

1768

June 4. CCC and Molly Darnall sign their marriage settlement.

June 5. CCC and Molly Darnall marry in Annapolis and set up housekeeping
there; CCA and Rachel Darnall move to Doohoragen, the Carrolls'
plantation at Elk Ridge.

1769

Apr. 3. Molly Carroll gives birth to a daughter, Elizabeth.

June 5. Robert Eden arrives in Maryland to replace Horatio Sharpe as
governor.

June 22. A Maryland provincial convention formally supports
nonimportation.

August. CCC and Molly Carroll's daughter Elizabeth dies.

1770

Mar. 5. The Boston Massacre.

Apr. 12. Parliament repeals the Townshend Acts, except for the tax on tea.

Sept. 2. Molly Carroll gives birth to a daughter, Mary.

Oct. 22. Maryland's tobacco inspection act and fee schedule expire.

Nov. 26. Gov. Robert Eden reinstates the fee schedule, prorogues the general assembly, and calls for new elections.

1771

Sept. 4. Frederick Calvert, sixth Lord Baltimore, dies, leaving the province of Maryland to his illegitimate son, Henry Harford.

1772

Apr. 21. Molly Carroll gives birth to a daughter, Louisa.

Fall. Effects of an international credit crisis and falling tobacco prices begin to be felt in Maryland.

Nov. 5. CCC and Molly Carroll's daughter Louisa dies.

1773

February–June. CCC (First Citizen) debates Daniel Dulany (Antilon) in the *Maryland Gazette.*

May 14–June 10. Voters elect delegates known to favor First Citizen's position to Maryland's lower house.

Dec. 16. The Boston Tea Party.

1774

March–May. Parliament passes the Coercive (Intolerable) Acts.

Apr. 19. Governor Eden prorogues the general assembly.

June 22–25. First Maryland convention meets in Annapolis; CCC is not a member.

Sept. 5–26. First Continental Congress convenes in Philadelphia; CCC arrives in the city on Sept. 6 and remains there for about two weeks but is not a delegate to Congress.

Oct. 19. Radical whigs burn the ship *Peggy Stewart* in Annapolis harbor.

Nov. 21–25. Second Maryland convention meets; CCC is a delegate for Anne Arundel Co.

Dec. 8–12. The third Maryland convention meets; CCC is a delegate for Anne Arundel Co.

1775

Mar. 2. Molly Carroll gives birth to a son, Charles.

Apr. 19. British troops and American militia exchange fire at Lexington and Concord.

Apr. 24–May 3. Fourth Maryland convention meets; CCC is a delegate for Anne Arundel Co.

May 10. Second Continental Congress convenes in Philadelphia.

July 26–Aug. 14. The fifth Maryland convention meets; CCC is a delegate for Anne Arundel Co.

Aug. 29–Oct. 21. CCC serves on the first Council of Safety.

Dec. 18–Jan. 18, 1776. The sixth Maryland convention meets, with CCC a delegate for Anne Arundel Co.

1776

Feb. 15. The Continental Congress appoints CCC, Benjamin Franklin, and Samuel Chase to conduct a diplomatic mission to Canada and asks CCC to persuade his cousin John Carroll to accompany them.

Mar. 2. CCC and John Carroll arrive in Philadelphia.

Mar. 26. CCC, John Carroll, Samuel Chase, and Benjamin Franklin leave Philadelphia for New York City.

Mar. 28. CCC and his fellow commissioners arrive in New York City.

Apr. 2. The commissioners to Canada leave New York City.

Apr. 7. CCC and his party arrive at Albany, N.Y.

Apr. 9–15. CCC is a guest at Old Saratoga, the summer home of Gen. and Mrs. Philip Schuyler.

Apr. 27. CCC and his fellow commissioners arrive at Fort St. Johns.

Apr. 29. The commissioners arrive at Montreal.

May 8–25. The seventh Maryland convention meets and on May 21 instructs delegates to Congress to vote against independence.

May 11. Benjamin Franklin and John Carroll leave Montreal; CCC and Samuel Chase remain.

May 31. CCC and Samuel Chase leave Montreal.

June 11. CCC and Samuel Chase arrive in Philadelphia and report to Congress.

June 21–July 6. The eighth Maryland convention meets.

by June 22. CCC returns to Annapolis and takes his seat in the eighth Maryland convention, where he composes "A Declaration of the Delegates of Maryland" in favor of declaring independence from Great Britain.

June 24. Gov. Robert Eden leaves Maryland for England.

June 28. Rescinding previous directions, Maryland's eighth convention instructs its delegates to Congress to vote for independence.

July 4. The Maryland convention appoints CCC a delegate to Congress.

July 17. CCC takes his seat in Congress and is appointed to the Board of War and Ordnance.

Aug. 2. CCC signs the Declaration of Independence.

Aug. 14–Nov. 11. Ninth Maryland convention meets; CCC is a delegate for Anne Arundel Co.

Aug. 17. The Maryland convention appoints CCC a member of the committee to draft a plan of government.

Nov. 8. The Maryland convention adopts the constitution prepared by CCC's committee.

Nov. 23. Molly Carroll gives birth to a daughter Ann Brooke, called "Nancy."

Dec. 9. CCC is elected a member of the Maryland Senate from the Western Shore, a position to which he will be continually reelected until 1800.

1777

Feb. 5. The government of the state of Maryland convenes with Thomas Johnson as governor.

Feb. 15. The Maryland legislature elects CCC a delegate to Congress.

Feb. 18. CCA declines his Feb. 15 election to the Executive Council.

Apr. 9. The Maryland legislature enacts a law making paper currency legal tender for payment of sterling debts; CCC files a formal protest against the measure.

May 5–c. July 21. CCC attends Congress.

c. Sept. 1. CCC begins a tour of Continental army posts on his way to Congress.

c. Sept. 15. The British raid the Carrolls' plantation on Poplar Island in Chesapeake Bay.

Sept. 26. The British occupy Philadelphia.

Sept. 27–c. Oct. 16. CCC attends Congress at York, Pa.

Oct. 17. Gen. John Burgoyne surrenders to Gen. Horatio Gates at Saratoga.

Dec. 5. The Maryland legislature again elects CCC a delegate to Congress.

1778

Jan. 17–21. CCC attends Congress until called home by the illness of his wife.

Feb. 6. France signs treaties of amity, commerce, and alliance with the United States.

Apr. 15–June 27. CCC attends Congress at York.

May 4. Congress ratifies the treaties with France.

Sept. 7. Ann (Nancy), daughter of CCC and Molly Carroll, dies.

Dec. 18. Molly Carroll gives birth to a daughter Catharine, called Kitty.

1779

July 15–Sept. 1. CCC and Molly Carroll visit the spa at Bath (Berkeley Springs), Va.

c. Sept. 10–19. Baroness Frederika von Riedesel and her children visit the Carrolls at Doohoragen Manor.

1780

Oct. 26. Molly Carroll gives birth to a daughter, Eliza.

Dec. 14. The Maryland legislature enacts a law that effectively repeals the legal tender act.

1781

May–February 1782. CCC and Samuel Chase clash in the pages of the

Maryland Gazette over the reasons for Chase's exclusion from Maryland's
congressional delegation in 1777.

Aug. 24. Rachel Darnall, Molly Carroll's mother (CCC's mother-in-law), dies.

Oct. 20. CCC translates for the public the comte de Grasse's letter reporting
Gen. Charles Cornwallis's surrender at Yorktown, Va.

1782

May 30. CCA dies in Annapolis.

June 10. Molly Carroll dies in Annapolis.

INTRODUCTION

· · ·
· ·
·

The letters of Charles Carroll of Carrollton (CCC), a Maryland signer of the Declaration of Independence, are a unique historical source. Deposited mainly at the Maryland Historical Society in Baltimore, this extensive personal correspondence provides a richly textured family history and offers vivid perspectives on the prominent business and political figures with whom the Carrolls associated. Besides chronicling CCC's childhood and youth in extraordinary detail, the documents from the first forty-five years of his life furnish compelling insights into the impact of the American Revolution on the colonial gentry and thus constitute, in the words of the late Merrill Jensen, one of the "most intriguing and valuable sources of data on the nature of the Revolutionary conflict." Moreover, because Carroll outlived all the other signers of the Declaration of Independence, dying at the age of ninety-five in 1832, the letters from his last half-century afford a rare opportunity to witness the economic, social, and political development of the American Republic from the viewpoint of one of its creators. The sheer sweep of time encompassed by CCC's correspondence, from the late colonial period down to the era of Andrew Jackson, together with the documents' human intimacy, presents an opportunity for examining events and people during the nation's formative period through an unusually complex, multifaceted lens.

The Carroll family papers as a whole span 150 years and cover five generations of the family beginning with CCC's grandfather Charles Carroll the Settler (1661–1720), who migrated to Maryland in 1688, and including Carroll's father, Charles Carroll of Annapolis (CCA; 1702–1782), CCC himself (1737–1832), his son Charles Carroll of Homewood (1775–1825), and CCC's grandchildren through the middle of the nineteenth century. These first three volumes of a projected six-volume edition of selected correspondence cover the first forty-five years of CCC's life, beginning in the late 1740s, when, as a boy of ten, he left Maryland to study abroad, through 1782, when his father, always his closest friend and most constant correspondent, died. The letters present a remarkably complete family history that portrays in detail a young boy's progress toward manhood within the context of his father's familial dreams and ambitions, a Roman Catholic outsider's integration into Maryland's ruling elite during the turmoil of the American Revolution, and the concurrent passing of the generational torch from father to son.

Deepened and enlarged by their Irish Catholic heritage, the Carrolls' story as presented in these manuscripts delineates the relationship of class and religion as it applied to Catholics and Protestants in Ireland and Maryland during the seventeenth and eighteenth centuries. Similarly, the Maryland Carrolls' understanding of the tragedy that befell the branches of their family that remained in Ireland and the emotional repercussions engendered by this knowledge suggest the complexity of forces that shaped human behavior in pre-Revolutionary America.

DESCRIPTION OF THE EDITION

The precise size of the corpus of manuscripts pertaining to CCC, his ancestors, and his descendants is impossible to estimate. Held in a variety of public repositories and in an unknown, though far smaller, number of private collections in the United States and abroad, these materials encompass a wide geographic and chronological sweep from the conflicts of the Gaelic O'Carrolls in the Irish midlands during the late medieval period through the family's struggle to survive in mid-eighteenth-century Ireland, their migrations to Maryland and St. Germain at the time of the Glorious Revolution, the reconstitution of the family's dynastic and economic fortunes in Maryland between 1688 and 1782, and the triumphal nineteenth-century reentry of CCC's granddaughters into the British society that had, 150 years before, punished their defiant ancestors as Catholic rebels and Jacobites.

Documents pertaining to the Carroll saga are located in the Republic of Ireland at the Public Genealogical Office, the National Archives, the Public Record Office, the Registry of Deeds, and Trinity College, all in Dublin; at various local repositories throughout counties Offaly and Tipperary; and in the private library of the earl and countess of Rosse at Birr Castle. In England, valuable materials concerning CCC's schooling in France can be found at Stonyhurst College, Hurst Green, Lancashire, and the West Sussex Records Office in Chichester holds the original manuscript of the Diary of John Baker of Horsham. Other pertinent materials are deposited at the British Library and the Public Record Office in London, and the Yorkshire Archaeological Society in Leeds and the library of the University of Southhampton each hold a wealth of manuscripts relating to CCC's internationally renowned granddaughters.

The most extensive group of manuscripts for the Carroll family from the late seventeenth to the early twentieth century is to be found in the United States, in the Manuscripts Division of the Library of the Maryland Historical Society, Baltimore. There are other important, though much smaller, collections in this country in Annapolis at the Maryland State Archives; in Baltimore at the Archives of the Archdiocese of Baltimore and in the Special Collections, Milton S. Eisenhower Library, the Johns Hopkins University; in New York City, in the Gilder-Lehrman

Collection and in the Manuscripts Division, both at the Pierpont Morgan Library, and in the Manuscripts Division of the New York Public Library; in San Francisco, in the Special Collections Division of the University of San Francisco Library; and in Washington, D.C., in the Special Collections Division of the Georgetown University Library and the Manuscripts Division of the Library of Congress.

The vast majority of the documents included in these three volumes are to be found in the Manuscripts Division of the Maryland Historical Society Library, which has been the major repository of such materials for 150 years. The core of this invaluable collection, known as the Carroll Papers, MS 206, consists of some 750 letters between CCA and CCC that were part of a trunkful of manuscripts secured from the Carroll family between 1855 and 1859 by Joshua I. Cohen, a Baltimore physician and a founder of the Society. In 1889, after Dr. Cohen's death, Mrs. Harriet Cohen deposited the documents with the Society, and in 1913 Mendes Cohen and Louis H. Dielman calendared the correspondence. Additional extensive collections at the Maryland Historical Society that are devoted primarily to CCC and his family include the Carroll-McTavish Papers, the Harper-Pennington Papers, the Carroll-Maccubbin Papers, and the Carroll-Harper Papers, and other important items are scattered through a variety of other collections at the Society.

In 1985, as part of the process of assembling materials for this collection, the Charles Carroll of Carrollton Papers staff, in conjunction with the Maryland State Archives, produced a microfilm edition of all documents pertaining to CCC and his family housed at the Maryland Historical Society. Entitled *The Charles Carroll of Carrollton Family Papers: A Microfilm Edition of Documents Located at the Maryland Historical Society, Baltimore* (Ronald Hoffman and Eleanor S. Darcy, eds.), this microfilm is composed of 7,058 items from more than a hundred different collections organized according to type — correspondence, land papers, business papers, etc. — and arranged in chronological order within each category. Approximately half of the material — some 3,237 items — consists of correspondence. For the period covered by these three volumes, 1749–1782, there are 1,023 letters, more than 60 percent of them between father and son.

PRINCIPLES OF SELECTION

In selecting documents for publication, the editors have placed their primary emphasis on the correspondence between CCA and CCC. Depicting in vivid detail the father-son relationship from the boy's eleventh year through the forty-fifth year of his adulthood, these letters provide the backbone of the edition. Far fewer in number are the letters to CCC from his mother; those found — seven out of the eleven known to have been written — are included here. A second tier of material has been chosen from documents that are not correspondence but that significantly pertain to members of the immediate family. Such items include two prenuptial agreements, marriage articles, six expense accounts, an inventory, a waiver of consanguinity, and three wills. Correspondence between CCC and CCA and persons not related to them constitute a third category of material. Here, selections have been made for the purpose of situating the intensely personal father-son relationship in the wider context of late colonial and Revolutionary Maryland and the emerging United States and keeping intact the continuum of family activity during periods when CCA and CCC were not writing to each other because they were living in the same house. Letters between CCC and his English friends beginning in 1765 record his readjustment to provincial life after an absence of sixteen years, his learning, under paternal tutelage, to master the familial responsibilities settled on him upon his return, his attempts at matrimony, and his earliest reactions to the imperial crisis. CCC and CCA resumed their correspondence in 1768, when the younger Carroll's marriage led father and son to separate their households into two establishments, one in Annapolis, where the newly wed couple lived, and the other at Doohoragen Manor, the family's plantation at Elk Ridge, some thirty-two miles west of the capital, which the elder Carroll chose as his principal residence. From CCC's debut on the political stage as First Citizen in 1773, through the War for Independence, letters selected from his correspondence and that of his father with other Revolutionary leaders in Maryland and beyond reveal the dimensions of the broader public arena within which the aims that the Carrolls vigorously delineated in their private exchanges failed or were brought to fruition.

A final category of documents has been chosen to round out the portrayal of the Carrolls' eighteenth-century world. These include excerpts from legislative proceedings involving CCA and CCC and samples of battles they fought through essays written for publication either in pamphlet form or in the press. In the latter case, the exchanges between CCC and Samuel Chase, reprinted from the *Maryland Gazette* between 1781 and 1782, constitute the only surviving record of the shattering of the leadership alliance that had brought Maryland safely through the turmoil of the American Revolution.

PRESENTATION OF THE DOCUMENTS

The documents in this edition are arranged in chronological order. They are introduced by headings that identify the author and recipient, in the case of correspondence, or that indicate, for other kinds of items, the nature of the document and the persons to whom it pertains. The format of the documents has been standardized, with the place or date in the upper right corner. An endnote follows each document and indicates its character (autograph letter, letterbook draft, etc.), its ownership (Maryland Historical Society, Library of Congress, etc.), and any other significant information about its transmission or reception (addresses, postmarks, endorsements, etc.), its physical condition, and other versions or copies of it that may exist. The symbols used in the endnotes are included in the list of abbreviations. The annotations for each document follow its endnote.

EDITORIAL METHOD

The documents printed in this collection have been prepared for publication according to the following procedures:

1. During the period 1748–1764, when the younger Carroll studied abroad, the Carrolls routinely made multiple copies of their correspondence to guarantee against loss and, in the case of the elder Carroll, as a record of his communication with his son. In such instances, the editors have printed the recipient's original copy or, if that is not available, the best extant copy. Any significant differences between multiple texts have been annotated.
2. Restored and conjectural material has been treated as follows:
    a. Brackets have been used to indicate text that does not appear in the original document. Missing material restored from other sources has been annotated, but not text inadvertently omitted by the author, illegibly written, or unintelligibly spelled.
    b. Missing material that could not be restored from other sources or conjectured has been indicated by three bracketed ellipses [. . .] for less than a line of missing text, and four [. . . .] for a line or more, with the extent of the loss explained in an annotation.
3. Brackets inserted by the authors are rendered as parentheses.
4. To present as readable a text as possible, the editors have silently incorporated marginal and interlinear material and author's corrections. Where relevant, the placement of such passages in the manuscript and any particularly interesting or significant material excised or overwritten by the author has been annotated.
5. Clerks' devices, such as using catchwords at the bottoms of pages and dashes to fill out shorter lines to the right margin have been silently eliminated.
6. Original spelling has been retained.
7. Original punctuation has been retained, with the following stipulations:
    a. Idiosyncratic marks occurring between complete sentences, the second of which begins with a capital letter, have been rendered as periods. Such marks preceding a phrase that does not begin with a capital letter have been rendered as dashes or colons.
    b. Superfluous dashes have been deleted, as noted in 5, above.

c. In the absence of other punctuation, flourishes following salutations have been rendered as commas.

d. All other punctuation inserted by the editors has been enclosed in brackets.

e. When more than one kind of end punctuation appears in the text—such as a period followed by a dash—only the first has been retained.

8. Original capitalization has been retained except that sentences beginning with lowercase letters have been silently corrected to begin with capital letters.

9. In letters of more than two manuscript pages written as a single paragraph, the editors have, on occasion, silently provided paragraph breaks for readability.

10. Underlining for emphasis by the author has been retained.

11. Text in languages other than English has been treated as follows:

a. Documents written in French have been presented in their original form followed by an English translation. Annotation numbers appear at the same places in both versions, and the annotations follow the translation. In instances where the author changes from one language to the other in a single document, only the portion in French is translated into English.

b. French phrases that appear in documents written in English and Latin phrases in documents written in French or English have been translated in the annotations.

c. Accents have been rendered as written. In cases where the author's intention could not be determined, the editors have accented the word correctly.

12. Abbreviations have been treated as follows:

a. Superscripts have been brought to the line.

b. The ampersand has been retained, but the tilde has not, nor has the abbreviation indicated by the tilde been expanded.

c. The thorn has been rendered th.

d. The tailed p has been rendered as per.

e. The lowercase m lined through has been rendered as thousand in figures.

f. The symbol ℔ has been rendered lb.

g. Eighteenth-century contractions such as "shou'd," "wou'd," "altho'," "thô," "thro'," and "t'is," have been retained as written.

h. Proper names of persons and forms of address have been retained with the author's punctuation.

i. Charles Carroll of Annapolis—Papa—has been referred to editorially as CCA. His son, Charley, has been designated CC—Charles Carroll—until August 1765, when he formally added the appellation "of Carrollton" to his name. Thereafter, the younger Carroll has been referred to as CCC.

13. Inadvertent repetitions by the author have been silently eliminated.

14. Archival notes in unknown scripts and random markings that appear on the manuscripts have not been reproduced.

15. Documents reprinted from published sources have been reproduced as published, typographical errors included, with the exception that the thorn has been rendered th.

ANNOTATION

The editors have sought to annotate these documents in a way that does not unduly burden the academic reader with information already well known but that gives the interested lay person enough specific knowledge to grasp the context of the Carrolls' lives without having to interrupt the enjoyment of the text to look up unfamiliar references. Annotations of individuals include birth and death dates and concise biographical information. Monographs and biographies used as sources are cited; dictionaries and encyclopedias are not. Annotations for books mentioned in the documents provide full bibliographic information, usually the earliest edition. Book lists enclosed in letters are printed and annotated in Appendix II. The *Catalogue of the Library of Charles Carroll of Carrollton . . . to Be Sold at Auction, Commencing on Monday Evening, December 5, 1864 . . .* (Maryland Room, McKeldin Library, University of Maryland, College Park) lists the books owned by the Carrolls at the time of that sale. When a book mentioned in a document is in the *Catalogue,* the item number and edition indicated therein follow the full citation. Information contained in the *Catalogue* is subject to the imperfections of most nineteenth-century printed bibliographies.

A NOTE ON DATING

The dating of documents written between 1748 and 1752 is complicated by the usage of two calendars. Roman Catholic countries like France, where the younger Carroll lived during this period, used the Gregorian or "new style" calendar. Promulgated by Pope Gregory XIII in 1582, the Gregorian calendar began the year on January 1, set its length at 365 days, added an extra day to every year exactly divisible by four, and decreed that years ending in hundreds could not be leap years unless they were divisible by 400. By contrast, Great Britain, a Protestant country, continued to employ the Julian or "old style" calendar, established by Julius Caesar in 46 B.C.E., which began the year on March 25 and fixed its length at 365 days, adding an extra day every fourth year. Great Britain finally mandated the use of the new style calendar throughout its dominions in 1752, but by this time an 11-day discrepancy existed between the two systems. To adjust this difference, 11 days were simply added to old style dates.[1] As a result, CC's old style birth date of September 8, 1737, became September 19, 1737 new style.[2] References to new style and old style dating in letters exchanged by CCA and CC prior to Great Britain's adoption of the Gregorian calendar are noted as they appear.

A NOTE ON APPENDIXES

Three appendixes appear at the end of Volume III of this edition. The first contains genealogical charts that explain the familial relationships among the Carrolls and those of their kin who figure prominently in these volumes. Appendix II offers an annotated compilation of the various lists of books that the Carrolls are known to have owned or acquired to the year 1782. This compendium confirms the intellectual prowess and range of both father and son and the breadth of their interest in and grasp of the literary and cultural dimensions of the age in which they lived. Finally, Appendix III provides all the surviving censuses made by the Carrolls of the persons they held as slaves during the period covered by these volumes, with appropriate annotation. These documents, among the most unique and valuable manuscripts within the corpus of Carroll material, present a rare, on-the-ground picture of the organizational structure of a thriving Chesapeake agricultural establishment and the bondmen and bondwomen whose lives and labor were the essential components of its operation and prosperity.

A NOTE ON PREVIOUS PRINTINGS OF
CARROLL CORRESPONDENCE

Although this collection is the first systematically compiled and edited edition of Carroll correspondence to be published, some letters have previously appeared in print. Kate Mason Rowland's two-volume biography, *The Life of Charles Car-*

---

1. This was accomplished by making the day that followed Wednesday, September 2, 1752, Thursday, September 14, 1752. Mark M. Smith, "Culture, Commerce, and Calendar Reform in Colonial America," *WMQ*, 3d Ser., LV (1998), 559. See also Robert Poole, " 'Give Us Our Eleven Days': Calendar Reform in Eighteenth-Century England," *Past and Present*, no. 149 (November 1995), 95–139.

2. Although birth dates were supposed to remain unchanged, according to the parliamentary statute that provided for calendar reform, the Carrolls, like others in Great Britain and her North American colonies, misunderstood and made the alteration. Smith, "Culture, Commerce, and Calendar Reform," *WMQ*, 3d Ser., LV (1998), 566.

{ INTRODUCTION }

roll of Carrollton, 1737–1832, with His Correspondence and Public Papers (New York, 1898), makes extensive use of Carroll manuscripts and includes in its text some of the pre-Revolutionary and Revolutionary documents used in these volumes. In 1902 a volume of Carroll letters spanning the years 1754–1832, compiled and edited by Thomas Meagher Field and entitled *Unpublished Letters of Charles Carroll of Carrollton, and of His Father, Charles Carroll of Doughoregan* was published in New York by the United States Catholic Historical Society. According to Field's introduction, he prepared this collection with the permission of Mrs. Charles Carroll McTavish, the widow of CCC's great-grandson, who possessed the original documents. The edition is seriously flawed by the misidentification of recipients, the silent excising of material, and the alteration of signatures. Comparison of Field's transcriptions with extant manuscripts reveals that occasionally he rewrote the text of a document. "Extracts from the Carroll Papers," consisting of correspondence between CCC and CCA between 1750 and 1774, appeared in the *Maryland Historical Magazine* between 1915 and 1921, but the name of the transcriber is not given. Finally, a Charles Carroll of Carrollton letterbook, transcribed and edited by J.G.D. Paul, was printed in the same journal in 1937, under the title "A Lost Copy-Book of Charles Carroll of Carrollton." This manuscript, as Paul's introductory note relates, was originally a part of the Cohen gift but became separated from the rest of the collection. Obtained by the Society following the sale of the estate of Miss Bertha Cohen in 1929, the manuscript is currently filed as Charles Carroll of Carrollton, Letterbook, 1770–1774, MS 203.2. Most of the letters printed by Rowland and Field can also be found among the Carroll collections at the Maryland Historical Society.

Dear Papa, Dear Charley

. . .
. .
.

VOLUME I

CHAPTER 1

Childhood and Adolescence
France, 1748–1759

· · ·
· ·
·

The liaison between Charles Carroll of Annapolis and his cousin Elizabeth Brooke (1709–1761) that produced the son who became Charles Carroll of Carrollton began in the mid-1730s. A daughter of Prince George's County planter Clement Brooke, Sr. (1676–1737), and his wife Jane Sewall Brooke (1680–1761), Elizabeth had become a member of the Carrolls' Annapolis household sometime between 1726 and 1730,[1] perhaps as a companion to her cousins Mary and Eleanor Carroll, CCA's younger sisters. After Eleanor's death in 1730 and Mary's departure in 1734 for a convent in Liège abrogated those responsibilities, Elizabeth continued to live with the Carrolls and to be actively involved in their affairs, witnessing various legal documents involving CCA, among them leases he executed with tenants and, in April 1734, the will of his brother Daniel (1707–1734), known since his marriage in 1728 as Daniel Carroll of Duddington.[2] The most dramatic and incontestable evidence of Elizabeth's presence occurred on September 19, 1737, when she gave birth, out of wedlock, to CCA's son, their beloved "Charley," the only child either of them ever had.

Little is known about the first decade of Charley's life. He was born in Annapolis, in the brick house his father had built beside Charles Carroll the Settler's commodious frame dwelling, where Madam Mary Carroll (1678–1742), the Settler's widow, continued to live, but his parents' correspondence indicates that he spent most of his time at the Carroll dwelling plantation, Doohoragen Manor, a thirteen-thousand-acre tract located at Elk Ridge, some thirty-two miles west of the capital.[3] By the time of CC's birth, CCA had already begun to acquire a formidable reputation as a defiant and outspoken Catholic single-mindedly bent on expanding his fortune. The arrival of his son initiated the second great undertaking of his life—the molding of an heir intellectually and morally capable of receiving and preserving the grand legacy of wealth he was building. Unwavering in his determination to succeed in this endeavor, "Papa," as he was known to the boy, transmitted his expectations to CC at a tender age and used a unique method to underscore what was at stake in fulfilling them. Until February 1757, he deliberately and

1

openly maintained a common law marriage with Elizabeth Brooke, his son's beloved "Mama." As CC clearly understood, any substantive deviation from the path CCA had decreed for him placed at risk the possibility of the legitimate union that would establish him as his father's legal heir.[4]

The documents included in this chapter provide telling evidence of this unusual domestic arrangement and of the genuine affection that CCA and Elizabeth Brooke had for each other and for their son. The separation that initiated the correspondence began just before CC's eleventh birthday. Because Maryland law forbade Catholics to maintain schools for their children in the colony, wealthy men sent their sons, and sometimes their daughters, to Europe to be educated. So it was that in August 1748 CC, along with several other Catholic lads of about the same age,[5] boarded a ship in Annapolis and set off on a transatlantic journey. Their final destination, by way of London, was the College of the English Jesuits at St. Omer, in Flanders, where CC began an educational odyssey that ultimately lasted for sixteen years.[6]

As CCA had planned, CC spent the first decade of his extensive schooling in various Jesuit institutions in France. After completing the course at St. Omers late in 1753, he spent a year at the college of the French Jesuits at Rheims and then moved on to the College of Louis le Grand in Paris in 1755, where he prepared and successfully defended a master's thesis in universal philosophy two years later. In late 1757 he enrolled at the University of Bourges for the study of civil law, but his dissatisfaction with that school led him to return to Paris after thirteen months to finish his work there. In September 1759 he left France for England.

The letters that cover this period of CC's life clearly delineate the pervasive role CCA played in shaping the boy's values and his perception of the world. Not even the watchful supervision of the priests to whom the lad had been entrusted could match that exerted by his father across the thousands of miles that lay between them. Through his letters, CCA oversaw every aspect of CC's mental, physical, and moral development. Cast far from home at a tender age, CC tried diligently to see his exile as an act of parental love, writing CCA wistfully in the spring of 1751, when he was thirteen and a half, "I can easily see the great affection you have for Me by sending me hear to a Colege, where I may not only be a learned man, but also be advanced in piety & devotion."[7] His natural desire for paternal approval intensified by reminders of his illegitimacy — until she married CCA, Elizabeth Brooke signed all her letters to CC with her maiden name — CC pledged that he would "continue to be a good boy" and that he was "much desiorus to obey" his father's commands.[8] His earnest apologies for his poor handwriting and spelling, which, lest CCA scold him, he promised to improve, indicate the depth of his receptivity to his father's expectations and instructions. By the time he reached the age of twenty, CC had learned his duty well: "You may be assured Dr. Papa I shall strive not to turn into an abuse the confidence you put in me. I shall endeavour to manage my little affaires with all the care and attention I am capable of by avoid-

{ CHILDHOOD & ADOLESCENCE, 1748–1759 }

ing the 2 extreames of affectation and meaness. I keep strick accounts and shall send them to you at the end of the year so you will be able to Judge yourself wether I have spent foolishly or no."[9]

Documenting, often with humor and poignancy, a boy's passage from childhood through adolescence to young manhood, the correspondence also reflects the gradual expansion of CC's world. Preparing him for the greater sophistication of life at Rheims after the cloistered existence at St. Omers, CCA delivered a lecture on social deportment that directed CC to "View every thing worth Notice carefully and with Attention, especially the behaviour of all about you, what may become a Man in one Country may be very ridiculous in another," and to "observe the Actions of others" before acting, for "none but brainless thoughtless People do otherwise."[10] When CC began at twenty to go into "company" at Bourges and communicated his initial awareness of the charms of women, CCA responded with an especially terse command: "Avoid any intimacy or familiarity with the Fair Sex especially Visits or Conversations without witnesses"![11]

Most memorable for CC of all his experiences in France were the months he spent in Paris with CCA between August and early December 1757. The reason for the elder Carroll's trip abroad was business rather than sentiment — new anti-Catholic measures passed by the Maryland legislature had spurred him to explore the possibility of quitting the province for the ostensibly more hospitable French colony of Louisiana — but he obviously welcomed the excuse that mission gave him for seeing his son. For CC, his father's visit provided so happy a respite from the emotional isolation of his exile that he found the parting that followed painful to bear. Grieved, but obedient, and consoled by his memories of "the agreable time we spent togeather in Paris," CC made the "slow dull and malancholey" journey to Bourges to continue the course CCA had set for him.[12] If he had hoped that his father would relent and allow him to return to Maryland, he was disappointed. And when he finished in France, he must look ahead to England, no matter how much he yearned for home.

1. The earliest mention of Elizabeth Brooke occurs in CCA's account of expenses associated with his sister Eleanor's funeral in 1730. Presumably, Elizabeth came to live with the Carrolls soon after Mary and Eleanor Carroll returned to Maryland from school in Liège in 1726. CCA, Account Book, c. 1730–1757, MS 211.1, MdHi; Charles Carroll, "An Old Cash Book and Accots: raised in 1749 with People indebted to John Digges whose Bonds are assigned to C: Carroll," fol. 9, DLC.

2. Prince George's Co. Land Records, Liber T, fols. 161–164, 269–270, 491–492, 518–519; Anne Arundel Co. Deeds, Liber R.D. no. 2, fol. 197; Prince George's Co. Wills, Liber 21, fol. 37, all MdAA.

3. See CCA to CC, July 26, 1756, and Elizabeth Brooke to CC, Sept. 8, 1756, both below. Doohoragen, from the Gaelic Dúiche Uí Riagáin, the ancestral territory of a neighboring sept, was one of four tracts, among the many he acquired between 1693 and 1720, to which Charles Carroll the Settler gave Irish place-names. As patented by the Settler in 1702,

Doohoragen covered seven thousand acres; by 1759, CCA had expanded the plantation to thirteen thousand. Ronald Hoffman, "'Marylando-Hibernus': Charles Carroll the Settler, 1660–1720," *WMQ*, 3d Ser., XLV (1988), 221, 235; CCA to CC, Apr. 16, 1759, below.

4. Pauline Maier has developed an interesting interpretation of the relationship between Carroll's illegitimacy and his conduct during the American Revolution. Although not persuaded by her analysis, the editors find her cogent essay imaginative and certainly worth considering. Maier, "Charles Carroll of Carrollton, Dutiful Son and Revolutionary Politician," in Maier, *The Old Revolutionaries: Political Lives in the Age of Samuel Adams* (New York, 1980), 201–268. In this regard, see also Sally D. Mason, "Charles Carroll of Carrollton and His Family, 1688–1832," in Van Devanter, *"Anywhere,"* 9–34; Mason, "Mama, Rachel, and Molly: Three Generations of Carroll Women," in Ronald Hoffman and Peter J. Albert, eds., *Women in the Age of the American Revolution* (Charlottesville, Va., 1989), 244–289; and Ronald Hoffman, *Princes of Ireland, Planters of Maryland: A Carroll Saga, 1500–1782* (Chapel Hill, N.C., 2000).

5. Among the boys who sailed with CC in August 1748 were his cousins John Carroll, Robert Darnall, and Walter Hoxton.

6. In eighteenth-century Europe and America, the English Jesuit College at St. Omer was known familiarly as St. Omers, a designation that has been used throughout this edition.

7. CC to CCA, March 1751, below.

8. CC to CCA, Mar. 22, Sept. 24, 1750, below.

9. CC to CCA, Feb. 4, 1758, below.

10. CCA to CC, Sept. 30, 1754, below.

11. CCA to CC, Aug. 30, 1758, below.

12. CC to CCA, Dec. 19, 1757, below.

· · ·
·

CC to CCA and Elizabeth Brooke

Blandike,[1] Sept. the 4th: 1749

Dear Papa. & Mama.

I cannot be better satisfied with a Place than this where I hope to accomplish my Studies to your greatest satisfaction. I receiv'd your desires with the greatest joy imaginable in staying in little figures another year, where I hope either to be 1st or 2nd.[2] I hope you & all my friends will excuse me for not writing for Yesterday falling down, I hurt my arm very much. I hope Dear Papa & Mama this will find you in a good state of health & desire you woud give my kind love & Service to all friends[.] I am, Dear Papa & Mama

Your ever loving Son
Charles Carroll[3]

ALS, Carroll Papers, MS 206, MdHi. Endorsed by CCA: "Blandike Sepr: 4: 1749 Cha: Carroll's Letter—Answerd." Financial calculations in CCA's hand not reproduced.

1. The English Jesuit College at St. Omer, to which CC was sent in late summer 1748,

was founded in 1593 by Father Robert Persons to circumvent penal laws that prohibited Roman Catholics from establishing schools in England. Initially a boarding school attached to the Walloon College, which served a local clientele, St. Omers became a separate entity staffed entirely by English Jesuits in 1614. Blandike or Blandyke is an anglicization of Blendecques, a village on the river Aa in Flanders, about an hour's walk from St. Omers. In 1626 the English Jesuits of St. Omers purchased a property there to provide a place where the students could spend their monthly holidays. This tradition, known as "Blendecques," "Blandikes," or "Blandykes," was preserved in some form at Jesuit academic institutions well into the nineteenth century, long after the original English College at St. Omer had been relocated to Lancashire, England, where it continues today as Stonyhurst College. T. E. Muir, *Stonyhurst College, 1593-1993* (London, 1992), 15-20, 29-30; John Gerard, *Stonyhurst College: Its Life beyond the Seas, 1592-1794, and on English Soil, 1794-1894* (Belfast, 1894), 26; Hubert Chadwick, *St. Omers to Stonyhurst: A History of Two Centuries* (London, 1962), 116.

2. The curriculum at St. Omers was a classical one presented in the manner prescribed by the *Ratio Studiorum*, a detailed pedagogical system initially conceived by Ignatius Loyola, founder of the Society of Jesus, and developed into its first published form by the Reverend Claudius Acquaviva, fifth general superior of the Society. Of the three main divisions in the course of study—literature or humanity, arts, and theology—it was the first, a six-year program beginning with the basic structure of Latin and progressing through grammar and syntax to poetry and rhetoric, that occupied CC at St. Omers. "Figures," a two-year course sometimes called "accidence" or "rudiments," introduced the students to elementary Latin, emphasizing grammatical devices such as word order and inflection. The initial year was devoted to "little" or "lower" figures, and a second year to "great" or "higher" figures. Competition for academic distinction was also an integral part of the curriculum at St. Omers, with prizes awarded for excellence in Greek and Latin prose and poetry and an extra holiday and dinner at Blandecques for the six students who achieved the highest scores on their year-end examinations. A.C.F. Beales, *Education under Penalty: English Catholic Education from the Reformation to the Fall of James II, 1547-1689* (London, 1963), 132, 146-148; Gerard, *Stonyhurst College,* 24; Thomas Hughes, *Loyola and the Educational System of the Jesuits* (New York, 1892); P. R. Harris, ed., *Douai College Documents, 1637-1794,* Catholic Record Society, LXIII (London, 1972), esp. 133-157; Muir, *Stonyhurst College,* 22-33, 157.

3. Preceding his final signature, CC wrote and struck through "Charles" and "C Carroll." The latter appears to have been written over another word.

CC to CCA

[Mar. 22, 1750]

Hon: Father,

I hope you wont be angry with me for not writing to you oftener than I do. You desir'd I should write to you at least twice a year. I assure you I shall obey your orders very punctually. This is the third letter.[1] So I have done pretty well, for I

Eighteenth-Century Flanders.
Courtesy Maurice Whitehead, University of Wales, Swansea. Photograph courtesy of University Photographic Service. The Brynmor Jones Library, University of Hull

think I have not been much above eighteen months out of Maryland. Cousin Carroll[2] got me to stay in little figures, and I believe it is better for me, for I hope to be always amongst the first, at least I promise you my endeavours shall not be wanting. I am very happy, my master is very good to me, and he says he will always be so If I continue to be a good boy, and I am resolvd to be so. I believe Cousin Jack Carroll[3] will make a good scholar, for he is often first. Most of our Merylandians do very well, and they are said to be as good as any, if not the best boys in the house: Bobby darnall[4] was put to business at Dunkirk, and is now come back to the College. I writ to Mr. Philpot[5] for two gunies[6] and an Ainsworth's Dictionary.[7] I thought you wou'd approve of it. He has sent me no answer as yet. Honourd Father I am your most dutiful Son.

Charles Carroll

22 Mar 1750[8]

Sir

I can't let this pass without assureing you that Master Charles is a very good youth & I hope he will deserve all the favours you bestow uppon him—I am Sir

Yr most obt humble Sert

Wm Newton[9]

ALS, Carroll Papers, MS 206, MdHi. Addressed by CC "To Charles Carroll Esq. of Anapolis Maryland," with William Newton's additional direction, "To be left with Mr Philpot at Mile End Green Merchant In London," and, in an unknown hand, "per Capt. Rigg 3.157." Endorsed by CCA: "1750 [new style] Mar: 22 Cha: Carroll's Letter—Ansd."

1. CC's first letter home, probably written in late September 1748, has not been found.

2. Born in Ireland, Antony Carroll, S.J. (1722–1794), nephew and heir of James Carroll of Anne Arundel Co. and CC's second cousin, studied at St. Omers from 1734 to 1744, when he entered the priesthood. Subsequently he studied at Liège and Rheims and taught at St. Omers before serving with the Jesuits in England. In 1774, after the suppression of the order, he traveled to America with his cousin John Carroll, returning the following year to England, where he spent the rest of his life. He died in September 1794 after being attacked in the streets of London. Holt, *St. Omers*, 59. See Appendix I, Chart B.

3. John Carroll (1735–1815), the youngest son of Eleanor Darnall Carroll and Daniel Carroll I of Upper Marlboro, studied at St. Omers from 1749 until 1753, when he entered the Jesuit novitiate at Watten. Upon the completion of his course of study there, he studied at Liège, was ordained to the priesthood in 1761, and then taught at various Jesuit schools in Flanders. Arrested briefly after Pope Clement XIV's suppression of the Jesuits in 1773, he accepted an offer of refuge from the English Catholic nobleman Lord Henry Arundell of Wardour and remained at Arundell's seat, Wardour Castle in Shaftesbury, Wiltshire, until the spring of 1774, when he returned to Maryland to reside with his mother at Rock Creek, in the section of Prince George's Co. that became Montgomery Co. in 1776. A member of the commission appointed by the Second Continental Congress to gain Canadian support for the American revolt, he journeyed to Montreal with his fellow commissioners— his cousin CC, by then known as "of Carrollton," Samuel Chase, and Benjamin Franklin —in the spring of 1776, but he left with Franklin in May before the termination of the unsuccessful venture. During the American Revolution he continued to live at Rock Creek, conducting services at St. John's Chapel on his brother Daniel's estate at Forest Glen and ministering to Catholics in the surrounding countryside. After the war his success in reorganizing Maryland's Jesuit clergy and improving its discipline and means of support brought him to the attention of Rome, and in 1784 he was designated superior of the missions in the United States. Within two years he had gained the funds and the authorization to found the Catholic academy that became Georgetown University. Keenly aware of his countrymen's antipathy toward the idea of a foreign body choosing a bishop for the United States, Carroll convinced Rome that the choice should be made by the American clergy subject to Rome's ratification. Accordingly, Carroll's nomination as first bishop in the United States was confirmed by Pope Pius VI on Nov. 6, 1789. He was consecrated at Lulworth Castle in Dorset, England, on Aug. 15, 1790, and convened his first synod in Baltimore in November of the following year. He became archbishop in 1808. An erudite man, he was a founder of the Baltimore Library Company in 1796 and served as its president until his death. He was well known as an outspoken advocate of religious liberty. On July 7, 1806, he laid the cornerstone for Baltimore's cathedral, the Basilica of the Assumption, which he had planned with Benjamin Henry Latrobe. Carroll died before the building was completed and is buried beneath its high altar. Joseph T. Durkin and Annabelle M. Melville, "Catholicism and the Carrolls in Early Maryland," in Van Devanter, *"Anywhere,"* 83–98; *Bio. Dic. Md. Legis.*, I, 199; Holt, *St. Omers*, 53. See Appendix I, Chart J.

4. Robert Darnall (c. 1728–1803), son of Henry Darnall III and Anne Talbott Darnall of Prince George's Co., was CC's second cousin. See Appendix I, Chart F.

5. Two London merchants named Philpot were active in the Chesapeake: Brian Philpot (?–1759) was in the tobacco trade as early as 1730; Thomas Philpot was probably his successor (Katharine A. Kellock, "London Merchants and the Pre-1776 American Debts," *Guildhall Studies in London History*, I [1974], 139–140). Payments for CC's educational expenses at St. Omers are recorded in Accounts of Fr. E. Galloway, October 1746–1753, Stonyhurst Manuscripts, D.I. 12, Stonyhurst College, Lancashire, England.

6. Guineas, English gold coins issued from 1663 until 1813. In 1717 the value of a guinea was fixed at twenty-one shillings.

7. Robert Ainsworth (1660–1743), *Thesaurus Linguae Latinae Compendiarius; or, A Compendius Dictionary of the Latin Tongue, Designed for the Use of the British Nations* (London, 1736). According to the 1864 catalog of their library, the Carrolls owned a two-volume edition (*Cat. Lib.*, no. 1182). Although the *Catalogue of the Library* cannot be considered a complete reference for the Carrolls' eighteenth-century collection of books, it frequently serves as a useful guide in identifying works the family purchased prior to 1782. For other lists of books bought by the Carrolls, see Appendix II.

8. This material appears on the back of CC's letter.

9. Jesuit William Newton (1683–1756), a native of Lincolnshire, served at St. Omers from 1745 to 1750 and from 1752 until his death. Henry Foley, ed., *Records of the English Province of the Society of Jesus . . .* (London, 1877–1883), VII, 546; Geoffrey Holt, *The English Jesuits, 1650–1829: A Biographical Dictionary*, Catholic Record Society, LXX (London, 1984), 178; Letterbook of London Procurator for St. Omers, 1732–1747, Stonyhurst MSS, D.I. 15.

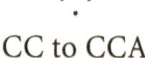

CC to CCA

[May 1750]

Dear Papa,

I take this opportunity of writing by Mr. Molinex[1] that I am well as I hope you are. I am sorry that you don't like my writing, but that letter was not my best, because I was in grate haste, for I did not know of the opportunity till it was almost pass'd, theirfore I beg to be excus'd. There is a writing school in the College[2] and I go there every day. I have not time to write to you a great deal[3] but only to acquaint you how affairs are. As to the rules of the house and studying hard I will do my best endavours for that end. Honour'd father I am your most dutiful son

Charles Carroll

ALS, Carroll Papers, MS 206, MdHi. Endorsed by CCA: "1750 May Cha: Carrolls Letter Answerd."

1. Although there were several Jesuits by the name of Molyneux active in England and

A Perspective View of the English College in Saint Omer.
Montbard, 1689. *Courtesy Stonyhurst College, Lancashire, England*

France at this time, this was probably Richard Molyneux (1696–1766) who, in 1746, during his service in Maryland, was brought before the provincial court on suspicion of "treasonable practices." CCA posted a security bond of one thousand pounds sterling for him. The case was dismissed on insufficient evidence, and Molyneux returned to England in 1749. Foley, ed., *Records*, VII, 514; Thomas Hughes, *History of the Society of Jesus in North America: Colonial and Federal* (London, 1907–1917), II, 528–529; *Arch. of Md.*, L, 53–55; Holt, *English Jesuits*, 167.

2. CC's stylized handwriting in this letter differs markedly from his penmanship in the two preceding, undoubtedly an effect of the "writing school."

3. The day at St. Omers began at 5:00 A.M., and by the time the students sat down for breakfast at 7:00, they had attended Mass and studied for an hour. Classes started at 7:30, followed at 10:15 by a 45-minute study period, lunch, an hour of recreation, and another study period. Formal instruction resumed at 1:45 P.M. and continued until 4:30. A fourth study period kept the boys busy until supper at 6:30, after which they were allowed an hour of recreation, a half-hour for study, and a quarter hour for prayers before going to bed at 9:00. This schedule operated only half a day on Tuesdays and Thursdays, and the Sunday routine included Mass and High Mass (7:00 and 10:00 A.M., respectively), vespers in the middle of the afternoon, and an evening service at 8:00 P.M. Muir, *Stonyhurst College*, 158.

CCA to CC

Sepr: 17: 1750

Dr Charly,

As the Bearer Mr Warring[1] goes from my House I could not omit Writing to You, to let You know that Yr Mama & I are well, & to Recommend Mr Warring to Yr Friendship & Assistance, which as he is a Stranger & A Marylandian I doubt not You will wth pleasure afford him.

I send You a letter from Your Mother & I shall soon write more at large to You being at Present very Busy. I have Recd: Yrs of Sepr: 4: 1749 & two wi[th] out date the 1st I su[pp]ose wrote last March & the othe[r las]t May; Always date Yr letters. I have two from Csn Antony of March 21st and May 25th 1750, & One from Mr Newton dated May 13th 1750;[2] Pray give my Compliments to those Gentlemen & let them know I intend to write to them soon. Give my love & Service to Csn Jacky, his Father[3] Mother[4] Br[5] & Sisters[6] are well. I wish You Health & Success in Yr Studies & I am My Dr Charly

Mo: Affly Yrs
Chars Carroll

ALS, Carroll Papers, MS 216, MdHi. Addressed by CCA to CC "By Mr Warring." CC's penmanship practice on verso not reproduced.

1. Richard Marsham Waring, Jr. (1733-1766), the oldest son of Richard Marsham Waring, Sr. By his will the elder Waring provided that his four sons should be raised in the Roman Catholic faith by their uncle Basil if their Protestant mother declined that responsibility. Following her death, Basil Waring took charge of his nephews and not long afterward sent Richard, Jr., to St. Omers. Bowie, *Prince George's*, 600-601; *Arch. of Md.*, L, 200.

2. Letters not found.

3. Daniel Carroll I of Upper Marlboro (1696-1751), a kinsman of CCA, had emigrated to Maryland about 1720. Settling in Upper Marlboro in Prince George's Co., he became a planter and a merchant. He and his wife, whom he married in Maryland, were the parents of seven children. Mary Virgina Geiger, *Daniel Carroll II: One Man and His Descendants, 1730-1978* (Baltimore, 1979), 4-12. See Appendix I, Charts A and J.

4. Eleanor Darnall Carroll (1703/4-1796).

5. Daniel Carroll II of Upper Marlboro (1730-1796), son of Daniel Carroll I of Upper Marlboro and Eleanor Darnall Carroll, was also known as Daniel Carroll of Rock Creek after 1776, and fondly to CC and CCA as Cousin Daniel. Educated at St. Omers between 1742 and 1748, Daniel married his cousin Eleanor Carroll (1731-1763), daughter of CCA's brother Daniel Carroll of Duddington and Ann Rozer Carroll, in 1751 and with her had two children, Daniel Carroll III and Mary Carroll Sim. A merchant and a planter, Daniel was barred from public office during the colonial period because of his Catholicism but embarked on a distinguished political career in 1777. He served on the Executive Coun-

cil (1777–1781) and as a senator from the Western Shore (1781–1789). He was a delegate to the Continental Congress (1781–1783) and to the Constitutional Convention (1789–1791). Elected to the House of Representatives in 1789, he was also appointed by George Washington to survey the District of Columbia and was a member of the district's first Board of Commissioners (1791–1795). At the time of his death he lived at Rock Creek in Montgomery Co. *Bio. Dic. Md. Legis.*, I, 199–200. See also Appendix I, Chart J.

6. John Carroll had four sisters: Ann (1733–1804), Eleanor (1737–by 1810), Mary (1742–1815), and Elizabeth (1745–1821). See Appendix I, Chart J.

CC to CCA

Sep: The 24: 1750

Dear Papa,

It is a long time since I received a letter from you and now I write as you commanded me, for I am extremely anxious to hear from you and am much desiorus to obey your commands. I have but a little ascended into great figures & I have got an extreme kind master, I study greek latin and the maps. I have got my dictionary, and I thank you for it & the 2 guineas, which I receiv'd from Mr. Philpot. I have hear'd that he is broke but I hope you have lost nothing by him. I have now just begun to dance, I assure you I will endeavour to make my self a learned man. Dear Papa I am your most dutiful son.

Charles Carroll

ALS, Carroll Papers, MS 206, MdHi. Endorsed by CCA.

Antony Carroll to CCA

Feb: 26th: 1751

Dr. Sr.,

I recd. yrs of the 6th. of October 1750.[1] I shall take care that Charly applies himself from time to time to the Maps, as you wou'd have it, not so as to hinder his other studies, but amuse him some half hours and quarters, which otherwise wou'd be spent unprofitably. This is no hard matter, for he is naturally curious. All those that converse with him are surpriz'd to see so much good sense in a child of his age; and yet the only Impediment, if any there be, to his advancement in his studies, is that he is giddy. This will perhaps seem odd to you, but it is not my opinion only, his Master is of the same way of thinking. And now that I have

Charles Carroll of Annapolis. By John Wollaston. 1753–1754.
Courtesy the present owner

mention'd his Master, I must tell you that he is remarkable for a bright genius, assiduity Piety, and good humour. In short, had I been the person to chuse a master for Charly, of all the young men I have known, Mr. Jenison[2] shou'd have been postponed to none. Carly is commonly, or rather always in the Six first. I have seldom seen him worse than 5th. which he is at present, but often better. However he cannot be call'd as yet a leader, because there are two or three that certainly out-top him. Tis a justice I must do Charly to inform you that he is in a strong School, which was form'd after the peace was concluded:[3] then Lads much older than he came over from latin Schools, being detain'd by fond Mothers, or for some other reason. I observe that such as outdo him are of this stamp, still there are a good number of 'em behind him. I return you a great many thanks for the kind offer you made me of being his Tutor at La fleche.[4] I find no natural repugnance to it, on the contrary an Inclination[.] I shou'd be glad to live some time in France, but particularly with Charley.

As for my Superior's consent, my private opinion is that there wou'd be no great difficulty in that regard; but my private opinion is [not] to be rely'd on. Tis proper I shou'd tell you that the English young Gentlemen [wh]o studied there lately, exclaim against the College, and say they were abus'd. [I wrot]e to one of ours, who lived there in quality of tutor 4 years, in order to be able [to g]ive you the Informations you desired. I will transcribe his words for your Curiosity.

If the Gentleman intends to have the Child under the Care of one of ours at la Fleche his Expences will amount to little less than £100 sterling per annum, and that with good management too. This was the least Allowance I, and several others had before, and at the same time with me at la Fleche; and we all found there was no living decently under that Sum. Besides this, I was likewise allow'd 15 or 20 lt.[5] for our excursions during the Vacancies. All which we found not too much.

In case the Gentleman shou'd think these expences too great, he may retrench them, by sending his Son without either tutor or Servt, and desire the Principal of the College to place him in a Chamber with two or three other Students there under the care of one of the French Jesuits: for by that means, the hireing and fur-niture of his Chamber, fire, candles, the maintenance of his tutor servant's wages, and several other expences will be equaly divided amongst them.

Lastly he may still provide for him in a cheaper way, by placing him in a com-mon chamber, as they call it: I.E. In a chamber together with 14 or 15 of his Fellow students. What will be the expences for his maintenance in this, or the former case, I can't justly tell, having had no experience that way. All that I can say is, that un-less his Son is very young, he will never be content to be upon either this or that footing.

What I have Say'd of la Flèche, the same may be applied to Paris, with this dif-ference, that upon whatever footing he puts his Son at Paris, the expences will amount to almost as much again, as they wou'd do to provide for him at la Flêche upon the same footing.

Dr. Sr. I am yr. most oblig'd and very afft. Kinsman

Anto: Carroll

ALS, Carroll Papers, MS 206, MdHi. Addressed by the author "For Charles Carroll Esqr," the letter also bears the additional notation "London March 1750/1 Reced & forwarded by Sr. Your humble Servt Willm. Perkins." Endorsed by CCA: "1751 N:S: Feb: 26. Anto: Carroll's [lett]er Relating to [Cha]rly's Character [& A]cct of Expences At La Fleche & Paris."

1. Not found.

2. Unlike other schools in which a master, aided by several assistants, presided over as many as half a dozen classes at once, St. Omers gave a master charge of one class from the time it entered the college until its members had completed their course of study. This system aimed to provide continuity and the development of strong ties between teachers and pupils. CC's master, English Jesuit John Jenison (1729–1792), entered the order in 1745. His relationship with CC was a mutually warm one that continued for nearly a decade after the boy left St. Omers. Described as "a brilliant classical scholar but restless and eccentric," Jenison spent the last years of his life in an asylum at Liège. Muir, *Stonyhurst College*, 28; Foley, ed., *Records*, VII, 399.

3. Probably the treaty of Aix-la-Chapelle, which marked the end of the War of the Austrian Succession in 1748.

4. "La Flèche" — "the spire" — was the familiar name for the Collège Henri IV de la Flèche, located in the town of that name in Sarthe. Founded in 1603, it became a famous Jesuit center of learning. CCA apparently considered enrolling CC there once the boy had completed his studies at St. Omers.

5. The French livre tournois was worth approximately 10d. sterling. John J. McCusker, *Money and Exchange in Europe and America, 1600–1775: A Handbook* (Chapel Hill, N.C., 1978), 97.

CC to CCA

[March 1751] [1]

Dear Papa

I recived a letter from you with a great deal of joy, dated 17th of October, & I recived one from my Mama,[2] by Mr. Warring. He is arived safe to the Colege & I hope he will do very well in his studyes. I am extream glad to hear that you are pleased with me & I assure you I will do all my endeavours that you may continue in the same sentiment. I can easily see the great affection you have for Me by sending me hear to a Colege, where I may not only be a learned man, but also be advanced in piety & devotion. I am now about the middle of great figuers, & I have got the fifth place in my school, among three & twenty boys. As for observing the meddows & pastors & all other things I will do with all cearfulness. I have got an excceding kind master, & we are to have an examen very soon, & I should have writ to you before had I not been employ'd in getting it. Give My kind service & love to my Cousin Charly,[3] all my freinds & relations. I hope you will not blame me for spelling ill for My Cousin Atony blames me very much for it. I am very sorry for Mrs. Hearn's death[4] she was a very pious & good woman. I hope she is happy. Cousin Watty Hoxton[5] & jacky Carroll give their service to you they are very well, & mightily beloved in the house. I am in great haste in getting my examen, & their fore I must conclued. I am your most dutiful Sone

Charles Carroll

ALS, Carroll Papers, MS 206, MdHi. Endorsed by CCA: "1750 [old style] March Charly Carrolls Letter."

1. The editors have rendered the date in new style.

2. Neither letter found.

3. Charles Carroll of Duddington (1729–1772), the only son of CCA's brother Daniel Carroll of Duddington and Ann Rozer Carroll, lived with his paternal grandmother, Mary Darnall Carroll, at her house in Annapolis from the time of his father's death until he left Maryland to attend St. Omers in 1742. When he returned to Maryland in 1748, his grand-mother Carroll had died, but he evidently remained in her Annapolis residence, which ad-joined that of his uncle CCA. As executor and trustee for the estate of his brother, as well as those of their parents, CCA managed the inheritances of his nephew, Charles, and Charles's sisters, Eleanor and Mary. In the late 1750s, Charles challenged CCA's administration of his legacies and contested the accuracy of his uncle's accounts. The difficulties precipitated by the confrontation led to bitter estrangements within the family and public embarrassment for CCA. The matter was finally resolved in 1774 through a settlement with Charles Car-roll of Duddington's widow, Mary Hill Carroll, whom he had married in 1763, in behalf of their three sons, Daniel, Charles, and Henry. See Onorio Razolini to CCA, Nov. 17, 1757, n. 5, below.

4. Probably the wife of Daniel Hearn, whose association with the Carrolls dated from the 1720s and whose name appeared on a 1756 list of Doohoragen Manor tenants. Anne Arundel Co. Deeds, Liber R.B. no. 1, fols. 569–570; CCA, Account Book, fol. 20.

5. CC's first cousin Walter Hoxton (?–1784), the son of Susanna Brooke Smith Hoxton and Hyde Hoxton, attended St. Omers 1748–c. 1754. Holt, *St. Omers*, 139. See Appendix I, Chart E.

CC to CCA

March the 23rd. 1751

Der. Papa,

I imbrace this oportunity to write to you by Mr. Henry Carroll,[1] but since I have but little time on account of the fiction[2] I must be short. Cousin Antony forced

Exercise Book of Charles Carroll. Cover and leaf 48.
Courtesy The Gilder Lehrman Collection on deposit at the
Pierpont Morgan Library, New York. GLC 600

me to write to you. I have very little to tell you onely that I am very wel. I am your most dutiful & obedient Son

Charles Carroll

Mr. Molien[3] desiers to be remember'd to you[.]

ALS, Carroll Papers, MS 206, MdHi. Endorsed by CCA, specifying the letter's date as "N.S." (new style).

1. Although both Carrolls usually refer to Capt. Henry Carroll (1727–1775) as "cousin," precise kinship lines have not been established. Captain Carroll lived in St. Mary's Co. and was master of the ship *Two Sisters* owned by William Perkins. *Bio. Dic. Md. Legis.*, I, 200; Rowland, *Carroll*, I, 65.

2. Probably the composition, one of the three examinations, two of which were written and the other oral, specified by the *Ratio Studiorum*. Muir, *Stonyhurst College*, 28.

3. Edward Molien (1700/1–1761), a native of Calais, entered the Society of Jesus in 1720 and served mainly at St. Omers. Foley, ed., *Records*, VII, 513.

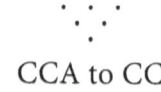

CCA to CC

Octobr 12th 1751.

Dr Charley

I receed yours of Sep 24 1750 March 23 1751. and one wt[hout] a date,[1] Do not forget to date your Lres They were all very w[el]come, and I hope you will continue to write to me at least twice a year. I am glad to find you are sensible of the adva[ntage] of being placed where you are, make good use of it, and as yo[u are] so happy [under][2] a good Master, shew by your deference to hi[m] & perfect respect for his Person that you are thoroughly sens[ible] of the Blessing. I lost nothing by Mr Philpot he is a very honest Man, paid his Debts punctually and is like to get into Trade again with Credit. Your Uncle Henry Brook[3] dye[d] the 10th Inst:[4] after a long sickness. Pray for him. I have wrote to Mr Galloway[5] to let you have two Guineas. I cannot omit always recommending to you a diligent applicatien to your Studies, Piety and due observation of the Rules of the Ho.[6] You are in make a good use of your ti[me] and you may lay in such a Stock of Virtue and Knowled[ge] as will give you more Credit and Comfort than the greates[t] Wealth. To save you sometime you need only direct Your Lres to me at the Top in the inside saying Dr Pap[a] & Mama so one Letter will serve us both I am Dr Charley

most Affec Yrs

Charles Carroll

LS, Carroll Papers, MS 216, MdHi. Addressed in clerk's hand. CC's practice signatures on verso not reproduced.

1. Undated letter not found.

2. This word is crossed out in the manuscript.

3. Henry Brooke (1703/4–1751) was the elder brother of CC's mother, Elizabeth Brooke. See Appendix I, Chart E.

4. The abbreviation "inst:" meaning "instant" designates the present or current month as opposed to "past," "ultimo," or "ult.," which indicate the month immediately preceding.

5. Edward Galloway (1706–1779) was born in London, studied at St. Omers, entered the Society of Jesus in 1724, and was ordained in 1735. His career included a long stint at the College of St. Ignatius in London. (Foley, ed., *Records*, V, 562 n. 43; VII, 285; Holt, *English Jesuits*, 98.) Anonymous handwritten notes on the flyleaf of the Letterbook of the London Procurator for St. Omers indicate that he was "an *agent* in Catholic administration" who acted as "the intermediary responsible for sending English boys to be educated at St. Omers, Bruges, and elsewhere on the continent. He was also a financial agent and bought bonds on behalf of many prominent people."

6. House.

CCA to CC

Octor: 9th. 1752.

Dear Charley

Since mine of the 12th of Octr: 1751. I have had the pleasure of Yors: of May 25th: Augt 26th Febry 22d. 1752.[1] The two first were very much interlined and Blotted, the last was more cor[rect] it is time for yo[u] now in all things to use Reflection Age quod Ages[.][2]

Your first by Mr Lancaster[3] who stayd in England did not reach me until last A[pril.] I am glad you are sensible of the happiness of having So good a Mar:[4] and study to make him to [be] your Friend, and to do so you need but do your Duty, pray present my Service and Complimen[ts.]

I hope you are not in earnest longing to return to Maryland, We should be as glad to see you as [you] would be to see us, but I flatter my Self that you have so much good Sense that if it were in [your] power to come you would chuse to stay to accomplish yourself as much as possible by pur[suing] your studies; what is a man without knowledge? and how is knowledge to be acquired but by [a] long Course of Study. Your Mamma has desired you to send her your Picture in Miniature[;] if there be good Hand in Town and it be agreeable to your Superiors comply wth her Reque[st.] I will make good her promise of reimbursing you.

You have now read Cicero's Epistles and are reading his Orations, & therefore I ho[pe to] find you improve in the Stile of your Letters. That you may be acquaintd [with such?] an Author I have desired Mr Galloway to send You his Life Wrote by Middleton[5] [& I sent?] you the Odyssy which you left behind you, Francis's Translation of Horace,[6] and Dryd[en's] Translation of Virgil[7] they will help you to understand those Authors well and to [enter] into the Spirit of them to aid your Judgment and form a taste in you. I have al[so] desired Mr Galloway to send you two Guineas, as to the Books carry them with [you] when you leave the Colledge, you will read them a few years hence with m[ore] pleasure than at present.

All the Letters I have or shall write to you or concerning you to any o[ne] are carefully entred in a Book so that in case you should be so unfortunate [as to] return not improvd in proportion to the Money Time and Care laid out on you [they] will at least be undeniable Testimonies of my Attention to your Welfare and a cons[tant] Reproach to you for not correspondg on your part to that attention, but to do you Justice from the Accots I have of yo[u] from Cousin Carroll Mr Newton & Mr Wappeler[8] I have no reason to apprehend your doing otherwise than Well, and I pray my Dear Charley make it your constant Study and Endeavour to deserve the contin[uance] of theirs and my Approbation.

I desire my Service to Cousin Jackey Mar: Hoxton and Mar Warrin[g. The] latters Uncle Basil[9] is lately married to Miss Susan Darnall;[10] Watty['s Father][11] &

Mother[12] are well Give my Compliments to Mr: Molien and be assurd that [I] am My Dear Charley

Yor most Affecly
Charles Carroll

LS, Carroll-McTavish Papers, MS 220, MdHi. Address in clerk's hand. Marked "Copy" by CCA. Right margin damaged. Penmanship practice on verso not reproduced.

1. Letters not found.

2. "Keep your mind on what you are doing."

3. Perhaps Capt. John Lancaster, Sr. (?–1760), who lived in St. Mary's Co. and was in 1734 co-owner of the thirty-five-ton schooner *Catherine*. Captain Lancaster's first wife, Elizabeth Neale, and CC's mother were second cousins. "Commission Book, 82," *Md. Hist. Mag.*, XXVI (1931), 141; Christopher Johnston, "Neale Family of Charles County," *Md. Gen.*, II, 258–259.

4. Master.

5. Conyers Middleton (1683–1750), *The History of the Life of Marcus Tullius Cicero* (London, 1741). CC received a three-volume 1750 edition published in London. *Cat. Lib.*, no. 705.

6. P[hilip] Francis (1708?–1773), *A Poetical Translation of the Works of Horace: With the Original Text . . .* (c. 1743). *Cat. Lib.* (no. 1316) lists a four-volume 1750 edition published in London.

7. The Carrolls owned a 1748 London edition of Virgil's *Pastorals and Georgics* translated by John Dryden (1631–1700) and probably part of his translation of *The Works of Virgil: Containing His Pastorals, Georgics, and Aeneis* (London, 1697). *Cat. Lib.*, no. 1111.

8. William Wappeler (1711–1781), a German Jesuit from Westphalia, lived at Newtown, the Roman Catholic mission in St. Mary's Co., from 1742 until 1748, when he returned to Europe. Weis, *Clergy*, 68; Foley, ed., *Records*, VII, 813–814.

9. Basil Waring, Sr. (1711–1793).

10. Susannah Darnall (1723–1806).

11. Hyde Hoxton (1703/4–1753).

12. Susanna Brooke Smith Hoxton (?–1767), CC's mother's sister, married Hyde Hoxton after the death of her first husband, Walter Smith, in 1734. Appendix I, Chart E.

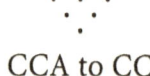

CCA to CC

Octobr: 10th: 1753.

Dr: Charley

I Receed your Several Letters of Augt. 30th. Decemr 20th 1752 & March 6th. 1753.[1] which were all most welcome to me, and althô a hurry of Business prevents my often Writing to you, you may be assured you are always in my thoughts, and that I most earnestly wish your happiness. As you have no such Avocations I desire I may often hear from you. Since you have not a good Dancing Mar: you was in the right to discontinue learning, but when you can meet with a good one you must resume it, for nothing contributes more to give a Gman a graceful and easy Carriage. You may some time hence meet with a good Painter, and then with your Mother I shall be glad to have your Picture in the Compass of 15 Inches by 12. Your opinion of Europe and the People there will be much alte'rd when you return to your Native Country: Fops are the objects of contempt and Ridicule every where, but it is from the fine Gentleman you are to take example. Dr: Child I long to see you, but I did not send you so far only to learn a little Greek and Latin, where you are you can only lay a foundation for other Studies which may hereafter be profitable to your Self and useful to Your Friends. When you have gone thro them, the rest of your Life will be a continued Scene of ease and Satisfaction, if you keep invariably in the Paths of Truth of Virtue. The Husbandman Annually repeats the Toil of Drying Plowing and Sowing for his Harvest. When you have compleated higher Studies Your Toil will be over, and Your Harvest will Daily and always come in, I am very glad to see you are so sensible of the Advantage of a Virtuous Education and that yo[u] are resolvd to make the best use of it. Mr Wappeler informs me you are third in your School which gives me great Pleasure and as your Judgment unfolds it self and ripens I expect to hear of your still Rising. Aut Cæsar aut Nullus.[2] The Ambition to excell in Virtue and Learning is laudable.

I do not doubt in Time to bring Dor Carroll[3] to Justice,[4] We are still threatned by our Assembly but I hope by the interposition of Our Friends in London it will not be in their Power to hurt us a continual Calm in Life is no more to be expected than on the Ocean.

Pray present my humble Service to Yor Mar: whose care of and kindness towards You deserve greater acknowledgments from me than I have in my Power to repay, I am under the same obligation to Mr Wappeler and Newton which pray let them know with my humble Service & Complimts: to them. I desire also my Compliments to Mr Falkner[5] and am very glad to hear he is contented in his Station, if you please he may be of Service to You in Arithmetic. Jacky I suppose is gone up the Hill,[6] remember me to Watty, Mr Warring and all the Marylandians. Your Mamma, Grand Mamma,[7] Aunt Jenny[8] and all your Friends in general are well, I hope the Books got safe to you and that Cicero's Life has in particular given you Pleasure.

You entred into the 17th Year of your Age the 19th of last Month being born the 8th of Septemr 1737. old Stile. Your Judgment therefore will enable you to enter into the Reason of the Rules and Lessons you are learning, Children learn like Parrots, Memory and Practice Aid them chiefly, but Men of Sense do not content themselves with knowing a thing but make themselves thoroughly acquainted with the Reasons on which their knowledge is founded. I beg you will carefully observe this in your present and future Studies, Memory may fail you, but when an impression is made by Reason it will last as long [as] You retain your Understanding.

I cannot wish to hear a better Accot of you than what I have from Messrs: Carroll, Wappeler and Newton, and I doubt not you will Daily merit it more & more; if you do so it will afford me the greatest Comfort and Satisfaction and increase the Love I have for You[.] I am Dr: Charley

most Affectly: Yors:

Cha: Carroll

LS, Carroll-Harper Papers, MS 1225, MdHi. Addressed by the clerk to CC "At Blandike."

1. Letters not found.

2. "Caesar or nobody."

3. Dr. Charles Carroll (1691–1755). Although their familial relationship is nowhere precisely specified, Dr. Carroll and CCA descended from closely related branches of the Irish O'Carrolls and referred to themselves as kinsmen. The son of Charles Carroll of County Offaly and Clare Dunn Carroll, Dr. Carroll studied medicine in Great Britain and emigrated to Maryland as a Roman Catholic in 1715. He settled in Annapolis and within a few years gave up doctoring for a varied career as a merchant, land speculator, shipbuilder, and planter. In 1731 he joined with CCA, Daniel Carroll of Duddington, Daniel Dulany, Sr., and Benjamin Tasker, Sr., in founding an ironworks, the Baltimore Company. By the late 1730s the doctor had forsaken his Catholicism and conformed to the Anglican Church, thereby making himself eligible to vote and to stand for public office. In 1738 he gained a seat in the lower house, where he became a vociferous proponent of anti-Catholic measures. He remained a member of the lower house until his death. Married twice, first to Dorothy Blake, daughter of Charles Blake and Henrietta Maria Lloyd Blake of Talbot Co., and second, probably to Ann Plater, daughter of George Plater and Ann Burford Doyne Plater of St. Mary's Co., Dr. Carroll fathered two sons, Charles Carroll, Barrister, and John Henry Carroll, and a daughter, Mary Clare Carroll Maccubbin. *Bio. Dic. Md. Legis.*, I, 193–194; Appendix I, Chart K; for Dr. Carroll's Irish background, see Brice McAdoo Clagett, "Butler Blood in Maryland Families through Dr. Charles Carroll," *Butler Journal: The Journal of the Butler Society*, III (1991), 352–362.

4. CCA is referring to his dispute with Dr. Carroll over the will of their kinsman James Carroll of Anne Arundel Co., of which they were co-executors. At issue was the residue of the funds James had left to be invested for the purpose of financing the education of several of his nephews. The sums involved were considerable — for Antony Carroll, his designated heir, alone, James had set aside one thousand pounds sterling. By 1750 all the legatees were of age and had completed their studies, and CCA, probably at Antony's request, called upon Dr. Carroll to return to them the balances from their uncle's bequests. Responding in a manner that tacitly acknowledged he had appropriated some of the money for his own use, Dr. Carroll offered to pay approximately half the amount due, maintaining that to do more would place a hardship on his family.

When CCA adamantly refused to accept anything less than payment in full and continued to press the claim vigorously, the doctor asserted that he was not obliged to restore the funds because the English penal statutes denied priests the right of inheritance. The claims of Antony and his cousins, all of whom were Jesuits, were therefore illegal. Underscoring the anti-Catholic threat implicit in this argument, the lower house's Committee on Aggrievances and Courts of Justice — of which Dr. Carroll was a member — issued a report on May 23, 1751, warning of a dangerous growth of popery in Maryland and recommending measures to curb "this spreading Evil."

The following day, an infuriated CCA posted a notice on the door of the lower house attacking Dr. Carroll and, in the view of the legislators, casting "scandalous and malicious Reflections upon the Proceedings of this House." Registering its profound disapproval of this action by a "powerful and leading Roman Catholic," the delegates ordered CCA taken into custody and confined until he made an acceptable apology to them and warned the governor of the alarming increase in Catholic influence. Encouraged by these developments, Dr. Carroll steadfastly refused to settle James's estate and continued to keep the Catholic issue before the lower house. Bills to limit the growth of popery were introduced annually between 1751 and 1753, and the committee on aggrievances presented two more reports on the subject. *Arch. of Md.,* XLVI, 550, 569, 572–573, 582–583, 593–594, 598, L, 41, 51–59, 198–205, 210, 249–250; James Carroll, will, 1729, Anne Arundel Co. Original Wills, Box C, folder 102; [George Hunter], "A short acct of ye state & condition of ye Roman Cath: in ye Province of Maryland . . . ," and [Hunter], "A short Account of ye proceedings of ye Assembly of Maryland in regard to ye Rom: Catholicks settled there . . . ," Special Collections Division, DGU.

5. Ralph Falkner (1736–?), son of Ralph Falkner of Charles Co., attended St. Omers from 1751 to 1755 and then went on to the English Jesuit College in Rome, eventually becoming a priest in the English mission. Edwin Warfield Beitzell, *The Jesuit Missions of St. Mary's County, Maryland,* 2d ed. rev. (Abell, Md., 1976), 316; Holt, *St. Omers,* 97.

6. "Up the Hill," refers to John Carroll's entering the Jesuit novitiate at Watten, seven miles from St. Omers, in 1753. Durkin and Melville, "Catholicism and the Carrolls," in Van Devanter, *"Anywhere,"* 86.

7. CC's maternal grandmother, Jane Sewall Brooke (1680–1761), was the daughter of Maj. Nicholas Sewall, stepson of Charles Calvert, third Lord Baltimore, and Susanna Burgess Sewall. In addition to CC's mother, Jane and her husband, Clement Brooke, Sr., were the parents of two other daughters and six sons. See Appendix I, Charts E and H.

8. No woman with a name for which Jenny seems a likely diminutive can be found in the Carroll, Brooke, or Sewall genealogies. References in the family correspondence to Aunt Jenny, who died unmarried in 1760, suggest that she was either a sister or maternal aunt of Elizabeth Brooke.

. . . .
. .

John Jenison to CCA

[November 1753][1]

Tho' I am not in a disposition of Writing Letters, having lost this morning the finest young man, in every respect, that ever enter'd the House, you will, perhaps, afterwards, have the pleasure of assuring yourself by experience that I've not exaggerated Charles Carroll's character in the foregoing lines. The Captain[2] will be able to give you, I hope, a satisfactory account of him. 'Tis very natural I should regret the loss of one who during the whole time he was under my care, never deserv'd, on any account, a single harsh word, and whose sweet temper rendered him equally agreeable both to equals and superiors, without ever making him degenerate into the mean character of a favorite which he always justly despis'd. His application to his Book and Devotions was constant and unchangeable, nor could we perceive the least difference in his conduct even after having read the news of his destination, which, you know, is very usual with young people here. This short character I owe to his deserts; — prejudice, I am convinc'd, has no share in it, as I find the public voice confirms my private sentiments. Both inclination and justice prompt me to say more, yet I rather chuse to leave the rest to Captain Carroll to inform you of by word of mouth.

Reprinted from "Autobiographic Sketch of Charles Carroll of Carrollton," in Brantz Mayer, *Journal of Charles Carroll of Carrollton during His Visit to Canada in 1776, as One of the Commissioners from Congress, with a Memoir and Notes* (Baltimore, 1876), 107–108. Mayer prefaces the document with the following note: "Another interesting biographical scrap in my collection, is contained in an envelope endorsed by Mr. Carroll's father: 'A Character of my Son: By Mr. Jenison his Master;' beneath which the modest son has written: 'I fear this letter was dictated by Mr. Jenison's partiality to me. I never found till this day (27th July, 1782) that he ever wrote to my Father about me.'"

1. Its contents suggest that John Jenison's letter was written just as CC departed from St. Omers for the Jesuit College at Rheims in late 1753.

2. Capt. Henry Carroll.

· · ·
·

Elizabeth Brooke to CC

Sepr. 30. 1754.

[Dr Ch]arly,

I have not recd. a Letter from you Since I wrote to you last, which was about this time twelve Month yr Papa has recd. two from you Since,[1] which gave us the greatest pleasure. I suppose you will be at Rimes[2] when this reaches you, let me know how yr Place agrees with you & how you like it I still insist on having yr Picture & imagine you wonte meet with any difficulty in geting it drawn where you are[.] Yr Papas love for you is so great & he is so well pleas[e]d with yr diligence improvement & good dispositions [that h]e is inclined to do every thing for yr Satisfaction [& a]dvantage & we have reason to believe that you'll [cont]inue to deserve our tenderness & care which gives [us] the greatest Comfort imaginable. Yr grand Mama Aunt Jenny & all other Friends are well & desire to be kindly Remember'd to you. I desire my Dear that you will be particular in writing to me, tel me yr Hight & whether you take care of yr Teeth as I requested of you some time ago, in Short any thing from you will be agreable. I am impatient to see you

& hope my Dear Charly as you do that a few Years more will bring us together. I have my Health I thank God very well & so has yr Papa, which I know will be agreable to you to hear. I pray God protect you. I am My Dr Child

Yrs Affecly.
Eliza. Brooke

ALS, Colonial Collection, MS 2018, MdHi. Addressed. Left margin damaged. CC's hand-writing practice not reproduced.

1. Not found.

2. The College of the French Jesuits at Reims apparently held its students to an even stricter schedule than St. Omers, with no afternoons off, formal instruction on Saturdays, and study periods on Sundays in addition to attendance at religious services. Walks or trips into town required the accompaniment of a prefect as chaperone — CC's chaperone and tutor may have been his cousin Antony Carroll who was studying theology at Reims in 1755. Boarding students paid four hundred livres tournois a year for housing and meals but were required to provide furnishings for their quarters. Those who employed servants or private tutors paid another five hundred livres tournois. The curriculum included geography, chronology, heraldry, religious and secular history, and various electives such as music, drawing, dancing, and writing. The school year ran from mid-fall to late summer and included a month's vacation. Pierre Delattre, ed., *Les établissements des Jésuites en France depuis quatre siècles: Répertoire topo-bibliographique* . . . (Enghien, 1949–1957), IV, 303–307; Holt, *English Jesuits*, 52.

CCA to CC

Septemr 30th. 1754.

Dr: Charly

I have this Year recieivd two Letters from You, one Dated Febry 13th 1754 the other without a Date,[1] but by the Contents I find it was Wrote before the oth[er] as in this you say you do not like Poetry nor Succeed in it as well as in your other Studies; But by yours of the 13th Febry I was well pleas'd to hear that as you entred into the beauties of it you liked it better and better and that you had [in] some Measure Surmounted it's difficulties with wch: You were at 1st: al[most] dismayed, let your success in this hereafter Animate you resolutely to pursue all your undertakings for you may be assured Resolution, diligen[ce] and a Genius will conquer almost impossibilities.

This will find you at Rheims where I hope you are well pleasd. As you will there enter upon a New stage and enjoy a greater degree of Liberty than you have hitherto had, I trust you will use it with that discretion that it may not be hurtful to your Self but that your Conduct may be instructive and edifying to your School-fellows whose Friendship and good Will I think you will study to deserve by a

Elizabeth Brooke Carroll. By John Wollaston. 1753–1754.
Founders Society Purchase, Mr. and Mrs. Walter Buhl Ford, II Fund. By permission
The Detroit Institute of Arts. Photograph The Detroit Institute of Arts

Polite behaviour[,] doing them all the little Services and good Offices in [your] power, studying carefully to avoid giving Offence to any of them, but suffer [not] an easiness of Nature or Complaisance to lead you with any of them into any Action inconsistent with probity, Honour, your Duty to God and your Superiors whose Friendship and good Will I am certain you will study to deserve. Sight with our other Senses is bestow'd on us by Providence for Our Benefit and happiness, but it mus[t] be kept under the Dominion of Reason, you must View every thing worth

Notice carefully and with Attention, especially the behaviour of all about you, what may become a Man in One Country may be very ridiculous in another, before you Act, observe the Actions of others none but brainless thoughtless People do otherwise, when you Copy the conduct, behaviou[r] and Air of those about you you will not incur Derision, but be not so Servile an Im[itator] as to let it be seen you Copy, but let your Actions be your Own, Natural, and Set easy o[n] you. You will now and hereafter have a Variety of Models on which to form your [beha]viour before your Eyes and I doubt not your good Sense will determine you only to imitate the fine Gentleman. I should swell this much beyond the Bulk of a Letter were I to expatiate on the many heads proper for you to be instructed in and to receive Advice on, but it gives me great pleasure that you are so exceedingly fortunate as to have your Cous[in] Antony with you who can so much better serve you, Cherish and be thankful for the blessin[g] and to shew that you are so: behave always with all possible respect towards him nev[er be] on the reserve with him or backward in Asking his Advice in every thing thô to you seemingly insignificant, look always upon him as your Friend and not as your Tutor, and so you will Daily more and more endear your Self to him and reap all the Advantages I propose you should by his instructions.

As I suppose you will at Rheims meet with a good Fencing and Dancing-Master, I desire you will apply your Self to those Exercises seriously, they both contribute greatly to a graceful Carriage. A Gentleman should know how to appear in an Assembly [&] Public to Advantage, and to defend himself if attacked, Continue to learn these [Ex]ercises to the end of Philosophy.

Your Mother is very desirous of having your Picture, and I hope you will gratify her if you can find a good Limner,[2] let the Sise of the Picture be about 15 Inches long and 10 Inches Wide.

You had good hair when a Child, if it continues so pray wear it, it will become you better than a Wig and beside you will be more in the fashion.

Your Mother sometime past prudently recommended it to you to take particular Care of your Teeth, I desire you will observe her recommendation, for want of such Care when I was young I have loss Several of my Teeth by the Scurvy in my Gums and have now others very loose, Wash your Mouth often with fair Water [e]specially after each Meal. Your Mother also desires an exact Accot of yr. height, [as] do I. You have not begun your Letters Dr. Papa & Mama, as I formerly [dir]ected, nor Wrote to your Mother this Year; Althô She is not, She has reason to be displeased. I attribute it to inattention, but for the future be more Considerate.

I hope you give some time to Geography and Arithmetic, would it not be very odd for a man to know Greek and Latin and not be able to describe the Position of any Noted place or Kingdom, or to Add, Multiply, or Divide a Sum.

I presume you have all the Letters I have Wrote to you by you, it may not be improper now and then to overlook them; I never Wrote to you as a Child, & [there]fore you may reap some advantage from a serious perusal of them. My Dear child I wish you Health, Success in your Studies and a Daily increase of Gods Grace [&] Blessings bestow'd on you and I am Dr Charly

most affety Yors
Cha: Carroll

LS, Carroll-McTavish Papers, MS 220, MdHi. Addressed by the clerk. Margins damaged.
1. Not found.
2. One who draws or paints.

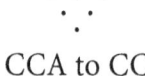

CCA to CC

July 26th. 1756.

Dr: Charly.

I have reced the 3 following Letters from you, Decemr: 14th. 1755. One without a Date Wrote as I suppose about the 10 of last Jany and the last Dated Feby 27th. 1756.[1] You may be assured they were all very welcome to me and yor Mama[.] I suppose you may buy Lock[2] and Newton[3] in Paris, if not, desire your Cousin Anthony to Write to Mr. Perkins[4] to send them to you or any other Books you may want: As War is declared,[5] I know not how you will get these Books, the Carriage thro' Holland will amount to more than the 1st Cost, if they could be sent to Rouen they would by the Sein reach you at little expence.

Thô we are threatned with the introduction of the English Penal Laws into this Province, they are not yet introduced, But last May a Law pass'd here to double Tax the Lands of all the Rom Caths.[6]

I Wrote to you the 16th of last Septr. and therein inclosd one from your Mama,[7] as yo[u] do not acknowledge the Receipt of the above letter I suppose yor Mamas Letter miscarried with it.

I am glad to hear you enjoy your health at Paris[8]—I sent your Letter to yor Cousin Walter Hoxton[.]

There was no final Decree against Dor: Carroll, as he died before the Case was ripe for a Trial, but I hope his Son[9] will be oblig'd in time to pay what his Father justly owed[.]

All your Letters give me reason to hope my Scheme[10] will succeed, I have wrote fully to Cousn Anthony to whom I refer you on this Head as I refer him to you for what follows.

You desire to know the Origin of Our American War, and the Events that have happened in the Course of it, I will endeavour to satisfy you in as clear and concise a manner as I can.

If the priority of Discovery was only to give a Title to Lands in America, the King of Spain alone would be entitled to all America, as neither ffrance or England would agree to such a Claim, each of them must found their Title to their several Dominions here, on possession[.]

The uncontested Possessions of the English seem to be from Kenebeki River, Southward to the River Savanna which is the Northern boundary of our new Colony of Georgia.

The Possessions of the French before the Treaty of Utrecht[11] were from the Kenebe[ki] to the Northward to include Acadie Isle Royal,[12] All Nova Scotia, New France or Cana[da] and Louisiana.

The 1st. Settlements of both Nations were upon the Shores of the Seas & Rivers that wash their several Territories.

As their Colonies increased the French extended their Settlements to the Eastward, the English theirs to the Westward.

The Settlements under the different Nations now approaching to each other, the Question is how far the English shall extend theirs to the Westward and the French theirs to the Eastward.

The English in many or most of their Grants extend the Western bounds of their Colonies to the South Sea, but maybe not with much Justice or Reason, for by this pretension they would not only swallow up all the ffrench Settlements on the Missisippi but new Mexico, which the Spaniards will hardly, consent to.

Nature seems to have pointed out other Boundaries to the two Nations which perhaps in the next Treaty of peace they may establish.

The ffrench are setled in St Lawrence and the Missisippi, I suppose claim all the Lands Watered by the several Rivers and Streams falling into the said Rivers[.]

The English by a parity of Reason may as justly claim all the Lands Laying on the several Rivers and Streams emptying themselves into the Atlantic Ocean[.]

This division of the Waters is made by the Apalathean Mountains which take their rise in the point of Florida and extend thence to the Northward inclining more or less to the Eastward and this Chain of Mountains as I said before may perhaps be hereafter agreed on as the common Boundary between the contending Powers.

The dispute about their Possessions to the Northward is of a more intricate Nature[.] The French were certainly the 1st. Setlers not only of Canada, but of Nova Scotia & Acadie which they contend to be two distinct Provinces.

The English on the contrary, contend that Nova Scotia includes all Accadie.

The Priority of the ffrench Possession of the aforesd Countries, I believe is undisputed and thô they were formerly disturbed in their possession of Nova Scotia, under which name I include Accadie, yet by Treaties Nova Scotia was always restored to them except by the Treaty of Utrecht[.]

By the Treaty of Utrecht, the French Ceded all Nova Scotia to England.

The Dispute at present between the two Nations is about the Bounds of Nova Scotia which the ffrench pretend to establish in such a Manner as to leave Out a great part of that Province to themselves under the Names of Accadie & Gaspesie.

As far as I have read, the English by the Treaty of Utrecht seem to have a Right to all Nova Scotia and Accadie. But as Princes and States, seldom think themselves bound by Treaties which unsuccesful Wars or a bad State of their Affairs force them to enter into, I imagine that France seeing the importance of Nova Scotia and Accadie not only to their Trade and Navigation but to their Colony of Canada are now endeavouring to avail themselves of a favourable time and Season to recover by Force Nova Scotia and Accadie which only Force and Necessity wrested from them.

Accordingly ever since the Treaty of Aix la Chapil, the French have been encroaching on the English in Nova Scotia they made some Settlement at St Johns River in the Bay of Fundy or as the French call it Baye Francoise, they erected Forts on the Peninsula between Baye Verte and Beaubason: The English last Summer took these places from the ffrench by Forces sent from New England with little loss and have recovered all the ffrench Neutrals in Nova Scotia some say to the Number of 12 or 15000 Souls to their different Colonies on the Continent where they have been treated with more or less Humanity. It has been the misfortune of 900 & odd of these poor People to be sent to Maryland,[13] where they have been intirely supported by privat Charity and the little they can get by their labour which for want of employment has been but a poor resource to them. Many of them would have met with very humane Treatment from the Rom: Caths here, but a real or pretended Jealousy inclined this Governmt: not to suffer them to live with Rom Caths, I offerd the Governr to take and support two Families consisting of 14 Souls, but was not permitted to do it.

The Case of these poor unhappy People is so hard that I wonder it has not been taken notice of by some of Our Political Writers in England.

They since the Treaty of Utrecht have been permitted to enjoy their Property and Possessions upon taking an Oath of Allegiance to the King of England: This Oath they say they have never Violated, the truth whereof seems to be confirmd by the Capitulation of the Forts at Beaubason by an Article whereof the Neutrals taken in those Forts were pardoned as being forced by the French under the pain of Military Execution to take up Arms — However their Fidelity was suspected and they have been Sacrificed to the security of Our Settlements in that part of the World. They have neither been treated as Subjects or Enemies, as Subjects they were intitled to the Benefit of our laws and ought to have been tried and found Guilty before they could be punished and to punish them all, All ought to have been tried and convicted. If they are deemed Enemies they ought to be treated as such and Maintaind as Prisoners of War but [no] Care has been taken here in that respect. These People for their Numbers were perhaps the most happy of any on the Globe, They manufactured all they wore and their Manufactures were good, they raisd in great plenty the Provisions they consumed, their Habitations were warm & comfortable, they were all upon a Level being all Husbandmen & consequently as void of Ambition as Human Nature can be, They appear to be very regular and

Religious and that from Principle and a perfect knowledge of their Duty wch convinces me that they were blessed with excellent Pastors.[14] But alas how is their Case altered! They were at once strippd of every thing but the Cloaths on their Backs, many have Died in consequence of their Sufferings, and the Survivors see no other prospect before them but Want and Misery.

Our 1st. Hostilities on the Ohio began in 1754. The Virginians attempted to build a Fort there which the French prevented, and Constructed one themselves called Fort Du Quisne. It was upon his March to this ffort that General Braddock was last year defeated and killed[.][15] The Victory was as compleat as could be, We lost at least 800 in the Field, the greatest part of our Train and Magazines fell into the Enemies hands, the rest was destroy'd to facilitate Our Retreat. What adds to Our Shame is that We sufferd this disgrace from between three and five hundred Indians. This information I had from an Officer of distinction, who I believe knew what he said to be fact and on whose Honr: and Veracity I have reason to rely. I hope for the Honr of the ffrench Nation that Indians only were concernd in this Action for the Wounded were all massacred, an inhumanity which I am confident French Officers or Soldiers would not be guilty of.

The next Action of Consequence was between the Troops under the command of the Generals Dieskau and Johnson near the Lake of the Sacrament,[16] the loss of Men on either side was very inconsiderable, I believe we lost most about 300. We were prevented from attacking Fort St Frederic, as were the ffrench from destroying General Shirleys Army at Oswego on Lake Ontario[17] by cutting off the communication between Albany and that Place. In Case Dieskau (who is still at New York and likely to live) had been Victorious Shirley must have surrendred himself and his Army and Oswego probably without striking a Stroke, Albany must also have surrendred, and New York perhaps might have been destroy'd which will give you a proper Idea of the importance of the lucky Stand made by General Johnson whose Service has been honourably and bountifully rewarded by his Maty.[18]

Since that Action both Nations seem to Act on a defensive Plan except that the ffrench by Parties have now and then surprized small Convoys of Provisions &c going to Oswego: Our Naval Force on Lake Ontario according to Our Gazettes consists of seven Armed Snows Brigantines, Sloops and schooners Carrying 22 = 6 pounders 52 = 4lb. pounders, & Eight Swivels and upwards of 230 Whale Boats Carrying each 10 Men. I know not what Vessels the French have here to oppose us[,] Their not attacking Oswego last Winter seems to point out their Weakness. This is all I know of the Events of the War to the Northward to this time except several Murthers committed by their Savages. From New York Southward since Braddocks defeat, the French have only attacked us by their Indians, who have and still continue to commit the most Shocking Barbarities on our Back Setlers in Pensilvania Maryland and Virginia, But I find these Our Sufferings are Vastly magnified in the English Papers[.] I do not believe these Provinces have lost to this time killd & [captured] 300 Souls two hundred in Pensilvania about 25 in Maryland, the rest in Virginia. The remotest of my Lands have not Suffered, and I think my Self and your Mama to be in no more danger than you are at Paris Maryland being in a great measure Screend by the more advancd Settlements of Pensilvania and Virginia. The Indians act as Wolves in small Parties and by surprize, and it is no wonder that the British Subjects intirely undisciplind should hitherto have Suffered, But Daily precautions are taking for Our security by erecting Lines of Forts on all our Frontier which will not only protect us but intercept the Savages on their retreat which they constantly make as soon as they have done any Damage. As We vastly exceed on this Continent the French in Numbers, and as they will force us into Discipline as the necessity of the thing will Oblige all our Colonies to a strict Union, and to Act in Concert,[19] as by our Superiority at Sea we shall often intercept the French Supplies and receive Our own hardly without a Risque, We doubt not but the Events of the War will be much in our favour.

Hitherto the Campain has not been opened by any Action, the Bulk of our Forces is assembled at and between Albany and the Lake of the Sacrament and the Provincial Forces exclusive of the Regulars are said to amount to 7000 Men; The French fforces at Fort St: Frederic We say amount to 3000 Besides the Regulars Shipt from England this Spring W[e] have 6 Regiments beside the Royal American Regiment to be raised and to consist of 4000, and its said 3 or 4 Regiments More are expected from Britain Lord Loudon who is to command in Chief[20] is hourly expected if not arriv'd. In appearance all these Forces will march against Fort St. Frederic and some of the ffrench Forts on Ontario or Erie Lakes[.]

We have lately taken a French 54 Gun Ship and a Store Ship of 400 Tons & 80 Men laden with Ammunition &c both bound for Louisburgh. The 1st. was taken by the Norwich of 50 Guns and another of 60 Guns. 11 more which had been in Company may fall into our hands as We have 13 Ships of War Cruising off of Louisburgh[.]

These Accots I give you to satisfy your Curiosity not to display my own Judgment for I never sat up as a Politician, but I have represented things as I conceive them, I maybe misinformd for every day brings new and contradictory Accots.

My Plantation where you lived[21] has been greatly improved by Beautiful Meadows, a fine Orchard of the choicest Fruits of all sorts, a very pretty Garden well Walled in &c &c. so as to make it as pleasant an inland Seat as any in Maryland but that and all my other possessions I am determined to Quit if I can meet with the Success I expect from my Scheme. I shall remove from a Setled and a well improvd Estate and in the Sale of which I expect to lose to the value of at least £10,000 Sterlg. But to procure Ease to my Self by flying from the pursuits of Envy and Malice and to procure a good establishment for You I am willing to undergo and struggle with all the difficulties and inconveniences attending on a new Settlement in a new Climate[.] There is but one Man in the Province whose Fortune equals mine.[22] Judge from this of the Love I bear you, but at the sametime be perswaded that my Affection towards you is greatly increased by the most agreeable Accots I receive of your

Pious, Prudent and Regular behaviour, of your sweet temper and disposition and of the proficiency and Figure you make in your Studies which gives me the strongest Reason to hope that you will in the Course of your Life no less distinguish your Self among men than you have hitherto done among your School fellows. Initium Sapientiæ timor Domini.[23] Always remember this and you will not only infallably secure happiness here and hereafter to your Self but you will be the Comfort of Yor Parents in their declining Years who are with the most tender affect Dr Charley

Yrs &c

Cha: Carroll

PS:

Your Mother is very well and gives her Love and Blessing to you[.]

LS, Carroll-McTavish Papers, MS 220, MdHi. Addressed by CCA: "A Monsr Monsr Crookshanks a l'Hotel de St: Louis Rue St: Antoine A Paris Pour faire tenir a Monsr: Cha: Carroll." Two other LS copies are filed with it, one bearing the same address and marked "Triplicate" by CCA, and the other marked "Copy" by CCA with no address.

1. Letters not found.

2. *Cat. Lib.,* no. 631, lists only one edition by John Locke (1632–1704) with a pre-1756 publication date — a three-volume set of *The Works of John Locke* published in London in 1727.

3. Sir Isaac Newton (1640–1727).

4. London merchant and shipowner who became CCA's cashier and special agent in the 1750s.

5. The hostilities that broke out in Europe between Great Britain and France in June 1756 extended the conflict between them over territory in North America that, as explained by CCA in this letter, began in 1754–1755. Known as the French and Indian War in the colonies and as the Seven Years' War abroad, the continental portion of the struggle pitted France and its allies — Austria, Sweden, a number of small German states, and Spain — against Prussia and Britain, with the sporadic involvement of Russia, which changed sides several times. The scope of the fighting was global: Britain and France engaged in naval battles in the Atlantic, the Caribbean, the Mediterranean, and the Indian Ocean and in land warfare in India as well as in Europe and North America. The outcome of the Seven Years' War reconfigured the colonial empires of the two principal adversaries. Emerging victorious, Great Britain gained through the Treaty of Paris (1763) most of France's holdings in India and the vast majority of its North American possessions — Canada, Cape Breton Island, and all of Louisiana east of the Mississippi River except New Orleans. Retaining only a few islands off Newfoundland and in the Caribbean, France also relinquished its claims to lands west of the Mississippi to Spain as compensation for that nation's loss of Florida to Britain. Although unforeseen in 1763, the most far-reaching consequence of the Seven Years' War lay in the policies Great Britain adopted to cover the cost of administering the additional expanse of North American territory it had acquired. These measures, begining with the Stamp Act in 1765, placed Britain's thirteen mainland colonies on the road to revolution.

6. By this time the animosity between Protestants and Roman Catholics had been an unpleasant characteristic of provincial life in Maryland for nearly a century. Despite the fact that the Glorious Revolution of 1688 and the subsequent establishment of the Protestant

succession to the British throne gave Maryland Protestants the political hegemony they had long sought, they never rested easily in their triumph. Even the exclusion of Roman Catholics from the political life of the colony after 1718 through the combined efforts of Gov. John Hart and the lower house of the assembly was not enough to allay the distrust and suspicion of the Protestant power structure, and anti-Catholic legislation appeared more or less routinely on the agenda of the lower house in succeeding years. During the 1740s and 1750s, as the possibility of open conflict with the Catholic French and their Indian allies intensified, the lower house was increasingly preoccupied with bills to "Prevent the Growth of Popery," and the perennial threat of invoking the penal laws—statutes first enacted during the reign of Elizabeth I that were aimed at punishing Catholic recusants—was resurrected. The double tax on Roman Catholic lands, long a familiar device of persecution to English Catholics, was a provision of a bill passed in May 1756, during a time of bitter wrangling between the upper and lower houses of the Maryland assembly over finances. French and Indian pressure on the frontier finally goaded the recalcitrant lower house into passing an act providing forty thousand pounds currency for defense, of which the double tax on Catholic landholders was a part. *Arch. of Md.*, L, LII; Charles A. Barker, *The Background of the Revolution in Maryland* (New Haven, Conn., 1940), 207–209, 240–242.

7. Not found.

8. CC entered the College of Louis le Grand at Paris in 1755. Located across from the Sorbonne and founded by French Jesuits in 1563 as the College of Clermont, the institution was renamed Louis le Grand in 1682 when it came under the protection of Louis XIV. One of the two best known Jesuit boarding schools in eighteenth-century France—the other being la Flèche—Louis le Grand accepted scholarship students, many of them from Ireland, as well as the sons of rich families. Although the school purported to treat all its students equally on the basis of ability rather than wealth, those on scholarships shared rooms with from three to fifteen others, wore distinctive dress, sometimes waited tables and swept courtyards, and were fed a different menu than their affluent classmates who, like CC, enjoyed private rooms, a more substantial and elegant cuisine, and the services of tutors, prefects, and valets. CC's lifestyle at Louis le Grand closely resembled that of students of means at la Flèche as described by his cousin Antony Carroll to CCA, Feb. 26, 1751, above. Delattre, *Les éstablissements des Jésuites*, III, 1232–1242.

9. Charles Carroll, Barrister (1723–1783), elder son of Dr. Charles Carroll and Dorothy Blake Carroll, was born in Annapolis and educated at the English school in Lisbon, Portugal, at Eton and Cambridge, and at the Middle Temple, one of the four Inns of Court, the legal societies that have the exclusive right to admit candidates to the practice of law in England. Despite his appellation, he never practiced law but concentrated instead on mercantile activities and various other business interests, including planting, flour milling, and the Baltimore Company. An Anglican like his father but without the doctor's religious prejudices, he sat in the lower house (1756–1761) and by the Revolutionary period had become a friend and political ally of his Catholic Carroll kinsmen. A member of all of the nine conventions that composed Maryland's provisional government (1774–1776) and of the first four councils of safety, the Barrister was also a delegate to the Continental Congress (1776–1777). Elected to the Maryland Senate from the Western Shore in 1777, he served there continually until his death. He married Margaret Tilghman, a daughter of Matthew Tilghman and Anne Lloyd Tilghman of Rich Neck, Queen Anne's Co., in 1763, and they re-

sided both in Annapolis and at Mount Clare, their country estate outside of Baltimore. His own children dying in infancy, the Barrister made his nephews Nicholas and James Maccubbin his principal legatees on condition that they legally adopt his surname, a proviso they fulfilled by act of assembly in 1783. It is not known whether the Barrister ever repaid his father's debt to James Carroll's heirs. *Bio. Dic. Md. Legis.*, I, 195–197, 200–202, 826. See Appendix I, Charts H and K.

10. The "scheme" was CCA's response to the increasing pressure placed on Catholics by the hostile actions of the lower house of the Maryland assembly during the 1750s. Determined to quit the province for a more hospitable locale, the elder Carroll initiated a series of secret negotiations with French officials through whom he hoped to acquire an estate in their colony of Louisiana that would be comparable to his Maryland holdings. Although CCA kept the particulars of those transactions from becoming generally known, he left little doubt that he was going somewhere. The May 27, 1756, issue of the *Md. Gaz.* carried his announcement that he intended to collect his debts and speedily "wind up his Affairs." In March of the following year, he placed a second notice in the same paper warning debtors "who have not yet settled with the Suscriber" that any accounts still outstanding in August 1758, when he returned from a trip to England, would immediately be placed in suit. Then, just before he embarked on that journey in June 1757, CCA prepared a longer advertisement for insertion in the *Pa. Gaz.* stating that he intended "to dispose of his Estate, both real and personal," giving a detailed description of his extensive lands and the improvements he had made upon them, and inviting interested persons to call on him at his house in Annapolis between May 1 and Aug. 31, 1758. *Pa. Gaz.*, July 21, 1757.

11. By the Treaty of Utrecht (1713), which ended Queen Anne's War, France ceded Acadia (Nova Scotia), Hudson Bay, and Newfoundland to Great Britain.

12. Cape Breton Island.

13. Four shiploads of Acadians had arrived in Annapolis by the first week of December 1755. Considering the refugees a social and economic burden, the Council allowed only one vessel to land its passengers in the capital and ordered the other three to proceed elsewhere in the colony. The government took no further action until the legislature convened the following spring, leaving the Acadians entirely dependent upon private charity for their maintenance over the winter. When the general assembly addressed the problem in April 1756, its members' ambivalent attitudes about whether the Acadians should be considered prisoners of war or neutrals, combined with the legislators' anxiety over the refugees being both French and Roman Catholic, led to the passage of a less than sympathetic bill directing the counties to provide only for those deemed "real Objects of Charity," to bind out as orphans all children whose parents could not support them, and to jail anyone who refused to work or traveled farther than ten miles from his or her abode without a pass. Basil Sollers, "Party of Acadians Who Sailed from the Potomac, Bound for the Mississippi," *Md. Hist. Mag.*, IV (1909), 1–21; Gregory A. Wood, *The French Presence in Maryland, 1524–1800* (Baltimore, 1978), 61–90; *Arch. of Md.*, LII, 542–544.

14. None of their priests were allowed to accompany the Acadians to Maryland. Wood, *French Presence*, 79.

15. On July 9, 1755, at the battle of the Monongahela, Maj. Gen. Edward Braddock (1695–1755) and his force of 1,400 British regulars and 450 colonials were routed by 900 Frenchmen and Indians. Braddock was killed, and his aide George Washington, whose contingent of

militia had suffered a similar defeat the previous year, led the remainder of the troops back to Virginia.

16. William Johnson (1715–1774), Irish immigrant, fur trader, landowner, and member of the council of New York from 1750, was appointed Indian agent to the Six Nations and ordered by Braddock in April 1755 to attack Fort St. Frédéric at Crown Point. By early September he had progressed only as far as the south end of lac du St. Sacrément, which he christened Lake George and where he paused to build Fort William Henry. There on Sept. 8 he was discovered by Baron Dieskau, the German commander of French troops in America. The colonials wounded and captured Dieskau and forced the French to retire, but Johnson was too weak to pursue. Lawrence Henry Gipson, *The Great War for the Empire: The Years of Defeat, 1754–1757,* The British Empire before the American Revolution (New York, 1958–1970), VI, 162–174.

17. William Shirley (1694–1771), governor of Massachusetts since 1741, was a major general and Braddock's second in command. In the campaign of 1755 he was to lead an expedition against Fort Niagara designed to oust the French intruders and protect the important trading post at Oswego. It was not until September that Shirley managed to collect his troops at Oswego, and though he determined on Sept. 18 to proceed with the attack on Fort Niagara, bad weather soon put an end to his plans for the season. Ibid., 127–161.

18. The crown awarded Johnson a baronetcy and made him superintendent of Indian affairs.

19. This proved too optimistic a view. The defeat of the Albany Plan of Union proposed by Benjamin Franklin in 1754 foretold more accurately the colonies' attitudes toward cooperative war efforts. The Maryland lower house, engaged in a protracted struggle against the proprietary prerogative, was chiefly interested in how it could manipulate war emergencies so as to extend its own authority into new areas. Barker, *Background of the Revolution,* 240.

20. Sir John Campbell, fourth earl of Loudoun (1705–1782), replaced Shirley as British commander in America on July 23, 1756.

21. Doohoragen Manor.

22. CCA is undoubtedly referring to Col. Edward Lloyd III (1711–1770) of Wye House, Talbot Co. A merchant and a planter, Lloyd and his two partners owned ships that traded to New England, Great Britain, and the Caribbean, and his landed interests encompassed some forty-three thousand acres, the greatest portion of which lay on Maryland's Eastern Shore. He served in the lower house (1738–1741) and became a member of the upper house and the Council, two bodies with identical membership but different responsibilities, in 1743, remaining in those positions until 1769. He was appointed to his most important provincial post—Lord Baltimore's agent and receiver general—in 1753, and, although his inattention to the duties of the office made his tenure unsatisfactory, his wealth and prestige secured him in the post until 1768, when he was persuaded to resign. Married in 1739 to Anne Rousby, Lloyd fathered two sons, Edward Lloyd IV and Richard Bennett Lloyd, and a daughter, Elizabeth. *Bio. Dic. Md. Legis.,* II, 535–537; Donnell MacClure Owings, *His Lordship's Patronage: Offices of Profit in Colonial Maryland* (Baltimore, 1953), 167.

23. "The beginning of wisdom is the fear of the Lord." Ps. 110:10.

Elizabeth Brooke to CC

Sepr. 8. 1756.

My Dr Charly

We have recd. four letters[1] from you since last Fall continue yr diligence my dear for nothing can Equal the pleasure I have in hearing from you. I wrote you a long letter last Augt or Sep[r] which I find has miscarry'd I am sorry for it [be]cause it Occations you uneasyness in being so long without hearing from me you was always an affectionate tender good Child & I find yo[u] are still the same that you have the same concern & care for me as useual which is no small Comfort to me[.] I have had my health perfectly well ever Since you left Maryland & they say I look as well now as I did then & not older I tell you this from the inquiry you made of Watty Hoxton about my looks[.] I saw yr letter to him & was mightly pleased with it I am glad to find that you & Watty keep up a Correspondance he is a good natured Youth a little rattling at present but I hope he will do very well as he do's not want good Sence, he has I am sure a very great regard for you — Yr Picture[2] is with me I set great Store by it for I think it has a great resemblance of you when y[ou] was here, yr Papa & most of yr acquaintance are of the same Opinion & most People think it like yr Papa I am one of the Number that thinks so I th[ink] it is not so handsome as you was & I [believe] what Mr Wappler says is true that the Limner has not done you justice.

It is a great pleasure to me to know that you are so well contented at Paris & that you injoy a good state of health there[.] I cou'd not help being greatly affected at the acct. Mr Carroll gave yr Papa of the disorder you were seized with on yr Travels, which I understand was a Severe fit of the Cholick, be carefull of yr Self my dr Charly & avoid every thing that you find disagrees with you or that may impair yr health for our greatest happyness, yr Papas & mine I mean depends upon yr welfare take this for granted that Our hearts is quite fixed on you & Our comfort is that you merit it. I hope the next letter I send you will be more Satisfactory to you then any you have yet had from me, for what may I not expect from yr Papas tenderness & affection which I have hitherto been happy Enough to preserve.

This Place[3] as I wrote you in mine that miscarry'd is greatly improved a fine flourishing young Orchard with variety of choice Fruit, the Garden inlarg'd & a Stone Wall round it, 2 fine large Meadows Several Houses Built[,] all this done Since you left it. It is realy a pretty Place, but I suppose it wou'd seem insipid to you after being at Paris & seeing le beau Monde[.][4]

Poor Mrs Croxall[5] yr good old Nurse died last March of a lingering illness, she was yr Cousen Anthony Carrolls Aunt. I went to see her & stay'd a week with [her a]bout a fortnight before she died, she said many tender things of you, called you her Boy, & said she hoped to live to see you come in again, she was a good Woman

& I believe she is very happy — Yr grand Mama notwithstanding her age which is 76 is quite hearty & well I saw her last June she charg'd me to give her Blessing to you whenever I wrote to you, all yr Relations & Friends desire to be kindly Re-member'd to you & yr Aunt Jenny in particular, she is with me every Winter, & I have Company pretty often of late I wish the time was come that I cou'd have yrs for I long my dear to see you & to have you with me. I am not under any apprehen-sion of the Indians nor in the least danger of falling in to their hands. I hope this will get [safe] to you & find you in good health & Spirits. Adieu [my] Dr. Charly I am

Mo: Affec[t] Yrs
Eliza. Bro[ok]e

PS

Pray give my Complyments to yr Cousen Carroll I shall always Regard him for his care & Tenderness of you[.]

ALS, Carroll Papers, MS 206, MdHi. Addressed by CCA. Marked "Copy" by Elizabeth Brooke.

1. Not found.

2. This portrait of CC has not been found.

3. Doohoragen Manor.

4. "Fashionable society."

5. CCA's first cousin, Joanna Carroll Croxall (?-1756), who came to Maryland from Ire-land about 1715 with her husband, Richard. See Appendix I, Chart B.

CCA to CC

Sepr: 14: 1756

Dr Charly,

I wrote to You the 26th: of last July a very long letter wh I doubt not has Reached You as I sent three Copies of it by different Ships: I all so wrote in the Same Manner to Csn: Antony — This incloses one from Yr Mama & an Extract from the Pensil-vania Gazet wh the Northern Post brought in last Night[.]

The French Cannot be less sensible of the importance of their Conquest of Oswego than we are of the Damage we must Suffer by the loss of it, what immedi-ately Affects us is that the Six Indian Nations by the French Called the Iroquois will Join wth them in destroying Our Frontiers in all Our Colonies — Pensilvania & Maryland have within 5 or 6 Weeks sufferd very much from the incursions of the Indians in Alliance wth the French & I apprehend will Suffer much more be-tween this & the Winter — Great Tracts of Ground & Many settlements have been Abandoned in Pensilvania & most of Our settlements at Conecochige[1] have been

Broken up entierly by the Cowardice & ill Conduct of our People who hardly make any Resistance, or unite to Oppose the Savages who Attack us in small Parties from 3 or 4 to thirty or 40 in a Party—I am in Hopes Our Men will soon be better disciplined & that their losses will inspier them wth Courage & Resentment[.]

I suspend my Belief about the Massacre of Our troops at Oswego,[2] if it be so, we are at a loss to Guess what Could have given the French a Pretence to treat us in so inhuman a Manner[.] I have allways entertained a high Opinion of the Generosity & Politeness of the French Nation Certainly the Air of Canada Cannot inspier different Sentiments—

We seem much dejected at this loss, It is thought here that the Siege of Fort St: Frederick will be laid aside for the Present at that Lord Loudon will only Act on the Defensive this Campain as the troops wh took Oswego will now be at liberty to Join the French at the Lakes Champlain & St Sacrament—Since I wrote to You I find the French were even Superior to us in their Marine on Lake Ontario[.] The French Constitution is better Calculated to Carry on a War than Ours, they are moved by only one Spring & they move wth Secrecy & Dispatch in all these we are deficient & May be they Serve their Prince with a Greater Sense of Honor & wth more Zeal & disinterestedness than we do Ours. I desier my Compliments to Csn Antony—Csn Harry Carroll is wth me & desiers his to You both—I am My Dear Charly

Yr Mo: Afft: Father[3]
Cha: Carroll

PS

It's said we had upwards of 100 Pieces of Cannon at Oswego for the defence of that Place the Vessells to be built, & other forts wh were intended to be erected in other Places, Beside a Compleat Train of Artillery &c. It is one instance of our good Management to trust So [ma]ny important deposits in a Place so [poor]ly Fortified & as I hear not [defend]able by it's Scituation[.]

ALS, Carroll Papers, MS 216, MdHi. Addressed by CCA to Mr. Crookshanks for delivery to CC.

1. Conococheague, later Williams Port, a settlement located on the Potomac River at the mouth of Conococheague Creek. To protect the inhabitants of this important but vulnerable outpost, Gov. Horatio Sharpe of Maryland ordered blockhouses built in late July 1755. However, the measure proved inadequate; early the next year, Col. George Washington reported to Lord Fairfax that "the whole settlement of Conococheague is fled, and but two families remain between here and Fredericktown." W. McCulloh Brown, "Fort Frederick," *Md. Hist. Mag.,* XVIII (1923), 101–102.

2. Fort Oswego, an important British trading post on Lake Ontario, contained 1,134 officers and men in the summer of 1756. Captured by the French on Aug. 14, the fort and all other habitations were destroyed. The British troops were not accorded the honors of war but were transported as prisoners to Montreal. Lieutenant Colonel Littlehales, who took over command of Fort Oswego during the battle, reported from Montreal that only 12 or 14

men were lost in defense of the position but that after surrendering "some of them having got in Liquor fell into Wrangling with the Indians & Several of them were Kill'd." Gipson, *Years of Defeat,* 199–200.

3. This is the only letter found that CCA closes with the phrase "Yr Mo: Afft: Father" prior to his marriage to CC's mother, Elizabeth Brooke, in February 1757.

. . .
. .
.

Articles of Agreement between CCA and Elizabeth Brooke

[Nov. 7, 1756]

Articles of agreement Indented had made Concluded & agreed upon this Seventh Day of November in the Year of our Lord One thousand Seven Hundred & Fifty Six Between Charles Carroll Esqr of the City of Annapolis in the Province of Maryland of the One Part and Elizabeth Brooke Daughter of Clement Brooke Esqr late of Prince Georges County in the Province aforesaid on the Other Part. Whereas a Mariage is by the Permission of God, Shortly to be had made & Solemnized Between the Said Charles Carroll & the Said Elizabeth Brooke It is therefore agreed by and between the Said Parties hereunto in Manner & form following That is to Say The said Charles Carroll in Consideration & Prospect of the said Marriage intended and for the Making a Proper Provision for the Said Elizabeth Brooke for her decent Support and Maintainance in Case She Should Outlive the Said Charles Carroll and in full Consideration of her the said Elizabeth Brooke's Right of Dower of in or to the Reall & Personall Estate of the Said Charles Carroll Doth hereby for him self his Heirs Executors & Administrators Covenant Grant and Agree to and with the said Elizabeth Brooke her Executors and Administrators That in Case the said intended Marriage shall take Effect & in Case the Said Cha: Carroll shall depart this life before the said Elizabeth Brooke That then and in such Case The Executors administrators or Assignes of the Said Charles Carroll Shall Pay or Cause to be paid to the Said Elizabeth Brooke her Executors administrators or Assignes Yearly and for so long a term as she shall Survive the said Charles Carroll The Sum of One Hundred Pounds Sterling Money of Great Brittain. And the Said Elizabeth Brooke in Consideration of the Marriage aforesaid intended to be made and Solemnized & in Consideration of the yearly Sum of One Hundred Pounds sterling herein before Stipulated to be Paid to the Said Elizabeth Brooke as a Maintainance in Case she should Survive the Said Charles Carroll Doth hereby for her herself her Heirs Executors Administrators and assignes Covenant and Agree to & with the Said Charles Carroll his Heirs Executors Administrators and assignes That she the Said Elizabeth Brooke will take the Said Yearly Sum of One Hundred Pounds sterling in full Satisfaction and Compensation of her Right of Dower of in or to the Reall or Personall Estate of the Said Charles Carroll And the Said Elizabeth Brooke Doth hereby for her self her Heirs Executors Administrators and Assignes in Consideration of the Said Annuall Sum of One Hundred Pounds sterling herein before Stipulated to be paid to the Said Elizabeth Brooke her Executors administrators or assignes, Renounce all Right Title Claim or Demand to any Dower out of the Reall or Personall Estate of the Said Charles Carroll or any Claim to Any Part of the Estate Reall or Personall of the Said Charles Carroll Saving the Yearly Sum of One Hundred Pounds sterling herein before Covenanted to be Paid to the Said Elizabeth Brooke her Executors Adminstrators or Assignes. In Wittness whereof the said Parties have hereunto set their hands and affixed their seals The day and Year first above Written

Cha: Carroll

Eliza: Brooke

Signed Sealed & Delivered in the Presence of

R. Croxall[1]

Henry Carroll

ADS, Colonial Collection, MS 2018, MdHi. Mislabeled on verso in unknown hand: "Chas. Carroll of Carollton's marriage." Faint residues of their seals appear after CCA's and Elizabeth Brooke's signatures.

1. Richard Croxall (?–1785), a son of CCA's first cousin Joanna Carroll Croxall and Richard Croxall, lived at the Garrison Farm in Baltimore Co. A devoted and trusted family retainer, he served from the late 1740s until the mid-1760s as manager of the Baltimore Company and was credited by CCA with greatly improving the ironworks' profitability. He and his wife, Eleanor Buchanan Croxall, had no children. Robert Barnes and Dawn F. Thomas, *The Green Spring Valley: Its History and Heritage* (Baltimore, 1978), I, 32-33, II, 29. See Appendix I, Chart B.

. . .

Certification of Marriage between CCA and Elizabeth Brooke[1]

[Feb. 15, 1757]

I Mathias Maners[2] a Priest of the Society of Jesus do hereby certify that I did on the 15th day of February in the year of our Lord 1757 marry Charles Carroll Esq: and Elizabeth Brooke Daughter of Clement Brooke Esq. late of Prince Georges county deceased.

In testimony whereof I have hereunto set my hand, and affixed my Seal the day and year first above mentioned.

testeth   Mathias Maners

Jane Brooke   S.J.

John Ireland[3]

ADS, Carroll-McTavish Papers, MS 220, MdHi. A remnant of Mathias Manners's seal follows his name.

1. According to notes made by William C. Pennington in 1885, the certificate attesting to the marriage of CCA and Elizabeth Brooke on Feb. 15, 1757, "was found in a bundle of old papers in a trunk loaned to me by Mrs. Chas. C. MacTavish." Pennington was related to the Carrolls by marriage as his wife, Emily Louisa Harper, was the daughter of CCC's grandson Charles Carroll Harper and Charlotte Hutchinson Chiffelle Harper. Mrs. Mac-Tavish, the former Marcella Scott, daughter of Gen. Winfield Scott, was the widow of CCC's grandson Charles Carroll McTavish. Pennington Papers, G5045, Genealogical Manuscripts Collections, MdHi; Dielman.

2. Mathias Manners, alias Sittensperger (1719-1775), a German Jesuit serving in Maryland, became superior at the Conewago Mission in 1754 and at Bohemia Manor in 1771. He held the latter position until his death. Maryland Province Archives, Box 3, folder 4½, Spec. Colls. Div., DGU; Catalogue of Members of the Maryland Mission of the Society of Jesus, 1634-1806, Spec. Colls. Div., DGU; Weis, *Clergy*, 55.

3. John Ireland was an overseer on Doohoragen Manor.

· · ·
·

Wrapper Containing Marriage Articles between CCA and Elizabeth Brooke[1]

[February 1757]

Cha: Carroll Esqr & Elizabeth Brooke
Mariage Articles
To be Delivered to my Son

AD, Carroll-McTavish Papers, MS 220, MdHi. Written in CCA's hand. Seal with Carroll crest, bird's wings closed.

1. This wrapper probably enclosed both the articles of agreement between CCA and Elizabeth Brooke, dated Nov. 7, 1756, and the certification of their marriage, dated Feb. 15, 1757.

· · ·
·

Eleanor Carroll[1] to CCA

April 8th 1757

Honrd Sir

It has given me great concern that you should imagine that I have been the cause of your intention of going home[2] &c being known and publickly talk'd of as I am sensible of the bad consequences that might from thence accrue it is true after the repeated Sollicitations of my mama[3] to know what scheme the Roman

Catholicks were upon and particularly yourself when she had given me her word of honour never to speak of it to any one I told her and was afterwards very uneasy that I had and begg'd her every time I saw her never to mention it and she as often promised me she would not and I believe did not even to her own son[4] till lately[.]

Since our return from Elkridge Mama has been here and says she never spoke to any one about it till after Cousin Digges[5] had been at her house and she ask'd where it was that you were going he took the map and shew'd her and after her asking him some questions whether some things were not to be as I had before told her (without letting him know she had heard it from me or any one else) he told her they were and let her into the whole affair then she told him she had heard it from me he told her it was no secret that Mr Henry Darnall[6] knew it for he had told him of it a few days before as he Came from Annapolis and said he had forgot to let you know how publick it was however Cousin Digges desired it might not be spoke of from him[.] I am Honrd Sir

Yr Most Dutifull & affect: Niece
E Carroll

ALS, Carroll-Maccubbin Papers, MS 219, MdHi. Endorsed by CCA.

1. Eleanor Carroll (1731–1763), the elder daughter of CCA's brother Daniel Carroll of Duddington and Ann Rozer Carroll. She married her cousin Daniel Carroll II of Upper Marlboro in 1751. (See Appendix I, Chart D.) Unlike her brother, Charles, Eleanor had no quarrel with CCA's management of her inheritance.

2. It is not immediately apparent what Eleanor Carroll means by the phrase "going home." Presumably, she is referring to Europe as a place of origin.

3. Widowed by CCA's younger brother, Daniel Carroll of Duddington, in 1734, Ann Rozer Carroll (1710–1764) married Benjamin Young within a year of her first husband's death. Young also left her a widow in 1754. The daughter of Notley Rozer and his first wife, Jane Digges Rozer, Ann was also the great-granddaughter of Charles Calvert, third Lord Baltimore, and his second wife, Jane Lowe Sewall, and the grandniece of Benedict Leonard Calvert, fourth Lord Baltimore. *Bio. Dic. Md. Legis.*, II, 707, 929. See Appendix I, Charts D and I.

4. The mother of three children from her first marriage—Charles Carroll of Duddington, Eleanor Carroll, and Mary Carroll—Ann Rozer Carroll Young had with Benjamin Young a son, Notley (1736/7–1802). *Bio. Dic. Md. Legis.*, II, 929. See Appendix I, Chart D.

5. Ignatius Digges (1707–1785), a wealthy Roman Catholic planter, married as his second wife Mary Carroll, Eleanor Carroll's younger sister, in 1752. They lived at Mellwood, a plantation near Upper Marlboro, in Prince George's Co. Although Digges had a daughter, Mary, from his first marriage to Elizabeth Parnham Craycroft, his union with Mary Carroll was childless. A leader, along with CCA, of Maryland's Catholic community, Digges fractured that alliance and caused a deep family rift when he supported his brother-in-law Charles Carroll of Duddington in questioning CCA's administration of the legacies devised

to Daniel Carroll of Duddington's three children. In 1761 Digges filed a suit in chancery seeking restoration of monies he believed due to him and Mary from the estates of which CCA was executor. CCA finally settled with Digges privately in 1775. Bowie, *Prince George's*, 272–275; Chancery Court (Records), Liber D.D., no. 1, fol. 15, MdAA; CCC to CCA, Apr. 3, 1773, n. 2, below. See also Appendix I, Chart I.

6. Henry Darnall III (1702/3–liv. 1783), CCA's first cousin, was the grandson of Charles Carroll the Settler's father-in-law and patron, Henry Darnall I. (See Appendix I, Chart F.) Educated at St. Omers (1714–1722), he conformed to the Anglican Church in order to circumvent the statutes that denied the franchise and the right to political office to Roman Catholics. However, his wife, Anne Talbott Darnall, and their six children—Henry IV, Robert, John, Mary, Katherine, and Ann—remained Catholic, Mass was regularly said in the chapel at the Woodyard, Darnall's Prince George's Co. seat, and one of the Darnall sons was sent to St. Omers. Although this readily observable religious duality made him unpopular and led the lower house to question intermittently the validity of his conversion, these circumstances did not prevent Darnall, who was related to the proprietary family, from obtaining an appointment as attorney general of Maryland in 1744. He remained in that office until he was "persuaded to resign" in 1756. In 1755 he had also become naval officer of Patuxent. This position, which he retained, required that he post a security bond of one thousand pounds sterling because of the large amount of revenue for which he would be responsible. His younger brother, John, and CCA together pledged the necessary funds. In the spring of 1761 a legislative investigation revealed that Henry Darnall III had failed to deposit considerable sums for the years 1757–1760. He fled the colony and took refuge in a convent in Liège, where he lived for a number of years. Nothing is known of the rest of his life. For CCA's efforts to recover the money he had advanced in Darnall's behalf, see CCA to CC, May 21, 1761, and June 22, 1761, below. *Arch. of Md.*, VI, 71–72, L, 52–53, LII, 159–160, 359, 385, LVI, lv–lviii; Owings, *His Lordship's Patronage*, 134; Bowie, *Prince George's*, 242–243; Holt, *St. Omers*, 83.

· · ·
·

An Excerpt of a Letter from Horatio Sharpe[1] to William Sharpe[2]

6th of July. 1757.

Dr Br

. . . I am glad to find by Your Letter as well as by One that I have received from Mr Calvert[3] that the Roman Catholicks of this Province have not so much Interest at home as they would have me beleive, His Ldp[4] has confirmed the Act agst. which they petitioned & for passing which they regard Me as a professed Enemy.[5] One Mr Charles Carroll who is at the Head of that Sect & is possessed of a Fortune of £30,000 or £40,000 Stg among Us has taken a passage to England in a Vessel that lately sailed hence & will probably be in London before this can be dld [delivered], What his Views or Intentions are in taking such a Voyage at this time I know not, It has been said that he has Thoughts of leaving Maryland & carrying his Fortune to Europe, He has a Son about 22 Years of Age now at Paris & if he should determine to spend the Remainder of His Life in Europe it is not improbable that he will take Up his Residence in some part of France as he seems by sending his Son to that Kingdom while he was very Young & by supporting him there since he has finished his Studies to prefer that Country. He is a sensible Man, has read much & is well acquainted with the Constitution & Strength of these American Colonies. If he is inclined to give the Enemy any Intelligence about our American Affairs None is more capable, but indeed I do not conceive that he has any such Inclination. He was heretofore a bitter Enemy to the Lord proprietary but having behaved with moderation since I came hither We was on good Terms till I incurred his Displeasure by assenting to an Act which I thought equitable & which You say appears to You in the same Light, since that time all Correspondence between Us has been broken off. I presume he will be much among the Merchants while he stays in London & in particular with his Friend Mr Philpot, Should he endeavour to do me any prejudice with my Ld or any one else during his Residence there I hope You will be able to render His Attempts abortive. . . .

I am with the greatest sincerity Dr Sr
Yr obliged & most affe Br

. . .

L, Governor and Council Letterbook, 1756-1768, MSA S 1075-3, fols. 93-94, MdAA. Courtesy of the Maryland State Archives.

1. A native of Hull, in Yorkshire, Horatio Sharpe (1718-1790) probably attained the governorship of Maryland, a post he held from 1753 until 1768, through the influence of his brother John, one of the guardians of Frederick Calvert, sixth Lord Baltimore, but he eventually lost the position to the proprietor's brother-in-law Robert Eden. Sharpe's military career included duty in the West Indies, and, while governor, he also acted as commander in chief, ex officio, of the Maryland militia. Prior to the arrival of Gen. Edward Braddock, Sharpe commanded the forces raised to defend against the French, and he endeavored to restore order in the west after Braddock's defeat. Never married, Sharpe maintained a residence in Annapolis and a country seat, Whitehall, about seven miles south of the capital. He returned to England in 1773 and lived there until his death. *Bio. Dic. Md. Legis.*, II, 726-728; Matilda Edgar, *A Colonial Governor in Maryland: Horatio Sharpe and His Times, 1753-1773* (London, 1912); Lewis Namier and John Brooke, *The House of Commons, 1754-1790* (New York, 1964), III, 428.

2. William Sharpe (1696-1767), the governor's brother, lived in London. In 1756 he was clerk of the Privy Council. *Bio. Dic. Md. Legis.*, II, 726; Edgar, *Colonial Governor*, 114; *Arch. of Md.*, VI, 13.

3. Cecilius Calvert (1702-1765), son of Benedict Leonard Calvert, fourth Lord Baltimore, and Lady Charlotte Lee, was the youngest brother of Charles Calvert, fifth Lord Baltimore. One of four guardians for his brother's son Frederick Calvert, sixth Lord Baltimore, Cecilius was appointed principal secretary of Maryland in 1751 and held that post until his death. As

his nephew took little interest in proprietary responsibilities, Cecilius enjoyed free rein and considerable power in administering the province. *Bio. Dic. Md. Legis.,* I, 188–189; Owings, *His Lordship's Patronage,* 36, 114.

4. Frederick Calvert, sixth Lord Baltimore (1731/2–1771), became proprietor of Maryland at the age of twenty. His union with Lady Diana Egerton, whom he married in 1753, was childless, but he fathered five illegitimate children, including one son, Henry Harford, to whom he willed the province of Maryland. In 1768 he was tried for rape and acquitted. Although he owned some 245,000 acres in Maryland and received annual revenues from the province well in excess of ten thousand pounds sterling, Frederick left administrative matters almost entirely in the hands of his uncle and principal adviser, Cecilius Calvert, and after Cecilius's death relied upon his successor, Hugh Hammersley. *Bio. Dic. Md. Legis.,* I, 189–190.

5. Horatio Sharpe had approved the May 1756 "Act for granting a Supply of Forty Thousand Pounds for his Majesty's Service," which included a provision mandating double taxation of Roman Catholic landowners.

CCA to CC

Portsmouth July 17: [1757]

Dr Charley

This is to Informe You that [I am] safe Arrived in England, Haveing Lan[ded] Yesterday on the Isle of White. I Prop[ose at] Present to Leave London for Paris abo[ut the last] of this Month or Beginning of the [Next. We] Were detained in Maryland by an [. . .] from the 15 of Aprill when the Ship was [set] to Saile to the 1st: of June. I left my [own] House the 2d & the Capes[1] the 8th. I have had a mo[st] Pleasant Passage. Yr Mother was perfect[ly] well & gives her love & Blessing to You[. She] has wrote to You wh I will Deliv[er.[2] I] have not time to Add but that I am Dr Charley

Yr Mo: Afft: Fat[her]

Cha: Carroll

PS

Pray Present my Sincerest Love & Compliments to Csn: Antony—

ALS, Carroll-McTavish Papers, MS 220, MdHi. Addressed by CCA to Mr. Crookshanks for delivery to CC. Right margin damaged. Figures in CCA's hand on verso not reproduced.

1. Cape Henry and Cape Charles, located at the entrance to the Chesapeake Bay.
2. Not found.

CC to CCA

[July 26, 1757]

Dr. Papa,

You c'ant concieve the anxiety your absence causes. T''is with the gratest im-patience I wait your arrival, I hoped to have the satisfaction of seeing you before this: but all my hopes are frustrated. I wait nothing but your arrival to leave the College; my studies are finnish'd; we broke up schools the 21 of this month: the 8th I sustained universall philosophy.[1] I know you are desirous to hear what suc-cess I met with: but it wou'd not become me to speak in my own praise; this I can only say that my auditors seem'd to be contented; the rest I leave to others. No man is a Judge in his own cause. You may easily imagin that time passes away but slowly since by [my] defension; before I was entirely taken up in preparing my-self; occupation serves to make the time pass away agreably; as I am not so much occupy'd at present I have more time to reflect et m'ennuyer[2] as the french say. Tho' I am not so much taken up as before my defension; I am not idle. I pass the gratest part of the time in reading and studying the french language: I have several other occupations which tho' the [they] can not make my present sejour[3] quite agreable serve to render [it] not entirely unprofitable. I hope you will remember to bring over the books I wrote for last year; You need not buy Mr. Lock's work it will be of no great service to me: I d'ont suppose you will make any great stay at London; pray write to me as soon as you arrive you will free me from a great deal of anxietude: t'is very natural I shou'd be in pain about you. Mr Hunter[4] is still in London; I do'nt doubt but what you intend to see him. He was some time at Paris, I had the plaisure[5] of accompanying him to Versailles: a great part of our discourse ran upon you: I was very much taken with him he seems to be a very honnest good meaning man. I have got numbers of things to tell you; but as I hope to enjoy your company soon I defer them to that occasion. I am very well; nothing is wanting to compleat my happiness but your presence. Pray send the enclosed to my Mama[6] she must be very malancholy since your departure: a letter from you and me at the same time will serve to raise up her spirits. I am Dr. papa your most loveing and obedient son

Charles Carroll.

July 26[7]

ALS, Carroll Papers, MS 206, MdHi. Addressed by CC. Endorsed by CCA: "1757 July 26 Cha: Carrolls Letter—."

1. A "public defense of all Philosophy" was undertaken after a student successfully com-pleted a course of study in the natural sciences or philosophy and passed an hour-long

preliminary disputation given by three examiners. The title of Master of Arts was conferred upon the graduate. Hughes, *Loyola*, 262–263.

2. "To be bored."

3. "Sojourn."

4. George Hunter (1713–1779), a Jesuit from Northumberland, came to Maryland in 1747 and settled at the Jesuit mission at St. Thomas Manor in Charles Co. He served at missions in that county, at Port Tobacco, and at St. Inigoes between 1749 and 1754 before becoming superior at St. Thomas in 1755. In 1756 he returned to England as a special emissary to the proprietor to speak in behalf of Maryland's Catholics. Hunter returned to Maryland in July 1759. For a discussion of his mission, see Beatriz Betancourt Hardy, "Papists in a Protestant Age: The Catholic Gentry and Community in Colonial Maryland, 1689–1776" (Ph.D. diss., University of Maryland, 1993), 295–301. Weis, *Clergy,* 49; Catalogue of Members of Md. Mission; Md. Province Arch., Box 3, folder 4½; Foley, ed., *Records,* VII, 384.

5. "Pleasure."

6. Not found.

7. In CCA's hand.

. . .
.

John Jenison to CC

Sept. the 6th. 1757.

Dr Charles,

Yr Cosen gives me this acceptable opportunity of acknowledging yr late obliging lines. 'Tis a most sensible pleasure to me to hear from others, that yr Father is satisfied with the progress you have hitherto made. I desire you will present him my compliments & sincere acknowledgemt for the regard he has been pleased to express for me. I can lay no other claim to it, than a most constant & unfeigned desire of serving him & you, as far in my power. The apprehension of danger in yr future situation, must be diminished by the consciousness of yr upright intentions, & a confidence in those powerfull graces, to which, I hope, you will ever prove faithfull. As to the means of supporting & strengthening such resolutions, you stand not in need of my advice: my best wishes & poor prayers shall always attend you. The reasons I have for always remembering one, whose whole behaviour gave me the greatest satisfaction without the very least allay of displeasure, would offend yr modesty, were I to mention them. Be persuaded that it is with the same sentiments of sincere esteem & friendship, I shall always remain Drst Charles—

yr Obedt Humble Servt

J Jenison.

I have lately seen my Br Tim at Gant who is well & desires to be kindly remembered to you; as do those at watten[.]

ALS, Carroll Papers, MS 206, MdHi.

. . .
.   .
.

John Carroll to CC

[c. Sept. 6, 1757][1]

Dr. Cousin.

Fr. Jenison, who is now at the villa, sends me a commission to scold you for not Sending us the directions to you. Pray how must I go about it? I believe you will mind very little, what I say to you, if I say it in a serious way. I never in my life remember to have been obligd to study so long to find out, what to write, as to day: I have neither political, domestic, or news of any other denomination to send you. Not one thought occurs to entertain you with; & I woud absolutely differ writing for some days, when I am to send a letter to your Papa from Mr. Niset,[2] who tells me he saw you at Rheims, if F. Jenison had not desird me to send of[f] this as soon as possible, he having one for F. Thorpe[3] to be inclosed in the same packet with this for Fr. Crookshanks,[4] to whom your inadvertency obliges us to trust this letter. I am Dr. Charles

Your affectionate Cousin &c

J. Carroll.

The otherside is for your Papa.[5]

ALS, Carroll Papers, MS 206, MdHi. Written on verso of John Jenison to CC, Sept. 6, 1757.

1. Dated from John Jenison's letter. Thomas O'Brien Hanley, editor of *The John Carroll Papers* ([Notre Dame, Ind., 1976], I, 3), dated this letter 1755, based on the comment that Mr. Niset had seen CC at Rheims, where the lad was in school from 1754 to 1755.

2. Niset may have been a French wine merchant. See CC to CCA, Oct. 11, 1763, below.

3. John Thorpe (1726–1792) studied at St. Omers and entered the Society of Jesus at Watten in 1747. He became agent for the English province of the Society in Rome in 1760. Foley, ed., *Records*, VII, 775–776.

4. Foley refers to two priests named Alexander Crookshanks. One, a Scottish Jesuit, was rector of the Scots college at Douai in January 1748 (ibid., 183). The other, born in 1709, took his vows in 1755 and was living in Paris in 1762 and serving as procurator for the missions of England and Scotland (ibid., 1461). John Carroll is probably referring to the latter.

5. The "otherside" contains Jenison's letter to CC of Sept. 6, 1757, printed above.

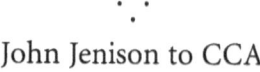

John Jenison to CCA

Sir,

You do me too much honour in acknowledging so particularly the little Services I have rendered, or rather wished to render yr Son. I am already more than sufficiently rewarded by the pleasure I constantly receive from his universal good character. 'Tis my sincerest daily wish, that he may always continue to give you equal satisfaction; as indeed there is all possible reason to hope and believe he will. I take the liberty to add a line to the inclosed from his Cousin, who obliges me sensibly by furnishing this occasion to assure yu, that I am Sr,

Yr most Obliged and Obedt Humble Servt

J Jenison

ALS, Carroll Papers, MS 206, MdHi. Addressed by the author. Endorsed by CCA: "1757 Octor: 20 John Carroll & Mr Jenisson's Letters."

Onorio Razolini[1] to CCA

Villa d'Asolo 9ber[2] 17t 1757

Dear Sir

Your favr of the 15 of 8ber[3] Last came to hand the 25t. of the same, & glad I am that one of mine came to yr. hand, & shall be glad to know if you have had the other.[4] I do not doubt that you did favour me every year, but certainly all the Letters were taken, & sorry am I that I had so bad Luck to be deprived of them, & of the Loss of your Tobacco.

When I wrote you in my Last that you would be heartly well come at our House, I realy wrote because it is so, & you'll find, if you will favour me, as heartly a well come, as is [in] my power to give you; Now as I suppose you are in England, & believe me the voyage from thence either is not attended with any fatigue; when I came over with my Wife I bought at Utrecht a small Chariot & came [Post?] in 16 travelling days from thence here but was obliged to have four Horses, & with my Stoping in all the principal Cities was two month, & we realy came without any fatigue, or trouble, but pleasure; If you will come I'll come to meet you as far as Ausburg which is nigh 3 hundred miles from here, so pray take courage, & come, I realy would not make any dificulty to come in the Spring to London, but at present can not Live [Leave] Italy, because if any accident should happen to my Brother, which God forbid, it would be of great damage to me & he is 76, you see that I honestly write how it is, & give you my reason for not coming, but I flatter myself that you have none[.]

As to what you tell me of your disapointment of the French, I realy do not wonder at it, & if you consider the thing well you'll find that England, take all things together, has few equalls, if any, as to me am persuaded of it, & if you come hear, you'll be of the same mind.

I am glad that Miss Brook that was, is now Mrs. Carrill, & beg of you to wish ioy [joy] from us, as we wish you the same; If you remember I told you that your Son would answer all your expectations, which is the greatest satisfaction you can have, & hope he will continue to behave to your content & to his honour. Pray what is become of yr. Nephe[w][5] I was in doubt If I should [ask] any thing about him or not but however you can not help it if he dont beheave as a Son of mr Del Carroll[6] ought.

The affairs of Europe are realy in a sad prospect, The King of Prussia has done wonders,[7] & it is almost a shame for almost all the greatest Pottentates of Europe to be obliged to unite to act against a Marquis of Brandenburg, I wish him success, & that he may be capable to make a tolerable Peace.

If you have any thing new from Maryland I hope you'll acquaint me with it, or any thing old that you think would be pleasant to me; You know we used to talk freely, & [I will] be glad to know how affairs goes on there.

Next week I shall write to Mr Calvert,[8] & hope there will soon be ships for that part of the world.

As to my way of Life it is pretty tolerable, & if you'll come you'll be witness that we may Live well if we wish, however I have not that pleasure that I should have had, at Least I think so, when in Maryland; the case is that there way of Life, conversation, humurs &c. &c., are quite different to what I have been used; The only thing that is better is the Climate, & we enjoy better health. Hope to hear soon from you, & believe that I sincerely am & shall be Dr sr Yr.

Most Hble Ob. Sevt.
Onorio Razolini

Pray acquaint me if Mr Calvert has built a House in the Country.[9]

ALS, Carroll Papers, MS 206, MdHi. Addressed by the author "To Charles Carroll Esq. at Mr. William Perkins Mercht. Mercers Hall London." Endorsed by CCA.

1. Protestant convert Onorio Razolini served as armorer of the province of Maryland from June 4, 1734, until August 1741, when he returned to Italy. With George Plater II he acted as guardian to Elizabeth Calvert, daughter of Charles Calvert, who was governor of Maryland from 1719/20 until 1729. Owings, *His Lordship's Patronage,* 48–49 n; *Bio. Dic. Md. Legis.,* I, 184–188.

2. The ninth month old style is November new style.

3. October.

4. Razolini apparently wrote at least two letters to CCA prior to this one. His letter of Sept. 25, 1757 (Carroll Papers, MS 206, MdHi), replied to correspondence he had received from CCA in late August, and he wrote again prior to Oct. 21 (not found).

5. Razolini is referring to Charles Carroll of Duddington's accusations regarding CCA's administration of the inheritances due him from the estates of several family members. At Charles's request, CCA's stewardship of his legacies had continued past 1750, the year in which the younger man reached the age of twenty-one. However, in the spring of 1757, CCA's plans for securing property in Louisiana during a year-long trip abroad led him to insist upon a new arrangement for Charles. The two men settled amicably the ownership of lands in which they had inherited a joint interest, but, after consultation with his brother-in-law Ignatius Digges, Charles unexpectedly repudiated the cash settlement he had originally accepted and contested the accuracy of his uncle's accounts. To resolve the disagreement, CCA proposed that the matter be placed in the hands of two arbitrators—his and Charles's cousin Clement Hill and Basil Waring—with both parties to the dispute binding themselves in the amount of one thousand pounds to accept Hill and Waring's decision. To the elder Carroll's surprise and considerable consternation, Hill and Waring decided in Charles Carroll of Duddington's favor in October 1761. CCA refused to comply and continued to argue his case. He finally settled with his nephew's widow in February 1774. See CCC to CCA, Apr. 3, 1773, n. 2, below.

6. Daniel Carroll of Duddington (1707–1734), CCA's younger brother, was educated at St. Omers c. 1718 and perhaps also at Douai. He returned to Maryland in 1726 and within a year had married Ann Rozer, a union that brought him the estates she had inherited, most notably Duddington Manor, which became the site of the U.S. Capitol. Daniel's will, drawn in the spring of 1734 just before his death, designated CCA as trustee and executor of his estate in behalf of his three minor children, Charles, Eleanor, and Mary. Holt, *St. Omers*, 59; Carroll, "Old Cash Book," fol. 9; Daniel Carroll, will, 1734, Prince George's Co. Wills, Box 4, folder 50. See Appendix I, Chart D.

7. Frederick II (1712–1786), the king of Prussia known as Frederick the Great, ruled from 1740 to 1786. He defeated the French and the Austrians at Rossbach on Nov. 5, 1757. Robert B. Asprey, *Frederick the Great: The Magnificent Enigma* (New York, 1986), 468–473.

8. Probably Benedict Calvert (c. 1724–1788). An illegitimate son of Charles Calvert, fifth Lord Baltimore, and known in his youth as Benedict Swingate, he was living in Maryland by 1742. In 1748 he married his "distant cousin" Elizabeth Calvert, who had been Razolini's ward. Bowie, *Prince George's*, 101; *Bio. Dic. Md. Legis.*, I, 184–185, II, 773–774.

9. In 1751 Benedict Calvert built a mansion on his estate, known as Mount Airy, located in Prince George's Co. Bowie, *Prince George's*, 101.

Elizabeth Carroll to CC

Novr. 30. 1757

My Dear Charly

I am now very impatient to hear from you I have not recd. a letter from you of a later date then Decr. 30. 1756.[1] which is too long to be without hearing from you, but I believe it is not yr fault, in War time, it is difficult for letters to Pass & I impute it to that[.] I imagine yr Papa will be with you when you receive this, his affairs I am afraid will detain him in Paris longer then he expected when he went from hence. Tell yr Papa my dear that altho' we had but few Apples in our Orchard at home, we got as many from Reeds & Selbys as made about fourteen hundred Gals. of Cyder, all put in my Cellers, he will be glad to hear that we are so well off. Send me by yr Papa if you can some good Rappee[2] to put in the Snuff Box you were to get for me. God preserve you & grant you health. I am My Dr. Child Yr Affect Mother

Eliza. Carroll

[Yr] Aunt Jenny desires to [be] tenderly Remember'd to you[.]

ALS, Carroll Papers, MS 206, MdHi. Addressed by Elizabeth Carroll. Letter's date repeated in CC's hand on verso.
1. Not found.
2. A moist, pungent snuff made from dark, rank tobacco leaves.

CC to CCA

Decemb. the 19th. 1757.

Dr Papa.

Your letter came to hand the 8th of Deb.[1] by which I see you stuck to your word of leaving Paris the wensday following. I believe you was extreamly glad to get away. That sejour after my departure must have been very dull and loanesom, at least I can say mine has been so hither too. Altho' I am well lodged, in a very discreat and regular family, altho' I am quite satisfied with my present situation yet all this has not as yet dispelled the grief I felt in parting with you; I think of you very often in the day and the agreable time we spent togeather in Paris perhaps my present solitude has enlivened those ideas for I may really call my present manner of living a true solitude. Tho' now I begin to make some acquaintance in town: I had the honnour of dining with the Intendant;[2] he seems to be a man of a great deal of wit and Judgement. I am to go to his house to morrow to carry him France's Horace,[3] which he has not as yet seen.

This town[4] is very big but not well peopled; the number of its inhabitants does not exceed 16 thousand souls. Yet notwithstanding there is a good deal of society and people of fashion. They delight in playing at cardes and that's their principal occupation: I dont much like that diversion; yet I must absoluetly know how to play to go in to company.

I dined a few days ago with Mr. Power[5] and his companions I was very well treated an very cordially. They are all my friends and I am persuaded very sincere ones. I have Jest begun the study of the civill law; you may be assured that I shall apply my self to it. The gentleman who is to instruct me is a doctor of the law; his name Champion; the duke of Norkfolk[6] knowes him very well; he stood godfather to one of Mr. Champion's children: if you shou'd see the Duke of Norkfoll you may put him in mind of it. I am to go thrice a week to Mr. Champion the lesson is to last an hour, and he demands a guinea a month. If you find it too dear pray let me know altho' I dont believe I can get a person to instruct me for much less:[7] besides Mr. Champion has lent me some law books and is very conveniently lodged for my purpose. I hope not to stand in need of his aid in 3 or 4 months time.

I question very much wether a 100 £S[8] a year will suffice. There are so many unforseen expences that occur; I believe I may do genteely with a hundred and 30, I shou'd be stinted too much with only a 100. However, be assured, I shall manage as well as I can and with the best oeconemy I am capable of. My Journey here cost 78 lt some sols:[9] my place alone and bagage cost 50 lt. Part of my linnen is cut out; there is enough to make in all 26 shirts. The woeman takes for making 'em 30 sols a piece: some of 'em must absolutely have work'd ruffles: for nobody here weares plain ones when he goes in to company. I d'ont as yet know how much that expence may amount to.

You may be assured that I shall not faill in writing to Mr. Liledieu;[10] I bear him to great an esteem to be defective in that point. I shall likewise punctually perform what you recommend to me in Your letter with regard to him. I did not arrive at Bourges till saturday; I never in my life made so slow dull and malancholey a Journey. I believe it will be the last time that I shall ever go in a publick coach. My Servant seems to be a good an honnest boy, but is very awkward and simple. If you meet with any english books that are curious and of late date and at the same time instructive you will do well to send 'em [to] me. The Intendant is a man that likes the belles lettres and is particularly diverted with english books; I know I shou'd do him a singular favour and sensible pleasure in lending him such books; by that means I may be able to insinuate my self into his favour, which is of no little consequence in this place. Every one payes his court to him; he is like a little king; every sunday and holy-day the principall people in town go to pay their respects to him. You may see by this that a person who is favoured with his friendship, must certainly be respected and considered in town.

This letter is pretty long and I think capable of letting you see in to my present situation. I shall lett you hear from me pretty often during your stay in London. I desire you will do the same yet I need not desire it, because I am certain your inclination and love for me are sufficient motives for your writing: pray let me know how my Mama does and what news she tells you in her letters. You may send her this letter; it will serve to amuse her and at the same time inform her how I am settled. I am Dr. Papa

Your most dutifull and loving Son

C: Carroll.

p:s:

I dined yesterday (the 18th.) with the Intendant I had been to carry the Horace I had promised him and he invited me to dine with [him]; there were 16 persons at table of whom 4 or 5 were ladys; after dinner they played at piquet;[11] but as there were 2 or 3 others that did not play I excused my self: they played for 12 sols the fish.

Mr. Power wou'd be glad to see the new translation of Pinder;[12] he desired me to write for it; it is only Just after so much pains taken to satisfy his curiousity in that point.

ALS, Carroll Papers, MS 206, MdHi. Endorsed by CCA. A notation in CCA's hand, "Ansd: Janu: 1st: 1758," appears at the top right of the letter's first page.

1. Not found.

2. Denis Dodart, the intendant for Bourges (1728–1767), was the son of Louis XV's doctor. Vivian R. Gruder, *The Royal Provincial Intendants: A Governing Elite in Eighteenth-Century France* (Ithaca, N.Y., 1968), 4–6, 17 n.

3. Philip Francis's translation of Horace.

4. CC was writing from Bourges, where he had enrolled at the university to study civil law.

5. James Power (1725–1788) was the elder of two Irish brothers, both of whom became Jesuits. James entered the Society of Jesus in France about 1741 and later held the position of professor of philosophy at the Jesuit College in Paris, where he was known as "a highly gifted scholar and profound mathematician." After 1763 he was apparently assigned to the London district of the Society. He died at Liège. (Foley, ed., *Records,* VII, 628, and addendum, 76.) On Sept. 23, 1757, Power wrote in French to CCA to discuss CC's forthcoming stay at Bourges and to assure the elder Carroll that he would introduce CC to all the most respectable men in the city. Carroll Papers, MS 206.

6. Edward Howard, ninth duke of Norfolk (1686–1777). L. G. Pine, ed., *Burke's Genealogical and Heraldic History of the Peerage, Baronetage, and Knightage,* 100th ed. (London, 1953), 1568.

7. In his Sept. 23 letter, Power reported that the private tutor he had arranged for CC would probably charge more for his services than the instructors who taught in the school. Carroll Papers, MS 206.

8. Pounds sterling.

9. A sol or sou was an old French coin equal to twelve deniers or one-twentieth livre. McCusker, *Money and Exchange*, 280.

10. Pierre de la Rue (b. 1688), known as l'abbé de l'Isle Dieu, was vicar general for all the French colonies until his retirement in 1776. The Carrolls' relationship with the abbé involved two matters: the plight of the French Acadians forcibly transported to Maryland and CCA's plan to acquire in Louisiana an estate comparable to his Maryland holdings.

11. A card game.

12. [Thomas Tyrwhitt], *Translations in Verse . . .* (London, 1752).

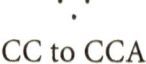

CC to CCA

Db. the 28th. 1757.

Dr. Papa,

I hope the letter I wrote you the 11th of this month[1] is safe arrived, by that you may give a guess how affairs stand with me. Nothing particular has happened since and this letter is only to wish you and My Mama a happy new year and many of e'm. If my wishes were fullfilled a long and happy old age wou'd be the least blessing; God grant you may live to see me at present your hope and Joy, the comfort of your declining age.

Of the 1200 lt[2] there is only at present remaining 447 lt 5 s ½; I have payed my pension that is 3 months of it; It began the 1rst. of this month. I have payed also for 6 pair of worked ruffles 60 lt, for a velvet Coat 172 lt and for a night gowne 57 lt. I bought the stuff and the velvet at the manufactury of the English established in town; the velvet cost 22 lt the french ell.[3] The making of my shirts will amount to 54 lt; the[y] go on very slowly; I wrote to Mr. de l'Liledieu some time ago; but have not as yet received an answer from him. Mr. Mat[4] my Master wrote me a very kind letter;[5] He seems and is I really believe my sincere friend; when I was at the College, he often desired me to procure him an english and french dictionary; to make him a present of one wou'd be genteel, and the least recompense I can make him for the esteem and friendship he allways shewed me. If you think proper to do so you may write to Mr. Crookshanks and he will buy him one at Paris. Since my last I have received a great number of visits from the gentlemen in town. I begin to get acquaintance by degrees, and consequently must keep company; but I believe my studies will hinder me from frequenting much company, twice a week will not be too much I believe but full enough. The study of the law is very dry and tedious it requires a good memory and common sense. I have allmost read the 1rst book of Justinian de institutionibus;[6] I make a little compendiun as I go along. Dr. Papa I wish you all health and happiness. I am

Your most dutifull and obedient Son
C: Carroll

The Song upon Port Mahon.[7] Par Mr. Collet.

Ces braves insulaires
qui sont qui font sur mer les corsaires
ailleurs ne tiennent gueres
Le Port mahon est pris il est pris (3 fois)
Ils en sont tous surpris
Il est pris il est pris
Les Forbans d'Angleterre
Ces fous ces fous ces foudres de guere
Sur mer comme sur terre
dés qu'ils sont combattus
Sont batus sont batus.

Anglois vos railleries
Ces traits ces mots, ces plaisanteries
Servient elles taries!
Tenez vous moins plaisans
Á present a present
Raillant ou Combattant
l'Anglois vaut tout autant
avec les mêmes graces
Il rit deffend et nous rend ses places

Ses lons mots ses menaces
Ont le meme succes
Apeupres apeupres apeupres.
Vos railleurs d'Angleterre
Nogent Melun le coche d'Auxerre
A vos vaisseaux de guerre
Ont pendant cet été
Resisté resisté resisté—
His? les ont maltraité
Notre flote d'eau douce
Vous voit vous Joint, combat, vous repouse
Et Jusques au moindre mousres
Tout est sur nos vaisseaux
des Heros des Heros des Heros. Finis

P:S:

Mr. Power gives his kind compliment[s] to you and wishes you a happy new year.

ALS, Carroll Papers, MS 206, MdHi. Addressed by CC: "For Charles Carroll Esqr. of Annapolis Recommended to the care of Mr. William Perkins Merchant In London." Endorsed by CCA.

1. Not found.

2. The editors have omitted the word "hundered," written after "1200 lt," as an inadvertent repetition.

3. The French ell equaled 1.2 meters.

4. Mr. Mat was presumably one of the priests associated with CC at the College of Louis le Grand in Paris.

5. Not found.

6. The *Institutes* was a part of the *Corpus Juris Civilis (The Body of Civil Law)* compiled at the direction of Emperor Justinian I (482–565). A summary of Roman law, it provided the legal framework for his Byzantine empire. John W. Barker, *Justinian and the Later Roman Empire* (Madison, Wis., 1966), 170–171.

7. "The Song upon Port Mahon" celebrates France's success in taking Minorca, of which Port Mahon is the capital, from Great Britain in the spring of 1756.

CCA to CC

Janu: 1st: 1758 London

Dr Charley,

I Received the Pleasure of yrs of the 19th Past this day, I need not tell you it was most Welcome to me. I wrote to You since my Arrivall here & acquainted you I had Severall letters from yr Mother & other Friends,[1] she is perfectly well & was so on the 6th of last Octor as I learn by a Gentn: who left Annapolis the 8th: My Affairs in Maryland were in as good a Scituation as I could Expect.

Yr letter is full & particular, a little time will reconcile You to yr Sollitude, it will not appear so, when you are well settled to yr Studies[.]

By all Means study to deserve the Countenance of Mr L'Intendant, you must Conforme to their amusements & learn to Play at Cards[.]

I do not think Mr Champion's demand of 12 Guineas out of the way, doe not lay him aside too Soon, I had rather you Should keep him 8 Months too long than that you should Discharge him one Month too soon, be well Convinced You doe not want a guide, before You lay Yrs aside.

I put too much confidence in yr discretion to tye you downe to £100 pr Annum, I only requier You to be frugall, I desier You Should be Genteel & decent, rather exceed than be Sordid or Mean, About the Middle of next Month you will be able to give me a better Acct, of what You think Yr Annuall Expences may Amount to—Keep strict accts. Since it is the Fashion You must get worked Ruffles.

I am Glad you resolve to write to the Abbe L'Isle Dieu, he well deserves that Complaisance I have wrote to him[2] from hence. I am sorry Your Journey was so disagreable & tedious. If I meet with any Books worth yr Perusall they shall be Sent, If you hear of any write to Mr Perkins for them & direct him how to send them to You, If by Communicateing them to Mr L'Intendant or by any other little Politesses[3] you can procure his Countenance it behoves you to doe it. I will send you the New translation of Pindar, Since Mr Power has the Curiosity to see it, I beg you to assure him it will give me a sensible pleasure to have it in my Power to oblige him, & You must not fail to present my sincerest respects to him.

I have been entierly taken up wth Business since my arrivall here wh I wrote you was on the 14th, past I have not had time yet to see a Play, before I leave London I will let You know which of the two stages I prefer.

Pray do not forget to Sollicit Mr Champion to put you into a proper Method of Framing a good & usefull Common Place Book, into wh You are to Enter the heads of yr Reading in the Civill Law, it is to Serve as an index to you hereafter — It ought to be a folio Book, what You do not fill wth yr Reading of the Civill Law, you may Compleat with the Common Law of England. Remember Arithmetick & Merchants Accts —

I Refer you to the Gazetts for Forreign news[.] The Report of the Generall officers appointed to enquier into the Causes of the failure of our late Secret Expedition was lately published it seems to Censure Genll: Mordaunt, but it is not apprehended he will suffer or be Disgraced.[4] Ld: Loudon[5] is Recalled & dayly expected in England, the Ministry is much displeased wth his Conduct & inactivity. With the 4000 troops sent last October to America its Computed we have 24 thousand Regular troops there & a very speedy embarkation of 10,000 more is strongly talked of, so that allmost in spight of ill luck Blunders &c we must Carry our Point there —

I pray to God to Grant You Health & Happyness & I assure You that I am Dear Charley

Yr Mo: Afft: Father
Cha: Carroll

PS
Let me know how to direct to you[.]

ALS, Carroll-McTavish Papers, MS 220, MdHi. Endorsed by CC.

1. Incoming correspondence not found.

2. CCA's draft of his letter to the Abbé de l'Isle Dieu of Dec. 26, 1757, mentions having "the most essential obligations to Mr le Normant" ("des Obligations tres essentielles a Mr le Normant") and professes pleasure at the "favorable sentiments" that gentleman has of CC ("Les sentiments favorables qu il a de mon fils me plat Beaucoup"). Pessimistic about chances for peace, CCA promises to "try as much as I possibly can, both by myself and with my friends, to assist those poor people with whom you have charged me" ("Je tacherai autant q'il m'est possible de soulager par moi meme et par mes amis les pauvres gens que vous m'avez recommandez") because of his inclination "to please you in all things" and as

proof of his gratitude and affection ("tant entierment disposé de vous plair en toutes Choses et de prouvez que je suis avec toute la Reconnaisance et la plus sincere attachment"). Carroll Papers, MS 206.

3. "Courtesies."

4. Gen. Sir John Mordaunt (1697–1780) commanded British amphibious forces in a surprise attack against the French naval base at Rochefort in September 1757. The mission was aborted after a series of ludicrous mishaps. Infuriated at the fiasco, which cost the government over a million pounds sterling, William Pitt, secretary of state for the southern department, ordered a court of inquiry. Lawrence Henry Gipson, *The Great War for the Empire: The Victorious Years, 1758–1760*, The British Empire before the American Revolution (New York, 1958–1970), VII, 122–124.

5. Although he had an outstanding military reputation at the time of his arrival in America, Lord Loudoun was also known as an extremely cautious man "whose greatest energies," according to his predecessor, "were put forth in getting ready to begin" (Samuel Eliot Morison, *The Oxford History of the American People* [New York, 1965], 164). Loudoun strongly disagreed with Pitt's determination to take Louisbourg, believing Quebec a more important objective. Nevertheless, he assembled a large force at Halifax in June 1757 and prepared to attack the fortress. He abandoned the effort, however, when he learned that the French navy had arrived to reinforce Louisbourg. His indecisiveness and equivocation led to his recall to England in the spring of 1758. Gipson, *Victorious Years*, 90–117.

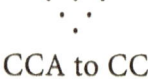

CCA to CC

L[ondon, Jan. 13, 1758][1]

[Dear] Ch[arle]y,

I wrote to You I think the 15th of Decr the day after my Arrivall here & Janu: 1st Acknowledging the Receit of Yrs of Decr: 19 & this is an answer to Yrs of Decr: the 28th. In Yr last you say you wrote to me the 11th of Decr if You did so that letter is not Come to hand. I hope my letters to You have not Miscarried But that the 1st Reached you in a few days after the date of yr last.

My Dear Child I thank You for yr Good Wishes, no thing Can happen to me more agreable than a Completion of them, However I beg you will be perswaded that in every step of myne Relating to you Yr Happyness only has been my aim, make use of the advantages I give you, improve yr time & in a few years you will Clearly see the advantages bestowed on you by a Provident & tender Father — I am well Pleasd you Consider how yr Money goes out, keeping regular Accts need not restrain you from things necessary & decent, it will rather enable you to procure them wth the Greater Satisfaction, as by a Review of yr Accts You will see whether yr Money has been well or needlessly expended[.] As to things Decent & necessary you must have them, I shall not begrudge my mony, if laid out in that [wyse?] & therefore You must draw on Mr Perkins [. . .] of Cash [. . .][2] Croo[kshanks] Should have money in his hands,[3] which I have hopes of. You did well to write to L'Isle Dieu, I have allso wrote to him. Pray write to Mr Crookshanks to get yr Master an English & French Dictionary do not Consult me on Such trifles; Pray present my Compliments to Messrs Mat, Fiteau[4] & any others to whome You think Yrself more Particularly obliged[.] I have Bought the Translation of Pindar for Mr Power wh shall be sent by the 1st safe Conveyance & I desier you will present my Sincerest Service & Compliments to him wishing him many happy new years[.] I advise You not to make too Generall an acquaintance, A return of Civilities is to be paid to all, an intimacy is not to be Contracted with any, untill You are well acquainted with their Characters, Manners & untill you are Convinced they are in the esteem of good Men. It is much easier to make acquaintance than to shake of[f] an acquaintance when made: Be nice in this Point & very Circumspect in the Choice of yr Friends, the Number that will deserve that name, I am Certain will be but small. Be Regular in the Distribution of yr Time, Relaxation is necessary, two afternoons in a week will not be too much. All Beginings are dificult, yr understanding will Open in Proportion to the Progress You make in Reading. By a Compendium you may probably mean what I mean by a Common Place Book wh I mentioned and Recommended in my last. [. . . .][5] of [l]ast Nov[r], he says he saw yr mother [. . .] she was very well & in high Spirits having Heared of my safe Arrivall. Capn Carroll Mr Croxall & Danll: Carroll all Desier their Compliments & Service to You.

Genll: Mordaunt has been acquitted by the Court Martiall, But with Genll Connoway[6] & another has been disgraced by his Majesty being struck out of the list of staff Officers; We have taken 3 or 4 French Frigates since my arrivall here & by the Papers of Yesterday a Frigate of 36 Guns Overset in Chaceing & every Soul perished, We have Beside taken a great number of Privateers & 3 transport Vessells wth Provisions & 1800 Souldiers bound to Louisburgh & we were in Pursuit of 3 more. Our Superiority at Sea is so great & our Attention to America is so much in Earnest 2000 Souldiers goeing thither immediately & 8,000 to follow in 6 Weeks, that we fl[a]tter Ourselves we shall not only be able to keep Downe the Marine of France, entierly destroy her Trade, But that we shall be able next Summer to distress her Greatly in America, while by Supplies to the K: of Prussia we shall keep her fully employed on the Continent.

I thank God I am very well, I Dayly Pray to him to keep you so, I wish you Many Many Happy New Years & I am Dr Charley

Yr Mo: Afft: Father

Cha: Carroll

PS

Another Secret Expedition is much talked of — I believe I shall not leave London before the 1st: of March[.]

ALS, Carroll-Harper Papers, MS 1225, MdHi. CC's endorsement partially obliterated. Tops of all pages damaged.

1. Date supplied from CC's letter of Feb. 4, 1758, below, which records his receipt of letters from his father dated Jan. 1 and Jan. 13, 1758, and alludes to CCA's plans to leave London on Mar. 1. The latter information is noted in the postscript to this letter but is not mentioned in that of Jan. 1.

2. Three-quarters of a line obliterated in the manuscript.

3. During his visit, CCA had placed a considerable sum of money in the hands of French officials, probably to facilitate the acquisition of property in Louisiana. He relied on Alexander Crookshanks to negotiate the return of these funds when the arrangements fell through. Crookshanks to CCA, Dec. 5, 1757, Carroll Papers, MS 206.

4. Possibly the Reverend Jean Matthieu Simon Fiteau (1716–?) who taught philosophy at Amiens and was rector of the College of Eu in 1762. Carlos Sommervogel, ed., *Bibliothèque de la Compagnie de Jésus* (Brussels, 1890–1932), III, 761.

5. One line obliterated in the manuscript.

6. Maj. Gen. Henry Seymour Conway (1721–1795) was co-commander with Sir John Mordaunt in the secret attack on Rochefort in September 1757.

. . .
.

CCA to CC

London, [Jan]u: 21st: 1758.

[Dr] Charley,

Since my Arrivall here I wrote to you Decr: 15th: Janu: 1st & 13th & I have not yet had the Satisfaction to know that any of them have reached You. I have Received yrs of Decr: 19th & 28th —

I have only been at 3 Plays yet But I Can tell You that the stages at Paris are not to be Compared to Ours. Our stages are not only much larger But infinitely better decorated, & I prefer Our Actors much to those at Paris, Garrick in Particular is both an Excellent Comedian & Tragedian.[1] The French Surpass us in their Dresses & Greatly in Dancing: Their stage is allso much more Chaste[.] The licentiousness of Ours is Realy shocking, I saw the Provoked wife[2] wh was only fit for an English audience & yet I Could not observe one Lady to Blush or be discomposed at the representation.

I suppose You will now & then write to Yr Cousin Antony & keep up a Correspondence with him this in gratitude You are Bound to doe, for althô he may have had some failings in his temper, You must be Convinced his Intentions were allways upright & that he all ways had Yr Interest & Wellfare most Sincerely at Heart[.]

As to Politicks we are preparing for a Vigorous Campain in America & Europe, To America (wth 2,000 Soldiers now goeing) we shall Send 10,000 [. . . re]inforcement will mak[e the nu]mber of Regulars there about 34,000, a force seemingly sufficient to insure success to wh You must add the Forces of the Colonies wh Cant be less than 10,000[.] By a Motion that was made Yesterday in the House of Commons by Mr Pit[3] The Kings Electorall Troops are to be taken into the Pay of Great

Britain,[4] Supposing the K: of Prussia should Come into a Plan of Operations & Measures projected by Our Court some say the Purport of the Motion was to Pay all the troops his Majesty should think fit to Employ in Germany, or as Others say a Round Sum of a Million sterling will be Granted without acct to that End. By this the Ministry seem to think that Vigorous Measures in Europe will facilitate & Greatly help Our Operations in America, wh Measure is Seemingly Contrary to their former Sentiments. We say that the Queen of Hungarys forces were 160,000 at the Begining of the Campain & that they are now reduced to 34,000 or 35,000[5] & that the Russian & French Troops are allso prodigiously deminished. The Ministry meet wth no opposition in Parliament, Publick Credit is in a flourishing Condition & Money is readily supplyed at an easy interest, wh: we hear is far from being the Case in France, their trade & Merchants are undone & allmost all their Ships of War wee meet with are taken[.]

I Believe I shall leave London about the 1st: of March a Convoy for the Maryland & Virginia [. . .] appointed the [. . .] & that time I hope to have the Pleasure of Severall [let]ters from You. Pray Present my Sincere Service to Mr Power, two Volumes of the Translation of Pindar in Octavo goes wth this to Mr Anto: Carroll, who has directions to send them to Mr Crookshanks who will forward them. I need not tell You that I wish You perfect Health & all Manner of Happyness. I am Dr Charley

Yr Mo: Afft: Father
Cha: Carroll

PS

I know not how to direct to You. I desier You will send me directions how I am to use the two sorts of Water for the Teeth wh Matton the Dentist sold me, I have forgot them[.]

ALS, Carroll-McTavish Papers, MS 220, MdHi. Addressed in the hand of Alexander Crookshanks to "Monsieur Carroll Gentilhomme Anglois a Bourges Berry." CC's endorsement partially obliterated.

1. David Garrick (1717–1779), the foremost thespian of his day.

2. A Restoration comedy written by Sir John Vanbrugh.

3. William Pitt (1708–1778) was born in Westminster and educated at Eton and at Trinity College, Oxford. First elected to the House of Commons in 1735, he served there until 1766 and quickly made his reputation as an orator. In 1756 he became secretary of state for the southern department. Dismissed and then reinstated by George II in 1757, Pitt successfully prosecuted the war and directed foreign affairs until 1761, when he resigned because of his failure to gain the support of George III and his favorite, Lord Bute, for a declaration of war against Spain. He continued to play a key role in the House of Commons and in 1763 opposed the surrender of parliamentary privilege in the John Wilkes case, despite his detestation of Wilkes's publication, the *North Briton*. He advocated the repeal of the Stamp Act and strongly defended the colonists' claim that Parliament had no right to tax them. Asked by the king to form a government in July 1766, Pitt did so but fatally undermined

his popularity as "the Great Commoner" by simultaneously accepting a peerage creating him earl of Chatham. Kept out of politics between 1767 and 1769 by ill health, he found his influence drastically reduced upon his return. As a member of the House of Lords he continued to oppose British policy toward America, but he also fought to retain the colonies because of the critical damage he believed granting their independence would inflict upon the monarchy. So diminished was his power after 1771 that he rarely attended Parliament. Namier and Brooke, *House of Commons*, III, 290–299.

4. The Hanoverians' accession to the British throne did not result in their relinquishing ties to their native duchy. To the jealous annoyance of many Britons, both George I, who occupied the British throne 1714–1727, and George II (1683–1760), who reigned from 1727 until his death, retained the title elector of Hanover, frequently visited there, and were actively committed to its defense. Although at one time vigorously opposed to giving financial aid to German principalities, William Pitt abandoned that position after becoming secretary of state in June 1757 and urged Parliament to grant large subsidies to Hanover, Prussia, and Hesse-Cassel for purposes of carrying on the war. Ibid., 291–292; Gipson, *Victorious Years*, 176; Carl William Eldon, *England's Subsidy Policy towards the Continent during the Seven Years' War* (Philadelphia, 1938), 93–121.

5. Maria Theresa (1717–1780), archduchess of Austria and queen of Hungary and Bohemia from 1740 until 1780. Her forces were routed by those of Frederick the Great at the battle of Leuthen in December 1757.

CC to CCA

Febry. the 4th. 1758.

Dr. Papa

I received the 2d. of this month tow [two] letters from you in one enclosed from Mr. Crookshanks.[1] the one dated the 1st. of January 1758 the other the 13th. of the same month. You may be assured they were both exceeding agreable and so much the more so as they freed me from all anxiety concerning your safe arrivall. I began to be apprehensive and uneasy having heared no news of you since your departure from Paris: for your letter of the 15th. of december did not come to hand being probably thrown overboard the packetboat taken the 23d. of Deb. Nothing gives me greater pleasure than to hear My Mama is well and in high spirits and that your affaires go on well. I am equally pleased to find my letter, I wrote you, full and satisfactory. I am of your opinion that i'ts better to keep Mr. Champion 8 months too long than discharge him one too soon. Alltho' the civill Law be a very dry and difficult studdy, I hope by my application and his assistance to acquire a sufficient knowledge of it in tow [two] years time. A Common place book is somewhat different from a Compendium, but a Compendium is more necessary for that part of the law I at present apply to [Vd?] the Institutes. The Institutes are a concinct picture or to speak more planely a most excellent epitome of the whole Roman

Law; consequently they must be somewhat obscure and difficult. The Compendium I make contains the principal articles, definitions, with some explication and remarkes. upon the most difficult parts in that work. I did not think a folio Book wou'd be convenient so I took one of a lesser size[,] when I come to the 2d. part of the civil law if you think proper I shou'd I will buy one in Folio.

You may be assured Dr. Papa I shall strive not to turn into an abuse the confidence you put in me. I shall endeavour to manage my little affaires with all the care and attention I am capable of by avoiding the 2 extreames of affectation and meaness. I keep strick accounts and shall send them to you at the end of the year so you will be able to Judge yourself wether I have spent foolishly or no.

Since my last to you, I have received tow [two] from Mr. L'iledieu.[2] I discover the same goodness the same affection in his letters that renders his conversation so agreable. By his last I am informed that 200 guineas are to be remitted this month to Mr. Crookshanks. Mr. L'iledieu desires to be remembered to you in the most kindest manner.

The books you intend to send me must be directed to Mr. Crookshanks at Paris: he when they are once arrived there can easily convey them to me[.] I know I shall oblige very much the Intendant by communciating them to him it was only with that Intent I wrote for them. I thank you kindly for the translation of Pindar, so does Mr. Power he presents you his kindest compliments[.] I live quite retired, see little or no company. I have 2 or 3 reasons for acting thus 1st. because there is no instruction to be reaped in those companies where they do nothing but play at Cards 2dly. because I c'ant go one night into company without going a 2d. a 3d. a 4th. and so on the whole week. Company is kept here regularly from 5 to 9 of the Clock one night in one Gentleman's house, another in another's. If I go to one I shall be invited to another and cant absent myself without committing an impolitess.[3] Frequenting thus regularly shuch company brings on a great loss of time. I went a few days ago to a ball given by the Intendant but did not danse. I was a perfect stranger and not well acquainted with their danses. I believe I shall take a dansing master for 4 or 5 months or thereabouts. The news you write is very interesting and agreable. In all likely hood we shall meet with more success in America than we have hithertoo done. I believe Spain will declare openly for France this spring. If you leave London the 1st. of March you w'ont be able to receive another letter from me before your departure. Dont faill I beg you to write to me when you set sail and immediately at your arrivall in Maryland. Embrace my Mama at your meeting a thousand times for me assure her of my love and affection et n'oubliez pas dans un moment si doux un fils qui vous aime tout deux de tout son Ceur et qui vous aimera toujours.[4] Farewell Dr. Papa, a happy voyage and all blessings attend you. I am

Your most affectionate and dutifull Son.
C. Carroll

P.S:

Direct to me thus A Mr. Monsieur Carroll chez mr. Carré Medecin pres la place des Carmes à Bourges[.]

I have taken a new Servant; my old one had not one good quality excepting honnesty and severall bads ones. Does Joshep remain with you will he follow you to Maryland: how did he get over his little trafick? Mrs. [Messrs.] Buttler Fitaux and Mat desire to be remembered to you. I sha'nt neglect your advise concerning Merchant's accounts and arithmetick; but all things in good time; who undertakes too much will do nothing.

ALS, Carroll Papers, MS 206, MdHi. Addressed by CC to his father in care of London merchant William Perkins. Endorsed by CCA.

1. Not found.
2. Not found.
3. "Rudeness."
4. "And do not forget in a moment such a gentle son who loves you both with all his heart and who will love you always."

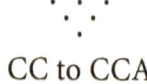

CC to CCA

Febry. the 11th. 1758.

Dr. Papa,

I wrote to you the 4th. of this month a very long and circumstantiall letter in answer to yours of the 1st. and 13th. of Janu[ry.] Yours of the 15th. of Debr. did not come to hand. This day I received another from you dated the 21st. of Janury. I am affraied this letter which is an answer to it will come too late. I intend to keep up a correspondance with my Cousin Antony I have wrote to him since my arrivall here. I am entirely persuaded he had allways my interest and wellfare and heart; Pray are people more particularly merry in England during shrove-tide[1] than at any other time. There are masquerades, danseing and God knowes [wh]at all in this place. I went masqued to a ball last shrove-tuesday night. I was mightily diverted with my own and other's ridiculous figure. I had the pleasure of accompaning and danseing with one of the most butifull young ladies I ever saw. D'ont be affraied now that I am fallen in love with her there is no danger; she is a going in few day's time to Paris to be married there to a handsom gentleman of a pretty fortune: her's is but very inconsiderable.

By what you write me and by what I hear ellsewhere the English seem really to be in earnest at last: I am of the Ministery's way of thinking videlicet[2] that the best way of forwarding our arms in America is to persue the war in Europe with the uttemost vigour. France will be more employed and consequently will not be able to fix her attention on her Colonies and settlements in America, or at most she will only be able to send but very moderate supplies which intercepted by the English squadrons at sea will entirely distress her in that part of the world. But after all I believe the French are not so easily to be distressed; they have innumerable resources and are a cunning warlike nation two qualites quite necessary in war, one of which we are entirely destitute of. The Queen of Hungary's forces are certainly greatly dimminished by the severall losses they have lately sustained but not so much as the English papers make them. I am surprised to hear that money is so easy to be had in England after shuch immense expences. Its certain that the commerce of France is nigh i'ts last gaspe but notwithstanding the King[3] stills finds as much money as he stands in need of.

Pray send me or desire Mr. Perkins to send me with the other books two little pocket Horaces of the Glascow edittion.[4] The books that may be allready bought or those that I may write for to Mr. Perkins must be sent to and directed to Mr. Crookshanks at Paris. I have received two or 3 letters from Mr. l'Isledieu he desires to be remembered to you in the kindest manner. 200 guineas are to be remitted to Mr. Crookshanks this month. I believe that sum will be sufficient to pay my expences during my stay in this town. Perhaps I shall be obliged to draw upon Mr. Perkins once on this side of the water in order to make a collection of all the Latin Classick authers. I have remaining by me of the 50 guineas 14 — I believe they will last me to Easter or ther[ea]bouts.

I left behind me at Paris a very pretty Collection of Rollin's mapps for the use and intelligence of ancient history.[5] I shou'd be glad to know wether you carried them away with you to London. I dont exactly remember how you are to use Mr. Muttons waters but I believe the rescription is more or less as follows. Wash your mouth at night with the red; take a teaspoon full of the saffron coloured every morning in a cup of lukewarm water and at the same time make use of the little brush up and down but not cross ways.

The inclosed is from Mr. Champion: be so good as to deliver it to the Duke of Norfolk. You must know that that nobleman came to Bourges some years ago where he made acquaintance with Mr. Champion and stood god father to one of his Children. Mr. Champion is an honnest worthy man and a merry one tho' not rich: two or 3 years ago he lossed 600 lt by a bankrupt; he has a numerous family to mentain; and I believe a present from the Duke of Norfolk wou'd be agreable to him in his present circumstances. If you see the duke and have an occasion you may, if you think proper, insinuate this to him: he was a particular friend of Mr. Champion's.

Your opinion of the English and French stage seems to be very Just; i'ts as I thought; but I did not really think there tragedies so obscene as you seem to mention. Mr. Power gives his kind compliments to you. Remember me to my Mama in the most affectionate manner do'nt forget to write to [me] immediately when you leave London and when you arrive in Maryland. I suppose you have all the letters I have wrote you from this place by you — they will be agreable to my Mama and may afford her somme satisfaction. Does not Cousin Antony go with [you] to Maryland?[6] I wish you a short and happy voyage and good health. My sincerest wishes to all my friends my Compliments to Mr Perkins. I am Dr. Papa

Your most dutifull and affectionate Son

C: Carroll.

P:S:

Be pleased to send me Sr David Hume's essays[7] 4 volu: in 12.[8] Remember me to Harry Carroll, when the war is at an end I suppose he will go to sea again, if so I hope I shall have the pleasure of seeing him in London in two or 3 years time; it will afford a great pleasure to see him at any time. I bear him a true affection and wish him all happiness. I desire you will give my compliments to Mr. Lawson[9] Mr. Croxall Charles[10] and D[ick] and Mr. Lyon.[11] Assure my Grand Mama of my love and affection for her all that's kind to my Aunt Genny. Vive et vale.[12]

ALS, Carroll Papers, MS 206, MdHi. CCA's endorsement indicates that he answered this letter on Mar. 1 "by Mr Duddle."

1. The three-day period immediately preceding Lent.

2. "To wit."

3. Louis XV (1710–1774), who reigned 1715–1774.

4. *Opera* (Glasgow, 1745).

5. Probably Jean Baptiste Bourgvignon d'Anville, *Twelve Maps of Antient Geography . . . Designed for the Explanation of Rollin's Antient History . . .* (London, 1757). Rollin (1661–1741) was professor of eloquence in the Royal College, University of Paris, and a member of the Royal Academy of Inscriptions and Belles-Lettres. *Cat. Lib.*, no. 1399, lists his *Histoire ancienne*, 13 vols., published in Paris in 1731.

6. There is no evidence that Antony Carroll visited Maryland before 1774. Foley, ed., *Records*, VII, 117–118.

7. David Hume (1711–1776), Scottish philosopher, historian, and essayist. The Carrolls owned a 1758 London edition of his *Essays and Treatises on Several Subjects . . . ,* 4 vols. (Edinburgh and London, 1753). *Cat. Lib.*, no. 522.

8. Duodecimo.

9. Alexander Lawson (1710–1760) was a wealthy ironmaster and at one time managed the Nottingham Ironworks in Baltimore Co. By 1738 he was serving as clerk to the Baltimore Company. His wife, Dorothy Smith Lawson, was the daughter of Elizabeth Carroll's sister Susanna Brooke Smith Hoxton and her first husband, Walter Smith (Appendix I, Chart E). The Lawson estate lay on the eastern side of present-day Baltimore's Druid Hill Park. Christopher Johnston, "Smith Family of Calvert County," in *Md. Gen.*, II, 379; William B. Marye, "The Old Indian Road," *Md. Hist. Mag.*, XV (1920), 210 n; " 'News' from the 'Maryland Gazette,' " *Md. Hist. Mag.*, XVIII (1923), 160; J. V. Kelly, *Druid Hill Park: The Land and Its People during the Period of Private Ownership*, Public Parks of Baltimore, no. 3 (Baltimore, 1928), 14–16.

10. CC's second cousin Charles Croxall (1724–1782). See Appendix I, Chart B.

11. Born in Perth, Scotland, William Lyon (1715–1794) immigrated to Baltimore in 1735, soon after receiving his medical degree. A partner in the town's first drugstore, Lyon's and

Philpot's, the doctor began to acquire land in the Green Spring Valley in 1745 and within a decade was living there. During the 1750s and 1760s he served as a justice of the Baltimore Co. court and as a Baltimore Town commissioner. In the late 1740s he returned briefly to Scotland where he married, over the objections of her parents, Jean Graham (Grahame) and brought her with him to Maryland. Barnes and Thomas, *Green Spring Valley*, I, 39–40, 366, II, 56–58; Lyons Genealogical Collection, G5034, Genealogical MS Colls., MdHi.

12. "Live on and fare well," a closing often used by Latin writers.

∴
∵

CC to CCA and Elizabeth Carroll

June the 14th. 1758.

Dr. Papa & Mama.

This is my second letter to you since your departure from London: my last was dated the 23d. of March: Yours of the 1st. & 8th of March & 1st. of Aprill are all come safe to hand.[1] The books you sent me from London are not as yet arrived. They remain still with Mr. Galloway at Ostend; but I hope to receive them in a short time. I advance on in the study of the civill law and as I advance it appeares more and more agreable. I have at length finnished the Institutes and have began to read Domat's civill laws:[2] a usefull and profitable book; I was obliged to buy it here being not able to borrow it; the price is 26 £. the advantage I hope to reap in the reading of it will answer the price.

The uniformity of my way of living can scarce furnish me with matter enough to fill up a letter. My chief nay my allmost only amusement is reading; I find no conversation more agreable than that of a Horace's a Virgil's a Racine's &c. their company is instructive and at the same time agreable, monent et mulcent.[3] Sometimes I forsake the Poets & prefer to the mellodious harmony of the muses the profitable and faithfull lessons of History; here I learn to be wise at the expence of other's and to attain to true glory by the example of the great, good, & Just. These and such like amusements are now and then interrupted by others of a quite different nature.

I lately made a little excursion into the adjacent country. I went from Bourges to Sancerre to see a Scotch Lord, who is established in that town a good, honnest, man, unhappy t'is true but worthy of a better fate. He was in the late rebellion[4] and lossed his estate of about 3 thousand pound Sterling a year. I dont ever in my life remember to have seen a finer country than the Sancerrois nor a more beautiful or a more extensive prospect. From a high eminence, on which the town is built you see before you as far as the eye can carry the view is only bounded by the horrison. On each side are hills adorned with vines and woods (the wine is exceeding good[)]. Between these hills layes wide and extensive meadows covered with flocks of sheep, herds of cattle, country seats &c. But nothing contributes more to the beauty and ornament of this so delightful a country than the River Loire. Charmed with the beauties of the place he peacefully glides along the meadows in so many and various meanders, that he often seems to return upon himself and quit this enchanting abode with reluctance. From this terrestrial Paradise I went to la Charité a little town in sight of Sancerre and 12 leagues from Bourges. Here I met with one Mr. Alcock an Englishman who has established at la Charité a factory of buttons. His method of making 'em is curious and amusing; but not half so amusing as his young pretty, witty daughter. After a day or two's stay I returned to Bourges in good health but a little dull and pensive.

There has lately been made a change in the Ministery. Moras has laid down his post, and has received from his Majesty as a recompense for his services done the state 40000 £ per Anu. Massiac an old experenced sea officer has succeeded him and Monr. le Norman is appointed his adjoint.[5] I wrote the latter a letter to compliment him upon his promotion. I likewise wrote as you directered me to Mr. l'Iledieu and endeavoured to season my letter with all the politeness and all the gratitude a grateful heart can be capable of: But as yet no answer. The 200 guineas are not as yet paid.[6] I have bought half a ticket in the Cologne Lottery & have allready gained to my share 10 £: a ticket costes 35 £. 11 S. I hope to acquaint you in my next of the acquisition of the gros lot. Amongst 5 tickets there are 3 prises, so you see I stand a chance of getting something. La lotterie est de 6 differentes tirages, et chaque tirage se fait chaque mois.[7]

I earnestly desire to hear often from you, nothing gives me greater satisfaction than to hear you are well. I humbly intreat my Mama to make her letters to me a little longer; she may be assured that any thing coming from her is agreable and welcome. When you write you wou'd oblige me in giving me an account of our American war. Pray have you as yet met with an offer for selling your lands? Or do you remain still determined to sell them? Does our ennimies still continue to persecute us? Their injustice and ungratefulness quite surprises me: what have we done to deserve such treatment from them? Their complaintes as well as their reasons I am convinced are entirely groundless. How did you find your affaires at your arrival? I doubt not but in a prosperous way: this is owing to the prudence of Mr. Croxall; my sincerest compliments to him and to his brother. My Mama I dare say made you a number of questions concerning me, I wish I cou'd satisfy them my self by my presence. I long to see you both with all my heart. I am Dr. Papa and Mama

Your most loving and obedient Son
C: Carroll

P:S:

I quite forgot the snuf-box. I shall repair my fault when I pass by Paris in my way to London: My love and duty to my Grand-Mama, my sincerest respects to my Aunt Genny compliments to Mr. & Mrs. Lawson & their children,[8] to doctor Lyon &c.

ALS, Carroll Papers, MS 206, MdHi. Endorsed by CCA.

1. Letters not found.

2. Jean Domat (1625–1696), *Les loix civiles, dans leur ordre naturel* (Paris, 1689).

3. "They instruct and they charm," probably a paraphrase of Horace *Ars poetica* 333–334.

4. In 1745 the "Young Pretender," James II's grandson Bonnie Prince Charlie, led Scottish highlanders in a short-lived revolt that was crushed, along with Stuart pretensions to the throne, on Apr. 16 at the battle of Culloden. During the uprising, the Maryland assembly pledged support to the house of Hanover. Scharf, *Maryland*, I, 435.

5. Peirinc de Moras served as French minister of marine, the agency responsible for administering France's colonies, from February 1757 until June 1758. He was succeeded by the marquis de Massiac, and Sébastien-François-Ange Le Normant de Mézy (1702–1791), who had served as intendant in Louisiana (1743–1748), was appointed Massiac's administrative officer. Ernest Lavisse, *Histoire de France depuis les origines justqu'a la Revolution* (1900–1911; reprint, New York, 1969), VIII, Pt. 2, 272; Lee Kennett, *The French Armies in the Seven Years' War: A Study in Military Organization and Administration* (Durham, N.C., 1967), 6 n; John G. Clark, *New Orleans, 1718–1812: An Economic History* (Baton Rouge, La., 1970), 117–121.

6. The material between "I wrote" and "yet paid" is bracketed in pencil in the manuscript. The editors have omitted the word "hundered," which follows the figure "200."

7. "The lottery has six different drawings, one each month."

8. Alexander Lawson and Dorothy Smith Lawson (1716–?) had nine children, six of whom were still living: Alexander (?–1798), Rachel (1738–by 1760), who had by this time married Lloyd Buchanan, Susanna (1743–1798), Rebecca (1752–1801), Isabella (?–1822), and Mary. Barnes, *Marriages and Deaths*, 111; *Bio. Dic. Md. Legis.*, I, 179–180, II, 936. See also Appendix I, Chart E.

CCA to CC

June 26th. 1758.

Dr Charley

I embrace the 1st opportunity to inform you of my safe Arrival the 11th Instant at my own house in Annapolis, the next Day yr Mama came to me from my Country Seat at Elk-ridge. You may more easily conceive then I can express the Joy & pleasure of our happy meeting. As I wrote you from Portsmouth I embarked the 1st of April we put into Torbay[1] from whence we took our Departure the 8th & on the 8th: of this Instt: we came into our Bay having that day 12 Month left the Capes for Europe. I have had the Satisfaction to find all our Friends in good Health & that my Interest has not suffered much in my Absence. Your Mama & I are I thank God in Perfect Health. As to news we have according to our Gazetts 30 Ships of the Line & 12 or 15 Frigates beside bombs & Fire Ships before Louisburg. Our Troops consisting of 14 thousand were expected to land the 3d Instt: in Gabarous Bay[2] about

2 Leagues from Louisburg. The French have 3 Men of War & 5 other Vessels there. Our Fleet & Transports left Halifax the 28th past. We daily take store Ships bound to Quebec & Louisburg. General Amhurst[3] commands agst: Louisburg. General Abercrombie has some time past marched from Albany with an Army of 22 thousand men[4] beside a great Number of Batteau[x m]en agst: Ticonderoga Crown Point &c. General Forbes with 7000 men is gone or on the point of going from the Back parts of Pensilvania agst: Fort du Quesne on the Ohio,[5] a considerable Datachment of his Troops have been out some time past Clearing the way. We compute at least 30 thousand Regular Troops now on this Continent,[6] & 15 or 16 Thousand Militia, wch may be augmented to what Number the Government at home think fit. We have the greatest plenty of all sorts of Provisions to Support much [m]ore numerous Armies. We do not apprehend that our Enemies can bring a Sufficient Force into the field to resist us & consequently we flatter our selves with Success in every Quarte[r.] Pray present my Sincere Service & Compliments to Mess[rs.] Power & De L'Isle Dieu[.] Yr: Mama & I join in our Blessing to you Praying God to Grant you Health & to keep you Innocent & Virtuous. I am My Dr: Charley

Yr Mo: Afft. Father
Cha: Carroll

PS

I shall write to you by all opportunities & I beg you will write to me at least Six times a Year & send Duplicates. Keep a Letter Book & let me know the Dates of all the Letters you write[.]

LS, Charles Carroll of Carrollton Collection, MS 1893, MdHi. Addressed by CCA: [first line of address obliterated] "Carré Medecin pres la Place des Carmes A Bourges," and marked "Triplicate."

1. A harbor located on the coast of Devon.

2. Gabarus Bay, on the east coast of Cape Breton Island.

3. Maj. Gen. Jeffery Amherst (1717–1797) was appointed the commander of British troops in America on Feb. 19, 1758.

4. Gen. James Abercromby (1706–1781) took the American command from Lord Loudoun on Dec. 30, 1757, but was shortly thereafter replaced by Amherst. Modern estimates of the size of Abercromby's force, as assembled at Lake George on July 1, 1758, in preparation for a march on Ticonderoga, number it at about twelve thousand men.

5. Between July and November 1758, Gen. John Forbes (1710–1759) moved along Gen. Edward Braddock's route through the Blue Ridge Mountains to engage the French at Fort Duquesne.

6. According to Theodore Ropp (*War in the Modern World* [Durham, N.C., 1959], 67), the British sent twenty thousand regular troops to America to fight alongside the same number of colonial soldiers.

CC to CCA and Elizabeth Carroll

Augst. 10th. 1758.

Dr. Papa and Mama,

Il y aujourd'huy un an que Je vous vis pour la 1re. fois apres 8 ans d'absence: que ce Jour est different de celui-lá! Quelle Joie ne sentois-je pas alors? il n'y manquoit rien pour être complette que d'etre d'une plus longue durée. Quand Je songe á ces momens agreables que nous passâmes ensemble, ces promenades que nous fîmes aux Thuileries, au Louvre, au Palais royal, ces petites courses dans les environs de Paris tout cela me frappe si vivement l'esprit que Je ne puis m'empecher de verser quelques larmes. Voila qui est bien foible me direz vous: soit: mais du moins vous devez aimer cette foiblesse, si vous m'aimez, puisque c'est vous qui en êtes la cause. Mais laissons-lá ces ideés et ce souvenir d'une Joie passagere qui ne laisse apres soi que du regret de n'en plus Jouir: cherchons en plutot quelque chose qui peut nous egayer.

Souvenez vous d'avoir vu Monr. Willougby,[1] c'est lui qui vous donnât á diner á Paris. Je l'ai rencontré dernierement á la Charité chez Monsieur Alcock (voyez ma derniere lettre) il y etoit lors que J'arrivois; oui il y etoit, mais á n'en point sortir si tot. Mademoiselle Alcock le tenoit enchainé, il l'aime eperduement, et elle le meprise: heureusement pour lui. Les Biens de mademoiselle Alcock sont tres mediocres ou pour mieux dire elle n'a d'autre bien que son esprit et sa beauté; les sienes sont considerables; cependant il etoit dans le dessein de l'epouser, si elle avoit voulu, et même sans le consentement de son Pere. Il est á la fin parti de la Charité, Je ne scais comment il a pu se ressoudre á quitter sa maitresse[.] Il lui est arrivé un peu avant son depart de la Charité un accident assez plaisant. La fantasie le prit d'accompagner Mademoiselle Alcock á Sancerre ville voisine et dont Je vous ai deja parlé. Ils y allerent donc, mais non pas seuls; y etant arrivé il va voir My Lord qui lui fait mille amities, le prie á souper, il s'excuse dabors; on le presse il se defend mal et enfin se rende tout a fais. Le voila á souper, il y cause beaucoup, mange de bon appétit et boit de même. Le souper etant deservi on apporte a large bowl of punche, il y en avoit assez pour noyer une armée presque entiere. Mon homme deja echauffé par le vin qu'il avoit bu, boit encore copieusement de ce liqueur seduisant. L'effet s'en suivît de prés; le voila grizé comme il faut; on le conduit dans sa chambre, et il s'endort mais son sommeil fut bientot interrompu. Le devoîment le prend tout d'un coup, il court aux commodités, au lieu des commodités il entre dans la chambre de la domestique, monte sur son lit croyant á coup sur trouver la ce qu'il cherchoit: elle etoit au lit. . . . Je vous laisse á deviner le reste.

Je m'applique toujours á l'etude des loix civiles et principalement á Monsieur Domat; c'est un auteur clair, net, et precis: J'espere et par son secours et par mon travail d'acquerir dans l'espace d'un an une coinoissance assez complette du droit civil. Apres un travail aussi continu et dans une matiere seche et ennuieuse vous penserez peutetre qu'il ne sera pas malápropos de prendre quelque relache et de se divertir un peu. C'est dans cette vue que Je me propose d'aller á Lyon dans quelque tems d'ici et peutetre plus loin si mes finances me le permettent. Monr. Power m'accompagnera; il seroit trop ennuieux de faire un si long chemin tout seul; il a la même envie de voir ce païs-lá que moi; Je l'obligerai beaucoup en le faisant compagnion de mon voyage; la politesse et la recoinoissance exigent de moi que Je le fasse: et J'ose me flatter que vous ne le trouverez pas mauvais. Á mon retour Je vous envoirer une longue relation bien detaillié de tout ce que J'ai vu de plus curieux et en même-tems le memoir de mes depenses pendant cette anneé.

J'ai reçû il n'y a pas long tems une lettre tres polie de Monr. le N.[2] malgré cette politesse il me donne tres peu d'esperance de voir votre projet reussir: il n'y faut pas penser seulement. On n'a pas encore remis á monsieur Crookshanks les 200 Louis d'or.[3] Quand seront-t'ils remis? C'est ce que Jignore. Momsieur de l'Isledieu ne me fait pas l'honneur de me repondre; Je lui ai pourtant ecrit deux lettrés de suite, il est difficile á deviner quelle soit la cause de son silence.[4]

Bourges commence á m'ennuier un peu: elle est toute propre á cela, point de spectacles, point de petites parties dè plaisir, point de promenades, c'est un païs isolé: il y faut Jouer aux cartes ou ne voir personne; J'aime mieux vivre en hermite ou comme Diogene sous un tonneau que de perdre tant de tems á Jouer aux cartes. Cela etant ainsi il est naturel á croire que Je souhaite d'être au bout de mon exil: cependant Je prendrai patience Jusqu'á ce tems-lá: patientiâ fit levius quid quid corrigere est nefas[5] comme dit fort bien Horace l'ami de bon sens.

Cette lettre (du moins Je l'espere) vous causera doublement du plaisir. 1. Vous verrez par-lá que Je commence a scavoir un peu le francois. 2. Vous aurez la peine á l'expliquer á ma tres chere Mere; cette peine sans doubte vous sera bien douce. Mais tandis que vous expliquerez cette lettre, n'oubliez pas celui qui l'a ecrit: il ne vous oublis pas: il vous aime, et ne pense qu'á vous. I am Drs. Papa and Mama

Your most dutifull and Loving Son
Charles Carroll.

P:S:

I desire to be remembered to my Grand Mama, to my Aunt Genny to the two Croxals, to Mr. and Mrs. Lawson, to Doctor Lyon; in general to all friends and relations.

ALS, Carroll Papers, MS 206, MdHi. Endorsed by CCA.

Translation*

Augst. 10th. 1758.

Dr. Papa and Mama,

It is just a year ago today that I saw you for the first time in 8 years: how different Today is from that! What Joy I felt then! To be complete it need only have lasted longer. When I think of those pleasant moments we spent together, the walks we took in the Thuileries, the Louvre, the Palais royal, those little excursions in the environs of Paris I remember it all so vividly that I can't help dropping several tears. You would tell me that is very weak: so be it: but at least you must love that weakness; if you love me, since you are its cause. But let's leave these thoughts and this memory of a fleeting Joy that leaves only regret for not having Lasted: instead let's look for something that might make us gay.

Do you remember Mr. Willougby,[1] it was he who entertained you at dinner in Paris. I ran into him recently at la Charité at Mr. Alcock's (see my last letter) he was there when I arrived; yes he was there but did not leave so early. Miss Alcock had captivated him, he loves her hopelessly, and she scorns him: fortunately for him. Miss Alcock's Wealth is very mediocre or to put it another way she has no wealth other than her wit and her beauty; his is considerable; neverthless it was his plan to marry her, if she had wished, even without the consent of his Father. He has finally left la Charité, I don't know how he was able to bring himself to leave his mistress[.] Shortly before his departure from la Charité a funny thing happened to him. He was seized by the whim to accompany Miss Alcock to Sancerre a nearby town that I have mentioned before. They went there, but not by themselves; upon arriving he goes to see My Lord who shows him a thousand kindnesses, begs him to stay for supper, he declines the invitation; they press him he resists a bit and finally surrenders completely. There he is at supper, he chats a good deal, eats with a hearty appetite and drinks with the same. The supper over they bring in a large bowl of punche, almost enough to drown an army. My man already overheated by the wine, continues to drink copiously of this seductive liquor. The effect was soon felt; there he is drunk as can be; he is led to his room, and he goes to sleep but his sleep is soon interrupted. Necessity suddenly grabs him, he runs to the commode, but instead of the commode he enters the maid's room, climbs on her bed thinking for sure that he has found what he was looking for: she was in the bed. . . . I leave you to guess the rest.

I am still studying civil law and principally Monsieur Domat; he is a clear author, accurate and precise: I hope both with his help and by my work to acquire in a year a fairly complete understanding of civil law. After such continuous work in a dry and boring subject you might think perhaps it would not be improper to take a little respite and to have some fun. It is in this spirit that I propose in a short time to go to Lyon and perhaps farther if my finances permit it. Mr. Power will accompany me; it would be too boring to make such a long journey alone; he wants to see this region as much as I; I will oblige him greatly in making him my traveling companion; courtesy and gratitude require that I do it: and I dare to flatter myself that you will not object. On my return I will send you a long detailed description of all the most interesting things I have seen and at the same time the record of the year's expenses.

I received not long ago a very polite letter from Monr. le N.[2] Despite his courtesy he gives me very little hope of seeing your project succeed: you should not think only of that. Mr. Crookshanks still has not been paid the 200 Louis d'or.[3] When will they be paid? That I don't know. Monsieur de l'Isledieu doesn't even do me the honour of answering; I nevertheless wrote him two letters in succession, it is difficult to figure out what might be the cause of his silence.[4]

Bourges begins to bore me a little: it is perfectly suited for that; there are no plays, no little pleasure parties, no promenades, it is an isolated region: one has to Play cards or see no one; I would rather live like a hermit or like Diogenes under a barrel than to lose so much time Playing cards. No wonder I wish I were at the end of my exile: however I will be patient Until that time comes: patientiâ fit levius quid quid corrigere est nefas[5] as Horace the friend of good sense says very well.

This letter (at least I hope so) will cause you double pleasure. 1st. you will see from it that I am beginning to know a little French. 2d. you will have the job of explaining it to my very dear Mother; that labour will surely be very sweet to you. But while you are explaining this letter, don't forget the one who wrote it: he does not forget you: he loves you, and thinks only of you. I am Drs. Papa and Mama

Your most dutifull and Loving Son
Charles Carroll

P:S:

I desire to be remembered to my Grand Mama, to my Aunt Genny to the two Croxals, to Mr. and Mrs. Lawson, to Doctor Lyon; in general to all friends and relations.

* Translated from the French by Philip Benedict and Eleanor S. Darcy.

1. Either Robert or Edward Willoughby, both of whom attended St. Omers with CC. Holt, *St. Omers,* 289–290.

2. Not found.

3. The Louis d'or was a French coin worth £1.02 sterling in 1758. McCusker, *Money and Exchange,* 11.

4. The first and last lines of this paragraph have been marked off by penciled lines at the left margin.

5. "Whatever we cannot change is made lighter by patience." Horace *Odes* 1.24.19–20.

. . .
.

Elizabeth Carroll to CC

[Aug. 29, 1758][1]

I can not express my dear Child the Joy I felt at meeting with yr Papa nor the Satisfaction & Comfort I recd. from his Conversation concerning you[.] I find his Opinion of you just to my wishes & I am Certain that no Parent can have a greater tenderness for his Child then yrs has for you, nor repose a greater Confidence nor be more at Ease at his Sons being at so great a distance, which are all Convincing proofs of yr Merit. I perused all yr letters to yr Papa & those to me with the utmost pleasure, they are so full of tenderness & affection for us that they cou'd not fail to delight & at the same time to draw Tears from me. Yr Relations & Friends are all well except yr Aunt Jenny who has been much indisposed for some time past with a Cancer in her Breast but it is now in a fair way of geting well, she is with me & gives her tender Love to you. Watty Hoxton came to see us about 3 weeks ago he told me he wou'd answer yr letter by the first opperty. I bid him inform you that he was a going to be Marrid he replyed it wou'd Scare you to hear that peice of News therefore he wou'd not mention it to you. I donte [. . . .][2] an agreable young [. . .] & a Roman Catholick I wish him happy but I think him quite to young to Marry.

You are always at heart my dear Charly & I am never tired asking yr Papa questions about you some times to tease, he answers me that you are a good for no thing Ugly little fellow, but when he Speaks his Real Sentiments of you there is not any thing can give me greater Comfort.

I daily pray to God to grant you his grace above all things & to take you under his protection. I have no thing more to add at present only that I am with the greatest tenderness.

Yr Affectionate & Loveing Mother
Eliza. Carroll

ALS, Carroll-McTavish Papers, MS 220, MdHi. Marked "Copy" in the author's hand. Top of page damaged.

1. Dated from CC to CCA, Jan. 17, 1759, below.

2. One line obliterated in the manuscript. The visible portions of the next line appear to refer to Walter Hoxton's fiancée.

CCA to CC

Augt: 30th: 1758[1]

Dr Charley

As this is the safest Conveyance I shall have for a long time (our Fleet sailing with Convoy) I with pleasure embrace it to inform you of my health. I often wish it was possible for me to inspect & direct your Conduct, I am sensible you entered into the World fully instructed as to yr: Duty to God & with a Sincere disposition to Comply with it & believe me the only way to Comply with it is not to omit on any Acct yr: daily Prayers to yr Creator, such is his infinite Goodness that he never abanons us unless we first abandon him: business Company late hours

&c gradually seem excuses for first Postponing & then neglecting our Prayers & this Rampart being once overthrown it's impossible to Enumerate the sad Train of Evils wch inevitably enter at the Breach. Prayer does not Consist in a set form of Words it is the Heart the Will the Attention & intention wch accompanies them that carries them like a pure Sacrifice to the Throne of the Almighty. A due sense of yr: own Misery & warts & of the power Mercy & infinite Goodness of God will move him to grant you those Graces & Blessings you stand in need of. Chuse yr Compa: with the greatest Circumspection, fly those whose Manners & Conversation is not Chaste & Pure[,] Evil Communication Corrupts good manners. Avoid any intimacy or familiarity with the Fair Sex especially Visits or Conversations without witnesses, I should chuse that Women should all most always make part of yr. Company they will contribute to soften & polish yr: Manners, a chearfull lively easy & polite Behaviour is no way inconsistent with Religion or yr Duty to God. Faith & Reason teaches us that God is every where present & that he sees & knows all our thoughts & actions how incumbent is it therefore on us to act with the greatest Circumspection before such a Judge & Witness. It is not only to promote yr Eternal wellfare that I write thus to you, nothing Contributes so much to our Comfort here as Innocence & a clear Conscience it heightens all the pleasures of Life & enables us to bear as we ought the Crosses & Afflictions incident to it.

You have now before you Models by wch to form yr. Cariage & Manners, the Advantages of a Graceful Carriage & deportment are inestimable[.] What strikes us at 1st Sight but a je ne scai quoi[2] in the Person & Manner of the Man that addresses us, hence a favourable prepossession wch if supported by good sense & judgment facilitates every thing he has to Sollicit. But this Cariage this Man[ne]r thô acquired must seem quite easy & natural, any affectation is disgusting & points out the Ape: Study to acquier this Manner this Cariage; I often told you of a little Stooping & pokeing out yr: head to wch you were Subject, it's a habit you contracted at School for no Child ever held him self up better than you did: Correct it, it is absolutely inconsistent with the Cariage I recommend a Constant reflection will mend it. I desier you will find time to learn to Ride it will greatly contribute to give you a habit of holding up yr: Head keeping you streight & erect & will Compleat you in yr: Exercises.

By the time this reaches you you will be able to inform me how long it may be necessary for you to read the Civil Law in order to acquier a competent knowledge of it, not such a knowledge as to enable you to teach it, But such a foundation in it as it might be sufficient to Commence Councillor or Advocate,[3] for they read & Study after they begin to Practice, you are Young & 6 8 or 12 Months must not be thought of, if necessary to the Study you are imployed in. As to yr: Expences I know not how to limit them; in yrs of Decr: 19th 1757 you tell me £130 will do genteely £5, 10, 15 or Twenty Pounds a year more or less are not sums of such Consequence as to be regarded, if they be necessary to yr: living or doing things Genteely But this requiers Judgment, for its certain a very trifle either spent or saved on particular occasions may make you be esteemed generous or stingy: if you happen to be with too expensive Company pay at the time yr: Money readily & chearfully but avoid the Occasion a second time, in short do everything with a good Grace. OEconomy & Generosity are so far from being inconsistent that it is by OEconomy we are enabled to be generous without hurting our Circumstances. If at certain times or on certain occasions you are obliged to be at an extraordinary Expence that Expence may be Ballanced by Retierment for a time & particular savings, out of some Articles of Expence a little ought to be saved for the poor. In short yr: Judgment & discretion must direct your Expences & you cannot Regulate yr: Expences with Judgment & Discretion without keeping a Regular Acct of them, & by often perusing & Considering that Acct. you will see what Articles of Expence may be avoided, an early habit of so doing will save you thousands in the Course of no long life[.]

Yr. Friends in General are well, Capt: Carroll married in my Absence One Miss Thompson[4] with a fortune of £2500 Sterl or thereabouts.

In the Postscript to a Copy of mine of July 26th.[5] I think I informed you that Louisbourgh was not in our hands the 25th past & that by our Bombs we had Burnt three French line of Battle Ships in the Harbour & that the French seemed to be pursuing the advantage gained over us at Ticondaroga or Carillon — We have been since informed that a [Co]nsiderable Body of them in 300 Batteaus [had] advanced to the head of lake George & that there have been some Skirmishes between small parties not to our Advantage & Private reports say that our Northern Militia there, are returned & returning to their several homes. So that Genl: Abercrombie will have only the Regulars with him, it is also reported that the Miscariage of our Attack at Carillon was owing to the Bad behaviour of our Militia.[6] Our Papers also say they have a prospect of a Bad Harvest in Canada & that part of our Troops agst Fort du Quesne had Crossed the Mountains & entrenched at the great Meadows the others being to follow immediately, But I think this Expedition goes on Heavily. We have at last an Acct that Louisburgh surrendered the 26th Past that 4500 Soldiers & Sailors were made Prisoners of War that the Inhabitants are to be sent to France that the Towne was almost reduced to Ashes before it Surrendered, that the Besieged lost 1500 Men the Besiegers only 300 that in the Course of the Siege 4 Capital Ships were Burnt, & one taken on the Surrender, the Rest (except a 74 Gun Ship & a Frigate which are said to have escaped) were either burnt or Sunk, You have heard of the French losses at Senegall on the Coast of Africa.[7] The French are not as we hear advancing on us from lake George. We have news from London to the 25th of June & are apprised of our Successes there & the pleasing Prospect of our own & the King of Prussias affairs[.] Our Ministry seems to Act with Vigour & to avail themselves of the great Superiority of their Naval Force wch threatens Ruin to the French Islands & Colonies in America.

I have wrote to Mr: L'abbe de L'Isle Dieu & Mr: Crookshanks by this Conveyance. My Sincere Compliments & Service to Mr: Power, I make bold to pay my hearty acknowledgements & Respects to Monsr: L'intendant for the Civilities he shews you & the Honr: he does you, it would give me infinite Pleasure to have it in my power to make a return to any one that is dear to him. I pray to God to preserve yr: Health & to Bless You & I am My Dr Charley

Yr: Mo: Afft: Father

Cha: Carroll

PS

You will see this letter was not wrote at one Setting[8] the acct of takeing Louisburgh is in our northern Gazets but not Confirmed by Authority —

LS, Carroll-McTavish Papers, MS 220, MdHi. Corrected by CCA and addressed by him to CC at Bourges. A second LS copy, identically addressed and marked "Copy" by CCA, is filed in the Carroll Papers, MS 206.

1. Date in CCA's hand.

2. "An indefinable something."

3. In eighteenth-century France, avocat, the bottom rung of the legal ladder, was the position for which graduates of the prescribed three-year course of legal study were eligible. After serving a two-year apprenticeship during which he was not allowed to argue cases, an avocat became "fully certified" and could stand for examination for the position of magistrate, a post that usually entailed serving as a conseiller (counselor) to a parlement. Gruder, *Royal Provincial Intendants*, 18–26.

4. Capt. Henry Carroll's bride was Araminta Thompson, a niece of Col. John Rousby II of Calvert Co. The Carrolls lived at the plantation Susquehanna on the Patuxent River in St. Mary's Co. Bowie, *Prince George's*, 246–247; Barnes, *Marriages and Deaths*, 28.

5. Three copies of CCA's letter of July 25, 1758 (not printed), exist, two in the Carroll-McTavish Papers, MS 220, and one in the Carroll Papers, MS 216, both MdHi. The letter is devoted to war news: the siege of Louisbourg, British losses at Ticonderoga, the campaign for Fort Duquesne, the superiority of the British navy, and the successes of the king of Prussia.

6. Gen. James Abercromby, with twelve thousand troops, including six thousand British regulars, launched an unsuccessful frontal assault on Fort Ticonderoga on July 8, 1758. Gipson, *Victorious Years*, 230–231.

7. On May 1, 1758, a small British naval force had penetrated the entrance to the Senegal River and, confronting the poorly armed French ships with overwhelming firepower, quickly secured the surrender of Fort Louis and all other French possessions there. Lawrence Henry Gipson, *The Great War for the Empire: The Culmination, 1760–1763*, The British Empire before the American Revolution (New York, 1958–1970), VIII, 174–176.

8. Text after "Setting" in CCA's hand.

CC's Account of Expenses

[November 1757–October 1758]

An account of money spent
from Nob. 1757 to the end of Octb. 1758.

[1]	£	S	D[1]
Given to Joseph your Servant	12	0	0
Spent in my Journey from Paris to Bourges	72	0	0
Paied to the Shoemaker	4	10	0
for a par á pluie[2]	18	0	0
Given to my Servant as an earnest[3]	3	0	0
payed my Servant of his wages	6	0	0
for the lineing of my coat	17	2	6
for clothing of my Servant	69	2	0
Paied a quarter of my pension[4]	250	0	0
for a pair of shoe's and galoshoe's	9	0	0
for ruffles	60	0	0
for a night-gown making included	57	2	0
for a velvet coat making included	172	3	0
for a new year's gift	21	0	0
Paied to the barber	3	0	0
for washing of silk-stockings	1	19	0
for a brush, comb, & port[5] of a letter	0	18	0
for the port of two letters	0	10	0
for an ink-horn	0	12	0
Paied to the washer-woeman	5	0	0
For my Servant's washing	1	0	0
For a pair of pump's	4	0	0
Paied my Servant of his wages	9	0	0
For Justinian's institutes pocket volume	2	0	0
Paied to the barber	3	0	0
For two tickets to be admitted to the ball	3	0	0
[2]	£	S	D
for a pair of gloves	0	15	0
For pometum[6] and port of a letter	0	11	0
For a washing bason	0	14	0
lossed at Cardes	3	0	0
Paied my Servant of his wages	5	0	0

	£	S	D
given to the poor	1	4	0
Given as an earnest to a new Servant	3	0	0
For port of letters & new year'a gift to the letterwoeman	1	4	0
For a pair of breeche's for my Servant	5	2	0
lossed at Cards	4	5	0
For two tickets	2	8	0
Paied to the washerwoeman	6	0	0
For my Servant's hat	4	0	0
port of a letter & lossed at cards	0	14	0
Paied to Mr. Champion	48	0	0
For a hair-bag[7]	2	0	0
For washing of silk stockings, letters &c	2	16	0
Paied to the barber	3	0	0
For shettlecock's[8]	0	12	0
For a writing desk	11	0	0
Given to the poor	0	12	0
for a pair of rackets	1	16	0
For the port of two volumes of Pindar from Paris to B:	1	4	0
For washing and mending silk stockings	2	10	0
Paied a quarter of my pension	250	0	0
Given to the poor	1	4	0
Paied to the washer woeman	5	0	0
Given to the poor	4	4	0
lossed at cards	0	12	0
For part of a ticket in the Cologne lottery	26	16	0
Given to the barber's boy	0	12	0

[3]	£	S	D
Paied to the dancing master	5	0	0
Given as an earnest to a new Servant	3	0	0
For washing of silk stockings	1	14	0
For port of letters & mending of stockings	1	11	0
Paied the washerwoeman	5	0	0
Paied to the Barber	3	0	0
for two pair of whight silk stockings	24	0	0
For Six handkerchiefs	21	0	0
For writing-paper	0	9	0
For Domat's civil lawes	29	16	0
For washing of silk stockings	0	18	0
For port of letters	2	15	0
lossed at play	0	10	0
lossed at play	1	16	6

	£	s	d
Paied to the barber	3	0	0
For the hiering of a horse	1	16	0
lossed at cards	2	6	0
Given to the barber's boy	0	12	0
lossed at play	0	12	0
Given to the poor	1	4	0
For a pair of bootes	16	0	0
For a pair of spurs	2	0	0
For a pair of pump's	4	10	0
For the hiering of a horse during a week	7	0	0
For his nurriture during that time	15	8	0
For other little expences during my absence	1	1	0
Paied to the washer woeman 2 months	10	0	0
Paied to the barber	3	0	0
For port of letters, mending & washing of stockings	2	7	0
lossed at cards	0	10	0

[4]	£	S	D
For a hairbag	1	13	0
For the lining of a coat	9	0	0
lossed at cards	0	10	0
For the port of a letter	0	14	0
For sealing wax	0	12	0
Paied to the barber	3	0	0
Given to the barber's boy	0	12	0
Given to the poor	0	12	0
For cutting my hair	1	4	0
Paied to the barber	3	0	0
lossed at play	1	6	0
For watch string	0	14	0
For pometum	0	6	0
Paied to Mr. Champion	96	0	0
lossed at play	1	6	0
For powder for the hair	0	6	0
Carriage paied from Paris to Bourges	1	4	0
Paied the washer woeman 2 months	11	0	0
Given to the barber's boy	1	4	0
For physick & other drugs during my sickness	16	0	0
For washing of silk stockings, port of letters	4	10	0
Paied the barber	3	0	0
for a portmanteau	10	0	0
For a comb	0	12	0

For port of letters & mending of stockings	0	15	0
Paied a quarter of my pension	250	0	0
Spent in my Journey	441	0	0
For a hair bag	1	19	0
Somme totale	2078	11	6[9]

AD, Carroll-Maccubbin Papers, MS 219, MdHi.

1. In this account £ stands for livres tournois, S for sols, and D for deniers.

2. "Umbrella."

3. Pledge or security, down payment.

4. Board.

5. Postage.

6. Pomatum or pomade.

7. Probably a hairnet, used when the hair was pulled back and tied.

8. Shuttlecocks.

9. CCA kept his own page-by-page total, in pencil, inserting the figures at various places on the document. The editors' total, 2,238lt. 8s. or £96 10s. 7d. sterling, differs from both father's (2,289lt. 13s. 15d.) and son's. The exchange rate is calculated from McCusker, *Money and Exchange*, 97.

· · ·
:

CC to CCA and Elizabeth Carroll

Nobr. the 7th. 1758.

Dr. Papa & Mama,

J'ai reçu votre lettre en date du 26 Juin le 7 de Sepb. et une autre en date du 25 Julier[1] avec un duplicata et un triplicata de la 1re. le 6 du Courant. Pour concevoir le plaisir qu'elles m'ont données, il faut concevoir l'amour que Je vous porte. Celleci fait ma 5eme. lettre depuis votre depart de Londres: la derniere etoit datée le 10 d'Aoust. J'espere que vous avez reçu si non toutes les 4 du moins quelquesunes: pour l'avenir Je vous enverrai des duplicata. Toutes mes lettres sont fidellement en registrées: il n'y a pas long tems que Je suis de retour á Bourges; J'ai été faire, comme Je vous ai mandé, un tour dans le midi de la France. Ce païs si beau par soimême et encore d'avantage par l'industrie de ses habitans. On peut rien voir de plus curieuse que le Canal de Languedoc: Jettez vos yieux un instant sur la Charte de la France, Je vais vous tracer ma tournée. J'allois de Bourges á Lyon par la Charité, Nevers, Moulins. De Lyon á Avinion, d'Avinion á Nimes, de Nimes á Montpellier, de Montpellier á Toulouse par Pozenas, Beziers, Narbonne, Carcassonne, Castelnaudari: De Toulouse á Montauban, de Montauban á Limoges par Cahors, de Limoges á Bourges Je ne me contenterai point de vous avoir dit simplement les noms des villes par oú J'ai passé, Je vous dirai dans mes lettres suivantes, ce que J'ai trouvé de plus curieux et de plus frappant dans Chacune.

Je me porte parfaitement bien: Je m'applique á mes devoirs et á l'etude du droit civil, Je ne scais si le succés repondera au travail. Il n'y a personne ici qui sache demoler avec ordre une matiere si compliquée, et mettre de la clarté necessaire, dans un cahos de difficultés et de tenebres. Monr. Champion, quoique tres honnête homme, et peu propre á cela. Il n'y a guerés d'autres qui soient plus habile que lui: que dis-je il n'y en a pas, qui soit aussi habile. L'université de Bourges est bien dechüe de son ancient splendeur, on n'y voit plus des Cujas[2] aujourd'hui: fuit Ilion et ingens gloria Dardanidum.[3] Desorte que Je me voie abandonné á moi-même. Neanmoins, avec le secours de Domat, et l'aide de Dieu, J'espere acquerir des coinnoissances dans cette matiere, et d'être assez instruit, pour commencer l'etude du droit public common law of England[.]

Je vous ai mandé dans ma derniere lettre, qu'il avoit eu depuis votre depart de ce païs-ci un changement dans le ministere: que Monr. de Moras avoit été contraint de se demettre de sa charge de Secretaire d'etat de la Marine, ou s'etoit demis volontairement: que Monr. Massiac et Monr. le Norman avoient succedé á l'emploie de ce Ministre. Il vient d'arriver toute á l'heur encore un autre change-ment. Messieurs Massiac et le Norman ont été remerciés. Monr. Bernier autrefois lieutenant de police, est actuellement secretaire d'etat de la marine.[4] On pretend qu'il y a des commissaires nommés pour examiner la conduit de Monr. de Moras, qui dit-on pendant son administration a sequestré 40 millions de 100 qu'il avoit reçu pour retablir et entretenir la Marine: si cela est on aura peu d'egards á tout ce qui a été fait pendant son ministêre: ainsi probablement les gratifications par lui accordées, pensions &c seront d'aucune validité.

Les 200 Louis d'or tant de fois demandés, tant de fois promis et Jamais payés ne le sont pas encore, et en toute probabilité ne le seront Jamais. Monr. del'Islidieu ne m'a pas encore fait l'honneur de me repondre. Nous voila dans l'oublie de tous les cotés. Promesses, paroles, assurances sunt verba et voces prætereaque nihil.[5]

Je vous demande en grace de m'envoyer une liste des livres francois que vous pouvez avoir chez vous: avec votre permission, J'acheterai avant mon depart de la France, quelques autres, comme par exemple, l'esprit des loix,[6] les comedies de Renard,[7] les tragedies de Monr. de Crebillion[8] les euvres de Monr. de Voltaire[9] &c. Il paroît ici un livre nouveau intitulé l'insprit;[10] on dit qu'il est ecrit avec beaucoup: mais c'est un esprit dangereux: le parlement faute d'Archeveque l'a excommunié comme contenant des principes contraires á la religion, et au gouvernement.

Le tems s'ecoule: me voici entré dans ma 2de. année scholastique qui est deja commencée depuis quelque tems. Je suppose que vous avez pris des arrangements avec Monsieur Perkins par rapport á ma pension, logements &c, ou du moins si vous ne l'avoit pas encore fait, J'espere que vous le ferai dans peu, á fin que Je puisse trouver tout en ordre et reglé á mon arrivé á Londres. Je ne saurois, etant tout á fais etranger dans païs-la prendre tous ces arrangements moimême.

Le Roi de Prusse couvert de gloire et des lauriers, et Jusqu'ici invincible, vient de perdre dans une bataille rangée contre le Marechal Daun le fruit de tant de travaux et de victoires, sans en perdre toutefois la gloire et la reputation d'un grand Capitaine: il a perdu 7 á 8000 hommes,[11] parmis lesquelles se trouvent le brave felt Marechal Keith,[12] le Prince Francois de Brunswick,[13] le Prince Anhalt-Desseau[14] bessé et fait prisonnier de guere, et plusieurs autres officies de marque on lui a enlevé 114 pieces de canon: sa retraite se fait en bon ordre on l'admire comme un chef d'euvre de l'art militaire, et pour to[ut] dire comme une de plus belles choses, qu'il ait fait Jusqu'á present.

Etes vous toujours dans la ferme resolution de quitter le Marylande ou irez vous pour être mieux? Si J'osois de vous conseiller un instant, Je vous dirois de n'en rien faire: ou du moins d'attendre Jusqu'á ce que les affaires soient eclaircies, et les troubles de l'Europe assoupis. Donnez moi le plus souvent que vous pouvez de vos nouvelles — Vous concevez pas, le plaisir et la Joie que vous me procurez en m'ecrivant. Dites á ma trés chere Mere de ma part tout ce que l'amour le plus tendre, le plus sinccre, et le plus affectionné peut vous suggerer. Adieu: aimez moi comme Je vous aime. I am Dr. Papa & Mama

Your most dutifull & loving Son
Char: Carroll.

P:S:

My love & duty to my Grand Mama & aunt Genny; my kindest compliments to my Friends especially to the 2 Croxals, to Mr. & Mrs. Lawson to Doctor Lyon &c.

ALS, Carroll Papers, MS 206, MdHi. Addressed by CC. Endorsed by CCA. A shorter version bearing the same date and address, marked "Copy" by CC and endorsed by CCA, is filed with this letter.

Translation*

Nobr. the 7th. 1758.

Dr. Papa & Mama,

I received your letter dated the 26 June the 7 of Sepb. and another dated the 25 of July[1] with a duplicate and a triplicate of the 1st. the 6 Instant. In order to conceive the pleasure they gave me, you would have to be able to conceive the love which I bear for you. This is my 5th. letter since your departure from London: the last was dated the 10 of August. I hope that you have received if not all 4 of them at least some of them: in the future I will send you some duplicates. All my letters are faithfully enregistered: I have been back in Bourges only a short while; I have made as I told you I would, a tour of the midi of France. This region so beautiful in itself and even more so because of the industry of its inhabitants. One cannot see anything more interesting than the Canal of Languedoc: Turn your eyes for an instant to the Map of France, I will trace my route for you. I went from Bourges to Lyon by la Charité, Nevers, Moulins. From Lyon to Avinion, from Avinion to Nimes, from Nimes to Montpellier, from Montpellier to Toulouse by Pezenas, Beziers, Narbonne, Carcassonne, Castelnaudari: From Toulouse to Montauban, from

Montauban to Limoges by Cahors, from Limoges to Bourges[.] I will not content myself simply with having told you the names of all the towns through which I passed, I will tell you in my following letters, what I found most interesting and most striking in Each one of them.

I am perfectly well: I am applying myself to my duties and to the study of civil law, I don't know if the success will equal the amount of work. There is no one here who knows how to figure out with order such a complicated subject, and to put the necessary clarity, into a chaos of difficulties and shadows. Mr. Champion, while a very honest man, is little suited for this. There are hardly any others who are cleverer than he: what am I saying there is none, who is as clever. The University of Bourges has deteriorated significantly from its ancient splendor, one no longer finds any Cujas[2] here: fuit Ilion et ingens gloria Dardanidum.[3] Thus I am abandoned to myself. Nevertheless, with the help of Domat, and the aid of God, I hope to acquire some understanding of this subject, and to be well enough instructed, to begin the study of public law common law of England[.]

I informed you in my last letter, that there has been since your departure from this country a change in the ministry: that Mr. de Moras has been forced to resign his charge as Secretary of state for the Navy, or quit voluntarily: that Mr. Massiac and Mr. le Norman have succeeded to the employ of this Ministry. Just now another change has taken place. Messrs. Massiac and le Norman have been thanked. Mr. Berrier previously the lieutenant of police, is now secretary of state for the navy.[4] It is thought that commissioners have been named to examine the conduct of Mr. de Moras, who it is said during his administration sequestered 40 million of the 100 which he had received to restore and maintain the Navy: if that is so people will care little for what was actually accomplished during his ministry: thus probably the gratifications accorded by him, pensions &c will be totally invalid.

The 200 Louis d'or so many times asked for, so many times promised and never paid still haven't been paid, and in all probability Never will be. Mr. del'Islidieu still hasn't done the honour of responding to me. Here we are forgotten by all sides. Promises, oaths, assurances sunt verba et voces prætereaque nihil.[5]

I ask you the kindness of sending me a list of the French books which you might have at your house: with your permission, I will buy before leaving France, some others, such as for example the spirit of the laws,[6] the comedies of Renard,[7] the tragedies of Mr. de Crebillion[8] the works of Mr. de Voltaire[9] &c. A new book appeared here entitled the spirit;[10] it is said that it was written with a great deal: but it is a dangerous spirit: the parlement in the absence of an Archbishop has excommunicated it on the grounds that it contains principles contrary to religion, and the government.

The time passes: here I am now entering my 2d. scholastic year which began a little while ago. I suppose that you have made arrangements with Mr. Perkins with regard to my board, lodging &c, or at least that if you have not done it already,

I hope that you will do it soon, so that I may find everything in order upon my arrival in London. I will not be able, being entirely foreign in that country to make all the arrangements myself.

The King of Prussia covered with glory and laurels, and Until now invincible, has just lost in a pitched battle against Marshall Daun the fruits of so much work and victories, without losing however the glory and reputation of a great Captain: he lost 7 to 8000 men,[11] among whom were the brave field Marshall Keith,[12] the Prince Francis of Brunswick,[13] the Prince Anhalt-Dessau[14] wounded and taken prisoner of war, and several other officers of mark[;] 114 pieces of cannon were taken: his retreat is taking place in good order[,] it is admired as a masterpiece of the military art, and all in all one of the most beautiful things, that he has Yet done.

Are you still firmly resolved to leave Maryland, where will you go to be better off? If I dared to counsel you a moment, I would tell you not to do anything: or at least to wait Until affairs are clearer, and the troubles in Europe are calmed. Send me your news as often as you possibly can. You don't know, the pleasure and the Joy that you give me when you write. Tell my very dear Mother on my part everything that the most tender love, the most sincere, and the most affectionate can suggest to you. Adieu: love me as I love you. I am Dr. Papa & Mama

Your most dutifull & loving Son

Char: Carroll

P:S:

My love & duty to my Grand Mama & aunt Genny; my kindest compliments to my Friends especially to the 2 Croxals, to Mr. & Mrs. Lawson to Doctor Lyon &c.

---

* Translated from the French by Philip Benedict and Eleanor S. Darcy.

1. This letter, of which three copies exist, two in the Carroll-McTavish Papers, and one in the Carroll Papers, MS 216, has not been printed. It is devoted entirely to war news that is largely repeated in CCA's letter of Aug. 30, 1758, above.

2. Jacques Cujas (1522–1590), professor of civil law at Bourges (1555–1557, 1575–1576).

3. "Troy and the immense glory of the Trojans is no more." Virgil *Aeneid* 2.325–326.

4. Nicholas-René Berryer (1703–1762), identified in the shorter version of this letter as the former police chief of Paris, succeeded the marquis de Massiac as minister of marine in November 1758 and continued in the post until October 1761. According to Lavisse, Berryer's leadership brought about the total collapse of the French navy. Lavisse, *Histoire de France*, XVII, Pt. 2, 272.

5. Promises, oaths, assurances "are words and voices and nothing more."

6. Charles-Louis de Secondat, baron de la Brède et de Montesquieu, *De l'esprit des loix* (Geveva, 1748). *Cat. Lib.*, nos. 1366, 1367, lists two copies of this work.

7. Jean François Regnard (1655–1709), often considered Molière's successor. *Cat. Lib.*, no. 1393, contains a listing for the works of Regnard in four volumes published at Paris in 1758.

8. Claude Prosper Jolyot, sieur de Crébillon (1674–1762). *Cat. Lib.*, no. 1258, lists a three-volume edition of de Crébillon's works (1751) published in Paris in 1754.

9. The only work of François-Marie Arouet de Voltaire (1694–1778) bearing a publication date of 1758 or earlier listed in *Cat. Lib.* is *Abrégé de l'histoire universelle . . .* (The Hague, 1753), printed in London in 1753 (no. 1426).

10. Claude Adrian Helvétius, *De l'Esprit* (1758).

11. During the night of Oct. 13, 1758, an Austrian force of ninety thousand men led by Marshall Leopold Josef von Daun (1705–1766) surrounded Frederick the Great's thirty-seven-thousand-man army near Hochkirk, some forty miles east of Dresden. Attacking on Oct. 14, Daun overwhelmed the Prussians, who retreated, leaving behind 9,500 men killed or captured and about one hundred guns. However, severe losses rendered Daun's army unable to pursue.

12. Field Marshal Jacob Keith (1696–1758), a Scotsman, left his country because he did not wish to serve its Hanoverian rulers. He became a close friend of Frederick the Great, who made him a field marshal and governor of Berlin. Pierre Gaxotte, *Frederick the Great*, trans. R. A. Bell (New Haven, Conn., 1942), 244.

13. Prince Francis of Brunswick (c. 1732–1758) was one of Frederick the Great's most capable generals. Gipson, *Victorious Years*, 139.

14. Prince Maurice of Anhalt-Dessau (?–1760).

CC to CCA

Janu. the 17th. 1759.

Dr. Papa,

I wrote you a very long letter in french from Bourges the 7th. of Novb. 1758. I write to you at present from Paris, where I intend to finnish my 2d. year of the civil law. I am lodged in the College of Louis le Grand;[1] I prefered living in that place than in town, as more conformable to your way of thinking & safer for myself. I shall enjoy as few perhaps fewer pleasures, certainly less liberty than at Bourges; my diet is not so good, & the manner less agreable: hence you may plainly see no desire of ease & pleasure determined me to this change; the only reason is my advantage & advancement in the law. I informed you in my last letter, and as you may see by a copy of it that accompanies this, that no proper person cou'd be found at Bourges to instruct me in the study of the Law: that Mr. Champion the only one capable at least willing to render me that service was inferiour to the task. Poor Champion is now no more. He died lately & suddenly of a violent pluresey. His death deprived me of all assistance: thereupon I resolved to quit Bourges & come to Paris; I executed my design by the advice of my friends, who are all of opinion that Bourges was the most improper place I cou'd be sent to in order to study the law. A few days after my arrival in Paris I agreed with a person of merit and capacity & well versed in the law to instruct me in that science: he demands 30 £ a month for his pains; I spend an hour with him every day: he is of opinion that I shall acquire a competent knowledge of the civil law in six month's time: however I propose to stay here 9 if not 10.

There is no such thing as a riding accademy at Bourges; I mention this, because you seemed desirous in your last letter of my learning to ride; at present I can comply if you think proper with your desire it will cost me 6 guineas the 1st. month and 3 the ensueing: certainly nothing can contribute more to form a genteel and easy carriage, of which I stand in great need. If you are willing to consent to this expence lett me know it as soon as possible: 3 or 4 month's exercise will be as much as I shall want.

I drew on Mr. Perkins some time ago for S £130; (as Mr. Crookshanks can by no means obtain the payment of the 200 guineas so often promised, & never intended to be paid) My expences will amount to more here than at Bourges; how much the[y] will amount to I cant exactly say. My chamber alone, that is the furniture of it will cost me 300£ but this is not losst money, as I intend to sell the furniture I have bought at my quitting the College, perhaps I may lose upon the whole near 60£. I shall endeavour to be as great an oeconemist as decency will permit. I hope you received the memoir I sent you of my last year's expences, and that you find them reasonable & are satisfied with my conduct. I continue to keep an exact & regular account of all the money I lay out.

I desired you in my last to send me a list of all the french books you have by you. I intend, with your leave, to buy their best authors, as for example Boileau,[2] Rouseau,[3] Voltaire; the latter has lately published a new & correct edition of all his works. I proposed likewise by your advice to get the Classicks of the 40. edition in usum Delphini;[4] but as they are so excessively dear (for I am informed they cost about a 100 guineas) I must go without 'em: perhaps they may be had at a better rate in England. It wou'd be ridiculous to have studied latin 6 years & forget it for want of books.

I received about a month ago your letter of August the 30th, with one from my Mama dated the 29th of the same instant, with a duplicate of the former & triplicate of the other two dated the 26th of Juin & 25th of July. It need not mention that they were all exceeding agreable, wellcome, & satisfactory. I thank you kindly & sincerely for the good advice contained in your last letter. If I practised what you teach, I shoud not only be a compleat gentleman but a good Christian, which is much the most important of the two. A good conscience & a virtuous life are certainly the greatest blessings we can enjoy on earth. I dont aim nor never did at cannonization; I detest scrued up devotion, distorted fa[c]es, & grimace. I equally abhor those, who laugh at all devotion, look upon our religion as a fiction, & its holy misteries as the greatest absurdities. I observe my religious duties, I trust in the mercy of God not my own merits, which are none, & hope he will pardon my daily offences. I retain as yet that salutary fear of his Justice which by the wisest of men is stiled initium sapientiæ.[5] I love him tho' far less than his infinite goodness deserves & I cou'd wish to do.

What shall I say to my Mama? My paper permits me to say but little; yet I have a great deal to say in answer to her kind letter, which has no other fault than that of being too short and concise: I intend to write her soon a long & curious letter even interesting; at least I flatter myself it will be such: in the meanwhile assure her of my love and duty not the least impaired by 11 year's absence. I can never leave off but against my will, when I once set down to write to you; yet my paper and time oblige me to call off my mind from a tender Parent, whose remembrance, love, & affection, for me makes my chief happiness. Farewell continue to love me, as long as I continue to deserve your love. I am Dr. Papa

Your most, affectionate dutifull & loving Son
C: Carroll

P:S:

I arrived at Paris the 8th. of January 1759. Pray present my love & duty to my Grand Mama; my love to my Aunt Genny; my kindest compliments to my friends in particular to Mr. Lawson & his wife, to the Croxals, to Doctor Lyon &c. —

ALS, Carroll Papers, MS 206, MdHi. Addressed by CC. Endorsed by CCA.

1. This is CC's second stay at the College of Louis le Grand in Paris, where he had studied from 1755 to 1757.

2. Nicholas Boileau-Despreaux (1636–1711). *Cat. Lib.,* no. 1199, lists volumes two and three of *OEuvres de Boileau* (Paris, 1757).

3. Jean Jacques Rousseau (1712–1778).

4. The "quarto edition for the use of the Dauphin" was the expurgated edition of the classics prepared for Louis de France (1661–1711), the only son of Louis XIV and Marie-Thérèse. The editor of the series was the dauphin's tutor, Pierre Daniel Huet. John Edwin Sandys, *A History of Classical Scholarship,* 3d ed. (Cambridge, 1908–1921), II, 292.

5. "The beginning of wisdom."

CCA to CC

Feby: 9th 1759

Dr Charley

I received yr: two letters of June 14th & Augst: the 10th the 12th of last Month. I realy began to be impatient, for I do not remember that since you left Maryland I have been so long without hearing from you. I need not tell you that they gave me & yr: Mother great Pleasure. I observe the advance you have made in reading the Civil Law, I would not advise you to read anything else but by way of amusement & Relaxation. Yr: description of Sancere & the Sancerrois is pretty & entertaining & I am well pleas'd to find that thô you give Miss Alcock the Merit of her wit & beauty you think yr: Friend Willoughby would have acted foolishly in marrying her, you judge right, such a Step is not to be made so early in life & hardly ever without the Consent of Parents —

I observe by our Papers that Mr Messiac soon gave way to another Minister of State for the Marine whose name I now forget, & very probably Mr: Le'Norman may have met with his Associates ill fortune. I approve of yr: writing to the latter, it is well to improve an acquaintance with such men even without any Interested view, Civility is due to his polite behaviour to you & me. I am surpriz'd that Monsr: L'Abbe de l'Isle Dieu does not answer yr: letters for in his to me of the 14th of Febry 1758 he writes Mr: Votre fils me fait l'honeur de m'Ecrire asses Souvent, notre Correspondance Jusque a present s'est asses bien Soutenüe, il est doux &c[.][1] Do not fatigue him with yr letters, gratitude prompts you to write but not to be troublesome consider his occupations to wch mere matters of form & Civility must give way & be persuded he is as well disposed as ever to serve you[.] Experience & yr: Knowledge of the goodness of his heart must evince this, make my sincere Compts to him when you write to him. If you shd: be disappointed in the Payment of the 4800 Li: wch: I destined towards yr: Support you must draw on Perkins, I am in hopes that money will not be lost[,] the Gentn: may at present be out of Cash, but I doubt not by the Assistance of yr: Friends Messrs Le'Norman & de L'Isle Dieu & in particular by Mr. Crookshanks care the money will be recover'd. I still persist in the Resolution to sell my Estate here, Since my Return I have sold to the Value of £2000 Ster: upon a peace I am in hopes my lands will go of[f] better & faster, what I have sold has not been under Value. The disposition of our Lower House of Assembly [is as] inveterate as ever[, it is true they do not succeed in their Attempts to distress us but who][2] would live among men of such dispositions that could live elsewhere.

I wrote to you that on my return I found my affairs in as prosperous a way as I could expect, I have let Mr. Croxall know the Compt: you pay him on that head. As I doubt not yr: serious & diligent application to yr Studies I am not agst: the agreeable Relaxation you propose of a Tour to Lions especially as you take Mr: Power with you, the choice of yr Companion is an Instance of yr: Prudence & Virtue. I present my sincerest Respects to him. I think no more of the Project I mentioned to you, & wch: I was fond of Fugaces lubuntur Anni[3] & the Success would depend much on my life. Yr: French letter is prettily wrote, I dont doubt but you will be a perfect Master of that Language.

As to news on the 25th of Novr: we took Possession of Fort du Quesne on the River Ohio or rather of the Spot on wch it stood the French having blown up & destroy'd the works. This the want of Provisions obliged them to & their want of Provisions proceeded from the loss of Fort Frontiniac & the Magazines there[,] had they been supply'd with provisions that Fort would have been still in their possession, for by the difficulty & length of the way our Troops were almost starving nor could they have got a Sufficient Supply to stay a week before the place[.] Our disappointment at Ticonderoga is imputed to the Misconduct of General Abercrombie[4] who it is said was not equal to the Command. When he found he could not force the French Entrenchments wch: was attempted by a Coup de Main[5] he shd: have made an immediate retreat & proceeded by a regular attack, insted of this he left his Troops some hours exposed to the murdering fire of our Enemies. Mr: Montcalms[6] disposition for a defence is as much censured by our Officers as Abercrombies Attack. They say that from a rising Ground with 2 or 3 peices of Cannon we could have drove the French from their works wch were so constructed as to be Enfiladed. These are little Anecdotes all the rest you may see in the Gazetts. Upon the whole our Campaign in America has been a glorious one, & we doubt not the Conquest of Canada next Campaigne, if the Efforts of this year be equal to the last wch we have no room to doubt: By our Superiority at Sea all supplies are cut of[f] from Quebec their Enterpot Louisburgh is in our hands the Isle of St Jean & several of their Settlements are destroy'd & the Inhabitants sent to [old] France,[7] Quebec will not only want their help [& the Provisions they supply'd her with but France will be burthened with the Maintenance of so many of her ruined Subjects.][8]

Things are in a quite opposite Situation with us, the pay of so many Troops, the Money laid out in provisions & providing Magazines &c for them circulates briskly among us, & we have plenty of Provisions for much more numerous Forces & more than enough beside to supply our West India Islands, so that the War wch at 1st as a new thing was terrible to us is now our Interest & desire. Beside by the Possession of Fort du Quesne the Western Frontier of Virginia Maryland & Pensilvania is secured agst the Cruelties of the Savages[.] At the same time we see the power of our Mother Country to be such that she awes, invades & terrifies the Coasts of France, ruins her Settlements in Africa whither she has sent a Squadron to secure them to ourselves & that she has sent out a Strong Squadron & a Considerable Number of Land forces to reduce some of the Islands belonging to the French in the West Indies. We know not yet where this Storm is to fall, nor have we yet any certain Acct of the arrival of our fleet at Barbadoes. It is true by our publick papers wch come down to the 7th of Novr: things go not so well with us & our Ally the K. of Prussia in Germany shd: France again Master the Electorate,[9] they may as some think have more than an Equivalent in their hands werewith to purchase such a peace as may be agreeable to them, while others think no Forreign Interest will hinder England from availing herself of the advantages she has & may reap by her Superiority at Sea & in America: This is a point wch I leave to time to clear up.

Yr: Mama & I join in our prayers to God to bless you, yr: Aunt Jenny loves you tenderly. Be regular & Virtuous & by being so secure to yr: self peace & happiness here & hereafter. I am Dr Charley

Yr: Mo: Afft: Father[10]

Cha: Carroll

LS, Carroll-McTavish Papers, MS 220, MdHi. Addressed by CCA to CC at Bourges. Another LS copy addressed by CCA to Mr. Crookshanks in Paris for delivery to CC is filed in the same collection. A third LS of this date, addressed to CC at Bourges and marked "Copy" by CCA, may be found in the Outerbridge Horsey Collection of Lee, Horsey, and Carroll Family Papers, MS 1974, MdHi.

1. "Monsieur your son does me the honor of writing fairly frequently, our correspondence holds up pretty well to date, he is a sweet fellow etc." Carroll Papers, MS 206.

2. Missing material supplied from the Outerbridge Horsey Collection of Lee, Horsey, and Carroll Family Papers (MS 1974, MdHi), copy.

3. "The fleeting years are slipping by." Horace *Odes* 2.14.1–2.

4. A number of factors contributed to Gen. James Abercromby's defeat at Ticonderoga on July 8, 1758, including his failure to make good use of his artillery and in particular not mounting cannon on high ground, known later as Mount Defiance, that commanded the fort. Gipson, *Victorious Years,* 213–231.

5. "A sudden vigorous attack."

6. Louis-Joseph, marquis de Montcalm de Saint-Veran (1712–1759), commanded the French troops at Ticonderoga.

7. Île St. Jean is now Prince Edward Island. By the terms of the surrender of Louisbourg, all inhabitants of Île St. Jean and Cape Breton Island were to become prisoners of war and to be transported to England on British ships. Gipson, *Victorious Years,* 206.

8. Supplied from the Outerbridge Horsey Coll. copy.

9. The French occupied Hanover after the battle of Hastenbeck in July 1757 until the following June when they retreated before the advancing forces of Ferdinand, duke of Brunswick. In early 1759, however, the French were again threatening the electorate from positions in Westphalia. Gipson, *Victorious Years,* 121, 126–127, 131, 287.

10. The copy of this letter in the Carroll-McTavish Papers contains the following postscript in CCA's hand: "I think this is Quadruple But am not Certain, as it was ready Copyed I send it."

$$\cdot \; \cdot \; \cdot$$

CC to CCA and Elizabeth Carroll

Febry. the 17th. 1759

Dr. Papa and Mama,

I lately received yours of Nobr. the 7th 1758,[1] which gave me the satisfaction to hear that you, my Mama and all my friends and relations are well. I wrote to you the 17th of last month; in that letter I informed you of my leaving Bourges and coming to Paris. Mr. Hunter wrote to me a few days ago from London that he proposed to set sail for Maryland with the fleet the 10th. of March. I cou'd not let slip so fair an oportunity of writing a line or two. In case my last letter shou'd miscarry you have here the substance of it. My reasons for quitting Bourges and coming to Paris are I believe well grounded & will meet with your approbation: but that I leave to your decission when you have considered them. My first and chief reason was the impossibility of finding a proper person to instruct me in the civil law, Mr Champion the most capable of such a task, and yet by no means sufficiently instructed to instruct others died sometime ago: indeed in case of necessity I might do with out any such helper, but it wou'd be far more Laborious and require more time and study; besides I shou'd be apt to forget what I read if not inculcated by word of mouth. I have met here with a man under whom I hope to make a considerable progress in the law, & be able in 7 or 8 month's time to commence the study of the common law, nay in a shorter space of time. I spend an hour a day with the above mentioned Person to wit from 7 a'clock in the morning till 8: I pay him 30£[2] a month. My second reason for abandoning Bourges, was the disagreableness of that sejour the stingy behaviour of my Landlady, and the difficulty of finding another convenient house to board in.

There is no such thing as a riding academy at Bourges; if you think proper I may go to the accademy while in Paris: it will cost me 6 guineas the first month and 3 the ensuing. But in that case I cant possibly leave Paris before next spring: besides I have little time to employ in such exercises and the College of Louis le Grand, where I am lodged at present, is at a great distance from the riding schooll: nothing indeed can contribute more to give me an easy and genteel carriage, which I am sensible, I stand in need of. I have lately taken a master of design at the rate of 18£ for 12 lessons, I believe I shall succeed, as I have allways had a taste and turn that way: its a pretty amusement, even usefull not to say necessary in several occasions. In about 6 or 9 month's time perhaps I may send you some of my performances.

My expences here will be more considerable than at Bourges; mine and my Servant's pension during the whole year will cost 1000£: his wages amount to 200£ a year. I reckon to lose upon the furniture of my chambre near a 100£ at the selling of it: besides I am to furnish myself with wood candells &cc; these Joined to other unforseen expences may amount to about 130 pounds Sterlin: I own I cost you a deal of money, more than ever I shall be worth. For supposing you had the power of the Ancient Romans <u>Jus vitæ et necis in Liberos</u>[3] and consequently of selling them I am certain you wou'd never get more for me than 10 or 12 pounds sterlin at most: for if I remember right a good lusty strong nigro only costs 30. Be it as it will I endeavour to manage with as much oeconnemy as is consistent with decency. Mr. Crookshank's has not as yet obtained the payment of 200 guineas, he has lately made a petition to that purpose, what will be the event I cant really say. Since my arrival at Paris I have been once or twice with Mr. de l'Isledieu: he talked a great deal in your commendation, praised the exactness & quickness with which you performed Made. Boison's affair, in short gave me the same demonstrations of zeal, friendship and cordiality as formerly, politely excused his not answering my letter, even cunningly. He desires his kindest compliments to you as likewise Mr. Buttler, Fiteau, and Crookshanks.

I find by the gazettes that General Forbes has at last made himself master of fort du Quesne: that the success of his entreprise was chiefly owing to the dispositions that reigned between the french Garrison and the Indians. There is no particular news stirring at Paris: the armies are preparing on all sides to enter into the field: I am affraid a great deal of innocent blood will be shed this campain.

The conspiracy formed against the king of Portugal makes a great noise. Pamphlets printed here and translated, at its said from the Portugeese accuses the jesuites of being the ringleaders of the conspiracy.[4] I attribute in great measure these reports spread out against them to the animosity of their ennemies. I dont really well know what to think of the affair, I suspend my Judgement till further confirmation. I promised in my last to write to my Mama but must defer it to another occasion: I have no time at present. Its needless to assure her of my Love and affection I pray God may grant you both all health and happiness—I am Dr. Papa and Mama

Your most loving & dutifull Son

C: Carroll

ALS, Carroll Papers, MS 206, MdHi. Addressed by CC. Endorsed by CCA.

1. Not printed. The complete LS document is filed in the Carroll-McTavish Papers; a copy of the final page, with a postscript in CCA's hand dated Nov. 18, 1758, may be found in the Outerbridge Horsey Coll. Its contents include a complaint about not hearing from CC, war news, and greetings from CC's mother and other Maryland friends.

2. In this letter, CC used the pound sterling symbol, £, to designate livres tournois and wrote "pounds Sterlin" when he meant English money.

3. "The power of life and death over one's children."

4. On Sept. 3, 1758, an attempt was made on the life of the king of Portugal, José I (?–1777). His prime minister, Sebastiao José de Carvalho e Mello, marquês de Pombal, used the incident to move against his political opponents among the nobility and to implicate the Jesuits with whom he had had bitter dealings over the administration of Portugal's South American colonies. Several members of the nobility were summarily tried and brutally executed, and, on Sept. 3, 1759, the Jesuits were expelled from Portugal. H. V. Livermore, *A New History of Portugal* (Cambridge, 1966), 212–238; R. W. Greaves, "Religion," in J. O. Lindsay, ed., *The Old Regime, 1713–63*, The New Cambridge Modern History (Cambridge, 1957), 123–125.

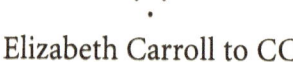

Elizabeth Carroll to CC

Ma[rch] 4 1759.

Dr Charly

We were transported at the receipt of yr letters dated June 13 & Agust the 10. We were exceeding impatient to hear from you not having had that pleasure since yr Papas arival in Maryland, untill the above mention'd letters, which came safe to hand about five weeks ago: Yr Papa is charm'd with yr manner of writing & so is every one that he has read yr letters to which has been to Several of his Friends, you will readily believe that I submit my judgement to theirs when it is in yr favour. I hope you have recd. a letter I wrote you last Sepr. which was a pretty long one. I find you complain of my short letters, the reason I made 'em so last Year, was because I expected yr Papa wou'd have been with you at the receipt [of t]hose letters & imagined you wou'd have seen mine [to] him which were more particular. Yr Aunt Jennys Breast is not well ye[t] but we are in hopes of its being cured next Summe[r.] She gives her tender love to you as dos yr Cousin Rachel Darnell, my Neece who now lives with u[s,][1] she is a very worthy agreable y[ou]ng Woma[n but] quite unfortunate in her Marriage, her [husband] is a worthless good for nothing Body,[2] [sp]ent [a for]tune in a very little time, & used h[. . .] respect, they have been Sep[arated] [. . .] 7 Years. She intends now I have introduced her to you, to write to you by next Opporty. Yr Papa has his Health Extreemly well & [is] grown fat Since his return to Maryland, as for my part I am quite [h]ardy & have as great a Share of health as I can desire to have[. I] heard from yr Grand Mama two or three days ago she was hearty & well, gives her Blessing to you, whenever I write to you & [d]esires you to Pray for her. Why did not you let us know whe[th]er you were grown any Taller Since yr Papa left you.

Watty Hoxton was Married last Novr.[3] His Wife [i]s a Virtuous good Girl, but I cante approve of his Mar[r]ying so Young & hope you wonte think of engaging in that [s]tate of Life yet a while, & never without yr Papas approbation [& a]dvice[. We] have great dependence on yr Conduct & Pru[den]ce[.] Mr Lawson & Croxall were both very much pleas'd with yr let[te]rs to them by yr Papa I heard them say that they wou'd answer ['e]m. We drink yr health every day I am very sure that all yr [Fr]iends & Acquaintence Sincerely wish it. We are in daily expectation of more letters from you, I wish we cou'd hear from you every Month no[t]hing wou'd give me more pleasure. I think I have told you every [thi]ng that has accured, perhaps I may have something new to inform you of in my next, till then my dear adieu, A mighty God protect you.

I am My Dear Child

Mo: Affecaly. Yrs
Eliza. Carroll

ALS, Carroll-McTavish Papers, MS 220, MdHi. Addressed by CCA. Manuscript damaged.

1. Rachel Brooke Darnall (1731–1781) was the only child of Elizabeth Carroll's brother, Clement Brooke, Jr., a sea captain who died on a voyage the year after Rachel's birth, and Mary Smith Brooke, who subsequently married Dr. Charles Neale and raised a second family. Rachel married Henry Darnall IV in the late 1740s and in 1749 gave birth to their only child, Mary. After Elizabeth Carroll's death in 1761, Rachel accepted CCA's offer to become his housekeeper and brought her daughter to live with her. Following Mary's marriage to CC in 1768, Rachel retired with CCA to Doohoragen Manor, which remained her princi-

pal residence for the rest of her life. Mason, "Mama, Rachel, and Molly," in Hoffman and Albert, eds., *Women in the Age of the American Revolution*, 262–271. See also Appendix I, Chart E.

2. Henry Darnall IV (c. 1725–1772), eldest son of Henry Darnall III and Anne Talbott Darnall, apparently lost most of his estate to a creditor, Samuel Roundell, who advertised the sale of Darnall's Prince George's Co. property in the *Md. Gaz.* on May 21 and Aug. 6, 1752. Darnall's subsequent career remains a mystery; for the sole reference to him in the family correspondence, see CCA to CCC, Sept. 6, 1772, below. For the kinship networks of which Darnall was a part, see Appendix I, Chart F.

3. Walter Hoxton married twice. His first wife was probably Anne Craycroft, daughter of Clement Craycroft of Anne Arundel Co. and Elizabeth Parnham Craycroft. His second wife was Susanna Harrison, daughter of Richard Harrison and Walter's half sister Rachel Smith Harrison. Legh W. Reid, "The English Ancestry of the Hoxtons of Maryland and Virginia," *VMHB*, LX (1952), 151–156. See Appendix I, Chart E.

．． ．
．
． ．

CCA to CC

[April 16th 1759][1]

[Dr. Charley]

In my last of the 9th of Febry I acknowledg'd the Receit of yr: two letters of June 14th & Augst: the 10th. I have since received yrs: of Novr: 7th & Janry 17th, they gave us great pleasure. I see you have taken a Tour to the South of France, & I hope it not only pleas'd but improv'd you, wch: is the reasonable end of Travelling, yr: Expences were so moderate that I do not think Mr: Power accompany'd you[,] I wonder you do not mention him. Inclosed is a list of the most valuable French Books I have,[2] I think you will not want any of them but L'Esprit des Lois however you are at liberty to get any of them you desire. Pray bring with you from Paris Pere Berruyer Histoire du Nouveaux Testament[3] & the 28th & the 29th. Vols: or more if Publish'd of the Lettres Edifiantes et Curieuses[4] if not already sent me by Mr: Crookshanks. I shall write to Mr: Perkins as you desire to take Chambers for you in the Temple[5] on yr Arrival in London, & untill they can be got, he will procure you other Lodgings, & he will take all other necessary precautions for yr: ease & Convenience, upon yr: giving him timely notice of the time you propose to be with him.

I realy think it will be to yr advantage, Comfort & Satisfaction to sell my Estate here, however I shall keep my Estate in & nigh Annapolis two large Seats of Land containing each about 13000 Acres[6] my Slaves & Iron Works[7] to the last so that you may chuse, but I doubt not you will think as I do if you should ever know our people—

I approve yr: return to Paris & the Residence you have chosen. My Compts to all I had the honour to know in that house, especially Mr: Galloway & his Pupil[8]—

I shall not at all begrudge the Expence of yr: Learning to Ride, you cannot expect to pay less than others, I doubt you will take care not to be imposed on by paying more, I hope you will not wait for this to begin—I receiv'd yr: Acct of yr: last years Expences wch is moderate & shews you to be frugal, you may purchase what Books you please, indeed if the Classicks in 40 in usum Delphini are so dear I would advise you to purchase only the most noted as Livys, Ciceroes, Horaces, Virgils Cæsars works of that Edition & to content yr. self with the rest in 80 [9] — Mr: Perkins advised me of yr. Bill on him for £130 Ster: & he will by my repeated orders answer any you may draw—I desired Mr. Crookshanks to take to his own use 10 Guineas out of the 1st. Money he receiv'd for you, if he has not done it, pray pay it to him, it is but a trifling acknowledgment for his Civilities & Services to you & me. Why dont you tell me he is well? My Sincere Compts. to him —

I sent under Cover to Monsr: de L'Isle Dieu Mrs: Manjans [10] Receit for the Money paid me in Paris by Mr: Buisson, I should be glad to hear it reached him, make my Compts: to Mr: L'Isle Dieu nothing will please me [more than to hear he is well. Unless Monsr: Mo: & Company are Quite Bank Rupts Mr: de L'Isle Dieu I am persuaded will do all he can to get you the 200 Louis Dors—] [11]

[By yr: last I perceive you designed to leave Paris in Novr: or Decr: next. In the Course of yr: Studies I] [12] doubt not but you will think it necessary to obtain a [p]retty good insight into the Constitution of France, so far at least as Concerns the Administration of Justice in Civil & Criminal matters, the method of Appeals from their inferior to their Superior Courts, & from their Provincial Parliaments [13] to that of Paris, wch I take to be the Dernier Resort, & how far the King by his Authority does or may Controul the proceedings of his Parliamts wch I take to be only Courts of Justice, or very little more. I also advise you to take another view of Versails & the Court, & such a one, as to be able to give a Tollerable Account of each, & I think by the account I have had & read of Chantilly you ought not to leave France without seeing it, the Park & Gardens with a Curious Eye: I know not whether Fountainbleau or Compiegne be so much worth yr: notice; I mention them as places the King honours with his presence. Should Excursions to these & yr: Studies detain you untill the latter end of Febry I should not be displeased, especially as you will avoid a Winters passage Cross the Chanel; wch I think almost as dangerous as a Voyage from England to Maryland, but this I leave to yr: self, I can hardly determine any thing at this Distance.

What has been the Real occasion of the Shocking Executions at Lisbon? The Lugging the Jesuites into the Plot makes me disbelieve what I see in our papers, I know the Envy their Superior Merit draws on them, they are not only too Virtuous but too wise to Engage in Assassinations however illy treated. Our news from Europe comes down to the 11th of Febry, I see great preparations on all sides for a Vigorous & bloody Campain, & that Don Carlos (who owes the Crowns he has possessed, & the Crown he is like to possess to France) [14] is like to side with us against her, what will not Ambition do? It is no wonder we have been so Successfull in America, our vast Superiority at Sea secured & will always secure our Successes here under such a Minister as Mr: Pitt—But I cannot Account for the figure France has hitherto made on the Continent. Here we promise ourselves no less this Campain than the Reduction of all Canada, & without Storms to ruin our Fleets, & Epidemical Distempers to destroy our Armies, I do not think our hopes too Sanguine. A powerfull Fleet & Army will go very early up St Lawrence to Attack Quebec, another Army will soon Attack Ticonderoga, Crown Point & Mount Reall,[15] we shall I believe only act on the Defensive on the Ohio, Rebuild, Inlarge & keep Possession of Fort du Quesne. We want no Provisions for our numerous Forces, while the people in Canada as we hear are Starving. Our latest Accts from the West Indies of Mar: 17th say that the French had not above 1000 White Men under Arms in Guardaloupe, & that it was imagined that Island must surrender by the 22d of last Month,[16] & that two of our Ships [had been at Dominica & destroyed the Forts there.[17] I forebear to mention our late Success at Goree on the Coast of Africa,[18] the inactivity of Lally in the East Indies[19] & the great reinforcements we are sending thither as you are better][20] & sooner infor[m'd o]f these than I can be[. In short] so flattering is our Prospect that unless Fr[a]nce is very fortunate this Summer on the Continent of Europe, we hope at the End of this Campain to prescribe such a peace as we please, & such a one as she must Submit to—

Your Mama & I are perfectly well, we tenderly love you & daily pray to God to bless you in every Sense, yr: Aunt Jenny presents her love to you, yr: Grandmama & all Friends are well & desire to be remembered to you particularly they whom you Salute—

Farewell & be assured that I am Dr. Charley

Yr: Mo: Afft: Father
Cha: Carroll

We are not yet Certainly informed whether Amherst has Crossed the Lake of the Sacrament its now said he has no more than 12,000 men with him & that Prideaux has between 6 & 7,000 & that he is going agt Niagara,[21] no stroke of any Consequence has been yet struck, Severall Skirmishes of little Consequence have happened at lake George & some on the Ohio, to the Advantage of our Enemies. Get a Compleat set of the Classicks in usum Delphini in 4o it's a Pity to have a Broken set—Our news from Europe is to the 10th of May—I see the French threaten us wth an invasion, they Certainly have it not in their Power to be in earnest. I am Dr Charly[22]

Yr Mo: Afft: Father
Cha: Carroll

LS, Carroll-McTavish Papers, MS 220, MdHi. The letter printed is addressed by CCA to Mr. Crookshanks at the Hotel St. Louis, rue St. Antoine, Paris, for delivery to CC. CCA marked this copy "Triplicate." CC's arithmetic has not been reproduced. An unaddressed LS copy is filed with the letter printed. Another LS copy, bearing the same address in CCA's hand and postmarked "Ostende," is located in the Outerbridge Horsey Collection of Lee, Horsey, and Carroll Family Papers, MS 1974, MdHi.

1. Dateline and salutation supplied from second Carroll-McTavish Papers copy.

2. The list of books is included in Appendix II. Manuscript copies are filed in the Carroll Papers, MS 206.

3. Probably part of the series by Isaac Joseph Berruyer (1681–1758), *Histoire du peuple de Dieu, depuis son origine, jusqu'à la naissance du Messie, tirée des seuls livres saints . . .* (Paris, 1728), *Histoire du peuple de Dieu, depuis la naissance du Messie jusqu'à la fin de la synagogue, tirée des seuls livres saints . . .* (Antwerp, 1754), *Histoire du peuple de Dieu, troisième partie; ou Paraphrase litterale des Épitres des Apôtres . . .* (The Hague, 1757) (*Cat. Lib.,* no. 1193, which lists volumes published in 1728, 1754, and 1757). The extremely controversial work was condemned by numerous French bishops, Jesuit superiors, the Sorbonne, and the parlement of Paris, and parts of it were consigned to the Index in 1732, 1754, and 1758.

4. *Lettres édifiantes et curieuses, écrites des missions étrangères par quelques missionnaires de la Compagnie de Jésus,* a collection of Jesuit missionary letters first published in 1697, with additional volumes appearing between 1702 and 1776. According to *Cat. Lib.,* no. 1340, the Carrolls owned a twenty-eight-volume set of the *Lettres* published at Paris in 1717.

5. The Temple refers to that area of London that served as the headquarters for the Knights Templars, a military and religious order active during the late Middle Ages. Since the fifteenth century, two of the four Inns of Court—the Inner Temple and the Middle Temple—have been located on this site.

6. Doohoragen Manor at Elk Ridge in Anne Arundel Co. and Carrollton Manor located between the Monocacy and Potomac Rivers in Frederick Co. Debt Books, Liber 2, Anne Arundel Co., 1759, fol. 8, and Liber 23, Frederick Co., 1759, fol. 7, MdAA.

7. The Baltimore Company, founded by CCA, his younger brother Daniel Carroll of Duddington, Dr. Charles Carroll, Benjamin Tasker, Sr., and Daniel Dulany, Sr., in 1731. The second ironworks to be organized in Maryland and the first to be financed entirely by principal investors without funds from abroad, the Baltimore Company was capitalized at thirty-five hundred pounds sterling, divided equally among each of the five partners. Benjamin Tasker, CCA, Daniel Dulany, Daniel Carroll of Duddington, and Dr. Charles Carroll, Oct. 1, 1731, Partnership Agreement, Colonial Collection, MS 2018, oversize, MdHi; Michael Warren Robbins, "The Principio Company: Iron-Making in Colonial Maryland, 1720–1781" (Ph.D. diss., George Washington University, 1972), 2–3, 24, 26.

8. Robert Edward, ninth Baron Petre (1741/2–1801), attended St. Omers in the mid-1750s. G.E.C. [George Edward Cokayne], *The Complete Peerage of England, Scotland, Ireland, Great Britain, and the United Kingdom, Extant, Extinct, or Dormant,* ed. Vicary Gibbs et al. (London, 1910–1959), X, 510; Holt, *St. Omers,* 204.

9. Octavo.

10. The widow Manjeant, an Acadian refugee for whom CCA conducted a financial transaction during his trip to Paris (see CCA to CC, Jan. [9], 1760, below), was living in Annapolis with her son Anselme and daughter-in-law Rose in 1763. Wood, *French Presence,* 187.

11. Supplied from the other Carroll-McTavish Papers copy.

12. Ibid.

13. Parlements.

14. Don Carlos of Naples (1716–1788), king of the two Sicilies from 1738 to 1759, became Charles III of Spain in 1759 and ruled that country until his death. His debt to France for his crowns is a reference to the first Family Compact, an agreement between the French and Spanish Bourbons signed in 1733 that allowed the Spanish Bourbons to regain Naples and Sicily as a patrimony for Don Carlos in the subsequent war of the Polish succession, 1733–1738. Stanley G. Payne, *A History of Spain and Portugal,* II (Madison, Wis., 1973), 359–361.

15. Montreal. The 1759 amphibious expedition against Quebec was one phase of William Pitt's three-part plan for defeating the French. In addition to the Quebec campaign (June–September), a siege was mounted against Fort Niagara (June–July) in an effort to sever western Canada from the St. Lawrence. At the same time, the British moved through the Champlain Valley against Ticonderoga and Crown Point.

16. Although repulsed at Martinique in January 1759, the British managed to take Guadaloupe after besieging it from February to April.

17. Dominica fell to the British in 1760.

18. Gorée, an island off Cape Verde on the West African coast, supplied slaves to the French West Indies. The British began a bombardment of Gorée in late December 1758, and the French garrison surrendered in short order. Gipson, *Culmination,* 174, 176–177.

19. CCA may be referring to Lally's inability to carry the French siege of Madras to a victorious conclusion. Thomas Arthur, comte de Lally (1702–1766), commander of French land forces at Madras, had breached the city wall, but the fierce British defense prevented his troops from storming through. After the arrival of British ships in mid-February 1759, he lifted the siege and threatened to resign. Ibid., 155–156.

20. Supplied from the second Carroll-McTavish Papers copy.

21. John Prideaux (1718–1759). Gen. Jeffery Amherst promoted him to brigadier general when he placed him in command of the expedition against Fort Niagara. Gipson, *Victorious Years,* 344.

22. This paragraph is in CCA's hand.

CC to CCA

Juin the 22d. 1759.

Dr. Papa,

Your long silence begins to make me uneasy; the last letter I received from you was dated the 7th. of Nobr. 1758, and the last I wrote you the 17th of Feb. 1759.

My expences will not mount so high as I first Imagined; I have dismissed my Servant, as little serviceable and extremely expensive; his wages alone wou'd have cost me 200 £ his pension 550 £.

(You may lay aside all hopes of ever getting the 200 guineas. Mr. Crookshanks has allways been put off with some indirect answer; there is no going to law with such people and in a country so far distant.) My dessigning master seems to be very contented with the progress I make in designing: I dont expect ever to be a Michel-Ange or a Raphael I shall be able to amuse my self & that's all I desire.

I hope you have not forgot to send me a list of your french books. Voltaire published some time ago a new and correct edition of all his works I shoud be glad to have them. I wou'd willingly buy Cicero, Vergil, Horace, Juvenal the in folio edition in usum Delphini. I must renounce bying all the Classicks (as you advised me) they cost near a 100 £ St.

I intend to leave Paris about the beginning of Sepb. I hope you have regulated upon what footing I am to be at London, with whom, wether with an attorney or privy-Counsellor, or in chambers; it woud be difficult being so little acquainted with London to take these arrangements myself and pitch upon the best.

The conspiracy in Portugal occasioned here for some time a prodigious uproar against the Jesuites infamous Libelles were published publicly; stories destitute of common sense invented to throw the odium upon them; they were said to be the ringleaders et pour parler françois l'ame de la conspiration.[1] At present one wou'd imagin that never any such thing had happened. The king of Portugal and Jesuites are quite forgot, which makes me apt to believe that what has been said against the Jesuites is mear calumny tho' at first it seem'd not quite destitute of probability. I have lately read a french pamphlet that attributes the Jesuite's disgrace in Portugal, the King's misfortune, the troubles in Paragay[2] to our national debts; this is certainly mounting quite to the source et gemino Trojanum bellum orditur ab ovo:[3] This strange Politician assertes after a positive manner that our formidable fleet that conquered the Isle of Daix in the year 57[4] was first destined to carry over into Portugal his royal highness the Duke of Cumberland, in order to be married to the Infanta and be proclaimed king after the present reign.[5] The Jesuites zeal for their religion the discontentment of the Nobility and People disappointed this wonderfull scheme. The Portugeese seem not to be less submissive than the frogs according to the fable

Loud thunder shook the bog
And the hoarse nation cried God save king log.

I have been informed that Mr. Hunter has met with success;[6] that our ministry & my Lord Baltimore are satisfied with the Catholick's conduct in Maryland, that orders have been given to your Governour and Assembly not to molest the Catholicks for the future. If this be true I suppose you will lay asside all thoughts of Leaving Maryland: This alteration must be agreab[le] I dare say to my Mama; she certainly prefers her native tho' uncivilised country, to any other. I have allready performed her commission; I have bought her a genteel and pretty snuff box à la mode de Paris et même à la plus nouvelle mode.[7] I shall send it by the 1st. oportunity I meet with after my arrival at London.

Pray give my duty to my Grand Mama my love to my Aunt Genny, I desire to be remembered to all my friends and in particular to Mr. & Mrs. Lawson to the two Croxalls, to Dr. Lyon &c. I am Dr. Papa & Mama

Your most loving and obedient Son
C: Carroll

ALS, Carroll Papers, MS 206, MdHi. Addressed by CC. Endorsed by CCA.

1. "And to speak French, the soul of the conspiracy."

2. The "troubles in Paragay" were the source of a bitter dispute between the Portuguese prime minister, the marquês de Pombal, and the Jesuits, who refused to relocate their missions, as ordered, to comply with a boundary treaty concluded between Spain and Portugal in 1750. Pombal blamed Jesuit intrigues for the subsequent Indian uprisings in the colony. Greaves, "Religion," in Lindsay, ed., *Old Regime,* VII, 123–125.

3. "And the Trojan war arises from a twin egg," a play on Horace (*Ars poetica* 147), who advises the would-be poet not to load his work with unnecessary detail by beginning the story of the Trojan war with the birth of Helen from a double-yolked egg.

4. The Ile d'Aix, a fortified island near the French naval base at Rochefort, was captured on Sept. 23, 1757, by the expedition under the direction of Gen. John Mordaunt. O. A. Sherrard, *Lord Chatham: Pitt and the Seven Years' War* (London, 1955), 224.

5. There is no verification of this rumor concerning William Augustus, duke of Cumberland (1721–1765), George II's third son, and the infanta, Maria (?–1816), who succeeded her father.

6. As a result of George Hunter's efforts, Cecilius Calvert ordered Gov. Horatio Sharpe and the upper house not to penalize Catholics "without Sufficient Cause of their Offence." Calvert to Sharpe, Mar. 30, 1759, *Arch. of Md.,* LVI, 526.

7. "In the Parisian style — the newest style."

CC to CCA

August the 14th. 1759.

Dr. Papa,

Since my last of the 22d. of June I have received two letters from you one dated the 9th of Feb. the other the 16th. of April, and one from my Mama the 4th. of March. They were all three extremely agreable & came very apropros; I was quite uneasy not having heared from you for a long time. (I have been obliged to draw lately on Mr. Perkins as it is impossible in the present situation of affairs to get the 4800 £.[1] The gentlemen are quite out of cash they are puzzeled how to find out money for their own use & necessary expences. In my opinion we shall never be paid; if we shou'd we must wait several years for the payment. I went a few days ago to see Monsr. de l'Isle-dieu, payed him your compliments after the most affectionate & politest manner my french will allow of. He is grown very cool, what can be the reason I will not really presume to say, unless that there is nothing more to be done pour son service. He received a long time ago Monr. Manjan's receit, I think you deserve at least a letter from him for your pains: how ever he desires his kindest compliments to you: you seem persuaded he will do all he can to get the 200 Louis dors paid; I am persuaded he thinks no more about it.)[2] Mr. Power accompanyed me in my Tour thrô the south of France, and prooved an agreable companion: my Journey was pleasant & instructive, I have made a Journal, when I have time to digest it I shall send it you.

I intend to leave Paris about the latter end of Sepb. or beginning of Octb. I shall write to Mr. Perkins before my departure from hence as you desire me. I proposed going once more to Versailles & Chantilly. I believe Mr. Crookshanks will accompany me thither; he seems desirous of seeing the latter. He thank's you kindly for the present of the 10 guineas; but I fancy I shall not be able to prevail upon him to accept them out of the money he received for me. He intends to wait for the payment of the 4800 £ which in my opinion is refusing to accept of them.

A good insight into the constitution of France concerning the administration of Justice in civil and criminal matters wou'd require 3 year's hard study; the administration of Justice both civil and criminal is different in every province each has its own coustoms (coutumes) and each coutume is commonly very different. Hence an able Lawer for example in the isle of France wou'd make an ignorant one in Languedoc where they follow the roman law (le droit cent). As to appealing from one parliament to another there is no such thing, each parliament is independant one of another and all depend upon the king: yet how far the king's authority may in Justice limit & controul his parliament's proceedings is hard to determin. Apply to a Parliamentarian for a solution he will restrain his Master's authority as much as possible: ask a Minister, his answer is ready at hand, Sr. the king's power is bound less because by this means he hopes his will be so too. What is certain you may appeal from any parliament (if not by fair means at least by foul) to the great councill (grand conseil).[3] This in french is not call'd appealing but évoquer du parlement au grand conseil. Ceci est un abus et n'a lieu que quand l'une des parties est assez puissante pour le faire; on pretend que celui qui a assez de credit pour faire évoquer ainsi son procès du parlement au grand conseil est sur de le gagner.[4] However there is one case when one may Justly appeal from the Parliament to the great councill videlicet when the Parliament issues out an arrêt[5] contrary to an express law: this even is termed in french se pouvoir en'cassation d'arrêt du parlement.[6] This expression was probably invented by some parliamentarian in order not to make use of the word <u>appealing</u> which denotes a superior court of Justice que messieurs du parlement ont été en tout tems bien fachés de recoinnaitre.[7] You seem to be vastly disgusted at our People; I am fully persuaded you have reason to be so. Perhaps the orders that have been sent from England to your Gouvernour may check their malice, they are not, I suppose, so audacious as to transgress them. Who knowes but that they will become milder & trectable, when they begin to grow more civilised, for I take 'em to be at present an uncultivated insolent rabble.

I thank you kindly for the list you sent me of your french books & the permission you give me of buying such as I think proper; I shall not make an ill use of it: I intend only to buy such as are usefull & entertaining & the most esteemed in the french language, for example their best Dramatick poets & some others as Boileau Rousseau &c. I have all ready bought a fine, new & correct in 40. edition of all Cicero's work's by l'abbè d'Olivet.[8] The edition in usum Delphini does not comprise all Cicero's works & is not near so much esteemed as what I have.

Immediately upon the reception of your letter I went to the Academy, it will not cost me so dear as I was informed; for a 162 £ I may acquire a sufficient knowledge in the art of riding I intend to continue as long as I stay here. I desire to be remembered to my Mama in the most affectionate manner; I shall answer her letter by the 1st. oportunity mine has allready passed the bounds of one. Assure her of my Love & duty, as also my Grand Mama & my Aunt Jenny: my kind compliments to the two Croxals to Mr. & Mrs. Lawson & their Children & to Dr. Lyon. I am Dr. Papa

Your most affectionate & dutifull Son
C: Carroll.

ALS, Carroll Papers, MS 206, MdHi. Endorsed by CCA.

1. The pound sterling symbol, £, represents livres tournois.

2. The material enclosed in parentheses is set off in brackets in the manuscript.

3. The "grand conseil" or conseil d'état was composed of the king, the chancellor, and several important ministers.

4. "To remove from the parlement to the great council. This is a writ of error and takes place only when one of the parties is powerful enough to do it. They claim that he who has enough influence to have his case removed from parlement to the great council will win it."

5. "A decree."

6. "To appeal a decision of parlement."

7. "What the members have always been loath to admit."

8. L'abbé Pierre-Joseph Thoulier d'Olivet (1682–1768), Voltaire's tutor and a member of the Académie française. This is probably the nine-volume Olivet translation of Cicero's works first published in 1740. *Cat. Lib.*, no. 1231.

• • •

CC's Account of Expenses

[November 1758–September 1759]

1	£	S	D
for drawing a tooth	3	0	0
lossed at cardes	1	10	0
for powder and pometum	0	15	0

	£	S	D
given to the barber's boy	1	1	0
paid to the barber	3	0	0
paid the dancing master	5	0	0
given to the poor	1	4	0
Postage	1	8	0
washing of silk stockings	1	14	0
given earnest to a new Servant	3	0	0
lossed at play	0	6	0
for two pair of double channeled pumps	9	10	0
for pair of clippers	4	10	0
Servant's wagers	27	0	0
2 pair of silk stockings	22	0	0
port of Letters	0	11	0
paid to the washer woman	12	0	0
for a Letter	0	15	0
for a pometum ball	0	6	0
pometum and powder	0	16	0
lossed at cardes	0	18	0
carriage of books from Paris to Bourges	1	4	0
given to the barber's boy	0	12	0
paid for washing	6	0	0
for powder	0	7	0
for a ticket in the Cologne Lottery	2	16	3
paid to the barber	3	0	0
paid a quarter of my pension	250	0	0
port of Letters washing silk stockings	1	18	0
powder for the teeth	1	16	0
given to the poor	2	8	0
for brown paper	0	2	0
	370	7	3

2	£	S	D
lossed at play	3	0	0
for writing paper	0	6	0
one month's pension	84	0	0
for reading the gazette	3	0	0
port of Letters	1	11	0
paid to my Servant	6	18	0
for thysan[1]	0	8	0
given to the barber's boy	1	4	0
given in new year's gifts	20	15	0
paid for the making my shirts	50	7	0

	£	S	D
paid for washing	6	0	0
paid to my Servant	13	4	0
paid to the barber	3	0	0
paid to the taylor	2	0	0
for dressing a hat	1	4	0
given to the Letter woman	1	4	0
carriage for trunck	27	4	0
for a place in the publick coach	25	0	0
spent during my Journey from B: to Paris	29	0	0
for a hackney coach	1	4	0
Spent in the Inn before entering into the College	7	0	0
for a bureau	33	0	0
pour un armoir[2]	63	0	0
pour un fourneau	8	0	0
donné aux Porteurs pour mes malles	1	4	0
donné au tailleur	0	15	0
pour un chapeau bordè	34	0	0
donné au tincturier pour des bas de soïe	0	12	0
pour des fers à frizer	1	10	0
payè à l'Ebeniste pour une bibliothèque	2	0	0
pour un ver à boir	0	10	0
une commission	0	6	0
	432	6	0

3	£	S	D
un bassin a barbe	0	12	0
poudre et pomade	1	1	0
un miroir	1	10	0
une brosse	1	10	0
des décrottoires	0	14	0
noir pour les soulliers	0	6	0
trois petits ballets	1	0	0
5 Livres de chandelle	2	15	0
du coton et poudre à papier	0	1	6
pour le fil de laton remis à bibliothèque	0	8	0
des doux	0	4	0
des allumettes, amadoux et pierre à fusil	0	3	0
une demie Livre de thè	4	0	0
sucre 3 Livres et ½ et 5 onces à 30s la livre	5	10	0
un goupillon	0	3	0
une brosse à peigne	0	8	0

	£	S	D
une grande et petite terrine	1	14	0
six tasses à 8 Sols	2	8	0
sucriere et theiere	2	0	0
pot et cafféthiere	0	16	0
un pot pour du lait	0	12	0
du lait	0	0	6
un couteau a guesne	3	0	0
du lait	0	0	6
etrênnes mignones	0	16	0
un baton à toupèe	0	8	0
une boëte pour du thè	0	18	0
6 millieres à caffé á 4 sols	1	4	0
du lait	0	0	6
une main de papier[3]	0	8	0
du lait	0	0	6
	34	11	6

4	£	S	D
un peigne	0	10	
un ruban pour un tablier	0	2	0
une Livre de caffeé	1	10	0
du lait	0	0	6
des epingles	0	3	0
un Jeu de piquet	0	7	0
du lait	0	0	6
du lait	0	0	6
blanchissage de 4 paires de bas de soie	1	0	0
donnè au rammoneur des chimineés	0	6	0
pour un cahier	0	10	0
perdu au Jeu	0	3	0
pour la fourniture de la chambre	234	0	0
port de Lettre	0	5	0
pour un fiacre	1	6	0
perdu au Jeu	0	8	0
port de lettre	0	5	0
pour la cire d'Espagne	0	11	0
perdu au Jeu	0	10	0
pour la tapisserie et boiserie de la chambre	138	0	0
un moulin à caffè	6	0	0
Port de Lettre	0	5	0
du lait	0	5	6

	£	S	D
une main de papier	0	8	0
5 Livres de chandelles	2	15	0
6 torchons façon et marques	4	0	0
2 paires de chaussons	1	18	0
une savonnette	2	5	0
du lait et un petit pain	0	9	0
pour 4 oeufs frais	0	8	0
une bourse à cheveux et ruban	2	12	0
raccommodage des pincettes	0	6	0
poudre et pomade	1	1	6
	402	8	6 [4]

5	£	S	D
souliers décrotés	0	1	0
du lait	0	5	6
un Pain de sucre de 5 L á 30 S la livre	7	10	0
port d'une lettre	0	5	0
prix d'un brochure	0	16	0
Port de deux Lettres	0	12	0
pour deux paires de souliers	12	0	0
pour un mois de gazette	1	10	0
un Jeux de piquet	0	7	0
2 bavaroises et deux petits pains	0	16	0
1 ruban	1	10	0
4 cahiers de papier d'Hollande [5] et d'ornidaire	1	18	0
des chandelles	2	15	0
Lait pour 8 jours	0	8	6
payè au blanchisseur	5	0	0
un chandellier	1	10	0
2 paires de bas de soie noire blanchies	1	0	0
1 paire de soie blanche	0	5	0
raccommodage de bas et chaussons	0	6	0
Perdu au Jeu	0	3	0
Lait de 6 Jours	0	6	0
perdu au Jeu de pomme [6]	2	9	0
pour la coupe de mes cheveux et frizure	3	0	0
depensé dans une partie de plaisir á cheval	7	15	0
port d'une Lettre	0	14	0
perdu au Jeu de pomme	0	19	0
perdu aux chartes	0	17	0
port de deux Lettres	0	14	0

	£	S	D
donnè pour voir un optique	0	12	0
pour une commission	0	4	0
payè au domestique	33	12	0
	90	0	0

6	£	S	D
fait decrotter les boïtes molles[7]	0	1	0
un 4eme. fer pour le fourneau et raccommodage	0	8	0
payé pour raccommodage et marques de linge	3	19	0
plus fait marquer 4 torchons	0	2	0
pour du lait	0	5	0
perdu aux chartes	0	5	3
port de deux Letres	0	10	0
donné aux pauvres	3	0	0
pour un foureau d'epeé	0	15	0
pour du papier d'Hollande	0	4	0
payè au maitre de dessein	18	4	0
pour la gazette	1	10	0
perdu à la pomme	0	8	0
pour un dictionnaire geographique historique	4	10	0
pour 7 aunes et ½ de Camelotte[8] à 9 £ l'aune	66	10	0
façon d'habit et doublure et soïe pour coudre	42	10	0
2 paires de Jarttieres une de soie l'autre d'argent	10	10	0
des bouttons pour l'habit et cullottes	12	0	0
pour une bavaroise	0	7	0
payê au Gazettier	0	9	0
payè au domestique	3	0	0
pour un Livre de caffé et du lait	1	12	0
payè au maitre de dessein	18	0	0
donnè aux pauvres	3	0	0
pr. un port crayon papier d'Hollande et crayons	1	7	0
payè au gazettier	2	5	0
perdu au Jeu de pomme	1	11	0
pour la relation de le bataille de Bergen[9]	0	8	0
payè un quartier de la pension et du domestique	213	10	0
pour du lois	45	0	0
pour du vin extraordinaire	30	0	0
	486	0	3

7			
perdu au Jeu de pomme	2	13	0
cahier	0	10	0

Port de Lettre	0	5	0
Pour de la braise	0	2	6
port d'une Letre	0	5	0
pour du charbon	0	3	6
	0	5	0
pour un briquet et pierre à fusil	0	5	0
pour du lait	0	11	0
payè à mon domestique	4	3	0
pour 5 L de chandelles	2	15	0
pour une commission	1	4	0
pour une commission	0	2	0
donnè au decrotteur	0	4	0
Pr. 5 L 5 onces de sucre à 30 sols La livre	8	0	0
payè à mon maitre de dessein	18	0	0
Port de deux Lettres	0	15	0
perdu au Jeu de pomme	2	18	0
Pour une commission	0	12	0
racommodage de fourneau	0	8	0
Payè au gazettier	1	10	0
P. deux paires d'escarpins	12	0	0
donnè au pauvres	3	0	0
Payè au blanchisseur	9	0	0
2 bavaroises	0	14	0
Perdu au Jeu	0	12	0
donnè au pauvres	0	10	0
Pr. une Labatierre	50	0	0
Pr. 5 petits pains et du lait	0	12	0
donnè au pauvres	6	0	0
Port de Lettres	0	17	0
	138	16	0[10]

8

perdu au Jeu de pomme	0	14	0
Pr. une commission	0	5	0
Payé au gazettier	1	10	0
Pr. deux paires de bas de fil	7	0	0
perdu au Jeu de pomme	1	10	6
P: une commission	0	12	0
Pr. des cerises	0	1	6
P. deux bouteilles de cidre et petits pains	0	10	6
pour une bavaroise	0	7	0
P: des commissions	0	8	0
P: du lait braise et charbon	2	6	0

Payè au domestique deux mois de gages	6	0	0
perdu au Jeu de pomme	1	16	0
P: deux bavaroises et 2 petits pains	0	18	0
P. deux boullions pendant ma maladie	3	15	0
P: un potage et un oeuf	1	3	0
P. un souper	0	15	0
Payè à mon maitre de dessein	18	0	0
depensè dans une partie de cheval	20	1	0
Donnè au garçon Peruquier	1	4	0
Perdu au Jeu de pomme	1	13	0
P: une commission	0	9	0
donné au domestique de la chambre	1	4	0
P. la gazette	0	1	6
P. une cinturon	2	10	0
P. Le cristal d'une montre	1	16	0
donnè au colporteur	1	4	0
Payè au gazettier	1	10	0
P: des cerises	0	3	0
	79	7	0

9

P: un cordon d'un fouët	0	18	0
P. une commission	0	12	0
Donnè au Calprenier de l'Accademie	18	0	0
Discours sur H: Eccl: de Mr. Fleury 4 volu: in 8o.[11]	9	0	0
Payè un mois de l'Accademie	48	0	0
P. un fouët	6	0	0
Payè à mon maitre de dessein	18	0	0
P: du caffè au lait	0	8	0
Estampes de La bourse de Londres St. Paul et Petersbourg	3	0	0
Payè à mon aggregè de droit pour six mois de Tems	180	0	0
P: le port de 3 Letres	1	1	0
Port d'un paquet venant de Bourges	1	6	0
P: un ¼ de thè	3	0	0
donnè au pauvres	3	0	0
payè a mon domestique	3	0	0
P: du lait, des cerises charbon et braise	1	8	3
Payè à mon Peruquier six mois	24	0	0
Pour une commission	0	8	0
perdu à la pomme	0	8	0
payè au Gazettier	1	10	0
P: un dejeunè	0	12	0
P: des pêches	0	10	0

P: un Virgile[12]	4	0	0
payè à mon maitre de dessein	18	0	0
perdu aux chartes	0	8	0
P: une commission	0	8	0
P: un carosse	1	6	0
P: une culotte newe	17	0	0
P: un habit tournè et raccommodè	14	0	0
P chapeau nettoyè	0	12	0
	361	15	3[13]

10

P: des pêches	0	17	0
blanchissage de mes bas de soie	4	11	0
P: le traitè de Westphalie 6 vo: in 120.[14]	13	10	0
Port dc Lettes	2	0	0
donnè P: des commissions	1	4	0
Depensé dans une partie à cheval	4	16	0
Perdu au Jeu	0	8	0
Pr. un carosse	4	4	0
Port de Letres	0	14	0
P. des commissions	1	4	0
Pr. une malle	37	4	0
Payè au maitre de dessein	21	0	0
Retraite spirituelle du Pére Bourdalauz[15]	2	10	0
deux paires d'escarpins	12	0	0
banchissage de six mois	12	0	0
P: deux rasoirs, caisson et cuir	7	13	0
Payè au gazettier	3	9	0
Pour une commission	0	7	0
Payè ma pension ¼	243	0	0
Donnè au Laytier	3	0	0
Payè à l'Apothéaire	4	0	0
Payè au tailleur	1	4	0
donnè au domestique de ma chambre	4	0	0
P. un botte de foine	0	12	0
Donnè au Porteur de mes malles	4	4	0
P: un carosse	1	4	0
P: de la toille circè	3	0	0
depensé dans un voyage à St. Cloud	4	0	0
Pour des cordes pour attacher les malle	5	0	0
Pr. un cheval pour mener la chaisse de post au College	3	0	0
Donnè à l'Homme de la chaisse pour avoir attaché les malles	2	0	0
	407	15	0[16]

AD, Carroll-Maccubbin Papers, MS 219, MdHi. Addressed by CC. Endorsed by CCA. This undated and unsigned ten-page account in CC's hand covers the remainder of his stay in France—the period from the end of October 1758, when he closed his previous record of expenses, until September 1759, when he left for England. The totals appear in livres tournois, sols, and deniers at the bottom of each manuscript page.

Translation*

for a wardrobe[2]	63	0	0
for a stove	8	0	0
given to the Porters for my trunks	1	4	0
given to the tailor	0	15	0
for a trimmed hat	34	0	0
given to the dyer for silk stockings	0	12	0
for curling irons	1	10	0
paid to the Cabinetmaker for a bookcase	2	0	0
for a drinking glass	0	10	0
an errand	0	6	0
	432	6	0

3	£	S	D
a shaving basin	0	12	0
powder and pomade	1	1	0
a mirror	1	10	0
a brush	1	10	0
shoebrushes	0	14	0
shoe polish	0	6	0
three small ballets	1	0	0
5 Pounds of candles	2	15	0
cotton and blotting sand	0	1	6
for replacing brass wire in the bookcase	0	8	0
candy	0	4	0
matches, kindling and flint	0	3	0
half a pound of tea	4	0	0
sugar 3 Pounds and ½ and 5 ounces at 30 S the pound	5	10	0
a bottle brush	0	3	0
a brush and comb	0	8	0
one large and one small pan	1	14	0
six cups at 8 Sols each	2	8	0
sugar bowl and teapot	2	0	0
pot and coffeepot	0	16	0
a milk jug	0	12	0

	£	s	D
milk	0	0	6
a knife	3	0	0
milk	0	0	6
small New Year's gifts	0	16	0
a curling iron	0	8	0
a teacaddy	0	18	0
6 coffee spoons at 4 sols each	1	4	0
milk	0	0	6
a quire of paper[3]	0	8	0
milk	0	0	6
	34	11	6

4	£	S	D
a comb	0	10	
tape for an apron	0	2	0
a Pound of coffee	1	10	0
milk	0	0	6
pins	0	3	0
a Game of piquet	0	7	0
milk	0	0	6
milk	0	0	6
laundering 4 pairs of silk stockings	1	0	0
given to the chimney sweep	0	6	0
for a notebook	0	10	0
lost at Play	0	3	0
for furnishing my room	234	0	0
Postage	0	5	0
for a hackney coach	1	6	0
lost at Play	0	8	0
Postage	0	5	0
for Spanish wax	0	11	0
lost at Play	0	10	0
for hangings and wainscotting in my room	138	0	0
a coffee grinder	6	0	0
Postage	0	5	0
milk	0	5	6
a quire of paper	0	8	0
5 Pounds of candles	2	15	0
6 dishcloths making and marks	4	0	0
2 pairs of slippers	1	18	0
a cake of soap	2	5	0

	£	S	D
milk and a roll	0	9	0
for 4 fresh eggs	0	8	0
a hair bag and ribbon	2	12	0
repairing the tongs	0	6	0
powder and pomade	1	1	6
	402	8	6 [4]

5	£	S	D
cleaning shoes	0	1	0
milk	0	5	6
a 5 Lb loaf of sugar at 30 S the pound	7	10	0
postage for one letter	0	5	0
price of a brochure	0	16	0
Postage for two Letters	0	12	0
for two pairs of shoes	12	0	0
for one month of the newspaper	1	10	0
a Pack of cards	0	7	0
2 Bavarian creams and two rolls	0	16	0
1 ribbon	1	10	0
4 quarter quires of Dutch [5] and ordinary paper	1	18	0
candles	2	15	0
Milk for 8 Days	0	8	6
paid to the laundryman	5	0	0
a candlestick	1	10	0
washing 2 pairs of black silk stockings	1	0	0
1 pair of white silk	0	5	0
mending stockings and slippers	0	6	0
Lost at Play	0	3	0
Milk for 6 Days	0	6	0
lost at Tennis [6]	2	9	0
for cutting and curling my hair	3	0	0
spent on a riding party	7	15	0
postage for one Letter	0	14	0
lost at Tennis	0	19	0
lost at cards	0	17	0
postage for two Letters	0	14	0
given to see a show box	0	12	0
for an errand	0	4	0
paid to the servant	33	12	0
	90	0	0

6

	£	S	D
for cleaning soft boots[7]	0	1	0
a fourth iron for the stove and repairs	0	8	0
paid for darning and marking linen	3	19	0
also for marking 4 dishcloths	0	2	0
for milk	0	5	0
lost at cards	0	5	3
postage for two Letters	0	10	0
given to the poor	3	0	0
for a scabbard	0	15	0
for Dutch paper	0	4	0
paid to the drawing master	18	4	0
for the newspaper	1	10	0
lost at tennis	0	8	0
for a geographical, historical dictionary	4	10	0
for 7½ ells of Camlet[8] at 9 £ an ell	66	10	0
making a coat and lining and silk for sewing	42	10	0
2 pairs of Garters one of silk the other of silver	10	10	0
buttons for the coat and breeches	12	0	0
for a Bavarian cream	0	7	0
paid to the Newsboy	0	9	0
paid to the servant	3	0	0
for a Pound of coffee and milk	1	12	0
paid to the drawing master	18	0	0
given to the poor	3	0	0
for a pencil box Dutch paper and pencils	1	7	0
paid to the newsboy	2	5	0
lost at Tennis	1	11	0
for the story of the battle of Bergen[9]	0	8	0
paid a quarter's room and board and for the servant	213	10	0
for laws	45	0	0
for some extraordinary wine	30	0	0
	486	0	3

7

lost at Tennis	2	13	0
notebook	0	10	0
Postage	0	5	0
For embers	0	2	6
postage for one Letter	0	5	0
for coal	0	3	6
	0	5	0
for a steel and flint	0	5	0

for milk	0	11	0
paid to my servant	4	3	0
for 5 Lb of candles	2	15	0
for an errand	1	4	0
for an errand	0	2	0
given to the shoeblack	0	4	0
For 5 Lb 5 ounces of sugar at 30 sols The pound	8	0	0
paid to my drawing master	18	0	0
Postage for two Letters	0	15	0
lost at Tennis	2	18	0
For an errand	0	12	0
repairing the stove	0	8	0
Paid to the newsboy	1	10	0
For two pairs of pumps	12	0	0
given to the poor	3	0	0
Paid to the laundryman	9	0	0
2 Bavarian creams	0	14	0
Lost at Play	0	12	0
given to the poor	0	10	0
For a snuff box	50	0	0
For 5 rolls and milk	0	12	0
given to the poor	6	0	0
Postage	0	17	0
	138	16	0[10]

8

lost at Tennis	0	14	0
For an errand	0	5	0
Paid to the newsboy	1	10	0
For two pairs of thread stockings	7	0	0
lost at Tennis	1	10	6
For an errand	0	12	0
For cherries	0	1	6
For two bottles of cider and rolls	0	10	6
for a Bavarian cream	0	7	0
For errands	0	8	0
For milk embers and coal	2	6	0
Paid to the servant two months' wages	6	0	0
lost at Tennis	1	16	0
For two Bavarian creams and 2 rolls	0	18	0
For two bouillons during my illness	3	15	0
For soup and an egg	1	3	0
For a supper	0	15	0

Paid to my drawing master	18	0	0
spent in a riding party	20	1	0
Given to the Barber's boy	1	4	0
Lost at Tennis	1	13	0
For an errand	0	9	0
given to the chambermaid	1	4	0
For the newspaper	0	1	6
For a belt	2	10	0
For a watch crystal	1	16	0
given to the peddler	1	4	0
Paid to the newsboy	1	10	0
for cherries	0	3	0
	79	7	0

9

For a whiplash	0	18	0
For an errand	0	12	0
Given to the Groom at the Academy	18	0	0
Discourse on Eccl: H: of Mr. Fleury 4 volu: in 8o.[11]	9	0	0
Paid for one month at the Academy	48	0	0
For a whip	6	0	0
Paid to my drawing master	18	0	0
For café au lait	0	8	0
Prints of the stock market of London St. Paul and Petersburg	3	0	0
Paid to my law teacher for six months of Time	180	0	0
For postage for 3 Letters	1	1	0
Carriage of a package from Bourges	1	6	0
For ¼ of tea	3	0	0
given to the poor	3	0	0
paid to my servant	3	0	0
For milk, cherries coal and embers	1	8	3
Paid to my Barber for six months	24	0	0
for an errand	0	8	0
lost at tennis	0	8	0
paid to the Newsboy	1	10	0
For a lunch	0	12	0
For peaches	0	10	0
For a Virgil[12]	4	0	0
paid to my drawing master	18	0	0
lost at cards	0	8	0
For an errand	0	8	0
For a coach	1	6	0

For new breeches	17	0	0
For turning and mending a coat	14	0	0
cleaning a hat	0	12	0
	361	15	3[13]

10

For peaches	0	17	0
washing my silk stockings	4	11	0
For the treaty of Westphalia 6 vo: in 120.[14]	13	10	0
Postage	2	0	0
given For errands	1	4	0
Spent in a riding party	4	16	0
Lost at Play	0	8	0
For a coach	4	4	0
Postage	0	14	0
For errands	1	4	0
For a trunk	37	4	0
Paid to the drawing master	21	0	0
Spiritual retreat of Father Bourdalauz[15]	2	10	0
two pairs of pumps	12	0	0
laundry for six months	12	0	0
For two razors, case and strop	7	13	0
Paid to the newsboy	3	9	0
For an errand	0	7	0
Paid ¼ of my room and board	243	0	0
Given to the box maker	3	0	0
Paid to the Apothecary	4	0	0
Paid to the tailor	1	4	0
given to my chambermaid	4	0	0
For a bale of hay	0	12	0
Given to the Porters for my trunks	4	4	0
For a carriage	1	4	0
For oil cloth	3	0	0
spent in a trip to St. Cloud	4	0	0
For straps to fasten the trunks	5	0	0
For a horse to lead the post chaise to the College	3	0	0
Given to the Man from the post chaise for loading the trunks	2	0	0
	407	15	0[16]

* Translated from the French by Eleanor S. Darcy.

1. "Tisane," an herb tea.

2. CC began writing in French with this entry.

3. Approximately two dozen sheets.

4. The correct total is 402.10.6.

5. Dutch paper is fine, handmade rag paper.

6. In French, CC consistently wrote pomme when he meant paume.

7. In French, a misspelling of bottes.

8. An expensive fabric of satin weave originally made in Asia of camel's hair. The European version was an imitation.

9. Possibly *An Authentick and Accurate Journal of the Siege of Bergen-op-Zoom, with a Plan of the Town . . . by an English Officer of Distinction* (London, 1747).

10. The correct total is 128.16.0.

11. *Discours sur l'histoire ecclésiastique* by Abbé Claude Fleury (1640–1723) was first published in 1691. *Cat. Lib.,* no. 1291, lists a thirty-four-volume edition published in Paris in 1722.

12. *Cat. Lib.* lists two copies of Virgil's *Opera* published in Paris before 1759, one published in 1722, the other in 1743 (nos. 1419, 1420).

13. The correct total is 379.15.3.

14. [Guillaume Hyacinthe] Bougeant (1690–1743), *Histoire des guerres et des négociations qui precederent le traité de Westphalie . . . ,* 2 vols. (Paris, 1727). *Cat. Lib.* no. 1202, lists an incomplete, five-volume set published in Paris in 1751.

15. The Reverend Louis Bourdaloue (1632–1704) was known as "le prédicateur des rois et le roi des prédicateurs" — "the preacher of kings and the king of preachers." His sermons became so famous that it was necessary to post guards at the churches where he preached in order to hold back the throngs. (Thomas J. Campbell, *The Jesuits, 1534–1921: A History of the Society of Jesus from Its Foundation to the Present Time,* I [New York, 1921], 364.) His *Retraite spirituelle à l'usage des communautez religieuses . . .* was published at Paris in 1721. *Cat. Lib.,* no. 1207, lists a 1747 Paris edition.

16. The grand total is 2811lt. 8s. 9d., which, using an average exchange rate of 30.87 pence sterling per ecu or three livres tournois, equals £120 10s. 10d. sterling. McCusker, *Money and Exchange,* 97.

CHAPTER 2

Young Manhood
England, 1759–1764

. . .
. .
.

In September 1759, Charles Carroll left France for England to begin five years of training in English law. As he immediately perceived, England, especially London where he was to live and study, was a vastly different world from any he had previously experienced. With the Jesuit presence that had circumscribed his life in France gone, he found himself "in an open sea, hitherto I have rode triumphantly; I have met with shoals & sands which tho' perhaps not avoided by me with all the skillfulness of an understanding pilot, have not occasioned a shipwreck."[1] Now he saw that life was infinitely more complex than he had ever imagined and that preserving virtue required far more than simply professing it. As he confessed with earnest candor in a letter written to Charles Carroll of Annapolis five months after his arrival in the English metropolis, a "young person's passions are strong of themselves & need no outward encouragement; but when roused by occasions, strengthened by example, fired with wine & Jovial company become almost irresistable. . . . the greatest resolution, prudence & virtue are requisite to protect me from such contagion. . . . Who can not promise not others but even himself, of remaining always virtuous"?[2]

The special dangers women posed for the naive and socially inexperienced frequently preoccupied both CC and CCA. Delightedly nervous, the young man wrote his father in January 1760: "I can't close this Letter without touching on that part of yours precautionning me against too great familiarities with women. A most necessary precaution indeed: for what so decieving, what so engaging as women! . . . the most beautiful are always the most powerful, at least with me."[3] Acknowledging that "the Strongest, wisest, best of men have been ensneared by women & brought to utter destruction," the younger Carroll wondered, "what then have I not to fear who am so week?"[4] CCA, in turn, not only worried about the wiles of proper girls who, having heard of the extent of the Carroll fortune, might trap CC into a "treaty of marriage without my Consent & previous knowledge"; he also fretted about "Women of the Town." "Avoid them," he warned his son tersely, "as you wou'd a Rattle Snake, by several Examples within my own knowledge they haved proved as fatally nay almost as suddenly venemous." Many a young man upon whose education large sums had been spent had been destroyed, the elder Carroll continued ominously, "by the poison reced from Prostitutes."[5]

Although father and son agreed about the necessity for guarding oneself against the abundant temptations of London society, other deeper and more subtle pressures unexpectedly emerged to threaten their relationship. CC rather quickly discovered that he hated studying the common law and expressed increasing resentment that he must endure "perpetual banishment"[6] in order to learn a profession his religion barred him from ever practicing. In addition, CCA's intermittent threats to quit Maryland for Louisiana where the social and political rights of Roman Catholics were not abridged unsettled CC, whose mental state had for years been conditioned by idealized memories of his home in Maryland. Equally disturbing reports that his mother's health had become uncertain intensified CC's anxiety, and he began to fear that he might never see her again.

CC's unhappiness reached the crisis stage in June 1761, when he received CCA's letter relating the details of Elizabeth Carroll's final illness and death in March. Stunned by the "afflicting news," CC cried out in anguish against the cruel fate that had robbed him of his mother. "May God almighty Dr. Papa preserve yr. health & grant you a long life: were you to leave me too, oh then I shou'd be compleatly miserable indeed."[7] Abjectly, twenty-four-year-old CC begged to be allowed to come home. CCA bore the melancholy despair expressed in his son's increasingly bitter complaints about the futility of his studies for a year before, "in my owne hand because I do not Care my Clerk should know that you still persist . . . to desier to Come in next Spring," he set his son straight: "Is a year to be Higgled for by a Man of yr Sense & Age? It gives me great uneasiness to think that what you seem to do so unwillingly you will not do well[.] You read the Civill law two years to facilitate the study of the Laws of England, are Six years of yr life to be flung away? If that should be the Case, I have done my duty, you will too late Repent yr not Corresponding with my Will & intention."[8] The taut leash held; CC's resistance collapsed, and he resigned himself to conforming to CCA's wishes: "Tho' I am impatient to return, I readily submit in obedience to your will to remain here this one year more, and my impatience shall not hinder my application to the Law."[9] However, in the future, he carefully justified his unwillingness to apply himself as assiduously as CCA expected by referring to the threat such close attention posed to his health: "I am persuaded you would not have me upon any account endanger my Constitution which tho' pretty good is none of the stoutest, and will not bear much fatigue; study may certainly be stiled such."[10] As he well knew, it was a rationale to which his father was acutely vulnerable.

In the fall of 1763, CC began to court a young English girl named Louisa Baker and entered into serious marriage negotiations with her father. The correspondence between CC and CCA through the course of these ultimately fruitless endeavors provides a humorous counterpoint to the tensions previously described.

CC's suit was rejected, a denouement he accepted with rather bad grace, and in September 1764 he sailed for America, his long exile at an end.

1. CC to CCA, Jan. 29, 1760, below.
2. Ibid.
3. Ibid.
4. Ibid., copy enclosed in CC to CCA, Feb. 30, 1760.
5. CCA to CC, Oct. 6, 1759, below.
6. CC to CCA, Apr. 10, 1760, below.
7. CC to CCA, June 10, 1761, below.
8. CCA to CC, July 24, 1762, below.
9. CC to CCA, Jan. 7, 1763, below.
10. CC to CCA, Jan. 31, 1763, below.

. . .
. .
.

CC's Account of Expenses

[September 1759]

Money spent in my Journey from Paris to London[1]

	£	S	D[2]
to a wheel mended	0	0	6
to a place in the Ghent Dilligence[3]	9	4	0
to the Customs house officers	1	16	0
to hiering a Post chaise	28	0	0
to living[4]	9	0	0
Post horses	69	10	0
Postillion's[5] vales[6]	20	5	0
to a glace broke in the chaise	5	0	0
supper at Lille	3	12	0
to the duty of my books	18	8	0
to carriage of baggage from Lille to Ghent	23	14	0
to the coachman	1	10	0
to a treat given to the Jesuites at Ghent	30	0	0
to the duty paid for my books	24	0	0
to hiering a chaise from Ghent to Bruskins[7]	30	0	0
to the coachman	3	0	0
for passage over the water from B: to Flushing[8]	4	8	4½
Sterlin money —			
Passage from Flushing to Dover	1	15	6
Passport from the English Consul at Flushing	0	10	6
to the custom house officers at Dover	1	1	0
From Dover to London	1	4	0

After my arrival in London till I got settled in my Chambers, I forgot to Set my expences: but during that interval I think I may have spent near 4 or 5 pounds in one thing or another; in going to the play bying different things: the carriage of my bagage from Dover to London cost me 1-15-6- besides 4S. & 6D given to Porters for bringing it to my Lodging. Besides I must have omitted several other Little expences during my Journey, which all together make up sum.[9]

AD, Carroll-Maccubbin Papers, MS 219, MdHi.

1. CC left Paris on Sept. 11, 1759, and arrived in London on Sept. 24.

2. CC began this account rendering his expenditures in livres, sols, and deniers. Then with the phrase "Sterlin money," he changed to pounds, shillings, and pence.

3. A diligence was a public stagecoach.

4. Personal maintenance.

5. The postilion rode the near horse of the lead pair when four or more horses were used to pull a carriage or post chaise or when two horses were used without a driver on the box.

6. Vails: a tip.

7. Breskens, a southwest-Netherlands ferry port for crossing the Western Sheldt River.

8. A port town located at the mouth of the Western Sheldt.

9. CC spent 281lt. 7s. 10½d. livres tournois and £4 11s. sterling, for a total of £16 7s. 5¼d. sterling. The conversion rate is from John J. McCusker, *Money and Exchange in Europe and America, 1600–1775: A Handbook* (Chapel Hill, N.C., 1978), 97.

· · ·
· ·

Elizabeth Carroll to CC

Sepr. 19. 1759.

Dear Charly

Yrs of June the 22 to yr Papa gave me great pleasure, nevertheless I was greatly disappointed that the long letter you promised me was not with it. I was impatient to have it & pleased my self with the thoughts of being highly entertained & of meeting with many deverting passages in it as you told me it wou'd be curious & interesting I am still in hopes of geting it. I suppose this will find you in London, where you probably are at this time if you kept yr Resolution of leaveing Paris the begining of this Month[.] I own I am pleas'd to hear it & glad of every thing that brings you nearer to me if I cante have the pleasure of seeing you as soon as I cou'd wish I shall have that of hearing oftener from you for I am sure you wonte miss any Opporty. of giving us that Comfort. You judge rite for I realy prefer my one Country to any other & hope after a little more time we shall all Live together in it, happily, & peaceably[.]

I am much pleas'd with yr larning to design it will c[ertain]ly afford you great amusement at yr Leasure hours I hop[e] to see some of yr Proformences as soon as you find a convenient Opporty. to send them[.] Yr Aunt Jenny begs you'll send her to keep to her Self some Comical little fancy of yr own in design she still continues ailing her Cancer not [yet] cured but we hope for the best she gives her tender love to y[ou.] Yr. Grand Mama is with us & has been here these two Months she is very hearty & well desires her Blessing to you & says she rejoyces with us at hearing from you. Yr Csn. Rachel Darnell gives her love to you I mention'd her to you in my last which I hope you got, it was dated either in Febry. or March —

I am oblig'd to you my dear for the Snuff Box you mention'd, you may assure yr Self that I shall think it very prett[y] as it is yr Choice for I am very apt to entertain a good opinion of yr judgment & fancy in every thing. We have just been drinking yr health & wishing you every thing thats good for this is yr Birth day. Almighty God grant you heal[th] & long Life & his grace to derect you in all yr undertakings[.] Adieu My Dr Charly I am

Mo: Affecly. Yrs
Eliza. Carroll

PS

Mr Mrs Lawson the two Croxalls & Docr. Lyon are vastly pleas'd at yr mentioning them particularly in yr letters, they have I believe a Sincere Regard & fri[end] Ship for you, if they knew that I was a writing to you I am sure they wou'd be much oblig'd to me to Remember 'em to y[ou] in the tenderest manner & so I believe would all the rest of yr [F]riends & Acquaintence.

ALS, Carroll-McTavish Papers, MS 220, MdHi. Endorsed in unknown hand. Margins damaged, ink extensively bled through.

CC to CCA and Elizabeth Carroll

Sepb. the 27th. 1759

Dr. Papa & Mama,

I take this oportunity of acquainting you of my safe arrival in London: I left Paris the 11 instant & arrived here the 24th. Mr. Diggs the bearer of this letter did me the favour of calling on me a day or two before he sett off for Maryland: I desire you to receive him civilly & politely but this admonition I am persuaded is unnessary.[1] I am at present exceeding busy in getting all things to rights, so I have not time to be so circumstanciall as I wou'd desire. I can only say I have all ready got into chambers I find them handsome & convenient, but of this Mr. Diggs will better inform you, he is actually with me: I am to pay £S40 a year.

My Journey hither has been very expensive on account of my heavy baggage & the duties I have been obliged to pay for my books and other things. Mr. Diggs will deliver you the 28th Lettre edifiante as likewise my Mama's Snuff-box. I hope it will please her; I think it a pretty one & of a very good taste its certainly the latest:

I have got by me le nouveau testament du Pere Beruyer as also his epistles; but as I have not as yet read 'em, & as I don't like to incommode Mr. Diggs with so many books, I shall send 'em by an other opportunity. I have bought a good number of french books[;] I shall give you a list of 'em, & lett you know what they cost. More money will be necessary in my present sejour, than in any I have hithertoo been how much I really cant determin, it depends upon the company I shall keep, if I get into the grand monde[2] it will be very expensive. I must keep a servant I begin to find one absolutely necessary.

I have a number of things to say, but time does not permit me. All your friends & acquaintance in Paris particularly Mr. Crookshanks give their kindest compliments to you. I had allmost forgot to tell you that Mr. Crookshanks & myself by a deal of trouble & bustle have at length obtained 1200 £[3] of the 4800; it was paid to Mr. Crookshanks in my presence the very day I left Paris, & he was promised to be payd the same sum the following week; they are not able to pay it all togeather, & really I dispair'd of its ever being payd. Mr. Diggs will tell you what the shortness of time will not permit me to do: the next letter I write shall be fuller & more satisfactory: in the mean while I remain Dr. Papa & Mama

Your most dutifull & affectionate Son
C: Carroll

ALS, Carroll Papers, MS 206, MdHi. Addressed by CC. Endorsed by CCA.
1. From the word "but" to the end of the sentence is interlineated.
2. "The fashionable world," i.e. society.
3. Livres tournois, not pounds sterling.

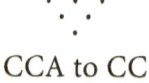

CCA to CC

Octr 6th 1759

Dr Charley

Had I expected you would have left Paris in the beginning of Septr: past as you advise in yr: last of the 22d of June I shd: before this have wrote much to the Purport of wt. follows. As to the settling you in the Temple I have been full enough to Mr: Perkins on that head, who I doubt not had Chambers ready for you on yr: Arrival if as you ought & as I directed in mine of the 16th of last April you gave him due notice of the time you proposed to be with him — If this meets you in London, it will meet you in an open & wide Ocean of danger: hitherto you have had friends to advise with, & good Example constantly before you, now you can only rely on Gods grace, yr: own prudence & the good principles instilled into you by a virtuous Education: I beg you will never fail daily & sincerely to implore the first without wch the other two can be of no Service. In yr Situation the greatest Resolution will be necessary to withstand the many Temptations you will be exposed to: so abandoned will you find most men as to be asham'd of even appearing Virtuous, I hope you will never be so mean. I do not desire to seclude you from Society or innocent pleasures, but I advise you to be very Circumspect in the choice of yr: Company, & to watch so that yr: amusements may not have any ill tendency. Relaxation is even necessary not only to yr health, but to a proper prosecution of yr: Studies, & such an application I expect & hope for from you, it is by such an application you will not only compleatly finish yr: Education, but by being imploy'd you will avoid many temptations wch by being Idle you will be exposed to, for nothing is more certain than that Idleness is the Root of all Evil.

Many reasons ought to incline you to a close & serious Study of the Law, it is a shame for a Gent: to be ignorant of the Laws of his Country & to be dependent on ev'ry dirty Petty fogger whose Intert: it may be to lead him by such a dependance into endless difficulties — On the other hand how commendable is it for a Gent: of an Independant fortune not only not to stand in need of Mercenary Advisers but to be able to advise & assist his friends, Relations & Neighbours of all sorts, wt weight must such a one have on the Circle of his Acquaintance? How endearing may he make himself to all by a Benevolent use of his knowledge[.] Suppose you shd: be called upon to act in any publick Character, wt an awkward figure would you make without the knowledge of the Law either as a Legislator, Judge or even an Arbitrator of differences among yr Neighbours & friends. The Law in England is not only a road to Riches but to the highest honours. How many great fortunes are made by it? How many are call'd to the Peerage by the knowledge of it? It is true as things now stand you are shut out from the Bar, but you are not debarred from acting as a Counsellor, & in that way many great fortunes have been made. But supposing you shd: not have so active a turn as to make the Law a Profession in order to accumulate a fortune, yet as I before observed the knowledge of it is absolutely necessary to ev'ry private Gent: of fortune who has the least Idea of being Independant. I do not send you to the Temple to spend (as many do) 4 or 5 Years to no purpose, I send you to Study & Labour, it is wt I expect from you do not disappoint my hopes, you have hitherto done well, all that you have done was but a preparation to do this well, finish worthyly, & apply as if yr: whole & sole Dependance was to be on the knowledge of the Law nihil nisi bene.[1]

When in London I met with one Mr: Twinyhoe of the Temple, I then mentioned you to him, & he very kindly, obligingly & politely promised me to advise you, Mr: Perkins will introduce you to him, he will instruct you how to begin & how to prosecute yr: Studies &c. I think all who study the Law have a Common place Book, such a Book is certainly very usefull & necessary, but I believe few agree in the Method of common placing, until you fix on one agreeable to yr: self common place yr: reading in loose sheets wch you may enter into yr: common place Book when you have fixed on a Method to yr: self clear & agreeable.

I understand that lately in one of our Universities there is a Chair Established for a Professor of the Common Law, this has been long wished for, whether the Professor or his method answers the Expectation of the publick I know not, but it is certainly worth yr: while to enquire whether you may not reap some advantage from it, & to judge yr self you may in Vacation time go to hear him. Books you must buy as you want, let them be good & of the best Editions, & be careful of them when bought. I recommend it to you to renew yr: Acquaintance with such of yr: school fellows as are men of family fortune & good morals, little Tours at proper times to their Country Seats will be a Relaxation & amusement: such acquaintance may in many other respects be very servicable:

Althô I still think it will be for yr Intert: & happiness to sell my Estates in Maryland yet I would not have you either decline or Sollicit an Acquaintance with Ld: Baltimore or his Uncle Mr: Cæcilius Calvert. If you shd: accidentally fall in their way you may when proper let them know that you are not unacquainted that yr: Grand father came into this Country[2] after a Regular Study of the Law in the Temple Attorney General, that he was Hond: with the Posts of Agent, Receiver General, Judge in Land Affairs, Naval Officer, & that he had the Appointmt: of the several Naval Officers & Land Surveyors of the Province that after he had served 3 Ld: Baltimores[3] for many years with Credit & Reputation, he was deprived by the late Ld: of his Posts to gratify a faction whose aim was to devest the family of their Government: you may also let them know you are not ignorant of the Laws made at that time & lately to deprive the Rom: Catholicks of their liberties & to distress & vex them, that the memory of the favours confer'd on yr: Grand Father will always incline you to promote the Intert: of the Proprietary family where you can do it with Honour & Justice, but remember the ill treatment yr: Grand father met with after so long a Series of Services, remember the cruel usage of the Rom: Catholicks by the late & present Ld: Baltimore, & let that so weigh with you as never to Sacrifice yr: own or yr: Country's Intt: to promote the Intt: or power of the Proprietary family. It is true they have it in their power to confer some places of profit & honour worth acceptance but as you cannot hold any of them as the Laws stand, & supposing that Impediment removed as I wou'd not wish you to hold any of them but upon Honble terms, I cannot think it will be worth yr: while to pay a Court there, or shew any other Respect than such a one as is due to them as Lds of the Country where yr: fortune lays —

You will meet with severall of yr: Countrymen in London, with some of them in the Temple or other Inns of Court, treat them politely & with Respect, if you shd: mention them in yr: Letters, let it be to their advantage, but with them as with all others be reserved until you know them. I expect from you all the Pamphlets worth my perusal you will be a good Judge as you may read them at the trifling expence of a small subscription[.] I also expect severall little Anecodotes & occurrences wch are not to be met with in the Common news papers. As to yr: Expences I will not tie you down to a certain sum, I am informed £200 or £250 a year at most will do very genteely[.] I wou'd not have you appear mean in anything, but I wou'd have you act with OEconomy: wt savings are made while you are confined to yr: Books & Chambers will enable you to make a figure when you are Rambling on Parties of pleasure & Amusement, Mr: Perkins is yr: Cashier & upon your shewing him this he will supply you with wt money you may want. You will see Messrs Corbie,[4] Pointz,[5] Baker[6] & Murphy[7] make my Compts to them.

I wrote to you so lately[8] that I have no news to tell you, but that by our latest Accts Wolf will not take Quebec wch he has almost reduced to ashes, but after laying the Country waste he will return to Louisbourgh & our Colonies.[9] Amherst seems to design nothing more than to secure his Conquests by erecting a Strong Fort at Crown Point & several small ones to keep up his Communication with our Colonies. Our Intelligence from England is as low as the 26 of July, we with impatience expect to hear the Event of the French preparations for an Invasion.

When at Paris I seriously exhorted you to make yourself a perfect Master of Arethmetic, I again recommend it as also to learn Surveying & Book keeping I know them all to be Essential, Instructors are plenty & I charge you to make use of them.

My Dr Child I cannot close this long letter without cautioning you in particular agst any familiarities with Women, I hope you will never enter into any treaty of marriage without my Consent & previous knowledge, & as to the Women of the Town avoid them as you wou'd a Rattle Snake, by several Examples within my own knowledge they haved proved as fatally nay almost as suddenly venemous, I have known some young men after as much time & Money spent on their Education as has been on yrs snatched from their Expecting Parents by the poison reced from Prostitutes, others I have known long to linger in a State of Rottenness & at last to die objects of horror, therefore if the more noble & pure Sentiments of Virtue & Duty should fail to keep you innocent, let a regard to yr: health deter you from a Crime wch may in this world make you most miserable. Yr: Mother & I offer our daily prayers to the God of Mercies to avert all Dangers from you to grant you health & every other blessing. We are both well & I am Dr Charley

Yr: Mo: Affte: Father
Cha Carroll

PS

Decr: 7th: 1759

Yr last was of the 22d of June[.] I send you this Postscript to Complain of yr neglect in writing. We are well & Give You our Blessing—I have nothing materiall to Communicate—

LS, Carroll-McTavish Papers, MS 220, MdHi. Marked "Triplicate" and corrected by CCA, with the postscript in his hand. A copy marked "Duplicate" by CCA and with margins badly damaged is filed with it. Another LS copy, also with margins damaged, may be found in the Charles Carroll of Carrollton Collection, MS 1893, MdHi.

1. "Nothing but well-done."

2. Charles Carroll the Settler (1661–1720) arrived in Maryland in October 1688. *Arch. of Md.*, VIII, 47–48.

3. Charles Calvert, third Lord Baltimore (1637–1714/5), who held the proprietorship from 1675 until his death, Benedict Leonard Calvert, fourth Lord Baltimore (1679–1715), who succeeded to the title on Feb. 21, 1714/5, but died shortly thereafter on Apr. 16, and Charles Calvert, fifth Lord Baltimore (1699–1751), whose term as proprietor began at his father's death and ended with his own.

4. Henry Corbie (Corby; 1700–1765) served as master of novices and rector at Watten (1745–1756) and as rector, i.e. provincial superior, of St. Ignatius College or the London district (1756–1762). Henry Foley, ed., *Records of the English Province of the Society of Jesus* (London, 1877–1883), VII, 168; Geoffrey Holt, *The English Jesuits in the Age of Reason* (Tunbridge Wells, Kent, 1993), 153.

5. John Pointz (Poyntz; 1709–1789) entered the Society of Jesus in 1732 and held the position of procurator of the province in London from about 1755 to 1766. Foley, ed., *Records*, VII, 629; Holt, *English Jesuits in the Age of Reason*, 153.

6. Bernard Baker (1698–1773), an Irish priest, spent the early part of his career teaching humanities and philosophy in Belgium. He served as rector of St. Ignatius College for a period up to 1766 and in 1772 became procurator in London. Foley, ed., *Records*, VII, 28.

7. Cornelius Murphy (1696–1766), a native of Ireland, entered the Society of Jesus in 1711 and moved to London about 1748 to begin an association with St. Ignatius College that continued until his death. Ibid., 533.

8. CCA's most recent letter to CC, dated Sept. 22, 1759, chided the young man for changing the time of his departure from Paris and for not writing as often as he had promised, inquired about French preparations for invading England, relayed news of the war from New York, and predicted that Montreal and Quebec would not be taken before the end of the year. Carroll-McTavish Papers, MS 220, MdHi.

9. Quebec fell to the British under Maj. Gen. James Wolfe (1727–1759), who died in the battle, on Sept. 13, 1759.

$$\cdot \; \cdot \; \cdot$$
$$\cdot$$

A Last Will and Testament of CCA [1]

[late 1759]

In the Name of God. Amen

I Charles Carroll of the City of Annapolis being at the Writing hereof in Perfect Health of Body and of Sound Memory and Understanding, for which I Humbly thank God. Do make and ordain this my last Will and Testament in the manner following—

Imprimis. I order all my just Debts to be paid which are but few and Small.

2. I order my Body to be Buried nigh my Fathers Remains,[2] if it should not prove Inconvenient to do so, by my dying at too great a Distance from my present place of Abode. I also positively and Expressly order my Body to be Buried as privately

as possible consistently with Decency, and I order Twenty Shillings to be paid to each of the Bearers—

3. Whereas my Nephew[3] and Neices[4] are Entitled to a Moiety of Several Lands Specified in a Schedule hereunto Annexed and Signed by me,[5] I do hereby Empower my Executor herein after Named to sell all the said Lands which I have not already Contracted for and to pay one Moiety of the Proceeds to my Nephew Charles Carroll and to his two Sisters. But in Case my Executor herein after Named shall not be in Maryland, I then Empower Daniel Carroll[6] to sell the said Lands and to pay my Son one half of the Proceeds, and to Divide the other half arising by such Sale in the manner above directed, and I hereby impower my Son or Daniel Carroll to Convey in Fee my Right to the Lands so sold or agreed by me to to be Sold—

4. I Bequeath to my Dear Wife Elizabeth Carroll during her Natural Life over and above what I have Engaged to give her by a Marriage Settlement my Dwelling House on Chance[7] or Doohoregan with all that Tract of Land called Chance by me Resurveyed with all the Buildings and Improvements thereon with so much of Doohoregan as is now cleared and makes part of my Dwelling Plantation, so as not to take in any part of Valentines, Jacobs[8] or John Reads Plantations or the Woods Adjacent thereto being part of Doohoregan—

5. I also Bequeath to my said Loving Wife all the Household Goods, Furniture and Kitchen Utensils in my said House and Kitchen thereto Adjacent, with all the Beds, Bedding, Rugs, Quilts, Blankets, Counterpanes, Sheets, Table Linen &ca: during her Natural Life—

6. Item. I Bequeath to my said Wife Fifty head of sortable Black Cattle, Fifty head of sortable Hogs, Fifty head of Sheep, Six good working Horses, two Yoke of Oxen, two Breeding Mares, two of my best Chair Horses, my Chair,[9] with the Geer, Collars, Yokes and Chains belonging to the working Horses and Oxen with two good Carts and all the Pots, Pans, Sifters and working Tools on the said Plantation called Chance—

7. Item. I Bequeath to my said Wife during her Natural Life Seven Negro Men and Seven Negro Women which Negroes shall not be above Forty or under Fifteen Years old and it is my Will that my said Dear Wife shall chuse as many of the Women as she shall think fit out of the House Slaves either at my said Dwelling House or at Mr: Irelands to make the Number of Seven Women.

8. Item. I Bequeath to my Dear Wife during her Natural Life one Negro Carpenter named Harry.[10] It is also my Will that my Executor herein after named in Case of the Death of any of the said Negroes shall put in their stead and Place others of like Age and Value in case the Increase shall not make good the said Number of working Slaves—

9. Item. I give and Bequeath to my Dear Wife one Hundred and Fifty Pounds Sterling during her Natural life to be paid her Annually by my Executor herein after

named over and above the one Hundred pounds Sterling Annually settled on my Wife by Marriage Articles—

10. Item. After the Death of my Dear Wife I Bequeath the Slaves and their Increase with all the Stock Goods &ca: Bequeathed to my Wife during her natural Life and which shall be then in my Dwelling House already mentioned and on my Plantation aforesaid unto my Executor herein after named.

11. Item. It is my Will that the Bequests herein before made to my Dear Wife shall be taken by her in full of any former Gifts or Engagements to her (Her Marriage Articles only Excepted) and also in full of any claim of Dower on any part of my Estate either Real or personal.

12. Item. All other my Estate, both Real and Personal of what kind or Nature so ever I give and Bequeath unto my Son Charles Carroll now a Student in the Temple in London to him I say and to his Heirs for ever in Fee Simple.

13. But whereas it may happen that my Son may die before me without having Issue or before he comes into Possession of my Estate hereby Bequeathed him, or without disposing of the same by Deed or Will after he comes into the Possession of the same: In any of these Cases it is my Will that all my Estate herein before Bequeathed to my Son and which he shall not have disposed of shall go to Daniel Carroll[11] the son of Daniel Carroll who married my Neice Eleanor Carroll and to his Heirs for Ever Subject nevertheless to an Annuity of Three hundred Pounds Sterling to be paid to my Neice Eleanor Carroll during her Life in Case of the Death of my Son as above mentioned. I also hereby further Declare that by this Limitation of my Estate to Daniel Carroll Son of Daniel Carroll by my Neice Eleanor Carroll I do not mean any way to create an Estate Tail of the Estate Bequeathed to my Son, but that my said Son may sell or dispose of the same in Fee Simple as to him shall seem meet—

14. I lastly Constitute and Appoint my Son Charles Carroll my Whole and Sole Executor of this my last Will and Testament and in Case of his Absence I Appoint my Dear Wife to be his Trustee and to Act in his Place and stead and to take out Letters Testamentary on this my Will on behalf of my Son. And I order no Appraisement shall be made of my Estate, but that my Wife for my Sons satisfaction shall cause an Inventory to be made of my Estate by any honest Men whom she shall appoint to make the said Inventory and Value the Articles contained in it, by which Inventory only she shall be obliged to Account with my Son or any other. I also desire my Wife to make an Exact List of all Moneys due to me by Mortgages, Bonds, Notes, Accompts or otherways which List shall be Signed as above—

15. Item. I do hereby order that all my Estate Negroes and Stock of all sorts and my Plantations shall be kept at the Risque and Profit of my Executor and that all advantages arising from my Estate Negroes and Stock shall be to his sole Benefit and Advantage, and that all Losses shall be to his Loss—

16. Lastly I declare this to be my last Will and Testament and I do hereby Revoke

all the Wills by me heretofore made. In Witness whereof I have hereunto set my
Hand and Seal this Day of Anno Domini
Signed, Sealed, Published and Declared
by Charles Carroll the Testator to be
his last Will and Testament in the
Presence of us the Subscribers

D, Carroll Papers, MS 206, MdHi.

1. This unexecuted document is the earliest will of CCA that has been found. It was
probably written in late 1759, after CCA learned that CC had arrived in England and settled
into his new quarters and course of study.

2. Charles Carroll the Settler was buried in the family graveyard, a hilltop plot of approximately two acres located on a tract called the Farm, about three miles from Annapolis.
The site fell into disrepair during the nineteenth century and was eventually obliterated by
commercial development. Louis Hoerner and Robert Worden, "Where Loved Ones Rest,"
St. Mary's Moorings, XIV, no. 3 (May 1983), 3–4; William Voss Elder III, "The Carroll House
in Annapolis and Doughoregan Manor," in Van Devanter, *"Anywhere,"* 60.

3. Charles Carroll of Duddington.

4. Eleanor Carroll Carroll and Mary Carroll Digges (1732/3–1825).

5. Not found.

6. Daniel Carroll II of Upper Marlboro.

7. A 969-acre tract adjacent to Doohoragen. Provincial Court, Deeds, Liber B.T. no. 1,
fol. 72, MdAA.

8. Valentine's and Jacob's were quarters on Doohoragen Manor.

9. A two-wheeled vehicle drawn by one horse.

10. For Carpenter Harry, who lived at Mr. Frost's, see Appendix III, "A List of Negroes —
on Doohoregan Manor taken in Familys with their Ages Decr. 1. 1773."

11. Daniel Carroll III (1752–1790), son of Daniel Carroll II of Upper Marlboro and CC's
first cousin Eleanor Carroll (Appendix I, Chart J). Enrolled at Bruges College in 1766, Daniel
surprised his father and other relatives by leaving without completing his course of study.
Pleading illness as his excuse, he returned home in the spring of 1771. CCA's assistance,
in the form of a five-hundred-pound-sterling line of credit, enabled Daniel III to establish himself as a merchant in Baltimore. In 1772 he married Elizabeth Digges, daughter of
William Digges of Warburton Manor, Prince George's Co., and Anne Attwood Digges, with
whom he had three children. Holt, *St. Omers,* 59; Mary Virgina Geiger, *Daniel Carroll II:
One Man and His Descendants, 1730–1978* (Baltimore, 1979), 57, Chart A; Daniel Carroll II of
Rock Creek to CCA, Apr. 14, 1771, Carroll Papers, MS 206, MdHi; CCA to John Buchanan,
Dec. 12, 1771, and to John Buchanan and Son, Aug. 6, 1772, Charles Carroll Letter-book,
1771–1833, Arents Collections, NN; CCA to CCC, Oct. 19, 1772, below; *Bio. Dic. Md. Legis.,* I,
199, 270.

CC to CCA and Elizabeth Carroll

Nob. the 13th. 1759.

Dr. Papa and Mama,

I hope Mr. Diggs has delivered you my letter & the last volume of the Lettres edifientes, and a snuff box for my Mama, which I hope will please her my compliments to Mr. Diggs and thank him from me for the trouble he has taken. I lately received a letter from you dated the 16th August,[1] which gives the most sensible satisfaction of hearing you are well: as to the news therein contained I allready knew, but am not the less obliged to you: I imagin you will now have no more news to write me, as our American war, will I dare say be finnish'd by the reduction of Quebec. I am allmost settled at present: as Mr. Twinhio is but lately come to town I have but Just begun to study the common law; I have bought by that gentleman's advice Wood's institutes[2] and Jacob's dictionary of law terms;[3] If you have any good law books, I think it wou'd not be improper to send me e'm, if of no use to you, by that means I shall avoid a considerable expence. I shou'd be glad to know wether you wou'd have me entered of the temple; as the Roman Catholick religion is an obstacle to my being call'd to the Bar, I don't see the necessity or need of it, especially as I cannot be entered as a member under 20 pounds.

I am not as yet able to determin how much my expences may amount to: and this greatly depends on the footing you intend I shou'd be upon. I have hitherto been without a servant but as a servant is absolutely necessary, I propose getting one soon: his cloths and board wagers will cost me 40 Pounds a year: my chambers cost me exactly that sum; my washing [(]a very dear article in London) will amount to 9 or 10 pounds: add to this, fewel, my own living, and other extraordinary expences such as buying law-books, parties of pleasure, riding into the country, going to the play (for these amusements are necessary and innocent) all this, I say, will come to a good deal of money especially in a country so extravagantly dear as this is. Pray let me know what you think will be genteel and sufficient, of this you are a better Judge than myself, and I am persuaded as you have allways acted with generosity in my regard, you will continue to do so: but let me take the liberty to remind you that it will be more necessary I shou'd appear in a proper genteel handsome way in my present station than in France, as you are much more known in one country than in the other: besides frequenting company will draw on expences, which a College life is exempt from.

My Present s[t]ation is widely different from any I have hitherto been in, and tho' I have been happy in all the different scenes thro' which I have passed, yet my present sejour promises to turn out the most agreable of all: my Chambers are genteel and convenient and in the most wholesome pleasant part of the temple.

The choice of good company is the most difficult & yet the most important article, in which the temple appears to be deficient, tho' extremely convenient in every other point. Few young gentlemen are here to be found of sound moralls[.] I cou'd pardon a little obscenety, provided it be not too barefaced and extended no farther than words: castum decet esse Poetam, says a chaste Latin Author, versiculos esse castos ō decet:[4] however this doctrine I am sensible is not too Christian and if a Jansenist shou'd chance to see this, I shou'd certainly fall under his censure, & be accused of having adopted la morale relacheé des Molinistes the most hideous of all crimes in a Jansenist's eye.[5] I am persuaded you foresaw this difficulty & having forseen it to expose me to such danger is paying me the highest compliment, which I cannot better answer than by not abusing the confidence you place in my good behaviour. Tho' indeed no place in itself can be the seat of virtue, as none can be secure from vice; and a person naturally inclined to be vitious and not able to subdue his passions, wou'd in the very cloistre seek to gratify em, and infalably succeed in his dessein, how soever great the difficulties he has to encounter and surmount, may be.

(Mr. Crookshanks has not been payed the 1200 livres as he was promised: the payment was postponed to another time.) The King of France has stop'd the interest for a year of money Lent him: this shews that his kingdom is reduced to the greatest extremety or else they wou'd never have consented to a remedy for their present exigencies so fatal to their credit and so serviceable to their ennemies: The King of Prussia notwithstanding his great losses keeps his ground, nay I think seems to be gaining ground upond the Austrians:[6] Politicians here are of opinion that the Russians have been bought off; how true I w'ont pretend to say; but really their slow way of acting after their victory seems to favour this opinion: tho' perhaps what we attribute to corruption may proceed from their policy;[7] They wou'd perhaps be glad to see the Prussians and Austrians so weakened by their mutual losses, as to be able to dictate to both what terms of peace they shou'd think proper for their own interest to empose.

I think I have said all I had to say: by the next time I write something new will occur & make the subject of as long & tedious a letter as this is: till then I remain Dr. Papa & Mama

Your affectionate and dutifull Son
C: Carroll.

P:S:

Be pleased to send by the 1st. oportunity 2 pounds of gentian root,[8] 2 red birds a mocking bird a live if possible, if not, preserved in his feathers and a dead humming bird preserved also and some of the best peach plants. My Love and duty to my Grand Mama & Aunt Genny my compliments to the Croxalls, to Mr. & Mrs. Lawson & to Dr. Lyon. Wou'd it be proper for me to go to visit Mr. Bladen[9] late governour of Maryland? Is there a good understanding between you? This I ask you because I remember few governours & you used to agree; I shou'd not care to pay such a compliment as a visit to any person you do'nt like or esteem.

ALS, Carroll Papers, MS 206, MdHi. Addressed by CC. Postmarked "New York" and "DE." Endorsed by CCA.

1. Actually a letter of Aug. 13, 1759 (Carroll-McTavish Papers). CCA reported British successes at Niagara, Ticonderoga, and Crown Point and Gen. James Wolfe's bombardment of Quebec.

2. Thomas Wood (1661-1722), *Institute of the Laws of England, or, The Laws of England in Their Natural Order, According to Common Use*, 2 vols. (1720). Several editions appeared over the next forty years.

3. Giles Jacob (1686-1744), *A New Law Dictionary* (1729).

4. "It becomes a poet to be chaste . . . [but] his verses need not be chaste" paraphrases Catullus *Poems* 16.5-6.

5. Molinists followed the teachings of Spanish Jesuit Luis Molina (1535-1600), who held that man was not intrinsically evil and that his impulses and desires were bad only when his reason did not control them. According to Molina, man was capable of good and could be saved simply by accepting fully the efficacy of God's grace. Jansenists, who flourished mainly in France during the seventeenth and eighteenth centuries, adhered to the doctrines of Cornelius Jansen (?-1538), who maintained that man was totally depraved, possessed of an innately perverse will, incapable of any good in and of himself, and totally dependent for his predestined salvation upon God's grace as personified in Jesus Christ. Any deviation from God's "absolute," "objective," and "inexorable" goodness was, for the Jansenists, inexcusable wickedness and a sign of moral laxity — "*la morale relachée.*" R. R. Palmer, *Catholics and Unbelievers in Eighteenth Century France*, 2d ed. (New York, 1961), 29, 31-32.

6. On Aug. 12, 1759, Frederick the Great suffered the greatest calamity of his career, losing twenty thousand men at the battle of Kunersdorf. He considered abdication but, after receiving reinforcements from Duke Ferdinand of Brunswick's Prussian-British army, began to reorganize his forces in the field. David Eggenberger, *A Dictionary of Battles* (New York, 1967), 224-225.

7. After the battle of Kunersdorf, the Russian forces retired from Prussia to their own frontier because of their inability to acquire sufficient food supplies.

8. The rhizome and roots of the yellow gentian were used as a stomachic and as a tonic.

9. Although related by marriage to the Calverts, Maryland's proprietary family, Thomas Bladen (1698-1780) was nevertheless dismissed as lieutenant governor of the province in 1746 after four years in office for "tactless and quarrelsome" behavior. The only native Marylander to have held that post, he returned the following spring to England, where he had lived for thirty years before becoming governor, and spent the rest of his life there. *Bio. Dic. Md. Legis.*, I, 135-136.

CC to CCA

Decb. the 10th. 1759.

Dr. Papa,

My last was dated the 13th of Nob. I have received several Letters from you since most of them copies[.] Yours of Sepb. 22d. came to hand a few days ago: you seem to complain of my not keeping my word of writing to you six times a year. This makes the 7th. Letter I wrote to you Janur. 17th. Febr. 17th. Juin the 22d. August the 14th Nob. 13th and one by Mr. Diggs upon my arrival in London. I must acknowledge that there appears some unsteadiness in my resolution of quitting Paris: but that is not to be attributed to me but the times. I had resolved upon setting out from Paris in the beginning of Sepb. but my friends persuaded me to lay asside that resolution, as it might expose me to dangers & difficulties supposed to be occasioned by an invasion. I cou'd not at first persuade myself the French were serious but the vigorous preparations that were carried on all along the sea-coast at last convinced me they intended to invade some part of the British dominion's:[1] but la Clue's[2] defeat put an end to their project; after that blow it was out of their power of attempting it, at least with any prospect of success. My silence in regard to these preparations proceeded not from neglect, but from thought & reason. Had I mentioned any thing concerning them, my Letters wou'd certainly have been stopped, perhaps something worse might have happened. Thus am I vindicated from neglect and unsteadiness: perhaps I may clear myself also of your reproach of my not being punctual in my promises. I really had promised my Mama a curious and interesting Letter and such I flatter myself it wou'd have been (for I am persuaded that any thing that regards me so nearly as that Letter did, wou'd have been agreable to her.) It was wrote by a gentleman of my acquaintance at Bourges to one of his: he therein gave his opinion of me so much the more freely as he thought it wou'd never have fallen into my hands: I unluckely lossed in packing up my papers at my departure from Bourges: I remember some particulars: but beg to be excused from mentioning them, I might exagerate some, diminuish others for how is it possible not to be partial when we are talking or writing of ourselves?

The letters you left with Mr. Crookshanks are still in his hands, the few that remained with me concerning that affair I burnt for greater security, as also the memorial you drew up to be presented to the M——. You Judged prudently in not giving up the 200 guineas for lost. I received yesterday a Letter from Mr. Crookshanks with the advice of his being paid the 4800 £.[3] I shall transcribe his words — I pleaded hard against the threatned stoppage I remembered you so much dreaded, and prevailed at length with much adoe. In so very critical times I dare not trust to any banker's bill here otherwise shou'd have remitted it to you. (You see by this how low publick credit is at present in France.[)] You know I cant have a more real pleasure than that of being serviceable to yourself or worthy Papa: pray assure him of my tenderest thoughts and best wishes, when you have occasion to write to him.[4]

I have drawn out an account of my expences from the time of the last account till my arrival in London. They expences of my Journey from Paris to London are not quite copied out, when they are I shall send them all togeather. How much my expences in London will amount to every year I am not able to determin even to guess at: this I know that to appear genteely and with credit, to pay my Lodgings, to keep a servant &c any thing under 300 £ St will be too stinting; but believe that sum a Just and handsom allowance.

This Letter is to go off to night: else I shou'd answer my Mama's Letter more at length: she seems to like Maryland better than any other country: i'ts natural; she has seen no other, knowes no other, and has friends in no other: Perhaps had she been as long absent from it, as I have been, that love so undeservedly bestowed on an ungreatfull country, wou'd be greatly dimminuished[.] I cant conceive how any Roman Catholick especially an Irish Roman Catholick can consent to Live in England or any the British dominions, if he is able to do otherwise. Its true we are quiet and unmolested at present, because the reigning king is not prejudiced against us: but the most tyranical laws are still subsisting, they can be put into execution to day to morrow, whenever it shall please the King for the parliament wou'd allways readily comply with such a demand. Now where is the man of spirit that can behold the rod lifted up, tremble, and kiss the hand of him that holds it? (At this thought and remembrance of all the wrongs we have unJustly suffered, I cou'd wish with Dido exoriare aliquis nostris ex ossibus ultor &c.)[5] Notwithstanding my natural aversion to all such oppressions, and to an humble, silent, groveling submission, I cou'd even rather bear all this, than be deprived of the pleasure and comfort of living happily togeather. I am Dr. Papa

Your most dutyfull and affectionate Son
C: Carroll

PS:

I shall take care to forward Monsieur de Buisson's Letter. I desire my Love and duty to my Grand-Mama to my Aunt Jenny, shall comply with her request of sending her a deseign of my own fancy; it will not be comical. I am of serious turn of mind & think grow more so daily. My compliments to Mr. Lawson; I have seen his son,[6] & think him a fine youth; he is set off for Camebridge & I dont doubt in the least of his doing well. I have received Mr. Croxall's Letter in answer to mine as also Mr. Lawson's: my compliments to the former & to Mrs. Lawson, to Dr. Lyon &c.

The king of Prussia, at least his forces have met with an other overthrow. Generals Finck & Wunch have with 20000 men been surrounded & taken Prisonners of war by Marchal Dawn, with the loss of all their artillery, bagage &c.[7] Great talks of a piece; the successes we have had will oblige the French to come into a very dishonnourable peace for them. Some Pretend to say that the Ministers of the respective powers at war have mett togeather at the Hague: wether true or not I cant say.

ALS, Carroll Papers, MS 206, MdHi. Addressed by CC. Endorsed by CCA.

1. The French plan for invading England in 1759 was a revival of a scheme conceived by Charles Fouquet, duc de Belle-Isle, in 1756 but laid aside. The French armada was to converge on the Clyde River, thereby securing access to the commercial and shipbuilding centers located at Glasgow. From Glasgow, French forces commanded by Armand Vignerot-Duplessis-Richelieu, duc d'Aiguillon, were to seize control of the Scottish lowlands and await support from the highlands, an area still believed to be disaffected despite the failure of the 1745 rebellion. To capitalize upon British consternation over the situation in the north, two French army corps totaling about twenty thousand men under Charles de Rohan, prince de Soubise, and François de Chevert were to cross the Channel in two flotillas made up of flatboats, each vessel capable of carrying four hundred men and two twenty-four pounders. The flotillas, one moving from Normandy and one from Flanders, were to land in southern England and move from there on London. Lawrence Henry Gipson, *The Great War for the Empire: The Culmination, 1760–1763*, The British Empire before the American Revolution (New York, 1958–1970), VIII, 6.

2. British ships commanded by Adm. Edward Boscawen (1711–1761) defeated twelve French ships of the line under Admiral de la Clue (?–1759) off the coast of Portugal in August 1759. Ibid., 12–16.

3. Actually 4,800 livres tournois, the equivalent of two hundred guineas in English money.

4. Text from "The letters you left with Mr. Crookshanks" through "occasion to write to him" is enclosed in brackets in a much darker ink; these brackets have not been reproduced.

5. "That some avenger might spring up from our bones" (Virgil *Aeneid* 4.625), Dido's curse on Aeneas and the Roman race.

6. Alexander Lawson, Jr., was admitted to the Middle Temple on Dec. 18, 1759, and on Jan. 29, 1760, enrolled at Cambridge. E. Alfred Jones, *American Members of the Inns of Court* (London, 1924), 122.

7. A Prussian detachment of twelve thousand men under generals Frederick von Finck and J. J. Wunsch was surrounded at Maxen by an Austrian army of forty-two thousand men under the command of Count Leopold von Daun. After trying for two days to break out, Finck surrendered on Nov. 20, 1759. Eggenberger, *Dictionary of Battles*, 270; Christopher Duffy, *The Army of Frederick the Great* (New York, 1974), 76.

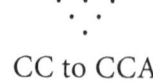

CC to CCA

Decb. 26th 1759.

Dr. Papa,

I am Just informed of an oportunity of writing to you a line or two: a convict ship is ready to set sail for Maryland, the captain is acquainted with you, I know his name, but know not how to write it, I think it is Macklorkley or some such thing. My last Letter was dated the 13th of last month: by that you have seen that Mr. Crookshanks has received at last the 4800 £. a sum a long while ago despaired of and gave over for lost by me.

I have nothing material to say at present: I am well hope you are, wish you a merry Christmass, a happy new year and many of them. This is particularly in answer to My Mama. I let her know by my last the reasons of my not sending the promised and so much wished for Letter; those reasons must certainly be found good, tho' perhaps they will not satisfy her curiosity, even may encrease it, when she finds by them, what the subject of that Letter was to be. Yet I can supply her with means to gratify that passion so natural to all women, namely curiosity. She may ask of others, as for example of Mr. Rozer[1] & Mr. Plater,[2] who both have seen me, their opinion, & by their reports, form her own. This will be the surest way not to be deceived: that Love so natural to Parents for their children, preJudice &c may make her too partial in my favour. Parents like Lovers are apt to be so much blinded as not to discover the faults of their Children, unless strongly pointed out, or perhaps to think those very faults good qualities. Turpia decipiunt cæcumvitia, aut etiam ipsa hæc delectant veluti Balbinum polypus Hagnæ.[3] I am not at all surprised at the great desire my Mama expresses of seing me; ti's natural; I shou'd be surprised if she had not that desire: if an enterview betwen us depended only on desires, as they are mutual, it wou'd along time ago have been brought about, I am as yet to undergo 3 or 4 year's bannishment, such is your will and such my inclination, as I know it conformable to yours, & beneficial to me.

My kindest compliments to my Cousin Rachael Darnell; I am touched at what she suffers or has suffered from an ungratefull husband, if I cou'd afford her any relief or comfort I wou'd do it with all my heart, not meerly as to a relation, but even as to an unfortunate person, undeserving of the ills she has undergone. All I can say is to recommend to her patience & resignation, the best tho' poor resource of the afflicted. My tender Love to my Grand Mama & to my Aunt Genny & the compliments of the season the same to all my friends, as to Mr. & Mrs. Lawson, the two Croxalls, Doctor Lyon &c. I am Dr. Papa and Mama

Your most affectionate and dutifull Son
Ch: Carroll

ALS, Carroll Papers, MS 206, MdHi. Addressed by CC. Endorsed by CCA. Filed with a second, slightly different ALS version sent because the ship carrying the original was reported lost; addressed by CC and endorsed by CCA: "1760 Janu: 29th Mr Chas: Carroll's Letter wth a Copy of his of Decr: 26th: 1759."

1. Henry Rozer (1726-1802) of Prince George's Co., whose sister Ann's first husband was CCA's younger brother, Daniel Carroll of Duddington (Appendix I, Chart D). Rozer, who married Eleanor Neale of Queen Anne's Co. and had four sons, was en route to Maryland from enrolling his sons in school in Germany. *Bio. Dic. Md. Legis.*, II, 929; Bowie, *Prince George's,* 572-574; Horatio Sharpe to William Sharpe, July 8, 1760, *Arch. of Md.*, IX, 443.

2. George Plater III (1735-1792) was the elder son of George Plater and Rebecca Addison Bowles Plater. A 1752 graduate of the College of William and Mary and evidently trained in the law at the Inns of Court, Plater was a planter and a lawyer and lived at Sotterly, his family's seat in St. Mary's Co. Elected to the lower house of the Maryland assembly in 1757, he served there almost continuously until 1766. Appointed naval officer of Patuxent in 1767, he remained in that post for the next decade. In 1771 he secured a seat in the upper house and on the Council. He held those positions until the coming of the American Revolution replaced Maryland's proprietary government with a series of nine conventions. A member of the seventh, eighth, and ninth conventions (1774-1776), Plater also sat on the third, fourth, and fifth Councils of Safety for the Western Shore (1776-1777) and was a delegate to the Continental Congress (1777-1780). He was chosen a senator from the Western Shore in Maryland's new state government and during his long tenure in that chamber (1777-1791) frequently served as its president. He ended his political career as governor of Maryland (1791-1792). Plater married twice, first in 1762 to Hannah Lee, who died the following year, and second in 1764 to Elizabeth Rousby, with whom he had a son and two daughters. *Bio. Dic. Md. Legis.*, II, 650-652.

3. "Her ugly defects escape his notice as if he were blind; rather they even delight him, as Hagna's wart did Balbinus." Horace *Satires* 1.3.39-40.

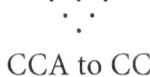

CCA to CC

Jan [9]th 1760

[Dr] Charley

I have at last had the pleasure of yr two Letters of Augst 14th & Septr: 27th. It gave us no small joy to hear by Mr Digges that you were safely arrived at London, we ask'd him many more Questions about you than he could answer & wish'd his acquaintance with you had been longer, however all he told us was pleasing & Satisfactory especially that Mr: Porter[1] spoke greatly in yr: Commendation may it ever be yr: Endeavour to merit the Approbation of good judges.

I desire at all events you may prevail on Mr: Crookshanks to accept of the ten Guineas, I hope he will not deprive me of the pleasure of testifying by so trifling a token my Gratitude for his many favours to you & me, I write from the Sincerity of my heart & wish him health & ev'ry other happiness wch pray let him know at the same time presenting my Service & Compts to him & to all my Acquaintance at Paris. I never despared of recovering the 4800£ I am sensible the streights people in France are reduced to makes the Discharge of Debts difficult & tedious: I am very unwilling to entertain the opinion you seem to have of Monsr: de L'Isle Dieu he may be one of those who cannot struggle with difficulties especially where they think their Credit or Interest not sufficient to carry wt they desire; he was under no obligation to me on Acct of Mr Buisson I was glad to do it to serve Manjan a poor Acadian here, wt will become of him or the rest of them God knows, the French seem to be so distressed ev'ry where, that upon a peace they cannot reasonably hope for relief from them[.] Thus will they fall Victims to our Cruelty, by wch they have been reduced from a state of ease & plenty to Misery, Poverty & Raggs.

We have long expected the interesting & curious Letter you promised yr: Mama, we supposed the Journal you promise us would be the Subject of it. What you say about the Administration of Justice in France, the Independence of the Parliaments on each other & the manner of Evoquing Causes from the Parliamts to the great Councill is said with Judgment & Perspicuity & is satisfactory. I am not more displeased with the Malice & Violence of our people than with the meanness & Injustice of our Proprietary & those acting under him, Gratitude if they had any would oblige them to protect & Countenance us. Pray let me know whether you took all the Lessons in Riding & whether you continue to be pleased with drawing: inform me in wt Court of the Temple you are & how to direct to you. I am glad to hear yr Chambers are handsome [convenient & that they please you. Mr] Perkins writes me that if [you like them & will have them for three Years more the owner] will paint them &c, I think you [must] stay at least 4 years in the Temple you cannot acquire a perfect knowledge of the Law in less if in so short a time, & that knowledge is Essential to you as I shall leave you to dispute many things of Consequence wch the present Injustice of the times will not permit me in prudence to contest, therefore endeavour to get yr: Chambers fitted up to please you by engaging to stay in the Chambers as long as you stay in the Temple & in case he will not fit them up on those terms agree to stay in them 3 years longer in case you live so long. We have not yet seen the Snuff Box or the 28th Lettre Edifiant, Mr: Digges not having his Baggage with him when he passed thrô Annapolis, however we thank you for both.

I have already wrote you that I could not determine exactly wt sum would be necessary for you in yr: present Sejour, I intimated the Sum I thought would be sufficient, it will depend much on yr: prudence & OEconomy, I would not have you appear mean in anything, the best Company is not the most Expensive if it be chosen with discretion: a Student who apply's as he ought is not supposed to be too often or too long from his Books: Prudence must direct you in this as well as on other occasions, the great point seems to be to get introduced into a proper Acquaintance, in this among others I would have you consult Messrs Corbie, Baker, Pointz & Murphy to whom I also refer you for yr: Spiritual Affairs, I hope you will pay a proper defference to their advice, & I desire most cordially to be remembred to them. You cannot do without a Servt: if he is not sober & orderly turn him away without Ceremony until you get such a one; As you become acquainted with the Town you will be better able to provide & chuse for yr self.

I have from time to time been concerned in Lotterys as you will perceive by the Inclosed Acct. As I have a good opinion of Mr: Perkins's Integrity I do not doubt but my Tickets turned out as express'd in the Credit side of the Acct, however as it is prudent to look carefully into ones own business, I desire you will without letting Perkins know it apply to some one of the Offices where they keep Registers of the Blanks & Prizes & satisfy yourself & me whether the inclosed Acct be agreeable to the Register, this I do, not only for my own Satisfaction but to give you a Lesson. I am yet ignorant of the fate of my last 10 Tickets as the drawing was last Novr: or Decr: I have hitherto play'd a loosing Game.

By my former Letters & by the Papers you are fully informed of our Successes in America. Our latest Accts from the Northward say that Monsr. Vaudreuil[2] intended to attempt to retake Quebec this Winter, & in [order to it] had ordered 20,000 p[air of Snow Shoes to be made:] he may be well supply'd with Snow Shoes, but in my [opinion] his Troops, his Magazines of Arms, Ammunition & Provisions are no ways equal to such an undertaking & all Canada for want of supplies must submit next Spring or Summer; Louisiana & the rest of their Islands may in all probability share the same fate if our Ministry think proper to avail themselves of the irresistable Superiority wch our Naval force gives us. I see by our latest Accts wch come as low as the 15th of Octr: that the French still threaten to invade England, it seems to me a pure Gasconade: if they did not dare stir out of their Ports when we had such powerfull Squadrons before Quebec & in the West Indies, will they attempt it upon the return of those Sqadrons wch will add so much to our Superiority? If they attempt it & Land, it must be miraculous, & I think 50000 Regulars will embarass us very much. You will be able to informe me whether the French ever seriously designed an Invasion, wt the Sentiments of the people at Paris were on the Subject & whether Prince Charles[3] was to accompany them, I do not see that they pretend to assist him or mention him, they must be very Sanguine if they proposed a Conquest.

Your Aunt Jenny has long laboured under a Cancer in her Breast, she is now at Deaths Door, God grant her a happy & easy Death. Your Mama since last Febry had a swelling & thought herself with Child, she has always been perfectly well, the swelling is now going of[f], & we have the strongest reasons to hope without the least Prejudice to her health. We both pray to God to bless you. I am Dr Charley,

Yr: Mo: Afft: Father
Cha: Carroll

LS, Carroll-McTavish Papers, MS 220, MdHi. Marked "Dupt:" by CCA; margins damaged. Filed with two other similarly damaged LS copies, one marked "Triplicate" by CCA. Text in brackets supplied from unmarked copy.

1. Probably Nicholas Porter (1724–1802), who completed his studies at St. Omers in 1741 and served in England from the mid-1750s into the 1760s. Foley, ed., *Records*, VII, 616; Holt, *St. Omers*, 211.

2. Pierre de Rigaud de Vaudreuil de Cavagnial, marquis de Vaudreuil (1698–1778), was the last French governor of Canada.

3. Prince Charles Edward (1720–1788), the Young Pretender, grandson of England's last Stuart king, James II.

CC to CCA

Janr. 29th 1760.

Dr. Papa,

I received a few days ago yours of the 6th of Octb. never was Letter more agreeable or more instructive. That my present situation is the most dangerous of any I have hitherto been in is evident: advice is necessary but most of all a sufficient resolution to put good advice in execution. Few are so blinded as not to see their duty; but how many[1] are there who follow it? Who is so profligate as not to love and esteem virtue? Yet how seldom is the man to be found who sticks up to its true principles? Young person's passions are strong of themselves & need no outward encouragement; but when roused by occasions, strengthened by example, fired with wine & Jovial company become almost irresistible. Ti's therefore with the greatest prudence and forecast you recommend to me the choise of my company a matter really difficult in London, but most so among young men. O tempora! O mores![2] Men ashamed of appearing virtuous I have seen none, but several guilty of criminal actions, who deemed them & least pretended to deem them indifferent. That the greatest resolution, prudence & virtue are requisite to protect me from such contagion is undoubted. Here is the place for protestations of the most heroic virtue: but such protestations are not comformable to my way of thinking, besides they emply presumption and too much self-confidence. I never like to promise unless morally certain of being able to fulfil my promise: and who can not promise not others but even himself, of remaining always virtuous.[3] I am now in an open sea, hitherto I have rode triumphantly; I have met with shoals & sands which tho' perhaps not avoided by me with all the skillfulness of an understanding pilot, have not occasioned a shipwreck.

The chair for a Professor of the common law is established at Oxford:[4] he is a man of parts, answers the expectation of the publick & believe will be very beneficial to those who profit of his lectures from the number of these I am excluded by my religion as it is only intended for the use & instruction of the Students at the University. Such an Institution was certainly very much wanted, and ti's to be wondered at why it was not thought of & executed sooner. The difficulty of the common law proceeds chiefly from i'ts want of a certain method & order, which perhaps this gentleman may introduce into it, at present it is a mere chaos, rudis indisgestaque moles,[5] which added to the natural dryness of this study, renders it almost insupportable to every beginner. However neither i'ts difficulty or dryness frightenen me; I am convinced of i'ts utility and therefore am resolved at all hazards to plunge into this Chaos, I expect to meet with no smaler difficulties than attended Satan on his voyage thro' the primeval one. But I shall not be alone & without a guide: Mr. Twinihoe will assist me as much as his affairs will permit him. I have begun to read Wood's institutes by the recommendation of that gentleman. As my Grand Father underwent[6] a regular study of the law in the temple he must have had a considerable number of law books; these I suppose, remain in a great measure in your hands: wou'd it be improper to send me such as are the most useful & necessary? Law books are extremely dear: this wou'd save a considerable expence: That a common place book if properly digested is useful, is I believe commonly allowed of not withstanding in my opinion no person ought to enter upon any such scheme, till he is pretty well versed in the law. The reason is obvious: if a raw beginner immediately undertakes to make remarks & commit them to paper, they must be trivial & of course not worth penning down.

You have laid a very heavy task upon me, but very undesignedly I dare say, I mean the reading of all the pamphlets that make their appearance in this town for a day or two, then die, are buried & forgotten. Without troubling myself with the perusal of such nonsense I shall be able to send you those that merit your reading; for such recommended by their own intrinsic value will be talked of by the Publick. There is at present one that has met with publick approbation, and very deservedly: but of this you will yourself be better able to Judge after having red it. I'ts entitled a Letter to two great men.[7] The end is particularly remarkable.

This naturaly leads me into some reflections started in your Letter. A change in our constitution is I think near at hand. Our dear-bought Liberty stands upon the brink of destruction. The reasons are pointed out in the above mentioned pamphlet.[8] Is such a change to be wished for by Roman Catholicks? They enjoy great peace and tranquility under his present Majesty. I mean in England. They may perhaps enjoy the same hereafter in Maryland: but men's minds and dispositions in that country must undergo a great change, before so favourable a revolution can happen. How is our Lord Proprietor disposed? If credit can be given to certain reports he is not master of his own will, but a mere weathercock to point out where the wind blows from. This is not my sentiment or private opinion. Nay I disbelieve it. As I have never seen his Lordship I am unable to form any idea of him, when I shall have that honour I really can't say, if ever the occasion presents itself, I shall embrace it. God be thank'd that I am borne to an independent fortune, for I never shou'd have acquired one by a servile dependence on the Great. I have too much pride to cringe and too much sincerity to flatter: both necessary to that Man whose hopes are grounded on Great men.

I can't close this Letter without touching on that part of yours precautionning me against too great familiarities with women. A most necessary precaution indeed: for what so decieving, what so engaging as women! I have often wondered why Providence has bestowed such art, such sagacity on that sex, and at the same time so much beauty. However set asside the charms of beauty, all their alluring inveigling arts will avail them little; for I have frequently remarked, that the most beautiful are always the most powerful, at least with me. I wou'd defy an uggly woman endowed with all the sagacity of a sphinx ever to entrap me.[9]

Your advice with regard to my countrymen here, shall be most scrupulously followed, melius enim est nihil, quam parum dicere[10] of such young gentlemen: by saying little it might be enterpreted that little is to be said in their favour, and as to saying a great deal — that I must decline, as I have neither time nor a turn for panegeryk. I think I may now safely end this overgrown Letter. I am Dr. Papa

Your most dutiful & Loving Son
C: Carroll.

ALS, Carroll Papers, MS 206, MdHi. Edited by CCA. Another ALS version of this letter bearing the same date is filed with it.

1. The word "few" in CCA's hand has been interlineated above "many" written in CC's hand but struck through.

2. "Oh the times! Oh the customs!" Cicero *In Catilinam* 1.1.1.

3. CCA edited this sentence to read: "and who can promise to others even to himself, to remain always virtuous."

4. The first person to hold this chair, established at Oxford in 1758, was the English jurist William Blackstone (1723–1780).

5. "An indistinct and confused mass." Ovid *Metamorphoses* 1.7.

6. CCA edited this passage to read: "As my Grand Father went thrô."

7. John Douglas's *Letter Addressed to Two Great Men on the Prospect of Peace; and on the Terms Necessary to Be Insisted upon in the Negociation* (London, 1760), was an appeal for ending the war directed to William Pitt and the duke of Newcastle. *Cat. Lib.*, no. 832; O. A. Sherrard, *Lord Chatham: Pitt and the Seven Years' War* (London, 1955), 362.

8. In Douglas's view, mounting war debt, power wielded collaboratively by political and military leaders, excessive ministerial influence over Parliament, and widespread corruption posed grave dangers to traditional British liberties.

9. In the other version of his letter, CC rendered this paragraph as follows: "I Can't close this Letter without touching on that part of yours precautionning me against too great familiarities with women: a most necessary precaution indeed for the Strongest, wisest, best of men have been ensneared by women & brought to utter destruction: what then have I not to fear who am so week? Great no doubt are the charms of that pleasing deceitfull sex, and surpassed by nothing but by their art in setting them off to the best advantage & in rendering them more fatel. The Celebrated Montesquiou in one of his persian Letters says

that the tears of a beautiful woman wou'd soften the very rocks themselves & move them to compassion? I have no Mentor to precipitate me headlong from of[f] the rock to secure me from the allurements of a Calipso[.] The remedy wou'd be indeed violent: how ever to be serious I hope to satisfy you in this point as on all others, & never will, you may depend on it, think of marriage without your previous consent & knowledge." Charles-Louis de Secondat, baron de la Brède et de Montesquieu (1689–1755) published *Lettres persanes* anonymously in 1721.

10. "It is better indeed to say nothing than not enough."

CC to CCA

Febr. 30th. 1760.

Dr. Papa,

The inclosed is a copy of my last. Mr. Stevens[1] was so obliging as to charge himself with this. I cou'd not let slip so fair an opportunity of writing a few lines. I say a few lines, for really since my last long Letter Little remains to be said: I intend to send by Mr. Perkin's ship a copy of this Letter together with the new testament of Pere Berruyer and his epistles, an account of my expences from the last to my arrival in England, the Letter addressed to two great men. The new Professor of the common law has published lately an Analysis of the laws of England with an introductory discourse on the usefulness of the study of those laws,[2] and a treaty on descents[3] all which I have bought.

I omitted in my last to answer that part of your Letter relating to my expences, not being then able to determin how much they wou'd amount to. At present I think I may give a good guess. 40 pounds for the rent of my chambers and 35-16-0 to my servant, his board wages included are 75£-16S-0D[.] Now putting my own Living at 60 pound's a year we have a 135-16-0, which Joined to 30 pounds expended in buying several little conveniencies for my chambers, as tables, a set of China cups & Saucers a few plates and dishes, glasses, punch bowls a dozen of silver tea spoons tongs &c (all which I assure you are necessary for no young gentleman that has a mind to appear to genteel can go without them) make 165-16-0 my expence in clothes will amount to 30, for I brought but two suits from France and those can be wore only on particular occasions; washing will cost 8 or 10 £ a year which if added to 165-16-0 we have in all 205-16-0[.] There remains out of 250 £, my allowance, but 44-4-0 a sum which I leave you to Judge, wether sufficient for private expences, as playing at cards, diversions, going to the play, riding out on parties of pleasure &c. I must own to have put the several articles of these expences at a round tho' no ways exagerated computation. What has been laid out this year in fournishing my chambers and in dress is a peculiar expence, incident to every setting out. Be persuaded of this that I shan't fool away my money; & shall endeavour to act with oeconomy and at the same time appear genteel, so as to avoid all imputation of meaness. Out of the 4800 Livres received of Mr. Crookshanks, 271-12-0 have been deducted (for expences at different times for payment 27 lt-18-0, for yr. order to Mr. Crookshanks 240-0, postage 3-14-0) thus there remains 4528£⁴-8-0, which has been remitted to me and makes of our money 190£-5S-1/3[.]

I have not enjoyed of Late as good a state of health as usual, I have been advised to keep a horse, but do'nt think proper so to do till I know yr. opinion of the matter, the keeping a horse (prime cost not included) will stand me in 35 pounds a year if not 40.

I shou'd be glad to know, if you think proper, how long you intend to keep me in London: three years in my opinion with all due defferance to yours, will be sufficient to acquire a competent knowledge of the law, so far as will be necessary & usefull to me. If you have a mind I shou'd thoroughly understand the law, and become another Lord Mansfield,⁵ a serious application of twenty years aided by a bright capacity will not enable me to attain to such perfection.

By yr. last you seem still resolved upon Leaving Maryland: I must own you have great reason to be displeased with the people: yet as much as I can learn concerning the country ut sic,⁶ you won't be able to exchange it for a better, and as the people become more civilised we may reasonably hope that their prejudices and animosity will wear off with time. True happiness on earth is not to be met with nihil ea o[mn]e parte beatum.⁷ We suffer at present in Maryland for our religion, that same religion exposes us in England to the very same oppression, which tho' not openly exercised, even suspended for the present may brake out a new whenever our government thinks proper. If you repair to France there you will only exchange religious for civil Tyranny, and In my opinion of the two the greatest evil. Civil oppression has nothing to console us; religious persecutions are always attended with this consolation at least, of not going unrewarded.

When I first took up my pen I was only to write a few lines, however I think I have made shift to compose a long Letter: before I end it I must beg a favour of you. I shall be much obliged to you if you can contrive to send me some good Madera wine, what we have here is so detestable that I can't drink it. As I drink no malt liquor and as cyder does not agree with me I am obliged to have recourse to wine & water. I desire my sincerest Love & duty to my Mama, shall write to her at Large when I send the copy of this Letter. I am Dr. Papa

Your most affectionate & dutifull Son
C: Carroll

P:S:

My Love & duty to my Grand Mama & Aunt Genny my compliments to Mrs & Mr. Lawson to the two Croxalls & Dr. Lyon.

ALS, Carroll Papers, MS 206, MdHi. Endorsed by CCA.

1. Probably William Stevenson (1739–1785) who resided at New Town, later Chester-

town, in Kent Co. George A. Hanson, *Old Kent: The Eastern Shore of Maryland; Notes Illustrative of the Most Ancient Records of Kent County, Maryland, and of the Parishes of St. Paul's, Shrewsbury, and I.U., and Genealogical Histories of Old and Distinguished Families of Maryland, and Their Connections by Marriage, &c.* (Baltimore, 1876), 79–81; *Bio. Dic. Md. Legis.,* II, 778.

2. William Blackstone published *Analysis of the Laws of England,* an outline of his proposed lectures, in 1754. His *Discourse on the Study of Law, Being an Introductory Lecture, Read in the Public Schools, 25th Oct. 1758,* appeared separately in 1758 but was included in later editions of his *Analysis. Cat. Lib.,* no. 104, lists a 1759 edition of the work.

3. Blackstone, *Treatise on the Law of Descents in Fee Simple* (1759).

4. Livres tournois.

5. William Murray, first earl of Mansfield (1705–1793), was appointed attorney general in 1754 and became lord chief justice of England in 1756. He was known for the lucidity of his arguments and his skill as an orator.

6. "As such."

7. "Nothing is altogether happy." Horace *Odes* 2.16.27–28.

CC to CCA

April 10th. 1760.

Dr. Papa,

This makes my 4th by this fleet; I have wrote by Mr. Stephenson a very modest Youth the highest commendation that can be bestowed upon a young man now a days: by Mr. Leornards,[1] & the present accompanies the account of my expences, which I put into the hands of Mss. Brown & Buchannon two of Mr. Perkin's Clerks.[2] As those gentlemen upon my arrival in London, behaved very politely to me, & were ready to render me all the Service that lay in their power, I beg it as a favour of you, to return their civilities, protect & recommend them.

In Your last of the 9th of January you seem to give some hints that new oppressive laws have been introduced against the RC — The passive indolence of our Proprietary offends you as much as the malice & injustice of our enemies. As I am perfectly ignorant of the Maryland government its laws, & power of the Proprietary, I am unable to determin wether he deserves the imputations of meaness & ingratitude. That I may be fully instructed herein you may make this the subject of your next Letter, and send me for my further instruction the Charter of Maryland you brought over with you to Paris. I have seen Mr. Calvert dined with him & my Lord Baltimore at Mr. Sharpe's,[3] brother to our governor & in appearance a worthy gentleman. Mr. Calvert has returned my visit. We had time to discourse at Large upon Maryland affairs; I reminded him of the unjust laws enacted against the Roman C-, hinted at the Proprietary's inactivity, not to use a more severe word, wondered that such tyrannical proceedings of a despicable vile mob, shou'd meet no check from lawful power; that they shou'd be tamely permitted to go on in making arbitrary laws, (if they may be call'd by that name) not leveled against the RC alone but also against the Proprietary family: Laws highly iniquitous in themselves and destructive of that Liberty of conscience which had been granted in the Charter of Maryland, & always exercised there without molestation from the 1st settlement of the Colony to the Revolution. He told me he was much offended at those laws & at the violence of our assembly & some Protestants who had painted the Proprietary in the blackest colours and th[r]own the most henious aspersions on him: that one Brooks had brought over & presented to my Lord Halifax a memorial loaded with the deepest & most severe complaints of the RC & Proprietary family:[4] That he knew full well their intentions; that in consequence of this memorial he had wrote to the Governor of Maryland to enquire after the conduct of the RC, to examin the Sheriffs of the different counties concerning their behaviour & deportment, that their depositions had been unanimous in our favour, that he had by him, & wou'd show to me these declarations signed by the sheriffs; that he had shown them to my Lord Halifax as a convincing proof [of] our innocence, and of the injustice done us by our enemies.[5] What reply cou'd I make to all this? Ought I to have asked why the Proprietary being convinced of our innocence permitted that very innocence to groan under oppression, why he approoved, or at least by not openly refusing his consent to laws so iniquitious even in his own opinion, tacitly approoved of them? I omitted to propose this question & am sorry for it.

My Chambers have been painted upon condition that I remain in them three years: you seem to think of keeping me longer here, tho' really I am of opinion that 3 years will suffice: what to attain a perfect knowledge of the law? No—but to get a tincture of it, so as to be able to study it, without being obliged to attend the courts of Judicature or the assistance of others: and this I may do as well in Maryland as in the temple, perhaps better. Besides several things, you say, of importance will be left me to be disputed, must I not be informed of their nature, of our right & title of the pleas of our adversaries? And by whom can I be informed & instructed in all this but by yourself? What must I live all my life time separated from you? What crime have I done to deserve perpetual banishment? But if it is your will & pleasure that I remain 4 years in London I readily submit. You have found me hitherto dutiful and obedient and hope you will always find me so in every respect. Since my arrival in England I have in a manner left off drawing not from disgust, but partly from want of time & a good & cheap master to instruct me. I have, I think I have, a turn for designing but it requires more time & practice, to attain a tolerable skill, than I am willing to bestow, since I can employ my leasure hours much more to my advantage, and even more to my amusement. I learnt to ride about a month & a half. I shall consult the Lottery register.

I am not acquainted with Mr. Bladen, nor do I desire to be since he is a gamester,

I detest gaming & gamesters; but this is not my only reason for declining his acquaintance. I have seen his daughters[6] at a ball.

My Mama's indisposition gives me great uneasiness; I was informed that she was with child, but cou'd not give credit to that report; I have been greatly apprehensive of i'ts turning to a dropsy, but hope my fears are vain, since the swelling is going off without any sensible alteration of her health. My Poor aunt Jenny! But why shou'd I pity her? Ti's I that am to be pitied who have lossed one who loved me & was dear to me. She certainly now enjoyes the reward of her virtue, sufferings & patience. My Love & duty to my Grand Mama. I am Dr. Papa

Your most dutiful & affectionate Son
C: Carroll

PS:

One Mr. Bird[7] a marble merchant, & a very nigh neighbour of mine, A Roman Catholick & a very honnest man, desires to know wether it wou'd be worth his while to send to Maryland marble chimny pieces & tables, if these can meet with a good & profitable debit, he desires also to be further informed of a proper intelligent person on whose honnesty he may depend & make his agent. Pray dont forget to answer this. I shou'd be glad to render Mr. Bird this little piece of service, as he has behaved in a very civil genteel manner to me.

ALS, Carroll Papers, MS 206, MdHi. Endorsed by CCA.

1. Frederick or Ferdinand Leonard (1728-1764), a German Jesuit, arrived in Maryland in June 1760. He subsequently served in Pennsylvania, returned to Maryland in 1763, and died at Port Tobacco. Maryland Province Archives, Box 3, folder 4½, Special Collections Division, DGU; Beatriz Betancourt Hardy, "Papists in a Protestant Age: The Catholic Gentry and Community in Colonial Maryland, 1689–1776" (Ph.D. diss., University of Maryland, 1993), 609–610.

2. William Brown and Thomas Buchanan became partners of William Perkins about 1763. Buchanan was the son of a wealthy Glasgow merchant. Katharine A. Kellock, "London Merchants and the Pre-1776 American Debts," *Guildhall Studies in London History*, I (1974), 139.

3. William Sharpe.

4. Dr. Richard Brooke (1716-1783) of Brookfield in Prince George's Co. probably presented his memorial to Lord Halifax (1716-1771) in 1752. It was apparently inspired by two unrelated events, the uprising in Scotland in 1745-1746 and the establishment of St. Mary's Church in Lancaster, Pa., in 1745 by the Reverend Richard Molyneux, superior of the Jesuit mission in the area. Molyneux was subsequently accused before the Maryland provincial court of being a French agent who was involved in nefarious dealings with the Indians. Halifax considered Brooke's memorial alarming enough to recommend it to the attention of both the Board of Trade and Parliament. Thomas Hughes, *History of the Society of Jesus in North America: Colonial and Federal* (London, 1907-1917), II, 528; *Bio. Dic. Md. Legis.*, I, 169–170.

5. Gov. Horatio Sharpe canvassed the Roman Catholics of Maryland twice—once, as instructed by the Council, in the wake of Gen. Edward Braddock's defeat in 1755, and, again, apparently of his own volition, at a later date. On both occasions he concluded that criticisms against them were unfounded. *Arch. of Md.,* IX, 315–318.

6. Harriet (?–1821) and Barbara Bladen.

7. Christopher Bird of White Friars.

• • •
•

CC to CCA

Porstmouth, [April] 15th 1760.

Dr. Papa,

I arrived here the 14th almost choked with dust, but have washed it down at last and am now preparing myself for all the wonders of Porsthmouth. I am informed the Belle Isle Captain Therrot's ship is in the harbour I propose going on board.

I have nothing particular to mention at present everything material has already been said in my foregoing Letters: Captain Kelty,[1] with whom Mr. Leonards a german missioner is to go, & who has a couple of Letters for you, desired me to give a line or two to introduce him to you.

Mr. Perkins is here with me & several gentlemen of my acquaintance all friends & good natured & chearful, so you may easily Imagin that the sho[rt] time we stay here, will be spent agreeably.

As to publick news I have nothing at all to im[part] to you: we have not heared as yet Lord George Sackville trial;[2] some pretend to say it will be degredation & that he will be rendered incapable of all employs.

There are now 500 highlanders in town going to be shiped off imediately for the east Indies; they grumble very much cawse all blunders & nonsense I scarce know what I say. My Love & duty to my Mama & my Grand Mama I am well & better than I have been for some time past. I am Dr. Papa

Your most dutiful & Loving Son
C: Carroll.

P:S.

Mr. Brown & Buchanon came down with me; they have Letters for you & can satisfy yr. curiosity in my regard as they know me well Mr. Perkins gives his kindest compliments to you.

ALS, Carroll Papers, MS 206, MdHi. Addressed by CC. Endorsed by CCA: "1760 Apr: 15 Mr Cha: Carroll's Letter Ansd: Augt: 4."

1. John Kelty (variously Kilty; ?–c. 1785). Like the Carrolls, he was a Roman Catholic and educated his son, born in 1756, at St. Omers. *Bio. Dic. Md. Legis.,* II, 510.

2. George Sackville Germain, first Viscount Sackville (1716–1785). Up to 1770 he was

known as Lord George Sackville and until 1782 as Lord George Germain. He was dismissed by his commander, Prince Ferdinand of Brunswick, after the battle of Minden on Aug. 1, 1759, for failing to execute orders promptly. Discharged from His Majesty's service on Sept. 10, Sackville demanded a hearing in the form of a court-martial in order to clear his name. The trial convened on Mar. 25, 1760. Sackville was judged guilty, and the king removed his name from the Privy Council book. Refusing to be cowed by treatment he deemed unfair, Sackville continued as a member of Parliament, to which he had first been elected in 1741 and in which he served until 1782, and within a decade he had regained power and influence. Appointed secretary of state for the colonies by Lord North in 1775, Germain directed the war against America until 1782, when he resigned from office. Failing health caused him to spend the last years of his life in retirement.

CCA to CC

May 1st: 1760[1]

Dr Charley

In mine of the 23d past[2] I acknowledged the Receit of yrs of Novr: 13th. & Decr: 10th I now answer them. I received from Mr: Digges the last Vol: of the Lettres Edifiantes & the Snuff Box, I think it genteel & yr: Mother is much pleas'd with it & thanks you for it the hand it comes from greatly enhances the Value of it. As you observe, I shall hence forward have very little news to write you, for if it be possible for the French in Canada to make any Resistance this summer, you will see the particulars in the English Papers before I shall hear them here for I find that most of the occurrences to the Northward of us are known in London sooner than to us. Inclosed is a List of such Law Books as I have by me[3] & I shall send them to you some time in April by Capt: Coolidge from Patuxent,[4] if any should want Binding or other Repairs you may get that done in London[.]

I would have you entered of the Temple & if I am to Judge of the Expence of yr: being so entered by what it cost yr: Grand father it cannot amount to nigh the sum you mention as you will see by the inclos'd Papers wch are Copies. However should it cost you £20 it is but that sum once spent & I desire you will take proper Testimonials of yr: Admission. You will see by my former letters what sum I thought might be a proper Allowance for yr: support, if more be necessary you must have it. Plays Parties of pleasure & Tours into Different parts of the Country I grant you, but these I grant you only at proper times as necessary Relaxations to enable you to prosecute the study of the Law with fresh vigour. When you consider the Croud you are in, the little notice taken of individuals by that Croud, & the folly of endeavouring to be taken notice of by such a Croud, you will judge a plain genteel Dress generally to be most Suitable: Yr: Expence need not be enhanced on my Acct. It is true I am known to our Tobo Merchts they are but Merchts & they can Consider me in no other light than as a good man (according to their phrase) that is as a man able to answer his Engagements. I may be personally known to a few of our Roman Cath: Gentry, to a few more by report, but not in such a manner as to lay you under the least necessity of an Extraordinary Expence; A laced Waste Coat may be necessary to introduce you to some Company, then wear a laced Waste Coat, but endeavour chiefly to keep such Company as will value you more for yr intrinsick than Extrinsick ornaments, by one set you may be amused, by the other instructed & improved — & if such Company cannot be found in the Temple seek it else where. You knew Sr: Thos: Webbs Sons[5] they may introduce to you their Acquaintance. Mr: Corbie Pointz &c may Recommend you to others, time, & Chance will bring you acquainted with others & I doubt not yr: own good sense, judgement & Virtue will at last procure you such Company, Friends & acquaintance as I could wish & as you may desire[. I have] as you observe a great Con[fidence] in yr: Discretion Prudence & Virtue but as evil Communication[s Corr]upt good manners avoid by all means the Company of Libertines who will end[ea]vour to laugh you out of yr Duty to yr: maker, nothing on Earth can be so Contemptible as such wretches. I have wrote you an Answer to what you say about Mr: Bla[de]n, he may possibly pay you a Visit, & I would have you return it —[6]

I have acknowledged the Receit of all the letters you mention in yrs of the 10th of Decr: & I own that by the 4 last you have made amends for the great gap between yrs of Feby: 17th & June the 22d. I challenge 6 Letters a year as a Debt by promise, if you will generously fling in a few more you will give yr: Mama & me great pleasure. Perhaps you took the little Rebuke I gave you about yr: unsteadiness as to the time of yr. Departure from Paris, yr: not mentioning any thing about the French preparations for an Invasion, & yr: not sending the Curious & interesting Letter a little too seriously,[7] I may perchance again now & then chide you, but you must know a tender parent is always more disposed to receive a Childs Apologies favourably than to censure him, but I cannot help being concer[ne]d for the Loss of that Interesting Letter as we are deprived of the Satisfaction it would have given us: How ever the Reasons for not giving us the particulars of it wch you remember are solid & become yr: Modesty —

I am glad to hear the Money you thought desperate has been paid & I am persuaded you owe the Receit of it to Mr: Crookshanks's Industry, diligence & prudence especially as there is such a stagnation of business & Credit in France; By one of yrs I take him to be under an Engagement of accepting the 10 Guineas out of this money & I beg he will no longer hesitate to take so insignificant a Token no way proportioned to the great obligations we are under to him, but at the same time I beg he may not measure my regard or Esteem for him by such a trifle. I am much obliged to him for his kind Remembrance of me, I shall always think of him with affection, & let him know I most sincerely wish him every thing that can Contribute to his happiness —

By yr: next I expect the Acct of yr: Expences until yr: arrival in London, not to be satisfy'd that you do not trifle away yr: money, but to accustom you (by keeping Accts) to know yr: self how yr: money goes & how to regulate yr: Expences. Pay no Bills or Accts without taking Receits, & when you have learned the Method of Book keeping[,] raise Accts with every one with whom you may have dealings & buy a Book to this purpose. I find you begin to think that neither Maryland or any of the British Dominions are a desirable Residence for a Roman Cath: without a Change in the Scene, they Certainly are not so. A change of Climate might shorten my Days, but when I have run my Course you may fix where you please —

I shall be glad to see the performance you have promised yr: Aunt Jenny, I expect it by the fleet, if yr: Genius leads you that way & you have a true taste for it follow yr: Inclination, it will help you to pass away many hours innocently & Pleasantly. If you have not perfected yr: self in the Art of Riding you may do it in London[, y]ou may also do the same in Fencing & Dancin[g. I] hope you have broke yr: sel[f of that s]tooping & Poking I formerly mentioned [to y]ou, unless you have grown [s]ince I saw you, you cannot afford to lose the least of yr: height: I remember you measured 5 feet 5 Inches, what do you measure now? I know not whether you have yet Studied Controversy,[8] I would have you at least acquainted with it in such a Degree as not only to satisfy yr: self but to be able to say something for yr: self when that Subject becomes a Topick of Conversation. In order to that I now send you 4 Vols: entitled Pruves de la Religion de Jesus Christ[9] with wch you may begin, I then recommend the Bishop of Meaux Histoire de Variations,[10] you may next read Englands Conversion & Reformation Compared[11] & you will find the shortest way to end Disputes to be a very solid thô a very little Book:[12] if yr Taste or Inclination should carry you farther, you have those at hand who will recommend other Books to you. By the 28th Vol: of the Edifying Letters I find a 29th Vol: is in the Press, pr[a]y let me have it as soon as possible. I know not whether you brought with you a large French Almanack containing an Acct of their Civil & Military Establishment &c &c[13] it is a large Octavo, if you have it not write to Mr: Crookshanks for one he will know what I mean —

I left with Timothy Rogers my Taylor 40 Coat & 36 Waste Coat Brandenburgs[14] in Gold the Coat I think at 3/ & the Waste Coat at 2/[15] each, if he has not sold them & paid Mr: Perkins take them to yr: own use if Fashionable. I left an order with Mr: Perkins on one Mr: Maccarty for £9.0.6 being so much won of him at Whist at Toms Coffee house, he lodged in Grays Inn, & his Finances Running low he retired into the Country, Mr: Pointz knew him & may inform you where he may be heard of, he is a short thick full-faced Gent: as it is a Debt of Honour I doubt not his paying it, if you can find where he is. My servt: Jos: Gallat owed me £11.7.1 Mr Jo: Edwards who is known to Mr: Perkins will let you know what part of this Sum is paid having had things Lodged in his hands as a Security. Yrs of Decr: 10th brought us the 1st: Acct of the trick Daun play'd the Generalls Fink &

Wunch, & it was looked upon as Popish news but unfortunately the Papers Confirmed it. I shall send you 2 lb of Ginseng[16] after the Season for Gathering it, wch will be next fall, I suppose you mean that, & not Gentian, & endeavour to procure you the Birds: it would be in vain to send you any Peach Trees unless I could send our sun with them, our finest Sorts come from England & are here improved in Richness & flavour by the Warmth of our Climate.

Mr: Lawson & those you Salute return you their Compts with great sincerity & it gives Mr: Lawson great pleasure to think his Son will have the good Luck to have you in the Temple to instruct, advise & introduce him into a good Acquaintance wch I am persuad'd you will do by Inclination. I desire my Respects & Service to Mr: Twynihoe, who I doubt not does [with p]leasure instruct you how to prosecute the Study of the Law in the most Methodical & advantag[eou]s manner, this can give him little or no trouble, nor is it my Intention you should give him any, thô from the little I saw of him & the Character I had of him I am persuaded he will not think that any trouble. Your own good sense will prompt you to consult other Competent Judges on this head as well as to explain to you the many difficulties & intricacys wch you will meet with in reading the Law.

You will probably meet with many Interested Civilities from the Merchts in our Trade, it might seem to be pride not to accept now & then their Invitations, but do it so seldom & in such a manner as not to make yrself cheap & that they may not have any room to think the Dinner they give is not more than paid for by the pleasure of yr Company & Conversation, Behave in this manner not only to the Merchts but to all others: when you have the least Grounds to surmise their Doors are not open to you by pu[re] good nature, esteem & Benevolence; there may be exceptions to this General advice yr: own Interest particular Circumstances & yr: Discretion will point them out to you —

Since I began this I reced yrs of the 26th of Decr: by Capt: Macgachan[17] the 21st of March you are a good boy for writing so often, but I see by it you do not keep a letter Book for it was in yrs of the 10th of Decr. you mentioned the Receit of the 4800 Livers, in yrs. of the 13th of Novr: you told me the Money was not paid. I would not advise you to keep a Letter Book if it were not to accustom you to a thing wch in the Course of yr life you will find usefull & even absolutely necessary & I again recommend it to you; To have the Subject of yr: letters to me always ready wch may be done if as thoughts occur to you you would minute them down & gradually digest them into order, by that means you would always have a letter or matter for a letter ready for us —

As yr: Mama knows the Subject of the Interesting Letter you promised her she bid me tell you she is the more uneasy at the Loss of it & wishes it could be recovered & may be it may be recovered by yr: writing to Bourges, she you may be assured will have Curiosity enough to enquire & hear what Messrs Rosier & Plater can say of you, but she thinks that they know you not so well as the Gent: who wrote that Letter, & may not have so good an opinion of their Discernment. Pray who was the Gent: who wrote that Letter? You see the trouble yr: Carelessness gives you & us—

Yr: Csn R Darnall presents her humble service to you & returns you many thanks for yr: kind Compassion & Concern for her—

I could not as I proposed send you all my Law Books by Capt: Coolidge, & I am not absolutely certain he will carry those which I mention to you with him as they are lent out to Mr: Darnall[18] who has promis'd to deliver them to Mr: Danl: Carroll at Marlbrô, who in [Case] he can get them will certainly ship them. The Books in the other List I will send by the 1st safe Conveyance with the 4 Vols: of the Pruves de la Religion de Jesus Christ. You will see by the Lists that there are Duplicates of many of the Law Books these & others you may sell in London & get new ones of later & better Editions—I would not have you spare Money & want a Compleat Collection of Law Books.

We are well, hope you are so & daily pray to God to keep you so, & that he would liberally bestow on you his Graces & Blessings, you have ours. & I am Dr Charley

Yr: Mo: Afft: Father

Cha: Carroll

PS[19]

May 5th: 1760.

I Yesterday Received Yrs of the 29th: of last January, I have not time now to answer it. You give us great Pleasure & oblige us beyond expression by writing so often—

[M]ay 28th

We are well. The Originall of this inclosed a letter from yr Mother[.][20]

LS, Carroll-McTavish Papers, MS 220, MdHi. Marked "Copy" by CCA. Margins damaged. Filed with another LS copy with no postscripts and margins damaged. Parts of a third LS copy are filed in two different collections: the first four pages, considerably damaged and silked out of sequence, may be found in the Carroll-McTavish Papers; the final page, with postscripts and addressed and marked "Copy" by CCA, is in the Outerbridge Horsey Collection of Lee, Horsey, and Carroll Family Papers, MS 1974, MdHi. Text in brackets supplied from second Carroll-McTavish Papers copy.

1. Dateline in CCA's hand.

2. CCA's correction "of February" instead of "past" is to be found in the second complete Carroll-McTavish copy.

3. Two lists of law books, "A List of Books" and "Law Books remaining by me," are printed in Appendix II.

4. Judson Coolidge (?–1784) was master of the *Patuxent,* a two-hundred-ton galley he owned jointly with John Buchanan. Annapolis Port of Entry Record Books, II, MS 21, MdHi.

5. The father of CC's schoolmates was Sir Thomas Webb (1703–1763), fourth baronet of Odstock, Canford, and Hatherop. His sons, John (1732–1797) and Joseph Webb (?–1787?),

were students at St. Omers from about 1748 to 1751. Burke and Burke, *Landed Gentry of Great Britain*, II, 1771; John Kirk, *Biographies of English Catholics in the Eighteenth Century*, ed. John Hungerford Pollen and Edwin Barton (London, 1909), 245; Holt, *St. Omers*, 280; *Obituaries*, Catholic Record Society, XII (London, 1913), 29, 31, 59.

6. The comment about Thomas Bladen does not appear in the second complete Carroll-McTavish Papers copy but is in the third incomplete version.

7. The rebuke, contained in CCA's letter of Sept. 22, 1759, reads as follows: "There appears some unsteadiness in yr Resolutions, by yr last I had Reason to think You would not Quit Paris before next Spring, & You are not quite Punctuall in yr Promises, yr Mother Puts You in mind of the letter You promised her & I remind You that You was to write to me at least 6 times a Year: From February 7th to June 22d is almost 5 Months A Silence much too long for Our Patience[.] I wonder You mention nothing of the great preparations wh Our Papers say are makeing along the Coasts of France for an invasion." Carroll-McTavish Papers.

8. Formal oral or written disputation between Catholics and non-Catholics, particularly Protestants. The term refers both to the art of conducting such a debate and to the branch of theology that informed it.

9. Laurent François, *Les preuves de la religion de Jésus-Christ, contre les spinosistes et les déistes* (1751). *Cat. Lib.*, no. 1385, lists a four-volume edition of this work published in Paris in 1751.

10. Jacques-Bénigne Bossuet (1627–1704), bishop of Meaux, *Histoire des variations des églises protestantes* (1688). *Cat. Lib.*, no. 1200, lists a four-volume edition published in Paris in 1747.

11. [Robert Manning], *England's Conversion and Reformation Compared; or, The Young Gentleman Directed in the Choice of His Religion; to Which Is Premised, a Brief Enquiry into the General Grounds of the Catholick Faith; in a Conversation between a Young Gentleman and His Preceptor; Divided into Four Dialogues* . . . (Antwerp, 1725).

12. Robert Manning, *The Shortest Way to End Disputes about Religion; in Two Parts* . . . ([London], 1716).

13. CCA is referring to the *Almanach royal*, which was issued annually between 1700 and 1792.

14. A brandenburg was a decoration for the breast of a coat. Common designs employed a frog with a loop or a broad horizontal stripe.

15. The slashes indicate shillings.

16. Ginseng root, a common ingredient of medicines with soothing properties but no curative powers.

17. Capt. William McGachan was master of the snow *Tryal*, owned by John Stewart. Annapolis Port of Entry Record Books, II.

18. Henry Darnall III.

19. Both postscripts are in CCA's hand.

20. The page of this letter filed in the Outerbridge Horsey Collection of Lee, Horsey, and Carroll Family Papers (MS 1974, MdHi), replaces the May 28 postscript with CCA's description dated June 3 of the current situation at Quebec.

Enclosure: Charles Carroll the Settler's Certificate of Admission to the Inner Temple

[May 7, 1685]

Interius Templum

Carolus Carroll Secundus filius Danielis Carroll de Ahagurton[1] in Reg Comitatu in Regno Hiberniæ Gen genaliter admissus est in Societat istius Coitire in Consideratione triu librar/ Sep Solid & octo Denar/ Pr: manibus Solut Septo die May Anno Dom 1685

Vera Copia Exam
per me Tho: Riggs
Sub: Trearr.[2]

Reced per me fees	o. 5.0	
Mr: Trearrs Clerk	o. 2.6	
Junr: Butler	o 4.0	
	0.11 6	

Mr: Minors

You are hereby to take notice that Charles Carroll Gen who is admitted of this Society hath now entred into Bond for Discharge of his Duties to the house & therefore you may admit him into Com[o]ns Given under my hand this Sixth Day of May Anno Dom 1685

To Mr: Wm: Minors chief
Butler of the honble Society
of the Inner Temple
London

D, Carroll Papers, MS 206, MdHi. In a clerk's hand. Marked "Copy" by CCA. Another copy, also in a clerk's hand, is filed in the Outerbridge Horsey Collection of Lee, Horsey, and Carroll Family Papers, MS 1974, MdHi.

1. For Daniel Carroll of Aghagurty (c. 1642–1688?), see Appendix I, Charts A and B.

2. This may be translated as follows:

Inner Temple

Charles Carroll Second son of Daniel Carroll of Aghagurty in King's County of Ireland Gent is generally Admitted into the Society of this body in Consideration of three pounds, Seven Shillings & eight Pence, paid by his hands on the seventh day of May in the year of Our Lord 1685

True Copy Examined
By me Tho: Riggs
Under Treasurer

Elizabeth Carroll to CC

May 5th. 1760.

Dr. Charly

I recd. yrs of Decr 26 with great pleasure you are very good in leting us hear so often from you it is the greatest Comfort we can have in yr absence. I was over joyed to hear by Mr Diggs of yr safe arival in London & that you were in good health & spirits, the S[n]uff Box you sent me by him I value greatly & every Body that sees it says its a very genteel pretty one & commends yr taste.

I donte doubt but you have recd. the letter from yr Papa that gives you an account of yr Poor Aunt Jenneys death, which I believe gave you great concern, her disorder was a Shocking one & we that were about her in the greatest uneasiness & grief to see her intolerable sufferings & Pain, yr Grand Mama was present the whole time & rejoced with us to see an end of her miserys here, as she always led a Virtuious good Life & seemingly made a pious end [I have no rea]son to doubt of her being in [. . .] the latter part of her illne[ss] [. . .] herself nor A[ny] others me[ntion you] without being in Tears, which proceeded from the tender affection she bore you & the thoughts of never seeing you again had it pleased God to have spared her Life & given health with it, she wou'd have been a great Comfort to me, for she realy was a Woman of good Sence & temper & we loved each other intirely. I long to hear from you again & hope we shall have that pleasure soon, as the Ships are dayly expected in. I shall be impatient to see Mr Rozier when I know he is arived tho' I donte expect so great a satisfaction from his report of you as I shou'd have had from the letter you mentioned if I had, had the good luck to have seen it, however what you have said concerning it convinces me that it was greatly to yr davantage & consequently must have been interesting & satisfactory to me.

Yr Cn. Rachel Darnell presents you her love & is much obliged to you for yr kind notice of her, she is an agreable Companion & seems quite contented & happy with us. We had the pleasure of yr Grand Mamas Company from the 14 of last July till the begining of March I heard from her a day or 2 ago, she was hearty & well, sends you her Blessing. Pray make my Complyments to Mrs Russel[1] & [fami]ly I hear you are often there [. . .] they [. . .] with great kindness & [. . .] to recommed to you to take care of yr health & to let you know that I have mine very well. How dos England agree with you, be particular when you write, any thing from you will be welcome & yr letters cante tire. Adieu My Dear Charly I am

Mo: Affecly. Yrs
Eliza. Carroll

ALS, Carroll-McTavish Papers, MS 220, MdHi. Addressed by CCA. Endorsed "5 May 1760" in unknown eighteenth-century hand. Margins damaged.

1. Ann Lee (c. 1711–1800), one of the seventeen children of Philip Lee, progenitor of the Virginia clan's Maryland branch. In the mid-1730s she married James Russell, a Scottish merchant who had recently immigrated to Maryland. Capitalizing on the Lees' extensive trading network made available to him by his marriage, James Russell built a firm that had by 1760 become "the most important house trading to Maryland" and "probably the biggest if not the richest trading to the Chesapeake." After the Russells moved to London in the early 1750s, Ann Lee Russell, like many other London merchants' wives, personally selected the fashionable items ordered by her husband's colonial clients. Her skill in executing this responsibility made her choices "the standard of Taste" in Annapolis. At the time CC visited them, the Russells resided at Jeffrey's Square, St. Mary Axe, with their two unmarried daughters, Eleanor and Ann. Jacob M. Price, "One Family's Empire: The Russell-Lee-Clerk Connection in Maryland, Britain, and India, 1707–1857," *Md. Hist. Mag.*, LXXII (1977), 168–179.

CC to CCA

May the 16th. 1760.

Dr. Papa,

Since the departure of the fleet your Letter of the 23d. Febry.[1] came to hand: it was extremely acceptable as all yours are: I am overjoyed to hear my Mama has her health: particularly as I was not a little apprehensive of the contrary: our sollicitude is always proportionable to our affection, absence even heightens our anxiety and makes us generally apprehend those evils, which we stand the most in dread of. Why shou'd you wonder at my silence upon our late glorious success at sea?[2] You must have heared that news before it cou'd possibly be conveyed to you in a Letter from me. Nothing can outstrip the speed of fame, mobilitate viget viresque acquirit eundo[3] says the Poet and it appears true by the account you received of Sr. Edward Hawke's destroying a 11 sail after the action.[4]

There must be a blindness (or to use the french gazette's expression) une fatalité attending their ministry which approaches to dulness and stupidity: how coud they ever hope to envade England with the least appearance of success in their flat-bottom boats, in opposition to so formidable a naval power as we then had at Sea? I was told when in Paris that the largest boats stood the government in a 1000 guineas a piece; how true this information may be I can't determin. Neither did they depend if we may credit the publick report, on any secret intelligence, interest, or insurrection in England. It is certain, there was not the least mention made of the Prince during the whole time their preparations lasted: Had he really been concerned in the scheme it wou'd have been difficult to have kept it entirely concealed from the Publick. Nor can we reasonably suppose they intended a conquest. Their view perhaps was (if I may once be allowed to turn Politician) to throw into this kingdom a force sufficient to destroy our naval stores, docks, shipping &c before any opposition cou'd be made: a force capable, even when we had collected all the troops we cou'd muster, to render the event of a pitch battle doubtful and precarious. The consequences of an overthrow cou'd not but proove fatel to this n[a]tion: wherefore it tis highly probable had the French landed in England with 50,000 men we shou'd have granted them their own terms and resigned what we have gained rather than run the risk of loseing all by the loss of one battle. What makes me inclined to believe they had no intention of restoring the exiled family, is because such a restoration, in my opinion, wou'd be inconsistent with their own interest, and the French will never act, at least knowingly, against that primum mobile of theirs. Risum teneatis amici?[5]

The unhappy Earl Ferrers was executed the 6th instant:[6] neither his riches or high birth cou'd exempt him from the ignominious death of a common malefactor they only contributed to render it more dishonourable. Tho' that unfortunate nobleman deserved some kind of pitty yet was this exercise of Justice highly commendable, necessary and instructive. Great men may see by this that the laws are not made only for the poorer sort, that they extend to all and can not be transgressed with impunity to no other cause was owing the ascendent the Spartan government had obtained throughout all the other states of Greece and the deference payed to its decisions. The Laws at Sparta ruled the Kings, and not they, the laws. The ancients thought, at least the wisest ancients, that the property, Liberty, and safety of individuals cou'd not be too secure from power and its natural ally, inJustice.

I have consulted the Lottery registers, & the account sent me is agreeable to the same. Yr. last years tickets are all blanks except Nos. c/1971, & 8974 each a prise of 20 £. Bar iron I am informed bears an exceeding good price and that no better commodity can be sent to market: if we come to a rupture with Prussia[7] it will still in all probability bear a better.

I propose next month going to see my old master; who lives at Wardour a seat of my Lord Arundel's[8] — he has been twice in town since my arrival; I saw him each time and our interviews, were as long as his stay in town, which was but short, and his business which was pressing wou'd permit. I leave you to conceive our mutual Joy & satisfaction at our first meeting after so long a separation: certainly no pleasure can equal that of conversing with a person, whom we love & esteem especially when such esteem is founded on true merit: nihil ego Jucundo contulerim sanus amico, says my old Friend Horace,[9] and Mr. Jenison is as deserving of the epithet Jucundus[10] as most men.

A Little before I left Paris a new, compleat, and correct Atlas was published price 10 guineas I had a great mind to buy one, but did not know wether you wou'd approve of it. If you do ti's not too late. Have you read Hume's history of the houses of Stuart and Tudor?[11] If not, you have a great satisfaction to come or I am mistaken. Mrs. [Messrs.] Corbey, Baker—Pointz & Crookshanks desire their compliments to you; mine to Mr. and Mrs. Lawson, to Dr. Lyon & the two Croxals: my Love & duty to my Mama & Grand Mama. I am Dr. Papa

Yr. affectionate & dutiful Son
C: Carroll

P:S:

Pray don't forget answering that part of my last Letter relating to Mr. [Bird] the marble merchant. My directions are to C: Carroll in the temple king's bench walks No. 5. but I think the safest way is to enclose my Letters to Mr. Perkins.

ALS, Carroll Papers, MS 206, MdHi. Addressed by CC. Endorsed by CCA.

1. Not found.

2. The battle of Quiberon Bay, Nov. 20–22, 1759, in which the British, commanded by Sir Edward Hawke (1705–1781), defeated the French under Hubert de Brienne-Conflans, comte de Conflans (c. 1690–1777), who was collecting armies and transports along the French coast in preparation for an invasion of England. Six French ships of the line were destroyed or captured and twenty-five hundred French sailors were killed; the British lost two ships. Stanley Ayling, *The Elder Pitt, Earl of Chatham* (New York, 1976), 266–267; Peter Douglas Brown, *William Pitt, Earl of Chatham: The Great Commoner* (London, 1978), 197–198.

3. "She grows strong in her speed and gains strength in the going." Virgil *Aeneid* 4.175.

4. During the night following his defeat at Quiberon Bay, Conflans inadvertently anchored his flagship, the *Soleil Royal,* in the midst of Hawke's squadron. When, at daybreak, he realized his error, Conflans ran his ship aground and set it on fire. Although Hawke destroyed at least one other grounded vessel on Nov. 22, 1759, a large number of French ships jettisoned their cannon and escaped up the Vilaine and Charente Rivers. Gipson, *Culmination,* 23–24.

5. "Could you, my friend, refrain from laughing?" Horace *Ars poetica* 5.

6. Laurence, fourth Earl Ferrers (1720–1760), was executed May 5, 1760, for the murder of his land steward. Burke and Burke, *Peerage,* 71st ed., I, 721.

7. By the end of 1759 Prussia's situation appeared increasingly bleak. Frederick the Great had suffered a series of severe military reversals, but he refused to alter his territorial ambitions or to mitigate his situation by yielding ground to his opponents. This intransigence, along with George II's failing health and the Prince of Wales's well-known support for peace, led Great Britain, Prussia's principal ally, to question seriously the wisdom of continuing the alliance. Eric Robson, "The Seven Years War," in J. O. Lindsay, ed., *The Old Regime, 1713–63,* The New Cambridge Modern History, VII (Cambridge, 1957), 481.

8. Henry, eighth Baron Arundell of Wardour (1740–1808). The Arundells, an old Roman Catholic family, were related to Maryland's proprietary family by the marriage of Cecilius Calvert, second Lord Baltimore, to Anne Arundell, daughter of Thomas, first Baron Arundell, and his second wife, Ann Philipson. Burke and Burke, *Peerage,* 71st ed., I, 122–123.

9. "I would compare nothing, while I keep my senses, to a pleasant friend," a paraphrase of Horace *Satires* 1.5.44.

10. "Pleasant."

11. David Hume's *History of England from the Invasion of Julius Caesar to the Revolution of 1688* was published under various titles between 1754 and 1763. The first four volumes

issued were devoted to the Tudors and the Stuarts. *Cat. Lib.*, no. 521, lists an edition of Hume's work entitled *History of England from the Invasion of Julius Caesar to the Accession of Henry VII*, 6 vols. (London, 1762).

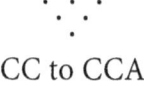

CC to CCA

May the 22d. 1760

Dr. Papa,

I take this opportunity of writing a few lines by Capt. James He[n]rick;[1] tho' I have already wrote a more circumstancial Letter which goes by the same gentleman—I refer you to that Letter as to what may regard me & my Little affairs: tho' if you expect to meet with any thing material or interesting you will be deceived. I am now with Mr. Perkins; who gives his kind compliments to you.

I desired you in a foregoing letter to send me some madeira wine—pray don't forget my commission if not too troublesom or otherwise inconvenient. I think of buying a horse to ride out, as that exercise is recommended to me for the preservation of my health, and as I can't well see the different parts of England without: and I believe you will not be against my making now & then some excursions & Jaunts of pleasure[.]

I propose, if you consent, to go over next summer that is next year, into Ireland: But of this scheme more will be said in an ensueing Letter—I shall only add at present that I am well & wish with all my heart that you are. My love to my Mama I am Dr. Papa

Yr. affectionate & dutiful Son
C: Carroll

ALS, Carroll Papers, MS 206, MdHi. Addressed by CC. Endorsed by CCA.

1. James Henrick (variously Hendrick or Hanrick), master of the ship *Dragon*, a 130-ton vessel owned by Chesapeake merchant Samuel Galloway. Annapolis Port of Entry Record Books, I.

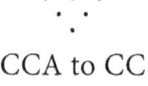

CCA to CC

July 14th 1760

Dr Charley

Since mine of the 1st of May I have yr. several Letters as per Margin,[1] & since that date I wrote you two short Letters relating to the Seige of Quebec wch were not worth Entring—Yrs by Mr: Leonards to yr: Mother is also come to hand.[2] Yrs of

King's Bench Walk, Inns of Court, London.
Photograph courtesy Jonathan Kelly

Charles Carroll's London Residence (No. 5).
Photograph courtesy Jonathan Kelly

the 29th of Janry: last is now before me. If you consult mine of Octor: 6th. 1759 you will see you were Mistaken in thinking I laid you under the Obligation of reading all the Pamphlets published in London, I only wanted those worth my perusal, & to such you will be directed in the manner you mention. I have been so full as to yr: Allowance that it is unnecessary to say more to you on that head than to tell you I think a Student in the Temple cannot apply himself properly to his Study's & spend above £300 a Year, whether you spend £250 or 300 a year, is to me immaterial, but to you it cannot be so, if by spending yr: Money you mispend yr: time, wch to you is more precious than Money. I do not mean by this admonition to imprison you in yr. Chambers, yr: health (wch is most dear to me) Requires a proper Relaxation & I am sorry to hear yrs in Febry was not so good as usual, & I should be alarmed at it, if I was not informed by Messrs Buchanan & Browne that you was very well & in good spirits when they left you. Mr: Perkins writes me he intended to take you with him a Tour into the Country I am much obliged to him as he thought it necessary for yr: Health. I think the Purchase & keeping of a Horse too Expensive & even unnecessary as you may hire when you want & be in general supply'd with pretty good ones by proper Management.

I intend you shall stay in the Temple full 4 years from the time you Entred, if you employ that time well you may acquire such a foundation as may be necessary for you readily hereafter to turn to proper Books & Cases on Occasion. You vainly at present fancy you might study here, might not every Gent: in the Temple say as much of his own home? The distractions & various Occupations of a man once Entred into the World make such a Scheme almost Chimerica but long series of years, Reason & Experience shew that it was necessary to have particular Places appointed for the Study of the Law, & that in such, a knowledge of it is soonest & best acquired, I might add that it is not to be acquired any other way[.] This I say from Experience, my Father directed I should go to the Temple, but he dying just as I had finish'd my Philosophy my Friends thought my presence necessary in Maryland & that I might study the Law here, I attempted it but to no purpose. You call the stay you are still to make in Europe a Banishment, had I listened to nature & been only guided by Inclination & a mistaken love, I should never [have parted with you. By the Course of Nature you are][3] long to survive me & therefore a sincere love guided by Reason prompts me to make the rest of yr: life happy, easy & Ornamental by giving you the best Education in my power & in particular by giving you an Opportunity of acquiring a perfect knowledge of the Law without wch I may say a Gent: is unfinished.

Pray how came you to dine with Mr: Sharpe? I hardly think you paid him a Visit: I conjecture our Govr: wrote to him to take notice of you, if so, it was kind & Genteel in him, he & I are at present on Good terms & were a Law now to be passed to double Tax the Rom: Caths: it would hardly meet with his Concurrence. You say Mr Calvert returned yr: Visit, this implies a previous Visit paid by you, & yet from what I wrote to you Octor: 6th 1759 I hardly think you took that step, this shews you cannot be too full, explicit & circumstantial in yr letters. What you said to Mr: Calvert was very proper, & what you omitted to say would still have been more proper, you cannot deal too freely with him provided you keep within the Bounds of Decency & Good Manners wch I am confident you will do; if he can bear truth with temper & patience he will profit by it, if he should prove shy on Acct of yr: frankness you will not be a loser. You have seen Ld: Baltimore, perhaps you have since seen him, if so, may be you can give me his Character. If our house of Commons could have their way, such is their Malice that they would not only deprive us of our Property but our Lives — Maryland was Granted to Cæcilius Ld: Baltimore[4] a Rom: Cath: all persons believing in Jesus Christ were by the Charter promised the Enjoyment not only of Religious but Civil Liberty & were entitled to all the Benefits of Lucrative places &c. It was Chiefly planted & peopled in the beginning by Rom: Caths: many of them were men of better families than their Proprietary, these priviledges were confirmed by a Fundamental & perpetual Law past here & all sects continued in a peaceable Enjoyment of these priviledges until the Revolution[5] when a Mob Encouraged by the Example set them by England Rebelled agst the Ld: Baltimore, stript him of his Governmt:, & his Officers of their places — Then the Crown assumed the Governmt:, the Tolleration Act as I may call it was Repeal'd,[6] & several Actts to hinder us from a free Exercise of our Religion past.

Benedict Ld: Baltimore upon conforming to the Established Church in the year 1714 was Restored to his Governmt: & died the same year, his Son Char: Ld: Baltimore the present Lds. father succeeded & the People here making a handle of the Rebellion in 1715[7] Enacted Laws injoining all the Oaths taken in England to be taken here & disqualify'd any person from voting for Members to Represent them in our assembly who would not take those Oaths & many other scandalous & oppressive Laws: to these the proprietary was not only mean enough [to assent, but he deprived several Rom: Caths: employed in the][8] Managemt: of his private Patrimony & Revenue, of their places, & among the Rest yr: Grand father who was his Agent & Receiver general &c & had held the former places under three Lords Baltimores, this no Act compelled him to do, & he did it to Cajole an insolent Rabble who were again aiming to deprive him of the Governmt: From that time to the Year 1751 we were unmolested, but then the Penal Laws of England were attempted to be introduced here,[9] & several Bills to this & the like purposes were past by our Lower House but rejected by the Upper House, at last in 1756 an Act was past by all the Branches of the Legislature here to double Tax us & to this Law our present Proprietary had the meanness to Assent thô he knew us innocent of the Calumnies raised agst us.

This is a Succinct Acct of Maryland as far as the present Subject requires. Our Constitution is similar to the English Vizt: the Govr:, Upper & lower Houses of Assembly, the Enacting Clauses of our Laws run, Be it Enacted by the Right Honble the Ld: Proprietary, By & with the Advice & Consent of his Lordships Govr: & the

Upper & Lower Houses of Assembly & the Authority of the same, by wch you will Observe that in fact we have 4 Branches to our Legislature, for notwithstanding the Govrs Assent to Laws the Proprietary may dissent. But the Proprietary's explicit Assent to our Laws is not necessary, as by usuage & Custom he is deemed to have Assented if in a reasonable time he does not Dissent, but it is yet undetermined what that Reasonable time is. The power of Enacting Laws & several other powers & priviledges granted to the Proprietary & people are derived from the Charter, a Copy whereof if I have time I will send you by the Fleet, at the same time I would send you a Body of our Laws if it were possible to get them & then you might see the several Laws by wch we are injured; But I question whether a Compleat set is to be found in Maryld: unless on Record. A private Gent: has offered to Collect them for the press & has spent a good deal of time & money to that End, but such is the meanness of our Assembly that it will not Encourage the Undertaker by a proper Gratuity to carry on the work. However I think I can procure you an Abridgmt: of them.[10]

From what I have said I leave you to Judge whether Maryland can be a tolerable Residence for a Rom: Cath: It is true Nature has been almost beyond Bounds bountifull to it, the Climate is very good, & every year improving as the Country is opened, the Soil in General is very fruitful & yeilds with very little Labour A plentifull increase of what ever is trusted to it, Cattle & Poultry of all sorts multiply surprisingly with moderate care & are Excellent in their kinds, a vast variety & succession of several sorts of Grain, pulse,[11] roots &c make a famine almost impossible: our fruits are delicious, add to these that no Country in the world is better watered & no wat[er]s more plentifully sto[cked] with a vast variety of [Excellent Fish . . .] Fowl with plenty of other Game: in sh[ort if] the people (who in fact & in general are ignorant mean & malicious) could be any way compared to the Country Maryland in time might be in reality what the most pleasant & delightfull Countries are described to have been by the fruitfull fancy of the best Poets — As it is, were I younger I would certainly quit it, at my Age (as I wrote you) a change of Climate would certainly shorten my Days, but I embrace ev'ry opportunity of getting rid of my Real Property, that if you please you may the sooner & with more ease & less loss leave it: however my most valuable Lands & slaves shall be kept to the last that you may chuse for yr: self & make yr: self as happy as possible, it is my greatest study & Concern to make you so.

By the War I am not well stocked with old Madeira Wine[.] I have therefore wrote to Mr: Betencourt my Correspondent there to ship you a Pipe[12] of choice Wine & to direct it to Mr: Perkins for yr: use, shew this to Mr: Perkins & desire him to answer Mr: Betencourts Bill for the Value; Do not trust the Wine in any Celler but Mr: Perkins's, when it is perfectly fine bottle it & husband it well. I find Cyder & water a palatable Liquor if yr: Cyder be pure may be in this way it may agree with you.

At yr: Request I shall speak to a Gent: who is building & if he wants Chimney Peices or Tables I will recommend him to Mr: Bird. I shall want a Marble slab & I shall direct Mr: Perkins to apply to Mr: Bird, I will enquire & consider whether it may be worth his while to send a small Venture by way of Tryal hither & advise by the Fleet.

Drawing is a pretty accomplishmt: & I wish you could spare time to attend to it, but let nothing divert you from Reading of the Law, nor break in upon yr: hours destined to that Study. I remember something of an old distribution of time laid down by Cook or Littleton Sex horas Somno &c yr Constitution may require Eight if so, take two from the quatuor orabis, if you employ not more than one in that Duty another hour is at yr: Disposal wch with what you may take from the Sacris Camænis will give you leisure for many things,[13] the waste of time is the worst sort of Prodigality: But I fancy when this Distribution of time was in fashion, there were no play houses, Coffee Houses, Renelaghs, Vauxhalls,[14] Routs, Operas &c &c because the old sage thô never so stiff & formal must have allotted now & then some hours to these Genteel & necessary Amusemts —

Messrs Browne & Buchanan are prudent, discreet deserving Young Gent, I am persuaded their trip to Maryland will be of great service to them & Answer Mr Perkins Expectations. My regard for Mr: Perkins & former Acquaintance with these Gent: & yr: Recommendation of them entitle them to every act of Friendship I can shew them. Mr: Stephenson is settled a great way from me at New Town on Chester River, I shall take a proper Notice of him when opportunity's offer. I have not yet seen Mr: Rozier who is [v]ery well.

Yr: Resignation to stay in the Temple as long as I shall appoint, is a Conti[nu]-ance of that Duty & Obedie[nce] you have always paid us & gives us a very sensible [Satisfaction; in return we will endeavour to make that][15] Duty always ea[s]y to you by requiring not[h]ing of you but what we shall be persu[a]ded will be for yr: true Intert: Your Mama is very well & much ple[as]ed with yr: Letter: her swelling is not quite gone of[f] but I realy think & hope it will not prejudice her Health, we love you as much as Parents can love a deserving Son, Bless you & pray to God to do the same. I am Dr Charley

Yr: Mo: Affect: Father
Cha: Carroll[16]

Part of Jo: Carroll's Letter from Liege Dated March 15th: 1760 to his Br Daniell Carroll in Maryland —

"My Cousin Cha: Carroll writes me from London wth all the Indifference of a Philosopher, that he is very unconcerned about news . . . Mediocritas[17] says he, is not that best? What Mr Carroll told You Concerning the Result of his voyage to Europe, is Conformable to what I understand from his Son when I saw him last Sepr, who told me his Father had not Succeeded at Paris. If it had been thought

Proper I should know the Motive of his [J]ourney, he would Probably have taken that Opportunity to tell me, But as he did not, I suppose it would not be, becoming in me to Push my Enquieries any farther. I went from Liege to Ghent to meet my Cousin Charly Carroll in his way from Par[i]s to London, Mr Rozier will give you an Acct of the Great improvement he has made in France, & his Elegant way of living in London[.]"

You see by the above that People are very Curious & Inquisitive, & learn from it, to trust no Man with a Secret without an absolute Necessity, especially if it be of any Consequence —

In yrs of the 10th of Aprill you say [y]ou are not acquainted [wth] Mr Bladen & that Y[ou do] not Desier to be acquainted w[ith h]im as he is a Ga[mes]ter & that __that__ is [not yr only Reason for declining his Acquaintance,] This is Misterious, [Wh]at other Reason [h]ave You? He was Civill to me when in London I hav[e] been long acquainted with him, His[18] & my Fathcr wcr[e] Neighbours and Acquaintance, I am intimate w[ith M]r Tasker[19] who Marryed his Sister,[20] therefore if he makes the 1st: Advance[s] be Polite & Civill, not Intimate —
July 31st —

LS, Carroll-McTavish Papers, MS 220, MdHi. Corrected by CCA and marked "C[o]py" in his hand. Margins damaged.

1. Entered at left margin: "1760 Feby: 30 April 10."

2. These three letters not found.

3. Phrase in brackets supplied from Field, _Carroll_, 45.

4. Charles I agreed to give George Calvert, first Lord Baltimore (1578/9–1632), several tracts of land in the Chesapeake during February and March 1631/2. However, George Calvert died on Apr. 15, 1632, and on June 20 the charter of Maryland was granted to his son Cecilius Calvert (1605–1675), who became second Lord Baltimore and first lord proprietor of the province of Maryland. Edward C. Papenfuse, "Introduction" to _The Charter of Maryland, June 20, 1632_ (Annapolis, 1982), n.p.

5. The Glorious Revolution of 1688, which brought William and Mary, the Protestant daughter of James II, to the throne of England.

6. Passed in 1649, "An Act concerning Religion" established the Christian religion in Maryland and provided penalties for molesting Christians on account of their beliefs. The act was annulled in 1654 by the Puritans during their brief period of hegemony in the province, but it appears to have been reactivated about 1660 at the time of the restoration of Charles II to the English throne. In 1692, soon after Lionel Copley arrived to assume the governorship of Maryland, the act was again annulled and the process of establishing the Church of England begun. The Anglican Church was legally established in the colony in 1702. Matthew Page Andrews, _The Founding of Maryland_ (New York, 1933), 330–331; Lois Green Carr and David William Jordan, _Maryland's Revolution of Government, 1689–1692_ (Ithaca, N.Y., 1974), 149, 203–204; Scharf, _Maryland_, I, 174–182, 198–215; Newton D. Mereness, _Maryland as a Proprietary Province_ (London, 1901), 423–440; _Arch. of Md._, I, 244–247, XIII, 425–430.

7. The 1715 Jacobite uprising in Scotland, which was led by John Erskine, earl of Mar. The "Old Pretender," James III, arrived in Scotland from France in December 1715 but hastily departed in February 1716 when his ill-prepared supporters were dispersed without a battle by troops under the command of John Campbell, duke of Argyle. The Jacobite leaders were arrested, and several were executed. Derek Jarrett, *Britain, 1688–1815* (New York, 1965), 153–154.

8. Phrase in brackets supplied in part from Rowland, *Carroll*, I, 42–43.

9. In 1751 the lower house's Committee on Grievances and Courts of Justice warned of the dangerous growth of "Popery" in the province and urged that, to combat it, the English penal statutes be fully enforced in Maryland. Browne et al., eds., *Arch. of Md.*, XLVI, 549–550.

10. The Reverend Thomas Bacon (1700–1768) apparently began his compilation of Maryland laws as early as 1757, but, although the need for such a collection had long been acknowledged by provincial officials, his request for financial support was received with a notable lack of enthusiasm by the lower house. Bacon's difficulty in securing backing for his work opened the way for James Bisset of Baltimore to publish his *Abridgment and Collection of the Acts of Assembly of the Province of Maryland, at Present in Force; with a Small Choice Collection of Precedents in Law and Conveyancing; Calculated for the Use of the Gentlemen of the Province* (Philadelphia, 1759), an unsatisfactory substitute. *Cat. Lib.,* nos. 61 and 95, lists both Bacon's compilation, without a publication date, and Bisset's abridgment. Lawrence C. Wroth, "A Maryland Merchant and His Friends in 1750," *Md. Hist. Mag.,* VI (1911), 235–236; *Arch. of Md.,* IX, 488–489.

11. The edible seed of leguminous crops such as peas and beans.

12. A large cask.

13. English jurist and legal author Sir Thomas Littleton (1422–1481) is chiefly known for his treatise on *Tenures* (c. 1481). The earliest survey of English land law to be printed, this short work served as a fundamental text in legal education for three hundred years and formed the basis for the four-volume commentary, *The First Part of the Institutes of the Lawes of England* (1628–1644), by Sir Edward Coke (1552–1634). Also a monumental contribution to legal history, Coke's compendium contained this prescription regarding the apportionment of time among life's duties:

> Sex horas somno, totidem des legibus aequis;
> Quatuor orabis, des epulisque duas;
> Quod superest ultra sacris largire Camoenis,

which may be translated as:

> Six hours to sleep, as many to righteous law;
> Four to your prayers, and two to fill your maw;
> The rest bestow upon the sacred Muses.

Institutes of the Lawes of England, Book II, chap. 1, sec. 85 (1628), as cited in Burton Stevenson, ed., *The MacMillan Book of Proverbs, Maxims, and Famous Phrases* (New York, 1948), 1187.

14. Ranelagh and Vauxhall were popular London gathering places offering light refreshment and musical entertainment.

15. Phrase in brackets supplied from Field, *Carroll*, 48.

16. The following text is in CCA's hand. Another copy of this material, also in CCA's hand and marked by him "Triplicate Sent in my letters of July 14: 1760," is filed in the Carroll Papers, MS 206. CCA appended another copy, also designated "Triplicate," to his letter of Aug. 4, 1760, below.

17. "Moderation."

18. William Bladen (1673–1718).

19. Benjamin Tasker, Sr. (c. 1690–1768). Born in Calvert Co., Tasker had moved to Annapolis by 1711, and shortly thereafter he embarked upon a distinguished public career. His various local positions included four terms as mayor of Annapolis. Among his important provincial posts were naval officer of Annapolis (1733–1742), rent roll keeper of the Western Shore (1733–1752), agent and receiver general (1742–1753), and commissary general (1754–1758). First elected to the lower house in 1715, Tasker served there almost continuously until 1722, when he was appointed to the upper house and the Council. He became president of the upper house in 1738 and held that post until his death. He also remained on the Council for the rest of his life and served as its president (1741–1768). *Bio. Dic. Md. Legis.*, II, 799–800.

20. Tasker married Anne Bladen (?–1775) in 1711. Ibid.

CCA to CC

Augst. 4th 1760

Dr Charley

I received yrs of the 15th of last April by [Cap]t: Kelty, the 30th of last Month. It gave us great Pleasure to hear [fr]om yourself, that you was well & much better than you had been [for] some time past. Mr: Rozer went from my House Yesterday, [his] stay was so short that I had not time to ask him half enough about you, he promises me a longer Visit soon. By him I learn that Mr: Calvert accidentally invited you to dine with Mr: Sharpe. I hear you have seen Mr: Jenisson wch must have given you great Satisfaction, Pray present my [Hu]mble & Sincere Service to him & to Mr: Crookshanks when ever you write to him. We are well & present our Love & Blessing to you. I am Dr Charley

Yr: Mo Afft: Father
Cha: Carroll

LS, Carroll-Harper Papers, MS 1225, MdHi. Marked "Copy" by CCA. CCA's triplicate copy of his postscript to his letter of July 14, 1760, printed above, is not reproduced here.

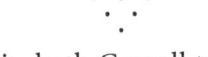

Elizabeth Carroll to CC

Sepr 10. 1760.

Dr. Charly

This go's by Mr. Brown who I find has a great regard & Friendship for you, which consequently makes him a favorite of ours, he is realy an agreable sweet temper'd young man & we may with Justice say the same of Mr Buchanan who I believe is equally yr friend, they are a good deal with us & you are often the subject of our Conversation they never mention yu but greatly to yr advantage. Mr. Rozier has also a high [o]pinion of you & we have the greatest Comfort imaginable from his account of you, in short every Body that [has] been in yr Company Speak well of you what must we feel my dear Charly at hearing so much said in yr favour, more then you c[a]n c[on]ceive or we express. I have no sort of uneasiness at present but about yr health which I flatter my Self you injoy better now then you did last Winter & Spring & that yr indisposition only proceeded from what is common to all upon their first going to London, which is geting great colds & coughs, how ever if you continue out of order ailing & puny let us know it, donte make the best of it for fear o[f] grieving us for [w]e may think of something that [may] relieve you, certainly yr [health is of] the greatest consequ[ence] to us & if you want that, we shall be unhappy, there fore avoid every thing you find or think may prejudice it—

Mr Lenards deliver'd me yr letter which I found intertaining & agreable. I am much plea[s]ed with yr open free manner of writing but take care what you say of the Ladys you may sometime or other meet with one that may make you pay for all the slights shewn to her Sex, by keeping you in her Chains & haveing no Mercy on you. You'll find when you return to Maryland many of yr Country Men of yr size I [am] not afraid of yr appearing among them in [a]ny respect to yr disadvantage neither am I afraid of yr [be]ing puzzled to get a Wife, if you have a min[d] for on[e] the only difficulty will be to get a good one, one of good [mi]n[d] & temper & every other way agreable to make you intirely happy, if you can meet with such a one about 3 or 4 Years hence I should be very glad to see you Marry'd I only wish you as happy in that State as yr [P]apa & I am.

Mr Brown will have a great deal to say to you when you see him, he can tell you how much I have you at heart & how I long to see you, that I am fat [&] hearty, with many other things &c I am sure he [w]onte forget to inform you how much he is Charmed with Maryland I suppose his friends will [find] it a hard matter to persuade him from returning H[ere] again. Just as I had wrote the above Capt. Henrick arrived with letters from you which gave us infinite pleasure especially as they brought an acct. of yr being in good health. Yr tender concern for my we[l]fare & health often puts me in minde of what you used to tell me, when a little Boy lolling & fondling a bout me, that you loved me dearly & always shou'd have the same fondness & affection for me, during Life, yr behaviour & the regard you have shewn me, hitherto, convinces me of the truth of those words, which I assure my de[ar g]ives me no small Comforte.

I was desired by Mr [T]asker in a kind friendly manner to present his Complyments to you. I dare say you remember him he gave you some Pocket Money when you went from hence, you promised him, when you returned to Maryland to give a Ball to the Genn. & Ladys of Annapolis which he says he has not forgot. I understand that yu. brought an Umbrello with you from Paris & that it is of no use to you in London, it wou'd be very exceptable to me shall be much oblig'd to you if you'll send it me by the [nex]t Oppo[rtunit]y I heard from yr grand Mama a few [day]s ago she was then very well & sends you her Blessing I intend to make her a Visit next Month —

Poor Mr Lawson has been dangerously ill with the flux,[1] but is now to the great Comfort of all his friends on the recovery he & Mrs Lawson Doc. Lyon the 2 Croxalls, with many other frnds. present their kindest Complyments to you. I wrote you the 5th of May which I hope you have recd. My best wish[es] & Blessing atend you. I am My Dear Charly

Mo[st] Affecly: Yrs
Eliza: Carroll

Pray my Complyments to Mrs Russel & Family & tell them they have my good wishes for their health & welfare. Yr Cn. Rachel Darnall desires in the tenderest manner to be remember'd to you, she proposed wri[ting to] you, but is too weak Occasion'd by fevers which she has but very lately got rid of.

ALS, Harper-Pennington Papers, MS 431, MdHi. Endorsed by CC: "Octor. 12, 1760 N:B: this the last Letter I received from my Mama." Margins damaged.

1. Severe diarrhea or dysentery.

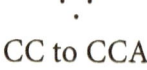

CC to CCA

Sepb. 16th. 1760.

Dr. Papa,

My last was dated the 16th of May. I have since received your several Letters of the 1st. May and 14th July and one from my Mama of the 5th. May. The books sent by Capt Coolidge are safe arrived: those that want binding I shall take care to get bound, those that are double or are of a bad or too old edition shall be sold and replaced by others of a later and better.

I propose entering myself of the Inner temple next term: the expence of entery may amount to 4£.0-0 or thereabouts: that of commons to 6 or 7 more yearly. Your observation on the Tobo. Merchants is well grounded: your advice concerning them and my dress Judicious: it shall be followed. The only thing I dislike in my present situation is want of company: good, I mean instructive company, is not easy to be met with: genteel company can not but be attended with great expence, great distractions and loss of time. No application, no study, without an undisturbed, serene, composed mind: independent of these objections the prodigious vacuum that reigns thro' the conversation of genteel company is insupportable to men of a certain stamp. I have not gained half a line since you saw me last, nor am I quite broke of my stooping.

Mr. Maccarty's finances are still ebbing, perhaps when the tide flows again it may bring him up to town with the £9-0-0[.] Jo: Gallot's pledge remains in Mr. Edwards hands, if its value be not adequate to the debt, his honesty will not hurry him to redeem it. I am informed he is servant to an officer of the militia, now in camp at Winchester. The Letter sent by Capt. Magachan, was wrote in haste: this prevented my referring to former Letters, which, as you desired, are all entered into a book[.]

I repent my having mentioned the interesting Letter, and its irrecoverable loss. Mr. Rozier, knows me as well as the gentleman, who wrote the Letter, and is as capable of delivering his opinion and with equal discernment. I shall make it my business to peruse seriously the books of controversy recommended to me: My dining with Mr. Sharpe was merely accidental. I happened to meet Mr. Calvert at Mr. Perkin's house: he politely invited me to come and see him: I accepted the invitation. Mss [Messrs.] Plater & Rozier accompanied me to his (Calvert) house: from whence we went all together to Mr. Sharpe's to dine: we were treated handsomely. To Judge from so short an acquaintance with Mr. Sharpe, I look upon him to be a well-behaved, sensible gentleman. Some months after my Lord Baltimore sent me an invitation to come to his country seat at Epsom[1] and to remain with him during the races: being preengaged I could not comply with the latter part of the invitation: however I dined with his Lordship the first day of the races; this was the second time, perhaps it will be the last I shall see his Lordship.

Forced by your reasons I must acknowledge the temple to be a more proper place to study the law in than my own home, where business or amusements (too often the Latter) engross our whole attention. Nothing but a sincere love guided by reason, I am perswaded, cou'd have kept me so long from you. The education you have given me, the care you have taken, the trouble and expence you have been at, are strong convincing proofs of this well regulated love. If I survive [you] the remainder of my life may be easy and ornamental but not happy: your remembrance will always be accompanied with grief: how shall I ever be able to think of you without shedding tears due to the memory of the best, the dearest, tenderest Parent? But wherefore do I anticipate pains which perhaps I shall never live to feel.

Your description of Maryland is quite picturesque: I believe a little Poetical. Pictoribus atque Poetis quid libet audendum[2] you have made some use of this permission: but by all accounts your encomiums are not unmerited. How displeasing then must the thought be of Leaving such a charming country to avoid the unjust the malicious prosecutions, of an ignorant, base, contemptible rabble[.] Yet time may perhaps polish and soften their manners; wealth acquired by their own industry may satiate their avarice, and correct at least moderate that eager longing after other men's property. But my chief hopes are founded on our Governors and upper house of Assembly. If we can be assured of always having governors as Just and as moderate as our present Governor, one not to be awed or over-ruled by the clamours of a mob we may laugh at and despise its insolence: its giddy fury will turn to its own shame. There are several gentlemen in the upper house, as such they are certainly of too disinterested, enlarged, and noble a way of thinking, than to suffer themselves to be lead into measures, mean, interested, and unjust. They may say, they ought to say, with the bold spirit of the Lyrick Poet odi profanum vulgus, et arceo.[3]

I question very much wether my Lord Coke stuck to his own distribution of time: he might have been, like many others, no follower of what he taught. I am perswaded, he frequently made as great a deduction from the quatuor orabis as you advise me to: and to Judge of the old gentleman by his rude uncouth style, the Sacræ Camenæ were no great favourites of his: of these and of history I am passionately fond: whatever time I can steel from druggery and necessary relaxation I consecrate to these. Without a perfect knowledge of history and Mankind, which latter is acquired from the study of History and personal experience, there is no possiblilty of excelling in the law. I might indeed be, what many Lawers are, to use some of Tully's words, Leguleius quidam cautus, et acutus præco actionum, cantor formularum, auceps syllabarum, an insignificant petty fogger groveling all my life in the mean but gainful application to all the little arts of chicane[.][4]

I spent the last month in the company of my old Master Mr. Jenison. After a stay of two weeks at Wardour, the place of his residence, we went to Bath, from thence to Bristol & to Oxford. Our Jant was extremely agreeable; the weather good, the country delightful. We parted at Oxford the 3d. instant much against our will. I reached London on the same day, he Wardour the day following[.] Thus ended in sorrow, the most agreeable, entertaining, pleasant Journey I ever made.

I return you many thanks for the Pipe of wine you have ordered for my use. As this letter is already too long I shall postpone answering my Mama's to the next oportunity. Assure her of my love and duty. I am over Joyed to hear her swelling has abated without impairing her health: tho' if I may credit some private information she was once in great danger; this I suppose you concealed from me de industriâ:[5] Pray do'nt deceive me for the future. In all your letters you mention her being in good health and that she sends me her blessing: why can't she tell me so in her own handwriting? It ti's but a line or two. Be pleased to give my love and duty to my Grand-Mama: I beg my compliments to my other relations and friends. I am Dr. Papa

Your most dutiful & loving Son
Ch: Carroll.

P:S:

This accompanies the news-papers & magazines that I take in, since Mr. Edward's removal to Hammersmith.

ALS, Carroll Papers, MS 206, MdHi. Endorsed by CCA on a separate sheet the verso of which contains an undated note to him from Richard Croxall.

1. Woodcote Park, located at Epsom in Surrey, about 14 miles southwest of London.

2. "Painters and poets have always had equal license to dare whatever they like." Horace *Ars poetica* 9-11.

3. "I hate the common herd and keep them afar." Horace *Odes* 3.1.1.

4. A stricter translation would read: "A kind of legal quibbler, cautious and sharp, a crier of court cases, a chanter of set pleas, a spyer-out of syllables" (Cicero *De oratore* 1.55.236). Marcus Tullius Cicero was sometimes known as Tully in the eighteenth century.

5. "On purpose."

· · ·
· ·
·

CCA to CC

Octor: 13th: 1760

Dr Charley,

In myne of the 15th Past[1] I acquainted you that I had sent you by Mr Browne two Dozen of Cain Spirits,[2] But as Capn: Hanrick importuned me very much for some of my old Madeira Wine & would not be Refused I have sent the Cain Spirits by him with an equall Quantity of Madeira Wine wh. you will Find to be very good —

Pray doe me the Favour to see that the inclosed be safely Conveyed & Write to Monsr Boison Acquainting him that you will take Care of any letters of his to Mrs Manjan, Send him yr Address & Present My Compliments to him & his Lady —

You Remember Old Mr Tasker & his son the Coll a very Worthy young Gentn[.] The Son is Dangerously ill & may not Recover in that case many Applications will be made for the Place he enjoys Vzt the Secretarys Office[.][3] Among the Rest I suppose Mr Hen: Darnall my 1st: Cousin by the whole Blood will not be so wanting to himself as not to lay in his Claim & in my Opinion ought to Succeed, if Merit, his being Related to my Lord Baltimore & Consequently to Mr Cæcilius Calvert,[4] his being descended from one of the Best families in the Country from a Family which early settled in this Province has made a very Considerable figure in it, has held the Chief Posts in it, has [been very] Serviceable [to it, has been remarkably serviceable to the Propri]etary Family, has Sufferd for it & whose Attachment to it has been Faithfull & so Constant that no one Act of theirs Can give the least Grounds to doubt it & yet Considering the little notice that has been lately Taken of him I think it more than Probable he will not Succeed, Thô I am Convinced it is Mr Calverts inclination to Serve him for as Soon as he Came into Power, to the Post of Attorney Generall wh Mr Darnall then held, he added that of Navall Officer of Patuxent, & orderd him to be made one of the Councill[.] [5] This Plainly shewed Mr Calvert thought him worthy of the highest Offices here & Consequently made him Enemies, who despairing of Preventing his Rise Branded him with being a Papist, Popishly Affected, disafected to the Government &c &c (for <u>what</u> will not malice faction Ambition & Envy prompt men to do) althô he had long Conformed to the Established Church & taken all the Oaths. The govr at the Same time was influenced by these men & I suppose Represented Mr Darnall to Mr Calvert in Such a light as to Put a stop to his intentions to Serve him, wh with Mr Calverts fears of being himself accused of being Popishly Afected, has made him fearfull of being Commonly Civill to him, that is of Answering his letters,[6] Thus has the Family for a long time Sacrificed us, Abandoned their Friends, Courted their Enemies by Bestowing all favours on them, A Policy as Weak & foolish, as it is Scandalous & ungratefull.

By yrs I see you have had some Discourse wth [Mr Calvert] About the Roman Catholicks[, this I took Notice of before & some passages] in myne to you of Aprill 16: 1759, Febru: 9: 1759, Octor: 6: 1759, Janu: 9: 1760, May 1st, 1760. July 14 1760, will shew you that no dependance is to be had on Peace for us here, Since in the last instance of the Act Double taxing us, my Lord thought Proper to Assent to it, tho he he knew us to be Innocent, & the Charges brought agt us to be false & Scandalous — I would never have You be ungratefull or Act Dishonorably by Opposing the Proprietary Family merely for Opposition Sake, (should You resolve to settle in Maryland agt my Opinion) But at the Same time I think You will act foolishly if from Principle You Espouse the Interests of a Family, who have Plainly shewed they have no Principle at all, or at least that Gratitude & Justice & Honour has no Influence on their Principles —

This Accompanys Mr Browne, my House has been his home & he well deserves the little Civilities I shewed him: He Cannot be Reconciled to Maryland, not withstanding yr Mothers Banter — He will Present my Service to Mr Perkins & his Uncle Jo:[7] & the Gentn: in that House, I hope You will doe the Same & to all my other Friends in Paris London &c — God Bless & Grant You Health. I am Dr Charly

Yr Mo: Afft: Father

Cha: Carroll

ALS, Carroll-McTavish Papers, MS 220, MdHi. Margins damaged. An LS copy, addressed by the clerk, marked "Copy" by CCA, margins damaged, is filed in the Carroll-Harper Papers, MS 1225, MdHi. Text in brackets supplied from the Carroll-Harper Papers copy.

1. Not found.

2. Probably rum.

3. Benjamin Tasker, Jr. (1720/1-1760), was the only son of Benjamin Tasker, Sr., and Anne Bladen Tasker to survive to adulthood. A planter active in breeding and racing thorough-bred horses, Tasker also held his father's share in the Baltimore Company and invested in the slave trade. His public career included a single term in the lower house (1742-1744), service in the upper house (1745-1760), and a number of proprietary positions, the most powerful and lucrative of these being the post of deputy secretary of Maryland, to which he was appointed in 1755. He died in office on Oct. 17, 1760. *Bio. Dic. Md. Legis.,* II, 801-802.

4. See Appendix I, Charts F, G, and I.

5. Secretary Cecilius Calvert did not actually appoint Henry Darnall III to the Council, although, to Gov. Horatio Sharpe's dismay, the idea was seriously considered in London. Sharpe feared, as he wrote Calvert on Oct. 26, 1755, that, if such an appointment were made, it would, given Darnall's enormous unpopularity, "Occasion great Uneasiness & Dissatis-faction among the People." *Arch. of Md.,* VI, 303; Donnell MacClure Owings, *His Lordship's Patronage: Offices of Profit in Colonial Maryland* (Baltimore, 1953), 134.

6. CCA's suspicions to the contrary, Governor Sharpe actually defended Darnall to Sec-retary Calvert on June 6, 1754, as "a well behaved sensible man," although lacking the legal training Sharpe believed requisite for the attorney general's post. Further, Sharpe persisted in trying to find Darnall a financially viable post to which he could be appointed with-out fanning the smoldering resentment of the populace to whom he was "obnoxious . . . on Account of his Family's being educated in a Religion against which it is the fashion to be clamorous" (to Calvert, Mar. 8, 1756). In Sharpe's view, the appropriate office was that of rent roll keeper, a position that Darnall uncooperatively refused to accept. Sharpe even defended Darnall to Calvert against the persistent accusations of the lower house that Darnall's conversion to the established church was spurious: "Mr. Darnall has received the Sacrament, taken the Several Oaths to the Government, repeated the Test & subscribed the Oath of Abjuration & Test, which being all that can be required obliges me to think favour-ably of him." Calvert himself, rather than Sharpe, appears to have been Darnall's detractor. *Arch of Md.,* VI, 71-72, 329, 355-356.

7. William Perkins's brother, John Perkins.

. . .
. .
.

CCA to CC

[Octor: 13: 1760]

[Dr Charley,]

I am very Solicitous [Mr] Darnall should succeed in the Application he Intends to make, & have therefore wrote you the letter of this Date wth a designe that You should shew it to [M]r Calvert wth the Paragraphs of the Severall letters referd to in it Relating to the Same Subject — Yr Manner of introducing the letter to Mr Calvert must be by telling him that yr wishes to have a Relation Succeed, who Ap-pears to be Dear to yr Father, had Prompted You to a step wh may be You ought in Prudence not have taken[.] It must not Appear to Mr Calvert that You shew him the letter by my order. It must Appear to be an Act of yr owne, & it will naturally appear so to him, When You shew him the other letters wh Speak the Same Sentiments, & Could not be Framed to answer the Present Purpose, as they were wrote Antecedent to the Event, the letter will appear in no other light to him then as Conveying an Article of news to You.

Its Possible the letter may help Mr Darnall, it Cannot hurt him — As to us it Cannot have any ill Efect, for wee need not give our selves the least Concern whether Mr Calvert be Pleased or displeased. In Case of the Colls Death, make yr Application on Receit of the Letter — I am Dr Charly

Yr Mo: Afft: Father
Cha: Carroll

PS

You may think the Severall letters You are directed to shew Mr Calvert, are Wrote too freely & may give Offence: They may give Offence, & should he shew the least Resentment either by Words or by his Behaviour, Ask him who has most reason to be Offen[ded, we who have been ungratefully treated & Persecuted without Offence Contrary to all Justice] & the Priv[i]ledges & liberty Promised by the Charter[1] & one of the 1st laws E[x]ecuted here,[2] in Violation of the Solemn Engage[me]nts & Promises made to us & Our Ancestors, by [his] Ancestors Proclamation, inviting & Encouraging Our Ancestors to settle here, or He who has Acknowledged to You that by Certificates from Persons in Power here, he was Convinced of Our Inocence, & Yet by Passing the law which Double taxes us, Consented to Oppress us — It is necessary on Some Occasions to be firm & Resolute & to shew a Proper Resentment, & I think Mr Calvert in Particular ought to be Treated in this Manner, & You are to Raise or lower yr Tone According to the Disposition You find him in[3] Cajole if that will doe — Enquier Dayly whether any news of Coll Taskers Recovery

ALS, Carroll-McTavish Papers, MS 220, MdHi. Top margin damaged. A second ALS copy considerably interlineated and endorsed by CCA "1760 Octor: 13 Copy To my Son" is filed in the Carroll Papers, MS 206, MdHi. Text in brackets supplied from Carroll Papers, MS 206, copy.

1. The Maryland charter assured colonists of their right to remain English subjects and prescribed that Maryland should be a "Christian" colony. However, the specific form of worship that would be used in the colony was to be chosen by the colonists themselves. The charter, therefore, cannot be said to have established toleration in a formal sense or to have denied it. In consideration of the religious sensibilities of the proprietary family, the document used the term "allegiance" to refer to the loyalties expected of the colonists toward the king of England and avoided the term "supremacy," which bore anti-Catholic overtones. Scharf, *Maryland*, I, 157–158.

2. Probably "An Act for the Liberties of the People," passed by the assembly in March 1638/9, which assured to "all the Inhabitants of this Province being Christians (Slaves ex-

cepted)" the possession and enjoyment of "all such rights liberties immunities privileges and free customs within this Province as any naturall born subject of England hath or ought to have or enjoy in the Realm of England by force or vertue of the common law or Statute Law of England (saveing in such Cases as the same are or may be altered or changed by the Laws and ordinances of this Province)." *Arch. of Md.*, I, 41.

3. In the other copy of this letter, CCA here wrote and then struck through the following: "As it's Possible Coll Tasker may Recover, do not apply untill You have advice of his Death, But desier Mr Perkins Russall &c to give you immediate notice of it."

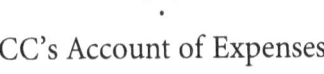

CCA to CC

Novr: 27th: 1760

Dr Charly,

As I wrote to You this day Mr Browne is still with me, so is Mr Buchanan. My House has been their home above 5 Months, this to me has been very troublesome & Inconvenient, I like to enjoy my owne family in Privacy & Retierment as much as Possible — Thinking Mr Browne would return in Sepr or Octr, I was willing to Put up wth the Inconvenience for some time & that they should be togeather while Mr Browne stayed, But on his Return finding Mr Buchanan did not think of takeing Private Lodgings, I Contrived that he should be Put in mind of it, He is now looking out But by their Behaviour, I see they are not well Pleased. I have I think payed them a very Great Compliment, But I am in the Case of every Man who endeavours to oblige that is I have Miscarried by not Continuing still to doe what is inconsistent with my owne ease & quiet. This is to Yr self, & I only mention it, least You should hear it from another quarter. I am Dr Charly

Yrs &c

Cha: Carroll

ALS, Carroll Papers, MS 206, MdHi. Endorsed as a copy by CCA.

CC's Account of Expenses

[October 1759–December 1760]

[1]	£	S	D
Octobr. 1759			
to hemming of shirts, breaches buccle, shoes blacking	0	1	10
to washing, blacking shoes and boots, Letters	0	1	5½

to Do.[1]	0	1	9½
to washing and dinner at a tavern	0	10	8½
to sand scrubbing brush and sope	0	1	2½
to shock buccle, watch chain and mourning buccles	0	12	6
to the play, Ansons voyage,[2] London Curiosities[3]	1	0	6
to spurs, powder and tooth brush	0	11	0
to seeing the curiosities of the town, and boot garters	0	7	0
to seeing the tower, hosseler[4] and Barber	0	10	10
to vales to servants and treat given to Mr. Perkins	1	7	1
to sugar loafes	0	13	3½
spent at a tavern	0	4	0
to vales to servants and to the Tennis	0	5	0
to beating the carpets, quills, one pound of candles	0	3	1½
to the play and supper at a tavern	0	8	4
to oat meal, blacking shoes, matches	0	0	4
to washing and dinner at a tavern	0	8	3
to the play and poor	0	7	6
to a dinner at a tavern	0	2	6
to Do.	0	3	4
to vales and washing	0	5	4
to milk pot and bason, cleaning my watch	0	5	9
to postage, coach hier, vales, loss at cards	0	11	10
to washing, cream, butter, vales, and to the play	0	13	7
to a chair, vales, mourning sword	0	11	0
to dressing my hat, butter, cream, washing, and french loafes	0	5	8
to coach hier, vales, loss at cards, washing	0	11	9½
to cream, candles, blacking shoes, vales, coach hier	0	4	10½
to 6 handkerchiefs making included	0	15	0
to vales and coach hier to washing candles, butter	0	9	3
to cream, chips for lighting the fire, blacking shoes	0	0	8
to coach hier, vales, loss at cards	0	13	0
to a hair, dressing and cutting my hair	0	8	3
to coach hier, vales to servants	0	4	0
to loss at cards, breakfast, washing	0	12	9
to cream, shoeblack — mending stockings	0	2	7½

[2]

Debr. 1759	£	S	D
to coach hier, vales to servants	0	2	0
to the shoemaker for shoes and boots	2	19	0

to tea table, tea chest, bason stand and tea board	4	3	0
to the Tennis Court and loss at cards	1	8	0
to subscription for reading books and list of books	0	11	0
to Dalrymple on feudal property[5]	0	5	0
to Hoyles games,[6] washing, and candles	0	6	7
to the shoe-black, to cream, french loafs	0	1	0
to Butter, loss at play, vales to servants	0	8	7
to coach hiere, vales, Christmass boxes[7]	0	16	0
to washing, Gellies, tarts and candles	0	9	6½
to the shoe-black, cream, bread, butter, sope	0	2	3½
to the poor loss at cards, to a chair	1	4	0
to vales, loss at cards	0	2	0
to 2 pair of laced ruffles	5	8	0
to making Do. furnishing tape and buttons	0	4	0
to washing, bread, cream, tarts and candles	0	5	7
to the shoe black, butter and Christmass box	0	4	4½
to turnpikes, butter, vales, to the play & loss at cards	0	8	3
to 2 pair of worsted stockings, 3 pair gause Do.	0	17	6
to 3 brushes, 3 pound of candles, 6 brass nobs 2 Lb. of sope	0	5	2
to a comb and blacking	0	1	7
to a chamber pot, bason, butter, bread, cream	0	1	2½
to pometum and curling Irons	0	2	5
to cream, bread, table matts corck sqrew	0	3	3
to washing, vales to servants to the opera	0	8	6
to the shortning the ruffles of 8 shirts & hemming	0	4	0
to cutting off ruffles and mending 13 Do.	0	2	0
to making 3 stocks	0	6	0
to half a year's dressing my hair	2	2	0
to 2 silk bags	0	7	0
to a treat given at my Chambers (at which Mr. Rozier was present)	4	15	8
to buck skin breaches fashion included	1	7	0
to the waiter from the Tavern	0	4	6
to vales cream & butter bread	0	2	1
to a leathern apron for my Servant & scrubbing brush	0	2	5
to candles and writing book	0	6	1
to my Landress for 4 months wages	2	2	0
to washing, vales to servants	0	3	7
to loss at cards, Wood's institutes & Jacobs Dictionary	2	15	0
to coach hire, writing Paper, 3 Lbs. of candles, and chips	0	5	9½

[3]

	£	S	D
to Christmass box newspaper and 5 plates	0	4	2½
to sand, powder, and sand glass	0	1	2
to knee buccles, to Balestone's great Charter[8]	0	16	10
to an Analysis of the law by Do.	0	4	6
to washing and quarters rent	10	2	1½
to the laws on descent by Blackstone	0	1	6
to vales, loss at cards, washing	0	12	9½
to cards, postage	0	2	6
to bread cream & butter during the week	0	1	9
to loss at cards, postage, riding out	1	0	8
to washing and week's breakfast, newspapers	0	2	9½
to cards, Lemon, bread & cream	0	2	0
to 3 pds of candles, milk and writing paper	0	2	1
to oatmeal, newspaper, & bread	0	0	7
to the young man's companion (a book of Arethmetick)[9]	0	2	6
to bread, cream, newspaper	0	0	3
to Do. to coffee and muffin	0	1	1½
to coach hire, bread, cream, newspaper	0	1	11
to Do. and salt and loss at cards	0	11	0½
to bread cream, paper, butter	0	1	2½
to 2 fowles	0	3	0
to 3 pds of candles, bread, milk, newspaper	0	1	10
to washing and sugar	0	7	5
to 2 Lb. of best Chocolate	0	11	0
to coach hire, vales to servants, loss at cards	1	4	6
to bread, cream, newspaper,	0	0	3
to oatmeal, flower, butter and greens	0	0	10
to 1 Lb. of Pruins and grapes	0	1	6
to cream, milk, newspaper, butter during the week	0	1	8
to half a pound of Bohee tea[10]	0	5	0
to loss at cards, vales, coach hire	0	7	6
to ½ a pound of cream a Tartar and to the play	0	6	0
to washing	0	4	5
to milk, paper, rice, bread, cream, butter	0	1	0
to Do. and to 3 pd of candles	0	3	0
to cream, newspaper, milk, butter and letters	0	2	10½
to Do. and to vales, to ribband for my hair	0	4	10
to Do. and slop bason and washing	0	3	4
to loss at play, to vales, to coach hire	0	12	0
to loss at cards, vales and Coach hire	0	9	0
to washing & newspaper	0	6	10½

to a stick, fish kettle, cream	0	5	11
to a basket, bread, cream, newspapers & butter	0	1	6
to bread, cream, milk, newspaper	0	0	4½

[4]

to slop bason, bread cream, paper	0	0	7
to Do. to postage, to 3 Lbs. of candles	0	2	9
to newspaper, butter and sope	0	2	1½
to bread, cream Paper salt and Barley	0	1	1½
to a watch chain, 2 raizors & case; shoe buccles, pencil	0	12	10
to Doe skin gloves	0	3	6
to tea, to hemming six shirts	0	13	0
to 6 stocks at 4 shillings each	1	4	0
to Pruins, vales, washing, bread, cream, news paper	0	5	5
to a frying pan	0	2	6
to bread, cream, butter, newspaper 2 Lb. of pouder	0	2	10
to Do. and pound of Barley	0	0	7½
to rum and milk, newspaper, butter during the week	0	6	7½
to postage, to the gardener, to loss at cards	0	4	9
to seeing Kingsinton Palace[11]	0	3	0
to a boat, coach hire, chease cakes	0	2	3
to bread, cream, Paper 1 pd of candles	0	1	0
to loss at cards	0	5	9
to coals and Coalmen	2	1	6
to newspaper & breakfast during the week	0	3	8
to sope, comb, and washing	0	6	6
spent in a Journey to Portsmouth	5	11	0
to washing, vales, to seeing Westm: abbey	0	7	8½
to gloves, coach hire, to scouring my Chambers	0	10	9
to a pound of sope, to the chimney sweeper	0	2	3
to beating the carpets and postage	0	2	4
to mending shoes, oil and lamp	0	2	7
to bread, newspaper, milk & butter, sope	0	3	6½
to the concert, to washing, sugar	0	13	5
to a nightgown	3	13	0
to vales, to bread, to cream, paper, butter	0	2	7
to the London Magazine	0	0	6
to washing and writing Paper	0	4	6
to loss at play, examining yr. Lottery tickets	0	10	0
to the Tennis court, & turnpikes	0	7	6
to washing, to a silver hilted sword	2	4	9
to an arm hat, to bread, cream, newspaper, butter	0	8	10

to washing silk stockings and oranges, to cream & Paper	0	3	2½
to water for taking out spots in Linnen	0	1	0
to the Tennis court, Journey to Rygate [12] & Epsom	0	15	6
to oranges, to breakfast, during the week	0	4	3
to washing, to 3 pds of candles	0	4	9

[5]

	£	S	D
to 2 pair of brown thread stockings	0	9	0
vales to Lord Baltimore's servants at Epsom	0	6	0
to the Carpenters for 2 chimney boards [13]	0	5	6
to the Tennis Court, washing & breakfast	0	10	0
to a pint of sweet oil	0	1	3
to washing, turnpikes, breakfast during the week	0	3	5
to dressing my hat, to the poor	0	2	7
to a supper given in my Chambers	1	3	0
to turnpikes, Ostelers, [14] spent at Vauxhall	1	0	0
to the gardiner, week's breakfast	0	4	7
to cards and candles	0	3	7
to a Pamphlet, 2 Lb. of powder for the hair	0	2	0
to a broom sand and blacking	0	0	5½
to washing	0	1	9½
to wine	6	13	0
to the Osteler, hay, corn, turnpikes	0	1	2
to loss at cards, to ½ Lb. of tea	0	6	4
to ½ a pound of green tea vales to servants	0	9	0
to washing to the London Magazine	0	4	6
to blacking, sope, sand, to breakfast	0	3	9
to coffee turnpike and Osteler	0	2	8½
to hire of a horse 3 days feading included	0	13	0
to turnpikes, washing, vales	0	5	6
to the week's breakfast	0	1	1½
to Dawson for buying a horse	0	10	6
to Do. for stable room	0	1	2
spent in a Jant to Colenbrook [15]	0	14	0
to Creech's Latin Lucretius [16]	0	4	0
to washing, silver shoe & knee buccles	0	18	3
to pollishing the teakettle and tinning	0	2	6
to whip & week's breakfast	0	4	9½
to a book and postage of Letters	0	4	6
to washing silk stocking to Osteler & turnpikes	0	4	9½
to the week's breakfast	0	1	6
to a ¼ rent for my Chambers	10	0	0

{ YOUNG MANHOOD, 1759-1764 }

	£	S	D
to corn, Ostler, turnpikes, Blacksmith	0	2	9½
Spent at Vauxhall	0	7	5
Spent in a Journey to Woolich[17]	0	5	0

	£	S	D
to coach hire [rulking?][18] shirts, weeks breakfast	0	11	8½
to leathern straps, Osteler and turnpikes	0	5	5
to hire of a horse, loss at cards, vales to Servants	0	8	6
to coach hire Lord Bolingbrook's Letters[19]	0	10	0
to a book think well on it[20]	0	1	0
to turnpikes, corn, & hay	0	2	6
to ½ pound of tea, washing, vales	0	8	2
to a pint of sweet oil, to the Blacksmith	0	2	3
to breakfast during the week	0	2	0
to 2 Doz of red port	1	16	0
to loss at cards	0	10	0
to turnpikes, Osteler, corn, hay	0	3	0
to a bottle of Renish wine	0	2	0
spent in a party of pleasure	0	7	6
to a prism, week's breakfast	0	10	2
Spent in a tour to Hampton Court, & Windsor, washing	1	17	5½
to hire of a horse for my servant	0	10	6
to vales, to 2 bottles of Burgundy	0	16	0
to [w]ashing the bed curtains and quilt	0	8	0
to washing, to the week's breakfast, vales	0	5	7½
to a birdcage & Caneira seed	0	6	6½
to washing, to Portmanteau, and straps	1	3	7
to a description of the roads in England[21]	0	4	0
to a pocket book & steel pencil case	0	3	5
to spent in my Journey to the West with Mr. Jenison	18	13	0
to a new hat, to postage	1	6	2
to the new testament, 2 Lbs. of Bohee tea	0	8	6
to the Tennis court & pouder for my hair	0	5	6
to 2 week's washing, Taylor's bill	8	10	6
to letter paper and Magazine	0	2	0
to a pound of pouder & matches	0	0	8
to 3 Lb. of candles, postage, week's breakfast	0	5	9½
to a ham, & longhair broom	0	11	1½
to a mop, matt, to sand & ashes	0	4	2
to the play, to the week's breakfast	0	5	4
to a key for my Chambers	0	11	0
to milk	0	0	8

	£	S	D
to Pometum	0	0	6
to candles, to gardiner, to the newspapers	0	2	9

[7]

	£	S	D
to loss at cards, vales, week's breakfast	0	16	8
to a supper at my Chambers	2	12	2
to the waiter, to coals, 2 weeks washing	0	9	6
to an oak stick	0	0	6
to keeping a horse at Livery stable, hire of Do. for 32 days	9	4	2
to 2 pillow cases, Lond. Maga: silk stockings washing	0	7	6
to sope, sand, washing, week's breakfast	0	6	0
to the Tennis Court	0	10	6
to pometum	0	0	8½
to silver tea spoons tongs &c with my crest ing[r]aved	3	8	7
to sugar, & weeke's breakfast	0	8	9½
spent in a tour to Dedtford[22]	0	18	0
to ¼ rent for my Chambers	10	0	0
to a horse	0	2	0
to carriage of Law book's	0	12	0
to 5 Chalds:[23] of coals 36S the Chal:	9	7	6
to ½ Lb. of Bohee tea	0	5	0
to stock buccle, sleave buttons, black crape hat band	0	3	10
to week's breakfast, coach hire, vales	0	8	0½
to 2 week's washing, to gloves, shamoe shoes	0	16	6
to 2 pair of single channeled Do.[24]	0	15	0
to washing, loss at cards	0	6	0½
to 6 Lb. of candles, breakfast during the week	0	5	4
to a dress mourning suit & grey frock	11	11	0
to weepers,[25] to coffee, to quart of Lamp oil	0	5	2
to a pound of rice, week's breakfast	0	1	9½

Nob. 21st.

	£	S	D
to 2 Doz of red	2	0	0
to the play, spent in a tour to Rygate	0	10	[1]
to week's breakfast, play, vales	0	11	1
to a Paper writing book	0	0	10
to Lond. Mag: week's breakfast, loss at cards	0	4	9½
to a Pamphlet, 3 Lb. of candles, week's breakfast	0	5	0
to postage, vales, loss at play, to the play, fire wood	0	9	10
to 2 week's washing, ½ a pound of Bohee tea	0	7	6
to salt, candles, fire wood, week's breakfast, loss at cards	0	8	0
to Gilbert's Tenures,[26] washing, spent at a tavern	0	15	6½

	£	S	D
to the poor	0	0	1
to Fitzherberts Natura brevium last Edition[27]	1	1	0
to coach hire, loss at cards, Christmass box	0	16	0
to the play, loss at cards, Christ. box, week's breakfast, Paper	1	7	0

[8]	£	S	D
to vales, to the Lond: Evening post ¼ paid	0	9	0
to mending the sconce to postage sealing wax	0	5	10
to one year's wages paid to my Servant	35	16	0
to ¼ rent for my Chambers	10	0	0
to 2 suits of cloaths	16	18	0
to superfine Blue great coat	3	2	0
to buying a horse	17	9	0
Spent in diet	23	9	10½
Sum total of my expences	333	8	0[28]
Money remitted from Paris by Mr. Crookshanks	190	5	2
Money received of Mr. Perkins	146	0	0
total	336	5	2
	333	8	0
Remains	002	17	2

My accounts come down to the 1st. of Jany. 1761. from
Octb. 1759. including one year & 3 months.

AD, Carroll-Maccubbin Papers, MS 219, MdHi. Endorsed by CCA: "1761 Janu: 1st An Account of my Sons Expences from Octor: 1759." This account was enclosed in CC to CCA, Mar. 28, 1761, below.

1. Ditto.

2. Baron George Anson (1697–1762), *A Voyage Round the World: In the Years MDCCXL, I, II, III, IV* . . . (London, 1748). *Cat. Lib.*, no. 37, lists a 1749 London edition.

3. David Henry, *An Historical Account of the Curiosities of London and Westminster* . . . (London, 1753).

4. Hostler, a groom.

5. Sir John Dalrymple (1726–1810), *An Essay towards a General History of Feudal Property in Great Britain* . . . (London, 1757).

6. Possibly [Edmond Hoyle (1672–1769)], *Mr. Hoyle's Games of Whist, Quadrille, Piquet, Chess, and Back-gammon* . . . (London, 1755).

7. Gratuities given to servants on Boxing Day, the day after Christmas.

8. William Blackstone, *The Great Charter and Charter of the Forest, with Other Authentic Instruments* . . . (Oxford, 1759). *Cat. Lib.*, no. 100, lists a 1769 London edition.

9. W[illiam] Mather, *The Young Man's Companion; or, Arithmetic Made Easy* . . . (London, 1752).

10. Bohea, a fine black tea.

11. Kensington Palace, which became a royal residence during the reign of William and Mary, 1689–1702.

12. Reigate, a market town, located in Surrey, south of London.

13. Planks used to close up a fireplace in the summer.

14. Hostlers.

15. Probably Colebrooke Park, a seat near Tonbridge, Kent.

16. Thomas Creech (1659–1700), ed., *Titi Lucretii Cari de rerum natura libri sex: quibus interpretationem et notas addidit Thomas Creech* (Oxford, 1695). *Cat. Lib.* lists both a 1717 Latin edition (no. 1345) and a 1715 edition of Creech's English translation (no. 642).

17. Woolwich, on the south bank of the Thames, eleven miles east of Charing Cross, was the site of the Royal Military Academy and the royal arsenal.

18. Possibly "rucking," to gather into small folds.

19. Henry St. John, Lord Viscount Bolingbroke (1678–1751), *A Letter to Sir William Windham; II. Some Reflections on the Present State of the Nation; III. A Letter to Mr. Pope* (London, 1753). *Cat. Lib.*, no. 113.

20. R[ichard] Challoner, *Think Well On't; or, Reflections on the Great Truths of the Christian Religion . . .* (London, 1728). Challoner was a Catholic prelate.

21. Possibly *A New and Accurate Description of the Present Great Roads, and the Principal Cross Roads of England and Wales* (London, 1759).

22. Deptford, four miles southeast of Charing Cross on the Thames south bank, was the site of the royal dockyard from 1513 until 1869.

23. A chaldron, a dry measure commonly used for coal, equal to thirty-six bushels.

24. A channel was a groove cut in the sole of a shoe into which was inserted the seam uniting the upper and the sole.

25. Strips of white linen or muslin worn on the cuff of a man's sleeve as badges of mourning.

26. Probably the *Treatise of Tenures, in Two Parts . . .* , 2d ed. (London, 1738), by Sir Geoffrey Gilbert (1674–1726), a judge and chief baron of the Irish exchequer.

27. *La nouel Natura breuium* ([London], 1534), a manual of legal procedures attributed to Sir Anthony Fitzherbert (1470–1538).

28. Actually £341 2s. 7d., leaving a debit of £4 17s. 5d.

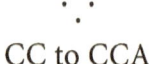

CC to CCA

Janry. 1st. 1761.

Dr. Papa,

I can not begin the new year better than by wishing you a happy one. God grant that you may live to see many: your alone can make them happy. Capt. Kelty and Henrick are arrived:[1] the latter has brought the Cain spirits and Madeira wine; which Is very good: I am much obliged to you and to the Captain, as it is no easy task to cheat the Custom house officers. Kelty has not as yet delivered his letters. By yours of Octb. 13th. 1760 and several other letters you seem highly disgusted with Maryland: you certainly have great cause of discontent I shou'd not chuse to settle in any place whatever, against yr. opinion & approbation: But the same reasons that make Maryland an uneligible abode, make England equally uneligible: to exchange a bad situation for a worse, or equally bad, wou'd argue want of Judgement. Besides the trouble and loss attending such a change, besides the prospect at least the hopes (and those probable too) of our enemies animosity abating (which are all reasons for remaining in Maryland) our importance there, woud determin me, if obliged to chuse between England & Maryland, to give the preference to the latter. Religious persecution, I own, is bad, but civil persecution is still more irksom: the one is quite insupportable, the other is alleviated by superior motives, which tho' they can not diminish the real evil, yet enable us to bear it with greater resignation. This makes me chuse to live under an english goverment rather than under any other: Catholick I mean: for I know of no Catholick country where that greatest blessing civil liberty, is enjoyed. . . . Whatever country I settle in, its welfare & my honour shall be the chief and sole principle of my actions. . . . shou'd I ever be so happy as to be able to protect the innocent, I wou'd not abandon them because weak nor court their enemies and mine with presents of slavery and fear —

15 months are now elapsed since my arrival in England[.] Notwithstanding a pretty serious application during this time, to the Law, I have made little or no advance in it. This must be owing to my incapacity, to the difficulty of the study and to want of instruction. Reading Law books & attending the courts is not sufficient to attain the knowledge of the Law unless assisted by the advice of, and conference with skillful Lawers. I know 2 or 3 young Roman Catholick gentlemen who study as Clerks, under the immediate direction of Hutton,[2] Wilmot,[3] & others, persons well versed in the law by long practice & great application: This in my opinion wou'd have been the best way for me to have studied: and this, I dare say was the course my Grand-father persued: There are many intricate passages, obscure reasons of Law, which certainly egent interpretre[4] often imaginary not real difficulties occur: these frighten the student, almost cast him into dispair and create an antipathy even to what he is most desirous of knowing.

I am sorry for young Tasker: I pity the father, who has sustained so great a loss: If Mr. Darnall shou'd stand competitor for the Secretary's office, I wish him success. I can only wish and hope: wou'd it were in my power to do more!

I have sent you the London Evening Posts & the Magazines with the considerations on the present German war, a new Pamphlet full of good sense:[5] this will confirm you in those notions, you undoubtedly have all along entertained of our continental connections: several scriblers have attacked the author, but their lame weak attempts plainly show the superior [for]ce of his reasoning and the truth of what he asserts. My Mama, I hope, is quite recovered of her indisposition & the swelling entirely gone off: Mr. Browne's not coming with the fleet is a great disappointment. I flattered myself with the pleasing hopes of many agreeable entretiens[6] about you both, my friends, and Maryland. Nothing can make me amends, but a very long letter from [my] Mama. I long to be with you: even this great Metropolis and all its ple[as]ures do not sufficiently attoane for your absence, they only serve to alleviate the desiderium patriæ[7] and pains of banishment. My duty to my Grand-Mama & service to my friends; the Croxalls, Dr. Lyon, Lawson & his Lady. I am Dr Papa

Yr. Most dutiful Son
Ch: Carroll.

P:S:

Mr. Crookshanks and other friends in London desire their compliments. I shall write to Mr. Boison: & take care to forward the letter when it comes to hand: it was not enclosed in yours of Octb. 13th that being only a copy: tho' you mention it in that Letter.

ALS, Carroll Papers, MS 206, MdHi. Addressed by CC. Endorsed by CCA.

1. James Henrick left Annapolis for London on Oct. 31, 1760; there is no record of Capt. John Kelty sailing for London from Annapolis during the fall of 1760. Annapolis Port of Entry Record Books, II.

2. Hutton may be the Roman Catholic conveyancer CC mentions in his letter of July 15, 1761, below.

3. Sir John Eardley Wilmot (1709–1792) studied law at Trinity Hall, Cambridge, and was called to the bar from the Inner Temple in 1732. In 1755 he became associate judge of the king's bench and served until 1765. He assumed the position of chief justice of the Court of Common Pleas and became a member of the Privy Council in 1766.

4. "They require an interpreter." Seneca On Benefits 4.16.3.

5. Israel Mauduit, Considerations on the Present German War (London, 1760).

6. "Conversations."

7. "Longing for one's country."

∴ ∴

CC to CCA

Febry. 13th. 1761.

Dr. Papa,

Immediately on the receipt of yr. Letter relating to Mr. Darnall I waited on Mr. Calvert: I came to the point in question by mentioning the premature death of Colonel Tasker; this naturally lead me to enquire who was to succeed him in his office of Secretary: I doubted not but that there wou'd be many compe[ti]tors, that Mr. Darnall certainly wou'd not be so wanting to himself as not put up for that post, which I hoped and wished him to obtain. His answer was somewhat to this purpot. He wished Mr. Darnall well was willing to serve him, but that strange reports were propagated against that gentleman. Then with great warmth & seeming emotion I can't conceive says he: how a man who has taken the oaths can be so base as to be Papistically affected or so deep a dissembler as to be a Papist at heart, a Protestant in appearance[.] Here he paused, looked big & stern, but his fire began to cool his ardour abated, he remembered, perhaps, his having been a Papist but his conscience accused him with no self-interested action (for which he seems to have a particular horror, for even the thought of a base a[c]tion had almost set him into a passion) in ceasing to be of that communion, nor since his change with any dissumalition or Paspistical affection: his conduct has Justified the last.

You may Judge by this he has not Mr. Darnall's interest very much at heart, at least I Judged so and urged no further. I turned off the di[sc]ourse to the late oppressive double-taxing law. I asked him how my Lord, or his advisers cou'd consent to a law which they knew to be an open breach of faith & since declared by the Attorney General subversive of the foundations of the Maryland constitution, most iniquitious and unjust by oppressing Men, by his own confession, innocent and undeserving of such treatment. His answer was this, I think very puerile, but poor Mr. Calvert who never did an interested selfish action designedly startled at the thought of having done one inadvertently; his surprise prevented him from giving a studied reason, & disclosed a short tho' true one. He (my Lord Baltimore) was advised to it: Besides the Roman Catholicks made not the least opposition to the bill while depending — therefore it was Just to double tax them or they were willing to be double taxed, is this a logical conclusion? However Mr. Calvert gave me a kind of promise, that no such laws if the Roman Catholicks did not give occasion to them by their disaffected behaviour, shou'd for the future meet with the Proprietary's approbation.

I return you many thanks for the Madeira and Cain spirits which are looked upon by the connoisseurs to be very good: the books are all come safe to hand: notwithstanding this supply I shall be put to a pretty great expence in buying others I stand in need of. Woud you advise me to buy the statutes at large? This is a very dear work. I shall take care to send the books you want by the fleet, if I can meet with them in London, if not they must be bought in Paris. I am surprised how Mr. Browne and Buchanan after so long a stay at your house, cou'd be displeased at yr. unwillingness to maintain them longer.

I have seen Mr. Macnamara:[1] you need not be apprehensive of too great an intimacy between us. The letters inclosed to me for Monsieur Boisson have been forwarded long ago[.] I wrote, as you desired, to Monsieur Boisson, to inform him, care shou'd be taken of his letters to his relations in Maryland, if conveyed to me. I intend to answer my Mama's letter, by the fleet; you may expect also by the same opportunity a longer and more circumstancial letter: this is wrote in haste, the ship it goes by, being to sail in 2 or 3 day's time. As you mention nothing in your letters of some pamphlets, the magazines, the Way to keep him a new comedy[2] & the news papers, I have some cause to think, that they have not been sent, or if sent not delivered. My Grand Mama's illness gives me great uneasiness, both on account of my affection for her, & the affliction her death will occasion to my Mama: so tender so good a mother, can not but be a tender affectionate daughter: try every expedient that may allay her grief. I desire my compliments to Poor Mr. Lawson's family: their loss is indeed great,[3] I think young Mr. Lawson (but this between us) is not so sensible of it as he shou'd be—I am almost sorry this reflection has esca[ped my] pen: pray remember to the Croxalls & Dr. Lyon.

There is no appearance of a peace this winter at least as [I] can see: we are raising recruits a pace for Germany: There is some talk of an expedition against the French forts in the Missisipi Martinico seems evidently threatned with an invasion. Marechal de Belle-isle died last month at Versailles in a very advanced age: it ti's not as yet known who is to succeed him in the post of Secretary of war.[4] Daun is to command the Austrian grand army, an Laudon an army of 35 thousand men in Silesia:[5] Mr. Keith has not been able to detach the empress of Russia from the grand alliance[6]—I am of opinion the king of Prussia will stand his ground again this campaign: which may be the occasion of another if the Powers at war can find means to maintain their forces.

AL, Carroll Papers, MS 206, MdHi. Addressed by CC. Marked "per Capt. Bryce [2 DC?]" in an unknown hand. Endorsed by CCA. A slightly different version of the first page appears on the verso of CC's July 20, 1761, letter to his father. Carroll Papers, MS 206.

1. Michael Macnemara (?-1767), son of CC's great aunt Margaret Carroll and Thomas Macnemara (see Appendix I, Chart B). Upon his father's death in 1720, Michael Macnemara became the ward of Daniel Dulany, Sr., who immediately sent him to London to study law at Gray's Inn, one of the four Inns of Court. Returning to Maryland about 1725, Michael secured employment in Dulany's law office where he handled most of the courtroom work for the older man. In October 1728 he became clerk of the lower house of assembly, a position he held more or less continuously for the rest of his life, and in 1752 he was commissioned clerk of the prerogative office. However, these posts did not satisfy Michael Macnemara's considerable ambition, and, in the fall of 1760, he resigned them and embarked for England in hopes of improving his fortunes. Not only did his efforts fail, but they also exhausted his resources. Unable to recover financially, he died in debtor's prison several years after his return to Maryland. An account of his misadventures in England can be found in his letters to CCA of Feb. 10, 1761, Carroll Papers, MS 206, and July 20, Oct. 29, 1761, Jan. 4, 1762, Carroll-McTavish Papers. Aubrey C. Land, *The Dulanys of Maryland: A Biographical Study of Daniel Dulany, the Elder (1685-1753), and Daniel Dulany, the Younger (1722-1797)* (Baltimore, 1968), 41, 96, 236; Jones, *American Members of the Inns of Court,* 150; Owings, *His Lordship's Patronage,* 138-139, 144.

2. Arthur Murphy, *The Way to Keep Him* (1760).

3. Alexander Lawson died in Baltimore in October 1760. Barnes, *Marriages and Deaths,* 111.

4. Charles Fouquet, duc de Belle-Isle (1684-1761), assumed the post of minister of war in March 1758 and held it until his death in January 1761. Lee Kennett, *The French Armies in the Seven Years' War: A Study in Military Organization and Administration* (Durham, N.C., 1967), 6.

5. Soldier of fortune Ernst Gideon Laudon (1717–1790) joined the Russian army as a cadet in 1732. He resigned from the Russian service in 1741 in order to join Frederick the Great, but, when he was not accepted, he turned to the Austrians and enlisted in a troop of light horse based in Vienna. By 1757 he had risen to the rank of major general of cavalry and soon began operating his forces in concert with Count Leopold von Daun. Trevor Nevitt Dupuy, *The Military Life of Frederick the Great of Prussia* (New York, 1969), 122, 126, 137–140.

6. Robert Keith (?–1774), a Scotsman, served as British minister at St. Petersburg (1758–1762) during the reign of the Czarina Elizabeth (1709–1762), who ruled from 1741 until her death. Russia and Austria had concluded a defensive alliance in 1746. In September 1755 Britain signed a preliminary treaty with Russia while at the same time secretly negotiating a treaty with Russia's archenemy Prussia to provide for the protection of Hanover, an arrangement confirmed by the convention of Westminster. Strongly displeased at this development, the czarina strengthened her ties with Austria and France and refused to sign the formal version of the proposed Russo-British agreement.

CCA to CC

March 22d 1761

Dr C[h]arley

Your Dr: Mama died the 12th Instt: having been confined to her Room since the 20th of last Decr: & to her Bed for at least the 3 last Weeks. She was to all Appearance in perfect health looked florid & well, her Complexion fine & clear when she was attacked with 3 or 4 very high fevers, these were Removed by a Blister & she was to all appearance in a fine way when she fell into a very deep Melancholy wch often affected her Senses & Understanding, a gentle Emetic contributed greatly to relieve her & restore her to her Senses, & it was repeated. In some days after the 2d Emetic she was taken with an obstinate Bilious Vomitting wch was very frequent & tormenting; from the 2d Vomit, wch I think was given on the 27th of Janry she never had a natural stool all her Evacuations downwards being procured by Clysters,[1] however her Vomitting was much abated, & little was apprehended from it, & wt: is very remarkable she was generally very temperate & had no sensible fevers until the 5th Instt: then she also began at times to ramble in her discourse & her fevers wch. could not be removed wore her away. If 4 Physicians could have saved her I shd: still be blessed with her. Our Loss is as great as such a loss can be, to you she was a most tender Mother, to me the best of wives being a Charming Woman in every sense, remarkable for her good Sense evenness & Sweetness of her temper. She bore her tedious Sickness with great patience & Resignation, & had all the Spiritual helps the Church can bestow in such Cases. Hence, & from the Regularity of her life we have the solid Comfort of a well grounded hope that her Death was precious in the Sight of God: Charity however to one so near &

dear to us prompts us to procure her ease from the pains she may suffer for such Transgressions as she may not have Attoned for in this life & therfore I desire you will apply 10 Guineas properly to that end, I have bestowed here a much larger Sum to the same purpose—

Nature can hardly support such Strokes Philosophy alone cannot administer any solid Com[fo]rt, for thô Death be the common Lot, thô many from the Creation have lost as tender mothers & dear wives & will continue to do so to the end of time, we do not find more Consolation from this Consideration than we shd: find ease in a fit of the Gout or any other disorder from the Reflection that many have & will [feel] as Excruciating pains as ours. Religion in such Cases is the only solid Comforter of the afflicted, by that we know, that the God who has Created us has a Right to dispose of us, that his Dispositions are just & mercyfull & that it is our Duty to submit to them, hence a Xtian,[2] by Resignation (wch is his Duty) finds that ease wch nothing else can give him, & is according to Gods infinite goodness rewarded with ease in Consequence of his Obedience, Submission & Resignation. I have dwelt so long on this melancholy Subject to soften if possible the 1st. impressions it must make on you, & to help you to bear yr. loss. You have before you an Affecting instance of Mortality, life is but as the Twinkling of the Eye to Eternity, the only serious business of life is to make that Eternity a happy one & the certainest pledge of a happy Eternity is a lively habitual faith, pray earnestly for this precious faith & cherish it; having it you cannot act so inconsistently & irrationally as to offend yr: God.

Farewell my Dear Child, I pray to God to bless you & to grant you perfect Health. I am my Dr Charley

Yr: Mo: Afft: Father
Cha: Carroll

PS

I have yrs of the 1st of Janry wch with yr: former I will answer soon—

LS, Carroll Papers, MS 206, MdHi. Addressed by the clerk. Margins damaged.
1. Enemas.
2. Christian.

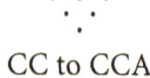

CC to CCA

March 28th. 1761.

Dr. Papa,

In my last of the 13th Febry. I acquainted you with the conversation I had had with Mr. Calvert relating to Mr. Darnall, and what little dependence that gentleman cou'd place on Mr. Calvert. I sincerely wish for mr. Darnall's sake that my arguments had been more peruasive, or Mr. Calvert's prejudices less violent not that I believe, Mr. Calvert's bears him any particular grudge or ill will; disaffection & Papistical inclinations seem to form his chief or only objection to Mr. Darnall.

You seemed desirous in one of last year's letters of my being entered of the temple: the expence of entry may come to near 4 £. the commons to pretty near seven pounds a'year: As my religion is an invincible obstacle to my being called to the Bar (and unless called to the Bar my being entered of the temple is of no signification or use) as attending the commons will infalibly expose me to the worst acquaintance & company, I have been so bold for once as to disobey yr. commands. But if these reasons appear insufficient (but I hope they will not) if you still persevere in yr. resolution, let me know it, and I will tho' unwillingly, obey.

I have bought of Mr. Lewis Croiset's moral reflexions:[1] I paid a crown for the 2 volus: this I am sensible is a great deal too much for such books, but the scarcity and the time and trouble of getting them from France, made me give this price: I shall look out for his exercises de pieté &c:[2] if not to be had in London, I shall write to Mr. Crookshanks for them. As Mr. Hume is continuing his history of England, I thought it wou'd be better to buy the whole entire work at once than by peace meals: this is the reason of my not sending by the fleet the 2 volus. already published. Pray let me have a list of yr. English books to prevent buying the same books over again.

My Lord Peter and his tutor Mr. Galloway are lately arrived in town from France: there is a report of my Lord's going to be married to the youngest Miss Aston:[3] perhaps his dancing at the Ridotto[4] with that young Lady the very night of his arrival, may have occasioned this report.

My Accounts of last year's expences accompany this I hope you will not think them exorbitant; all my care, all my study is to please and satisfy you, if my endeavours prove successful, I am happy and sufficiently recompensed. Mr. Macnamara informs me you have sold the large tract of land at Monoccasy[5] for 12500£ sterling: this piece of information surprised me not a little, as you intimated to me in one of your Letters yr. design of keeping the largest tracts of Land till my arrival in Maryland, that then I might be able to chuse either to settle there or leave that country. I do not mention this with a view to blame yr. measures, which I am fully persuaded are always prudent, or that I am dissatisfied at yr. selling that land, but only to know wether the good bargain or some other particular reason prevailed upon you to part with it.

Mr. Bird has sent by the fleet a venture of some marble tables; I hope the event will answer his expectation: as I have a value for the gentleman, and he deserves my esteem both by his Character, & polite, friendly behaviour to me. The marble slab, you ordered, goes with the tables: by the bill you will see it tis charged at 7S. a foot: 5 shillings is the common price; the 2 shillings extraordinary are owing to the double thickness.

I have had no intelligence of the Pipe of Madiera wine you commissioned by yr. Correspondent at the Madeiras to send. Mr. Crookshanks in a Letter of 2d. of Febry[6] writes as follows: Affairs in Portugal are at a stand; Carvallo having pretty nigh accomplished his ends to wit the separation from Rome and overturn of Religion: affairs of religion here, in the same fluctuating state you lelft them.

I intend to follow yr. advice of making a tour thro' Holland: I may execute this scheme some time next summer; towards the latter end of this I propose visiting the northern parts of England: I must lay asside the thoughts of going over to Ireland: the present situation of that Isleland, will only renew the memory of past wrongs. . . . Fuit Ilion, et ingens gloria Dardanidum[7]. . . . how unavailing to remember what we can not revenge! How melancholy to behold, ancient, noble, and once flourishing families now reduced to beggary!

Joseph Gallot called upon me a fortnight ago to pay his debt: as Mr. Edwards was entrusted to receive the money, and with some of Gallot's merchandise for security of payment, I ordered him to pay the money to Mr. Edwards he has not yet called upon him: his place, by his account, is worth 50 guineas a year. Mr. Crookshanks has been so obliging as to compose an Atlass of the best maps by several different Authors: the maps cost 269 lt. 3 S. the binding 48 lt. They are bound in 2 volus. as you advised.

For Public news I refer you to the newspapers & the London Magazin[es],[8] which I send by this opportunity. I pray God to grant you health and happiness: my best wishes to my friends: my duty to my Grand Mama. I am Dr. Papa

Yr. dutiful & affectionate Son

C: Carroll

P:S:

March 29th. 1761.

I received this day yr. short letter of the 3d. of Febry.[9] I must confess you have some little reason of complaint; I acknowledge my fault, am sorry, & will attone for it by writing oftener: but then you must not expect letters of this length. I hope my Grand Mama has exchanged this frail mortal life, for a glorious happy immortality. Her death, I knew too well, wou'd deeply affect my Mama: I do not blame her tears: they are the tenderest acknowledgement of humanity: not to be affected at the death of a Parent wou'd argue insensibility: But immoderate grief is unreasonable and unbecoming: to the pious, Just & good death is comfortable, sweet an easy: ti's the term the end of misery, the commencement of never ending happiness: is it not therefore unreasonably to lament their death? The decrees of God are irrevocable he has doomed all mankind to die: shou'd we not then humbly submit to his omnipotent, holy, irresistable will? These & such like arguments, I dare say, you made use of to allay my Mama's sorrows: I am overjoyed to hear she begins to get the better of her grief & that her spirits revive: company is the best preservative against melancholy: Pray remind her of our love and for our sakes at least, let her be careful of her health, than which nothing can be dearer to me.

ALS, Carroll Papers, MS 206, MdHi. Addressed by CC. Endorsed by CCA.

1. Probably *Réflexions chrétiennes sur divers sujets de morale,* a two-volume work by the Jesuit theologian and ascetic Jean Croiset (?–1738).

2. The Carrolls owned an eighteen-volume edition of Croiset's *Exercises de piété pour tous les jours de l'année . . . ,* 5th ed. (Lyon, 1745). *Cat. Lib.,* no. 1242.

3. Their brief flirtation notwithstanding, Lord Petre and Barbara Aston (1744–?) did not marry.

4. A social gathering featuring music and dancing.

5. Carrollton Manor.

6. Not found.

7. See CC to CCA and Elizabeth Carroll, Nov. 7, 1758, n. 3, above.

8. *The London Magazine; or, Gentleman's Monthly Chronologer,* published from 1732 until 1785.

9. Not found.

∴

CC to CCA

March 30th 1761.

Dr. Papa,

Capt. Kilty seeming very desirous of a Letter from me, I cou'd not but comply with his request. I have nothing material or new to add to my last. I commissioned Kilty to bring over some of yr winter Pears. They ought to be packed up in Moss the best preservative against their rotting: I gave him a nother commission for some hams: they must be newly cured else by the time they get here they will be good for little or nothing. Have you any flowers peculiar to Maryland? If there be such pray Let me have some of the seed.

By the newspapers you will find how the French have been forced to abandon the Land graviat of Hesse Cassel, after leaving garrisons in the Capital & other tenable towns: They being now reinforced by the troops from the Lower Rhine are marching forwards in order to raise the siege of Cassel & the other towns besieged or blockaded by the Allies.[1] By the last Holland mail we have an account of an advantage gained by the French over the Hereditary Prince,[2] who ti's reported has had 2600 men taken prisoners with the loss of 13 pieces of cannon, the number of the killed is inconsiderable: we are in hourly expectation of a general engagement between the two main armies: the event will determin the fate of the landgraviat, & perhaps if uncessful to the French may bring on a peace.

You will find amongst my letters by Capt. Hanson[3] one from Mr. Rozalini:

Mr. Perkins sent it to me; on opening it I soon discovered the mistake, to prevent which for the future Mr. Rozalini had better direct to you at Annapolis. Pray remember me to the Croxalls, Henry Carroll, & my other friends. I am Dr. Papa

Yr affectionate & dutiful Son

Ch: Carroll.

P:S:

April 2d.

Messieurs Corbey and Pointz present their compliments to you: I am not certain wether this letter will go by Kilty or no, as I understand he has already fallen down the river. No accounts from Germany later than the 28th of March: prayers have been said for my Grand Mama. Mr. Bladen has sent me this day an invitation to dine with him next tuesday 7th of April. . . . I have not seen him since my arrival in London: he dines very late a little before 4 o'clock I think his servant told me. My objection to an acquaintance with Mr. Bladen proceeds only from what you mentioned to me: I imagin they play high to which I am very averse: as I have no great inclination for cards & am unluckly. Mr. Plater goes with this fleet: we were acquainted, and had I esteemed the company he kept [as?] much I do him, our acquaintance had been greater. I am Dr. Papa

Yr. affectionate Son

C: Carroll.

All the books you sent me are come safe: I thank you for the abridgment of the acts of Assembly in Maryland.

ALS, Carroll Papers, MS 206, MdHi. Addressed by CC to CCA in Annapolis "p favour Capt. Kilty." Endorsed by CCA.

1. The town of Hesse, held by the French, was invested by forces allied with Frederick the Great during the winter of 1761, but by the end of March the French had successfully reestablished their control. The landgrave, Frederick II, a Catholic convert, was suspected of having French sympathies. Reginald Savory, *His Britannic Majesty's Army in Germany during the Seven Years War* (Oxford, 1966), 290, 433–434.

2. Karl Wilhelm Ferdinand of Brunswick (1735–1806).

3. Capt. Halbert Hanson's ship, the *Baltimore,* of 170 tons, arrived in Annapolis on June 25, 1761. Annapolis Port of Entry Record Books, I.

CC to Elizabeth Carroll

March 31st. 1761.

Dr. Mama,

This is an answer to your last letter of the 10th. of Sepb. 1760. I was greatly disappointed at Mr. Browne's not arriving with the fleet & sorry to learn his stay was occasioned by sickness: Pray remember me to his fellow traveler Mr. Buchanan. Be not uneasy about my health: I enjoy it pretty well: frequent colds, sometimes attended with a diziness & swimming of the head are my only ailment: These I attribute to the dampniss of the air. I am much obliged to Messieurs Browne Rozier, Buchanan & others for their character and opinion of me: I am too sensible it ti's owing more to their good nature & friendship, than to any rea[l me]rit of mine. I wou'd not have you believe all that is reported: few are sincere enough to speak their thoughts especially if disagreeable to those they value and regard: you will be greatly disappointed at my arrival in Maryland to see how undeserving I am of such encomiums: tho' parental love & prejudice may even then conceal a number of faults: what I say is not dictated by an affected modesty, worse than pride; ti's the sentiment of my mind: I detest dissumulation and dissemblers.

If ever any expression slighting or disrespectful of the ladies escaped my pen, I humbly crave their pardon; my heart, I am sure, was innocent and not of intelligence with my hand. No one can be a greater admirer of the fair sex than I am. What happiness on earth without the Ladies? They pollish, correct and soften our manners: in their company the Englishman, such is the force of beauty and of wit, slights his tobacco pipe and coffee house politics, reduced to defend his own heart he forgets his bloody speculative battles, trade, Liberty and property are all forgot: to enjoy the sweets of women's conversation the airy, gallant frenchman, bids adue to war and glory: even the unmannerly freeborn Dutchman glories in being their slave, and for once endeavours to please and be polite. What can resist the wiles the winning arts of women? For my own part I can't conceive how my heart remains still unsubdued. No Lady at least can boast an entire conquest: I can give no other reason for this Phoenomenon, but that no one ever thought it worth her while: But shou'd some fair witty maid captivate my heart I might often attemp[t to] shake off my fetters, for even now I am frighted at the clincking of matrimonial chains; those are never to be broke. . . .

My expressions of love and tenderness for you when a boy were the language of native simplicity: the dictates of a heart that cou'd not then, nor will now dissemble its real sentiments: these are unalterably the same: my love, my affection, my tender concern for my Parents are not diminished by length of time and place: they are only strengthened and confirmed by reason which teaches me to acknowledge and be grateful for the greatest obligations from the best of Parents.

Pray return my kind compliments to Mr. Tasker; I remember his daughter,[1] the present he gave me, but not the promise of a ball at my return to Annapolis. The umbrello, I brought with me from Paris, I made a present of to a Lady some months before the receipt of yours. I wish you had let me known sooner that you wanted one: I shall embrace the first opportunity that presents itself, to get another from Paris: Mr. Lawson's death gave me a real concern: his loss is great to his widow and family I pray my best wishes to them: Young Mr. Lawson was, when I saw him last in good health and spirits. I desire to be tenderly remembered to my Cousin Rachael Darnall: I wait with impatience the long promised favour of a Letter from her: I am sorry to have been thus long deprived of this satisfaction, but particularly to hear her delay has been occasioned by illness: I wish her an entire recovery of her health and all possible happiness. I am Dr. Mama

Your most du[ti]ful & loving Son
Ch: Carroll.

ALS, Carroll-McTavish Papers, MS 220, MdHi. Addressed by CC. Endorsed by CCA: "1761 March 31 My Sons Letter To his Mama."

1. Benjamin Tasker, Sr., and his wife, Anne Bladen Tasker, had four daughters: Anne (1723–1817), Rebecca (1724–1822), Elizabeth (1726–1789), and Frances (1738?–1787). CC is probably referring to Frances. *Bio. Dic. Md. Legis.*, II, 799.

CCA to CC

April 16th 1761

Dr Charley

This is in answer to yrs of Sept: 16th 1760 & Janry 1st 1761 but as our Provincial Court is sitting as I am hindred by Company & Business, I must be short. I shd: be glad to know by name those with whome you are most intimate & with whom you chiefly Converse. All sorts of Company must be kept occasionally & in particular genteel Company, how ever insipid or disagreeable, a knowledge of mankind is not otherwise to be attained. You must not forget the Money due from Maccarty & Gallot, it may be got by degrees. Pray my Compts to Mr: Jeneson & all other friends as if particularly named. I hope you have long since reced the Pipe of Wine I ordered you. I see by yrs of the 1st of Janry that you reced wt: I sent you by Capt: Henrick. As I have often given you reasons to shew Maryland to be no desirable Residence for a Rom: Cath:, & as you have as often shewn it to be as much so as most others, you are quite at liberty to fix where you please. If a country life shd: be yr: taste you may be happy here with yr: Books & the amusements wch Farming &c afford.

I am sorry to hear you think you have made little or no advance in the Law, I know it is not for want of Capacity, if instruction is wanting it is yr: own fault, for I always understood there are always men in all the Inns of Court capable & willing to instruct Young Men how to pursue the Study of the Law, to solve their doubts & clear up their difficulties for a moderate yearly Stipend: Can yr: Money be better laid out than in Employing such a one? The thing is to make a good choice. Besides in the Society there are Exercises wch I think are called Mootings wch must be great helps to the Students, but above all, it's hard if by a prudent affable & engaging Behaviour you do not so far conciliate the Esteem & friendship of some men sufficiently skilled in the Law, as to induce them readily to help & instruct you. To study as you say as a Clerk [under] some Eminent Lawyer may be an Eligible way to lead a [man mo]re directly into the practick part of the Law, [but] I do not [. . . .][1] [as you have been in a Singular Course of Studies is neither necessary or becoming. If I am not mistaken you are too stiff & reserved. In essential things] a man can hardly be too reserved, but a prudent reserve shd: be always hid by a well dissembled shew of Candor, affability, Openness & unreserve, would you not wish that all men would act with Candor affability openness & unreserve towards you? How can you expect it, if you do not endeavour to appear to behave so to all men? To suit yr: self to the world, in non Essentials you must give up yr: Opinion, Sacrafice yr: time ease & inclinations, this is a sure way to be loved, esteemed & served. I mention yr: Reserve because I find you are so even to me, to whom nothing that you know or think shd: be a secret, but yr: sins; I do not mention this without a good foundation, to wt: else can I impute yr: not answering particularly my letters in my own hand writing of July 14th & Octo: 13th 1760 to the last without assigning any reason for yr: Silence. Is it enough to say you wish the Gent: I recommended to you Success & that you can only wish & hope? Ought you not to have informed me, why you could not do more? I have so good an opinion of yr: Judgment & discretion as to believe you can well account for wt: you say or do, or do not do: But then I think you shd: give me as circumstantial an account as possible of wt: I desire to know & wt: I recommend to you. I desire'd you would learn Surveying & Book keeping, I have mentioned in the Course of my letters I think some other things wch I think you take no notice of. Pray be punctual in answering wt: ever I write to you: I will not recommend to you to do wt: you cannot do, or wt: I do not think Essential that you shd: do.

When you take in the London Evening posts & Magazines put them up carefully & regularly that Mr: perkins may have them at the shortest warning. Since the sailing of the Fleet I have only had the London Evening Posts from Sept: 23d to Novr: 25th those from April to Septr: are missing. The pamphlet you sent me Vizt: Considerations on the German War gave me & many others much pleasure. Do not yr: politicians furnish Annually above one pamphlet worth reading?

I love you entirely & my present lonesome condition added to that love might (if any thing could) incline me to call you home, but no Consideration althô there are many pressing ones can influence me to call you from the Study of the Law:

Hence judge how necessary I think the knowledge of it is to you, & let me not suffer so cruel an Absence without answering the end for wch alone I submit to it.

Mrs Darnall yr Mothers Neice is with me & keeps my House & presents her Love & Service to you. Mr. Richd: Croxall & Capt: Carroll desired their Compts the 1st time I wrote to you. God grant you Health may he bestow his Choicest B[less]ings & Graces on you may you always answer those Graces. These are the [Constant] wishes & Prayers of Dr Charley

[Yr: Mo:] Afft: Father
[Cha: Carroll] [2]

LS, Carroll-McTavish Papers, MS 220, MdHi. Addressed by CCA. Margins damaged. Another LS copy, also with margins damaged and marked "Triplicate" by CCA, is located in the Taylor Family Papers, No. 9965, ViU. Missing text has been supplied from that copy.

    1. Approximately three lines are missing in both manuscripts.

    2. Signature obliterated.

. . .
.

CCA to CC

Aprill 17: 1761

Dr Charley,

Mr Danll: Dulany[1] our late Commissary Generall & Present Secretary talks of g[oin]g some time in June to England for the Recovery of his Health. Upon his Arivall I would have you visit him & invite him to Sup or dine wth you, if he Repays yr Visit Continue to treat him Politely & with a Seeming Openness, it may hereafter be of Service to you. He is a Man of Great Parts, of Generall knowledge indisputably the best Lawer on this Continent, a very entertaining Companion when he Pleases, But wth this weakness that his Veracity is Questioned, He is very Vain Proud & designing & so much a Politician as not to be over Scrupulous in the Measures he takes to answer his Ends. From this Sketch you will know how to behave towards him & I give you these Hints now, Because should I write by him I shall say nothing that I need seal up. I am Dr Charly

Yrs &c
C: C:

Duplicate sent by Mr Jo: Semples ship to Glasgow — Triplicate made out —

ALS, Carroll Papers, MS 206, MdHi. Endorsed by CCA: "1761 Aprill 17 Copys To my Son."

    1. Daniel Dulany, Jr. (1722–1797), the eldest son of Daniel Dulany, Sr., an Irish Protestant who emigrated to Maryland as an indentured servant in 1703 and made himself one of

the province's wealthiest and most powerful men, and Rebecca Smith. Born in Annapolis, Daniel, Jr., lived there until 1776. He was educated at Eton and Clare College, Cambridge, and called to the bar from the Middle Temple in 1746, an unusual distinction for an American. In addition to practicing law, a profession he no longer actively pursued after 1763, the junior Dulany was a planter and a stockholder, with his brother Walter, in the Baltimore Company ironworks. He began his provincial political career in the lower house of the Maryland assembly where he represented Frederick Co. (1751–1754) and Annapolis (1756–1757). Following his father's death in 1753, Dulany began a concerted drive to make himself a principal player in Maryland. Appointed commissary general jointly with his father-in-law, Benjamin Tasker, Sr., in 1754, he resigned the post in 1756 but held it again 1759–1761. In 1757 he gained a seat in the upper house and on the Council and continued in both until 1776. Dulany's success in securing the office of deputy secretary of Maryland in 1761 gave him almost as much power as the colony's chief executive and allowed him to consolidate his family's position to a degree that considerably alarmed Gov. Horatio Sharpe. A strong supporter of the proprietary government, Dulany defended actions taken by Sharpe's successor, Gov. Robert Eden, in a series of articles that appeared in the local press under the pseudonym "Antilon" in 1773. The unexpected response these essays inspired from CC, by then known as Charles Carroll of Carrollton (CCC) but writing as "First Citizen," surprised Dulany and placed Carroll at the center of the political stage. Although Dulany argued publicly against the Stamp Act in 1765, he nevertheless vigorously opposed extra-legal protests, and when the American Revolution abolished his posts along with the rest of Maryland's proprietary government, he retired to the Dulanys' Baltimore Co. estate, Hunting Ridge, and sat out the war as a neutral. When Hunting Ridge, the ownership of which he had transferred to his loyalist son Daniel III prior to 1775, was confiscated and sold as British property, Daniel Dulany, Jr., moved to Baltimore where he lived for the rest of his life. Besides Daniel III, Dulany and his wife, Rebecca Tasker, whom he married in 1747, had another son, Benjamin Tasker Dulany, and a daughter, Ann. The definitive study of the Dulany family remains Land's *Dulanys of Maryland.* For a complete list of Daniel Dulany, Jr.'s offices and tenures, see *Bio. Dic. Md. Legis.,* I, 287.

CC to CCA

May 15th. 1761.

Dr. Papa,

You are indebted to Mr. Macnamara for this letter: who informed me of an opportunity of writing by Capt. Creamer.[1] Since my last letters by the fleet little or nothing has occurred worth yr. notice: Joseph Gallot has in deed prooved himself honester than I thought him: he has paid me the money he owed you: I wish Maccarty may have as much honour as Gallot has honesty: My Lord Arundel is expected over every day: his Lordship has been so obliging as to charge himself with my Atlass and the royal Almenack for 61.

Before this comes to hand you will, I hope, have had the pleasure of seeing

Mr. Plater: he lived in the temple & pretty near me: we were acquainted tho' little together: tho' I valued & esteemed Mr. Plater I disliked his company: sed digito compesce labellum.[2] My Cousin Antony Carroll was lately in town: he is now at Lincoln till further orders that place is to be his sejour.

A life so uniform so retired as mine Can afford nothing interesting: scarce subject for chit chat. The books I read are so dry that they seem to have communicated their schèresse[3] even to the reader. The premises, the habendum tenendum of a deed, writts of Attorney, fines sur cognisance &c are certainly very entertaining: The barbarous language most our Law books are wrote in, is in my opinion a great disadvantage to the Laws: terms of art are necessary to every science: but why cannot good sense & knowledge be delivered in good language: Law must be wrote in an unintelligible Jargon: & a Judge condemned to ware a full-bottomed wig: affectation of wisdom implies the want of it.

Our new Monarch[4] seems to please all parties: There have indeed been some complaints of his countenancing the Scots: My Lord Bute's favour may create Jealousies at Court:[5] Courtiers will grumble: if he is prudent, if modest in prosperity, if he abuses not the confidence of his Sovereign these heartburnings will be confined to the court & to the dependents of Courtiers.

Ti's not as yet known when the coronation is to be: single front seats, I am told, will let for 12 guineas each. Some friends have advised me to throw away so much money to gratify my curiousity: but you are the best adviser what is yr. advice? Pray let me know it by the 1st. oppertunity: That I may act accordingly.

I propose to taking a Jant for 3 or 4 weeks time as soon as next Hilary term is ended: Mr. Bird's son[6] will favour me with his company: Our plan is not yet settled. In all probability we shall go into the northern counties & return home thro' the eastern ones: but this is only guess work.

I hope my Mama enjoys her health and has recovered her spirits: I long to see you both, & to see Maryland I have more reasons than one for returning home: . . . .

I sincerely wish you health & happiness: I am Dr. Papa

Yr. dutiful & affectionate Son

Ch: Carroll.

P:S:

No news from Bellsile:[7] I wrote you yesterday a letter[8] from Mr. Perkins house: ti's the substance of this: he told Capt. Creamer was to set off that very evening.

ALS, Carroll Papers, MS 206, MdHi. Addressed by CC. Postmarked New York and marked "2/0" and "Sh 4, 16" in an unknown hand. Endorsed by CCA.

1. Matthew Craymer, master of the *Dolphin*, a 230-ton French prize owned by John Stewart and Duncan Campbell, and of the *Thetis*, a 200-ton French prize owned by John Stewart, was active in the Chesapeake trade between 1759 and 1763. Annapolis Port of Entry Record Books, I, II.

2. Loosely, "but mum's the word." Juvenal *Satires* 1.160.

3. "Sécheresse" — "dryness."

4. George III (1738–1820) succeeded to the British throne on Oct. 25, 1760, upon the death of his grandfather, and ruled until 1820.

5. Two days after his ascension to the throne, George III appointed John Stuart, third earl of Bute (1713–1792), to the Privy Council and on Nov. 15, 1760, made him groom of the stole and first gentleman of the bedchamber. The constant companion and confidant of the future monarch throughout the 1750s, Bute became by virtue of these positions the conduit for communicating with the king. Such power made it impossible for him to serve without a public office, and on Mar. 25, 1761, he became secretary of state for the northern department. Bute's relationship with the king and his Scottish nationality made him enormously unpopular both at court and with the general public. In 1762 he took the position of first lord of the treasury, selecting George Grenville as his successor as secretary of state, but he retired from office in February 1763, upon the conclusion of peace with France. Despite a deteriorating relationship with Grenville, Bute remained close to the king until 1765, when, at Grenville's insistence, he lost his remaining influence. A member of the House of Lords since 1737, Bute attended sporadically until 1780, when he permanently withdrew from public life.

6. Christopher Chapman Bird (1737–1810).

7. Belle-Isle or Belle-Île-en-Mer was strategically located in the Bay of Biscay. Planning for the island's seizure began in the fall of 1760, and military operations commenced in April 1761. The French surrendered on June 7. Gipson, *Culmination*, 178–185.

8. CC to CCA, May 14, 1761, Carroll Papers, MS 206.

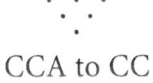

CCA to CC

May 21[st 1]761

[Dr Char]ley

I wrote to you the 16th past, a Copy whereof you will receive with this. I have since the pleasure & Satisfaction of yrs of the 13th of Febry 1761 — You acted very prudently in yr: Application to Mr: Calvert; but I am surprized he shd: tell you that the Rom: Caths: made not the least opposition to the Bill here, while depending — I cannot suppose a man of his family & station in Life would stoop to advance a falsity, I must then conclude he has been imposed on, or at least that he has not had so plain & faithfull an Acct of the Transactions Relating to the Act of Assembly double Taxing us, as I think he ought to have had from hence & therefore pray present my Compts: to him, read to him wt: I have wrote & further tell him that whoever informed him that the Rom: Caths: made not the least opposition to the Bill while depending here, told him a most notorious Lye, For the Ro: Caths: petitioned the Upper House 1st & then the Govr: agst: the Bill; Their petitions were long, circumstantial & very remarkable, that especially to the Govr: for it is from that petition, the Upper House was furnished with the remarkable passages inserted in their Message to the Lower House in the Session of Assembly begun the 28th of March 1758 wch Message, that is, the part of it wch relates to the Ro: Caths: Mr: Calvert will find in the Pages 65, 66, & 67 of the printed Proceedings.[1] I do not care to mortify Mr. Calvert who can urge nothing to excuse his Familys ingratitude to the Ro: Caths: & therefore I drop this Subject —

If I forget not in a former Letter I advised you to furnish yr: self with a Compleat Collection of Law Books among them you must have the Statutes at large, a Curious Collection of wch I am informed has been Published since I left England.[2] It was an instance of yr: Duty to desire my advice whether you shd. buy them, & in that very agreeable to me, but in order that on such occasions you may not lose time by waiting my Answers, buy any Books you may like or think deserving a place in a Gents: Collection or Library, yr: Money will be well laid out if you [are] carefull of them when bought for they are the best & most agreeable Pabulum Animæ.[3]

Pray give my Service to Csn: Macnemara & tell him his Sons are well,[4] & that I would have wrote him on the Subject he desired, had there been ground given — Upon Receipt of yrs wch I [am] now answering I conclude[d Capt: Mc]Gachen was intrusted with the pamphlets &c you mention, I [spoke] to him & he told me they were sent from his Ship in Patowmack by a Sloop bound to Annapolis & Patapsco, in short they are lost; let this instruct you never to send anything without mentioning in yr: letter wt: you have sent & by whom, an immediate enquiry can then be made for it & a loss prevented.

You say this is wrote in haste the Ship it goes by being to Sail in 2 or 3 days, it seems it was so, for you do not conclude or sign it. Dr: Charley never write to me in haste, unless you are surprized with notice of a Vessells Sailing when you happen to be in the City, & then I will not only excuse Brevity but be obliged to you for letting me know you are well by two or three lines. I have repeated it to you to minute down thoughts as they occur that you may always have a letter or at least the Subject of a letter ready for me, & I again beg you again in this to observe what I recommend[.]

In a Postscript to my last letter I think I informed you that I had hopes I shd: secure the £1000 Sterg: I have been obliged to pay as Security for that ungratefull H: Darnall who you know I was endeavouring to serve,[5] his Lands by a Marriage Settlemt: are entailed on his Issue Male & their Male Issue, he has two Sons marry'd, neither of them without the Death of their Wifes have a prospect of Issue Male.[6] The Father & Eldest Son have joined in a Deed for my Security to cut of[f] the Entail, considering the little Chance the youngest Son has to inherit & to transmit the inheritance to his Heirs I doubted not he would readily Convey also to me, especially as his Uncle Jo: Darnall[7] is not only jointly bound with me for his Father, but is beside bound to me with & for his Father for £213.0.0 wch must ruin him unless the Money can be raised out of the Lands. H: Darnalls Lands are worth £2000. We have a Collateral Security of about £350. We can hold the Lands during the Lives of the Father & Eldest Son at least, by wch we can so destroy them as to make the 2d sons Chance of the Reversion not worth any thing. We have beside the Reversion in Fee for want of Issue Male of the two Brors. Under these Circumstances we offer the Lands to the 2d son whose Intert: it is to purchase at a Rate wch will idemnify us, & who because it is his Intert: will I think purchase, & who I think would do nothing to save his Uncle from Ruin & me from sustaining so great a loss occasioned by his Fathers Villany if he was not prompted by his Intert: to do it—

I observe wt. you say about the Young Gents. not being so sensible of his Loss as he should be, it indicates a very unfeeling Disposition or a bad Heart, but such instances are too frequent. This I know is far from yr: Case, & I wish this may find you not only resigned but in some measure composed under our great M[isfortu]ne of the loss of yr: Dr Mama: you have not such images before you [as] constantly to bring & keep her in yr thoughts: I have, & yet I wo[ul]d not have it otherways for there is a sort of a dolefull pleasure & Satisfaction in continually thinking of one I loved so tenderly especially as my thoughts are accompany'd with the comfortable & Animating hope of enjoying her in a happy Endless Eternity. You are left the Pledge of our Love & friendship, in you my whole Satisfaction is centred, you are the Object of all my Cares & here it occurs to me to acquaint you that I have a Will[8] executed constantly by me, by wch everything I have (Trifles excepted) is yours, I mention this least you shd: have a moments uneasiness on that Acct, you shall never feel any that can be prevented by the constant Care & attention of Dr Charley

Yr: Mo: Afft: Father
Cha: Carroll

LS, Carroll-McTavish Papers, MS 220, MdHi. Addressed and marked "Copy" by CCA. Margins damaged. Filed with a second LS copy, also addressed by CCA and with margins damaged.

1. In his "List of Papers Sent to England in Defense of the Roman Catholic's Of Maryland," CCA mentioned "The Petition of the Roman Catholics against the said Bill to the Upper House" and "The Petition of the Roman Catholics to the Governor against the Said Bill," both dated 1756 (Spec. Colls. Div., DGU). For the message from the upper house that was drawn from the petition to the governor, see *Arch. of Md.*, LV, 485, 507–512, and *Votes and Proceedings of the Lower House of Assembly of the Province of Maryland*, Mar. sess., 1758 [Annapolis, 1758], 29, 65–67.

2. Possibly *The Statutes at Large from Magna Carta to 30th Geo. II*, comp. John Cay (1758).

3. "Food for the mind."

4. Michael or Micky (?–liv. 1781) and Tommy Macnemara (?–liv. 1771). Their mother's name is unknown; at this time Michael Macnemara was evidently a widower. Michael Macnemara to CCA, Feb. 4, 1761, Carroll-McTavish Papers. See Appendix I, Chart B.

5. In the spring of 1761, an audit of loan office accounts by a joint committee of the Maryland assembly discovered that Henry Darnall III had embezzled sixteen hundred pounds

sterling from the Patuxent naval office revenues for which he was responsible. Further investigation revised the amount of the default upward to nearly two thousand pounds sterling. As Darnall's securities, CCA and John Darnall were required to forfeit the one thousand pounds sterling bond that they had posted in 1755 to enable their kinsman to assume the office. *Arch. of Md.*, LVI, lv–lviii.

6. Of Henry Darnall III's two married sons, Henry Darnall IV was estranged both from his wife, Rachel Brooke Darnall, and from their only child, Molly, and Robert Darnall had no children by either his first wife, Sarah Muir, or his second, Sarah Rider. The third son, John Darnall (c. 1730–1819), was a bachelor. Bowie, *Prince George's*, 242; Marion B. Wood et al., comps., *The Darnall, Darnell Family, Including Darneal, Darneille, Darnielle, Darnold, Dernall, Durnall, Durnell, and Names Variously Spelled with Allied Families* (n.p., n.d.), I, 20. See also Appendix I, Chart F.

7. John Darnall (1708–1768). See Appendix I, Chart F.

8. Not found.

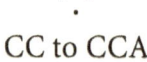

CC to CCA

June 10th. 1761.

Dr Papa,

I received yesterday the afflicting news of my dear Mama's death. Yr. Letter, if any thing cou'd, wou'd have given some comfort: but what comfort can there be for so great a loss. I loved my Mama most tenderly: how strong how cogent were the motives of my love! How affectionate, how tender, how loving a mother was she to me! What fond delusive hopes have I entertained of seeing her again! I was too credulous: all my imaginary Joys are vanished in an instant: they are succeeded by the bitter cruel thought of never seeing more my loved lost Mother: the greatest blessing I wished for in this life was to see to enjoy my Parents after so long a separation to comfort to support them in an advanced age: one is for ever snatched from me! May God almighty Dr. Papa preserve yr. health & grant you a long life: were you to leave me too, oh then I shou'd be compleatly miserable indeed: death wou'd then be the only comforter of a sad, distressed, unhappy son. Pray Let not yr. loss affect you too deeply: it may impair yr. health: remember you are now my only consolation in this world.

You do not mention in yr. letter my Mama's speaking of me in her last sickness: I must certainly often have been the object of her thoughts & subject of her conversation: did she not frequently wish to see me? Did she not so much as say remember me to my dr. absent son? How little does he now think of his dying mother! What grief what affliction will my death give him! Oh had I seen her in her last moments to take a last farewell that had been some sad relief: even this was denied me. But I must no longer dwell upon this melancholy subject: yet tho' I leave off writing I can not leave off thinking of her: now all the little occurrences [o]f my infancy, those happy days spent at Elk-ridge in her sweet company, our lonely retirement and mutual fondness pass in remembrance before me. I shall never see such days again. I wish you wou'd permit me to return to Maryland in the next fleet. I am only doing here what I cou'd do as well at home. I am persuaded I can apply as closely to the Law in yr. house as in the temple: what more distractions shall I meet with in Annapolis than in London? There are certainly more amuse-ments more avocations here: but I am not so fond of these amusements as many young men are: I do not like much company: I love to live retired: 12 or 13th. years spent in application has Given me a relish for retirement and study. Mr. Maire,[1] Mr. Hutton are even married yet they carry on a great deal of business. Besides yr. company & instructions wou'd be more serviceable to me than all the Law & Lawers put together. I am utterly unacquainted with business you might form me to it. I may now and then have a Law suit to maintain or carry on: tho' ever so great a Lawer myself I must be at the mercy of another. The intelligence & proper management of my own affairs is of an indispensible & absolute necessity & not to be acquired with out help, time, & experience: If I shou'd Lose you too, which God forbid, who is there to help me? What experience have I? none: time? That depends on God. Consider how short & uncertain life is: alive to day & dead to morrow: we have before us a most afflicting instance of its precariousness: I wish these reasons may prevail upon you to send for me over: I ardently long to be with you. Pray write to me by every oppertunity: you cannot conceive what pleasure it gives me to hear from you. I am Dr. Papa

Yr. most dutiful & affectionate Son
C[h:] Carroll.

P:S:

This goes by Mr. Athawes[2] a young gentleman of my acquaintance whom I beg you will treat with civility. Pray Let me know my Mama's age & my own.

ALS, Carroll Papers, MS 206, MdHi. Addressed by CC. Endorsed by CCA.

1. A son of Thomas Maire of Lartington, Yorkshire, John Maire (1703–1771) was admitted to Gray's Inn in 1727. He subsequently became a conveyancer, that is, one involved in titles and their transference. Although a Roman Catholic, Maire could undertake such work be-cause it did not require being called to the bar. Joseph Foster, ed., *Register of Admissions to Gray's Inn, 1521–1889* . . . , Collectanea Genealogica, II, no. 1 (London, 1889), 368.

2. Probably Samuel Athawes, the son of Edward Athawes, a London merchant active in the Virginia tobacco trade. Price, *Johnson's Letterbook*, xii; Rutland, *Mason*, I, xxxi.

CCA to CC

[22d. June 1761]

Dr Charley

I wrote to you the 21st past a Duplicate & Triplicate of wch has been sent you. I saw Capt: Hendrick lately by him I have the great pleasure to hear that you looked hearty & well. This goes in the Wilson[1] with Mr: Dulany, to whom I doubt not you will shew all the Civilities in yr: power. Give my Love & Service to Csn: Macnemara if he is still in London. I inclosed one to him in my last to you & sent him a letter from his Son wch I hope has not miscarry'd, especially that wch covered a letter from his Son. Both his Children are well. I would write to him but have nothing material to communicate to him, & indeed I know not whether he is not in his way home in the Fleet. The last Acct I have of Hen: Darnall is that he went to Hampton in Virginia to take his passage in a Vessell Bound to the West Indies, but either thrô impatience or a want of Resolution, he returned home, & is since gone to Virginia to take his passage for England, he there intends as it's said to apply to Lady Petres[2] & others for a support to pass the Remainder of his days in Retirement in Flanders. Unless he has sunk very large Sums of Money in some way wch no one here can guess at, he stands in no need of any Assistance, he certainly deserves none, but Charity forbids us to expose him, my own security may oblige me to it, if I am not secured by his Lands & Negroes made over to me; the Negroes were made over to Lady Petres in Trust & to cheat me & to provide for his Daughters,[3] he intends to endeavour to prevail on Lady Petres to Convey them to his Daughters: you may heare more of this according as my Security may turn out here.

You will hardly believe we have Horses in Maryland that sell for 150 Guineas or more Coll: Tasker's stud was lately sold, 1 Horse 4 year old sold for 150 Guineas, A Mare 4 year old for £150 Ster: A two year old Colt for £187.0.0 Ster a Yearling Filly for £81 Ster. A Mare 15 years old with a Colt dropt this Spring for £101.0.0 Ster[.] These are thorough Bred Horses from Horses imported by Coll: Tasker from England.[4] I have some not entirely of the whole Blood Vizt: 4 Mares, 1 Horse 8 years old & a Colt 2 year old wch promises to make a fine Horse & wch I destine for you. I have [. . .] for 40 guin[ea]s, I hope in a few ye[ars] to be well stocke[d] at all my plantations.

You remember I got the Genealogy of our Family Translated from the Irish when I was at Paris,[5] But I know not from wch of the Branches our Family is descended, but I shd: think from the family of Danl: of Adamstown, but by the inclosed Print[6] you will see yr: Grand father stiles himself 2d Son of Danl: Carroll of Litter lorna. His Elder Bror: was Antony,[7] yr: Csn: Antonys Grand father, who I suppose was born about the Year 1630. His Son Michael[8] was living a few years past & may be still living & from him by the means of yr: Csn: Anto: or from others you may trace our Branch of the family Back to 1500 or higher if you can, & in as Distinct a manner as you can, & I desire you will do it. Beside the family of Adamstown, I find the family's of Birr, Kilcomin, Killmean or Kilmeanesm, Britstown, Mecyremmch, Bullagh, Curra Chaverine, Culoge, Chran O Gianagh, Bealash, Tullagh, Chran Eaghaill, Nenagh, Cullin, Newtown, Cuill No Vinnoge, Cuill no Cræ, Cuill No Girrour, Boss Curmah, Ballynoclog, Seanra, Youghall, Liniogn, Lisanma, Ely O Carroll &c[.] [9] I find by History as well as by the Genealogy, that the Country of Ely O Carroll & Dirgaill which comprehends most of the Kings & Queens County's were the Territories of the O Carrolls & that they were Princes thereof: you may as things are now Circumstanced & considering the low Estate to wch all the Branches of our family are Reduced by the struggles the Antient Irish maintained for the support of their Religion, Rights & Properties & wch Reced their finishing stroke at the Revolution, think my Enquiery an Idle one, but I do not think so. If I am not right the folly may be excused by its being a General one, & I hope for your own & my sake you will gratify me in making as carefull an Enquiery as possible & giving me wt: lights you can on the Subject. As soon as there is a peace I will send you the Genealogy in Irish & English & I desire you will then get our family in particular traced to its Origin—

In my last I acquainted you that I always kept a Will by me, the Circumstance of yr: Dr Mothers Death induced me to make a new one, of wch you have here with a Copy.[10] If it is not expressed as clearly as it shd: be according to my meaning, I desire you will advise me wherein you may think it proper to make any alteration. [. . . .] [11] This accompany[s] Mr: Brown who has [enjoyed?] so poor a State of health here, that he has not much rea[son] to be pleased with Maryland. I hope his Native Air wi[ll] agree much better with him[.] I am My Dr Charley

Yr: Mo: Afft: Father.
Cha: Carroll

PS [12]

July 14th

Mr Browne is still here, His Health will not yet Permit to goe to Sea.

LS, Outerbridge Horsey Collection of Lee, Horsey, and Carroll Family Papers, MS 1974, MdHi. Addressed by CCA. Endorsed by CC: "1761 22d. June." Margins damaged.

1. The *Wilson* was captained by William Johnson. Land, *Dulanys of Maryland,* 237.

2. Catherine Walmesley Petre Stourton (1697–1785). Widowed by Robert, 7th Baron Petre, in 1712/3, after a year of marriage and the birth of a son, Lady Petre, the grandmother of CC's St. Omers classmate, Robert Edward Petre, the 9th baron, did not remarry until 1733. Although her second husband, Charles Stourton, became the 15th Baron Stourton during the 1740s, she apparently continued to be known as Lady Petre and evidently functioned as a sort of grande dame in the English Catholic community. As the sole heir of her brother, Francis Walmesley, she was an extremely wealthy woman. (G.E.C. [George

Edward Cokayne], *The Complete Peerage of England, Scotland, Ireland, Great Britain, and the United Kingdom, Extant, Extinct, or Dormant,* ed. Vicary Gibbs et al. [London, 1910–1959], X, 507–510, XII, 310–313.) In appealing to Lady Petre, Henry Darnall III was following in the footsteps of his father: in 1740, in an attempt to evade his creditors, Henry Darnall II assigned eight slaves to "the right Honourable Catherine Lady Petre" and her husband. Prince George's Co. Land Records, Liber Y, 1739–1743, fol. 212, MdAA.

3. Mary Darnall, Katherine Darnall (?–1807), and Ann Darnall (?–1788). See Appendix I, Chart F.

4. Benjamin Tasker, Sr., was a leading importer of English thoroughbred stock and one of provincial Maryland's foremost horse breeders and racing enthusiasts.

5. This small manuscript volume, written in Gaelic with an English translation on the facing pages, traces the origins of the O'Carrolls back to Adam. "Genealogy of O Carroll," Carroll-O'Carroll Genealogies, MS 1998, MdHi.

6. Not found.

7. For Anthony Carroll of Lisheenboy (by 1660–1724), see Appendix I, Charts A and B.

8. For Michael Carroll of Lisheenboy (?–by 1762), see Appendix I, Chart B.

9. CCA appears to have culled these Irish place-names from the "Genealogy of O Carroll," Carroll-O'Carroll Genealogies.

10. Not found. According to a codicil CCA made in 1771, he drew a will on June 15, 1761. Carroll Papers, MS 206.

11. An entire line missing.

12. Postscript in CCA's hand.

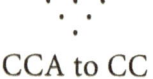

CCA to CC

[July 10, 1761][1]

[Dr Charley,]

I acknowledge the Receipt of yrs of Mar: 28th 1761 with a Pos[ts]cript of the 29th. Mar: 30th with a Post. S. of April 2d & yrs to yr: Mama of Mar: 31st. I proceed to answer the two to me. Is it not some Satisfaction to you to see by the Certificate I sent you that yr Grandfather was entered of the Temple, as the Law [is a] Liberal profession being entred of the Temple is a proof of Gentility & may not yr: Grandson be as well pleased to see that you was of the Temple as you are to know that yr. Grandfather belonged to that Society, the Expence you mention of Entry & Commons is but a trifle & you need only pay yr: Commons & not attend them, shd: the attendance of them expose you either to bad or Disagreeable Company[.] If to save money you decline being entred of the Temple do not mind the Expence, if you must in Consequence of yr: being entred of the Temple keep bad or disagreeable Company decline it. Is it not possible by a gratuity properly placed or by some other expedient, to be called to the Bar without taking the Oaths? Have there not been instances of this sort? Enquire carefully—

I have reced Croisets Moral Reflections, I shall expect his Exercises de Pietate & Humes History when compleat. You take no notice of the Lettres Edifiantes nor of the large French Almanack I wrote for, & for wch I desired you would apply to Mr: Crookshanks (to whom present my sincerest Respects). Send me annually Millans or the Gentns Register.[2] Inclosed you have a List of my Eng: Books.[3] Mr Meighan[4] p[ro]mised to send me O Connors Transl[a]tion of Keating History of Ireland[5] with upwards of 160 Coats of Arms of Antient Irish noble families & their Genealogy's among wch are some of the O Carrolls, this Book was to be bought at 2d hand, put him in mind of it. If O Connors Translation be a faithfull & full one, Keating I think does not deserve the Merit given him by many. Notwithstanding the Ravages & Revolutions in Ireland the Destruction of their Records & Histories, I think materials enough have escaped the jaws of Ruin to compile a more Compleat & coherent His: of Ireland than has yet fallen into my hands or knowledge, the Duty all Irish men owe to the Glory & Honour of their Country shd: prompt them to pro[m]ote & encourage such a Work. But the difficulty would be I apprehend greater to find an impartial than an able hand: If the author shd: be supported by the Descendants of the Antient Irish the ill treatment their Ancestors met with might if possible be exagerated, if he shd: be Patronized by the present Possessors, we may suppose truth would at least be veiled to conceal their Original meanness & the unjust, shocking & barbarous treatmt: of the Antient Possrs so that I fear such a History cannot reasonably be hoped for—

As to yr: Acct I shall remark that it appears by it that you have not according to my advice & desire yet had any one to instruct you in Book keeping for 1st I find but two Dates in yr: Acct Vizt: Octo: 1759 & Janry 1st 1761. 2dly There are but two Articles of Cr: Vizt: £190.5.2 & £146[.] Now as I find you charge all the Money you lose at Cards you ought to Cr: wt: you win, for I cannot [suppo]se you so unfortunate as not to win sometimes. You ou[ght therefore, to . . . the Balance . . . Article either to your Debit or Credit of . . . subject and by . . . money or play . . . y]ou will at [any time] see the profit or loss in that Article. [3dly] You are not part[icu]lar enough [in your] charges for Example To hire of [a] horse for my Ser[vant I]t ought [to have] been expressed To so many days horse hire, or To h[or]se hier from s[uch a] place to such a place. Althô yr. Acct is not dated I ca[n s]ee yr: Charges are made at the time they happened for you charge To Dawso[n] for Buying a horse 10/6 three pages before you charge the Price of the Horse. The several Columns of yr: Acct are not cast up. Thus far you see I object not to the Substance but to the form of yr: Acct, & I shd: not have had any reason to do this had you as I desired learnt to keep Accts. Now as to the Substance of yr: Acct I have but the following Remark to make; you charge £9.4.2 for keeping a horse at a Livery Stable & hire of Do: for 32 Days wch is I think 5/9 a Day wch multiply'd by 365 days makes £104.18.9 a Year, wch plainly points out that you were greatly imposed on in this Article, & if yr: keeping a horse shd: be proportionably Dear I submit it to you whether it will be prudent to keep one. I shd: think it best when you intend a Tour of a Month or more to buy horses for yr: self & Servt: & to sell them at yr: return, at a loss if you cannot do better & to hier for accidental Rides — As to the Rest I have no Objection to yr: Accts & I trust entirely to yr: Prudence & OEconomy —

I have not sold my large Tract at Monocasy, Mr: McNemara might have heard that I was offered £12500 & from thence conclude I sold it. I wish Mr: Birds Venture may Answer his Expectations, I cannot yet say anything on that head a little time will shew — I have again wrote about yr: Pipe of Wine. When you make yr: Tour to Holland I doubt not you will take the Precaution to procure some Letters of Recommendation to persons of Credit & figure there, this is a Step you shd: take even in yr: lesser Tours, yr: Business is to see men as well as things & the knowledge of things is best acquired from m[en] of figure & Experience. When you are in Holland you wont be far from Antwerp & Brussels they are worth seeing.

You ought to have taken wt: ever Money Gallot would have pay'd you & given an order to Mr: Edwards to Cr: him so much & to deliver the Goods on Paymt: of the Ballce, make it a Maxim never to refuse Money d[ue] to you for fear of its not being again offered wch may be the Case with Gall[ot] —

I hope you will keep the Resolution mentioned in yr: Postscript of writing oftner, for as all yr. Letters give me joy & put me in Spirits, so yr Silence makes me very anxious & uneasy. It cannot be an unpleasing task to write to me, to write often & Long Letters to me, I who one Day with another write & am confined for yr: sake to my Books of Accts & Papers for at least 6 hours, can & do find time to write to you & generally long Letters, are you more occupied? I am certain you do not want affection, Be not Lazy or Indolent —

If I shd: have any Pears worth sending you shall have them by Hanson, Kelty is at too great a Distance. As to Hams, we kill our hogs generally about the Beginning of Janry, our Bacon is Cured about the last of Mar: if a Convenient opportunity shd: then happen I will send you some Hams, it is flinging them away to send them in the summer. As I shall send Mr: Webb[6] some Seeds &c I shall desire him to spare you a few of such sorts as you may chuse. I have hitherto been disappointed of the Jensang, but I am still promised it. It is not worth while to desire Mr: R[az]olini to alter the direction of his Letters, I have no Secr[e]ts wch I would conce[al from] you.

[. . . .][7] Cap[t.] Carroll [. . .] & Mrs: Laws[on, desire their Compliments to you; if you had no] oth[e]r Objection to an Acquain[tance] with [Mr. Bladen] than that of his being a Gamester, why do [you s]ay in yrs of the 10th of April 1760, that that is not the only Reason for declin[ing] his Acquaintance, you must have wrote these last words without [a]ny meaning or you mean some thing wch you do not care to communi[ca]te — Pray no Reserve with me. You ought in playing to limit yr: self to a Stake the loss of wch will not give you any uneasiness, for its carrying Complaisance too far to Sacrifice yr: Money & resolutions to the inclinations of others. Let yr: Esteem be never so great for any particular person drop yr: Acquaintance with him rather than Associate for his Sake with Company you do not like; I am pleased to see you judge so rightly on this head, for an ill judged Complaisance & easiness of temper in this point has laid the foundation of many hopefull Young Mens Loss of innocence, Health, fortune & Honour—I again seriously recommend it to you to learn the Art of Book-keeping, ½ an hour a day spent with a Master 4 or 6 Months will be Sufficient to Raise the form of a Set of Books. I shall want yr: help to keep mine, you will want that knowledge to keep yr: own, it will be too late to learn when you come here, Learn Arithmatick also methodically, Surveying with a Compass & Chain will not take so much time as Book-keeping & the knowledge of it & cast up the Contents of any Survey is absolutely necessary to every landed Gent. here, I therefore again press you to learn these things & I hope to hear from you that you will follow my Advice, the Money paid to yr Instructors will be very well laid out—

I have a Collection of the Maps of all the Counties in England & Wales By Bowen & Kitchen [8] [ex]cept those mentioned in the inclosed List,[9] wch I desire you will get for me, the Size when Bound in an Atlas (as those are wch I have[)] is a feet & ½ an Inch long & 17 Inches & ½ Wide—Shd: there be any Maps of the Several Counties of Scotland & Ireland published, buy them for yr: own use with a General Map of each Kingdom & get them bound in an Atlas.

I desired Mr: Perkins to inform you I had secured all the Money I was likely to lose by Hen: Darnall, I have not only done this but I have also secured his Bror: Jo: who was jointly bound with me for his Brors due Execution of his Office as Naval Officer. John was bound to pay me for his B[r]o: Hen: £213.12.11 Ster: this I have also secured, in short I have secured for Jo: Darnall & myself £1266.1. Sterg by Conveying my Right to H: Darnalls Lands & Chattles to his S[o]n Robt: As to H: Darnall he lately took his passage from Virga: to London wt: Schemes he may have I know not: Avoid him but do not expose him, may God grant him a Sincere Repentance.

Yr: mention of yr: Mama to me & yr: Letter to her softened me, time will give us more fortitude: Let her have our daily prayers, thô I [f]irmly hope she wants them not, Deviate not from the Paths of Virtue & H[ono]ur that we may meet her in Heaven, if there were a Blessing beyond that I [wo]uld wish it to you: I am My Dr Charley

Yr: Mo: Afft: Father
Cha: Carroll

PS

Rachel Darnall presents he[r] Co[m]pts & Love to you—

LS, Carroll-McTavish Papers, MS 220, MdHi. Margins damaged. Text in brackets, with the exception of the dateline, supplied from Field, *Carroll*, 61–62.

1. Dated from CCA to CC, Sept. 9, 1761, below.

2. *Millan's Universal Register of Court and City-Offices* . . . published annually in Lon-

don from 1752 until 1766, and *The Court and City Kalendar; or, Gentleman's Register . . .* published annually from 1745 until 1769. *Cat. Lib.,* no. 576, lists several editions of the latter.

3. Appendix II.

4. Patrick Meighan, bookseller, leased space at Holborn gate, Gray's Inn, in February 1719/20. Presumably the Carrolls dealt with one of his descendants. Reginald J. F. Fletcher, ed., *The Pension Book of Gray's Inn (Records of the Honourable Society),* II, *1669–1800* (London, 1910), 175.

5. Geoffrey Keating (1570?–1644?), *The General History of Ireland . . . ,* trans. Dermo'd O'Connor (fl. 1712–1729) (Dublin, 1723).

6. John Webb, a seedsman located on Parliament St. in Westminster. CCA to West and Hobson, Oct. 8, 1771, Charles Carroll, Letter-book, fol. 4, Arents Colls., NN.

7. At least one line missing.

8. Emmanuel Bowen and Thomas Kitchen, *The Large English Atlas; or, A New Set of Maps of All the Counties in England and Wales . . . with a General Description of the County, Its Cities, Borough, and Market Towns, the Number of Members Returned to Parliament . . .* (London, [1760?]).

9. Not found.

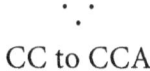

CC to CCA

July 15th. 1761.

Dr. Papa,

This answers yours of the 16th. April: I will endeavour to be as full & circumstancial as possible: I am intimate with nobody. The Persons whose company I most frequent are as follow Mr. Bird and his family worthy good people. Mr. Will Perkins his Brother & Mr. Eure[1] a most amiable gentleman: I used to be pretty often at Mr. Russel's: but my visits there are not so frequent as they formerly were: not from disgust or any dislike to the family I am always civilly received & made welcome: but a too great intimacy in a family where there young ladies may give room to idle reports & familiarity with the sex is immediately construed into love: I must not forget Mr: Ludwell in this list, a Virg[i]nia gentleman & one of the council in that Province:[2] his company & friendship is desireable; his esteem wou'd redound to my praise; ti's glorious to be esteemed by men of worth: amongst these Mr. Ludwell ought to be ranked if true politeness, solid sense, a virtuous mind & a good heart deserve this appellation. These are they whose company I most frequent, to whom I may add Mr. Maire & Hutton R C conveyancers: I intend to cultivate my acquaintance with the Latter; his advice may be serviceable to me: But these gentlemen have little time to spare from business. The company I keep, you may perceive, is neither low nor great: the genteelest company is confined to the upper end of the town at a great distance from the temple independent of this inconveniency that sort of company is not the most suitable to a student of the Law, the expence & dissipation attending it quite opposite to close application and to my inclinations: I never was fond of great companies. I am naturally timid & bashful: this timidity may occasion my dislike to company; my forbearance may have confirmed this timidity & propensity to silence & retirement. Innocuas amo delicias doctamque quietem.[3] Rural amusements such as farming & other country occupations united to Philosophy (its best allies) form that plan of life wh to me appears of all others the most eligible: the Laws of my country exclude me from acting in any public capacity I must endeavour then to be esteemed in private life. I own I am too stiff & reserved I can only be free and open with an intimate friend; yet I know how necessary a seeming openness & affability are towards conciliating the goodwill of mankind: something more substantial is required to procure their esteem: yet the one leads to the other; or their esteem is rested from them by violence & great very great merit. I have not been so lucky as to find out a proper person (nor is such a one easily to be found) to instruct me in the Law: undoubtedly there are many very capable, but such persons can scarce find time for their own business and are above such an employment & a pecuniary reward: There are Law lectures in Gray's Inn but [in] no great repute: The method I am advised to pursue (& wh all young gentlemen, who study the Law, follow) is to attend the courts at Westm: a regular & diligent attendance, I am told will let me into the practice of the Law & imprint in mind what I learn by private reading: My Lord Coke recommends this method to all who study the Law & are desirous of being proficiants in that useful science.

I hope you have received before now my letter of the 13th. Febry.[4] & that you find it a full & satisfactory answer to yours relating to Mr. Darnall: but for fear of miscarriage I here, send you a copy of it. The news-papers have been regularly filed & sent from the time I began to send them: I sent you the Letter to two great men & the way to keep him a comedy wrote by Mr Murphey,[5] whose reputation as an author has suffered by some Latter productions[.] The Letter to 2 great men & the Considerations &c are the only Pamplets I have seen and thought worth yr. perusals. Yours of Febry. 13th.[6] is Just come to hand.

(I know of no memorial published by the Jesuits: The troubles in Portugal so far as they relate to the Jesuits are as much a secret here as with you. Some Italian letters have been published, written, as is said, by the Pope's nephew in vindication of that order.[7] But this I am told by Mr. Jenison to whom I sent them is a general vindication & does not unfold the mysteries of Lisbon & of course is far from being satisfactory. I shall transcribe his (Jenison's) words. The Italian apologies do not lay open the mysteries of Lisbon, but set the Character of the sufferers in a favourable light, vindicates them from the imputation of trade, ambition & rebellion: do you not think that a short essay on the subject wou'd be favourably received or prove serviceable to yr. friends? I have such a one by me from a good hand & wish you had a sight of it and yr. sentiments of an edition. . . . I intend to write to Mr. Jenison soon & shall desire him to send me the copy of the essay he mentions: I beg you wou'd not communicate this part of my letter to any one).

My Lord Baltimore is seldom to be seen: he now & then entirely disappears. I visit Mr. Calvert now and then; he returns my visits & we converse amicably & freely together. I am looking out for a master to instruct me in Arithmetic, book-keeping, & surveying: I know how necessary ti's to be master of them: you may depend upon my application: I propose setting off the 1st. week in August for Yorck. I may be absent from London about 6 or 7 weeks: when I return I shall begin immediately to learn Arithmetic &c. In my last of the 10th. June I desired you to call me home: you say you have pressing reasons for so doing: I gave you mine in the above mentioned letter: I am still of the same way of thinking: I wish my arguments may have influence enough to prevail upon you to recall me. The loss of my dear mother still sets heavy on my heart: but as my grief is unavailing and prejudicial to myself I endeavour to get the better of it: (The money you ordered has been paid: and Masses said for her in our Chappels: at some I assisted: I always remember her in my prayers but I hope she does not stand in need of them): did she die in her senses? Did she recommend any thing particular to me before her death? She certainly must have often thought of me during her illness.

When Mr. Dulany arrives in town I shall wait upon him as you advise me. I hear from Mr. Macnamara, & he from Mr. Calvert, that you have lost a 1000£. sterling by Mr. Darnall by being his security: I think that gentleman's behaviour unaccountable if what is reported of him be true, that he has converted to his own use the public money. But I suspend my Judgement till I am well informed of the truth of this report: I hear Mr. Darnall is confined to a prison: if his misfortune can be imputed to chance & unforseen accidents he is to be pitied: but if he has brought upon himself this calamity by his imprudence or extravagance ti's his own fault & he scarce deserves compassion. . . . money given to the industrious & good, tho' indigent man is well bestowed: but to an idle extravagant man, meerly thrown away—I never knew an idle man that was good for any thing unless to entertain company at a feast: he may be a Joyous merry companion but no more. Witt without vertue and Judgement is dangerous to the witty man & to his acquaintance. I must conclude this letter wh I hope you will find satisfactory. I am Dr. Papa

Yr. most dutiful & loving Son
Ch: Carroll.

P:S:

16th

I called upon Mr. Calvert this morning: he read to me the Govenor's Letter to Mr. Bordley,[8] his answer, & some other letters relative to Mr. Darnall[9] whereby I see you have been obliged to pay a 1000£:

ALS, Carroll Papers, MS 206, MdHi. Addressed in an unknown hand. Endorsed by CCA.

1. Mr. Eure may have worked for William Perkins. See CCC to Perkins, Buchanan, and Brown, Oct. 5. 1765, below.

2. Philip Ludwell III (1716–1767) was a native of James City Co., Va., where he owned a plantation called Greenspring. A member of the Virginia Council from 1751, he went to England in 1760 and remained there for the rest of his life. Abbot, *Washington: Colonial Series*, I, 71 n, II, 105 n, VII, 39 n.

3. "I love harmless delights and learned repose."

4. Carroll Papers, MS 206.

5. Arthur Murphy (1727–1805), an Irish playwright, was educated at St. Omers.

6. Not found.

7. Probably *Reflections of a Portuguese upon the Memorial Presented by the Jesuits to His Present Holiness Pope Clement XIII; Translated from the Copy Printed by Authority at Lisbon; to Which Is Added, the Opinion of the Congregation of Cardinals, to Whom the Said Memorial Was Referred by the Pope* . . . (London, 1760). Pope Clement XIII's (1693–1769) nephew Carlo Rezzonico was created a cardinal in 1758.

8. Stephen Bordley (1710–1764), an Annapolis attorney whose abilities were said to equal those of Daniel Dulany, Jr., received his formal legal training at the Inner Temple, to which he was admitted in 1729. Bordley returned to Maryland in 1733. He was elected to the lower house in 1745 and served three additional terms in that body. With the support of Gov. Horatio Sharpe, Bordley succeeded Henry Darnall III as attorney general in 1756 and simultaneously held the post of naval officer of Annapolis. In 1759 he gained a seat in the upper house and on the Council. When Benjamin Tasker, Jr.'s death in the fall of 1760 left open the office of deputy secretary, Bordley let it be known that he intended to apply. Cecilius Calvert was willing to make the appointment if Bordley agreed to pay a "saddle"—a kickback—of £300 per annum. Although willing to comply, Bordley had no sooner received the offer than it was withdrawn because Daniel Dulany, Jr., had persuaded Lord Baltimore to award the position to him. In 1762 Bordley accepted Dulany's old post of commissary general as a consolation prize, but within eighteen months he suffered the incapacitating stroke that brought about his death in December 1764. *Bio. Dic. Md. Legis.*, I, 146–147; Land, *Dulanys of Maryland*, 233–236; *Arch. of Md.*, IX, 460–461, 467, 478–479, 497–498; Owings, *His Lordship's Patronage*, 132.

9. Gov. Horatio Sharpe's letters to Secretary Cecilius Calvert and to Lord Baltimore about Darnall's malfeasance are in *Arch. of Md.*, IX, 511–516.

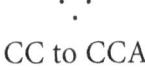

CC to CCA

July 23d. 1761

Dr. Papa,

Yesterday yours of the 21st. May came to hand[.] As Mr. Nelson[1] by whom this is to go, Leaves London to morrow you must not expect a full answer to yr. letter. This I defer doing till the next opportunity: but can not help [taking?] notice of a few passages in yr. letter. Knowing you wou'd not be against it, & tempted by the cheapness I have subscribed to a new edition of the statutes at Large now going forward.[2] The[y] are to be in 27 Octavo volus. the price 6 guineas in sheets to subscribers: I prefer this Edition to any other; the octavo volus. being much more handy & commodious that the infolios. I always send the Papers to Mr. Perkins: I am acquainted with few of the Captains of ships: MGachen was much to blame in sending the papers committed to his care in the negligent & careless manner you mention. You never informed me in any preceeding Letter or Postscript, of the 1000£ you were obliged to pay as security for the ungrateful Mr. Darnall. Yr. prudence & discretion will direct you to persue the shortest & safest manner of endemnifying yourself for the loss sustained. If the 2d. Son is of age (wh I suppose he is by his being married) as his reversion is worth little, shou'd he Join in the deed for cutting of[f] the entail, this wou'd be the surest & most afectual method by barring even the possibility of the reversion to him [&] his male issue, & by leaving the fee [simple] in us without any entermediate estate: in this case you might sell the Lands to the best bidder as the Purchaser's title wou'd then be quite secure. But this he will not do: & yet may be unable to redeem his Father's lands at the rate you offer & their real value.

I still feel & shall long continue to feel my dear Mama's death: The Earnest vehement desire I had of seeing her & the present impossibility of gratifying this desire is most cruel & afflicting. If I survive you I shall never think of so dear a Parent without blessing his memory: you have been to me the best the tenderest Father: my constant endeavour will be to make a suitable return & to please you. I shall [never] be able to repay the care & pains you taken of my education, but yr. love for me is already repaid by mine I love you most tenderly: my daily prayers are that we may long live happy together: Pray do not talk of leaving me: there is nothing after yr. displeasure I so much dread as yr. death: you are my only support my almost only friend in Maryland: The disposal of yr. affairs never gave me the least uneasiness: My kind compliments & service to Mrs. Darnall: the same to Capt. Carroll & Mr. Croxall[.] I am Dr. Papa

Your most dutiful & affectionate Son

Ch: Carroll.

ALS, Carroll Papers, MS 206, MdHi. Addressed by CC.

1. Thomas Nelson (1738–1789) was returning to Virginia with Samuel Athawes from study at Christ's College, Cambridge.

2. Probably Danby Pickering, *The Statutes at Large, from Magna Carta to the End of the Eleventh Parliament of Great Britain,* 24 vols. (Cambridge, 1762–1769), rather than the Cay's edition suggested by CCA.

· · ·
  ·   ·
    ·

CCA to CC

Sepr: 9th: 1761

Dr Charley,

I wrote to you Febru: 13th: 1761, March 22d, Aprill 16th, May 21, June 22, & July 10th in the last I acknowledged the Receit of yrs of Mar: 28th, March 30th & March 31st: This will be Deliver'd to you by Capn: Carroll: I am Perswaded it will give you a Sensible Satisfaction to see him, as he Can say much to you Relating to me my Affairs & Health wh God be Praised I enjoy as well as most People of my Age, being now in my 60th year — I shall therefore in this only write to you about the Inclosed Cases, wh I have sent you not only for your information, But that you may by them see how Essentiall it will be to you to know the Law well. Yr Estate for this Part of the World will be a Considerable one & of Course lyable to Many disputes, Especially as A Roman Catholick stands but a Poor Chance for Justice with Our Juries in Particular —

The Browne paper Role or Packet Directed to Mr Dulany you are to Deliver to him, it Contains a Transcript of the Record in my Case wth: Clifton[1] as well as a state of that Case as you will see by my letter to Mr Dulany which I have left Open for yr Perusall, you having done so seal it & Deliver it[.] I have sent for yr owne use a state of the Case allready Mentioned, & a state of a Case which arises from the Former between me & My Partners in I[ron] Works,[2] these you will keep Care fully & [consid]er —

Pray Present my Humble service & Respects to Messrs Corby, Pointz, Baker, Galloway, Jennisson, Mr Crookshanks &c[.] If the Abbé de L'Isle Dieu be still living Pray write him a small Billet under Cover to Mr Crookshank let him know I desierd it to Testify my Respect & Esteem for him this is the least Return I can make for his Civilities to us —

You may know Mr Webb the Seedsman[.] Give my Service to him & let him know that if I do not send him any Seeds, its owing to a great Hurry of Business & the Fleets Sailing sooner than we Expected. This also obliges me to be at present so short to you. God Bless You I am My Dr Charley

Yr Mo: Afft: Father
Cha: Carroll

PS

My Compliments to Mr Bird & tell him I am fearfull his Venture will meet wth a slow Sale, of this Mr Maccubbin[3] will write him more at large — Desier Mr Perkins to forward the inclosed[.]

ALS, Carroll-McTavish Papers, MS 220, MdHi. Endorsed by CC. A second LS copy, addressed and marked "Copy" by CCA, may be found in Carroll Papers, MS 216, MdHi.

1. William Clifton (?–1770), a descendant of an old English Catholic family, emigrated to Maryland in the early years of the eighteenth century and eventually settled in Stafford Co., Va. He subsequently married his cousin Elizabeth Brent, a daughter of Robert Brent of Stafford Co., and this union strengthened his ties to the Carrolls, who were also related to the Brents. (Appendix I, Chart J; David M. French, *The Brent Family; Carroll Families of Colonial Maryland* [Alexandria, Va., 1981], 56, 58, chart 5.) Although CCA's transactions with Clifton were numerous and protracted, the lawsuit to which he refers here concerned a series of complicated loans that he had originally made to Clifton but that ultimately involved other parties. Particularly at issue was the amount of interest CCA had charged and his method of calculating it. See CC to CCA, July 4, 1762, below.

2. The second case involved a slave at the Baltimore Company that three Stafford Co. men — Clifton, Peter Hedgeman, and John Mercer — claimed had been mortgaged to them and was being unlawfully detained at the ironworks. CCA contended that the Negro belonged to the company and refused to comply with the request that the slave be returned. Mercer sued, and on Oct. 12, 1756, the Stafford Co. court found for him and ordered CCA to pay £300 10s. 6d. Maryland currency. Declining to accept the decision, CCA responded by suing Clifton. Although the Virginia court ruled in CCA's favor in April 1760, he was dissatisfied with the decision because he considered the sum awarded to him only a third of what he was due. He further maintained that because the Negro at issue belonged to the Baltimore Company, his ironworks partners, including Daniel Dulany, should bear proportionate shares not only of the expense of the suit but also of the financial losses he sustained when, during the course of the litigation, Clifton stopped paying interest on other debts he owed the Carrolls. This legal battle dragged on for many years and was not finally settled until 1791, long after most of the original litigants had died. The outcome partially vindicated CCA's position: because they had approved his actions, his Baltimore Company partners were held liable for the costs CCA had sustained in bringing suit over the slave, but they were judged not responsible for the expenses he had incurred in his dispute with Clifton over unpaid interest. In the first instance, the executors of the deceased litigants were ordered to pay CCC £208 11s. 10d. each. The Papers of the Carroll Family, MS 3072, DLC; *CCC v. Daniel Dulany and others*, June 27, 1791, Chancery Court decree, Cooke Papers, MS 195, MdHi.

3. Richard Mackubin (?–1778), an Annapolis merchant. *Md. Gaz.*, July 9, 1761.

CCA to CC

Sepr: 17th: 1761

Dr Charley,

I leave the inclosed to Sr Thos: Webb Open for yr Perusall, Having done that, you will seal & Deliver it, as I presume you are acquainted wth him, If you are not acquainted wth: him get Mr Perkins to Deliver it. I shall send a Duplicate & triplicate of this to you, If one be Deliverd it will be Sufficient: keep the others by you.[1] By my letter to Sr Thos: you will see that I have formerly Solicited him in favour of Mr Ireland; I Proposed he should Advance 4 or £500 To Purchase him a Seat of Land some slaves & to Enable him to Build & improve the Land. You must know that Mr Ireland is Related to Sr Thos who was his Guardian, that he had an Estate in Yorkshire of 4 or £500 a year which he indiscreetly Run thrô having Maryed Before he was 18 Year old, & Having been Severall years in the French and austrian Service, the latter he Quitted in 1745 for a Particular Reason: He is a Polite well bred & very Agreable Gentleman, & althô his former Conduct may have Given Sr Thomas reason to be Displeased with him, His Present wants & fruitless indus-try deserves his Compassion — I have also formerly sollicited Lord Montague[2] in favour of Mr Ireland, His Lordship was So Polite & Condescending as to answer My letters & to express a desier to Serve Mr Ireland, But his Ability not being Equall to his Inclination He gave me Hopes he would use his Interest with Sr Thos in Mr Irelands favour. If you have the Honr to be acquainted wth his Lordship Pray put him in Mind of this — I also sollicited Mr Molineux Sr Thomas's Chaplain, He is an old Acquaintance of myne & Promised to use what Interest he had to Serve Mr Ireland Pray Put him in Mind of this Presenting my Respects to him, & let me know what steps he Took in Complyance with his Promise[.]

I am sorry I Cannot give you an Agreable acct of Mr Birds Venture wh was greatly to large, Mr McCubbin told me he has only sold two Tables, He says slabs for Chimneys would have sold much Quicker, I am Satisfyed no Industry was want-ing to get them off: They have been Advertised in Our Gazet[3] & Exposed to sight in the most Publick part of the Towne[.]

Mr Browne went this Day hence to take his Passage for England[.] Perhaps it would have been better if he had stayed in London: He is young & wants Judge-ment & Discretion, he lately was taken in too deeply I fear at the Hazard Tables, it will Puzzle him to settle the Acct of that loss with his Uncle[.]

Cousin Macnemara is not Returned to us, If he is still in London what is he doeing, what Success has he had, or had he any Prospect of Success —

You are no doubt acquainted wth Mr Dulany thô I suppose not often with him, Many here think he will Come in Govr, that he will try for it if he sees any Prospect of Success I doubt not: How little doe we understand our true Happyness, In Case of Success he will be Miserable for he Cannot bear Contradiction or Opposition & that he will Certainly meet with —

In the fore part of this letter you see what I wish to be done for Mr Ireland, you are Acquainted wth Sr Thomas's Sons they were yr Fellow Collegians You may Per-chance influence them to incline their Father to Assist him, neither they or their Father will Miss 4 or £500 Pounds, that Sum would make Ireland Happy & Inde-pendant it is shocking to see a Gentn: Reduced to Hard Labour Especially when he is a Man of Great Merit — I have Advanced a Great Deal of Money to Purchase a Pretty seat of Land for Mr Ireland within two Miles of my House at Elk Ridge[.] I have Built Convenient Houses on it & I lately Bought two negroes for him I Can-not aford to give a way Such Sums But Sr Thomas may. You are not to let Sr Thos:

know what I have done for Mr Ireland least he should be less sollicitous to Serve him — Mr Ireland has for two years Past Overlooked all my Plantations at Elkridge to my Great Satisfaction & Interest, He is an E[x]cellent Manager very Obliging active & Diligent, His Integrity is Such that I am quite at ease as to everything I have Committed to his Care[.] He lives where Shalmerdine Lived & its a great Pleasure to me to have so agreable a Companion when I visit that Estate. You may from what I have said see how much I have it at Heart to Serve him & Consequently will not Omit any thing in yr Power to answer my Intention, Capn Carroll knows him well & Can give you a more ample Acct of him. God Bless you & Grant You Health. I am Dr Charley

Yr Mo: Afft: Father
Cha: Carroll

PS

    I leave my letter to Mr Bladen Open for yr Perusall, having done that Seal & Deliver it[.] The young Ladys say you have the Polish of a French Education[.]

    ALS, Carroll-McTavish Papers, MS 220, MdHi. Endorsed by CC. An LS copy, addressed by CCA and with the postscript in his hand, may be found in the Outerbridge Horsey Collection of Lee, Horsey, and Carroll Family Papers, MS 1974, MdHi.
    1. Not found.
    2. Anthony Browne, sixth Viscount Montagu (1686–1767). In 1720 Montagu married Barbara Webb, third daughter of Sir John Webb and sister of Sir Thomas Webb. [Cokayne], *Complete Peerage*, ed. Gibbes et al., IX, 102; Burke and Burke, *Landed Gentry of Great Britain*, II, 1771.
    3. The *Md. Gaz.* was edited and printed by Jonas Green of Annapolis and his descendants from 1745 until 1839. Richard Mackubin's advertisement appeared in the July 9, 1761, issue.

CC to CCA

Octbr. 13th. 1761

Dr. Papa,

    This is to acknowledge the receipt of yr. several letters of June 22d. July 10th. & twenty 1st. May a copy. The last I have already answered, one paragraph excepted, in mine of July 23d. by Mr. Nelson. I then omitted for an obvious reason to return an answer to that part of yr. letter. It cannot be supposed that Mr. Calvert was ignorant of the double taxing act or misinformed in any of the circumstances and transactions relative thereunto as the chief nay all the Proprietary's business passes thro' his hands. He was hard pressed & to avoid the imputation of countenancing injustice, was glad to find any excuse to palliate his own injustice & pusillanimity.

For whoever can & won't protect innocence when oppressed is himself unjust. You desire me to read yr. letter to him: this I think wou'd not only be unserviceable but improper at so long an interval as has passed from the time of our conversation to the receipt of yr. letter. He may disown his ever having said the Roman Cath: made no opposition to the act.

When Mr. Dulany arrived in town I was out upon my Journey before my return he was gone to Bath for the recover[y] of his health. When we meet I shall shew him all the civility in my power. Henry Darnall is gone over to the continent to live in retirement in what place ti's not known he will fix his abode. Mr. Titchburn[1] who was his master at St. Omers saw him lately, & foretold to him when a boy what wou'd happen & has happened if he did not correct his indolent easy character. I am pleased to hear you have horses of such value, but surprised at the extravagant prices they were sold at. I am extremely obliged to you in reserving for me the 2 year old colt. I take great pleasure in a good & fine horse. Keeping a horse at a livery stable comes to 8S. 4D a week and to 21£. 13S. per an: a sum prodigiously short of what you mention; had I paid 9£.4.2 for 32 days keeping & hire of a horse for Do. I had been most grossly imposed upon. Yr. mistake lays in imagining so much money was paid for 32 days keeping & 32 days hire: where as my horse stood near 3 months at the livery stable as you may see my the inclosed bill.[2]

I shall do my best endeavours to get all the ecclaircisements[3] that, can be had, concerning our family by applying to my Cousn. Antony. Such a curiosity is not only satisfactory & natural to all men but laudable & instructive. The sending a copy of yr. will, tho' it proves how much you love me, was an unnecessary step if with an intent to remove any apprehensions or disquiet I might feel on that subject. I have been all along per[sua]ded, that yr. good sense, steady conduct, & our mutual love were a sufficient security against any disposition of yr estate that might greatly prejudice me. If I survive, you may depend on a due & entire execution of all you recommend or order to be done: the will, I think, can not be drawn up with more precision & greater perspicuity.

My only objection to being entered of the temple arose from its inutility & the danger of frequenting loose company. The expence is not worth mentioning. I must acknowledge I feel some satisfaction in my Grandfathers being a member of that society, of wh I intend soon to be that my grandson may not be deprived of the same satisfaction. This is the only advantage that can accrue to either of us from my entery. There is no possibility of being called to the bar without taking the oaths: supposing such a scheme not impossible & that by a well timed gratuity I might be called to the bar, yet I coud never act as counsellor without assuming a double & ignominious character. All counsellors are supposed at least to have taken the oaths a necessary qualification to all, who bear any post, office, charge or trust & act in a public capacity. (I expect Pere Croiset's exercises de pieté from Paris in a short time). I have by me the Almanacks for 60 & 61 they will accompany this. Millan's register shall be sent annually according to desire. I wrote to Mr. Crookshanks to send regularly the lettres edifiantes as they are published, but intend writing again to him soon in order to refresh his memory & to get a circumstantial account of the Parlts. proceedings against the Jesuits & the pleadings pro & con: in the late lawsuit in wh they were cast & the whole body made answerable for the debts of every particular house.[4]

Mr. Meighan is involved in great distresses: his daughter has filed a bill in chancery against him to recover the money left her by her grandfather: he can no other ways avoid her claim than by disowning her for his daughter or by assertaining the illegitimatecy of her birth: but as his marriage with the mother can be clearly proved, ti's thought this affair will entirely ruin him: The trial is to come on next term: be that as it will I shall remind Mr. Meighan of his word: I never read any Irish history: an impartial history of that country I am affraid is not to be had, perhaps never will such a one be published for those very reasons you have assigned.

I am now looking on for a proper person to teach me arithmetick & bookkeeping. A gentleman of my acquaintance has recommended to me one, who taught him: his salary is a guinea a month he attends his schollars thrice a week at their lodgings. The gentleman who recommended the above mentioned person will be this week in town; he promised to conduct me to the person, & if we agree I shall immediately begin to learn Arith: bookkeeping, surveying &c. I know their utility & how necessary ti's for a gentleman to be master of all these & shall apply accordingly. A certain gentleman's being a gamester, is I think a sufficient reason to decline his company. . . . I meant no more by saying <u>that was not the only reason</u> than that by frequenting his house I might fall a victim to his daughter: she is remarkably handsom; upon a stricter acquaintance I might discover qualities wh have more influence on a man of sense than beauty. I have already got the maps of the counties you wanted: The 13 counties make but 5 maps too few to be bound in an Atlass. You may have them bound up with yours: There are no maps of the different counties of Scotland & Ireland: I have a general map of each kingdom in the Atlass sent me from Paris. I am glad to hear you have secured the money you was bound to pay as a security for Henr. Darnall: has his son Robert already paid in the 1266£.1.10 for the transfer made to him of yr. right to his father's lands? I have been informed that Darnall sunk more public money that his securities were bound to pay. (If so will not the government seise his lands & Chattels to make up the defiency and come in before his securities & other creditors?)

My Journey has been pleasant, instructive, & agreeable: the melancholy circumstance of my Mothers death often threw a damp upon my spirits even in the midst of company: time only can wear off the impression her death has made on my mind: you may expect by the fleet a Journal of my rout containing an account of my adventures & of the most curious places, & things I have seen upon my Journey. I beg my compliments to Mrs. Lawson, Docr. Lyon & in particular to Richd. Croxall. Present my love to my Coun. Rach: Darnall I shall always bear her a sincere affection, for the great care & tender concern she shewed for my Dear Mother in her last sickness. I wish you with all my heart health & happiness. I am Dr. Papa

Yr. most affectionate Son

C: Carroll

ALS, Carroll Papers, MS 206, MdHi. Endorsed by CCA: "1761 Octor: 13th: & 22d: My Sons Letters Ansd: Aprill 8: 1762."

1. John Tichborne (1694–1772).

2. Not found.

3. "Elucidations."

4. Antoine La Valette, a French Jesuit and superior of the mission in Martinique from 1753, borrowed a large sum from a Marseilles bank that he then used to develop sugar and coffee plantations and to speculate in foreign trade. From 1755 on he also raised money in England through John Pointz. When ships carrying coffee and sugar worth between six hundred thousand and two million livres were captured by the British in 1756, the bank failed and the creditors took the Jesuits to court. The parlement de Paris subsequently upheld a decision that the entire Society was responsible for the debts. Holt, *English Jesuits in the Age of Reason,* 151–153.

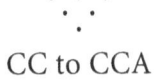

CC to CCA

Octb. 22d. 1761.

Dr. Papa,

Since I wrote my letter there has been published a Pamphlet with an account of the late Parliamentary proceedings against the Jesuits in France:[1] As it contains The french kign's declaration and the decree of the Parliament of Paris against the Jesuits, with some curious anecdotes I thought it woud not be unacceptable & have sent it for yr. perusal. You will see several bulls relating to the Society, several letters of i'ts general's, several extracts of i'ts constitutions, wh explain the nature of the Institute & discover the extensive <u>too</u> extensive priveleges confer'd by former Popes on that order. If these bulls, constitutions & letters are faithfully quoted I can not but concide with the Parliat: in Judging dangerous to the state a body of men who implictly believe the dictates of one Superior, & are <u>carried on to the execution of his orders with a blind impetuosity of will & eagerness to obey without the least enquiry or examination.</u> Reason was not given to man merely to restrain his passions, or merely to regulate his own actions, but to weigh & examin wether the actions he is sollicited or commanded by others to perform, are such as can stand the scrutiny & sentence of an unerring, if unprejudiced, Judge. The force & permanency given to their constitutions by the Bull dum indefessæ &c[2] in declaring them no ways subject to be repealed limited or derogated from, either by the author of the bull, or any his successors, and the many other too extensive priveleges in particular the exemption from the power & Jurisdiction of the ordinaries, are certainly an empeachment of that policy wh distinguishes the court of Rome; those immunities that independency may be attended with bad consequences and are contrary to the true spirit & discipline of the Catholic Church. No one has a greater regard for the Jesuits than myself; I revere the virtue, I esteem the learning, I respect the apostollic labours of individuals but am forced to acknowledge their institute & plan of goverment liable to great abuses: let it be granted, that no such abuses have as yet crept into it, that its members are disinterested, unambitious, strict observers of their vow of poverty & that other vow, wh secludes them from all wordly concerns, from power, from sway, from the intrigues of courts & ministerial influence. Abuses are easier to be prevented, than when once introduced, eradicated. I have said enough, perhaps too much on this subject. I have entrusted my thoughts to none but you; be true to yr trust, & as my deposit is of such a nature as not to be restored to its owner, do not at least make it over to another.

By the newspapers wh accompany this, you will be made acquainted with the late great changes in our ministry. Mr. Pitt's resignation[3] has cast a sudden gloom on all well wishers to their country. The cause & motives of his resignation can not be better explained than in his own letter to Mr. Beckford,[4] wh is inserted in the newspapers. The debates in council run very high: ti's thought the result of all these deliberations will be a Spanish war & the reinstating of Mr. Pitt in his former office.

Mr. Meighan was with me this very morning: he presents his compliments to you, & desired me to tell you that he has not by him at present O'Connor's translation of Kea[ti]ng's History, but will look out f[or] one, & the very first he lights upon will send it to me: the price is from 18 to 20 shillings: the performance but indifferent. There is now publishing at Paris a history of Ireland in french wrote by an Irish [a]bbè:[5] wh[a]t are the merits or demerits of this work, what suce[ss] it has met with, or may des[erve] I cannot pretend to say. The French Almanacks, (the [Pr]oceedings against the Jesuits of France) the newspapers & magazines, & the maps you wrote for, all go in the ship, by wh this letter goes. The Magazine for Augst. may not perhaps be sent by the same opportunity, I have lent it to a gentleman & he has not as yet returned it. I am Dr. Papa

Yr. most loving & dutiful Son
Ch: Carroll

ALS, Carroll Papers, MS 206, MdHi. Addressed by CC. Endorsed by CCA: "1761 Octor: 13th: & 22d: My Sons Letters Ansd: April 8: 1762."

1. Possibly *The Authentic Proceedings of the French King and His Parliament against the Jesuits of France* . . . (Paris and London, 1761).

2. The 1571 papal bull *Dum indefessae* granted the Jesuits complete and irrevocable immunity from all ecclesiastical sanctions, including excommunication. Francisco Gaude, ed., *Bullarum, Diplomatum et Privilegiorum Sanctorum Romanorum Pontificum . . .* , VII (Naples, 1882), 923–926.

3. William Pitt had served as secretary of state with supreme direction of the war and of foreign affairs since June 29, 1757. With the accession of George III, however, he encountered opposition from the monarch's confidant and adviser, Lord Bute, who disagreed with the secretary's policies and pressed for an end to the war. Pitt had no desire for peace until France had been totally humiliated and, in pursuit of that objective, he proposed in September 1761 that Britain commence hostilities against Spain because of her ties to France through the Bourbon Family Compact, an alliance concluded by those two countries on Aug. 15. Between Sept. 15 and 21 Pitt argued his case in the cabinet; unable to win agreement for his position, he resigned on Oct. 5. Ayling, *Elder Pitt*, 286–291.

4. William Beckford (1709–1770). Born in Jamaica, Beckford was educated in England and became a wealthy merchant. He was elected several times to Parliament (1754–1768), where he was an ally of William Pitt, and he served twice as Lord Mayor of London (1762–1763, 1769–1770). Gerrit P. Judd, *Members of Parliament, 1734–1832* (New Haven, Conn., 1955), 118.

5. [James] MacGeoghegan (1702–1763), *Histoire d'Irlande ancienne et moderne . . .* , 3 vols. (Paris, 1758–1762). *Cat. Lib.*, no. 1350.

∴ ∴

CCA to CC

Novr: 10th 1761

Dr Charley

Last night I Reced yr. most wellcome Letters of May 14th,[1] June 10th July 15th 20th[2] & 23d 1761 by Messrs: Athawes & Nelson. You will see by my last how impatient I was to hear from you. Pray desire Mr: Perkins to put you in a way to dispatch yr: Letters as soon as they are wrote, beside the Packets[3] to New York Ships often come to Philadelphia & Virginia, he may cover them to Gent: in those Provinces with a desire to forward them by the Post —

I have only time to take notice of yrs of the 10th of June relating to yr: Dr: Mother, you were always in her thoughts, she spoke often to Mrs Darnall about you in the most tender manner, desired to be remembred to you with the affection you may better conceive than I can express, & suffered for the grief & sorrow you would feel on Acct of her Death. I could not say less as you desired to be informed as to these particulars, I cannot say more the Subject being too moving. From a tenderness for each other we seldom [menti]oned you. If she was speaking to Mrs: Darnall about you upon my coming into the Room she was Silent. For the future let us mention her as seldom as possible, we can never cease to think of her & pray for her. She was Christened May 17th 1709 & born I think the 9th: you was born Sept: 8th 1737. I was born April 2d 1702 (all old Stile) & I thank God enjoy perfect health—

Pray my kind service to Capt: Carroll & tell him I heard a few days past that his Wife & Child were perfectly well. That his Warrant is renewed & in my hands & that I will take care it shall be again Renewed in April. I pray to God to Bless you & grant you health. I am My Dr Charley

Yr: Mo: Afft: Father
Cha: Carroll

PS

Return the inclosed to me if Mr: Macnemara is on his way home—

LS, Carroll Papers, MS 206, MdHi. Addressed by CCA. CC's penmanship practice and the following notes in his hand appear on verso:

My Mother 1760 died

    1709. born
    .51 aged.

my Father 1763

    1702
    .61

    my Age 1763
    born 8 Septbr. 1737
    26

1. Not printed (Carroll Papers, MS 206). The letter comments on the cost of seats for the coronation and plans for the war.

2. Not printed (ibid.). The letter is a fragment of a copy made to replace a lost original.

3. Mail ships operated by post office authorities.

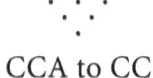

CCA to CC

[Dec. 7, 1761]

[. . . .][1] have whatever [M]oney you want for [all necess]aries & a genteel support confiding in yr: prudence & OEco[no]my.

I could not give my Advice in time about yr. laying out 12 Guineas to see the Coronation, if you have done so it is agreeable to me. I am glad to hear Gallot has paid [his] Debt & I doubt not you will press Mr: Maccarty by letters to pay his, Debt to all appearance desperate are often secured by assiduity & care—Pray my sincere Compts & thanks to Mr: Crook[sha]nks for the Royal Almanack, I suppose the 29th Vol: of the Lettres Edifiantes &c is not yet published as he has not sent it to you. My Compts. to Csn: Anto: when you write to him.

In my last I said as much as I could say relating to yr: Dr: Mama, I shall only add, that she had every Sentiment in regard to you wch the best the fondest Parent could have for a deserving dutifull Son: she died in her Senses. Grief as you say is unavailing it is not only prudent it is our Duty to suppress it — My Dr: Charley I am sensible that yr. love & fondness for me is sincere, but accustom yr:self to expect my Death, I must in the Course of nature go before you, yr. Concern & anxiety will not retard my fate[.] I seriously endeavour to prepare for that hour, & I desire yr: Prayers that my Endeavours may not prove fruitless, Unexpected misfortunes are the most shocking, frequent thoughts on this Subject accompany'd with Acts of Resignation to the Divine will, are the best precautions agst: immoderate grief & will help you most efficaciou[s]ly to bear yr: loss. It may happen tomorrow or several years hence for I am in a good habit of Body & perfect health, whenever it happens cover yr:self with the shield of reason & fortitude[.] Neither the consideration of the possibility of this Event before you have gone thro the time I have appointed for you to read the Law nor the disadvantages you may in that Case be under, nor my love & fondness can make me alter my Resolution, judge from hence of the importance I think the knowledge of the Law will be to you. As I formerly wrote to you, you vainly imagine you could apply to the Study of it here, other occupations will engross yr: time. Should you ever be in my circumstances follow my Example, let no self love disguised by the appearances of great advantages or the fears of losses or disadvantages induce you to alter a well laid s[c]heme for the Education of yr: Children, nothing of consequence can be brought to a happy Issue without diligence steadiness & Resolution. About this time 2 years yr: 4 years Study of the Law will be over, it will take you the winter Months to prepare for yr: Voyage for I would not have [. . . .]²

I approve t[he] C[ompany you] keep they may [. . .] now & then I think y[r:] Circle shd: be enlarged not [to] seek intimacy bu[t to] know men & the world & the persons & Characters of such as seem to [have] the greatest weight & to be the principal Actors in the Political management of the Court & [Pa]rliament — You judge well in cultivating an acquaintance with Mr: Hutton for the reason you mention, he & others may clear up difficulties & make the study of the Law easier & pleasanter to you. It's certain the stile of our Law Books is disgusting & that most forms & fashions are ridiculous, but we must bear things as we find them & endeavour to turn the follies of Mankind to our advantage — Shake off that timidity & bashfullness you say you are subject to, il faut se faire Valoir,³ this [is a] Lesson I would not give a Coxcomb, the Maxim is never abused by a man of Sense, it shd: be prudently practiced by men of Merit, we must by a proper assurance command the Respect due to us. Have you not renewed an acquaintance with any of yr: Schoolfellows? I suppose there were many Young Gent: of family & fortune at the College in yr: t[i]me. An Acquaintance shd: never be dropt, if it can be kept up without prejudice & with Conveniency, Events may happen to make it beneficial. The plan of life you seem to have chalked out to yr:self is not only prudent & innocent, but above all others I think most agreeable, I enjoy it as oft as I can.

As you are sensible how necessary a seeming openness & affability are towards conciliating the good will of mankind, make it yr: Study to appear so, a gaiety & chearfullness of temper in Co: is almo[st] the thing, I have seen men who come into Company with so solemn [a] face as to be stupid & almost to make every one else so —

If nothing more can be had I shall be glad to have the Translation of the Italian Letters in favour of the Jesuits. If you are at Liberty to communicate the Essay you mention on this Subject, you will oblige me by sending it. I see by an Article in the news Papers about the last of Sept: that the Parliament of Paris is prosecuting the Jesuits & that they have offered a vast Sum to stop the Prosecution, I suppose there is no foundation for this, but shd: it prove true it will not surprize me, for it sometimes happens that a Transcendant Merit by exciting the passions of Envy, Malice & Hatred has drawn on the innocent as cruel Treatment as has been due to the worst of Malefactors —

You are in the right to keep up a Correspondence with Mr: Calvert on the terms you hold it & an acquaintance with my Ld: Baltimore if it can be done without fawning, however insignificant he may be. I am glad to hear you propose to learn Arithmetick, Book-keeping & surveying they will not take up much time, & you will find them [. . .]⁴ of their destination. You cannot expect any[th]ing int[. . .] on N. America Canada being reduced. You may hear some[thin]g of the Politicks relating to Maryland as Mr: Dulany is wi[th y]ou, who it is here said aimes at the Government of Maryland, [or] at least to get Mr: Ridout⁵ the present Commissary General removed & his Bror: Mr: Walter Dulany⁶ appointed in his sted or in case he shd: not succeed in that, to get him named to the Naval Office of Patuxent in the place of Mr: Ross⁷ who succeeded the unhappy Mr: Darnall, this is to yr:self. You may possibly be able to write me something relating to these transactions & to acquaint me wt: is become of poor Mr: Darnall, his scheme as I apprehend was to go to Watten or some such place to spend the remainder of his days, I wish he may succeed in it, his friends in that case will I believe contribute to pay for his board & Cloaths. I cannot find he has carry'd any Money with him, althô it is impossible to conceive how he has Squandered the sums wch: have past thrô his hands.

Mrs: Darnall presents her Compts & Hum: Service to you so does Mr: Croxall, Csn: Jo: Darnall⁸ has a sincere esteem & value for you, he is a man of strict Honr: his sons⁹ are worthy Youths, it may in time be in yr: power to serve them & I wish you to do it, & upon the strength of wt: I have wrote, I hope you will in yr: next letter desire to be remembred to him & them. I have lately built on Doohoregan a Brick stable 66 feet long & 42 feet wide, it will contain commodiously 34 horses, it is not showey on the outside but I intend to finnish it compleatly within, a very usefull & profitable discovery of several Quarries of Lime stone on my Land makes building cheap & easy to me there.

You will see by mine of Octo: 26¹⁰ how uneasy I was by not hearing from you, But by yr: 6 Letters 5 of wch came to hand the same day, I see with Satisfaction that you was not to blame for not writing, the fault was in not contriving to send yr: Letters as soon as they were wrote: In this Mr: Perkins must for the future assist you. He has a Correspondence at Glasgow, Bristol &c [.] He may know when Vessells are sailing from those ports. Mr: Glasford[11] at Glasgow will forward any letters under Cover to Mr: Robt: Petre at Bladensburgh by any Ships bound to Patowmack, & by any Ships bound up our Bay or to Patuxent from the sam[e] Port Letters will come to my Address, Letters by the Way of Bristol will come safe by any Vessel up the Bay directed to myself. Beside the Packets there are opportunities to Philadelphia & to Virginia[,] Letters under cover to Coll Hunter[12] at Hampton in that Colony will be forwarded by him, I shall not begrudge Postage. I know it is out of yr: way to forward your Letters & there fore I again say you must desire Mr: Perkins to do you & me that favour. Adieu my Dr Charley God grant you Health & every Blessing. I am Dr Charley

yr: M[o:] Afft: Father

Cha: Carroll

LS, Taylor Family Papers, No. 9965, ViU. Marked "Trip" by the clerk. Endorsed by CC: "7 Decb. 1761." Page containing the salutation missing; margins damaged.

1. At least one page missing.

2. Several lines missing.

3. "One must put oneself forward."

4. At least one line missing.

5. John Ridout (1732–1797). Born in Dorsetshire, England, and educated at Oxford, John Ridout emigrated to Maryland in 1753 as secretary to Gov. Horatio Sharpe whose patronage he enjoyed. In 1761 Ridout was Sharpe's candidate for the post of deputy secretary and served briefly before the appointment went to Daniel Dulany, Jr. Although disappointed in that respect, Ridout was already a member of the upper house and the Council, where he remained until 1776, and for a short while he also held the office of commissary general. He finally settled on the position of naval officer of Annapolis in 1762 and continued in it until 1777. He married Mary Ogle, daughter of former Maryland governor Samuel Ogle and Anne Tasker Ogle, in 1764, and with her had two sons and two daughters. When Horatio Sharpe returned to England in 1773, he left Ridout in charge of his affairs in Maryland and gave him the use of Whitehall, his Anne Arundel Co. estate, which Ridout bought in 1782. Although he signed the Oath of Fidelity before the July 25, 1778, deadline, Ridout was widely viewed as a loyalist during the American Revolution. The Ridouts' Annapolis home was on Duke of Gloucester Street, a few doors from the Carrolls' residence. *Bio. Dic. Md. Legis.*, II, 691–692.

6. Walter Dulany (?–1773). Apprenticed to a merchant in Philadelphia, Walter Dulany received a much more modest education than his older brother, Daniel, and became a merchant and a businessman. First elected to the lower house in 1745, he served there almost continuously for the next twenty years and during the same period filled a number of local offices such as deputy commissary for Anne Arundel Co. and councilman for Annapolis. Although Daniel Dulany, Jr., gained the deputy secretaryship of Maryland in 1761, Walter did not benefit from his brother's rise until 1765, when the younger man became naval offi-

cer of Patuxent. Thereafter, Walter's political fortunes rapidly improved: he became commissary general and a member of the Council in 1767 and took a seat in the upper house the following year, positions he continued to hold until his death. Married in 1745 to Mary Grafton, daughter of wealthy New Castle, Del., merchant Richard Grafton, Walter fathered three sons and four daughters. Ibid., I, 287–289.

7. John Ross (?–1766) of Annapolis was first appointed naval officer of Patuxent in 1727, but he resigned in 1729 when he was made clerk of the Council, a position he held for the next thirty-five years. After Henry Darnall III's abrupt departure in April 1761, Ross again assumed the naval officer's post at Patuxent and served until June 1765. Owings, *His Lordship's Patronage*, 136, 160.

8. Henry Darnall III's brother.

9. William Darnall (liv. 1749), John Darnall, Jr. (?–1796), Henry Darnall (?–1809), and Thomas Darnall (?–1798). Appendix I, Chart F.

10. Not found.

11. Probably John Glassford (1715–1783), founder of John Glassford and Company, a Glasgow mercantile firm trading to the Chesapeake, principally to ports on the Potomac River and Maryland's Eastern Shore. T. M. Devine, *The Tobacco Lords: A Study of the Tobacco Merchants of Glasgow and Their Trading Activities, c. 1740–90* (Edinburgh, 1975), 187; Edward C. Papenfuse, *In Pursuit of Profit: The Annapolis Merchants in the Era of the American Revolution, 1763–1805* (Baltimore, 1975), 38, 41.

12. Probably John Hunter (1733–1795), a merchant living at Little England, near Hampton, Va. Rutland, *Mason*, I, lxxi–lxiii.

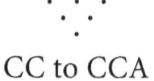

CC to CCA

Decb. 16th. 1761.

Dr. Papa,

I am informed by Mr. Perkins that a ship will sail for Maryland in a few days: as you desire me to write by every oportunity I wou'd not let slip this occasion of acquainting you that I am well. The fleet is arrived: it was separated some time after leaving the Capes in a hard gale of wind: one division came in with the Assistance man of war at 15 days interval the remainder under convoy of the postillion put into Plymouth. Kapt. Kelty was taken by a privateer in the chops of the chanel: the ship was ransomed at 2,000 guineas: she was insured at £4000. Kelty has since been obliged to put into Falmouth by stress of weather: Capt. Carroll wrote to me from thence: he is well: Mr. Brown is arrived in town and in good health.

I have received yr. letter of the 17th. Sepb. with the inclosed to Mr. Bladen and Sir Thomas Web. I am not acquainted with the latter: his younger son was my schoolfellow[.] When I was down in the west, I paid him a visit at Hadropth a country seat of his father's in Oxfordshire,[1] where he still resides. I shall inform myself wether Mr. Molineux is still with Sir Thomas: in that case, I propose waiting upon him with yr. letter & by his means to get introduced to Sir Thomas: I will do all in my power to assist Mr. Ireland as he is so deserving of it, & has gained yr. esteem wh he cou'd not have done without sufficient merit. I shall take to deliver Mr. Bladen's letter. Mr. Dulany is still at Bath: but I am told he receives but little benefit [from the] waters: the report of his returning Governor of Maryland, I take to be mere surmise: I never heard it mentioned: yet perhaps the report may prove true. I have taken a master of Arithmetick & have had him this month & better & am got to decimal fractions: Arithmetick takes up more of my time than I imagined it woud: but I am convinced its utility well deserves the time, labour, & expence I bestow on acquiring so necessary a knowledge: My Master gives me two lessons a week; his salary is a guinea a month.

My last letter was dated the 13th. of Octb. I sent you by the same oportunity the proceedings of the Parliatment of Paris against the Jesuits, the Almanacks & the maps you wrote for. Pere Croiset's exercises de pieté pour toute l'anneé et pour les fêtes et dimanches are come to hand: there are in all 18 volumes: the prime cost & carriage will come to 4 or 5 pounds. Mr. Crookshanks desires to be remembered to you in the kindest manner[.] In his last letter of the 12th. Sepb. he writes as follows: . . . . Tis hard to tell how they the Jesuits, will weather this storm: their enemies being so powerful & so violent, even to that degree that hitherto they have hindered them to print or publish any thing in their own Justification, while at the same time libells dayly appear loading them with all the infamy malice can invent & in some measure authorised by our Judge & party, for their place of sale & distribution is the sale de Palais.

I have bought Hume's History, wh is now compleated. I shall send this, Croiset's works, & the memorial of the late negotiations [2] [by] the fleet. Our Cousin Macnemara is a strange man: he has [little? thou]ght & no prudence. He came over to sollicit some employ in Maryland: he has as yet obtained nothing but assurances & promises: he has sold to Mr. Lawson or wants to sell his office of surveyor of the customs of Micocomico & Munni:[3] I say wants to sell for if Mr. Lawson or some one in his stead will not advance the money, Macnemara will not get the commission made out: for our Cousin wants ready money: he is much out of humour with the Merchants for not opening their purses. I have lent 10 guineas: he has given me his note of hand payable in 10 days: he tells me you have a good & sufficient security of his in yr. hands for a much larger debt. If he can not get ready money by some means or other, he will certainly be arrested for debt. By his own confession he owes upwards of £30. I shall advance him no more money & have told him as much.

I have received my Cousin Rach: Darnall's letter,[4] wh I shall answer by the fleet. In the mean while assure her of my love. She expresses so great a value, so sincere an affection for my dear Mama, such unfeigned sorrow at her death, that I love her tho' I have never seen her. I cou'd not refrain from tears on reading over that part of her letter in wh she mentions yr. last separation from my dying mother. I felt all yr. anguish & sorrow: I still feel the severe blow that has been given us. I must expect from time that remedy wh greater firmness than I am possessed of might, and Christian resignation ought to administer. I am Dr. Papa

Yr: most loving & dutiful Son
Ch: Carroll

ALS, Carroll Papers, MS 206, MdHi. Endorsed by CCA.

1. Hatherop is in Gloucestershire.

2. A compilation of the diplomatic documents exchanged between France and Great Britain relative to the possession of Canada, Newfoundland, Guadeloupe, and other territories at issue in the Seven Years' War appeared originally in French, but an English translation entitled *An Historical Memorial of the Negotiations of France and England from the 26th of March 1761 to the 20th of September of the Same Year, with the Vouchers* was published in London in 1761.

3. Macnemara had assumed the office of riding surveyor of Wicomico and Monie on Sept. 30, 1746. In December 1761 he succeeded in selling the post to William Bacon of Somerset Co. Owings, *His Lordship's Patronage*, 185.

4. Not found.

∴∵

CC to CCA

Decb. [19]th 1761

Dr. Papa,

I am Just returned from Si[r Thoma]s Webb[.] I sent my servant with your letter, he was told Sir Thomas woud call upon me: I thought it properer to wait upon him & prevent a 1st. visit. £30 have been paid to Mr. Pointz 10 whereof are appropriated to bear the charge of young Ireland's[1] passage to Maryland — Sir Thomas desired me to acquaint Mr. Ireland not to draw any more upon him as his bills will be sent back protested and at the same time told me he wou'd annually pay to Mr. Pointz on the 23d of Nob. each year 30 pounds, & 10 pounds apart for his son. If Mr. Ireland drew for £40 on Sir Thomas, as you seem to intimate, he must not be surprised to see his bill sent back protested, as that money for the year 61 has been advanced to Mr. Pointz & I suppose Mr. Ireland has received it before this. Mr. Ireland must put up with the charges of the protests: he had once the indiscretion to draw upon Sir Thomas for £100[.] His bill's being protested last year was oweing to his benefactor's absence, who was down in Gloucestershire with his younger son. Young Ireland is to return with the next fleet, he is now with his uncle an Apothecary in Wapping; he appears to be of a mild & tractable disposition, but utterly ignorant of wordly concerns & quite unexperienced. It was ill Judged to keep him so long at St. Omers. That education is only fit for Priests:

the little lattin he knows, for he knows but little, will be of no service to him in the capacity of a Planter and Mr Ireland's fortune will not permit him to act in a higher sphere. Had he been ta[k]en from St. Omers in Grammar and bound [to] some business he might by application & industry ha[ve se]cured a decent lively hood & been of great ass[istance to] his father, where as things are now circumstanced, he will, I fear, be a charge to him at least for some time. But let not this discourage Mr Ireland his son is young, tractable, sober, & indowed with sufficient sense. I have not the honour of knowing Lord Montague. I am acquainted with Sir Thomas's younger son but not intimately enough to sollicit by letter (our distance barrs all other communication) his influence & good will in Mr. Ireland's favour. £400 or 500 is a considerable sum of money: Mr. Ireland is not the only poor [re]lation who stands in need of assistance from Sir Thomas, & who is supported by his charity & munificence[.] You certainly rather wished, than hoped, the advancement of such a sum. I did not so much as mention it, a request of that sort wou'd have been ill timed & perhaps displeasing. I hope Mr. Ireland by means of the £30 conditional not settled annunity, by the little assistance you may lend him, & by his own industry, will be enabled to live comfortably, & to leave his Son a competent livelyhood.

We have no very interesting news. The fate of Colberg is yet undecided. By the last accounts General Romanzoff was still before that place:[2] The Parlt. is unanimous in supporting the measures of our late great Minister & seems determined to prosecute the German war with the utmost vigour. According to our papers 12000 men are to be sent over to Germany early in the spring. We begin to find the scarity of money & men. An additional tax is laid upon windows, & one (as is said,[)] is to be laid on dogs. Our Cousin Macnemara was with me this afternoo[n] as I was busy in writing he staid but a minute or two & then took his leave seemingly in an ill humour. I conducted him to the door where stopping short, he with some emotion desired me, as I was writing to my father, to inform him, that he shoud return soon to Maryland that you need not give yourself any pain or concern about him; that he was the best Judge of his own affairs, that he hoped to transact them in such a manner as to give satisfaction to himself & to his friends: Is this style suitable & becoming a man who a few days ago was under the strongest apprehensions of being arrested for a debt of 3 or 4 pounds? Pray give my compliments to Richard Croxall & to his brother: to Mrs. Lawson & Doct. Lyon. I am Dr. Papa

Most affectionately Yours

Ch: Carroll

ALS, Carroll Papers, MS 206, MdHi. Addressed by CC. Endorsed by CCA.

1. John Ireland, who attended St. Omers from 1753 until 1760. Holt, *St. Omers,* 144.

2. Late in 1761 the fortified town of Kolberg, located on the Baltic Sea at the mouth of the Prosnica River, fell to the Russians. Gipson, *Culmination,* 61.

CC's Account of Expenses

Accots. of Ch: Carroll Jur—

P: 1

1761			£	S	D
Jany.	1st.	To sope, pouder 3 lb. of candles	2	11	
	2d.	To the magazine, weekly bill, 2 weeks washing		7	
	Do.	to loss at play, mahogony Table & bottle stands	3	5	6
	7	Paid to my Servant residu of his wagers for 60	4	5	
		to an Iron scraper & Decantors & washing		12	
		to tea Bohea ½ lb. at 10s per lb.		0	5
		to Sugar		6	5
		to the weekly bill to Candles 3 lb.		4	9
Jany.	13th.	to ¼ rent due 25th. Deb. 1760	10		
	Do.	to vales & loss at cards		17	
		to the weekly bill. to a bag for my hair, coach hire		6	11½
		to vales to the Play		5	6
Do.	26	to a dinner to 5 persons	1	2	10
		to a Ball given by the Marylanders my quota	6	6	
Do.	27	to weekly bill, pometum, washing sweeping chymnys		10	
	Do.	to the Play		3	
	28	to the Gardiners Bill, to the Play		6	5
		to pouder for my hair & biscuits, weekly bill		2	9
	9	to 6 lb. of candles to blacking the stove & Lemons		4	11½
		to a Chanty Concert & Opera		15	6
		to Vales & Coach hire		1	6
Feby.	1st.	to the weekly Bill, magazines, riband,¹ fire wood		7	1
		to 2 weeks washing to vales, loss at Cards		11	6
	5th.	to the Play, Washing, weekly bill		6	1
	6	to ½ lb. of Bohea Tea at 10S per lb., dying silk stockings		10	

			£	S	D
	Do.	to mending the same & coach hire		2	
Febry. 16		to Mr. Coles Bill for a Supper	2	5	
	Do.	to one lb. of sope, loss at Cards		2	7
	17	to Charges for the Medeira wine & Cain Spirits		10	6
		to loss at Cards, vales to Servants		12	6
		to washing, weekly Bill & Letter		3	9
	26	Paid to my Servant	1	1	
	Do.	to loss at Cards		3	
March 2d.		to washing, Vales, weekly Bill to a pair of gloves		8	6½
Do.	7	to My Servant	1	1	
	9	to washing, 6 lb. of Candles, weekly Bill		8	3½
		to loss at Cards		5	6
		to Croisets Reflextions 2 volus. 80.		5	
		to the Oratorio		3	6
	16	to the weekly Bill, to vales, Charity		8	6
	24	to Washing, Vales, fire wood, weekly bill		5	
	Do.	to my Servant	1	1	
			53		4[2]

[2]

			£	S	D
	Do.	to my Servant		8	
March 26		Paid to keeping a Mare at grass 18 weeks	1	16	
		to shoeing Do. to Vales to the Servants at Iver[3]		12	
		to turnpikes			4
Do.	29	Paid to my Servant	3	3	
		to boat, Chanty, Letters, loss at Cards		2	9
April	1st.	To the weekly Bill, to Sope, beating Carpets		3	8½
		to the Porters		2	
	2d.	Paid to Mr. Bird for 2 chests of Florence wine	8	5	
	Do.	to loss at Cards, ½ lb. of Bohea Tea		8	
		to washing, vales, Tennis Court, turnpikes		12	11
		to Coach hire & vales		4	
Do.	8	to My Servant	1	1	
		To Waddington a horse dealer		4	
		To the Weekly Bill, collar, comb & spunge		5	1½
		To the Magazine, to a key to a Cive & measure		4	6

			£	s.	d.
		To a staple & ring, salt, flower of Brimstone[4] & Antimony[5]		1	7
		to a Chair to Mr. Bladen's & vales to Dos. servants		6	6
		to Bleeding my Mare			9
Do.	11	to ¼ Rent (Repairs deducted[)]	7	10	6
		to hire of a horse		4	6
		to mounting a Tortoise shell snuff box sent from Paris	2	2	
		to vales, coach hire, pometum, pouder		2	10
		to the Lawers Magazine,[6] Chimney Sweepers, stirups Irons		4	1½
		to a Halter, Black Smith, powdering ingien[7]		2	10
		to the weekly Bill, loss at Cards, washing		8	6
Do.	14	Paid to ¼ for the London Evening Posts		6	6
		to the Tennis Court, vales, party of pleasure in the country	1		
		To the weekly Bill, bleeding my Mare		2	
		to the Carpenters Bill, washing, loss at Cards		13	8½
		to vales, Sugar loaf 8 lb. 11 oz. at 10d per lb.		8	3
		To the Roseiad[8] a Poem, Taylor, coffee, to a Tragedy	1	10	6
		To the Practice of the Kings Bench & Com: Pleas 2 volus.[9]		12	
Do.	26	to washing, weekly Bill, flower of Brim: & Antimony		5	2½
		to the Play, Cards, vales, coa[c]h hire, dish of coffee		11	6
May	1st.	to shoes, vales	1	2	6
	2d.	Paid to my Servant	1	1	
		to the weekly Bill to Bran, 3 lb. of candles		7	6
		to Anti: & flower of Brimstone		1	
		to shoeing my Mare		2	4
Do.	7	to the Window tax for 1 year & a half		13	6
	11	To Coffee, 2 weeks washing, weekly bill, shoeing horn		7	6½
		Postage, ½ lb. of Bohea tea, hire of a horse, vales, turnpikes		12	8
	13	To the weekly Bill, writing bookes, bleading my Mare, stuffing the saddle		10	3½
	14	Spent in taking a ride into the Country		10	

			£	S	D
Do.	20	Paid to Mr. Crookshanks for the Atlass & snuff box	18	2	5½
			57	16	11

			£	S	D
		Spent at Vaux hall[10]		18	4
May	25	to washing, weekly bill, coach hire		11	5½
		to a Poem, to the play		6	
Do.	29	Paid to my Servant	2	2	
		To the Carpenter, weekly bill, bran, loss at cards		15	2½
		To the magazine, turnpikes, Ostler		2	
June	6th.	Paid to my Landress her wages	4	14	6
		to the weekly bill, seeing Chelsea Gardens[11]		3	9½
		to 2 weeks washing & 2 caps		7	11
	10th.	Given to Mr. Chapman[12] to offer prayers for my Mother	5	5	
		To Zutart the Juggler		4	
		To vales to ¼ of lb. of green tea at S 16 the lb.		5	
		To Bran, pometum, weekly bill, vales, coffee		5	7
Do.	16	To washing, Jant to Woolwich		11	½
	21	Subscribed to the cold Bath for ¼ of a year[13]		14	
		Washing, weekly bill, a picker, broom, turnpikes		6	11½
	24	to a pair of silk stocking breatches seating another	1	2	6
	25	Spent in a Journey to Ryegate in Surry		9	1
	30	To washing, beating the Carpets, Mop, weekly bill		6	10
July	1st.	Paid to ¼ rent due at midsummer 1761	10		
	Do.	To vales, Farriers bill	1	19	6
	2d.	Spent in a party to Vauxhall		8	
Do.	4th.	Given to Mr. Baker to offer up prayers	5	5	
	5th.	To Coach hire, Vales, washing, weekly bill		13	8½
Do.	10	Paid to my Servant ½ a years wages	7	8	
		To Vales & spent in going into the Country		12	6
	14	spent during 4 day's stay at Ryegate in Surry	1		
	15	To washing		2	2
Do.	23	To the weekly bill, riding out, to vales		16	3
		To ½ lb. of Bohea Tea at 10s per lb.		5	

			£	S	D
28	To the Taylor, to lamp Oil, to riding out, Ostlers &c			6	
Do.	To a pair of Sheets making included		1	6	8
	To 2 weeks washing			5	4
29	Bought a new horse		12	12	
	To vales, pouder, soleing my boots, 2 lb. of sope			7	
	To the Weekly Bill			2	5½
	To a pair of Doe skin breeches		1	11	6
31st.	To my quota for a Servant's horse		4	11	
	To glove tops to feeding the horses & vales at Rygate			7	5
	To pair of shoe Buckles my quota of a Portmanteau			9	8
Augst 2d.	To washing the Bed curtains & quilt			7	6
	To washing & mending weekly bill			6	8½
	To ¼ of the London Evening Post			6	6
	To Turnpikes, straps & Ostler			3	1½
			71	4	2½

[4]

		£	S	D
Augst. 3d.	Paid to my Servant	2	2	
Do.	To sope box & brush		3	4
	To the Magazine			6
Octob. 11th.	To loss at Cards		6	
Do.	To a horse at Livery stable 2 nights hay & Corn		3	
10	To turnpikes, dinner, vales, coach hire		5	6
13	To ¼ rent for my Chambers due Sepb. 19th	10		
15	To Diag: of the Dead,[14] Melmoth transla: of Cicero's Letters[15]		19	
Do.	To the Maps of Several counties in England & Wales		7	6
16	To Vales, coach hire, loss at Cards to the play	1		6
	To 2 bushel of Coals		2	2
17	To the Magazine, 2 quire of Paper, 6 lb. of candles		6	4
Do.	To mending the Stable fork pair of thread stockings		4	
18	to ¼ Evening Post, blacking turnpikes		8	11

	19	to 2 China cups, weekly bill, vales, 2 week's washing		10	9½
Do.	Do.	To feeding a Cat		2	3
	20	To mending stockings, Carpet, Sheets		3	6
	23	To the play, playbook, coffee, fruit &c		7	10
Do.	24	To My Journey absent 9 weeks 3 days	35	10	
	25	To letter, vales, 2 weeks washing weekly bill		5	
	27	to Sugar 8 lb. 13 oz at 10d per lb. of double refined		7	4
	Do.	To keeping of a horse from 28 March Octb. 27th	6	8	
Nob.	1st.	To keeping a horse 2 nights at livery stable		6	2
	Do.	to turnpikes		1	6
	4	Paid for a supper given at my Chambers		17	11
	6	Paid to my Servant	2	2	
	Do.	To shoeing my horse weekly bill, 2 weeks washing		10	5½
	10	To mending, ribanding, ruffling 2 shirts		4	10
	Do.	To the Negotiations of a peace		2	6
		By mistake gave ½ a guinea for 6d.		10	6
	17	To my Servant	1	1	
	18	To 2 weekly bills		7	2½
	20	To loss at Cards, to vales		6	
Deb.	1st.	To 3 weeks washing		6	6
	Do.	To the Play spent at Ryegate		16	
	2d.	To 2 weekly bills, coach hire, ½ lb. of Tea, To the Taylor		13	5
	3d.	To 3 lb. of candles, to the play, to a pair of worsted stockings		11	10
	Do.	To vales & Coach hire		2	2
	4	To 6 volus. in Quarto of Hume's Hist: of England	4	9	
	Do.	Law Catalogue, Doc: & Shed: Cowel's Institutes[16]		8	6
	6	To my Arith: Master	1	1	
		To an Arith: book		2	
	9	Subscribed to Sheridan's lectures on Elocution[17]	1	1	
			76	4	11½

		£	S	D
Do.	To Riding out, vales, & coach hire		9	
10th	To a chair, loss at cards		4	
11	To cutting & curling my hair lost at the Tennis Court		13	
12	To the Taylors bill		7	
13	To 2 weekly bills		3	10
Do.	To 3 lb. of candles		1	10
Do.	To the magazine, sope, pometum		[2	6]
14	To 3 lb. of candles for my Servant		1	10
Do.	To the Black Smith		1	
19	To my Servant		1	1
Do.	To Coach hire to Sir Tho: Webb's		4	
21	To one weekly bill		2	2
Do.	To the Carpenter & 2 lb. of pouder at 6 per Do.		2	
24	To the Gardiner's bill for cutting the Jessamine &c		3	8
Do.	To vales		1	
28	To the weekly bill 3 lb. of candles		3	11
Do.	To a Mop, firemen, Chimney Sweeper		5	6
Do.	To soft pometum [. . .]ing		9	4
Do.	To loss at Cards & vales		5	6
29	To Christmas boxes	3	3	
30	To Coach hire & Vales		2	6
	Spent in diet during the year 1761	31	9	3½
		39	15	10½
	Sum Total	298	5	3½ [18]
	Remains	5	4	8½

The enclosed[19] was sent to me By Mr. Crookshanks In order to forward it to you that you might procure if possible the mortuary bill: it relates to some of the French Neutrals & perhaps those at Annapolis may give you the necessary lights upon the subject: a speedy answer is desired—

AD, Carroll-Maccubbin Papers, MS 219, MdHi. Endorsed by CCA: "1761 Decemr: 30 My Sons Expences from January 1st."
  1. A ribbon used especially as a decoration.
  2. CC totaled his figures at the bottom of each page.
  3. Iver is located near Heathrow.

4. Flour of brimstone, a form of sulphur, was used as a tonic.

5. Antimony is an emetic and diaphoretic.

6. *The Lawyers Magazine, or, Attorneys and Solicitors Universal Library.*

7. Probably a powdering "engine," a device for dusting powder on the hair or on a wig.

8. [Charles Churchill], *The Rosciad* (London, 1761).

9. [William Brown], *The Practice of the Courts of the Kings Bench and Common Pleas . . .* (London, 1696).

10. This entry is listed twice but the expenditures only once.

11. The "Phisick" or "Botanick" Garden in Chelsea was established in the seventeenth century.

12. Probably Francis Chapman (1704-?), a native of Warwickshire and a Franciscan who had studied at Douai. Foley, *Records,* VI, 471-472.

13. CC's subscription to "the cold Bath" is the first evidence of a practice he was to follow throughout his life. After his return to Maryland, he supervised the construction of a cold bath at Doohoragen Manor, and his use of it became in his later years an indispensable part of his daily regimen.

14. [George Lyttelton, Baron Lyttelton], *Dialogues of the Dead* (London, 1760).

15. William Melmoth's (1710-1799) translation of Cicero's *The Letters of Marcus Tullius Cicero to Several of His Friends* appeared in three volumes in 1753. A London edition of 1753 and a Dublin edition of the same year appear in *Cat. Lib.,* nos. 214, 215.

16. Johanne Cowello [John Cowell] (1554-1611), *Institutiones Juris Anglicani ad Methodum et Seriem Institutionum Imperialium Compositae et Digestae . . .* (Cambridge, 1605), was translated into English as *The Institutes of the Lawes of England, Digested into the Method of the Civill or Imperiall Institutions . . .* (London, 1651).

17. Thomas Sheridan (1719-1788), *A Course of Lectures on Elocution . . .* (London, 1762). *Cat. Lib.,* no. 992.

18. Actually £298 2s. 3½d., leaving a balance of £5 7s. 8½d.

19. Enclosed were an official copy of Jean Bequet's baptismal certificate dated Feb. 18, 1696, and a copy of a deposition attesting to Bequet's death about 1748. Carroll Papers, MS 206.

CC to CCA

Janry. 5th. 1762.

Dr. Papa,

I embrace with pleasure this opportunity of presenting you with my sincerest and most ardent wishes for your good health and happiness during the course of this and many succeeding years: whatever is like to alter or disturb the one or the other gives me the greatest concern. Your present difficulties and embroils, may, I fear, hurt your health but yr. happiness founded on virtue and conscious innocence is secure from envy and superiour to the base arts of Malice: will not a family dispute[1] attended with such rancour and animosity bring upon you much vexation and trouble? Is it not better to yield up a few points, tho' Just, than to be involved in a long, expensive, and troublesome law suit. Too close application to business may impair your health, which is most dear to me, and for my sake, if not for your own, ought to be to you. Harry[2] has been with me twice or thrice: each time our discourse run entirely upon Maryland affairs: he has given me some little insight into them: and if things are fairly stated & truely represented by him, I think, my presence in Maryland necessary, and a longer than one year's absence from this time, prejudicial to my Interest. I can study the Law at home as well as in the Temple: Reading alone, is not sufficient to know the Law, it must be Joined to practice, and of doeing this I can have no opportunity till I come to the management of my own affairs.

I have seen the famous Dulaney: he came to town from Bath a few days before Christmas; I had wrote to him & enclosed yr. letter in mine, not knowing of his being come to town. He proposes returning to Bath in Febury: his brother[3] is there at present and will take Care of the letter. Mr. Dulaney the day I saw him was very much out of order; he received me politely and promised to return the visit when able; said he shou'd be glad to see me whenever I came that way: we had some little discourse about the Law suit with Clifton & Mercer.[4] He seemed to . Intimate that you thought yourself more Injured than you really were & imparted to me this very remarkable piece of intelligence, wh he had received from Mercer: much to this purpot. That Mercer's Lawer consented and even wanted the decree to be reversed in full confidence of obtaining one much more favourable to his Client, and to use Dulaney's words, that he might smash your Father, meaning you. I sent my servant with the packet the same day: when I mentioned my having such a packet by me, he told me his present ill state of health rendered him unfit for business, and incapable of serious reading and close application. However he wou'd employ some other person to examin the proceedings, if his health woud not permit him to take that trouble upon himself.

This feasting visiting time has prevented my studying the cases you have drawn; they seem intricate and demand a good deal of thought and consideration. I am to dine the 7th. Instant at Mr. Bladen's: Dulaney and several others, my countrymen are to be of the party. This day war against Spain is to be proclaimed. Ireland will be the bearer of this: he is innocent, modest, and does not want for sense, encourage & excite him to be industrious. Several news papers, 2 magazines, and the memorial of the late negotiations between France and England go with him. In my letter of the 19th Decb. I informed you of my waiting upon Sir Thomas Webb & of what passed between us, a repetition wou'd be tiresome & is unnecessary as Mr. Ireland can by word of mouth acquaint you with every particular. Sir Thomas has been so obliging as to return my visit. We hear nothing further of the proceedings of the Parliament against the Jesuits.

A Law suit is now depending in Chancery between Mr. Pointz and one Brome-field and others for a very large fortune. Bromfield is heir at Law to an old woman, who died about a year ago in the 80th. year of her age, and left all her fortune some trifling legacies to her relations excepted, to Mr. Pointz[.] Pointz had transacted her business for several years before her death: & had at her death in his hands a considerable part of her fortune to the amount, as set forth in the bill, of 10 or 12000 pounds Sterling: Mrs. Row the testatrix has granted to Mr. Pointz In her last will a release & discharge of all accounts: The plaintiff prays Mr. Pointz may be made accountable: Pointz pleaded the release & discharge: his plea was overruled & he is to account. . . . He will give in his answer in this next or the term after. I am Dr. Papa

Yr. most affectionate and Dutiful Son
Cha: Carroll

P:S:

My compliments to Mr. Richard Croxall

ALS, Carroll Papers, MS 206, MdHi. Endorsed by CCA.

1. The "family dispute" was a continuation of the disagreement that began in 1757 when Charles Carroll of Duddington contested CCA's administration of estates from which the younger man was to receive an inheritance.

2. Capt. Henry Carroll.

3. Lloyd Dulany (1742–1782), the son of Daniel Dulany, Sr., and his third wife, Henri-etta Maria Lloyd Chew Dulany, was only eleven at his father's death and grew up under the guardianship of his brother, Daniel Dulany, Jr. Admitted to Clare College, Cambridge, in 1760, Lloyd entered the Middle Temple the following year. Upon his return to Maryland he married Elizabeth Brice, the daughter of John Brice II and Sarah Frisby Brice, became a leading figure on the Annapolis social scene, and spent liberally in building himself an im-pressive brick house on Conduit Street. In 1773 he was co-president of the Maryland Jockey Club. An active loyalist, he left Maryland in 1775 for London, carrying letters from Gov. Robert Eden to the earl of Dartmouth, the colonial secretary. In 1782 Lloyd Dulany was killed in a duel in Hyde Park by the Reverend Bennet Allen, a longtime family antagonist. Land, *Dulanys of Maryland*, 166, 217–219, 296–297, 317–318, 324, 328–329; James Haw, "The Patronage Follies: Bennet Allen, John Morton Jordan, and the Fall of Horatio Sharpe," *Md. Hist. Mag.*, LXXI (1976), 139–144.

4. John Mercer (1704–1768), a native of Dublin, immigrated to Virginia in 1720 and settled in Stafford Co. In 1728, after spending several years in mercantile activity, he entered the practice of law. His compilation of Virginia statutes, entitled *An Exact Abridgment of All the Public Acts of Assembly, of Virginia* . . . was published in Williamsburg in 1737. Ex-tensively involved in land speculation and business in both Virginia and Ireland, Mercer subsequently served as secretary of the Ohio Company. Rutland, *Mason*, I, lxxix.

CC to CCA

Jany. 8th. 1762.

Dr. Papa,

My old play fellow, Mr. Lawson insisted upon my writing a line or 2 by him: without which sanction he shou'd be ashamed, he said, to see you. Ti's merely to comply with his request that I write this, having nothing new or material to add to what has been already imparted to you, in my preceeding letters. Yesterday I dined at Mr. Bladen's; we came away about 6 o'clock: Dulaney was so much indisposed with a cold attended with a swelling in his face and throat that he cou'd not venture out. I delivered your letter to Mr. Bladen who politely enquired after you: he bears his age extreamly well, looks fresh and Jolly. I am astonished two such fine young ladies have remained so long, and still remain single: if beauty and sense improved by the best education, command esteem & inspire love, no lady was ever better entitled to both than the Miss Bladens: very few of our young gentrey, if any, are deserving of them: They themselves are not sensible enough of their own worth, to entertain such a thought; possessed of every advantage, every amiable endowment of the fair, they are without that almost common fault to all, a too great sense & opinion of their own charms.

Warlike preparations are carried on briskly in every department: but for publick news I refer you to the papers. The war seems likely to spread still further: it will, ti's imagined, extend to Italy: Unless Denmark Joins Prussia this next campaign, that great Hero,[1] must fall under the united efforts of such powerful allies . . . Take care of yr. health if you love me. . I am Dr. Papa

Yr. most affectionate and Dutiful Son
Ch: Carroll.

ALS, Carroll Papers, MS 206, MdHi. Addressed by CC. Endorsed by CCA.
1. Frederick the Great.

CC to CCA

17th. March 1762

Dr. Papa,

My last was dated the 5th. of Januy: you have no doubt received my several letters of the 13 Octb. 16, & 19 Dob. they will inform you what steps I have taken to serve Mr. Ireland & with what success: But Mr. Ireland has I hope already had the satisfaction of learning all this from his Son who left England at least London 3 months ago. I have received yr. letters of the 26 Octb.[1] Nob. 11.[2] Deb. 7th. I write to you almost every month: the oportunities of a speedy & safe conveyance are very rare & precarious few Merchants caring to trust their ships upon so long a voya. without convoy. Independent of yr. commands, wh I always make it my study to obey, I find too great a pleasure in writing to you to deprive myself of that satisfaction: Mr. Perkins tells me he seldom or ever knows of ships sailing from Bristol or the other outward ports.

I coud indulge my grief in dwelling upon a melancholy subject were it not for fear the tender feelings of an over flowing heart might soften yours, and provoke fresh tears. Capt. Carroll is pretty often with [me]; I like his company as you generally are the topic of our conversation. His accounts of Maryland in as much as they concern me are very unfavourable. I may lead a happy life in my native country tho' the prospect seems unpromising. But as I expect little happiness, So if I meet with difficulties I shall not be disappointed & unprepared. Mr. Dulaney has told Capt. Carroll his health will not permit him to examin the papers sent him; he told me as much when they were 1st delivered, but added that shoud his indisposition wh hindered his application to buysiness, continue he wou'd give them to some other Lawer to revise them: This he has not done. I have called upon him several times but can never meet with him at his Lodgings. I shall desire him to return the Packet that I may consult Mr. Hutton or some one else upon the case in question & ask his opinion wether an appeal will lay against that decree. Perhaps this may give offence to Mr. Dulaney but I shall take care to manage the affair in such a manner as to remove all suspicion of diffidence or disgust.

30 books & other pieces containing the constitution & doctrines of the Jesuites have been publickly burnt at Rhoüen persuant to an arrêt of the Parlt. of Normandy issued the 12th. Febry., by wh the Jesuites are enjoined to evacuate their houses before the 1st. of July next & to retire wither they shall think proper, there to live in a clerical way under the authority of the Bishops; their estates & effects of whatever kind they may be will be put under the care of Administrators. I have desired Mr. Jenison to translate such passages of the Italian letters, as to him appear the most material & interesting. I have not as yet seen the essay.

Are all the Law books sent from Maryland yours? I ask this because some have my Grandfather's coat of arms & others have not, in some I find Daniel Carroll's name written: several want new binding but they will scarce answer the expence being old & bad editions. Maccarty has taken the benefit of the Insolvent Act he has quitted his Chambers in Gray's Inn but cannot learn wither he has removed to. The Pipe of Madeira is at last arrived. I have not as yet tasted it: but doubt not of its being good If I may Judge from the price. I wou'd willingly enlarge the circle of my acquaintance; but to get acquainted with men of such eminence & influence is extremely difficult if not impossible to one in my station. The frequenting of company in high life wou'd be attended with great expence & loss of time, & other inconveniencies; without any other advantage than the knowledge of such persons, their follies vices & extravagancies.

I have begun to learn the Italian method of book keeping.[3] It is certainly useful & ought to be known by all Merchants & men in buysiness. It gives me real satisfaction to hear you enjoy yr. health & a good habit of body. Yr life is dear to me beyond any thing in this world: yr. death wou'd be the greatest misfortune that can befall me. I daily pray to God that whenever he pleases to take you from me you may be found duly prepared to appear before yr. Omnipotent, Just & merciful Judge. Frequent thoughts on this melancholy subject accompanied with proper acts of resignation to the divine will might soften the 1st. impressions of grief. But the remedy is worse than the evil. I shoud thus anticipate my unhappiness and bewail as present what may be & I hope is still at a great distance. Whenever I lose you my loss will be exceeding great: shoud that fatal day be near at hand, shoud you be snatched from me in my absence to what difficulties woud you leave me exposed? without experience perhaps without a friend, surrounded with enemies, engaged in hereditary quarrels, bewildered in the labarynths of Law, obliged to dive into old an intricate accounts & to rummage for papers, wh I shou'd not know where to look for: besides encumbered with the management of a large estate and unacquainted with buysiness an utter stranger to the people, country, & situation of my affairs. A year or two's experience and yr. assistance wou'd prevent all these inconveniencies; you wou'd soon make me acquainted with the true state of the disputes you are engaged in, with the character, disposition and temper of those with whom it might be my interest to be connected, or of those whom it wou'd [be] adviseable to shun: You woud instruct me to manage the estate, as you have done with prudence & oeconomy: Yet I must forego all these advantages to compleat the term of years destined to my reading the Law: of what great advantage will the knowledge of the law be to me? I can't be called to the bar & of course can not practice & Lawers do not care to [be] instructed by those who employ them: I believe you have experienced this more than once to be true. If other occupations in Maryland will hinder my further application to the Law of what service will 4 years study be? If you still adhere to yr. former resolution I readily submit to it & will endeavour to make the best use of my time.

I desire to be remembered in the kindest Manner to Mr. Croxall & my Cousin John Darnall for both whom I entertain a sincere regard as worthy men, yours and, I hope, my friends. My compliments to Mrs. Darnall. I am Dr. Papa

Yr. most affectionate & dutiful Son
Ch: Carroll

P:S:

I have enclosed & sent by this oportunity to Mr. Harden at Philadelphia[4] the papers relative to the late rupture with Spain: I have read & found them interesting: If I am not mistaken they will afford you some instruction at least pleasure.

The death of the late Czarina will, ti's generally thought, alter the system of her Court: the new Emperor, if credit can be given to our papers, is desirous of peace & will conclude a peace with the king of Prussia:[5] That Monarch is making great preparations to sustain the last efforts of the Empress queen: wh in all probability will prove abortive, if the Russians as ti's reported withdraw & become spectators instead of actors in these fresh scenes of slaughter & inhumanity. Portugal will be obliged in all likelyhood against its interest & inclination to take part in the present war & declare against Spain: My Lord Tyrawley[6] is gone to Lisbon, he will command the English forces wh are to be sent to the relief of the king of Portugal: warlike stores are shipped on board all the vessels bound to that kingdom. Marshal Broglio is in disgrace: D'Etreès in conjunction with Soubise is to command the french troops in Germany this campaign.[7]

ALS, Carroll Papers, MS 206, MdHi. Endorsed by CCA. List of names in unknown hand not reproduced.

1. Not found.

2. Presumably the letter of Nov. 10, 1761, above.

3. Double-entry bookkeeping.

4. Probably Harding, a Philadelphia merchant.

5. Upon becoming czar in January 1762 on the death of his aunt, the Czarina Elizabeth, Peter III (1728–1762), a staunch admirer of Frederick the Great, moved quickly to terminate Russia's alliance with Austria and to ally instead with Prussia.

6. James O'Hara, Baron Kilmaine and second Baron Tyrawley (1690–1773).

7. Charles de Rohan, prince de Soubise (1715–1787) and Louis-Charles-César, duc d'Estrées (1697–1774), replaced Victor-François, duc de Broglie (1718–1804), as commanders of the French armies in 1762. Gipson, *Culmination,* 63.

CCA to CC

April 8 [1762][1]

[Dr Charley,]

The 10th of last Month I desired Mr: Perkins to acquaint you that I had reced yr: two letters of the 13th & 22d of Octo: wch: were brought by one Capt: Ramsay[2] who arrived here about the middle of last Janry & did not deliver the letters until the 8th: of last Month. Had Mr: Perkins observed my directions & sent me a single letter advising that I had a Packet & Packages on Board, this delay could not have happened, & I shd: not have rebuked you as I did in mine of the 30th of Janry 1762.[3] Our Merchts: are eager to get business, but very careless to deserve it by doing any little services out of the beaten path of Trade, this you will find to be true unless they much alter their Conduct—

You did prudently in not abruptly communicating my letter to Mr Calvert, but shd: that subject at any time be again started in Conversation, it may not be improper perhaps to let him know wt: I say —

Yr: Colt Nimble will I think make a fine horse, he is 3 years old this Grass & is 14 hands 2 Inches & ½ high, I expect he will rise to at least 15 hands. Cannot you adroitly come at a thorough bred Horse or Mare among some of yr: Country acquaintance at an easy rate? In that Case Capt: Carroll would be carefull of them, think of it between this & his next Voyage —

If I made any mistake about yr: Horse hire & keeping, I apprehend that upon inspecting yr: Acct you will find you led me into it —

I never meant that you shd: act as a Counsellor even provided you could by any means consistent with Honr: & Conscience be called to the Barr if the Title of Barrister could be so obtained, it might not be improper to get it. I am pleased with yr: Sentiments & shall be ever far from advising you to any step wch: may expose yr: Honr: or sincerity to Censure.

I am glad to hear you are Resolved to learn Book-keeping &c, & I again strongly recommend it to you to carry yr: Resolution into Execution.

A Gamester is certainly not an Eligible Companion but an Acquaintance without an intimacy may I think be kept up with such a one without running into the dangers you seem to apprehend, & wch: I would have you by all means avoid. I have formerly explained my motives for yr: being at least polite to him.

As no judgment was obtained agst Darnall & his sureties, & as his Lands were made over to me, they cannot be liable to wt: he owes the Publick, which amounts at least to £13 or £1400 Ster: The money I advanced on his Acct is in a great measure paid & the Ballce is very secure.

It gives me pleasure to hear that yr: Jaunt proved instructive, pleasant & agreeable to you, & it will be a great satisfaction to me to receive yr. Journal. Is it too much to tell you, you owe me the Journals of all yr: Tours but one.

I have not fail'd to pay yr: Complts: to those you desired to be remembred to —

I see how severely the Jesuits have been handled by the Parliamt: of Paris, particular Members of that Society may be indiscreet, they may be wicked, Judas was numbred among the 12. But is it not inconsistent with the Rules of Justice [. . .] [4] [this, if the Body should] not be [liable] to the Co[ntracts of Individuals in a business? transaction, because] it is the Body that is trusted, [as Individuals are known to] have no property. But the Parliament seems to [me to have] exceeded the Bounds of their Jurisdiction in censuring the opinions of their Authors, wch I shd: think only fall properly under the Cognizance of an Ecclesiastical Tribunal: moreover wt: may not any Author be made to say if particular propositions or sentences be extracted from his Writings without paying a just regard to the whole Tenor of his Doctrine? Is it not by such means that every sect of Xtians adapt the Scriptures to their opinions? And are not those Sacred Oracles made to countenance the most impious & blasphemous Doctrines? It is true their Constitutions

& the Bulls & priviledges granted them & the Doctrine of their Obedience may contain things not to be supported & therefore not dangerous, for wt: ever a man may grant, wt: ever Rules he may lay down, wt: ever Doctrines he may profess, if they be inconsistent with reason & Contrary to Morality Justice & Religion they are in themselves void & can have no ill Effect, & this has been the Case in all the instances mentioned for has any Evil resulted from the Bulls, their Constitutions or Doctrine? My meaning may be explained in some measure by the following instance wch: I acknowledge not to be quite apposite as the point is still Controverted. Upon the Restoration every Church in England sounded with the Doctrine of Passive Obedience & Non Resistance wch: was much more effectively refuted by practice than supported by Argument. The Popes extravagant priviledges to the Society amount to no more than an Expression of their sense of their great merit, they were not so ignorant as not to know the power of their Successors would be equal to their own. The implicit Obedience professed by the Jesuits cannot be meant by common Sense & Justice to extend beyond things innocent, indifferent & Just. Have they murdered, burnt or destroy'd in virtue of their Obedience? I say it as my Sentiment their Eminen[t] Merit & Virtue has provoked this persecution. The figure they make in the Church, in their Schools, the notice taken of them by the several Rom: Cath: Courts in Europe excites the Envy of even the other Religious orders, who perhaps with complacency see them distressed not considering Proximus ardet.[5] I have I thank God been bred among them, & if you do wt: they have taught you & nothing contrary to it, you will be happy here & hereafter: Can there be a stronger instance of the King of France's weakness than to suffer the Parliamt: to carry their insolence & wickedness to such unwarrantable lengths, but Delirant Reges plectuntur Achivi—[6]

I find we have a Spanish War, & that Mr: Pit is not reinstated: however successfull the Nation has been under his Administration, it's certain he must fall into Contempt with all honest men. Who more averse to Continental Connexions? Who with a more lavish hand has squandered the national Treasure on the Continent? A truly virtuous man cannot be guilty of such inconsistencies. If Government cannot be carry'd on without corruption there is an end of the Constitution, the keeping up of forms may deceive the multitude. Virtue has abandoned us & liberty is gone with it. I see the Parliamt: raised last year nigh 20 Millions, wt: must the Supplies of this year amount to? Will not Holland follow the Example of Spain? Have they[. . . .][7]

I have never seen [an authentic? story of Irela]nd [of] any Value, let me have that published or publishing at [Paris.] My Ld. Castlemains Cath: Apology[8] thô in a very uncouth State & Ire[la]nds Case stated[9] may in point of History & truth be usefull to you & worth yr: perusal—

You have no doubt heard that we have Conquered Martinico.[10] Who shall prescribe limits to our Conquests by Sea if we only mind the Interest of England. But are we able to bear the growing Expence? A Kingdom may be Bankrupt. If there be a Lottery wch: you like, take 10 Tickets for me but in yr: own name: but whether fortunate or otherways sell out immediately. Let this be a standing order to you subject to yr: discretion — Mr: Croxall desired that whenever I wrote to you, I would present his Service & Compts: to you, yr: Csn: Darnall gives her love to you, I give you my blessing & daily pray for yr: health & wellfare, no parent can wish both to a Child more sincerely than

Yr: Mo: Afft: Father
Cha: Carroll

PS

If Csn: Macnemara is still with you remember me to him & tell him Tommy dined with me last Sunday & that he & his Son Michl: are well —

LS, Carroll-McTavish Papers, MS 220, MdHi. Addressed and marked "Trip" by clerk. Top margins damaged. Text in brackets, with the exception of year in dateline, supplied from Field, *Carroll*, 65, 67.

1. Dated from CC to CCA, Aug. 6, 1762, below.

2. Alexander Ramsay, master of the *Maryland Packet*, arrived in Annapolis on Jan. 14, 1762. Annapolis Port of Entry Record Books, I.

3. Not found.

4. Approximately a line and a half missing.

5. "Your neighbor['s wall] is burning." Horace *Epistles* 1.18.84.

6. "Whenever their kings rave, the Acheans receive the blows" refers to the suffering of the Greeks in the Trojan war. Ibid., 1.2.14.

7. Two lines missing.

8. [Roger Palmer, earl of Castlemaine] (1634–1705), *A Reply to the Answer of the Catholique Apology; or, A Cleere Vindication of the Catholiques of England from All Matter of Fact Charg'd against Them by Their Enemyes* ([London?], 1668), was a vindication of the loyalty of Roman Catholics in the wake of the London fire of 1666, a calamity for which Catholics were blamed. A devout Catholic, Castlemaine, whose wife, Barbara Villiers, was the mistress of Charles II, was an adviser of James II and became a member of the Privy Council in 1687. After James's flight, Castlemaine was accused of treason and eventually exiled. A copy of the *Catholique Apology* dated 1674 is listed in *Cat. Lib.*, no. 196.

9. William Molyneux, *The Case of Ireland's Being Bound by Acts of Parliament in England, Stated* (Dublin, 1698). The edition owned by the Carrolls was published in London in 1720. *Cat. Lib.*, no. 725.

10. The British took Martinique, the most important French stronghold in the Lesser Antilles, on Feb. 15, 1762.

CC to CCA

26 April 1762

Dr. Papa,

This goes by Capt. Kelty, whom, I beg. you will treat civilly: He is an honest, sober, industrious man & merits encouragement: He invited Harry Carroll & myself twice to his house & gave us a very good dinner. Pray invite Capt. Hanson to dine with you he deserves yr. notice. Since mine of the 11th. Instant[1] I have recd. yr. short letter of the 30 of Januy.[2] It gives me real concern & no smal mortification to hear I lost such an oportunity of writing which was owing to my being wholy ignorant of it. This is the more surprising as I was then in town: for the future I shall take care to enquire myself, of ships sailing to Maryland or Pensilvania & not trust to other intelligence[.] I hope you have recd. my several letters of the 13 Octb. . . . . Deb. 16 & 19, 5 Jany. & 17 March. I refer you to the newspapers for news[.] These you will find in the box with the books & magazines: The papers taken in since, the Magazine for April, & a book lately published containing some discoveries made by the Russians on the northwest Coast of America[3] go by Capt. Kelty.

Yesterday the proceedings in the chancery suit Between Clifton yourself & others was sent to my chambers from Tom's coffee house, unsealed & only rapt round with a scanty piece of brown paper Dulany gave it to Macnamara to deliver it to me: The manner of returning the packet might have been more genteel so might Dulany's behaviour to me: common civility required a return of the visits I paid him: to be wanting in civility thro' indolence bespeaks illbreeding; thro' mean pride or childish vanity implies the want of good sense. Perhaps Dulany has wrote to you concerning the appeal: if not pray let me know what steps I must take in the affair: If you want to obtain an appeal, I must apply to some able Counsellor to know wether it can be obtained, & this application will be attended with no little expense. The proceedings are pretty voluminous & the cause knotty: the case you have drawn may assist & save some trouble to the Lawer but is not explicit enough to make him understand the true state of the question or enable him to give his opinion.

Macnamara has avoided me as much as possible since he got the 10 guineas: I was often plagued with his company before. I saw him this morning 2d of May: he can't pay me: I send you here inclosed his note of hand for £10..10 so much money borrowed of me wh he will pay unto you: I suppose he is indebted to you in a much Larger sum.

Capt. Carroll returns with Kelty: the London air does not suit his constitution: I hope all his complaints will be removed by a change of climate. His company has been very agreeable: The reasons & arguments advanced in some of my letters to hasten my return home will, I hope, seconded by Harry have such influence as to persuade you to recall me next spring. I am most heartily tired of my present situation, & I wish you cou'd be convinced, as I am, that its continuance to the time you mentioned, will not only be unserviceable but prejudicial perhaps to my health, most certainly to my interest. I desire my compliments to my Cousin Rach: Darnall: I shou'd have answered her letter by this fleet, but the sudden departure of Capt. Carroll for Portsmouth, & a slight indisposition for these few days past has prevented me. Assure John Darnall & Richard Croxall of my sincere regard for them. I am Dr. Papa

Yr. most affectionate & Dutiful Son
Ch: Carroll

ALS, Carroll Papers, MS 206, MdHi. Addressed by CC. Endorsed by CCA.

1. Not found.

2. Not found.

3. [Gerhard Friedrich Mueller], *Voyages from Asia to America, for Completing the Discoveries of the NorthWest Coast of America; to Which Is Prefixed, a Summary of the Voyages Made by the Russians on the Frozen Sea, in Search of a Northeast Passage . . .* , trans. Thomas Jefferys (London, 1761). *Cat. Lib.,* no. 754.

. . .
.

CCA to CC

May 12: 1762

Dr Charly,

I am not at all surprized at what you write Concerning Mr Macnemaras Behaviour; He has a very unhappy temper His Conduct is thoughtless, by that he runs him self into difficulties & necessities, & his Pride is Such, that he Cannot acknowledge as he ought obligations & gratefull. I have a letter from him dated the 4th of last January after he had Behaved to you in the Manner you Mention in wh far from taking Notice of what he said to You he Plainly Represents his pressing necessities & Earnestly Beggs my Assistance, But I Cannot in Prudence do more than I have done for him —

I Communicated yr letter where in you mention the Miss Bladens so much to their advantage, to Mr Tasker, who in all Probability will let Mr Bladen know what You say. A man Can loose nothing by a little Complaisance of that Sort & Custom[1] has made it all most necessary thô it has at the Same time Established Such Politesses to be looked upon as things of Course & sans Consequence. Adieu my Dr Child I am

Yrs &c
C: C:

ALS, Carroll Papers, MS 206, MdHi. Endorsed by CCA: "1762 May 12 Copy of my letter to my son."

1. CCA wrote and then struck through "the World."

CCA to CC

June 29th 1762

Dr Charley

My last to you was of the 12th past. A few days since I Reced yrs: of the 17th of March 1762. Mr: Perkins you tell me says he seldom or ever knows of Ships sailing from the Out ports,[1] a Mercht: may easily acquire that knowledge by en-quiery. All Out port Ships sail without Convoy, the packets to New York sail at stated times, & if I mistake not the Merchts: are acquainted with those times, so that without giving himself much trouble Mr: Perkins might acquaint you with frequent opportunities of forwarding yr: letters to me.

Troubles & difficulties are as certain Concomitants of a large share of property as Envy is of Merit. Poverty will not screen you from trouble & perplexity, thô the want of merit may free you from Envy. If Mr: Dulany for his own sake will not consider the case as far as it relates to Mercer, I shd: be sorry you gave yr: self any trouble about it, you may have observed by my Letter to him wch: accompany'd the Case that it was upon that footing I wrote to him. The latter part of the Case wch: concerns us, is to know, whether we are not entitled to a Recovery of such Damages from our Co: as we have sustained by Mercers Attachment & Suit. I am persuaded you will not give Mr: Dulany any offence, I am rather apprehensive you will be too complaisant, it is not the way to succeed with him & for this reason I told you to treat him civilly if he returned yr: Visit &c. He has not thought it worth his while to answer my Letter.

I am concerned for the Jesuits, & I shd: pity France were we not at War with her for having such a King — All the Books I sent you belong to me, dispose of them as you please, but remember I desired you to get a compleat collection of Law Books. I am sensible it is almost impossible for you to get a personal acquaintance with Ministers of State Dukes &c, but I do not think it difficult to know their Char-acters & persons: they frequent particular Coffee houses & other publick places, they resort to each House of Parliament, they are frequently the Subject of conver-sation, shd: you for Example be asked on yr: Return wt: sort of a man is Mr: Pitt who were his Seconds & chief supporters in the Administration & in each House of Parliament & you shd: say you never saw him & knew nothing of the matter, after a stay of 4 years in London, might you not be looked upon as incurious & stupid, as if you could not give an Acct of Westminster Bridge or St: Pauls & the places they stand in. We live in the world & ought to know it, that knowledge gives us weight in it, & makes us agreeable in Company & Conversation, some time & some money ought to be sacrificed to that end. I am glad to hear you have begun to learn the Italian method of Book-keeping, it is a qualification not unbecoming the greatest Peer in England. Be perfect in Arithmatick & learn Surveying, believe me they are all Essential to you & that makes me so often mention them.

Dr Charley I am convinced you would be sincerely concerned for my Death, I know in that case you would sustain a great loss, but not nigh so great as you represent it to yr: self, Mr: Croxall time & application would soon let you into a thorô knowledge of my affairs & yr: Interest: instead of dreading my death, thank God that I have lived until you have attained an Age & knowledge to act for yourself. It is true a year or two's instruction from me would be of great advantage & make things much easier to you. But that case that advantage unless God is pleased to spare me cannot be obtained but by a greater disadvantage, the disadvantage of quitting the Study of the Law. You see things in so partial a light, you have it so much at heart to return, that yr reasoning is unbecoming yr: good Sense. I have always told you I never intended you shd: practise the Law, will therefore the knowledge of it be unprofitable to you, would it not be of infinite advantage to England if every man of property who serves in parliament were a Sound Lawyer & well acquainted with the Constitution? Will not the knowledge of the Law enable you to transact yr: affairs with ease & Security? Will it not enable you to state yr: own Cases, to instruct those you employ & if you find them ignorant, knavish or conceited direct you to employ others? It is true I have met with some of these Characters, but had I been a Lawyer or deemed such, it's more than probable they would not have ventured to have imposed on me. Althô other occupations here will hinder you from such an application to the Law as to give you a knowledge of it, yet certainly after four years Study & close application to it in London some spare hours here may conduce to improve yr: knowledge, the Path will be beaten & easy & you will certainly know how to turn to proper Books & Cases upon occasion, or your time & money must be wasted to no purpose. I never expected you to Rival a Talbot[2] or a Murray,[3] but I have always hoped from yr: Capacity & application that you would make a Sound Lawyer: I endeavour to convince, I would always avoid the harshness of a command, & I hope you will be persuaded that yr: Wellfare, Interest & happiness only induce me agst. my natural fondness & propensity to see you & have you with me, not to alter my Resolution in this Respect. I have paid yr: Compts: as desired.

As far as I can judge this year will add new & important Conquests to England, & laurels to her Admirals & Generals, I name our Admirals 1st because every Success is evidently owing to our unbounded power at Sea. What have the French to hope for from the Hero of Rosback, for by Papers of a later Date than yr. Letter I see D'Etreè has refused the Command. The Empress Queen I apprehend deserted by Russia will be reduced to act on the Defensive. I suppose Spain would not have quarelled with us, had she not resolved to attempt again to annex Portugal to her

Dominion, at so great a distance I cannot see wt: can hinder her Success but the want of good Officers & a prudent Conduct, but she may pay the full purchase by the loss of Cuba, Hispaniola &c &c.

I have a letter from Mr: Thos: Waller[4] with 2 Magazines & his proposals, I have communicated his Magazines & proposals to some of my acquaintance but with little prospect of Success, let Mr: Waller know this & present my Compts to him. Pray remember me to Mr: Crookshanks, Corbie, Pointz, Jennison &c. We expect the fleet daily I am not impatient for any thing but your Letters & to see Capt: Carroll from whom I expect a more circumstantial Acct of you than they will give me, you are allways in my thoughts, you are the Object of all my cares, & I am Dr Charley

Yr: Mo Afft: Father
Cha: Carroll

LS, Carroll-McTavish Papers, MS 220, MdHi. Marked "Copy" by CCA. Endorsed by CC.
1. Any British port other than London.
2. Sir William Talbot (?-1633), a prominent Dublin attorney.
3. William Murray, Lord Mansfield.
4. Probably a London bookseller.

CC to CCA

4 July 1762

Dr. Papa,

The new York packet is to sail the 10th. instant. I take this oportunity the first since the departure of the fleet of letting you hear from me. I hope you have re-ceivd. my letters by Hanson & Kelty & have had the pleasure of our Cousin Harry's company: Pray remember me to him in the kindest manner & put him in mind of his promise to write to me and let me know how he enjoys his health: I hope Mary-land agrees with him better than London. I have perused some part of the papers & proceedings in the Law suit betwixt you and Clifton. You seemed desirous of obtaining an appeal & sent the papers to Dulany to have his opinion wether an appeal cou'd be obtained. I have no instructions to meddle in the affair and shall not take upon me to proceed in a case of such importance without your order. I must observe that Law charges, besides the trouble and fatigue, are very heavy. You know by experience to what a tedious length Law suits are generally spun out. It ought therefore to be a concern of great weight wh shoud prevail upon one, who thinks himself injured by an unjust decree, to sollicit an appeal; He ought to be well convinced of the Justice of his cause, of a well grounded probality of success, of his own impartiality, before he lanches out into new expences & submits his suit to the final determination of a tribunal without appeal. In reading over the proceedings the following difficulties have occurred wh if worth your notice and time pray remove in your answer to this.

The 16 Octb. 1752 you obliged Clifton to execute a bond to Igna: Diggs for the payt. of £634..5..4 sterling. Now I can not conceive how Clifton at that time cou'd be indebted to you in so large a sum. The 19 Octb. 1738 you lent him £66 wh with the Interest at 6 per Ct. for 12 years amounts to £113. . . . 3d; I say for 12 years because you stoped in your own hands £7..16..5 being 2 years interest of the £66, wh said sum of £7..16..5 W: Brent[1] had directed you to pay to Clifton. You lent to the same gentleman the 13 Augst. 1740 the further sum of £50: This with the Interest at the above mentioned rate for 12 years and 2 months comes to £86..10S..[.] The 15 Octb. 1741 you lent to W: Brent £216..7..4 upon Clifton's becoming Brent's security. The Interest with the principal to the 16 Octb. 1752, being 11 years amounts to £359..3..5½. On that very day Clifton executed to Ign: Diggs the bond of £634..5..4. Now the 3 above mentioned sums added together make £559..3..5½. The difference is £75..1..10½ a surprising one indeed and which by no means I can account for. Indeed the 14 Octb. 1744, Clifton, as he says, was forced to become bound to you in a Judgt. Bond conditioned for the payt. of £257..14..6¾. But the legality of this bond and of yr. demand appears to be but ill founded. Particularly if what Clifton advances, be true, that you insisted upon his executing that bond without any manner of consideration whatsoever, but under a pretence that as he was Brent's security he must & shou'd pay you the said £216..7..4 Sterling with <u>compound</u> Interest for the same &c &c.

You cannot be ignorant that compd. Interest is deemed usury: the Law looks upon it in that light & has endeavoured to restrain that illegal practice by severe & heavy penalties. I can scarce think a man intitled to compd. Interest even in equity; for this reason: All property is regulated and protected by Law. Descents, the different species of estates, the manner of transferring them from one to another is fixed by the Common & Statute Laws. This is evident from the difference of hereditary succession in different kingdoms. The regulating of interest is undoubtedly as much the object & proper concern of the Law as anyone thing besides: hence the frequent statutes for fixing the Interest of money: hence the difference of Legal interest in different countries: In England the legal interest is 5 per Ct. In Maryland 6. If it be the proper province of the legislature to settle the Interest of money, most certainly the prescribing in what manner Interest is to be taken is equally so — nam qui majus habet habet et minus, et principale ducit accessoriu[2] are known maxims of the civil & Common Law. The Inference from this reasoning is too obvious, it woud be too gross an impeachment of your sense to draw it at full length.

One more observation on the proceedings and I have done. You recovered 13 July 1743 against Peter Hedgman[3] by Judgt. of the county Court of Stafford £235..5..11. I think you have been somewhat injured by this decree, it has deprived you of £3..15..9¼. From the 15 Octb. 1741 to 13 July 1743 is one year 9 months:

the Interest for that space of time amounts to £22..14..4¼ with the Principal is £239..1..8¼. Nor do I in the least understand the method used by the county Court in computing that Interest: I refer you to the proceedings and desire an ecclaircisement. Clifton pretends that you have no legal demand for any Interest on that Sum from the time Mercer filed his bill in order to stop the same in the hands of Hedgman. Are his pretensions unjust? Ought not the money from the time it was so stop'd to be deemed a kind of deposition a security or indemnity for Mercer till a final decree cou'd be obtained? And thus as neither Mercer or Clifton cou'd make any use of the money during the attachment and pending the Suit it may appear somewhat hard to charge either of them with the Interest. I have tired myself and fear I have tired you with these prolix perhaps futile objections. I'll drop this subject at present: you may expect on some other occasion farther observations on the proceedings.

The sudden change of Russian politics will in all probability bring about a peace in Germany if not thro' all Europe[.] Those very Russians who a few months ago were auxiliaries to the Austrians, the very General who commanded those auxiliaries have by this Joined the Prussian army in Silesia to act in opposition to their late friends. This conduct has determined Sweden to follow the Russian Emperor's example & to make peace with Prussia. The King of Denmark is unwilling to give up Holstein and yet affraid to rest his cause and right upon the decision of war.[4] The contest wou'd be very unequal and as the king of Denmark is esteemed a wise & politic Prince; he will avoid it if possible. He has extorted a loan from the city of Hamburgh of £ St 150000 paying or promising to pay 4 per Ct. Interest.

The 25 of June Prince Ferdinand[5] surprised the French army commanded by the Marshalls D'Etrees and Soubise in their camp at Graebenstein. The attack discovered the approach of the enemy: The French had not time to draw up in line of battle they retreated precipitately & in the utmost confusion. A total overthrow wou'd have ensued had not Stainville[6] with a body of troops the flower of the army thrown himself into a wood. This brave resolution cost him dear: his whole corps was cut to pieces, taken, or dispersed: he himself is said to have fallen in the field. The Allies have taken between 2 and 3 thousand prisoners and amongst these upwards of 200 officers: The enemy's army retreated under the Canon of Cassel & a great part of it passed very hastily over the Fulda: we wait with impatience the consequences of this event[.] The greatest part of this account is taken from the gazette extraordinary[.]

Perhaps a few lines concerning myself will not now be unacceptable. I am well tho' thin. I have learnt Arithmetic & am now, & have been for some time learning the Italian method of bookeeping tho' I am not as yet master of it, but with time, patience, & practice hope to be. I apply to the Law but can not apply with that assiduity I cou'd wish: my constitution will not bare much fatigue & no fatigue can be greater than the intense application of the mind to difficult & abstruse knowledge. I recd. some while ago your letter of the 8th. April wh as all yours was most welcome. I shall answer it by the next oportunity. I go to Margate[7] to morrow morning to breath the country air, to bathe & for a little relaxation: my stay there will not be longer than a week. I am Dr. Papa

Yr. most affectionate & loving Son

Ch: Carroll

P:S:

My kind compliments to Rich: Croxall John: Darnall & Sons, Rach: Darnall, & Harry Carroll

ALS, Carroll Papers, MS 206, MdHi. Addressed by CC. Endorsed by CCA.

1. William Brent, Sr. (1710–1742), of Richland, Stafford Co., Va. Lothrop Withington and H. F. Waters, "Virginia Gleanings in England," *VMHB*, XI (1903–1904), 70.

2. "For he who has more has less; and the principal thing draws the accessory to itself."

3. Peter Hedgeman (?–1765), a Stafford Co. lawyer, member of the Virginia House of Burgesses, and executor of the estate of William Brent. Rutland, *Mason*, I, lx.

4. Both King Frederick V (1723–1766) of Denmark and Norway and Czar Peter III of Russia claimed the duchy of Holstein in 1762 and were preparing to fight for it. Gipson, *Culmination*, 62–63.

5. Prince Ferdinand, duke of Brunswick (1721–1792), brother-in-law of Frederick the Great.

6. The comte de Stainville, brother of Etienne François, duc de Choiseul, the chief minister of France. Savory, *His Britannic Majesty's Army*, 334; Gipson, *Culmination*, 40.

7. A popular seaside resort about seventy-five miles east of London.

. . .
.

CCA to CC

July 24th 1762

Dr Charley

I have yr: two Letters of the 11th & 26th of last April with all the Books & Papers mentioned in them, for wch: I thank you, they were very acceptable. I realy believe that neither France & Spain or even all Europe Confederated can put a stop to our Victorious Arms, if we confine ourselves to such operations as can be effectually promoted by our Fleets, the Taking Havannah & the Reduction of Cuba wch: we have the greatest reason to expect to hear daily will be a strong proof of this, & if we can find men this will be the fate of all their American & Asiatick Dominions. Lewis the 14th[1] was sincerely disposed to restore the Exiled family. Since his Death the Chevalier[2] & his Son have been but Cats Paws in the hands of France who may now have good reason to repent their double dealing with that unfortunate family—I am the more astonished that the King of France has abandoned the Jesuits as I cannot see in the Arrets of Parliament & other Papers published by them

& others agst: them anything but Gross barefaced Calumny unsupported by facts or reason. Inscrutable are the ways of God Quos vult perdere primô dementat—[3]

In my Letter to Dulany of the 10th of Sept: 61 among other things I wrote him as follows "I submit to you (if an Appeal can be obtained) whether it will not be the most Eligible way to you & my other partners of terminating my claim on you & yr: claims on me"—I did suppose you would have kept a Copy of that letter, you would have seen by it, I sent the proceedings to Dulany at his own Request, however give yr: self no further Concern about him, & if he continues to behave to you as he has done, despise him—

It gives me pleasure to hear you have been at Mr: [H]uddlestones & that y[ou] was very well. In a former Letter I advised you to renew yr: acquaintance with yr: old school fellows[4] where it could be done without inconvenience. I cant tell whether I ought not to condemn yr: want of Relish for the Races at Newmarket,[5] the seeing Horses Run may not be very amusing, but to see such Company as meets at the Races would I think be very entertaining to any young man of Curiosity, the world must be known by going into it, a knowledge of it in theory you will find very defective.

I Reced all yr: Letters mentioned in yrs: of the 26 of April. In a former letter I let you know how yr: Letter of the 13th of Octo: by Capt: Ramsay happened to be kept from me so long. In yrs: of the 13th of last Octo: you promised me a Journal of yr: Tour to the North by the Fleet, you promised to write to Mrs: Darnall, a Gent: shd: take care to keep his word, you procrastinate too much, never put off untill to morrow wt: can be done to day, to morrow brings on its own business. I formerly told you to minute down things as they occur to you, by so doing you will always have sufficient matter for a Letter ready: you may write yr: letters as you have leisure the Date may be the last thing—

I was much pleased with the Russian Voyages from Asia to America, by a note in the 2d Page I find there is just ready for the press the Natural & Civil History of Kamtschatka translated from the Russian,[6] Pray send it to me when published. In a former Letter I told you, you need not concern yr: self about any part of the Proceedings sent you but wt: relates to my claim on my partners agst: whom I shall shortly file a Bill in Chancery—

I find poor McNemara has made a very broken Voyage, 5 days before he came home his House was burnt a great Loss & shock to him, his own bad conduct without misfortunes is enough to ruin him. I Reced his Note for £10.10.0[.] Capt: Carroll has spent 2 nights with m[e w]hen ever we were alo[ne] you was chiefly the Subject of our conversation. I hear you have promis'd to spare Dulany a ¼ Cask of Madeira I wonder how he could ask it of you, you were in the Right to let him have it, for merit must not always be the motive of our Beneficence, but I suppose you will take care to make him pay his part of Frt: Duty & all other Charges[.]

Last winter was a very severe one with us. Being constantly confined by the weather & business I had a small Swelling in my legs towards my Ancles, it some times leaves me, & is not nigh so much now as in the Winter. I do not find nor am I apprehensive of any ill Consequences from it, I have a very good Appetite & am hearty & well. Pray continue to let me know all the steps taken agst the Jesuits in France. God Bless you. I am Dr Charley

Yr: Mo: Afft: Father
Cha: Carroll

LS, Carroll-McTavish Papers, MS 220, MdHi. Corrected by CCA.

1. Louis XIV, king of France (1638–1715).

2. The "Old Pretender," James Francis Edward Stuart (1688–1766), was recognized in France until 1713 as James III. After that date he was referred to as the chevalier de Saint Georges. Ragnhild Hatton, ed., *Louis XIV and Europe* (Columbus, Ohio, 1976), 306–307.

3. "Those whom [He] wishes to destroy [He] first drives mad."

4. Three sons of the Huddleston family of Sawston Hall near Cambridge attended St. Omers during the time CC was a student there: Ferdinand (1737–1808), Thomas (1740–1799), and Richard (1742–1801). Holt, *St. Omers,* 139–140; Burke and Burke, *Landed Gentry of Great Britain,* I, 866.

5. A horse-racing center from the seventeenth century.

6. [Stepan Petrovich Krasheninnikov], *The History of Kamtschatka, and the Kurilski Islands, with the Countries Adjacent . . . ,* trans. James Grieve (London, 1755). *Cat. Lib.,* no. 431, lists a 1764 Gloucester edition.

CCA to CC

July 24: 1762

Dr Charly,

This is in my owne hand because I do not Care my Clerk should know that you still persist after what I have Said to you to desier to Come in next Spring, were I to Consent to it, would not that Consent make us ridiculous in the Eyes of think-ing Men? Should not a man who has had yr Education Crowne it with the Study & acquierment of some Liberall Profession? Can any other knowledge be more use-full to or becommin[g] a Gentn: than the knowledge of the Law? Can less than 4 years be bestowed in acquiering that knowledge? Is a year to be Higgled for by a Man of yr Sense & Age? It gives me great uneasiness to think that what you seem to do so unwillingly you will not do well[.] You read the Civill law two years to facilitate the study of the Laws of England, are Six years of yr life to be flung away? If that should be the Case, I have done my duty, you will too late Repent yr not Corresponding with my Will & intention.

If the air of London disagrees with you take lodgings in some of the adjacent Villages & read there. If fasting & keeping lent impares yr Constitution, you ought not to fast, yr Confessor upon such a Report from your Dor: will order you not to fast & you ought to Pay an Obedience to his orders[.]

I understand Mr Perkins sometimes is not so Ready as he ought to be in supplying you with Cash, if that is the Case, the 1st time he serves you so & you think yrself ill used, let him know you have orders to Call for a supply Elsewhere & Apply to Mr Thos: Philpot first & in Case of a Refusall to Mr Jo: Philpot they I doubt not will Readily supply you on yr shewing them this letter & I will take Care immediately to make them full Remittances. I am My Dr Charly

Yr Mo: Afft: Father

AL, Carroll Papers, MS 206, MdHi. Endorsed by CCA: "1762 July 24 A Copy of my Letter to my Son."

CC to CCA

Augst. 6. 1762

Dr. Papa,

I wrote to you the 4 of last month: in that letter I started some difficulties in your lawsuit with Clifton which as that letter may have miscarried I shall here repeat. In reading over the proceedings the following difficulties have occurred wh if worth yr. notice and time pray remove in your answer to this. The 16 Octob. 1752 you obliged Clifton to execute a bond to Ign: Diggs for the payment of £634..5..4 Sterling. Now I can't conceive how Clifton at that time coud owe you so large a sum: the 19 Octb. 1738 you lent him £66 which with the Interest at 6 p Ct. for 12 years comes to £113..—.3d. I say for 12 years, because you stopped in your own hands £7..16..5 being 2 years Interest, wh said sum Wm. Brent had directed you to pay to Clifton. You lent to the <u>same gentleman</u> the 13 August 1740 the further sum of £50, this with the Interest at the above mentioned rate for 12 years & 2 months amounts to £86..10[.] The 15 Octb. 1741 you lent Wm. Brent £216..7..4 upon Clifton's becoming Brent's security. The Interest with the Principal to the 16 Octb. 52 being 11 years amounts to £359..3..2½: these several sums added together come to £559..3..5½. Clifton executed a bond to Ign: Diggs the 16 Octb. 1752 for the payt. of £634..5..4: the difference is £75..1..10½. A striking difference in deed and which I can no ways account for. Indeed the 14 Octb. 1744 Clifton, as he says, was compelled to become bound to you in a Judgement bond conditioned for the payt. of £257..14..6¾. But the legality of this bond and of your demand, as far as I can see appear to be but ill founded: upon what grounds cou'd you exact that sum since your debt had been settled by a Judgement of the county Court of Stafford in virtue whereof you recovered only £235..5..11¾ & by my method of computing, a rong one perhaps, you only ought to have recovered the further sum of £3..15..9¼.

I dont think you complained of any inJustice done you by that decree since you ordered Peter Hedgeman to pay the money to Clifton & if you abide by part of the decree you abide by the whole. Moreover Clifton affirms that you insisted upon his executing the above mentioned bond without any manner of consideration what-soever but under a Pretence that as he was Brents security he must and shou'd pay you the £216..7..4 with compound Interest for the same. You can not be ignorant that compound Interest is deemed usury; the Law looks upon it in that light and has endeavoured to restrain that illegal practice by severe & heavy penalties by for-feiture, If I am not mistaken, of treble value of the money lent: another observation and I have done. The 13 July 1743 you recovered against Peter Hedgeman by Judge-ment of the county court of Stafford £235..5..11. I think you have been somewhat inJured by that decree as it deprived you of £3..15..9¼. From the 15 Octb. 1741 to 13 July 1743 is one year 9 months: the Interest for that time amounts to £22..14..4¼ with the Principal is £239..1..8¼. Nor do in the least understand the method used by the County court in computing that Interest; I refer you to the proceedings and desire an ecclaircisement. Clifton pretends that you have no legal demand for any Interest on that sum from the time that Mercer filed his bill in order to stop the same in the hands of Peter Hedgeman. Are his pretensions altogether so unjust? Ought not the money from the time it was so attached to be deemed a kind of deposition, a security for Mercer till a final decree cou'd be obtained: and thus as neither Clifton nor Mercer cou'd make any use of the money during the attachment and pending the suit it may not seem Just to charge either with the Interest.

I have tired myself and I fear I have tired you with the length and futility of these objections: I shall drop this subject at present to resume it on some other occasion and proceed to answer yr. letter of the 8th April the last I have received. I am pleased to hear Nimble is like to turn out a fine horse. It woud be no very difficult task to procure a thorough bred Stallion, the chief difficulty lies in the price and risks of a long Passage: a thorough bred Mare may be come at at a pretty easy rate, tho' I shoud be glad to know what you think an easy rate: When I was down at Wardour I saw a Stallion belonging to a Farmer in the neighbourhood for whom he gave £300: the owner did not think his purchase dear at that Price.

No degree at Law can be obtained without being called to the bar. The being entered of the temple and going to Commons is a necessary, previous, & prepara-tory step to that ceremony wh tho' a ceremony is an opening to all preferments in the Law; ti's attended with no other advantage but many and great inconvenien-cies, the chiefest is the frequenting loose and dissolute company: for this reason I have resolved not to enter myself of the temple; to what purpose? Why shou'd I expose myself to danger and be at a needless tho' small expence without any view or hopes of profit and advantage —

I owe you (and with some shame I acknowledge it) all the Journalls of my sev-eral tours. A Prodigious debt! I shall certainly be a bankrupt: Let us compound matters; better receive a shilling in the pound than nothing. I promise to give you the Journal of my last northern expedition on condition of a general discharge & release from all other Journalls. . . . I am still going on with my Italian bookkeeping. I think it a too tedious and prolix a method for a gentleman: the multiplicity and intricacy of a Merchant's transactions require greater method and the nicest exactness—

Mr. Lewis the bookseller has promised to procure me Gahagan's history of Ireland wh was publishing when I was at Paris. He tells me you bought of him O'Connors translation of Keating: I fancy he must be mistaken or else you woud not have desired me to send it you. Pray let me know wether you have it by you.

You desired me in one of your letters to trace our branch of the family back to 1500 by means of Cousin Antony or some one else: he is the only one to whom I coud apply for information or any other lights on this subject: I wrote to him and have received his answer which for your satisfaction I shal transcribe verbatim— I shall do all in my power to procure the information both you and your father desire tho' it seems pretty certai[n] I can not do much considering how matters stand at this time: the last letter I had from Ireland gave an account of the death of Mr. Alexander Carroll,[1] Cæsar's father; Mr. John Carroll, the Colonel's brother; & uncle Micha[el] I scarce know any one that I can expect intelligence from. When I was a boy we had Dr. Keaten's Irish history in MS in which I remember to have heared say that our genealogy was preserved but that as well as other things disappeared before I left the kingdom. This I mention to let you see how hard it will be to get any satisfactory account of our extirpated family. It does not make to the present purpose, but it is proper to know, that in Cambden's account of the county of Gallway[2] mention is made of the chief of our name, who was defeated, with some other leaders at the battle of Knoc-tee, by Gerald Earl of Kildare, anno 1516. The same author in his account of the county of Tipperary tells you ti's bounded on the North with the territory of the o'Carrolls, which I am confident is to this day called Carroll's Isle, at least there is, I know, a place so called in that part of the country. So far the letter—

I shall follow the advice you have given concerning Lottery tickets; there is to be no Lottery this year. In my last I gave you an account of the surprise at Grebenstein: the enemy's loss in killed wounded and prisoners did not exceed 5000 men; if the consequences of that action had not been much greater than the loss of 5000 men, the Allies woud have acquired great honour but no real advantage. The French have since lost several magazines, they have been driven from several important posts; their communication with Franckfort is cut off and that city is under the greatest apprehension of a visit from the allied army: these are the natural consequences [of the rout at Grebenstein: on the] 23 July the french were again defeated [in the neighbourhood of Cas]sel. Prince Ferdinand ordered general Gilsac[3] to attack the enemy's right wing composed chiefly of Saxons under Count de Lusace[4] in their intrenched camp at Lutternburg[.] The attack succeeded and the enemy driven from their post with slaughter a whole regiment of Saxon horse was taken or cut to pieces; above a 1000 prisoners fell into the victors hands besides 13 pieces of cannon & 3 standards: our loss did not exceed 200 men. During this attack Count de Stainville, who saved the french army at Grebenstein, marched out of his lines that cover Cassel with 10,000 men to support the Saxons & cover their retreat: Prince Frederic of Brunswick who was watching his motions immediately took possession of those important intrenchments: Count de Stainville perceiving this threw himself into Cassel: this is our latest intelligence from that quarter.

A surprising and sudden revolution has happened in Russia. The Emperor is dethroned and his Consort Catherine second of the name[5] is now seated on that throne which her Royal Husband so lately occupied[.] She was proclaimed the 10th of July sole Empress of all the Russias & the succession settled on her son the Grand Duke Paul:[6] She has published a manifesto explaining the motives of this great & sudden change. They are reduced to three. 1st. tis said the fundamentals of the orthodox greek religion have been shaken, her traditions exposed to total ruin by endeavours made to introduce a foreign religion. 2dly. the glory of Russia acquired by the effusion of so much blood has been trampled under foot by the peace lately concluded with her greatest enemy: these are the very words of the manifesto. 3dly. the interiour arrangements on which the welfare of the country depends have been totally subverted: the late Emperor is supposed to be confined in some strong fortress together with his nephew Prince George of Holstein Gottorp. . . We have no very interesting accounts from Silesia: Daun has been obliged to retire into the confines of Bohemia; his communciation with Shweidnitz is cut off. The Prussian parties have made some excursions upon the borders of Bohemia & Moravia. You have no doubt heared of the taking of the Hermoine a very rich spanish register ship: My sincerest compliments to Cousin Henry, & to Mr. Croxall & John Darnall & Sons: remember me to my Cousin Rachael. I am Dr. P:

your most affectionate and dutiful Son

Ch: Carroll

P:S:

I intend setting out in a few days time for Tunbridge wells:[7] Mr. Jennings, son to the Mr. Jennings[8] of Maryland goes with me: We were down at Margate; he is a sensible, sober, discreet well behaved young man: We shall make Tunbridge our head quarters and from thence make excursions round about the adjacent count[r]y. I had almost forgot to tell you that the English Jesuits in France are like to meet with no better treatment than their brethren: centinels are placed over their College and an Inventory has been taken of all the moveables belonging to that House. You rember Pere Power to whose care you recommended me while at Bourges: upon the dissolution of his order in France he got admitted of the English province & is now in England: I have not had the pleasure of his company as yet, but he is to dine with me to morrow; I expect from him a satisfactory accot. of the late troubles.

ALS, Outerbridge Horsey Collection of Lee, Horsey, and Carroll Family Papers, MS 1974, MdHi.

1. Alexander Carroll (?–by 1762) of Kilfadda, County Tipperary.

2. Probably [William Camden (1551–1623)], *Annales Rerum Anglicarum, et Hibernicarum, Regnante Elizabetha, ad Annum Salutis MDLXXXIX* (London, 1615), a history of England and Ireland.

3. Major General von Gilsa.

4. Prince Xavier of Saxony, known as the comte de Lusace to the French, commanded Saxon troops in the French army. Savory, *His Britannic Majesty's Army,* xxi.

5. Czarina Catherine II, "the Great" (1729–1796), ruled Russia from 1762 until her death.

6. Czar Paul I (1754–1801).

7. A fashionable spa in Kent patronized by such notables as Samuel Johnson and David Garrick.

8. Born in Maryland, where his father served several terms as deputy secretary, Edmund Jenings (1731–1819) went to England in 1737 with his parents, Edmund Jenings (1703–1756) and Ariana Vanderheyden Frisby Bordley Jenings, and lived there for the rest of his life, except for the years 1778–1783, which he spent in Paris and Brussels. Educated at Eton and Cambridge, Jenings trained in law at the Middle Temple but did not have to rely on a legal practice for his livelihood because he enjoyed a comfortable income from holdings in both America and England. Although he never returned to his native land, Jenings's affection for it remained strong, and he appears to have consistently supported the Americans' position throughout the Revolutionary period. He had family ties to both sides: his sister, Ariana, married the Virginia loyalist John Randolph, and he frequently corresponded with his second cousins Arthur and William Lee and involved himself in their European affairs. Between 1779 and 1784 Jenings regularly exchanged letters with John Adams, who became his unwavering defender against Henry Laurens's charges of misconduct and double-dealing in the early 1780s and also gained Jenings's admission to the American Academy of Arts and Sciences in 1788. *Bio. Dic. Md. Legis.,* II, 487; Elizabeth B. Gibson, *Biographical Sketches of the Bordley Family, of Maryland, for Their Descendants . . .* (Philadelphia, 1865), 25–26; James H. Hutson, ed., *Letters from a Distinguished American: Twelve Essays by John Adams on American Foreign Policy, 1780* (Washington, D.C., 1978), x–xx, 51–66.

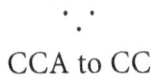

CCA to CC

Sepr: 1st: 1762

Dr Charly,

At yr Age it is Naturall to think of Establishing yr self in the World by Mariage. Whenever you do this yr Future Happyness will depend on the Choice you make. Without yr Wife be Virtuous, Sensible, good natured, Complaisant, Complying & of a Chearfull Disposition, you will not find a Marryed state a Happy one. Next to these Family & Fortune Come under Consideration[.] As to family there is not one in England wh would be disparaged by bestowing a Daughter on you: It is true our Family is not now Decked wth. Titles, But we derive our Descent from Princes & untill the Revolution notwithstanding Our Sufferings under Elizabeth[1] & Cromwell[2] We were in Affluent Circumstances & Respected & we intermarryed wth the best Families in the Kingdom of Ireland. As to fortune, Without Exageration & without improbable & unforseen Accidents I shall leave you worth at least Sixty Thousand Pounds sterling, & (I fancy) there are not many Roman Catholick Families in the Kings Dominions wh Could give their Daughters fortunes Proportioned to yours, & I Earnestly Recommend it to you on no Consideration to Marry a Protestant, for beside the risque yr Offspring will Run, it is Certain there Cannot be any Solid Happyness without an union of Sentiments in all Matters Especially in Religion.

Beauty is not to be under valued, But it is too transient & Lyable to too many Accidents to be a Substantiall motive to Mariage, & yet it Affects Our Propensity to Lust so strongly, that it makes most Matches, & most of those Matches Miserable unless when Beauty is gone, Virtue, good Sense good Nature, Complaisance & Chearfullness Compensate the loss. An Agreable Genteel & Neat Woman wth these Qualities is therefore to be sought by a Man of Sense; But how is she to be found? First of all by not being in love, that is by not letting our Passion Blind our Understanding, By not letting her know you have the least designe on her as a Wife, untill you know her: The Sex are the most Artfull Dissemblers, But Nature will shew it self. By her Generall Character from disinterested Persons; A too great stress ought not to be laid on this, However if it Concurs with yr owne Opinion & Observation, it is in some measure to be Relyed on.[3] If her Parents be Persons of Good Sense & Understanding, it is likely their Daughter may not want the Same good Qualities, If they are OEconomists their Children will not be Bred in Idleness. Girls confined Early to their Book Needle & Works Sutable to their Station & Properly instructed in the Principles of Religion, may be presumed will make good Wives, But if they have been Humoured when young & Bred in Dissipation & inattention to things necessary & Laudable, the Contrary is much to be dreaded: The Character therefore of the Father & Mother & the Regularity of the Family are Seriously to be Weighed, for you will not geather Grapes from Thorns. It will be an advantage if the Lady should have been bred in a monastery, early good impressions are very l[a]sting—

It is of Importance to the Offspring that a Man & Woman should be of a good Size well Proportioned & free from the naturall defects of Lameness Deafness Squinting stammering stuttering, from Hereditary disorders Such as the Gout Gravell,[4] Consumption &c, Madness also runs in the Blood. A nobleman would not suffer an undersized Pyebaled Walleyed Spavined Mare in his Stud, & he shall Urge his Son to Marry a Humpbacked Puny Woman with a great fortune: Has he not a greater Afection for his Beasts than his Family?

Having Pointed out to you what sort of a Wife is most likely to make you happy,

& the Precautions necessary to get Such a one, the last thing in my Opinion is the fortune, Not that a fortune in Prudence ought to be overlooked, But it ought not to be Prefered or even put in Competition wth the other good Qualities I have taken Notice of & wh I wish you may find in a Wife. By what Yr owne fortune will be, you may Judge of the fortune you have a right to Expect wth a Wife, (your Education & Personall Merit is not to be left out of the Scale)⁵[.] If you Should Condescend to take a Woman unequall to you in Point of fortune I hope that inequality will be Compensated in Point of Family, by her Virtue & the other good Qualities of her mind & Person. It often Happens that there is a very disagreable train of Hangers on & dependants brought into a family either by the Husband or Wife or both: It will not be so on yr Side as you are an only Son, & should you Marry in England, those (if any) on the Side of yr Wife will be left behind you. I shall never perswade or influence you to Marry against yr inclinations, Should you marry in Maryland I expect you will not marry against myne, But I assure you I will [n]ot deny my Consent unless I think the Match Dishonorable or like to Prove unhappy, this I think I have not the least Reason to fear from the Opinion I have of yr good Sense & Prudence. If you should Marry in England (wh I Consent to if you think yr so doing will Conduce to Yr Happyness) I must trust you to Yr owne Judgement & May you be Happy: In that Case the Distance I am at will not admit me to Join in the Marria[g]e Articles or Settlement on yr Wife, However I hereby bind my self to settle on yr Wife as a Dower Si[x] Pounds a year during her life if She Survive you, for every Hundred Pounds she shall bring you as a fortune.⁶ But I desier you will not Marry without Makeing a Settlement on yr Wife, If you Omit it & she Survive you she may Carry a third of yr Fortune by a Second Mariage or otherways into a strange Family—

Thus Dr Charly you are allways in my mind, Whether you Marry or do not Marry keep this by you, what I have Said may be of Service to you it Cannot Hurt you: These are but Hints but they Open a vast field of Matter for thought & Reflection. May you in all things embrace what is best. I am Dr Charly

Yr Mo: Afft: Father

Cha: Carroll

ALS, Carroll Papers, MS 206, MdHi. An AL copy endorsed by CCA as a copy is filed in the same manuscript collection.

1. Elizabeth I of England (1533–1603) ruled from 1558 until her death. Her reign marked the stringent enforcement of the penal statutes that deprived Roman Catholics of civil and political rights and the garrisoning and planting with Protestant settlers of areas of Ireland that included part of the Carrolls' ancestral lands. Ronald Hoffman, *Princes of Ireland, Planters of Maryland: A Carroll Saga, 1500–1782* (Chapel Hill, N.C., 2000), chap. 1.

2. Oliver Cromwell (1599–1658) ruled England as Lord Protector from 1653 until 1658. A leader of the Parliamentary forces during the English Civil War, Cromwell served in 1649 as commander in chief and lord lieutenant of Ireland, where he was responsible for several

brutal massacres. Following the defeat of the Irish by the commanders who succeeded him in the field, Cromwell initiated a policy of land confiscation that drastically reduced the holdings of rebellious Catholics like the Carrolls. Ibid.

3. Here CCA indicated an insertion. In the original document the text comprising the remainder of this paragraph is written following his signature.

4. Kidney stones.

5. Parenthetical phrase interlineated in original.

6. Remainder of paragraph interlineated in original.

CCA to CC

Sept: 2d 1762

Dr: Charley

I sit down to write to you not knowing with wt: to fill this letter. As Capt: Carroll has altered his scheme, I know not whether it will be worth yr: while to look out for any Mares as we cannot depend upon a carefull Capt: to bring them over & as the Risque by that means will be greatly increased, & nothing in my opinion shd: induce us to attempt it but the goodness of the breed, beauty & cheapness of the Mares. The Accidents to them of lameness, loss of an Eye or other blemishes wch: I mentioned in a former letter will not make them the less valuable to us as they are designed only for Breeding. If you shd: be tempted by the lowness of the price to get one or two, they ought to be shiped in May or June getting them 1st. covered by some Top Horse, in a Ship lightly loaded the freight would be easy, the Expence of Water Casks, Hay, Oates, slings &c may be computed; a common Ostler or Groom shd: be provided to take care of them on the passage, such a one may be induced to serve 4 or 5 years by employing a Crimp[1] without yearly Wages, or upon very low Wages, the Mares shd: never be put into the Slings but upon very bad Weather, they ought to stand in the Hold upon fine Shingle Ballast & have room enough to lay down, other necessary considerations relative to them may occur to you. But supposing every difficulty of procuring them &c removed, do not trouble yr: self with them if that trouble shd: be attended with the least uneasiness to you, in short please yourself & do as you will, but shd. you send them procure their Pedigrees properly attested & of the Horse covering them.

I killed 6 Hogs early in last Winter in order to send you the Hams & Shoulders in the Spring but I could not find an opportunity, to send them now they would be of no value to you, as they would be quite stale & as salt as Brine by the time they reached you.

I desired Mr: Perkins to send me two Guns to be bought of Turvey, he sent me 2 ungenteel ones bought of one Stanton. Pray let me know if Turvey the Gunsmith be living, nothing but his Death can excuse Mr: Perkins for not complying with my orders—In running over the 25th Vol: of the Monthly Review² fol: 454 I came across a Book wch: may be of service to you as you have a taste for drawing & may build in time, the short title of it is, Kerbys perspective of Architecture³ in 2 Vol: folio price £3.3.0 in Sheets, you may see the Volumes & judge for yourself.

I have the 2d: Vol: in folio of Collin Campbells Vitruvious Britanicus⁴ & I shd: be glad to have the 1st, its probable yr: Bookseller may get the 1st. I gave Mr: Meighan a Mo: about it, but I suppose he has forgot it.

Before you come in, if you have not got them already I would have you bespeak presses or proper Book Cases for yr: Books, but pack yr: Books in Chests, for the weight of yr: Books would very probably break yr: Book presses especially if they be not well cased—

I recommended it to you on yr: going into the Temple to make a common place Book, you assigned reasons for not doing it then, but I suppose you have one now, as the reasons you assigned no longer subsist. I also recommended to you to hire a pson to instruct you in yr: reading the Law, yr: Objection to this was, that no one properly Qualify'd could be got for Wages, I have been since informed that you was mistaken: As you will have little more than a year to stay in the Temple after the Receit of this you may possibly think it too late to make use of such a one, of this you are now the best judge; but I guess yr: not getting one at 1st was owing to a too great delicacy you have in making an Acquaintance with men whose temper or something else might prove disagreeable to you but in that case are not such men easily shook off—

You have informed me that in pursance of my Advice you intended to learn Surveying, you have not yet acquainted me that you have begun to do so, I again recommend it to you as a thing very Essential to you, & you will find a thorough knowledge of Arithmatick & Book-keeping still more necessary. I suppose in the Course of these two little branches of knowledge you reduce yr: Lessons into Books, & that in Book-keeping you will be made to raise a Day Book Journall & Leidger that is a short form of Books,⁵ these I would have you bring in with you to refresh yr: memory. When you come in do not forget to look out in time for a good Stock of Bristol Water⁶ you will find it the most necessary & agreeable part of yr: Sea Store as the Ships Water is hardly drinkable, at least very disgusting: two gross will be as little as you ought to have, & if you shd: have fellow passengers put them in mind to store themselves, if they neglect it, they will have the less reason to expect you shd: share yrs: with them. Let it be shiped to you in time from Bristol, it will come much cheaper than to buy it in London, & as the bottles make almost the whole Cost, desire yr: Servt: to be carefull of them & pack them away as they are emptyd for they will be very usefull here.

Several Gent: in England have Game keepers who supply their Tables with Gibier,⁷ I suppose the Wages of such a one would not exceed the Wages of a footman, if you can get such a one who can shoot well flying he may be placed at Elk ridge from whence he may supply us with Growse, Pheasants Woodcocks &c.

Some of yr: acquaintance in the Country may recommend such a Servt: to you & he shd: be Indented to serve 5 years for his stipulated wages, but you ought to be well informed that he is a good Marksman.

I understand you dress plainly, I commend you for it, but as dress introduces a stranger into most Companies perhaps with stronger Impressions than the best Recommendations, I think you shd: have Cloths suitable to such occasions & upon yr: first appearance among us some shew may not be improper. You may contrive to be supply'd with 2 or 3 Waste coats, Silk for two genteel Summer Suits, Velvets &c from France at the best hand & in the newest Taste, after yr: 1st Appearance you may be as plain as you please. I would have you also bring with you a Genteel set of Horse furniture,[8] you need not by Pistols as I have a very neat pair mounted with Silver wch: are at yr: Service. I mention these things now as they now occur to me I might forget them at a time when it might be more proper to put you in mind of them, you may make this letter suit that time by keeping it & then consulting it.

Poor Mrs Manjan a French Neutral has not heard from her Daughter & Son in Law Mr: Boisson since my return from Paris, should I inclose a letter from her to them or one of them forward it & at the Bottom of it give yr: Address to Boisson telling him you will forward any letters to them. I intend if a peace happens before you leave London to send you wt: family pictures I have wch: are done by shocking hands in order to have the likeness taken by the best hand in London & to have them new dressed. Mr: Thos: Buchanan returns with this Fleet, he has behaved here with a great deal of prudence diligence & discretion, & if Mr: Perkins will be guided by his Advice I doubt not he will find his Business increase here. Pray remember me in a particular manner to Messrs Crookshanks, Corbie, Pointz, Murphy & Baker & to our friends in Lime Street. God Grant you health & every Blessing wch may not be prejudicial to yr: Eternall Wellfare, it is my daily Prayer. I am Dr Charley

Yr: Mo: Afft: Father
Cha. Carroll

PS

Csn: John Darnall & Mr: Richd: Croxall present their Service to you, they esteem & love you. Pray present my Service & Compts: to Mr: Jenisson. I desire you will get yr Picture drawn by the best hand in London, let it be a three Quarters length, let it be put in a Genteel gilt frame & sent me by the next fleet carefully Cased & packed—

LS, Carroll-McTavish Papers, MS 220, MdHi.

1. A person who entrapped or forced men into sea duty or military service.

2. *The Monthly Review; or, Literary Journal* was published from 1749 until December 1844.

3. John Joshua Kirby (1716–1774), *The Perspective of Architecture; in Two Parts; a Work*

Entirely New; Deduced from the Principles of Dr. Brook Taylor; and Performed by Two Rules Only of Universal Application . . . (London, 1761). Kirby was a teacher of perspective to the Prince of Wales who, after he became George III, underwrote the cost of the plates for Kirby's book.

4. Colin Campbell (?–1729), *Vitruvius Britannicus; or, The British Architect, Containing the Plans, Elevations, and Sections of the Regular Buildings, Both Publick and Private in Great Britain, with Variety of New Designs . . .* (London, 1715–1725). *Cat. Lib.*, no. 187, lists a five-volume edition published in London in 1761.

5. A daybook or journal is a book for entering daily transactions in the order of their occurrence. The ledger is the principal book of the set used in keeping mercantile records and contains all debtor/creditor accounts.

6. Bristol water, taken from the warm springs at Clifton, near Bristol, was known for its quality and medicinal uses.

7. A French term meaning game or wild fowl.

8. Equipment, especially harnesses, for draft horses.

CCA to CC

Octor: 1st 1762

Dr Charley

I wrote to you the 2d of last Month, but as the Ships stay longer than I expected I with pleasure embrace the opportunity of writing to you again. But I am sorry I must complain & with reason that you do not seem to take the same pleasure in writing to me for yr: last was by the Fleet & Dated the 26 of April. I recommended it to you to write by every opportunity, & I particularly mention'd the New York Packet, two have sailed for New York since the Fleet, the last Arrived very lately, but no letter from you, are you not much to blame? That you might always have a letter for me ready, I told you to minute down yr: thoughts of such things as it might be proper for you to communicate to me, I told you never to write to me in a hurry & in order to avoid it to prepare a letter for me at different times, I think you ought not only to observe these directions, but that you ought to have acquainted me you would observe them, & I again desire you will observe them. What can prevent yr: writing to me? I might excuse my not writing to you by a multiplicity of business, but yet you see I often write to you. Devote ½ an hour a day to think of & set down wt: you may say to me, that makes 15 hours a Month a time more than sufficient for yr: Correspondence with me. I cannot doubt yr: love & affection for me, yr: Neglect must therefore proceed from an indolent & post-poning disposition, but that Habit & disposition must be got over, otherways, you will never be able to carry on yr. affairs to yr: own advantage or the Satisfaction of those you may be concerned with. It is so disagreeable to me to say anything

Chiding to you, that I shall for the future suffer yr: silence with patience rather than complain again on this head, especially as I see my many former admonitions have not had a proper Effect —

By the time you [will] receive this, you will enter into yr: 4th year of yr: reading the Law, a year wch: with proper Application will be more Essential & advantageous to you than the 3 you have past. At 1st yr: study was intricate, dry & disgusting, I doubt not you gradually find it clearer & more agreeable, & now I hope yr: Reason & Judgmt: will be satisfy'd, & that you will be able to comprehend & digest your reading so as to answer the end intended; I look upon this year as an Essential one, & I shd: reckon the others as flung away if this was not added to them, you must certainly upon reflection think as I do —

Mr: Jo: Darnall & Capt: Carroll are with me & desire their Service & Compts: to you, Mr: Croxall is well & by a standing order to me desires his. I am well & am My Dr Charley

Yr: Mo: Afft: Father

Cha: Carroll

LS, Outerbridge Horsey Collection of Lee, Horsey, and Carroll Family Papers, MS 1974, MdHi. Addressed in the clerk's hand "To Charles Carroll Esqr: Kings Bench Walks Temple near the Water London." Marked "Copy" in CCA's hand.

CC to CCA

11th. Nobr. 1762.

Dr. Papa

The last letter I reced. from you was dated the 29 of June, the preceeding Letter of the 12 May never came to hand. About the middle of Augst. I went down to Tunbridge wells spent there the remainder of that month and all the next: Mr. Jennings our countryman bore me company; we kept house together, lived regularly, friendly & sociably. We found Mr. Dulany at the Wells, he remained there till within a week of our departure for London: he dined with us 3 or 4 times and we with him as often: we some times rode out together; in one of our morning airings the discourse happened to fall upon your Law suit with Mercer & Clifton: he let drop in persueing this topic that the Company wou'd readily bare their proportion of the Negroe's Price and wages but thought it unjust in you to insist upon their baring such proportion of the damages incurred by Mercer's attacht. Dulany has an easy, fluent and persuasive tongue; is bold in asserting positive in his assertions, ready to contradict, impatient of contradiction, imperious, decisive & dogmatical. I chose rather to drop the subject than insist on the Justice and legality of your demand, of wh I have but a partial and imperfect knowledge. To Judge from the stated cases you sent me (but I own my Judgt. may be prejudiced by self love) it appears to me reasonable and Just that your Partners shou'd bare their proportion of the damages you have suffered by Mercer's suit & attacht. of your money in Clifton's hands, and that in equity you are entitled to a recovery of such damages against the Company. Indeed from the whole tenor of their conduct your Pa[r]tners seem to have acted a shuffling and dishonourable part. From the stated case sent me and from the several letters therein referred to it appears that upon the demand made by Mercer of the Negroe Will you consulted your Partners and in consequence of their approbation and promise of indemnification you put in your answer to Mercer's Bill. Your Letters to the Co. & their answers are only referred to and not given at Length 3 or 4 excepted, I can't possibly determin how binding the Company's promises maybe unless I see the letters, in which those promises are contained: I make no doubt you have the originals by you as a proof of their approbation of the steps you persued & of their promises of indemnification. By your Letter to Dulany of the 7th. Janry. 1761 you seemed determined not to apply the money reced. of Frazier and Wright to the purchase of Pimlico, but to apply it to the reimbursement of such charges & damages as were brought upon you by Mercer's suit and attachment. In case of non compliance with his arbitrary demand, Dulany threatnens you with a Lawsuit: how are these disputes and mutual claims settled? Or are they as yet settled or like to be? Do you Intend to sollicit an appeal? By your desiring me not to give myself any further trouble about it I suppose you have laid aside that intention; then I apprehend you must abide by the several decrees of the Virginia Courts. If the Co. remains intractible and will not defray their part of the expence you have been put to by supporting a common cause, will it not be necessary to commence a suit against them in order to do yourself that Justice which you must not expect from their honour or uprightness. You will oblige me in letting me know what steps you have taken or intend to take, and wether you will stand by Hill's arbitration;[1] I am affraid that affair will involve you in much trouble and perplexity. If you reject the arbitration is not the bond for performance of the award forfeited? Unless indeed manifest partiality or corruption can be proved.

In my last of the 6th Augt. I enformed you that I had applied to Cousin Antony Carroll as the properest Person from whom you might receive the Intelligence you desire concerning our family: he wrote to his sisters[2] in Ireland for information: their accounts are very unsatisfactory. One of his Sisters sent him a scrap of Paper in Irish relative to our family & as he believes taken from Keeting's History: I have given it to a person to be translated, when returned shall send it you by the 1st. oportunity. I know not whom to apply to for further information, if you can point out a method of obtaining better intelligence, I will readily persue it.

Mr. Lewis has sent me in the 1st volu: of Gahagan's Irish history: the second and third volums. are not as yet published: the whole work, I am told, is to be comprised in 3 volus. in 4o. at 12S per volu: in sheets. . . . The English Jesuites have been obliged, in consequence of the dissolution of their order in France to quit St. omers; their College is now in the Possession of the Secular Priests of Douay: The Students and Jesuites have removed to Bruges by an invitation from that city and from the Empress Queen[3] who promises them her protection. But I refer you to Mr. Hunter for further particulars who undoubtedly has ere this received a circumstantial account of the whole affair. Mr. Kenedy to whom you applied to get the genealogy of our family translated, is in town; he desires his compliments to you & has promised to procure me all the memorials Published by the french Jesuites in their defence and in vindication of their innocence. I expect them shortly and shall send by the fleet or sooner if a safe oportunity is offered.

The Preliminaries of a peace between England France and Spain were signed at Fontainbleau the third Instant they are not as yet published by authority, but are said to be as follows. All Canada and that Part of Louisiana situate on the east side of the Mississipi to be ceded to England: thus that River is to be the boundary of the British and French colonies upon that continent: The Havanna to be restored to Spain, in return all Florida to be given up to England and the Spaniards & French to evacuate Portugal; our right of cutting logwood established their claim to a share of Newfoundland fishery relinquished. The French are admitted to fish between the capes Raz & Bonavista[4] only, & to have the Ports of Miquelon & St. Peters;[5] in the last mentioned Isleland they may erect a fort and keep a small garrison but under the Inspection of an English commissary. Guadaloupe, Martinico, St: Lucia, Marigalante[6] to be restored to France[,] the other Islelands to remain in our Possession. Senegal we keep and give up Goree, and Belleile for Minorca. The French are at Liberty to rebuild Pondicherry, & are allowed 2 or 3 factories in Bengal. I have given you the substance of what are said to be the Preliminaries, but forgot to mention that the French and English armies are to withdraw from Germany, and in case the war continues between Prussia & Austria the French and English are to assist their allies according to treaty. The French are to evacuate Ostend and Newport & to demolish the fortifications of Dunkirk.

I do not make the progress I coud wish in the Law owing to the want of a good method & proper Instructor and still more to my being out of the way of Business & the practice of the Courts. I still continue to apply & am not disheartned with the difficulties I meet with Persuaded as I am of the necessity of understanding the Law well. I desire my kindest complts. to Harry Carroll from whom I long to hear: pray rembr. me to Mr. Croxall & John Darnall whom I much esteem & to my Cousin Rach: Darnall. I am Dr. Papa

your most affectionate & dutiful Son
Ch: Carroll

ALS, Carroll Papers, MS 206, MdHi. Addressed in an unknown hand. Endorsed by CCA.

1. CC is inquiring about Clement Hill's (1707–1782) arbitration in CCA's dispute with Charles Carroll of Duddington.

2. Margaret Carroll Biggs (?–liv. 1762) and Mary Carroll Ashton (?–liv. 1762). See Appendix I, Chart B.

3. Maria Theresa. By the treaty of Aix-la-Chapelle, which ended the war of the Austrian Succession in 1748, Bruges and the rest of present-day Belgium were awarded to Austria.

4. Pointe du Raz, in western France near Brest, and Cape Bonavista, in Newfoundland.

5. The important cod-fishing ports of Miquelon and St. Pierre are located on islands off the southern coast of Newfoundland near the Grand Banks.

6. Marie-Galante, an island in the French West Indies.

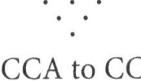

CCA to CC

Decr: 24: 1762

Dr Charly,[1]

Perhaps you Mistake what Compound Intt. is to Illustrate it I state the following Acct

1760 A.B .... Dr	1761 Ca	Cr
Janu: 1st To yr Bond £100:0:0	Janu: 1st By Balla: Chargd prCa.	£106:0:0
1761		
Janu: 1st To 1 yrs Intt thereon	6:0:0	
Do .... Dr	106:0:0	
do To Balla: pr Ca	106:0:0	
1762		
Janu: 1 To 1 yrs Intt thereon	6:7:2¼	
	112:7:2¼	

Do You Call this Compound interest? If you do I think our law dos not, for it Says you Shall not take for mony lent more than 6 pr Ct V: Bissetts Abridgement sent you. Is this taking more than 6 pr Ct Is not the 1st yrs Intt: if not paid Money lent? Is it more agreable to law that the Borrower should make an Interest of the 1st yrs Intt: than the Lender. Money is Supposed to Carry an Interest in whatever hand it lays & Does not the Borrower who makes an interest on the £6 by not paying it to the lender Cheat the Lender of that Interest? Can the Law Countenance that Cheat? The Law is founded on reasone Do not our Proprietors in the Funds Receive their Interest every half year? Is this Contrary to law? Might not more Interest be made this way than Can be made in the Manner Stated in the Above Acct. Before Commerce was Carryed to nigh its Present Pitch & Consequently before the Value of Money was so well knowne to Carry its Price any Intt: by the

Canon Law as I have been informed was deemed usury. In Equity I am informed Compound Intt: is allowed on Mortgages, if so why not on Bonds? If not on Bonds is not the Distinction without a Difference. In Conscience Justice & Reason[2] I am Clear I am entitled to take Intt: in the Manner above stated. I should be glad to know from you after you are well informed whether upon our Law I am liable to any Penalty [for] takeing Interest in the above Manner & whether the Law does look upon Intt taken in the above Manner to be taking Compound Interest. Have any Penalties been recovered for takeing intt: in the above Manner? I have never heard of Such a Recovery & I doubt not but that if Persons were lyable to Penalties for takeing Intt: in the above Manner that Prosecutions Would often be Brought for the Recovery of Such Penalties & the Reason why I apprehend no Penalty is incurred by taking Intt: in the Above Manner is, because the Lender in the Above Manner does not take more than 6 pr Ct on Money lent. But should a lender take £6:10:0 pr Ct on Money lent I doubt not but he might & would be Prosecuted for the Penalties[.]

PS

If a Man was to Compute his Intt Monthly & Charge intt on the Balla or that Intt this I apprehend is Charging Compound Intt Because he takes more than 6 pr Ct pr Annum on Mony lent —

AL, Carroll Papers, MS 206, MdHi. Endorsed by CCA: "1762 Decr: 24 Copy To my Son." Two ALS copies, both designated "Copy" and with margins badly damaged, are filed in the Carroll-McTavish Papers, MS 220, MdHi.

1. Following the salutation CCA wrote and then struck out the following: "This is in my owne hand as I did not Care my Clerk should be Acquainted with what you say about Compound Intt: in Yrs of July 4th & Augt: 6th." The line does not appear in either of the ALS copies.

2. Both ALS copies read "In Conscience Equity & Reason."

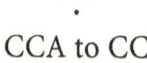

CCA to CC

Dec: 26 17[6]2

Dr Charley

I have at last Reced yr: two long wished for letters of July 4th & Augst 6th 1762, the 1st Via Virginia came to hand the 22d & the last by the N. York Packet the 9th Inst: These letters Mr: Perkins might have sent as I wrote you sooner Viz: by the Packets wch: Sailed in July & Augst: & then they would have come to hand in Sept: & Octor:

I am sorry you have given yrself any concern about my Cause with Clifton &

Mercer any further than to Consider & judge from that Transaction whether we are intitled to recover of my Partners in the Iron Works according to the particular state of the Case relating to them wch: I sent you. You may consider that Case for yr: own Satisfaction, but it is not necessary you shd: say more to me upon it than shortly to give me yr: opinion upon it. Cliftons allegations of his being forced to execute the Bonds for £634.5.4 & £257.14.6¾ are destitute of truth. An allegation in a Bill is but a Charge, those allegations in my Answer are deny'd, & an Answer is Evidence if not contradicted by superior Evidence wch: I am certain does not appear in the proceedings or elsewhere. I had nothing to do with the Recovery agst Hedgman, I was only a nominal person in that Action, the Recovery was for the Benefit & Security of Clifton who was Brents Security & to whom the Mony was paid. Cliftons pretensions would not appear destitute of reason if he had been ready & willing to pay the Mony, the whole proceedings shew the Contrary, & that he kept all his Crs: out of their money as long as he could, & that his lands were at last sold to pay them & moreover that he had other large Sums of mine in his hands, & if I forget not the proceedings the Attachment was droped & the Mony paid by Hedgman to Clifton—

I shall remember you to Capt: Carroll, he proposed to write to you by the Fleet & I doubt not he has done so; He was [. . .] last [. . .] him. You give me [the great]est pleasure by acquainting me you are well, you cannot be thinner than I was at yr: age, I was also subject to little lurking fevers, such a habit obliged me to be very temperate in my Youth & that temperance hath brought me to 60.

I have wrote to you formerly on the Subject of a Horse & Mares, a horse as I told you is not wanting & such Mares as I described I think may be got on very easy terms if you think it worth yr: trouble to get them. I acquiesce to yr: Resolution of not entering yr: self of the Temple. I Compound with you as you desire, but run not again in Debt, let me not only have the Journall of yr: Northern Tour but of all yr: Tours subsequent to that. I beg you will not think the Italian method of Book-keeping too tedious & prolix, rely in this particular on my judgment & Experience, I wish I had kept all my Accts in that manner, I did not know how to do it, it was not laziness that made me think that method too tedious or prolix. Why shd: not a Gentns: affairs & Books be kept in as clear a manner as a Merchts:? Mony affairs must be kept so & you will not have a very small share of that to keep so. Do not forget Surveying.

I did not purchase O Connors Translation of Keating of Mr Lewis. I again desire for yr: own sake that you will by Csn: Anto: or by any other means trace our family up to 1500. Csn: Carroll is right about the Country of the O'Carrolls, it was by the Latin Authors called Elia Carolina commonly Ely O Carroll. Your Grand-father gave that name to one of the Seats of Land he took up here.[1] Let us try to be fortunate in the next Lottery. All yr: News is stale by the long laying & passage of yr. letters. I have thought of an Expedient to make you a more regular & punctual Correspondent, it is not to write to you but when I receive letters from you & I think it a good one. The Ships to Philadelphia put up for freight at the Pensilvania Coffee house, you may easily know [. . . .]² come safe to me. Neglect no[t the] N. York Packets. I hope y[r]: Tour to Tunbridge has been pleasant & agreeable to you. Pray present my sincere Service to Mr Power, I most sincerely condole his & his Brethrens misfortunes, I think they must soon be reinstated. The usefullness of their Schools only will oblige the K. of France to recall them, his Parliament as well as the English have made a Cypher of him. Remember me kindly to Mr: Jennison & all the Gent: in London.

Pray make it yr: business to be well informed at wt: yearly allowance Mr: Hen: Darnall is supported abroad & by whom. He sollicits supplies from hence, & his friends who are not many of them in Circumstances to support themselves con- tribute, his Temper & Disposition is such as to Squander any Sums foolishly, if he has enough to support him as a person in his Circumstances shd: be supported, that is barely with necessaries, it is unjust he shd: raise Contributions on his friends here, it is for this reason I desire to be as fully informed as possible —

Your old acquaintance Mr: Lawson is within a few days going to commit Matri- mony.³ I have presented yr: Compts: to those you mentioned & you may be assured they would send you theirs if they knew of my writing. Rachel Darnall desires to be affectionately remembered to you. Wishing & daily praying for yr: health & Happiness I am my Dr Charley

Yr: Mo: Affte: Father
Cha: Carroll

PS

Some years past some Mathematicians were sent from France & Spain to So: America to measure a Degree on the Earth, among them was one Uloa who has published some Acct or Memoires of America,⁴ I shd: be glad to have them. I have seen a Vindication of the Jesuits said to be publish'd at Rennes Entitled Memoire concernant &c⁵ it is very plain & not at all labour'd but very full & Convincing[.]

LS, Carroll-McTavish Papers, MS 220, MdHi. Another LS copy, with date, salutation, and part of the first line missing, is filed with it.

1. Surveyed for Charles Carroll the Settler in January 1695/6, the one-thousand-acre Baltimore Co. tract Ely O'Carroll lay in what is today the Green Spring Valley.

2. One line missing.

3. Alexander Lawson, Jr., married Elisabeth Brown of Queen Anne's Co.

4. Don Antonio de Ulloa (1716–1795) and Don George Juan (?–1773), *A Voyage to South-America: Describing at Large the Spanish Cities, Towns, Provinces, etc., on That Extensive Continent; Interspersed Throughout with Reflections on the Genius, Customs, Manners, and Trade of the Inhabitants; Together with the Natural History of the Country; and an Account of Their Gold and Silver Mines . . .* , 2 vols. (London, 1758). *Cat. Lib.*, no. 113, lists a two-volume 1760 London edition.

5. [Henri Griffet], *Mémoire concernant l'Institut, la doctrine et l'établissement des Jésuites en France* (Avignon, 1761; Rennes, 1762).

CC's Account of Expenses

[January–December 1762]

1

Jany 1762			£	S	D
		to ¼ of the London Evening Post		7	6
		to loss at Cards, coach hire Christmass boxes	1	14	6
	5th.	to the Bricklayers Bill		3	6
	do.	to ¼ Rent due the 25 Decb. 1761	10		
	8	to my Arithmetick master	1	1	
		to a subscription Ball	1	6	
		to loss at Cards, Vales, Coach hire, & Supper at the Tavern	1	4	8
		to loss at Cards	1		
		to 2 weeks washing & the Waterman's Vales		10	4
		to soheing my horse to postage Magasines 2 weekly bills		5	6x
do.	15	Paid to Mr. Pointz for books & Carriage	3		2
		to cutting my hair to the play		4	11
		to loss at cards to washing to a filet¹ for my hair		9	
		to the Robin Hood society²		1	
	20	to the play vales & Coach hire		3	6
		to 2 weekly Bills		3	8
		to a letter, halter for my horse ½lb. of tea at 10s per lb.		5	10
		to 6lb. of Candles to mending the bed hinges		6	2
		to 2lb. of Sope to dinners from the Tavern		12	
		to one weeks washing		2	7
		to the Poor & loss at cards		14	6
Febry. 1st.					
		to my Arithmetick master	1	5	8
		to vales & Coach hire		4	
	2d.	to my Servant	3	3	
		to the play & weekly Bill		11	8½
		to one loaf of Sugar 7lb. 7oz at 10d per lb.		6	2½
		to loss at Cards to the poor	1	11	6

			£	S	D
8	to	Do.		14	6
	to 2 weekly Bills to the Magazines to a bed hinge			5	1½
	to shoeing my horse to salt to 3 week's washing			12	½
	to a pair of yarn stockings			2	1
17	to 1 Chaldron of Coals			2	5
	to the play to vales			6	6
	to washing &			4	2
25	to my Servant		3	3	
	to 2 weekly Bills to a door hinge 2lb. of pouder			5	5½
	to 3lb. of candles to a quire of Paper			3	11
	to 3lb. of Do. for my Servant			1	9
			36	15	4½ [3]

2

		£	S	D
Feby. 26	to the Porters, 2lb. of Rice & Inkglass		3	
	to the Oratorio		3	6
March 2d.	to my Arithmetick master	1	1	
	to the Chimney sweepers		6	
	to loss at Cards		4	
	Paid to my Servant	5	6	
	to one weekly Bill		3	1
	to the Taylors Boy to chair hire to go to Court		7	6
	to Chestnuts, loss at cards, 1 week's washing		15	½
	to loss at Cards to vales 2lb. of candles baking pans		5	9
	to one weekly Bill		4	6½
	to one week's washing to the Poor		14	5
	to one weekly Bill ½lb. of Bohee tea		6	2
	to the Gazette, salt, washing silk stockings		3	2
	to 9lb. of candles at 7d per lb.		5	
	to coach hire & coffee		4	11
	to ¼ rent	10		
	to cutting & loss at cards		5	6
	to my Arithm: Master	1	1	
	to the American Negotiator [4]		5	
	to the Farrier's Bill		15	2

			£	s	d
		to 1 weekly Bill & magasines		3	8
April	5th.				
		to 2 weeks washing		5	3½
		to ¼ London Evening Post		6	6
		to a holy week book		5	
		to the Poor to coffee		11	
April	17	to my Journey to Sawson Mr. Huddlestone's seat	2	19	3
	.	to a weekly Bill shoeing my horse		5	8
		to a new hat	1	1	
		to 4 pair of brown thread stockings		18	
		to 2 weeks washing to mop, matt & cleaning windows		9	1½
	21	spent in a Journey to Ryegate		13	6
		to memoirs of Brandenburgh[5] & new discoveries		8	6
May	1st.	to loss at Cards & Bleeding the arm		7	6
		to the weekly Bill coffee a Bottle of mountain[6]		9	10½
		to 1 Loaf of sugar Weit 6lb. 3oz at 10d per lb.		5	2
			32	11	8½[7]

3

			£	S	D
May	4th.	to the Poor, 1 weekly Bill, to coffee & vales		5	½
	10	to ½ Chaldron of coals at 44s per Chaldron	2	2	
		to shooting Do.			6
		to loss at cards		7	6
		to Vales to Mrs. Anderson's son	1	2	
	14	to loss at cards		7	
		to the Bricklayer's Bill		8	6
		to the cutting my hair		2	6
		to a Philet for my hair		4	
	17	to the Weekly Bill		1	4
		to shoeing my firewood		4	½
		to 4 weeks washing		10	
		to coffee		1	3
	19	to my Servant	5	5	
		to loss at Cards		11	
	21	to my Arithmetick master	1	1	

Date		Description	£	s	d
		to the weekly Bill		1	5
		to 2lb. of powder for my hair & blacking		1	6
		to coffee & loss at cards		2	6
	25	to Waller's Bill for Books	16	3	
		to vales		2	
		to the window tax being 1 years assessment		9	
		to Vauxall gardens		6	
		to loss at cards & seeing the Pictures at Spring gardens[8]		11	6
June	1st.	to one weekly Bill 2 week's washing		7	4½
		spent at the Tavern	1	8	6
		to loss at cards		5	
		to Rhenalagh house		7	
June	4	to my Servant	2	2	
		to Sadlers wells[9] & supper at the Tavern		4	
		to one weekly Bill, coffee, blacking, magazines, salt		5	9½
		to washing silk stockings		2	
	9	to rebinding Coke Littl: & Wingates Arithmetick		8	6
		to postage		0	10
		spent at Vauxhall		11	
	14	to shoeing my one weekly Bill, & Jellies		5	5
		to coffee & weekly Bill		5	3
	21	to Sheppards Touchstone[10] & a writing book		12	6
	Do.	to sundry other Law books		15	
		to coach hire		2	
			38	11	9

4

Date		Description	£	S	D
June	26	to 3 pair of thread stockings at 4..6 per pair		13	6
		to a Journey to Ryegate, one weekly Bill		9	½
		to paper, quills, 2lb. of candles		2	5½
		to one truss of straw to the Blacksmith		3	1½
		to vales & coffee		3	3½
July	2d.	to my Arithmetick master	1	3	6
	do.	to my Servant	1	1	
		to vales, to the watermen		2	2
		to turnpikes, & horse charges		8	
	19	to ¼ subscription to the cold bath		13	

	to the History of the Arians[11] Ostler & turnpikes		3	2
	to 6 weeks washing, 1 weekly Bill, coach hire		18	11½
21	to ¼ rent due midsummer's day	10		
	to a pair of gloves & vales		2	6
25	Spent in a tour to Margate absent fortnight	14	5	6
	spent at Ryegate absent 3 days		15	
	to 1 weekly Bill, beating carpets, ½lb. of tea, bottle of wine		7	8
	to mending cloaths, chips, postage		5	1
	to coffee		2	5
31	to my Servant	1	1	
do.	spent at Vauxhall		5	
Augst. 4	to one weekly Bill, flower of Brimstone		2	10
	to Blacksmith & Porters, coffee		7	6
7	to 2 waiscoats, to the poor	2	4	6
	to my Landress one years wages	4	4	
10	to shooting coals, head Porter		11	6
	to 6 stocks[12] at 4s.. per stock	1	4	
	to the play, 2 weekly Bills, 6lb. of candles		13	1
	to sope, blacking, pometum, coffee, 4 weeks washing		15	3
17	to my Servant	1	1	
Octobr. 2d.	Spent at Tunbridge Wells in 44 days	43	17	3
do.	to servants wages extraordinary for 44 days at 1..6 per day	3	6	
do.	to horse hire for 44 days at 2s..6 per day	5	12	6
	to washing		7	3
5.	spent at Ryegate	1	4	3
	to the play		4	
do.	to ¼ rent due 29 Septb. 1762	10		
	to a ring		1	8
	to breakfast at the coffee house 4 times		2	8
		110	1	9½[13]

5th.

		£	S	D
Octb. 9.	to loss at cards		9	2
	to a weekly Bill, to a letter, blacking, salt, pometum		5	½

Date	Description	£	s	d
	to vales & loss at cards		10	
	to the play, & shoemaker	3	8	2
	to the Saddlers Bill, to the play, waterman & vales		17	3
Octbr. 18.	to mending shoes, pouder for the hair		4	7
	to a weekly Bill, to Sugar, coffee, loss at cards		13	4½
19	to 5 Chald: of coals at 34s per Chaldron	8	10	
do.	to metage[14] & Lighterage[15]		10	
	to washing & mending leather breeches		5	
22	to my Servant	1	1	
	to loss at cards, weekly Bill, 3lb. candles, 1lb. sope, 1lb. Butter		5	6
	to washing bed hangings & blankets		14	3
	to 6 weeks washing		15	9
	to collering shirts, sweeping chimneys, a mop, coach hire		10	11
27	to my Servant	1	1	
Nobr. 1st.				
	to the play, to washing, weekly Bill, shoeing my horse		10	7½
	to ½ years news papers		16	3
	to vales, loss at cards, coach hire, cutting my hair		8	
8	to washing, weekly Bill, coffee, vales		8	11
13	to my Servant	3	3	
	to the weekly Bill, to 6lb. candles, washing		7	11½
18	to ¼ subscription to the cold Bath		13	
	to vales, Arithmetick master, play, loss at cards	1	10	
	to the weekly Bill, Taylor, Iron scrues, washing		7	5½
23	to 3 pair of stockings at 4s..6 per pair		13	6
	to vales, play, coffee, weekly Bill		14	4½
	to ½lb. of tea at 10s per lb.		5	
	to a broom, flower, coach hire, vales, & loss at cards		19	11
Decbr 1st.	to mending the chimney		16	1
	to the play, weekly Bill, 3lb. candles		7	4
9	to my Servant	2	2	
	to 3 weeks washing, & Opera		18	7

		£	S	D
16	to my Servant	1	1	
	to the play		5	
		36	9	

		£	S	D
Decbr. 17	to my Arithm: Master	1	1	
	to 2 weekly Bills, brooms, pack of cards, washing stockings		11	
	to 2lb. sope, chips, Paper books, 3lb. candles		6	
	to vales, coach hire, play		8	
29	to one weekly Bill, 3lb. candles,		3	7
	to dressing two hatts		3	6
	to charity	1	1	
30	to ¼ news Papers 39 Papers at 2d ½ per Paper		8	1½
31	to vales & coach hire		3	
	to diet	24	15	3½
		29		6
		£254	9	7½
	Sum total	283	10	1½ [16]
	Received	295	14	

N:B: This account begins from the 1st. January 1762 and ends at the 30 Decebr.; the 27 of that month I took up twenty five Pounds 4 shillings: but little of this last sum is accounted for in the present accot. . thus is the deficiency of £12 explained.

AD, Carroll-Maccubbin Papers, MS 219, MdHi. Endorsed by CCA: "1762 My Sons Expences from Janu: 1st to Decr 30th."

1. A net with a square mesh.

2. A tavern debating club.

3. Actually £36 19s. 4½d. CC totaled his expenditures at the bottom of each page.

4. John Wright, *The American Negotiator: or, The Various Currencies of the British Colonies in America . . . Reduced into English Money . . .* (London, 1761). *Cat. Lib.,* no. 1175.

5. Frederick the Great, *Memoirs of the House of Brandenburg. . . . Cat. Lib.,* no. 838, may possibly be the 1748 London edition, signed by CCA, now at the George Peabody Library of the Johns Hopkins University, Baltimore, Md. *Cat. Lib.,* no. 1358, is a 1751 Berlin edition, published in French.

6. Wine from the mountains of Malaga, a province in southern Spain.

7. Actually £32 8s. 9½d.

8. Beginning in 1761 a number of leading artists, calling themselves "The Society of

Artists of Great Britain," organized exhibitions of their work at Spring Gardens in Charing Cross.

9. Eighteenth-century Sadlers Wells was a pleasure garden offering food and entertainment.

10. William Sheppard (?–1675?), *The Touchstone of Common Assurances . . .* (London, 1648). *Cat. Lib.,* no. 991. Sheppard was a legal writer and judge.

11. Louis Maimbourg, *The History of Arianism Shewing Its Influence upon Civil Affairs . . .* (London, 1728–1729), trans. William Webster.

12. Probably close-fitting neckcloths.

13. Actually £110 10s. 11½d.

14. The duty paid for determining the official weight of a load of grain, coal, or a like commodity.

15. The charge levied for the transfer of goods from a seagoing vessel into a flat-bottomed harbor barge or lighter.

16. Actually £284 4½d.

· · ·
·

CCA's Inventory of Doohoregan

[1762]

Inventory of Goods in the Hall — 1762

new Chairs	10
old Do.	7
Tables	8
Backgammond Tables	1
Great Chairs	3
Screwtores[1]	1
Lookinglass	1
Hand Irons[2]	2
Shovels	2
Tongues[3]	2 pr.
Picturs	1
Cloth brush	1
Hair brooms[4]	3
Middle Closset	
Chinea Soop plates	11
Chinea Plates	24
Old Do. Do.	9
Chinea Patties[5]	12
Do. Broke	2
Custard Cups	12

Old Do. Do.	5
Old Do. Broke	1
New Chinea Dishes	4
Chinea Soop Dish	1
Do. fruit Do	4
Do. Do. Broke	1
White Stone Patties	3
new Pewter plates	[?]
Do. Do. Dishes	2
Old Pewter Soop Dishes	2
other Dishes	8
Plates	36
Soop plates	6
Collender	1
Pewter Basons	7
Tin Pans	6
Water Plates[6]	6
Dish Covers	6
Tin slice[7]	1
Knifes	11
Forks	11
Brass Candle Sticks	8
Stone mugs	2
Pr. Steel snuffers	1
Stone mustard Pot	1
Box Irons[8]	2
Heathers[9]	5
flat Irons	6
Iron Graits	3
Brass Cheffing Dishes	2
Platewarmer	1
Tea Kettle	1
Plate Basket	1
Lawn Sifter[10]	1
Coffie mill	1
Dish mats	5
Stone pitcher	1
Vinegar Cruets	2
knife Basket	1
Goods in the Tea Closset	
Plate Salvers[11]	3
Castors[12]	3

Coffie Pots	1
Sauce Boat	1
Cups	3
Snuffers & Case	1
Tea Cannester	1
Salt Sellers	2
Candle Sticks	1
Large Soop Spoon	1
Small Do.	15
Tea Spoons	13
Tea Tongues	1
Strainers	2
Snuff box	1
Tea Closset	
Red & white Chinea Cups	10
Caussers [13]	10
Coffie Cups	6
Tea Pot	1
Tea Cannester	1
Cream Pot	1
Spoon Boat	1
Sugar Dish & Cover	1
Plate for the Tea Pot	1
Cake plates	2
Slop Bowl [14]	1
Bleu & white Chinea	
Bowls	5
Bro[ke?]	[?]
Coffie [Cups]	[?]
Tea Cu[ps]	3
Saucers	3
Tea Pot & plate	1
White Stone Tea Pots	3
Wine glasses	24
Ale Do.	4
Tumblers	3
Dicanters	2
Alter Cruets [15]	2
wine Cranes [16]	3
Bellows	1
hand Coffie mills	2
Truss	1

Glass lamp	1
Pipkin[17]	1
Earthen Dish	1
Cork Screw	1
Nutmeg graiters	2
Sugar Boxes	2
Cannesters	8
Tea Chest	1
Parlour Closset	
Box of Candles	1
Sope Tub	1
Bottle Brush	1
Tea Cannesters	9
In the Screw Tore	
Mass Book	1
½ Manuels	2
Preparation for a happy Death[18]	2
Introduction to a Divote life[19]	1
a Roman Catholiks Reason's why he Cannot conform	
to the Protest Religion[20]	2
Grounds of the Catholick Doctrin[21]	7
Cathecisms	2
Christian perfections[22]	1
new version of Psalms[23]	1
Histoire de Virginie[24]	1
Dunciad[25]	1
a select Collection of Novels[26]	1
Collection of Novels & Tales[27]	1
works of Sheakspier Vollums	3
English Grammer	1
Play Books	[4?]
Guys Fables[28]	2
Lattin Book	1
le Sicle de Louis 14th Vollums[29]	2
London Magazis	28
a Youngmans Diversion	1
French & English Dictionary	1
R[em]arks on Bishop Burne History[30]	1
Pr: of Pistols	
Brass Cocks	3
Gun Chargers	3
[P]owder horns	[?]

Shaving box and Brush	[?]
a Hone[31]	1
Strap	1
Pruning knife	1
Ink bottles	2
Box of Wavers[32] & Seal	1
Shoe Horn	1
Razors	6

Green Room

new Table Cloths	14
new Damask napkins	12
old Diaper[33] Table Cloths	5
Huckerback[34] Do.	5
old Damask napkins	12
Huckerback Do.	8
Do. Towels	14
old Pillow Cases	15
new Do. Do	12
Shaving Cloths	2
Sheeting linnen towels	5
Ozenbrig[35] Towels	5
new Holland[36] Sheets	7 pr
old Do. Do.	8 pr
1 set of Bed Curtains	
4 window Curtains	
Stockings	1 pr.
Cheek	13 Yards
Bed Ticking	3 Do.
Masks	3
Basket	1
Cannester of Coffie	1
Tea Cannester	1
Curtains & Valiants	
Chest of Drawers	1
Chairs	3
Table	1
Cots	2
Bedsteads	1
Feather Beds	3
Matrasses	2
Bolsters	3
Pillows	6

Countrepins	4
Quilts	4
Blankets	4
Yallow Room	
Feather Beds	1
Matrasses	1
Blankitts	2
Quilts	1
Countrepins	2
Bed Curtains & Valiants	
Bolsters	1
Pillows	2
Chairs	3
hand Irons	2
Shovel & Tongues	
Lookinglass	1
Comb Case	1
Cricket[37]	1
Chamber Pots	11
Pitcher	1
Trunks	3
old Boxes	4
Table	1
Red Room	
Feather Beds	1
Matrasses	1
Bolster	1
Pillows	2
Blanketts	2
Quilts	1
Countrepin	1
Bedstead	1
Lookingglasses	1
Tables	1
hand Irons	2
Shovel & Tongues	
Chairs	2
Curtains & Valiants	
Closestool[38] box & pan	1
warming pan	1
In the Cellar	
Bottles	28 Dozen

Snuf Bottles	7
Apple Chests	3
Casks	5
Soap Jars	3
Small beer Barrel	1
in the Kictchen	
Larg Copper Kettle	1
Fish Do.	1
Frying Pan	1
Irons Pots	4
Pestle & Mortar	1
Skillets	2
Spits	3
Iron Ladle	1
Flesh Fork	1
Skimmer	1
Shovel	1
Tongues	1
hand Iron[s]	2
Iron Rack	1
Crain	1
Water Pails	2
washing Tubs	2
a Cooler	1
Dripping pan	1
a Griddle	1
Grid Iron [39]	1
Trivet [40]	1
Chaving Dish	1
Iron Scewers	7

D, Carroll Papers, MS 206, MdHi. Endorsed by CCA: "1762 An Inventory of Goods &c i[n] my House at Doohoregan."

1. Escritoires — writing desks.

2. Andirons.

3. Tongs.

4. A broom made of hair or having a hairlike texture.

5. Small pastry pans.

6. Dishes to be filled with hot water and set under dinner plates to keep food warm.

7. Any of a variety of flat cooking utensils.

8. Irons for pressing clothes.

9. Probably heaters, removable blocks used to maintain the temperature of a box iron.

10. A fine sieve, often made of linen or silk.

11. Trays.

12. Small vessels with perforated tops, similar to salt and pepper shakers, used for condiments.

13. Saucers.

14. A receptacle for waste at the tea table.

15. Containers for wine or water used in celebrating the Eucharist.

16. Siphons.

17. A small earthenware dish.

18. Possibly *Preparation for Death; or, Acts of Graces and Pious Exercises; in Order to a Happy End* . . . (Edinburgh, 1731), a translation of Jacques-Bénigne Bossuet's *Préparation à la mort.*

19. Francis de Sales, *An Introduction to a Devout Life* . . . (London, 1616).

20. Richard Challoner, *A Roman Catholick's Reasons Why He Cannot Conform to the Protestant Religion* [London?, 1735?].

21. *The Grounds of the Catholick Doctrine* . . . (London, 1736), a later edition of Challoner's *Profession of Catholick Faith, Extracted Out of the Council of Trent by Pope Pius IV* . . . (London, 1732).

22. William Henry, *Christian Perfection; A Sermon Preached in the Cathedral Church of Derry; on the Tenth Day of September, 1751* . . . (Dublin, 1752).

23. Possibly [Nicholas Brady and Nahum Tate], *An Essay of a New Version of the Psalms of David: Consisting of the First Twenty Fitted to the Tunes Used in Churches* (London, 1695), or Brady and Tate, *A New Version of the Psalms of David, Fitted to the Tunes Used in the Churches* (London, 1698).

24. *Cat. Lib.,* no. 1313, lists "Historie de la Virginie" (Amsterdam, 1707), probably a translation of Robert Beverley's *History of the Present State of Virginia, by a Native and Inhabitant of the Place* (London, 1705).

25. Alexander Pope, *The Dunciad* . . . (London, 1728). *Cat. Lib.,* no. 882.

26. S[amuel] C[roxall], comp., *A Select Collection of Novels in Six Volumes Written by the Most Celebrated Authors in Several Languages* . . . (London, 1720–1722).

27. Possibly Samuel Humphreys, ed., *Tales and Novels in Verse; from the French of La Fontaine; by Several Hands* (Edinburgh, 1762). *Cat. Lib.,* no. 1326, however, lists a two-volume French edition of la Fontaine published in Paris in 1759.

28. [John] Gay (c. 1685–1732), *Fables* . . . (London, 1727–1738).

29. Voltaire, *Le siècle de Louis XIV* . . . (Berlin, 1751).

30. John Cockburn, *A Specimen of Some Free and Impartial Remarks on Publick Affairs and Particular Persons, Especially Relating to Scotland; Occasion'd by Dr. Burnet's History of His Own Times* (London, [1724]).

31. A whetstone used especially for razors and fine-edged tools.

32. Wafers upon which a seal might be imprinted, used for securing letters.

33. A soft linen or cotton fabric.

34. Huckaback, a strong, rough-surfaced linen fabric.

35. Osnaburg, a coarse, durable cotton fabric.

36. Linen cloth, made originally in the Holland province of the Netherlands.

37. A footstool.

38. An enclosed chamber pot.

39. A grill placed over a fire for cooking meat.

40. A three-footed metal surface that could be fastened to a grate for cooking and heating over a fire.

CC to CCA

1763 Jany. 7th.

Dr. Papa,

Accept of my sincere wishes for your health and happiness during the course of this new year and many succeeding years. This I hope will be the last I shall pass in absence from you: tho' I am impatient to return, I readily submit in obedience to your will to remain here this one year more, and my impatience shall not hinder my application to the Law.

The Preliminary articles have received the Sanction of Parliat.;[1] warm debates it was imagined wou'd ensue: the expectations of the publick have however been deceived. Both houses voted an address of thanks to his Majesty for obtaining a safe advantageous and honourable peace: The House of Commons divided; but the division, tis said, was only intended to shew the opposition their weakness and unimportance. Mr. Pitt had prudently withdrawn before the division came on: his friends wish he had not appeared in the house that day or at least had not spoke in it: his Eloquence failed him: his mind partook of the infirmities of his body: the Vehement the Impetuous Pitt was for once dull, tedious, & insipid: he spoke as one cautious of offending, unwilling to approve, fearful of disapproving: the real sentiments of his mind seem'd sacrificed to his Interest, the dictates of his Conscience or of his passion, to his pension. Notwithstanding the great majority in favour of the present ministry and of their measures, there have been many and considerable resignations: The list may surprise you particularly as several have resigned very lucrative employments; cou'd a Concurrence with the leading party have procured a continuance of those employments in the former Possessors the list of the <u>Outs</u> wou'd have been much shorter. The King of Prussia is endeavouring to force the Princes of the Empire to a neutrality: his forces have invaded and pilaged Franconia[2] Peace between that Monarch & the Empress Queen seems still distant:

I shall now answer your letter of the second of Sepb. the last I have received: As I knew Captain Carroll had laid aside the thoughts of going to sea again, I gave myself no further concern about the Mares. I intend bringing over a Couple with me if they can be had at a reasonable rate: wou'd not a thorough bread Stallion be of greater advantage? I am creditably informed that there are People in Maryland & Virginia who make £200 or 300 a year by their Stallions. If this be true should mine arrive safe in the Country he will amply repay me his purchase, passage & other Additional charges. I should be glad to know how much it would be proper to allow a groom for his taking care of the horses upon their Passage: as also the wages of a Gamekeeper, a footman's (I suppose) would nearly amount to the same[.] I don't imagin a good and trusty Servant woud transport himself to a forreign country for the same pay he could receive in his own. Mr. Dulaney tells me that Wight Servants seldom turn out well in Maryland; that they disagree with the Negroes & will not eat with them. Wou'd it be better for me to provide my Servant or let him provide himself with Cloaths, and encrease his wages proportionably? I should chuse the 1st. and allow a livery suit and Frock[3] yearly —

I shall take particular care to lay in a good stock of Bristol water for my Voya. to get book cases and whatever else you recommend to me to bring over, as genteel cloaths, horsefurniture &c[.] I thank you for the present of the Pistols, and for reminding me of the necessaries of the Voya. It tis a further proof of that affection you have always bore me and on which I set the greatest value. My picture shall be drawn according to directions and sent by the fleet. Mr. Key[4] proposes to return home very soon: I shall send by him the Magazines, newspapers, and 3 french Pamphlets relative to the french Jesuits; as likewise the tryal of the Rom: Catholicks in Ireland[5] lately published and wh will please you much. The Guns Mr. Perkins sent you were made by the Person, who on Turvey's death, succeeding him in his business. My Bookseller tells me there are 3 volus. of Cambell's Vitruvius Britannicus: if so you want the 1st and 3d. volumes; he fears it will be impossible to procure the odd volus. without buying the whole work.

I have begun a Common Place book: But Bacon's new abridgt. of the Law comprised in 4 volus. Folio[6] which I have got, is much better than any Common place Book I am able to make. The Whole body of the Law is there alphabetically digested under proper heads with references to the year Books, Statutes, & reports. The new Edition of the Statutes to which I have subscribed, will I hope be finished before I leave England. 2 or 3 volus. are already published. If I had known how to procure a person to instruct me in the Law or where such a person was to be found, I should not have neglected doing it. . . . but indeed such a one is not easily to be met with: The best way to become a good Lawyer is to be under an Attorney not as his Clerk, that wou'd not be so proper for a gentleman, but to be in his office on the footing of a gentleman by allowing him a handsom gratification: I should then have known the practical part of the Law, by which knowledge many difficulties wou'd be removed which for want of it are Now insurmountable. Most of our great Lawyer's have been brought up under Attorneys. The great Lord Hardwick[7] is a recent instance of that method's being the best for forming a sound Lawyer. Nothing can be more absurd than the usual manner of young gentleman's studying the Law: They come from the university, take chambers in the temple, read Coke Little: whom they cannot possibly understand, frequent the Courts whose practice they are ignorant of; they are soon disgusted with the difficulties and dryness of the study; the Law books are thrown aside dissipation succeeds to study, immorality to virtue; one night plunges them in ruin, misery, and disease!

I think I understand the theory of Italian book keeping and am able to follow that method if need be, in the transacting of my own business. I shall soon discharge my Master. I have agreed with Mr. Cowley Professor of Mathematics at Woolich to teach me surveying: he is to have 2 guineas entrance money, a guinea per month the month to consist of 8 Lessens: I begin the 18 instant. My Accomptant Master has taught me to raise a form of books consisting of Waste Book,[8] Journal, & Ledger: wh I shall not fail to keep by me, as they will be of use here after.

Mr. Crookshanks upon the dissolution, was obliged to leave Paris; I have now no Correspondent there. I remember Boisson made some scruple about paying the Postage of a letter from his relations, tho' he was only charged with the Postage from England to France; his affection can not be very great, or his necessities are very pressing. Mr. Kenedy returns soon to Paris; I shall write a line or two by him to Mr. Boisson letting him know my address & that I will forward his letters to Maryland. I don't find any provision made or indemnification stipulated by the Preliminaries for the Poor Neutrals: I am affraid they will be overlooked in the definitive treaty & their redress sacrificed to more important Interests. In looking over yr. list of English Books I am surprised not to meet with Shakespear's works. If I remember well you had e'm when I was in Maryland.

The negotiations are going on: there seems to be a demurrer about the Evacuation of Cleves & Gueldres:[9] the french want to give up those places to the Austrians: the English insist upon their being put into the hands of the king of Prussia. In my next, I shall answer the Letter in your own hand writing: I beg my Compliments to Cousin Joh: Darnall & his Sons, to Mr. Croxall & Harry Carroll & to Cousin Rachael Darnall: I am dr. Papa

yr. most dutiful & Loving Son
Ch: Carroll

ALS, Dreer Collection, PHi. Addressed by CC. Endorsed by CCA. Below the endorsement is the following note: "This letter to his father from Charles Carroll of Carrollton the surviving Signer of the Decl. of Independence, now in his 95 year, was given me by *him* in 1831 Robert Gilmor."

1. The proposed peace settlement, placed before Parliament on Nov. 29, 1762, was debated on Dec. 9. William Pitt, although ill, spoke in opposition and William Petty, earl of Shelburne, in support of the treaty. The House of Commons approved the articles by a vote of 319 to 64; opposition in the House of Lords was negligible. Gipson, *Culmination,* 307–309.

2. In October 1762 Frederick the Great's brother, Prince Henry, led his victorious forces through Bohemia, Saxony, and Franconia. Ibid., 286.

3. A coat with long skirts.

4. Edmund Key (?–1766) of St. Mary's Co., the younger son of Philip Key and Susannah Gardiner, had already been admitted to the Charles Co. court (1756), the mayor's court of Annapolis (1757), the provincial court (1757), and the chancery court (1757) and served briefly in the lower house of the Maryland assembly (1758–1759) before leaving the province to study law in England. He was admitted to the Middle Temple in 1758 and to the Inner Temple in 1762. After his return to Maryland in 1762, he was again elected to the lower house and from 1764 until his death held the post of attorney general. Never married, he willed money to support a female child until she reached the age of eight that the Widow Cumming of Annapolis swore to be his. *Bio. Dic. Md. Legis.*, I, 338–339.

5. Henry Brooke, *The Tryal of the Roman Catholicks* (Dublin and London, 1762). Brooke was an Irish writer.

6. [Matthew Bacon], *A New Abridgement of the Law . . .*, 5 vols. (London, 1736–1766). *Cat. Lib.,* no. 769, lists a four-volume edition (1762).

7. Philip Yorke, first earl of Hardwicke (1690–1764), was a leader in systematizing equity law in England. He was appointed solicitor general in 1720, attorney general in 1724, elevated to the peerage and made lord chief justice of England in 1733, and served as lord high chancellor of Great Britain in 1736 and 1737. He began his legal training with two years in the office of a London solicitor, was admitted to the Middle Temple in 1708, and was called to the bar in 1715.

8. A rough account in which transactions of any kind—purchases, sales, payments, receipts, and the like—were entered as they occurred to be posted later in a formal book.

9. Cleves and Guelders were retained by Prussia at the end of the Seven Years' War. Gipson, *Culmination,* 304.

CC to CCA

1763 Jany 31.

Dr. Papa,

I can't Let slip the present oportunity by Captain Hamilton[1] tho' I have nothing new or material to communicate but what is contained in my letter of the 7th Instant. In that I enformed you I had agreed with Mr. Cowley Professor of Mathemactics at the Academy of Woolich to teach me surveying. I have received 5 or 6 lessons: I then thought the previous knowledge of Geometry & Trigonometry wou'd be necessary in order to understand surveying: my conjectures were right in part: Certain problems must be learnt before I can proceed to survey: unless I chuse to be a meer mechanical surveyor, & of course a very inacurate one, unacquainted with the first principles and ignorant of the reasons on which the several operations of surveying are grounded. My Master has brought me a Book of Geometry composed by Mr. Simpson his predecessor in the same office: ti's a thin octavo:[2] I must go thro' the 1st. and 6th. Books; certain problems & theorems scattered up & down the other books are likewise to be learnt. It will require time & study to learn these; not less than 2 hours a day: you see my reading the Law will be somewhat interrupted at least for some while. My health will not permit me to apply as closely and as long as I could wish; and I am persuaded you would not have me upon any account endanger my Constitution which tho' pretty good is none of the stoutest, and will not bear much fatigue; study may certainly be stiled such. There is no fatigue greater than that of the mind. When I have learnt the theory of surveying I shall be taught the practice: my Master will go out with me and survey grounds about London or recommend me to skilful men employed in that business. If you have not by you the Instruments proper for surveying I must bring them over with me, if you have, and they are well conditioned, it will be unnecessary. Therefore pray Let me know as soon as possible what Instruments you have got.

Mr Buchanan arrived in town aday or two ago from Ireland; the fleet was forced by easterly winds, wh have long prevailed to put into Corke where they are still detained. I have the satisfaction to learn from Mr. Buchanan that you enjoy a good state of health and even better than some time ago my own experience has taught me that a too sedantary life is no friend to a Constitution. I wou'd advise you to take proper exercise particularly in the winter: since from the want of exercise last winter the swelling in your legs probably proceeded. If the weather is fair tho' the cold shou'd be severe, you might fence against that by putting on a warm great Coat: an hour's walk every day, I am certain, wou'd be of great service to you.

It gives me real concern that my Letters miscarry or are not sent off in proper time; when finished I deliver them to the care of Mr. Perkins and desire him to forward them by the 1st. oportunity. By the following dates you will see I write to you every other month; consequently what you complain of is not owing to any negligence of mine. I wrote to you the 4th. of July, the 6th. of August, the 11th. of Nobr. and the 7th. of Januy. What can I do more? Tell me and I will do it. As I intend writing again in about a months time by Mr Key I shall be brief.

The denifitive [definitive] treaty is not yet concluded: the negotiations between the Courts of Berlin and Austria are in a precarious way & as likely not to succeed as to suceed if credit can be given to the Papers. The old Chevalier de St. George lays at the point of death: ti's said he has left by will all his Jwels and other effects to his eldest Son. Yesterday came on before the board of trade the Cause or rather complaint of the Virginia Merchant's against the great emission of paper money in that Colony:[3] by which they say their trade has suffered greatly and is likely to suffer more: wether they will meet with redress or what redress is yet unknown:

one of the Merchants in expatiating upon these grievances entered upon a topick foreign to his subject and of a too delicate nature to be treated by a Merchant: He remarked the growing independency of the Colony: the Little deference paid to his Majesty's orders and even the contempt shewn them: another observed, to what purpose do we protect the Colonies and expend such sums in their defence if we are ultimately to be undone by them, and their trade instead of being beneficial to great Britain is detrimental to, and only an incumbrance on i'ts Merchants? I think I cou'd observe a smile on the Countenances of the gentlemen who presided at the Board occasioned, no doubt, by the solidity of those remarks: Mr. Montague[4] in his defence of the General Assembly artfully put the following question; gentlemen is there any one here who is not as ready to transact business & receive Commissions since the emission of Paper money as before? He was answered by an eminent Merchant in the negative: that he could not nor would not give further credit while the present grievance remained unredressed. I have mentioned these particulars not that I think they will afford either instruction or entertainment, but merely to fill up, and to shew I am not averse to writing long Letters and frequently as by the dates in this Letter specified, will appear. Pray present my kind compliments and my excuses to my Cousin Rach: Darnall & tell her she shall certainly hear from me by the next oport[uni]ty[.] I desire to be remembered to Cousin John Darnall and his Sons, to Mr. Richard Croxall and to Capt. Carroll from whom I expect to receive a Letter by Kelty.

Dulaney is still at Bath: when he 1st. desired me to spare him a quarter cask of my Medeira he offered to pay for it as also the charges of freight and duty: he sometime ago wrote to Mr. Perkins with his Compliments to me desiring I wou'd send him down to Bath 2 doz of Bottles. They have been sent long since, but neither Perkins or myself have reced an answer acknowledging the receipt: I think common civility requires at least a Letter of thanks. . . . C'est un homme bizarre: voila tout ce qu'on en peut dire.[5] Boison's Letter shall be entrusted to Mr. Kenedy, who will take care to deliver it to him. Since Mr. Crookshank's departure from Paris my correspondence with him has been broke off: I intend keeping up a correspondence with Mr. Kenedy, a well bred sensible and honest Man. I am Dr. P:

Your most affectionate & dutiful Son
Cha: Carroll

ALS, Carroll Papers, MS 206, MdHi. Endorsed by CCA.

1. Either Capt. George Hamilton, co-owner of the 100-ton snow *King George,* or Capt. William Hamilton, master of the 280-ton ship *Four Friends,* owned by James Makin and Company. Both were involved in the Chesapeake trade. Annapolis Port of Entry Record Books, II.

2. Thomas Simpson (1710–1761), *Elements of Plane Geometry; to Which Are Added, an Essay on the Maxima and Minima of Geometrical Quantities, and a Brief Treatise of Regular*

Solids; Also, the Mensuration of Both Superficies and Solids, Together with the Construction of a Large Variety of Geometrical Problems (London, 1747).

3. The continual complaints of London merchants that Virginia planters were using their colony's depreciated paper currency to pay private debts eventually led Parliament, on the recommendation of the Board of Trade and the Privy Council, to enact the Currency Act of 1764. This measure prohibited the issuance of paper money as legal tender in all the American colonies, a ban in effect for the New England colonies since 1751. Merrill Jensen, *The Founding of a Nation: A History of the American Revolution, 1763–1776* (New York, 1968), 51–55.

4. Edward Montague, the London agent for the Virginia House of Burgesses. David John Mays, *Edmund Pendleton, 1721–1803: A Biography,* I (Cambridge, Mass., 1952), 331.

5. "He is a strange man: that is all one can say."

. . .
.

CC to CCA

Febry. 19. 1763.

Dr. Papa,

Before the receipt of the letter I am now answering matrimony took up but little of my thoughts. The rules you lay down for my conduct in this important affair are as sensible as affectionate & if adhered to will ensure to me that happiness which most married men expect but too few experience: the reasons for being of the same Religion are so strong that no consideration whatever shall prevail upon me to marry a protestant. If my family & fortune alone entitled me to a good wife I have [the] reason to hope and expect such: A chearful sensible virtuous, good natured woman is rara avis in terris[1] a Prodigy, a miracle, a deviation from the general & fixed laws: not one in 10000 is endowed with all those good qualities: my choice is confined to a very small number & therefore the improbability of my succeeding the greater: But shoud I be so lucky as to meet with this lady can I expect her to leave her Home, her friends & relations & follow me to a barbarous uncivilised country: what lady of family will be prevailed upon to make so great a sacrifice: I mention not fortune that is quite out of the question; no woman of a considerable fortune, can now be induced to live in the country: their love of pleasure is stronger than their love of riches. I know of no R: Cath: lady that will suit me: I have never as yet seen the woman I shou'd chuse to marry: I have never been in love & hope I never shall be. I can not here help expressing my gratitude for the liberty of choice you allow me, a liberty which denied has prooved often the source of great unhappiness: to force a child's inclination in a concern of such importance is the highest cruelty a father can be guilty of; & yet how often do we see it practiced by Parents and as often followed by such fatal consequences as should deter others from imitating their example. For my own part I had rather be disinherited than obliged to marry against my inclination & wou'd not hesitate a moment if the alternative was left at my option. As I am left to my own choice the trust you have reposed in me shall not be abused: I here solemnly promise as long as you live, which I hope will be long, never to marry without your full & free consent & approbation. I am Dr. Papa

Your most dutiful & affectionate Son
Cha: Carroll

ALS, Carroll Papers, MS 206, MdHi. Enclosed in CC's letter of Mar. 22, 1763, below. Endorsed by CCA: "1763 Febru. 19 My Sons Letter Came to hand June 1st Ansd June 22d."

1. "A rare bird on earth," an allusion to Juvenal *Satires* 6.165.

CC to CCA

March 22d. 1763.

Dr. Papa,

I wrote to you the 5th. instant[1] & 19 Febry. by Capt. Brookes,[2] enclosed is a copy of that letter. Capt. Brooks had the misfortune to lose his ship she was drove on shore near Deal: the greatest part of her Cargo is saved, Perkin's letters, I know, are; but my packet, I am affraid is lost: it contained the magazines & newspapers, 3 french Pamphlets relative to the Jesuites, the Tryal of the Rom: Cath: in Ireland: I regret most the loss of the Pamphlets; the tryal of the R:C: shall be sent by the fleet. The Pamphlets were curious & enteresting & if lost (for I am not certain that they are) you will be deprived of a great pleasure; but yr. pleasure shall be only postponed; I will procure others. This goes by the same Capt. enquire of him wether a brown paper packet, corderd, sealed, directed to you, & given him in charge by Mr. Perkins or his Clerks was saved with Perkin's letters; & if not, why it was not saved, being not so voluminous as Perkin's box of letters. Brooks has got another ship & is to sail to morrow morning. My Servant will deliver him this & has particular orders to enquire about the packet: I wou'd see the Capt. myself but really have not time. I am to set at 1 o'clock being the second time, for my picture. Mr. Cowley comes at 12: my Portrait without the frame will come to 25 guineas, an extravagant price but you desired it shoud be done by the best hand: & 25 guineas is a fixed price for a ¾. . . . Late last night I received your letter of the 24 Decerb. I have not time to answer it now.

Peace is to be proclaimed this day:[3] I have at last been favoured with a visit from Dulany: He had concluded with Mr. Hyde[4] to buy his land for £500: Hyde approved the price; the deeds were to be drawn & executed: Dulany waited on him the next day with the rough draft: he then desired 14 days to consider of it: alledging that it was better to take time than repent, when too late, a hasty bargain: thus

I am affraid the affair will come to nothing; especially if what Dulany says be true that a bargain has never as yet been struck with Mr. Hyde; that he mistrusts every man's integrity & his own understanding: ti's difficult to come to any agreement with such Men.

I wrote[5] to Cousin Rach: Darnall by Capt. Brooks: the letter was enclosed in yours & yours in the brown paper packet. I shoud send by the present oportunity a copy of that letter had I time, but I am really hard pressed: therefore beg leave to conclude being Dr. Papa

your most dutiful & affectionate Son

Cha: Carroll

ALS, Carroll Papers, MS 206, MdHi. Addressed by CC. Endorsed by CCA: "1763 March 22 My Sons Letter Came to Hand June 1st Ansd June 21st."

1. Probably CC's letter of Feb. 5, 1763. Carroll Papers, MS 206.

2. Probably Capt. Leonard Brooke (1728–1785). Christopher Johnston, "The Brooke Family," in *Md. Gen.*, I, 108.

3. The Treaty of Paris, signed on Feb. 10, 1763, after long and difficult negotiations, ended the hostilities between Great Britain, France, Spain, and Portugal. Prussia and Austria settled their differences on Feb. 15, 1763, in the Treaty of Hubertusberg.

4. Probably London merchant John Hyde (?–1771), son of Jane Calvert and Col. John Hyde. Daniel Dulany purchased the one-thousand-acre tract "Peirces Incouragement" from Hyde for the Baltimore Company in early April 1763. Mrs. Russel Hastings, "Calvert and Darnall Gleanings from English Wills," *Md. Hist. Mag.*, XXII (1927), 339–340 n; Charles Carroll, Barrister, to William Anderson, June 24, 1761, Sept. 2, 1763, "Letters of Charles Carroll, Barrister," *Md. Hist. Mag.*, XXXIII (1938), 196, 377.

5. Not found.

CCA to CC

[April 28th,] 1763[1]

[Dr] Cha[rle]y

The 10th Inst: I Reced yrs: of the 11th of last Novr: Before that I had a Cover from you to a letter directed to James Maccollum without a Date, Maccollum is in Philadelphia extreamly poor, he Mortgaged his Land & ran away from this Province in debt. I do not take the young man to be Maccollum's son, I think he had no Son, an Orphan Boy lived with him who as I apprehend run away from him & I suppose to be the same who gave you the trouble to forward the letter—[2]

I find you know Mr: Dulany pretty well. Dulany before he left Maryland Sued me for his part of the Mony I Reced of Wright & Frazier, the Suit hangs as he filed no Declaration. If on his return he does not drop the Action, & he & my other Partners do not pay me the damages I have suffered by Mercers Suit, I shall prefer a Bill in Chancery agst: them — Since my Partners do not advise me to it, I do not think it worth my while singly to appeal agst: the Decree in favour of Clifton & Mercer —

I do not intend to abide by Clemt: Hill & Basil Warings Award in favour of my Nephew, I have prepared a Bill in Chancery agst: them & my Nephew wch: is under the Consideration of Council & will be filed by next Sept: & I am not in the least fear of not succeeding to set aside the Award —

If by Csn: Anto: & by such Relations in Ireland as he may point out to you, you cannot trace our family as I formerly directed, I know not what other directions to give you. You see by the Coat of Arms I sent you that yr: Grandfather stiles himself the 2d Son of Danl: Carroll Esqr: of Litterlona in the Kings County; May not Csn: Antos: Mother,[3] Sisters or some of Michl: Carrolls Children[4] or some of their Relations trace up our Bra[nch] to [. . .] You may [perhaps] hereafter wish more earnestly [than] you do at present that this had been done. I shall be glad to see the Irish Hist: when compleated. Do not refer me to Accts I may Receive from others of the proceedings agst: the Jesuits, such Accts if sent may not be Communicated to me: you are on the Spot & may procure & transmit as perfect information as any one. I doubt not you Reced Mr: Keneday kindly, & shewed him proper Civilities, if he transmits to you the Papers he promised he will lay an Additional Obligation on me, & if you shd: write to him present my Respects to him. It pleases me much to hear you are not dishearten'd with the difficulties you meet with in the Study of the Law, but I think you have been unfortunate in not meeting with any one to direct you in the most profitable Method of reading it & instructing you in yr: difficulties, if you could not by friendship, I think you might by Mony have procured such a one.

I have made yr: Compts: as desired, I saw Capt: Carroll a few days past, Csn: Jo: Darnall is now with me, they, Rachel Darnall & Mr: Croxall desire to be kindly remembered by you —

My last to you bore Date Decr: 24th 1762, in wch: I acknowledged the Receit of yrs: of Augst: 6th 1762. You see I keep my Resolution of not writing oftner to you than you write to me. On the 13th Inst: my Neice Eleanor Carroll the Wife of Danl: Carroll died, I sincerely regret the Loss of her, for she was in ev'ry Respect a very worthy & valuable Woman. My Nephew who is not capable of doing a wise thing, has lately done the foolishest thing he ever did, for he has taken to himself a Wife, the Daughter of Mr: Hen: Hill —[5]

The 22d Inst: I put in yr: Horse Nimble for the 4 year old purse, I shall give you the Event in the words of our Gazette. Mr: Carrolls Horse Nimble won the 2 first heats, but in Running the 3d to save his distance only, the foolish Rider endeavoured to get before & ran within one of the Poles — Nimble will I think make a fine horse, he is allowed by all to have a very good Bottom —[6]

[. . .] will continu[e yr: St]udy of the Law [. . .] in Feb: you will prepare for yr: Voyage, & I shall expect [you] some time in the May following. Do not come in a Ship with Fellons or Servants, & it will be agreeable to you not to be crowded with Cabin Passengers 2 or 3 you will find to be Company enough, try to get a neat Capt: & one who loves to live well. Be very inquisitive as to the Age of the Ship, & whether she be sound & strong, & well found. About this time twelve Month I shall be as impatient as you have been for a long time past, I shall then long to see you, for I am My Dr Charley

Yr: Mo: Afft: Father
Cha: Carroll

PS

I have been offered £100 for Nimble & refused it —

LS, Carroll-Harper Papers, MS 1225, MdHi. Addressed and marked "Copy" by CCA. Margins damaged.

1. Date supplied by Rowland (*Carroll*, I, 55-58) and confirmed by CCA to CC, Oct. 3, 1763, below.

2. CC's undated covering letter (Carroll Papers, MS 206) relates his meeting a young man claiming to be Maccollum's son and asks CCA to assist him.

3. Mary Browne Carroll. See Appendix I, Chart B.

4. Two of Michael's sons may have been alive at this time, Daniel Carroll and Henry Carroll, S.J. (1720-liv. 1741).

5. Charles Carroll of Duddington married Mary Hill (1744-1822), daughter of Henry Hill (?-1796) and Anne Haskins Hill of Prince George's Co. Bowie, *Prince George's*, 428-429.

6. Spirit or staying power. William Woodward, "The Thoroughbred Horse and Maryland," *Md. Hist. Mag.*, XVII (1922), 154.

∴
∴

CC to CCA

29 April 1763.

Dr. Papa,

This in answer to yours of the 24 Decbr. the last letter I have received from you. By compd. Interest I understood what you understand & have exemplified: to such interest I am clear you have no legal claim; and tho' the charging compd. Interest is not usury within the Statute and consequently not liable to the penalty, yet the borrower is not obliged to pay interest thus computed: to clear up & remove all yr. objections I shall here transcribe a short case to be met with in Salkelds reports[1] Pag: 449. The case indeed relates to mortgages, but I take the Law to be the same on bonds. . . . A mortgage was made with proviso, that if the interest was behind six months, that then the interest shou'd be accounted principal & carry interest; this by my Lord Cowper[2] was decreed to be a vain clause and of no use & he said that no precedent had ever carried the advance of interest so far: and that an agreemt. made at the time of the mortgage, will not be sufficient to make future interest principal, but to make interest principal it is requisite that interest be first grown due, and then an agreement concerning it, may make it principal. . . . Here ti's expressly holden that even when interest is become due, without an express agreement, it cannot be made principal, that an agreement made, before interest accrued, to make it principal is void; a fortiori without any such agreement neither future or accrued interest are to be deemed Principal: your reasons are of weight if the mere equity or conscientiousness of the charge be solely considered; they establish no legal claim whatever. If the interest be not punctually paid you have your remedy at Law[:] you may take a new bond in which the interest become due may be made Principal; or you may sue for it at yr. election. You say you are informed that compd. interest is allowed on mortgages; I wish yr. author had pointed in what cases and where those cases are to be met with: I shall consider more at my leisure of the case between you and yr. Parter. in the Iron works: but indeed I am affraid I shall be unable to form any opinion for want of the original letters that passed between you & them, particularly as I am not well acquainted with the full extent of your claims. My application to the Law has been interrupted by learning surveying; I am almost sufficiently advanced in Geometry to comprehend the principles of surveying: the elements of every science are dry and difficult; they require time and application to be well understood: Geometry is much more entertaining than the Law; the mind is convinced strengthened, & instructed by the strict reasoning of the former, puzeled, perplexed, and dismayed by the incertainty, and obscurity of the latter science, founded upon, and still subsisting by villany.

I have some thoughts of going to Holland this summer and perhaps from thence to Berlin: Mr. Graves,[3] a master in Chancery talks of bearing me company: should he alter his mind, I shall confine myself to Holland. I have wrote to my Cousin at Liège[4] for an account of Mr Darnall's conduct & manner of living at Ghent; I have also wrote to Boison; Mr. Kenedy will deliver our letters to him: sometime ago Mr. Kenedy wrote to Ireland concerning the pedigree of our family: he has since red. an answer, of wh the enclosed is a copy: as the person to whom he applied bears the character of an honest man, and from a long attendance in the Herald's office in Dublin well qualified to give us the best information, I have remitted him 5 guineas to defray the expence of examining the records & to pay the clerks their customary fees: to get our pedigree traced back to 1500 & properly authenticated, will come to near £40: for Mr. Kenedy, informs me, one pound is charged upon every descent: the sealing with the Lord lieutenants' seal costs 4 or 5 guineas: besides Mr. Whitten is to be rewarded for his trouble: if this gentleman upon searching the records and other memorials can find proper materials for making out our pedigree, it will be worth while to bestow £30 or £40 upon it: thus, and thus only your curiousity can be satisfied.

In Easter week I went down to my friend's Mr. Huddlestone; we went over to the races; my intention was to look out for some brood Mares; I saw none to my liking: I was asked £50 for a Mare & £100 for a Stallion: but neither appeared to be worth the money: there is the greatest danger of being cheated in such purchases: If I buy any Mares I shall rely on the Judgt. & integrity of some understanding gentleman: a honest sober & experienced groom is scarce to be met with: should such a one, contrary to my expectation, be found, he would no doubt expect large wages for going to Maryland: I shou'd be glad to know what wages it wou'd be proper to allow him: Pray inform me of this.

My picture is finished & will go by Hanson. It costs 25 guineas, the frame 3 guineas & a half; the likeness is pretty well taken. I have bought no lottery tickets, the very first day they were delivered out, they sold at the advanced & extravagant price of £13 some odd money: you will see in one of the Papers a sketch of this lottery & I believe you will not blame my conduct. I have sent by Hanson besides the Papers & magazines the following books vide: Millers[5] Register: tryal of the R. C in Ireland: 1st. volume of Warners Irish History;[6] 1st. volu: of the same in French by Gahagan: Uloas voya. to South America 2 volus. in Octo.

In my last of the 22d. March I informed you that Mr.————[7] had taken 15 days to consider of the sale of his land to the Baltimore Co: Mr. Dulaney soon after went out of town, I have not seen him since: he returns with the fleet; you may learn from him what steps have been taken in that affair. Have you filed a bill in chancery against your Parteners as you intended? How does yr: law suit with Diggs go on? I wish that dispute cou'd be compromised: It must breed great ill will & occasion many severe reflections: Relations if possible, should avoid such unhappy differences: is yr. Law suit with Howard come to any conclusion?[8] If you can not meet with Justice in Maryland you will, I suppose appeal to the King in council: yr. claims upon Howard must amount to more than £500, the sum to wh, I understand, appeals are limited. I desire to be kindly remembered to John Darnall & sons & to Mr. Croxal. I am Dr. Papa &.c.

Cha: Carroll

Copy of Mr. Whitten's letter to Mr. Kenedy.[9]

I have no doubt but it may be practible to make out Mr. Carroll's pedigree, as I believe there is mention of them in several offices; & also in the County where I was born viz the King's county, as they had very large property there, are still stiled by the ancient Inhabitants Princes of Ely o'Carroll: Yr. friend to make the query more clear, should fill up the blanks by mentioning his father & Mother Grand father & Grand Mother &c. so that by going back as far as he can, very possible he might Join some of the different Branches on Record. There is another thing wanting, wh is some little credit in Dublin as you well know there is no information to be had in any office, without being at some little expence therefore when that is provided for, I shall be ready to give my trouble. Thus far Mr. Whitten.

N:B: As to filling up the blanks that I thought quite unnecessary: besides I coud not go higher than my Grand father as he was the 1st. of our branch who settled in Maryland; I desired Mr. Kenedy to write to Mr. Whitten & inform him in what year my Grand father lelft Europe, & that the pedigree need not be brought lower down than my Grandfather. I coud not precisely determin in what year my Grand-father left England: by his Certificate I see he was entered of the Temple in 1685, by allowing 4 years for his stay in London I may suppose he went over to Mary-land in 1689: there is another difficulty: in the certificate he is stiled second Son of Daniel Carroll of Ahagurton: in the coat of arms he styles himself second Son of Daniel Carroll of Litterlouna[.] I have sent one of the prints to Mr. Whitten with an account of this difference wh he may perhaps clear up.

If you are determined to have the Pedigree made [out &] willing to have yoursef & me inserted; please to let me know it as soon as possible; also inform me when my Grandfather was married & to whom: when you & I were born.

ALS, Carroll Papers, MS 206, MdHi. Addressed by CC. Endorsed by CCA.

1. William Salkeld (1677–1715), *Reports of Cases Adjudg'd in the Court of King's Bench . . . from the First Year of K. William and Q. Mary to the Tenth Year of Queen Anne* (London, 1717–1718).

2. William Cowper, first Earl Cowper (?–1723), studied law at the Middle Temple and was called to the bar in 1688. He became king's counsel in 1694 and was renewed in that posi-tion by Queen Anne in 1702. Elected to Parliament in 1695, he was raised to the peerage in 1706. He served on the commission that negotiated the Act of Union with Scotland and was subsequently appointed the first lord high chancellor of Great Britain, a post he resigned in 1710 but held again (1714–1718) under George I. Although recognized as a skillful and persuasive orator, Cowper was also regarded as undistinguished in terms of his reasoning ability and command of the law.

3. William Graves (1724–1801) was the eldest son of Rear Adm. Thomas Graves and his second wife, Elizabeth. Educated at Balliol, Oxford, and at the Middle Temple, he became a master in chancery (an assistant to the lord chancellor) in 1761 and was elected to Par-liament in 1768, where he served from 1768 to 1782 and from 1796 to 1798. He and CC maintained their correspondence until the time of the American Revolution, and Carroll wrote to Graves at least once after the war. Lewis Namier and John Brooke, *The House of Commons, 1754–1790* (New York, 1964), II, 534; *Debrett's Peerage of the United Kingdom of Great Britain and Ireland,* 18th ed. (London, 1829), 347; CCC to Wallace, Johnson, and Muir, Mar. 8, 1784, Arents Colls., NN.

4. After completing his training as a Jesuit scholastic at Watten, CC's cousin John Car-roll taught at Liège during the late 1750s and early 1760s. Annabelle M. Melville, *John Carroll of Baltimore, Founder of the American Catholic Hierarchy* (New York, 1955), 15.

5. Probably "Millan's."

6. Ferd[inand]o Warner (1703–1768), *The History of Ireland* (London, 1763). *Cat. Lib.,* no. 1133.

7. Blank in original.

8. From the 1750s until 1772, the Carrolls were engaged in land disputes with the Howard family. One suit, which had been stalled in the courts for some time, seems to have come to

an end with the death of the elder Samuel Howard in 1766. Another, involving the younger Samuel Howard, flared up in the early 1770s (see CCA to CCC, Aug. 26, 1771, n. 1, below). Newman, *Early Families,* II, 232–236, 238–241; Chancery Court (Records), Liber IR no. 5, fols. 1161–1162, Liber BT no. 1, fols. 6, 252, 256, Liber DD no. 1, MdAA.

9. Edward Whitten's letter of Apr. 2, 1763, from which CC copied this extract, is filed in the Outerbridge Horsey Collection of Lee, Horsey, and Carroll Family Papers, MS 1974, MdHi.

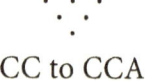

CC to CCA

London May 14th 1763

Dear Papa,

I can now with pleasure Inform you that I am recovered from the Small Pox, so far at least as in my own my Physician & Apothocary's opinion, as to be out of all danger. Dr. Reeves the President of the Colledge of Physicians recommended by Mr Etherington — my Apothocary attended me, to there Care Judgment & assiduity, I owe under the Divine providence my Recovery, I cannot but mention Mr. Etherington with a Sence of gratitude for his friendly care & diligent attendance, the Tender & Friendly assistance Receiv'd from Mr Bird's family can not be too sufficiently express't, who have given me an Invitation to there Country house as soon as my Physician & Apothy. thinks it proper[.] This Sickness hath prevented sending the Journall I Intended, but on my Recovery it shall be forwarded without fail my kind esteem & respect attends Hy. Carroll to whome I desire to be sincerely Recommended, likewise to Mr Croxall, & John Darnell & Sons[.] I am Dear Papa with tenders of most Sincere affection

your Dutifull Son.
Charles Carroll

PS.

Mr Delaney called upon me a few Days before, & In my Illness

LS, Carroll Papers, MS 206, MdHi. Addressed. Endorsed by CCA.

CC to CCA

May 15. 1763.

Dr. Papa,

Captain Kelty has been so assiduous in calling to see me during my sickness & so earnest of having a letter from me that I cou'd not refuse him his request. He will deliver you another letter wrote by a different hand but signed by me: in that you was made acquainted that I was out of all danger. I am mending apace; find myself in good spirit[s] & very hearty considering all things. I fancy I shall enjoy a better state of health than ever: God send you may. The 18 I take Physick[1] for the 1st. time, I shall take 4 or 5 Dozes. I shall not be much pitted with the small pox, tho' I have had them very plentifully. I shall be obliged to cut off my hair & ware a wig; a wig will not be so becoming but much more convenient. I must reccommend Kap: Kelty to you he deserves yr. notice. I write this in bed & must be short I am very well: Adieu Dr. Papa. I am

yr. most dutiful & Loving Son
Cha: Carroll.

ALS, Carroll Papers, MS 206, MdHi. Endorsed by CCA.
1. A purge or cathartic.

CC to CCA

14 June 1763.

Dr. Papa,

I am quite impatient to hear from you; your last was dated the 24 Decbr. I returned yesterday from Ryegate where I was friendly entertained by Mrs. Bird, Mr. Bird sister at her country house: I have found great benefit from the country air & have quite recovered my strength, & am now in much better spirits & health than I have been for this twelvemonth past. Mr. Bird & his sister kindly endeavoured to prevail upon me to continue a week longer, but I have already lost too much time by my sickness, I want to be master of surveying; my time is but short. I shall set out with Mr. Graves for Dunkirk the 20 of July or thereabouts: we have changed our intended Journey to Berlin for the following reasons; the Journey to Berlin wou'd require more time than either of us can well spare; Germany at all times a bad country to travel in must certainly at present be worse than ever when over & above the bad accomodations the roads are infested with robbers and Banditti. From Dunkirk we shall proceed to Brussels and Antwerp from thence thro' Holland we shall take Liege in our way: we have thoughts of going to Paris where I shall furnish myself with the waiscoats & silk suits you mentioned in one of yr. Letters. I have by me a very handsom suit of cut velvet for the winter as good as new wh I brought with me from Paris.

A gentleman of my acquaintance has lent me 3 Pamphlets all in favour of the Jesuits one of wh is entitled memoires presenteés au Roy par Monsieur d'Equilles President du Parlement d'Aix contre les arrêts et arrêtés de sa compagnie dans l'affaire des Jesuites.[1] This memorial is couched in the strongest terms; it points out the ambitious views of the Parliamts., their disregard & contempt of the Royal authority, the injustice, violence, & precipitancy in their proceedins against and condemnation of the Jesuits. In the Parliat. of Aix there was only a majority of two votes, 29 against 27: the 29 to make use of Monsieur d'Equilles own words oserent en oter de leur places les 27 qui aevient declaré ne pouvoir & ne vouloir juger une affaire de cette importance, sans aucune sorte d'instructions, sans aucun compte rendu par des commissaires, et sans aucun examen des constitutions.[2] I see by the newspapers the Majority has since proceeded to more violent measures against the dissenting members; they have banished the President d'Equilles for life, fined him 3000 livres, l'abbé de Montvallon his near relation is also banished & fined & several other members. You will be astonished to hear by what an inconsiderable majority throughout all the Parliaments the ruin of the Jesuites has been affected. You may depend upon what follows, ti's extracted from a Pamphlet stiled mes doubtes sur la mort des Jesuites[3] a Pamphlet wh the Parliats. have burnt, but not answered. In the Parliat. of Roüen there were 20 against the Jesuites 15 for them: in that of Rennes 31 against 28, of Toulouse 41 against 39, of Aix 29 against 27 of Bourdeaux 23 against 18, of Perpignan 5 against 4; thus a majority of 18 votes only, in open defiance of the King's edict, has subverted an order confirmed by several Popes, approved of by the council of Trent & patronised by all the present Bishops of France, one only excepted, Fitz James Bishop of Soissons.[4]

I recd. the inclosed letter the other day from Mr. Whitten[5] at Dublin: perhaps you can furnish him with some new lights. He imagins our Branch is descended from Charles the last mentioned person in the extract of the Carrolls of Ely: is his opinion well grounded? If you have reason to be of a different opinion let me know it as soon as possible, & wether you are willing to get the Pedigree made out at the expence mentioned in my last.

Mr. Wilkes[6] continues to be the subject of discourse in most conversations: what will be the event is uncertain; he is countenanced by men of the greatest influence & popularity. The name of Liberty as well as of Religion has often covered the worst designs. If the welfare of England & the liberty of the subject were the true motives of Mr. Wilke's conduct I shou'd wish him well: but who is so blind as not to discover the secret designs of a disappointed party, grasping at power & willing to obtain it, at the expence of the peace & happiness of their fellow subjects. But perhaps from a conscientiousness of their superiour abilities they are only desirous of serving their country & not themselves; such patriotic statesmen shou'd be careful how they overate their capacity for government & remember that unanimity is the greatest blessing a free People can enjoy. You have no doubt your Wilkes, Pitts, & Temples;[7] ti's impossible for all men to be in place, & those who are out will grumble & strive to thrust themselves in. Among all the disadvantages a Rom: Catho: labours under there is still this advantage; he may be honourable, honest, independent. Where is the Placeman, I do not say who is himself endowed with these virtues, but who does not hate them in others. If then posts of dignity &

profit are almost incompatible with virtue they are not desireable & their Posses-sors or rather slaves more worthy of hatred than envy. Socrates the wisest & most virtuous of the Heathens declined all offices of state from a persuasion that a man cou'd not long be great & virtuous. But these thoughts wou'd lead me too far they have already made me exceed the bounds of a letter, wh I can not end better than with the sincerest assurances of my being Dr. Papa

Yr. most dutiful & Loving Son
Cha: Carroll:

P:S:

Pray give my kind complits. to Rich: Croxall, John Darnall & Sons, to Csn: Rach: Darnall & to Capt. Carroll.

ALS, Carroll Papers, MS 206, MdHi. Addressed by CC. Endorsed by CCA.

1. *Mémoires présentés du Roi par M. d'Éguilles, Président du Parlement d'Aix, contre les arrêts et arrêtés de sa compagnie dans l'affaire des Jésuites* (Notes presented to the king by Monsieur d'Eguilles, president of the parlement at Aix, against the judgments of and decrees against his company in the affair of the Jesuits) (n.p., 1762).

2. "Dared to deprive of their places the 27 who had just declared that they were unable and did not wish to judge a matter of such importance without instructions of any kind, without an account from the commissioners, and without an examination of the establish-ments."

3. *Mes doutes sur la mort des Jésuites* (My doubts on the death of the Jesuits) (n. p., 1762). The pamphlet was published anonymously by a priest named Pierre Cabut.

4. François de Fitz-James (1709–1764), bishop of Soissons, a leading Jansenist and oppo-nent of the Jesuits. Thomas J. Campbell, *The Jesuits, 1534–1921: A History of the Society of Jesus from Its Foundation to the Present Time,* I (New York, 1921), 487.

5. Not printed. Edward Whitten postulated a descent for Charles Carroll the Settler that differed significantly from the Gaelic "Genealogy of O'Carroll" that the Settler had brought with him to Maryland. Whitten's errors, which gained some currency, were eventually cor-rected in Frederick John O'Carroll, "Stemmata Carrollana, Being the True Version of the Pedigree of Carroll of Carrollton, and Correcting that Erroneously Traced by Sir William Betham, Late Ulster King-of-Arms," *Journal of the Royal Historical and Archaeological Asso-ciation of Ireland,* 4th Ser., VI (1883), 187–194.

6. John Wilkes (1727–1797) was elected to Parliament in 1761 as a supporter of William Pitt and developed a close association with Pitt's brother-in-law Lord Temple. Wilkes hoped his connections would secure him a foreign service post, but, when that did not occur, he blamed the influence of Lord Bute. In June 1762, with the backing of Lord Temple, Wilkes began to publish his views in a series of critical and satirical pamphlets entitled *The North Briton,* in direct opposition to *The Briton,* a periodical designed to defend Bute. The in-famous *North Briton,* no. 45, casting aspersions on the king's integrity, was published on Apr. 23, 1763, and so enraged the monarch and the court that charges of seditious libel, based on evidence obtained through the use of a general search warrant, were brought against Wilkes. Arrested and then released on a writ of habeas corpus, Wilkes fled to France and remained there for five years, making periodic demands for compensation. Nearly desti-

tute, he returned to England in 1768 and attempted to get elected to Parliament. Defeated in London, he then stood for Middlesex and won. In 1779 he secured the rich post of chamberlain of the city of London, a position that allowed him to recover financially. For more than a decade, the legal and constitutional uproar initiated by official treatment of Wilkes attracted wide popular attention in both Great Britain and her American colonies, where he became a symbol of individual liberty. Jensen, *Founding of a Nation*, 155–158; Namier and Brooke, *House of Commons*, III, 639–640.

7. Richard Temple Grenville, Earl Temple (1711–1779). A member of Parliament (1734–1752), Temple served as lord privy seal (1757–1761) in Pitt's first administration, but he refused to join the second and instead became one of Pitt's most vicious opponents.

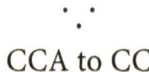

CCA to CC

June 22: 1763

Dr Charley,

This is an answer to Yrs of the 19th: of last Febru: [I] am Convinced You Entertain an Opinion by far too disadvantageous of Women: What not one Chearfull Sensible Virtuous Good Natured Woman in 10,000; Pray How many Chearfull Sensible Virtuous goodnatured Men do you Reckon in a like Number. To do the Sex Justice they would outnumber us in good Qualities. A Woman Sensible of yr Merit & fortune, I Believe would have no Objection or Dificulty of Accompanying you to America, I should be sorry You should ever Happen to like a Woman so Silly as to make Such an objection. Domestick Happyness is the great Comfort in a marryed State & that may be enjoyed as fully in Maryland as in London. I Plainly see you do not at Present think of Matrimony, (I have never been in Love & hope I never shall be) I shall not therefore press it upon You, I never will Press it upon you: But many Men talk as you do untill they are far Advanced in years, Some untill they are past their Grand Climacterick[1] & then become fond Doting Husbands. Wishing whatever you do May Conduce to yr Temporall and Eternall Happyness I am Dr Charley

Yr Mo: Afft: Father
Cha: Carroll

ALS, Carroll Papers, MS 206, MdHi. Endorsed as a copy by CCA. Another AL copy is filed in the Taylor Family Papers, no. 9965, ViU.

1. A climacteric, a period of life during which a person is supposedly especially vulnerable to alterations in health or fortune, was calculated on the basis of multiples of seven and nine. The grand climacteric was the sixty-third year—seven times nine—and was considered particularly critical.

CC to CCA

July 2d. 1763.

Dr. Papa,

I wrote to you the 14 of last month by the new York packet: by the newspapers I see there is another packet to sail the 9th. instant. I coud not let slip this oportunity of informing you that I continue in perfect health: my acquaintance think I am grown fatter tho' I don't perceive it myself.

I have procured by means of Mr. Panting[1] several interesting pamphlets in vindication of his much injured Brethren. These shall be sent you by the first safe oportunity.

I shall soon set out on my Tour to Holland and the low countries. Mr Graves, who is to accompany me is at present somewhat indisposed: if his health permits our departure is fixed to the 17 instant. In all probability we shall make some stay at Paris: we shall be absent about 3 months: our expences may amount to £150 each person. I hope you will not think the time too long, nor the expence too great: my health & studies require relaxation: nor ought this to be thought entirely lost time: the knowledge of men and of the manners of different countries polishes and improves the understanding. In the opinion of Horace, whose opinion is of great weight with me utile proposuit nobis exemplar Ulysses, qui domitor Trojæ multorum providus urbes, et mores hominum inspesit.[2] Can I follow a better example than what is set me by the wise Ulysses? I am not indeed endowed with his wisdom or experience therefore my travels will not be so improving as his were, but I hope they will be attended with fewer dangers and with less fatigue.

I have begun Trigonometry: and one more month's close application I hope will make me master of surveying. I have taken great pains with Geometry, & my pains have been rewarded by the pleasure resulting from the strictness of Geometrical demonstrations and from the thorough conviction of their truth: wou'd there were the same certainty, the same fixed principles in the Law! I am disgusted with its subtilities and perplexed by its intricacy particularly from want of knowing its practice: how much is it to be lamented that the knavery of mankind shoud render this knowledge necessary! But it must be confessed that knavery has introduced all those subtilities, those mean arts, which disgrace the science, obstruct justice, and disgust a liberal mind.

Sir Thomas Webb died a few days ago many will feel his loss, I wish Mr. Ireland may not. Sir John Webb[3] bares an odd character. If credit can be given to report (for I am no ways acquainted with him) liberality is not to be found in the list of his virtues. God is the Judge of these, time will make us Judges of that. Pray present my kind compliments to Mr. Darnall & Sons, to Mr. Croxall & my Cousin Rach: Darnall & to Capt. Carroll. I am Dr. Papa

Yr. dutiful & Loving Son

Cha: Carroll

P.S.

July 6th.

The following is an extract from Mr. Whitten's Letter to Mr: Kenedy. . . . In my search in the College of Dublin I have found out three good families the Carrolls married into, viz Roger Prince of Ely, whose son Teige deceased in the year 1407, was married to Jane daughter of the second Earl of Ormond, whose Son married a daughter of O'Dempsy, who had a son John who had a Son Donagh, who married a daughter of the Earl of Kildare. I am informed that Daniel Carroll of Ahagurty married a daughter of O'Dun,[4] & ti's very possible that Kean was his eldest son,[5] who claimed that denomination before the Trustees for Irish forfeitures upon the Revolution in 1688, & Charles his second Son, as mentioned in the Print. Vide the Print I sent you with Whitten's Letter inclosed in my last.[6]

ALS, Carroll Papers, MS 206, MdHi. Addressed by CC. Postmarked New York. Endorsed by CCA.

1. John Panting, S.J. (1732–1783), served the English Province. Geoffrey Holt, *The English Jesuits, 1650–1829: A Biographical Dictionary,* Catholic Record Society, LXX ([London], 1984), 184.

2. "Ulysses set us a useful example when, after his victory over Troy, he took the opportunity to study the cities and customs of many men."

3. Sir Thomas Webb died June 29, 1763, and was succeeded by his elder son, John. Burke and Burke, *Landed Gentry of Great Britain,* II, 1771.

4. For the Carrolls' Irish ancestry, see Appendix I, Chart A.

5. Keane Carroll of Aghagurty (?–liv. 1700), a son of Daniel Carroll of Ballimooney and the grandfather of Daniel Carroll II of Upper Marlboro. The Settler's elder brother was Anthony Carroll of Lisheenboy.

6. Print not found.

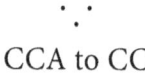

CCA to CC

July 20th: 1763

Dr Charley

Capn: Anson[1] brought in a mare for Mr Tasker thorough Bred, She is full 15 hands & I think Handsome & a very Clever Mare to Breed from[.] In training She hurt her Coffin Bone & would not stand her Exercise in Keeping. Many Mares meet wth Such or like Accidents & May be Bought very Cheap, Witness Mr Taskers Mare wh Cost only £25. He told me this as a Secret & therefore You have it in my

Owne Writing, for he knows that everything is generally Valued According to what it Costs, not for its Intrinsick Value, & that the Colts from his Mare would not sell at a high Rate, if it were knowne she Cost only £25. By looking out Properly Such mares are often to be met with. Mr Tasker has her Pedigree. My Man Heeson took Care of her on the Passage, she Came in as good order as Could be Expected, & Mr Tasker made him a Present of three Guineas for his trouble. I shall in some future letter let you know the Totall Charge of her Passage[.] Mr Perkins Charged him £15 for Freight, wh I think £9 too much; Had Perkins left out goods upon the Freight of wh he Could have made £15, Or if the Mare, Her Water & Provisions took up as Much roome as Could have stowed Common Course Goods to the Value [of the Freig]ht, The Freigh[t] Charged might be Deemed Reasonable. I mention this for Yr Information & Notice. If you should Bring or Send in Mares, May not there be Servts Passengers in the ship who may take Care of yr Mares as Heeson took Care of Mr Taskers. If Mr Webb should send me One or more Gardeners, May they not take Care of yr Mares? I am My Dr Charley

Yrs &c
Cha: Carroll

ALS, Carroll-McTavish Papers, MS 220, MdHi.
1. Possibly Halbert Hanson.

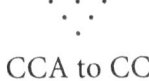

CCA to CC

[Jul]y 20th 1763

D[r] Charley

I have yrs: of the 29th of April by Hanson, May 12th & 15th by Kelty & the Mo: Kelty took relating to you the 19th of May.[1] How vastly fortunate & Happy am I in yr: recovery, & in hearing yr: recovery without knowing that you was ill; as I am bound so I do return the Almighty my most sincere & humble thanks for this & all others his blessings & favours confered on us. It happened very luckily that Kelty had a shorter passage & arrived before the other Ships & came to me the 17th Inst: the other Ships appeared in sight the 18th, 19th & some this Day. I & yr: Dr: Mama were convinced you had the disorder at Elk-ridge as it was in the family & you had a fever with several Eruptions, this prepossession prevented yr: being innoculated[2] before you left Maryland & made me perfectly easy as to the Small Pox.

I shall expect a particular Acct of yr: Tour to Holland & Prussia. As to Mr: Whittens letter about our Genealogy yr Grand fathers name was Chas:, yr: great Grand fathers name you see by the Arms was Danl: My Fathers eldest Brothers name was Antony his eldest sons name was Danl:[3] who was yr: Csn: Antos: Father, I know nothing of my Grand fathers or Uncle Antos: Wives, or into wt: families they married. As to any Expence do not begrudge wt: you think proper. Yr: Grand father left Europe & arrived in Maryland Octo: 1st 1688 with the Commission of Attorney Genl:, he on the 19th of Feb: 1693 marry'd Mary Darnall[4] the Daughter of Coll: Henry Darnall.[5] I know not how my Father came to stile himself of Ahagurton & afterwards of Litterlorma. I was born April 2d 1702. Yr: Mother was the Daughter of Clemt: Brooke Esqr: of Prince Georges County, you was born Sept: 8th 1737, this is as much as I can furnish towards our Pedigree with the Translation I obtained in Paris & wch: I will send you by the 1st safe hand.

Yr: Picture is a good one but whether like you or not I cannot determine. The price to me seems exorbitant, but if you are convinced you pay no more than oth[e]rs, there is no room to [. . .][6] I take yr: Picture to be a [B]ust, a ¾ length I apprehended was a Portrait to the knees, you do not mention the Painters name.

Since you did not for the reasons you mention think proper to take any Tickets in the lotte[r]y I am content. I have prepared but not filed a Bill agst: my Partners, I shall 1[st] speak to Danl: Dulany who is arrived & in nigh the same State of health he left us. As to the other Suits you mention they will not be ripe for a Decision until you have been long with me.

You may be assured I am obliged as fully as I ought to be to Dor: Reeves & Mr: Etherington, Mr: Bird & his family & I sincerely wish I had an opportunity of convincing them that wt: I say comes from my heart. I will not omit any opportunity of serving Capt: Kelty, he has a general Invitation to my Table when his business calls him to Annapolis. Pray let yr: hair grow again, hair is much more troublesome than a Wig, but infinitely more becoming a young man.

Heeson the Gardiner sent me by Mr: Webb left in charge with one Mandro at the Sign of the Ship in London Lane nigh Execution Dock a Trunk & Bundle value upwards of £5, Mandro without orders delivered them to a Porter who cannot be found, Mandro is lyable to Heeson, Heeson says you have a Mo: about it; if the Goods or anything in Satisfaction for them can be obtained pray try to serve the Man. Heeson appears to be a man who would have suited me very well but the Incumbrance of a Wife obliges me to put him at a Plantation where as a Farmer its possible he may be of Service. My Compts: to Mr: Webb, & let him know this & that I shd: be obliged to him if he could provide me with one or 2 such Gardiners as Heeson, but they must be single men. I Reced his letter & will endeavour to send the things he desires, & Heeson shall have ground enought to raise wt: ever plants or Flowers he pleases for Mr: Webb.

The Indians continue their murders & Invasions on our remote Settlements from the Lakes to the Southward on the back of all our Colonies. They gave us notice before they committed Hostilities that they would not suffer us to settle & that they would not sell the back Lands. [. . .][7] & to concur in these[. . .]. While the Fren[ch shar]ed the Continent with us the Indians found themselves to have some w[ei]ght, at present they see themselves at our Mercy & we have never shewn any disposition to favour them. This War[8] will put the Governmt: to a great Expence in Marching Troops to the Frontiers & supplying the Out posts & Forts with Provisions & Amunition &c. But that being done, & the Indians present Stock of Amunition being spent & it being as I apprehend impossible for them to procure fresh Supplies, they must submit & Retire, for however groundless our pretence may be to their Lands our power is sufficient to obtain the possession of them, & have the Indians more reason to complain than any other Nation? Is there a Prince in the Xan[9] World who would not treat his Neighbours as we treat the Indians if he was as secure of success.

When you leave England take care to leave yr: Measure with 2 Taylors & lasts with 2 Shoemakers & charge them to be carefull of them. By yr: next I hope to hear that yr: health is perfectly Reestablished, you know that it will give me the greatest pleasure & Satisfaction for I am Dr. Charley

Yr: Mo: Affte: Father
Cha: Carroll

LS, Outerbridge Horsey Collection of Lee, Horsey, and Carroll Family Papers, MS 1974, MdHi. Addressed by the clerk. Marked "Copy" by CCA. Endorsed by CC. Top margins damaged.

1. Not found.

2. Beginning about 1720, a preventive technique known as variolation or smallpox inoculation was used as a defense against the disease. It involved "transplanting pus from the pustules of a smallpox victim into an incision or puncture in the skin of a healthy person. The resultant infection was usually mild and chances of survival were far greater than in cases of infection through ordinary contact." First used in the American colonies during a Boston epidemic in 1721, variolation became a subject of heated controversy, but its success in mitigating the fatal effects of the disease popularized its use, and it was widely employed well into the nineteenth century. John Duffy, *Epidemics in Colonial America* (Baton Rouge, La., 1953), 16, 24, 63–112.

3. Daniel Carroll of Killecregane (?-1724). Appendix I, Chart B.

4. Mary Darnall (1678-1742), daughter of Henry Darnall I and Elinor Hatton Brooke Darnall, was fifteen when she married Charles Carroll the Settler. During the course of their marriage, she bore him ten children, but only one, CCA, outlived her. She was the Settler's second wife. His first, Martha Ridgely Underwood, whom he wed in November 1689, about a year after his arrival in Maryland, died in childbirth in 1690. Her infant son succumbed three days later. Charles Carroll, Bible records, no. 48735, Filing Case A, Library, MdHi. See Appendix I, Chart C.

5. Henry Darnall I (c. 1645-1711), a native of Hertfordshire, England, had emigrated to Maryland by 1664. A cousin of Charles Calvert, third Lord Baltimore, Darnall capitalized on this connection to become the wealthiest and most powerful Catholic in the province. He sat briefly in the lower house (1674), then served on the Council and as a provincial court justice for a decade (1679-1689), held a seat in the upper house (1681-1688), acted as joint chancellor and commissary general (1682/3-1685), and was a member of the Land Council (1684-1689). From 1685 until 1689, he was rent roll keeper and chancellor. A lead-

ing defender of the proprietor in the 1689 rebellion, Darnall, like other Roman Catholics, lost his lucrative public offices in the aftermath of that struggle, but he continued to act as Lord Baltimore's agent and receiver general, with primary responsibility for protecting the proprietor's interests and collecting his revenues, and to amass wealth as a planter and merchant. His patronage was the foundation of Charles Carroll the Settler's material success. *Bio. Dic. Md. Legis.*, I, 250–251; Hoffman, *Princes of Ireland*, chap. 3.

6. One line missing.

7. One line missing.

8. Displeased by the transfer of western territories to Great Britain that resulted from France's defeat in the Seven Years' War, Indians on the frontier renewed hostilities against the British in the spring of 1763. Led by the Ottawa chief Pontiac, they captured most of the British military posts that defined the perimeter of settlement but failed to take forts Pitt, Niagara, and Detroit, the last of which was critical to their campaign and which they besieged from May through November. All real fighting ended in the summer of 1764, when a large number of tribes signed treaties of peace, but Pontiac himself did not submit until July 24, 1766, when he concluded an agreement with the British authorities at Oswego. Howard H. Peckham, *Pontiac and the Indian Uprising* (Princeton, N.J., 1947), chaps. 7, 9, 11, 17.

9. Christian.

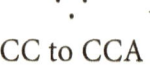

CC to CCA

Rotterdam 8 Augst. 1763.

Dr: Papa,

I received yesterday yours of 31 May;[1] it gives me the greatest satisfaction to hear you enjoy a good state of health & I sincerely wish a long continuance of it & beg you will neglect no means that may insure so great a blessing. Tis along while since Mr. Perkins sold the pig iron. I do not remember what price Iron bore at that time, but I remember Perkins was then complaining of its little worth: he wou'd have parted with it long before upon better terms (as he said) had he not been tied up to a certain price: if at that very time more money was given for iron not better than yours, Perkins is innexcusable for selling yours at an under value: Tis a hard matter to form a right Judgment of man's circumstances from appearances. I never heared Perkins credit suspected, and as to his manner of living it bears all the marks of oeconomy: he is of a timorous & distrustful temper & this disposition hurts his business wh wou'd otherwise be more extensive, but the Little business he has I believe is good & I have not the least room to suspect his integrity. I am very glad to hear my Cousin Nancy Cooke[2] is well recovered of the small pox, & I hope her beauty is not impaired by a distemper so fatal to the charms of the fair Sex.

You will perhaps be surprised to see my letter dated from Rotterdam: I left London the 17 July; arrived the 19 at Calais & the next day went to Dunkirk. The French are demolishing the works that were made during the war in that town: the Cunette is half filled up. The bason is yet untouched but is to share the same fate: this is a most noble & expensive work: ships of 50 guns may ride here in safety; the whole is lined & paved with freestone. At Dunkirk & Calais I saw several of the flat bottom boats; never more clumsy & unwieldy machines were invented; they can not keep the seas in a high wind, & seem intended merely for the canals of Holland & Flanders: from Dunkirk I proceeded to Bruges where I found my old Preceptors removed from St. Omers. They are at present settled in the vieux gouvernement an old an[d] roomy building but never intended for a College & therefore notwithstanding all their contrivances their situation is inconvenient: they are waiting to see what turn affairs are likely to take: shoud the King of France live much longer they may give up all thoughts of returning into that kingdom: the Parliaments are aiming to subvert the present govermt. and to limit the King's power: shuch a design however difficult may be executed: the chief opposition is to be apprehended from the army the never failing support of despotisem: to obviate this difficulty the Parliats. have substituted to the Jesuites men of republican principles who will not fail to inspire the youth with the Love of liberty. Thus in 20 years time Loyalty will be no more the characteristick of the french nation: the nobility will be Patriots instead of Courtiers from slaves to Kings transformed to friends of Liberty. . . .

Tho' I passed thro' Ghent I did not call upon Mr. Darnall; my cousin Jacky Carroll whom I met at Anterwp informs me that Mr. Darnall is assured of no more than £ St 30 per annum & that upon so precarious a bottom, as renders him very uneasy under his present circumstances. I keep a Journal of my Journey, wh when finished I shall send to you by the first oportunity. I arrived here the 7 instant, I sett off to morrow for the Hague. I intend going to Amsterdam, Nimeguen, Cleves, Dusseldorp; Liege, Aix la Chapelle, spa: I shall enter France by Champagne & center at Paris: after some stay in that metropolis I shall return to Calais by Lille & St. Omers: I am in perfect health & upon the best terms with my fellow traveller[.] You may expect to hear from me again when I get to Paris[.] I desire my kind compliments [to all] my friends, but have not time to name them particularly. The enclosed is from Boisson I am Dr. Papa

Yr. dutiful & affectionate Son
Ch: Carroll.

ALS, Carroll Papers, MS 206, MdHi. Addressed by CC. Endorsed by CCA.
1. Not found.
2. For Anna Maria Cooke, CC's first cousin once removed, see Appendix I, Chart H.

CCA to CC

Sept: 20th 1763

Dr Charley

My last to you was Dated the 20th of July in Answer to yrs: by Hanson & Kelty. I yesterday Reced a Copy of yrs of July 2d 1763 the original & yrs of the 14th of June are not come to hand. I need not tell you it gives me the greatest Pleasure to hear you are in perfect health. The Pamphlets you mention in Vindication of the Jesuits will be very wellcome. Those you sent me by Brooke were lost, pray replace them. I think 3 Months a long vacation & as you are well acquainted with Paris a Tour to Berlin would I think be better, but in this I am quite indifferent, so you are pleased, it is well. I shall write to Sir Jo: Webb in favour of Mr: Ireland althô from wt: you say of him I have no great reason to expect my writing Will be of Service. I have presented yr: Compts as desired. Ra: Darnall & the Gent: desire theirs to you.

It is very probable my Grand father Danl: Carroll was living in 1688, it is certain my Unkle Anto: was, & consequently Kean Carroll mentioned in Mr: Whittens letter to Mr: Kenedy could not be an Ancestor of ours in a direct line. You may get a fresh plate of our Arms stiling yourself the only Son of Cha: Carroll Esqr: of the City of Annapolis in the Province of Maryland & great Grandson of Danl: Carroll of Litterlorma Esqr: in the Kings County in the Kingdom of Ireland, & get at least 1000 Stamps from the plate to be pasted in all yr: Books. I shall send you by Kelty or Hanson the Genealogy of our Family as Copy'd from the Irish original & translated at Paris into English, this may be Copy'd & sent to Mr: Whitten. Those acquainted with Heraldry may trace the several families by this & make out the Genealogy's if this cannot be done while you are in London, you may possibly get some one who may be trusted to see it done, but do not part with the Book.

Pray bring with you a continuation of the Hist: of Ireland by Warner & McGeogan. I am much pleased with the Tryal of the Irish: Rom: Caths:, bring one well bound with you, & indeed every Book of any value shd: be well bound, it is flinging Mony away to have Books half bound for they are soon torn to pieces. I formerly wrote to you to bring a Choice & compleat collection of Law Books with you. Your outset in Books, Cloaths &c will be expensive I shall try to make Remittances accordingly. Kelty is very desirous you shd: be his Passenger, in that case send your Books & heavy Baggage by Hanson as most convenient to yr: home. Whoever you come with lay in Plentifully for a 12 weeks p[as]sage[.]

I send you by Hanson 6 Doz: of Cane Spirits, 4 Doz: are designed for you & 2 Doz: for Mr: Bird, present them to him with 2 Doz: of your Madeira Wine in my Name & as a small acknowledgement of the many Civilities he & Mrs: Bird has shewed you.

Mr: Dulany who speaks very genteely of you says you may purchase Filly's of the Best Broods in England from 20 to 25 Guineas provided they be undersized so as not to be able, or promise to carry 12 Stone. Among others he instanced the Duke of Devonshires[1] Brood of Horses as the best in England whose Stud is nigh Chatsworth in Derbyshire. As Mr Perkins is well acquainted in Derbyshire he may get you by a Friend 2 Fillys 3 years old for it is at that age they Judge of their Size. You must if you conclude to bring any get their Pedigrees attested properly. If you bring or order any Fillys to be shiped for Maryland, they must not be brought in Slings but stand in the Hold of the Ship on Shingle Ballast, they will naturally humour the motion of the Ship, Slings may be provided in case of very violent weather, but even in such weather I question whether it will be necessary to use them. Mr: Dulany brought over a Mare in Slings, she was shiped in fine order & was Landed a Skeleton; Mr Taskers Mare was very poor when shiped, she was not put in Slings & was Landed in good order. Inclosed you have an Estimate of the charges attending the passage of a Horse or Mare for yr: direction. If you shd: purchase aged Mares with any blemishes by Accidents (Mr Dulany gave me many Instances of such, & of the best Blood being bought for 20 Guineas) let them be covered by some noted Horse before they are shiped.

You forgot to send me the natural Hist: of Kamskatska, I suppose it was not then published. Pitch upon some Judicious friend to supply you with Books, Pamphlets &c & give Mr: Perkins directions to pay the Cost of them, & desire Mr: Perkins to send me the London Evening Posts & Magazine by all opportunities. Pray some time before you leave London wait on my Ld: Baltimore, Mr: Calvert, the Governors Brothers & Mr: Bladen to receive their Commands. I think I wrote to you to leave yr: Measure with yr: Taylor Shoemaker & Hosier. I wrote to you to enquire how Mr: Darnall was supported in Flanders, My Lady Sturton, Mr: Wild, my Ld. Stafford[2] & the Earl of Shrewsberry[3] contributed to his Support. I do not Want to know how he lives but wt: he receives for I am persuaded he would Squander away any Sums given & beside distress his friends here by begging from them wt: they cannot afford to give him wch: is the case. He writes he will come in next Spring & a sum of mony is to be remitted to him to enable him to do so, in that case I hope you will not be a fellow passenger with him. On the 30th of Augst: I was overset in my Chaise, by the fall I sprained my right wrist so badly that I now only begin to write, it is still very weak, but I hope time will restore its strength. I am Dr Charley

Yr: Mo: Aff: Father
Cha: Carroll

PS

Kelty will deliver you the Genealogy[.]

6 Best Butts[4] to contain at least 130 Galls: will cost with Iron   £4.16. 0
hoops from 12/ to 16 per Butt & will contain 780 Galls: of
Water wch: at 8 Galls: per Day will last 97 days

These Butts will be worth their cost in Maryland & care shd: be
   taken to have them filled at the last Port

25 Bushs: of Oats at 2/ per Bush: at a Peck a day will last 100 days	2.10. 0
1600 of Hay at 2/ per Ct: at 14 lb. per Day will last 114 days	1.12. 0
1 Load of Straw of Litter	1.12. 0
The Straw & Hay must be made up in Trusses	
5 Bush of Bran for Mashes	0. 5. 0
Slings &c	1.16. 0
	12.11. 0
Cost of Mare	25. 0
	37 11:
Freight 2½ per Ct: ad Valorem wch: is a full	1.17.11
	39 8 11

consideration if goods be not left [ou]t to carry the Mare & in that
  case a Ship must be Employ'd wch: is not fully Loaded[.]

LS, Outerbridge Horsey Collection of Lee, Horsey, and Carroll Family Papers, MS 1974, MdHi.

   1. William Cavendish, fourth duke of Devonshire (1720-1764), served as lord lieutenant and general governor of Ireland (1754-1756) and as prime minister of Great Britain (1756-1757).

   2. John Paul Stafford-Howard, fourth earl of Stafford (?-1762). Burke, *Peerage*, 15th ed., 935.

   3. George Talbot, fourteenth earl of Shrewsbury (1719-1787). [Cokayne], *Complete Peerage*, ed. Gibbes et al., XI, 725.

   4. A large cask.

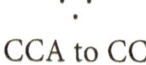

CCA to CC

Octo: 3d 1763

Dr Charley

   I answered yrs: of July the 2d by mine of the 20th past & in mine of the 24th past[1] I acquainted you I had received yrs: of June 14th. The reasons you assign in yr: last for not going to Birlin are such as I approve. If a safe opportunity has offered I doubt not I shall receive the Pamphlets you mention relating to the Jesuits as well as those lost by Brooke, & that you will bring with you all the curious Pamphlets you can collect relating to so interesting a Subject. It seems to me the K. of France is not sincerely a friend to the Jesuits, considering how small the Majority in the several Parliamts: was agst: them, could not he, if in earnest have commanded a great Majority in their favour? It is natural to suppose Pompadour[2] not to be their friend & the surprizing influence she has, I doubt not has been exerted agst: them, in short it is no wonder a K. of France who gives up his Authority by suffering the Executive part of Governmt: to be exercised by such Parliamts: shd: connive at their unjust & unprecedented proceedings agst: the Jesuits: Lewis the 14th or any King of Spirit would have chastized their villainy & Insolence —

By the Genealogy of the family sent you by Kelty I doubt not Mr: Whitten may be enabled to make out our Genealogy to the present time & if it can be done with certainty I shall not begrudge the Expence. I believe all sensible disinterested men look on Wilkes as a bold wrongheaded man & a fit Tool to those who patronize him, I see by the Papers the Printers h[ave] recovered Damages agst: the Messengers, things seem to be tending hasti[ly] to Anarchy in England, Corruption & freedom cannot long subsit togeather, that the 1st has long universally prevailed we here must give for granted since every Party when out has acknowledged & asserted it, for my part I think an absolute Governmt: preferable to one that is only apparently free & this must be the case of yr: present constitution if it be true that whoever Presides in the Treasury can command in Parliamt:

It is true I did not write to you from the 24th of Decr: 17[62] Until the 28th of April 1763 I was provoked & discouraged by not receiving yr: letters in time; but I wonder the last letter did not reach you before the 2d of July. I have since wrote to you May 31st, June 21st,[3] July 8th,[4] July 20th, Sept: 20th Sept: 24th. The inclosed to Sr: Jo: Webb I beg you will deliver after you have perused & sealed it, from wt: you say of him I expect little fruit from it, however if you have an opportunity or can see any prospect of success pray back it & endeavour to serve Mr: Ireland.

Pray bring with you a convenient Crucifix to be put into the hands of a dying person & two Registers for large Missalls. Mr: John Darnall, Richd: Croxall & Capt: Carroll have within a few days past been with me, they desire their Compts: to you so does yr: Csn: Rach: Darnall. My hand mends I have wrote the rough draft of this without much difficulty, it was on the 30th of July I sprained my wrist & not on the 30th of Augst: as I wrote you. I am making an Addition to my house at Elk-ridge I want to stucco it, but we have not here a workman who can do it, I wish you could by yr: self or by a Crimp procure such a one, I would be content he shd: only serve 2 years for the charges of his passage &c. But let him procure a Certificate from some Master builder or undertaker that he is a good workman, if he can not be got on other terms I would pay his Passage if he would work for me on reasonable terms & you may assure him he would not want good business here. The Cane Spirits I sent you by Hanson are designed for yr: Sea Store, when you are in the Downes[5] or if you stop at any Port get an Anchor[6] of Brandy that you may now & then bestow a Bottle on the Sailors with the Capts: leave, it is common for Gent: Passengers to do this —

Mr: Warner in his explanation of his Authorities mentions Dissertations on the Antient Hist: of Ireland — No Name — By Cha: O Connor Esqr: 8vo. I shd: be glad to have it, it was published in 1753.[7] It is probable before this reaches, you, you will see Mr: Cha: Digges[8] a particular favourite of mine, a young Gent: of great Merit & esteemed here by every man of Sense who has the pleasure to know him, I therefore hope you will shew him all the Civilities in yr: power. I suppose at the [writ]ing of this you are on y[r: retu]rn to London & that you will [immed]iately write to me wch: I may probably receive in the Beginning of Decr: Wishing & daily praying for yr: health & Happiness I am Dr Charley

Yr: Mo: Affte Father

Cha: Carroll

LS, Outerbridge Horsey Collection of Lee, Horsey, and Carroll Family Papers, MS 1974, MdHi. Addressed by the clerk. Endorsed by CC. Margins damaged. A second LS copy misdated Sept. 3, 1763, is filed in the Carroll-McTavish Papers, MS 220, MdHi.

1. Not found.

2. Jeanne Antoinette Poisson, marquise de Pompadour (1721–1764), Louis XV's mistress.

3. Actually CCA's letter of June 22, 1763.

4. Not found.

5. An eight-mile stretch of protected anchorage in the English Channel off the coast of Kent.

6. An anker, an old Dutch or German measure for wine or other spirits or the cask used for storing these liquids. It held between eight and ten gallons.

7. Charles O'Connor (1710–1791), *Dissertations on the Ancient History of Ireland* (1753).

8. Charles Digges of Warburton (1740–1769) was the American partner of London merchant Thomas Philpot. Bowie, *Prince George's,* 256. See also Appendix I, Chart I.

CC to CCA

Paris 3 October 1763.

Dr. Papa,

I[n] my last from Rotterdam I promised to write to you again from Paris, you see I am as good as my word. At that time I little thought I shou'd have occasion to write on the following subject. My friend & yours Mr. Crookshanks has lately introduced me to a young lady[1] of 17 of an agreeable person and good natured: as to her temper & amiable qualities I can at present only depend upon Mr. Crookshank's report who I am confident wou'd not willingly deceive me in a matter of such importance. The young lady is the only daughter & sole heiress of a West India gentleman of great fortune: his name is Baker:[2] She is now at the Ursilin nuns: her fortune her person, her education are unexceptionable: provided I can obtain the Father's & the daughter's consent I flatter myself you can have no objection to the match. I expect to be in London about the 5 of Nobr. Upon my arrival I shall immediately wait upon Mr. Baker and disclose to him my affection for his daughter and beg his leave to visit her in the Convent: if leave be granted I shall immediately return to Paris and pay my addresses to the young Lady: her inexperience will favour my design: unpractised in the wiles & artifices of worldly women her genuine candour & simplicity will lay open her real character, her good qualities and her defects.

You have permitted me to settle on my wife if I marry in Europe at the rate of 6 per Ct. Shoud the Lady's fortune amount to £ St 30000 then in this case upon my death she wou'd be entiteled to a yearly Jointure of 1800 pounds: will our estate be equal to so heavy an incumbrance? If I die young, which is not improbable as I am of a weak constitution, my widow may marry a second Husband & carry the greatest part of the estate into a nother family: this difficulty is perplexing; I wish I were assisted with your advice upon this point: I shall consult the best in London. Shoud Mr. Baker approve of me for his Son in Law I shall then trust the drawing up the marriage settlement to one or two gentlemen upon whose honour I can rely, & whose experience & knowledge will enable them to treat with the Father most to my advantage. It will not become me to appear personally in the transacting of this affair: it woud be difficult to avoid the imputation of selfishness the most even in an interested lover to be concealed: but this is far from being my case: if upon further acquaintance with the young lady I shou'd change my mind & think the match not suitable her fortune however great shall not tempt me to sacrifice mine or her happiness to ambition or avarice.

I have seen our worthy & estimable friend de l'Isledieu[.] The good old man coud not conceal his Joy at our meeting; he immediately & most affectionately enquired after you; your name was never pronounced but with the warmest expressions of gratitude affection & esteem: he has promised me to write you a long letter before my departure from Paris which I shall forward by the first oportunity after my arival in London. I have desired Mr. Crookshanks to get me the several arrêts & remonstrances of the Parliaments to the late Edicts as likewise the arrêts relating to the Jesuits. It wou'd take me up too much time & labour to give you a circumstantial & Judicious account of the present critical situation of affairs in this kingdom. Perhaps it wou'd not be safe to dwel upon them with that liberty & freedom that satisfies & becomes an englishman. The Pretender certainly resides at Bouillon[3] the seat of the Dukes of that name. I was within 20 french leagues of the Place. The account given me by some french officers of his Character was so little favourable that it quite damped the curiosity I had to see a personage who has made so much noise in the world: now indeed as much forgotten as once celebrated & famous. His mind is unable to bear the weight of his misfortunes. He endeavours to drown their remembrance in wine & is now so utterly abandoned to that vice qu'il est (to make use of the french officers expression) entirement abrutis.[4]

I shall leave Paris in about 12 days time & return to Calais thro' Normandy a province I have never seen. Since my departure from London I have drawn the following bills two on Perkins one of £30 the other of £100 and a third on Mr. Bird for 50 in all 180 pounds: out of this I have provided myself with a good stock of Linnen & 5 suits of cloaths of wh two are silk. If I am successful in the main point neither time or money are lost. That you may see me happily married, enjoy your health & be happy is the sincere & ardent wish of Dr Papa

yr: affectionate Son

Cha: Carroll

ALS, Carroll Papers, MS 206, MdHi.

1. Martha Baker (1747–1809), referred to by her father as Patty and by CC as Louisa. Diary of John Baker of Horsham, Lytton MSS 533, West Sussex Records Office, Chichester, England; Philip C. Yorke, ed., *The Diary of John Baker, Barrister of the Middle Temple, Solicitor-General of the Leeward Islands, Being Extracts Therefrom* (London, 1931).

2. John Baker (1712–1779) maintained residences in London and at Grove Place, near Southhampton, and owned two sugar plantations on St. Croix. See CC to CCA, Jan. 27, 1764, and Enclosure 2: Nicholas Tuite's Account of John Baker's Wealth, [Dec. 22, 1763], below.

3. Located in present-day southeast Belgium, the town of Bouillon was a part of France in 1763.

4. "He is . . . entirely besotted."

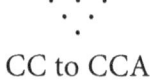

CC to CCA

Paris 11 Octobr. 176[3].[1]

Dr. Papa,

In my last letter from Rotterdam I promised to write to you again from Paris. At that time I little thought of writing on the following subject. Mr. Crookshanks has lately introduced me to a young lady of 17 of an agreeable person & good tempered if I may rely on Mr. Crookshanks who I am confident wou'd not deceive me in a matter of this importance. She is the only daughter & sole heiress of a west India gentleman of great fortune his name is Baker: Mr. Crookshanks is not acquainted with his circumstances but Judges he must be a man of great wealth by the unlimited credit he allows his daughter: She is now in the Convent of the Ursilin nuns in this city: if upon better enquiry the Father really turns out to be a man of great fortune there is one point gained: I only am to except to her person & temper: you can have no objection to her education: I therefore flatter myself If I can obtain the Father's & the lady's consent you will not refuse me yours.

Immediately upon my return to London I shall wait upon Mr. Baker; disclose to him my affection for his daughter & desire leave to visit her in the Convent: if he grants me leave I shall immediately set out for Paris pay my addresses to the young lady & strive to make a conquest of her heart: her youth & inexperience will I hope smooth the path of victory: the first addresses of a young lover may make some impression on a heart unpractised in the wiles & artifices of worldly women: her genuine candour & simplicity will unfold her true character, all her virtues, & her imperfections. It will require time to sound the lady's inclinations, to know her well, & to settle matters with the father: precipitation where one's whole happiness depends wou'd be madness: If I meet with success in this enterprise it will be absolutely impossible for me to return to Maryland this next spring: I am afraid that my voyage must be put off to the spring following: nothing I assure you can be more contrary to my own inclinations; but in all we do there is a mixture of pain & pleasure.

You have given me leave to settle on my wife if I marr[y] in Europe at the rate of 6 per Ct.: supposing that my wife's fortune amounts to 30000 then the interest will be 1800 per annum. Shou'd I die young this wou'd be a heavy incumbrance on the estate is it able to support so great a burthen? In case of my death my widow may marry again & by so considerable a Jointure carry off the greatest part of the estate to another family: these difficulties are perplexing but I shall leave them to be adjusted between Mr. Baker & one or two gentlemen in whose honour & capacity I shall confide the drawing up the marriage settlement. Mr. Baker may have some objections to my living in America; but if he is a man of sense I think he must approve of my full & settled determination of residing in a country where I have so large a property[.] Miss Baker no doubt will have stronger objections than her Father to my settling in Maryland: but when once the knot is tied & her affection fixed, my interest will prevail over her inclinations to remain in Europe where she has no deep connections nor particular acquaintances: all I have said must be understood conditionally; if upon our being better acquainted I approve of the young Lady & she approves of me; for to insure our happiness our love must be mutual[.]

The enclosed paper contains the different prices of Mon Nisett's wines. I can answer for the Chambertin's [2] being excellent: I was nearly tempted to give Mr. Nisett a commission to send you a pipe: let me advise you, if you buy french wines always buy the best.

I have seen our worthy & estimable friend L'Abbé de l'Isle-dieu: time has made no alteration in his affection & esteem for you: he is the only frenchman I ever knew succeptible of friendship.

I shall leave Paris in about 2 or three days time. Mr. Crookshanks has promised to procure me the several arrêts of Parliament relating to the late edicts & to the Jesu[its] they will give you much more insight into the affairs of this kingdom & its present critical situation than I can: it wou'd take me up infinite time & labour to enter into a long narrative of the present transactions & to make you thoroughly acquainted with them.

Pray give my sincere respects to all my friends I am dr. P:

your Most affectionate Son
C: Carroll.

Since my departure from London I have drawn for 180 St: out of this I have provided myself with a pretty good stock of linen & 4 suits of cloaths two of which are silk.

ALS, Carroll Papers, MS 206, MdHi. Addressed by CC. Endorsed by CCA: "1763 Octor: 11th My Sons Letter Ansd Janu: the 9th: & 10th 1764."
1. Misdated 1761 by CC.
2. A wine produced in the Côte de Beaune section of Burgundy.

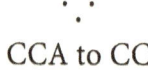

CCA to CC

No[v]r: 7th: 1763

Dr Charly,

I have the Pleasure of Yrs of the 8th of Last Augt from Roterdam & I am perswaded the Tour You tell me You Proposed to take will be Both improving & Agreable But I Suppose you see Paris again in Complaisance to Mr Graves. I shall depend on yr Journall: you do not Acknowledge the Receit of myne of Aprill 28th: 1763, I think it must have Reached you. As by yr Tour & Outset for Maryland yr Expences will be very Considerably enhanced, I have Prepared Accordingly, for to this Date I have Remitted Mr Perkins upwards of £2000 & I shall Probably Remit £4 or £500 More to Answer My owne & your Calls — I was not Surprised to see yr Letter Dated from Rotterdam as I was preadvised that you intended to Holland &c[.] Anny Acct of yr old Preceptors is agreable But as I am perfectly acquainted wth: their Merit, I feel very sensibly the injustice done them & I am Convinced whatever Appearances the King of France may Put on, that he is Consenting & Premoting the stepps taken agt the Jesuits, I have Since Lewis the 14ths: Majority looked upon the Parlia[m]ents of France as almost m[ee]r Courts of Jus[tice], & in Matters of State as Obliged when the King says Sic Volo[1] to Comply, & that without the Danger of the Least Convulsion in the state Every Member of the Present Parliaments might be Discarded & New ones Substituted in their sted & this Lewis the 15th would do if he did not approve what his Parliamts have done — I think you did Prudently in not seeing Mr Darnall. If he would live as I think he ought to live, that is Board him self in some Monastery in the Country £30 pr Annum would

Prove an Ample Support, But as I wrote to you I understand he Intends Back & has for that Purpose sollicited Remittances.

I inclose you two letters from Mr Ireland Pray seal & forward them, or if you have any Encouragement from my letter to Sr John You may Deliver Mr Irelands letter. If my Lord Montague Should be in Towne Deliver the letter to him & Present my Mo: Hum: Respects to his Lordship—

In the London Magazine of Febru: 1763 I see an Acct of Wards Paste[2] for A fistula & His Dropsy purging Powders, Get me 4 lb. of the Paste & 12 Parcells of the Powders with Directions for using Both. I have had a Fistula upwards of 30 Years wh has not been nor is Painfull to me, & as the swelling in my Ancles may Return I am willing to be Provided with Remedies wh may possibly [be of] Service to me[.]

The Indians still Continue to Commit Murders on the Frontiers of all Our Provinces & it is thought Our People at Fort Detroit will be obliged to Surrender for want of Provisions: They have hitherto Behaved with Bravery & More Discipline & Prudence than we thought them Capable of, Hence it is Surmised they have French Officers among them, But I have not heared of one Instance to Justify Such a Surmise. I am well, so is yr Csn Darnall & her Daughter[3] they Salute you I pray to God to Bless you & am Dr Charly

Yr Mo: Afft: Father

Cha: Carroll

ALS, Carroll-McTavish Papers, MS 220, MdHi. Addressed by CCA. Endorsed by CC. Top margins damaged. A second LS copy addressed and marked "Copy" by CCA is also filed in the Carroll-McTavish Papers.

1. "I wish it so."

2. Ward's paste was a preparation containing arsenic.

3. Mary Darnall (1749–1782), who came to be known as Molly, was the only child of Rachel Brooke Darnall and Henry Darnall IV. After Elizabeth Brooke Carroll's death in 1761, Molly came to live with Rachel Darnall at CCA's house. See Appendix I, Charts E and F.

CC to CCA

12 Novembr. 1763.

Dr. Papa,

This is to let you know I arrived safe in London the 6 instant: ever since, I have been in the greatest expectations of a letter from Mr. Crookshanks, who has promised me to get me introduced to Mr. Baker: wether I shall obtain that gentlemam's consent to Marry his daughter seems very doubtful: he may perhaps object to my living in north America: if he does I must lay asside all thoughts of Miss Baker: the situation of our affairs absolutely require my residence in Maryland: and I can not sacrifice the future aggrandisement of our family to a woman: America is a growing country: in time it will & must be independent. As soon as I am introduced to Mr. Baker & know his determination I shall make you acquainted with it.

Very good brood Mares I make no doubt can be had for 25 or thirty pound: the most difficult task is to procure a good, sober, understanding groom: the having a gardiner or other servant to take care of them on their passage will be merely accidental, besides unsafe, as either the ignorance or sloth of such a fellow might be fatal to the Mares. If I can procure two good Mares I intend to get them covered:

My picture was done by Reynolds:[1] tis a ¾ length a half length wou'd come down to the knees. The price is fixed: I payed no more than what others pay:

I shall take care to deliver yr. message to Mr. Webb: or leave at his house an extract of that part of yr. letter that relates to him. My friends think I look full as well in a wig as in my own hair.

I shall endeavour to right Heeson if possible: but I am affraid all my trouble will be to no purpose. I wish you the enjoyment of yr. health & pray to God for it. I am Dr. Papa

yr. affectionate Son
Cha: Carroll.

ALS, Carroll Papers, MS 206, MdHi. Addressed by CC. Postmarked New York. Endorsed by CCA.

1. Sir Joshua Reynolds (1723-1792). The portrait, which appears herein, is now owned by Yale University.

CC to CCA

8 Decemb: 1763.

Dr. Papa,

Mr. Perkins has informed me that a packet is to sail for new York next saturday: & tho' I wrote to you the 12 of last month & have nothing new or material to say yet as my letters seem to afford you some pleasure I am willing you should enjoy it as often as possible.

Capts. Kelty & Hanson are arrived: the Cane Spirits have been delivered for wh I return you my thanks my fate is yet undecided. I wrote this very day to Mr. Baker at Southampton: I should have wrote sooner but the expectation of a letter from Mr. Crookshanks wh is not yet come to hand, made me put it off till now. Mr. Baker I hear has had two wives & Children by both, his daughter therefore will not probably have so great a fortune as Mr. Crookshanks imagined: the probability of my

Charles Carroll. By Joshua Reynolds. 1763.
Courtesy The Yale Center for British Art, Paul Mellon Collection

succeeding is the greater: women entitled to large fortunes are not easily persuaded to leave England.

My Lady Webb[1] has had the generosity & benevolence to continue to Mr. Ireland the annuity paid by her Husbd. Sir Thomas: instead of £30 she will remit annually to Mr. Ireland by Mr. Perkins 30 guineas.[2] I am well acquainted with Jo[s]: Webb her youngest Son who has promised at my desire to introduce me to his mother. I shall return her Mr. Irelands thanks for the continuation of the charity & if an oportunity offers endeavour to get the additional sum of 10 guineas paid to his Son.

In yours of the 20 Septbr. you promised to send me by Kelty the Genealogy. I have seen Kelty, but I forgot to ask him for it & perhaps he forgot to deliver it to me. I have recd. no letters this long time from Mr. Whitten I shall write to him soon and send him the copy of the genealogy if it is arrived with an extract of that part of yr. letter which relates to Kean Carroll. You may expect by Hanson the continuation of Geogans & Warner's irish histories as also the natural history of Kamkatska if they are published: I have acquainted Mr. Webb the seedsman with yr. commission: your instructions for my Voya. & about the Mares if they can be had at a reasonable rate shall be punctually followed: I have given a country gentleman of my acquaintance a commission to loo[k] out two for me at £25 each: their pedigrees to be well attested &c. Before the receit of yr. last I had a plate of our arms ingraved & 200 stamps with only my name at the bottom, & had ordered 400 more. I shall leave the plate with the ingraver to supply me with more stamps if wanted: the plate is too short to have the words you direct insert[ed]. Mr. Bird thanks you kindly for the Cane spirits; I could not spare him the 2 Doz of Madeira as I have but a small quantity lelft which will be serviceable on ship board. I shall make Mr. Bird some other return for his civilities to me.

Mr. Graves my fellow traveller has introduced me to the company he generally dines with: they are most of them Parliat. men, lawyers, or have had a law education and are men of sense. Their conversation is instructive & entertaining, & tho' the Tavern bills are pretty high, our quota generally amounting to 8S 6d a head, it would be foolish & mean to decline their company on that account. One of these gentlemen got me twice admittance into the house of commons: the first debate I heared, arrose upon a motion for an address to his Majesty on his most gracious speech:[3] Mr. Beckford the most violent of the opposition said he should consider the speech not as the King's but as the Minister's: that he had been all along & still was of opinion that the peace was inglorious & inadequate to our successes: words directly con[tra]dictory of those made use of in the Speech:[4] he severely reflected on the proclamation for settling our new acquisitions: he openly declared the present ministry incapable of governing, ignorant of geography, arbitrary & despotick. Mr. Pitt made a long speech not less severe but more cautious: the peace he thought inadequate: that the greatest advantages had been given up to the French without an equivalent: that a total exclusion from the Newfoundland fishery should have been insisted on: for his part whatever notions people might entertain, he could safely say he did not censure for the sake of censuring or from any ill humour: that he entertained the highest opinion of those ministers who could derive advantages from a peace from which he himself could not foresee any: far from being fond of power or a ministerial influence he was resolved to shun both: it ti's but just that those ministers who made the peace should be continued in office to improve their own work: Should I, contrary to my wish, once more assume the cares of government a disapointed nation would attribute to my partiality & dislike to the peace the small advantages derived to their country in proportion to the vast expense of blood & treasure. He very artfully touched upon the present divisions & distracted state of the nation. . . I am really of opinion we are divided more by names than things: there was a time & that too not very distant (meaning his own administration) when the nation was all unanimity. To what is the present disunion owing? Are not the principles of men now in power the same with those out of power? Are they not revolution principles, the principles of liberty, agreeable to this constitution? Let there be a kind of political test established, let it require the highest veneration for Magna Charrta, express the strongest aversion to false imprisonment, a profound regard for the Habeas corpus Act the great protector on english liberty, is there even a Minister who would scruple to subscribe such a test? And if he does what danger is to be apprehended from his administration, unless his hand subscribes what his heart, what his conduct disclaims. Mr. Pitt's manner of speaking is deliberate yet animated, his voice distinct tho' not loud, his words bold, sometimes too pompous, his thoughts deep, his imagination truly sublime.

The House of Commons has come to the following resolutions: the North Briton No. 45 voted a seditious libel tending to raise traiterous insurrections: a member of Parliat. writing a seditious libel has no privilege: the North Briton No. 45 to be burnt by the hands of the common hangman. It was accordingly burnt some days ago, the mob rose, insulted & slightly wounded Mr. Harley the Sheriff & rescued a part of the paper from the flames: this affair is now under the consideration of both houses. One of Mr. Wilke's actions against Wood was yesterday determined in the Court of Common Pleas.[5] After 15 hours hearing the Jury which was special withdrew & brought in their verdict for the Plaintiff with £1000 damages & full costs of suit. Mr. Wilkes is out of danger but will not be able to attend the house these 3 weeks: the majority will not proceed against him any further till he can attend in his place. I say no further for certainly the above resolutions affect Mr. Wilkes: if he is proved the author of the North Briton he will be expelled the house, and no one here makes the least but that he will be expelled: his story is pregnant with incidents: every day brings something fresh: yesterday One Mac Dun was taken into custody for intending to assassinate Mr. Wilkes: he is a Scotsman & a madman and lately let loose from a private mad house: he will be brought to day to the bar of the house of Commons:

The Accot. Capt. Kelty gives me of yr. health affords me great satisfaction: I hope your wrist is quite recovered: The Capt. told me how sensibly you was affected at hearing I had the small pox: during my illness what gave me the most pain till I was out of danger, was the thoughts what sorrow and affliction you would feel at the news of my death: I am now enjoy my health very well & wishing you a continuation of yours I am Dr. Papa

Yr. affectionate & dutiful Son
Ch: Carroll.

P:S:

Pray give my complits. to Mrs. Darnall: I congratulate with her upon the recovery of her daughter from the small pox. I desire to be remember to John Darnall Ric: Croxall & to Capt. Carroll: tell him I thank him for his useful letter: but that in these times of liberty he should fill up his words: a dash is unnecessary.

ALS, Carroll Papers, MS 206, MdHi. Endorsed by CCA.

1. Sir Thomas Webb's widow, Anne (?-1777), the daughter of Thomas Gibson of Welford, Northants. G.E.C. [George Edward Cokayne], ed., *Complete Baronetage*, II (Exeter, 1900-1909), 221.

2. A 5 percent increase.

3. George III's address of Nov. 13, 1763, opening Parliament.

4. In his speech the king had maintained that the treaty of Paris ending the Seven Years' War was a notable achievement.

5. Lord Temple had filed suits in John Wilkes's name against Lord Halifax, the secretary of state, and his assistant Robert Wood (1717-1771), who were chiefly responsible for the seizure of Wilkes's papers. The case against Wood was tried in November 1763, and a verdict in favor of Wilkes was rendered on Dec. 6. Jarrett, *Britain,* 282-283.

CCA to CC

Janry 9th 1764

Dr Charley

I yesterday Evening Reced yrs: of the 11th of Octo: past from Paris, & as it is on a very Interesting Subject I cannot delay answering it. I hope Miss Baker may be endowed with all the good sense & good nature you say she has. Giving this for granted, you have my full Consent to pay yr: Addresses to her, but as you value yr: own happiness endeavour to be well informed whether Miss Baker is that sensible, sweet tempered Lady you represent her to be. Believe me, these are Essential to yr: future happiness, for without Domestick peace & Content Matrimony must prove a Curse insted of a Blessing. You have reason from her Education to place a Confidence in her Virtue. As to her fortune, wt:ever it may be, you know it does not with me enter into any sort of Comparison with Virtue, good nature & good sense. I was so full to you on this Subject in my letters of the 1st of Sept: 1762 & June 22d 1763 that I must beg you to refer to them, I only add, that I hereby again bind myself to comply with wt: I promised in the 1st relating to the Settlement to be made on yr: Wife, knowing this letter will be as binding on me as any Bond or Settlemt: executed by me. Should the Lady bring you a Considerable fortune, wch: you say you have reason to expect from the Manner of her Education, you need not apprehend yr: Children or family will be hurt by the Settlement I propose in Case the Lady shd: survive you, unless you shd: turn out a Spend thrift, wch: from yr: past Conduct I have not the least Grounds to surmise: for the growing Interest on the Lady's fortune with the principal will be a very sufficient fund for the Payment of the Dower[1] to be stipulated, & I consent that my whole Estate if necessary may be bound to make good such Settlemt: Only note, that if hereafter you shd: incline to leave Maryland, the Lands may not be so bound as to prevent a Sa[le] of them, in wch: Case it may be Covenanted that the Mony's arising by such Sale shd: be vested in other Purchases, & that such Purchases shd: be lyable to make good the settlemt: And that Mr: Baker may be Convinced I am capable of securing wt: ever fortune he may think proper to give his Daughter I hereby give you a short Abstract of the Value of my Estate.

40000 Acres of Land, two Seats alone containing each upwards of 12000 A[2] would now sell at 20/[3] Ster: per Acre	£40000.0.0
⅕ of an Iron Work Consisting of the most Convenient Furnace in America, with two forges built, a third Erecting with all Convenient Buildings, 150 Slaves young & old, Teams, Carts &c & 30000 A of Land belonging to the Works a very growing Estate wch: produces to my 5th Annually at least £400 Ster at 25 years purchase	10000.0.0
20 Lots in Annapolis with the houses thereon	4000.0.0
285 Slaves on my different Plantations[4] at £30 Ster: each in an Average	8550.0.0
Cattle, Horses & Stock of all sorts on my Plantations with working Tools &c	1000.0.0
Silver Household Plate	600.0.0
Debts outstanding at Interest in 1762 when I Ballanced my Books	24230.9.7
	88380.9.7

You must not suppose my Annual Income to equal the Interest of the Value of my Estate, many of my Lands are unimproved, but I compute I have a clear Revenue of at least £1800 per Annum & the Value of my Estate is Annually increasing by the increase of the value of my Lands.

A thing of so much importance as Matrimony is not to be precipitated but as you took it into yr: head last Octo: I hope if you proceed you may finish it so as to be with me next summer or at farthest in the Fall. You have long been impatient to be with me, for yr: Good I have long deprived myself of that pleasure, but as next April I shall enter into my Grand Climacterick you must not wonder that in my turn I shd: grow impatient. I long to see Miss Baker with you as you paint her in so amiable a light, But see you I must & when my Eyes are closed live where you please; I think Maryland more agreeable to solid happiness than any Country I have seen, it is plentifull & the Climate charming.

If I can find a likelyhood of an Established Correspondence to Holland I will write to Mr: Nizet for Wines, at present such a one does not exist. It was with great pleasure I heard that Monsr: L'Abbe de L'Isle Dieu was well, I loved him the Moment I saw him, his Virtue is so conspicuous, his Manner so engaging that a man must be insensible not to Esteem him on the slightest acquaintance, tell him I am not accustomed to make Compts: that it would be ridiculous to endeavour to impose upon him by such at 1200 Leagues Distance, that these are the Sentiments of my heart, that I love & Esteem him & that I wish him health & every happiness.

I expect by the 1st Ships after yr: Return from Paris every Paper & Pamphlet relating to the Jesuits & the Journal of yr: Tour. God grant you health & an Accomplishment of all yr: Wishes wch: may conduce to his Glory & yr: reall happiness being My Dr Charley

Yr: Mo: Affte: Father
Cha: Carroll

LS, Outerbridge Horsey Collection of Lee, Horsey, and Carroll Family Papers, MS 1974, MdHi. Marked "Copy" and corrected by CCA. Endorsed by CC. An AL copy, endorsed by CCA, is filed in the Carroll Papers, MS 206, MdHi.

1. The portion of a husband's estate reserved by law to his widow for the rest of her life.

2. CCA's landholdings in 1764 encompassed some 37,888 acres. The largest of these tracts, one of the two "Seats" referred to here, was the 10,000-acre Carrollton Manor and the 2,553-acre "Addition to Carrollton" in Frederick Co. (Debt Books, Liber 24, Frederick Co., 1763, fol. 28, MdAA). His second seat, located in Anne Arundel Co., consisted of his dwelling plantation, the 10,000-acre Doohoragen Manor, and part of Chance, a contiguous tract of 1,339 acres. CCA owned an additional 3,604 acres in Anne Arundel Co., bringing his total acreage in the county to 15,035 (ibid., Liber 3, Anne Arundel Co., 1764, fol. 9). Other large holdings included 2,026 acres in Prince George's Co., of which the most extensive tract was the 919-acre Outlet (ibid., Liber 34, Prince George's Co., 1763-1764, fol. 21), and the 1,000-acre Poplar Island in the Chesapeake Bay, listed at this time within the bounds of Queen Anne's Co. (ibid., Liber 38, Queen Anne's Co., 1763, fol. 17). In St. Mary's Co., CCA claimed ownership of 2,475 acres in 1764 (ibid., Liber 40, St. Mary's Co., 1764, fol. 36), but his title to a 1,725-acre portion of St. Clement's Manor was not clear.

3. Shillings.

4. Most of these slaves were quartered in family groups at Doohoragen Manor, with smaller numbers lodged at the Poplar Island plantation, Annapolis quarter, and the house on Spa Creek in Annapolis. Carroll slave inventories made in the 1770s are printed in Appendix III.

CCA to CC

Janu: 10th: 1764

Dr. Charly,

I did not in myne of yesterday Mention good Mr Crookshanks as it might not there have been Proper to Acknowledge the fresh obligation You & I are under to him for Introducing You to Miss Baker, I Cannot express the true Regard & Afection I bear him therefore only tell him I love & Esteem him, most Sincerely that I wish him Health & Happyness here & His Virtue insures it to him hereafter. I am Persuaded he would not have made Such an Overture to You had he not thought You deserved the Lady & that she was deserving of You[.] A View to yr Mutuall Happyness I am Convinced induced him to propose her to You—He as You tell me Candidly told You he was not Acquainted with Mr Bakers Circumstances but Judged he must be a Man of Great Wealth by the Unlimited Credit he allows his Daughter; yr Prudence there fore I doubt not direct[e]d you to Enquier into his Circumstances before you Waited on him. You will be informed whether his fortune Consists in Plantations & Negroes in the Islands or in Cash. If in Cash the settlement I think Should only be for the Fortune paid downe, If he Proposes beside a fortune in hand to Settle on his Daughter after his Death his Lands & Negroes it would be well if they Could be settled at least on her Male Issue by You [&] the enjoyment in Case of yr Death to the Lady during life, in wh Case no Security Can be Requierd for the Reall Estate or settlement Stipulated by you for the Same. If you find it will not be Prudent to make Such a Proposall you must wait a future time to make it to the Lady in Case you Marry her. I know not Mr Bakers age Even if old he may Marry again, this Consideration will incline you (if you Can adroitly) to get his Estate settled on the Lady. At this distance were I acquainted with Every Circumstance I Could but advise & my advice in all Probability may Come too late, Incidents may arise wh I Cannot foresee there fore I must leave all to Yr Prudence & Discretion Praying God to Direct You & wishing you Health & Happyness I again Assure you that I am My Dr Charly

Yr Mo: Afft: Father

C: C:

ALS, Carroll Papers, MS 206, MdHi.

CCA to CC

Janry 16th 1764

Dr Charley

You no doubt will by every opportunity write to me on the Subject of yrs of the 11th of Octor: from Paris, & let me know whether things turn out as you imagined as to Mr. Bakers Circumstances &c. I am Dr Charley

Yr: Mo. Affte Father

L, Carroll Papers, MS 206, MdHi. Endorsed by CCA: "1764 Janu 16 Copy To my Son."

CC to CCA

27. Janury. 1764.

Dr Papa,

In my last of the 8 Decembr. I let you know of my having wrote to Mr. Baker: a week after I received the enclosed answer.[1] I repaired immediately to Bath; my Physician had advised me to drink the waters, and I think I find myself benefited by them: for this some time past I have felt a gradual decay of strength and wasting of flesh attended with unusual low spirits: my nerves are week and my whole frame very delicate, tho' my lungs are not the least affected: my Bath Physician has ordered a regimen which I am to stick to for 5 or 6 weeks & he doubts not of my being restored again to my usual strength. I am to drink every morning in bed a pint of asses milk, to breakfast & sup on milk & to use the cold bath twice a week: pray dont let my indisposition give you any concern as it is thought not the least dangerous & I find myself growing better.

Mr. Baker left Bath 2 or three days after my arrival: he gave me an invitation to come and see him at his seat near Southampton: I accepted the invitation and went from Bath to Grove Place where I remained a full fortnight.[2] Mr. Baker is a man of sense and honour: his second wife[3] the mother of the young lady is living, she is no favourite of mine, nor I of hers. If the daughter's temper ressembles the mother's I shall leave England next May or June: Miss Baker will come to England in April: my returning to Paris is therefore unnecessary. Mr. Baker proposes going next May or June to St. Crux, in which Island his estate lays: in his absence Mr. Tuite[4] with whom he is much connected, will be intrusted and empowered to act in his stead; from the enclosed paper[5] which is in Mr. Tuite's own hand writing you will be able to form some judgt. of Mr. Baker's circumstances, for Tuite is as well acquainted with them as Baker himself. In talking of the settlement, in case the match takes place, Mr. Baker told me he intended to leave his estate real & personal equally divided among all his children his 4 sons and daughter: that gentleman's affairs at present are somewhat embarrassed: he owes £ St. 10000 which he was obliged to take up to clear, settle, and plant his sugar lands: this he himself acknowledged; from this circumstance and from several other hints I plainly understood I was not to expect any ready money with his daughter at least no considerable sum: he hinted that if you should not be contented with an equal division between all the children to take place at his death, a certain sum might be agreed upon, as a portion for the young lady, to carry interest till the principal should be payed off. He will undoubtedly expect a great part of yr. estate to be settled on me and the issue of the marriage, but these matters I leave entirely to yr. own discretion & pleasure. I shall just here insert a few general terms which Mr. Graves at my request was so obliging as to set down upon paper:[6] I have shewn them to Baker, he read them & said he would return an answer when I received one to my letter from Paris: as I wrote in the latter end of Septbr. and sent a copy of that letter in the beginning of Octobr. I may expect an answer from you in Febuary or march.[7]

I think I mentioned in my last the company or set Mr. Graves has introduced me to: perhaps you may be desirous to know who they are: the following are the principal men: Mr. Hussey[8] attorney general to the queen: Mr. Barington[9] my lord Barington's[10] brother and one of the welch Judges, Mr. Prat[11] member of Parlt. and nephew to the chief Justice,[12] Mr. Camphion[13] membr. of Parlt. and sometimes Doctor Hay[14] favours us with his company. Mr. Hussey has desired me when I return to Maryland to send the company a buck: as I shall be detained here longer than he imagins I should be greatly obliged to you if you could send me one by the first oportunity; it must be cut up into several joints, each joint covered with bay salt[15] and closely packed in a separate box: he says he has eat many sent from Virginia in that manner which proved exceeding good. I desire my cousin Rach: Darnall may be intrusted with this commission[.] Pray present her with my compliments and aknowledgt. for the regard and tender concern she seems to bare me. I shall answer her letter which I have just received by Hanson:

You no doubt have heared of Mr. Wilke's fate: he has been expelled the house of commons. but took care previously to withdraw to France. It was said great wagers were laid wether he would return or not before the meeting of the Parliat. I would like to have laid a considerable sum that he would not return so persuaded was I that he never intended to return.

N:B: The 6 per Ct. will not be thought a sufficient settlement I am told that settlements are frequently made at the rate of 8 per Ct. The going to America will no doubt be made a reason for demanding a larger settlement on my Wife in case of my death: a woman that abandons father, mother, & all her relations out of love for her husband deserves a handsom jointure.[16]

I beg to be remembered to my friends in particular to John Darnall, Rich: Croxall & Capt: Carroll. I have sent you a copy of Mr. Baker's letter not caring to part with the original. I have not as yet seen Mr. Diggs as I am but lately arrived in town, you may depend on my treating him with that civility which is due to a gentleman you esteem. I have spoke to Mr. Bird about the stoko man: he will endeavour to find one out to go on the terms proposed: but he doubts wether a good workma[n] can be engaged to leave England on such terms, as they earn a great deal of money & have constant employt. Kelty has delivered the Pedigree it shall be copied & sent to Mr. Whitten by some safe oportunity: I have received no letters from that gentleman this long while. I am Dr. Papa

Yr. affectionate & dutifull Son

Cha: Carro[ll]

ALS, Carroll Papers, MS 206, MdHi.

1. See enclosure 1, below.

2. The Diary of John Baker notes his receipt of two letters from CC, dated Dec. 8 and Dec. 17, 1763, and that the two of them met on three successive days in Bath, Dec. 20–22. CC subsequently stayed at Baker's estate, Grove Place, from Jan. 9 through Jan. 22, 1764.

3. Baker's second wife, Mary Ryan (?–1774), was a daughter of Thomas Ryan of the Leeward Island Montserrat, who held considerable property both on that island and on St. Croix. The family originated in Ireland. Yorke, ed., *Diary of John Baker,* 10–11.

4. Nicholas Tuite (1705–1772), a close friend of Baker's, was largely responsible for the development of St. Croix as a producer of sugar, rum, coffee, and cotton. He had close ties with the Danish royal house, serving the king as lord chamberlain, and kept a mercantile office and a residence in London and a house in Bath. Ibid., 62–63 n.

5. See enclosure 2, below.

6. See enclosure 3, below.

7. Following this paragraph in the original manuscript, CC wrote "*General terms,*" perhaps with the intention of writing out William Graves's notes. However, he ultimately included Graves's remarks as a separate enclosure.

8. Richard Hussey (1715?–1770) served as attorney general to Queen Charlotte after the accession of George III. Called to the bar from the Middle Temple, he represented a Cornish district in Parliament from 1761 until his death.

9. Daines Barrington (1727–1800).

10. William Wildman Barrington, second Viscount Barrington (1717–1793).

11. Robert Pratt (c. 1728–1775) was a member of Parliament for Horsham (1763–1774). Judd, *Members of Parliament,* 312.

12. Sir Charles Pratt, first Earl Camden (1714–1794), attended Eton and King's College, Cambridge, and was called to the bar from the Middle Temple in 1738. In 1755 he became king's counsel and attorney general to the Prince of Wales, and when his friend William Pitt came to power in July 1757, Pratt was named attorney general, a position he relinquished in December 1761 upon being knighted and appointed chief justice of the court of common pleas. As chief justice he played an important part in the Wilkes affair, maintaining the illegality of general warrants and the privilege of Parliament, and earned great popularity for his position. When he took his seat in the House of Lords in December 1765, having been created Baron Camden the previous summer, he denounced the Stamp Act as uncon-

stitutional in his maiden speech. Named lord chancellor in July 1766, he resigned as chief justice.

13. Anthony Champion (1725–1801) served in Parliament from 1754 until 1768. Judd, *Members of Parliament,* 147.

14. Probably Sir George Hay (1715–1778), who served in Parliament more or less continuously from 1754 until his death. Ibid., 224.

15. Large crystals of salt obtained from sea water by using the heat of the sun.

16. A freehold estate limited to the wife for the duration of her life, effective upon the death of her husband, and intended to bar her exercise of dower rights.

Enclosure 1: John Baker to CC

Bath Thursday 15 Decemr. 1763.

Sr.

It was not till late last night at my return from Bristol to this place that I was honoured with yours of the 8 instant, which was sent me from my house near Southampton, else good manners would not have suffered you to wait so long for an answer to it.

Tis true Sr. I have not the pleasure of personally knowing you tho' I am from being altogether a stranger to the name of yr. family; but it is impossible for me to give a precise answer to yr. proposal, tho' such satisfaction as I can give you, I will.

As to what you suggest of my having perhaps already pitched upon some other Gentleman for my daughter, believe me Sr. ti's a matter I had not yet begun to think of and perhaps but for so unexpected an incident as the present should not for a long time to come have at all thought about it, she being now but in her seventeenth year, which I think upon the whole, rather too early to engage in the married state: so that on this particular head I can give you, I believe all the satisfaction you desire: neither her mother or my self having ever turned our thoughts on any particular gentleman, or indeed considered the matter as yet calling for our attention; and I have great reason to believe her own affections to be as utterly disengaged as they were ten years ago.

As to your fortune Sr. I have some reason to suppose it such as I could have no objection to, and indeed to be far more considerable than my daughter might be (what the world calls) intitled to: so that should every other circumstance be agreeable to both parties, the objection on that article is more likely, as I take it to proceed from yr. part than from mine, and even if the great liking you seem to have conceived for her should be powerful enough to induce yourself to dispense with what another would insist on, what certainty is there that your father would so easily be brought to dispense with it too? Yr. father Sr. who is at so considerable a distance & yet without whose approbation I dare say neither would you yourself nor on any the most advantageous terms woud I, chuse to have effected what you seem so desirous of.

Thus you Sr. (which is all that yet can be) I am not as yet sensible of any objections I should have to your proposal: what may hereafter arise from a farther enquiry into each other's situation & character or from a personal conference or from her liking or not liking your person, or you from a farther knowledge & acquaintance not continuing to like hers, it is impossible now to say. All I can assure you is that I should not affect to raise any: and will even ingenuously own to you that I seem to observe in yr. manner of writing certain marks of candour & worth that rather incline me to wish I might not find any; nor can I be wholly without sentiments of gratitude for one who appears to have entertained so sincere & disinterested regard for a daughter who from her infancy has been so exceeding dear to me. I have the honour to be

signed John Baker

L, Carroll Papers, MS 206, MdHi. In CC's hand and endorsed by him: "copy of Mr. Baker's letter." Addressed to CCA in unknown hand. Endorsed by CCA, with mathematical calculations in his hand.

Enclosure 2: Nicholas Tuite's Account of John Baker's Wealth

[Dec. 22, 1763]

a list or valuation of the Estates of Jno Baker Esqr. in the
Island of St Croix in america

vzt.

a Plantation called Concordia [at?] 480 Acres of Land with Buildings proper for making Sugr & Rum. about 150. Negroes. 30 to 40 head of cattle & mules. & now in a Condition to make communibus annis.[1] 300. hhds Sugr & 150 hhds of Rum. but yearly improveg. & will I suppose in the Space of 4. or 5. years make at Least 400 hhds of Sugr. & 200. hhds of Rum

a nother Plantation called Plessens. in wch. Mr Baker is one moyety concerned. The whole contains 900 Acres of Land. with Buildings Proper for making Sugr & Rum. about 300. to 350. Negroes. about 40 head of mules & Cattle & now in a condition to make in the whole 500. hhds Sugr. & 250 hhds of Rum. but yearly improveg. & will I suppose in the Space of 4. or 5. years be capable of makeg. at least 700 to 800 hhds of Sugr. & 350. to 400. hhds of Rum. So that Mr. Bakers moyety being added. to his. own Produce will be as follows. vzt.

The Produce of Concordia at psnt 450 hhds of Sugr. & Rum at 7£.

Sterg. per hhd clear of fraight Insurrance[2] & commission [&ca]   £3150.0.0

one moyety of the Produce of Plessens[3] at psent 375. hhds Sugr.

& Rum at 7£. Sterg. per hhd clear of charges   2625

5775

out of wch. you are to deduct the annual charges of Each Planta.

vzt. for overseers wages taxes Doctors fees mortality of negroes

& Cattle. feeding the negroes. Boards Staves & hoopes & all
other charges. about 2000£ Sterg for both Estates in there
pressent condition. deduct—   2000.
                                                                  _____
nett produce yearly in the pressent condition.   3775

But as the Plantations are not as yet come to their full perfection & that in case
of war. the nett value of Sugr. & Rum may be 10£. per hhd or upwards. I think
the nett produce of the whole may be justly rated at Four thousand five Hundred
pounds Sterg. per annum communibus annis for the next Twenty years to come
& may be much more

Bath 22d. Dber 1763

The foregoing is a just & true accot. or valuation of the Estates or Plantations of
Jno Baker Esqr. in the Island of St Croix. to the Best of my Knowledge wch. I will
at any time confirm on Oath if required witness my hand

N. Tuite

ADS, Carroll Papers, MS 206, MdHi.
1. "In ordinary years."
2. CC interlineated "rance."
3. CC struck through "Concordia" and interlineated "Plessens."

Enclosure 3: William Graves's General Terms

[January 1764]

Some General Terms.

It being supposed that Mr. B: after every debt payed is worth £St 50,000 and that
he has but 5 Children and intends to make them all equal in their fortunes

What sum as a portion to his daughter will Mr. B absolutely secure on her
marriage to carry interest from that time & untill the principal be payed

And what further fortune may she reasonably expect at his death under his
promise to make her equal to any other child?

In consideration of the above supposing Mr. C's father to be worth £St 60,000

What portion thereof will Mr. B expect to be settled on the marriage?

And of what shall be so settled how much for life upon the wife (if She survive)
as a Jointure—& how much upon the younger Child or Children?

And Provided there be no son of such marriage but one or more daughters how
much of the above settlement to go to such Daur or daurs & how much thereof to
revert to the disposal of Mr. C.?

D, Carroll Papers, MS 206, MdHi. In CC's hand and designated "General terms" by him on verso.

CCA to CC

Febru: 27: 1764

Dr Charley,

Yrs of the 11th: of Octor: 1763 I answer[d] the 9th & 10th of Janu: Immediately on the Receit of it. I have Since yrs of the 12th of Novr: wh I was in hopes before I opened it would have informed me whether You had Mr Bakers Consent to Pay yr Addresses[1] to his Daughter & whether he was the Man of that Fortune you expected: This you might have knowne from the 6th: to the 12th of Novr. You might have also informed me why you did not Bring Mr Crookshanks Recommendatory[2] letter with You. You ought to have mentioned the Dates of Such of my letters as had Reached you[.] Dr Charley if You would give Yrself time to Reflect what my Concern & Anxiety must be, you would have been as Particular as it was in Yr Power to be. Should Mr Bakers Objection be against his Daughters leaving him, If he be a good natured Sensible Man, He may Come with his Daughter & Retier with me to Elk Ridge where we may Pass the Remainder of Our lives in an easy Retierment, Becoming & I think agreable to Old Men: In that Case I shall Surrender to You my House in Annapolis to You, Being desierous on my Part to Remove every Dificulty or Objection that may have the Appearance of Reason to Promote yr Happyness. I write but little because You may at this time be Preparing for Yr Voyage to Maryland, in that Case I pray to God to Grant you a Safe & Pleasant One[.] I am Dr Charley

Yr Mo: Afft: Father
Cha: Carroll

ALS, Carroll-McTavish Papers, MS 220, MdHi. Addressed by CCA. There is a second ALS, addressed and marked "Copy" by CCA, filed with it. A third L copy, endorsed by CCA "1764 Febru: 27 Copy to my Son," may be found in the Carroll Papers, MS 206, MdHi.
1. "Respects" in the other copies.
2. "Introductory" in the other copies.

CC to CCA

27 Feby. 1764.

Dr. Papa,

My last was dated the 27 of Jany.: this goes by Capt Macgachan, by whom you will receive the news-papers & magazines. Mr. Lee[1] proposes to return soon to Maryland, he will be so obliging as to bring with him Ward's medecines & the long-promised french Pamphlets: but I hope you will not be under a necessity of making use of the medecines. I find myself much mend[ed] since my last & in better spirits. I keep at present a couple of horses: my Phya. recommended riding & as I find that exercise suits best my constitution, I shall continue to keep horses as long as I remain in England.

By the news papers you will learn the fate of Mr. Wilkes, and the event of the debates in the house of Commons subseqt. to that gentleman's expulsion and in consequence of a complaint made by him while [a] member of a breach of Privilege on being arrested and his papers seized by the Secretary's warrant: the complt. againt Webb[2] & Wood was discharged: the legality of the warrant as the house sat till 6 next morning was adjourn'd to the friday following: each party mustered all their force for that important day. The house ressembled more a hospital than a Senate. Sr. Lawrence Dundass was brot. upon a couch into the house just before the division & carried out in the same manner when he divided with the ministry:[3] the division was upon the previous question being put; the ministry not daring to go into the general question concerning the legality or illegality of the warrant: that question has been adjourned for 4 months, that is entirely put off: A Bill will soon be brot. into the house for taxing America: ti's said a duty will be laid upon stamped paper.[4] Mr. Baker is in town I am impatient to receive yr answer: wishing you health I am Dr. Papa

yr. loving Son
Ch: Carroll.

ALS, Carroll Papers, MS 206, MdHi. Addressed by CC. Endorsed by CCA.

1. Philip Thomas Lee (1738-1778), elder son of Richard Lee of Blenheim, Charles Co., and Grace Ashton Lee of Virginia. Sent to England for schooling in 1753, he attended Eton and Christ's College, Cambridge, entered the Middle Temple in 1756, and was called to the bar on Feb. 10, 1764. After a brief stay in Maryland in 1764, he returned to England and married his first cousin Ann Russell, a daughter of James Russell and Ann Lee Russell. In 1773 he brought his family with him to Maryland and embarked on a public career, serving in the upper house (1773-1774) and on the Council (1773-1776), as a justice on the provincial court, and as naval officer of North Potomac (1774-1777). Although he signed the Oath of Fidelity in 1778, Lee had previously been taxed as a loyalist. His death in December 1778

has traditionally been attributed to his distress over the break between mother country and colonies. *Bio. Dic. Md. Legis.*, II, 527–528.

2. Philip Carteret Webb (1700–1770), a London lawyer and politician, led the prosecution of John Wilkes in 1763.

3. Sir Lawrence Dundass (c. 1710–1781) represented Newcastle-under-Lyme in Parliament from 1762 until 1768. A supporter of the ministry under Grenville, Dundass was brought from his sickbed to vote on the legality of general warrants, an issue central to the Wilkes case, on Feb. 17, 1764. Namier and Brooke, *House of Commons,* II, 357–361.

4. On Mar. 22 and 23, 1764, the House of Commons passed the Revenue Act of 1764, a measure aimed at raising revenue in North America and the West Indies. Popularly known as the Sugar Act, the legislation lowered the existing duty on foreign molasses, raised the tariff on other foreign goods while also levying new duties, provided a series of complex regulations for the loading and unloading of cargoes in colonial ports, and instituted changes in criminal proceedings for persons accused of violating the customs laws. However, the Commons postponed for a year the enactment of a provision calling for the imposition of a stamp tax. Lawrence Henry Gipson, *The Coming of the Revolution, 1763–1775* (New York, 1954), 65 n, 69; Jensen, *Founding of a Nation,* 47–49, 60.

CCA to CC

Febru 28: 1764

Dr Charley,

This is only to informe You I this day Received yrs of the 8th of Decr: If you like the Lady I hope her merit may in a great Measure make up for what her fortune may fall short of yr Expectation. Act with Caution: May God direct You, What you say about Mr Ireland will be most Welcome News to him & he will thank Lady Webb — As Mr. Baker has other Children my Invitation to him to Come here is at an end. You leave me in the Greatest State of Uncertainty, Could you not learn what Mr Baker is supposed to be Worth Where his Estate lays of what it Consists, what Sum You Suppose he may, or may be able to give his Daughter. I suppose you had some Information as to these Particulars & to Many more before you wrote to him. I Cannot write to you as fully as I would do were you more Explicit. I am My Dr Charly

Yr Mo: Afft: Father
Cha: Carroll

ALS, Carroll-McTavish Papers, MS 220, MdHi. Addressed by CCA. A second ALS copy, addressed and marked "Copy" by CCA, is filed with it. A third L copy, endorsed by CCA, may be found in the Carroll Papers, MS 206, MdHi.

CC to CCA

21 March 1764

Dr. Papa,

Capt. Kelty will deliver you this and the following books & Pamphlets: the natural history of Kamschatska: Orme's history of Indoustan lately published:[1] the second volume of Warner's Irish history is not yet come out: Gahagan's cannot be had at present there being none in town. Lord Clives letter,[2] 2 numbers of the votes of the house of Commons, the newspapers & one magazine: the royal french Almanack, 6 Pamphlets relative to the Jesuites: I shall send by Mr. Lee or Capt. Hanson Wards medicines as also my journal,[3] Accounts,[4] & the dissertations upon the Irish history you wrote for.

I have greatly exceeded this last year my allowance of £300 by my journey to Holland & France, but I expect to be amply repaid the expence of that expedition in the possession of a sensible, agreeable, & virtuous woman.

I have just purchased for 15 guineas a theodolyte[5] the compleatest instrument for surveying that can be had: if I should have large tracts of land to survey a wheel will be necessary: the price is 5 guineas: however it will be time enough when by experience I have found a wheel to be necessary, to order one in.

I have got the Genealogy copied & am waiting for an oportunity to get it conveyed to Mr. Whitten. By the newspapers you will see the french Jesuites have received the finishing stroke.[6]

By the votes Sent you, you will see the different taxes that have just been laid on the colonies: the Merchants have petitioned against the taking off the drawbacks upon coarse linens[7] alledging it to be of great detriment to the trade of this kingdom that it will occasion the setting up linen manufactures in north America: I am informed that Mr. Grenville[8] said in answer to the Merchants that the grievances complained of should be examined into and if found liable to the above exceptions, some other tax less detrimental might be substituted in its stead.

Should my marriage with Miss Baker not take place I shall leave England in the Autumn: I impatiently wish to be with you. I am rather of opinion that I shall not succeed with miss Baker, supposing even upon a better acquaintance I should find she answers the character all her friends give her: the going to America is a prodigious objection to young ladies: should Miss Baker's good sense & inclinations overcome this objection, her mother will never be brought to consent to her daughter's parting from her especially as there will be little hope of their ever meeting again in this life: had I known the mother before I opened the affair to Mr. Baker I should have entirely dropt the thoughts of that marriage.

I have sent you the gentleman's register instead of Millers, as it is much more perfect & correct. Pray present my kind compliments to my Cousin Rach: Darnall & to her daughter: remember me to Jhon Darnall & Rich: Croxall: I am Dr. P.

Yr. most affectionate & dutiful Son
Ch: Carroll.

p:s:

March 23. 1764.

I had just finished the above when I received your long & much expected letter of the 9 Jany.: in mine of the 27 of the same month you have as full and as circumstantial an account as I can give of Mr. Baker's circumstances & family: all I could say upon that subject at present would be useless repetition. Mr. Baker & his Lady will be in town in about a fortnight: but not to lose time I shall write to him & inclose a copy of your letter or at least of such parts as I judge most proper to be communicated: matrimony is an affair of too much weight & importance to be precipitated: it will require some time to know the young lady's temper & dispositions: but you may be assured I shall use all the expedition consistent with prudence & decency to bring the affair to a speedy conclusion. I have always been and still am as desirous as ever to return: and as soon as the match is concluded or broke off that minute will I prepare for my voya. I told Mr. Baker at our first enterview that my interest and more particularly my inclination led me to live in America; he hinted that during your life there was no necessity for my returning home: I made him this answer: You know little of me, Sir, and do me injustice to imagin that I can be prevailed on to live absent from a father, whom I most tenderly love, to whose company & conversation I would willingly sacrifice every other enjoyt. Should I not discover the utmost ingratitude & cruelty in complying with so unnatural a proposal, even supposing my Father's consent to it could be obtained? & indeed, Sir, his consent would give me great concern & uneasiness as it would betray a cool indifference, which I should merit, were I even to suffer such a proposal to be made.

This short & firm reply convinced Mr. Baker he must adopt this alternative either to lose his daughter if the match should take place, or brake it off immediately. As he did not think proper to do the latter, he was then willing to make a sacrifice of his fondness to his daughter's welfare & happiness: But since my acquaintance with Mrs. Baker wether influenced by her or by a discovery of something disagreeable in me, he has shewn rather too much indifference to be thought desirous of the marriage: this may be only surmise or perhaps owing to his temper, or to care & disapointments: be it as it will in my letter I shall acquaint him of the settlement you propose to make, the necessity of my returning to Maryland and that too as soon as possible after the marriage: and desire him to recommend to the earnest consideration of his Lady wether she can sacrifice maternal fondness to her daughters inclinations: wether or no I can prevail upon the young lady to accompany me to America will depend upon her affection for, or her dislike to me:

But if the mother thinks she is not mistress of sufficient resolution to surmount the parting with her daughter, the affair is at an end & you may expect me in this next summer or in the fall: I chuse rather to forego my own happiness than make a Parent miserable. Believe me to be Dr. Papa

Yr. most affectionate and dutiful Son

Ch: Carroll.

ALS, Carroll Papers, MS 206, MdHi. Endorsed by CCA.

1. [Robert Orme] (1728–1801), *A History of the Military Transactions of the British Nation in Indostan, from the Year MDCCXLV* . . . , 2 vols. (London, 1763-1778).

2. Robert Clive, Lord Clive (1725–1774), a general and a statesman, played a key military and political role in establishing British supremacy in India during the Seven Years' War. Returning to England in 1760, Clive was elected to Parliament in 1761 and served until his death. A man of considerable influence in the East India Company, in which he held a substantial amount of stock, Clive published *A Letter to the Proprietors of the East India Stock* . . . in London in 1764. *Cat. Lib.,* no. 832.

3. Not found.

4. Not found.

5. A portable surveying instrument used to measure angles.

6. In 1764 Louis XV approved the actions taken against the Jesuits between 1761 and 1763, paving the way for the expulsion of the order.

7. A "drawback" was a refund of a duty on a commodity. The Revenue Act of 1764, as passed by the House of Commons in March, provided for significantly lower duties on linens than those specified in the legislation initially presented to the House. Gipson, *Coming of the Revolution,* 65 n.

8. George Grenville (1712–1770) was educated at Eton and Christ Church, Oxford, and called to the bar from the Inner Temple in 1735. First elected to Parliament in 1741 from Buckingham, he held that seat until his death. He began his political career by opposing the ministry of Robert Walpole and by 1745 had allied himself with William Pitt. In 1754, the year his sister Hester married Pitt, Grenville became treasurer of the navy and a member of the Privy Council. By 1761, however, his increasing association with Pitt's opponent Lord Bute had begun to cause a rift between the brothers-in-law. Grenville succeeded Bute as first lord of the treasury and chancellor of the exchequer in 1763 and led the ministry until political events in England forced his resignation in 1765. For the rest of his life Grenville remained an adamant defender of Parliament's right to tax the colonies, and he vigorously opposed repealing any of the measures enacted during his administration to raise revenues in North America. Jarrett, *Britain,* 277–280; Jensen, *Founding of a Nation,* 41, 69, 164–169.

CCA to CC

April 10th 1764

Dr Charley

The 4th Inst: I received yrs: of the 27th of last Janry. Yours of Octo: 11th, Novr: 12th, Decr: 8th 1763 I answered by mine of Janry 9th, 10th & 16th Febry 27th & 28th 1764. I beg you will always acknowledge the Receit of my Letters by mentioning their Dates. I wonder in particular you take no notice of mine of the 8th of last July[1] relating to the Acadians & of Sept: 24th relating to Mr: Reresby,[2] you have too good a heart not to have done wt: was incumbent on you as to both, I must therefore attribute yr silence to forgetfulness —

As to yrs: of the 27th of last Janry, Mr: Bakers Letter to you speaks him to be a man of Sense & Honr: I would not have you insist on a larger Sum in hand with the Lady than it may be convenient to him to lay down as he is willing to pay Intert: for the fortune he may agree to give his Daughter until he can pay the Principal, & as he moreover promises at his Death to make his Daughter share equally his Estate real & personal with his Sons —

I approve the General Terms given to Mr: Baker, but take care that by the Settlement you do not give a certainty for an uncertainty, that is, that the Settlement be not Binding but in Proportion to the Sum you may now or hereafter receive with the Lady & that a proper distinction be made in the [Se]ttlemt: between the Jointure to be made for the Sum paid in hand or the Intert: to be paid you Annually on such Sum, & the Jointure to be made on wt: may fall to you at Mr: Bakers Death, the difference being very obvious — In this you will make similar Cases the Rule to direct you.

Considering the low Intert: on our Funds I think 6 per Ct: an ample Settlemt: especially if you shd: have Issue by the Lady, for I think a Mother shd: as well as a Father contribute to the Establishment of her children, but if Mr: Baker shd: insist on 8 [per Ct] to make you happy I co[n]sent to it — In mine of the 9th of Janry 1764 I told you I was willing if the Lady's Fortune could demand it to make my whole Fortune Lyable to the Settlemt & Jointure[.] This I confirm & I leave it entirely to you to act, what is reasonable according to the Advice of your Friends —

I proposed upon yr: coming into Maryland to convey to you my Mannor of Carrollton 10000 Acres & the Addition thereto called Addition to Carrollton, 2700 Acres now producing Annually £250 Sterg: & greatly improving as not nigh half of the 12700 A is let, & wt: is let, is let to Tenants at Will[3] & my Share of the Iron Works producing at least Annually £400 Ster:

If this shd: not be deemed a Sufficient Settlemt: & Gift to you & Security for the Lady's Jointure I am willing to add on my Death my Mannor of Doohoregan 10000

A & 1425 A called Chance adjacent thereto on wch: Seats the Bulk of Negroes are settled —

If you shd: Marry Miss Baker & not have Issue Male by her I think it would not be prudent to engage yr: Real Estate to Daughters as out of yr: personal Estate you may make a Settlemt: on yr: Daughters proportioned to their Mothers fortune —

In case you shd: survive Miss Baker you will take care not so to engage as to lay yr:self under unreasonable Covenants detrimental to yr: future ease and happiness —

As I have said upon yr: Return to Maryland I will give you my Mannor of Carrollton & the Addition thereto & my Share of the Works, I will also settle on you my Mannor of Doohoregan & Chance & the Slaves thereon on my Death. As you are my only Child you will of Course have all the Residue of my Estate on my Death —

In short to obviate as much as it is in my power every objection & to hasten the Match & yr: Return to me wch. I hope may be in the next fall, I hereby bind myself to confirm by any Articles wch: may be sent me what I have engaged to do by this & my letter of the 9th of last Janry & I desire this & that Letter may be lodged with Mr: Baker or Mr: Tuite as a Security for my so doing. If anything more shd: be required from us wch: you & those you may consult may think reasonable to be done, I leave you at liberty to engage to do it & I think Mr: Baker may confide in any engagemt: you will enter into as my whole Estate will fall to you at my Death —

I much approve the Company you keep. I shall endeavour to oblige Mr: Hussey with a Buck, but I cannot absolutely promise it, as I could not in the last Season procure for myself more than two fine Haunches — I have presented yr: Compts: as desired. I am well, but yr complaints give me pain, I hope they in a great measure proceed from the Anxiety yr: passion for Miss Baker gives you[.] I wish a happy issue to it that yr: health may be perfect & that God will Bless you in everything wch: may contribute to [yr:] Temporal & Eternal wellfare. I am My Dr Charley

Yr: Mo: Affte Father

Cha: Carroll

LS, Carroll-McTavish Papers, MS 220, MdHi. Addressed and marked "Copy" by CCA. Filed with a second LS copy addressed and marked "Triplicate" by CCA. A third, unaddressed L copy without salutation and endorsed by CCA as a "Copy To my Son" may be found in the Carroll Papers, MS 206, MdHi.

1. Not found.
2. John Reresby was CCA's clerk.
3. Tenants at will held leases at the pleasure of the landlord.

CC to CCA

19 April 1764.

Dr. Papa,

In my last by Kelty I acknowledged the receipt of yr. letter of the 9 Janry. I wrote to Mr. Baker upon the occasion & sent him enclosed a copy of yr. letter what follows was the substance of mine to that gentleman.

That as I had received yr. consent to pay my addresses to his daughter, there now remained only two things to be settled: the marriage settlemt. & the young ladys going to America, which if she refused or her Parents should have an objection to, I then must lay aside all thoughts of the match: that if Mrs. Baker could not bare the thoughts of parting with her daughter, & was determined not to part with her, it would be improper to introduce me to the young lady, since it would be impossible contrary to her mother's will to persuade Miss Baker to accompany me to America: that tho' it were possible I should not chuse to persue my own happiness in opposition to a Parent's will, nor wish to suceed if my success should make that Parent retched & unhappy.

Mr. Baker returned no answer to my letter as he was upon the point of coming to town when he received it. Upon his arrival I waited on him to know his determination. He advised me to return as soon as possible to Maryland, since you seemed so desirous of my returning as it was very natural you should: his daughter, he said, would be over in May or June: that if I thought proper, I might see her, and if upon a further acquaintance, we should like each other, I might return 3 or 4 years hence (for that would be time enough) & marry his daughter: he mentioned not one word about the settlemt., but I know he thinks it insufficient, and indeed so does a lawyer of my acquaintance with whom I talked upon that subject.

But had Baker had no other objection to the match but the quantum of the settlt. to be made on his daughter, he would have had some conversation with me on that head: but I could plainly see, by the above speech & by his manner, that he was not very desirous of its taking place: and I am sure I am not, upon the condition of returning three or 4 years hence to Europe on a wild goose chase. What certainty is there that the lady will remain for 4 years of the same opinion? Or rather how probable is it she will not? I do not care to entangle myself in any such engagement: in short I have dropt all thoughts of Miss Baker, whom I wish extremely well to & married to a man worthy of her.

I hope to be with you about the latter end of Septbr. I do not chuse to arrive sooner in Maryland on account of the heats: the remainder of my time here I shall spend in perfecting myself in the practical part of surveying & making necessary preparations for my voyage. I have sent you over the American Act,[1] and a Pamphlet intituled consideration on the penal laws against Rom: Catholicks:[2] I sent by

Mr. Lee Wards medicines & gave him the instructions in writing for taking those medicines. I have been indisposed all this last week with a cold attended with a feaver & cough: my feaver is entirely gone off, there remains a little cough: these colds are very rife at present: had it not been for this indisposition I should have finished the journal of my last Tour: as I only took short notes of things as I went along to refresh my memory it requires time to enlarge them & to dispose them in such order as may give some little entertainment in the reading: If I cannot finish the Journal time enough to send it by Hanson, I shall send it by some other ship or bring it in with me. Pray present my compliments to my cousin Rach: Darnall & her daughter, to Mr. John Darnall & Sons & to Rich: Croxall. I am dear Father

Yr. most loving Son

Ch: Carroll.

P:S:

This letter was ready to go by Hanson: but Mr. Perkins gave me no notice of his sailing: he told me indeed a week before Hanson sailed, that he imagined he would sail in about a fortnight's time: how easy was it for Mr. Perkins to have sent me word by a penny post letter or by his Ser[vant] that his ship was ready to sail? The only excuse for t[his] neglect is that he imagined as I had wrote so lately by Kelty I had no letters or parcels to send: I am not certain how this letter will go: perhaps by the new York packet. Mr. Buchanan tells there is a ship going in a fortnight: I shall send by the capt. of that ship; the Pamphlets, news papers, & magazines; & my accounts.

ALS, Carroll Papers, MS 206, MdHi. Endorsed by CCA.

1. The Revenue Act of 1764.

2. [Charles Howard of Greystoke], *Considerations on the Penal Laws against Roman Catholics in England, and the New Acquired Colonies in America* (London, 1764). *Cat. Lib.*, no. 832.

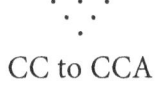

CC to CCA

1 May 1764.

Dr. Papa,

I wrote to you the 19 of last month and in that letter informed you of my having laid aside all thoughts of Miss Baker: as that letter may miscarry I shall here give you the substance of it.

When I communicated yr. letter to Mr. Baker, wether dissatisfied with the settlement you proposed to make or unwilling to part with his daughter, he advised me to return as soon as possible: he added, to soften, I suppose, this piece of advice, that if upon a further acquaintance I continued to like his daughter, & she me, that I might return to England 4 or 5 years hence:

By this you plainly see Mr Baker is averse to the match: is it probable that a young lady will retain her affection 4 years for a gentleman with whom she can be[1] but slightly acquainted, & from whom she will be separated by the Atlantick? Besides it would be imprudent in me to enter into any such engagement: I may meet with some young lady in Maryland whom I may like, & in that case I should chuse to settle without loss of time: the sooner, the better, for then I might live to bring up my children: if I stay till I attain the age of 36, the chances of my living so long, are against me as I am of a thin & puny habit of body. 6 per Ct. is too slender a settlement: A Lawyer of my acquaintan[ce] told me it was common to settle upon the wife at the rate of 8 per Ct. & sometimes 10: this holds where the wife brings with her no very considerable fortune: but when her fortune is large, it is then usual to settle part of her own fortune upon her.

I hope, Deo juvante,[2] to be with you about the latter end of Septbr. I am willing to perfect myself in the practical part of surveying before my departure: besides, I am apprehensive of the summer heats & am desirous of avoiding them in coming in: I shall be gradually prepared for the heat of the summer following.

I can not get my Journal finished to send it by this oportunity: I have wrote out my Accts. but find such a deficiency or rather difference between my expences & receipts that I am ashamed to send them. I cannot otherwise account for this great deficiency which amounts to near £60 but by my negligence, & by my forgetting to set down regularly my expences: however the main articles of expence are all set down: I shall bring them in with me, as also the acot. of what I spent in my late tour thro' Holland & France.

I sent you by Mr. Lee Wards medicines & the directions for taking of them: but as Mr. Lee may have lost those directions, I shall here insert a copy of them:

For the fistula paste[:] Take the bigness of a nutmeg night & morning and two tea spoonfuls of sweet oil immediately after, no visible operation, to live as usual.

The dropsy powders; one to be taken every two days; such as have not taken them before, are to begin with half a powder to be taken in a little mountain, after every operation drink a little broth or water gruel, the less they drink the better.

This accompanys the magazines, news papers, the American act, & the considerations on the penal laws against the Ro: Cath: I desire my compliments to Mrs. Darnall, Mr. Darnall & Sons, Rich: Croxall, & Harry Carroll. I am Dr. Papa
Yr. most affectionat[e &] loving Son
Ch: Carro[ll].

ALS, Carroll Papers, MS 206, MdHi. Addressed by CC. Endorsed by CCA.
1. "Is" struck through here and "can be" interlineated.
2. "God willing."

CC to CCA

May 30 1764.

Dr. Papa,

This goes by Capt. Lewis:[1] I had some thoughts of [sailing] with him, but could not get ready for th[e time] of his departure; and indeed if I could ha[ve] been ready, I should not have chose to have sa[il]ed so soon, as I should then have got in the ve[ry] midst of the hottest weather.

I have not as yet been able to go out into the [fie]lds to learn the practice of surveying: Mr. B[a]teman the Surveyor, whom Mr. Cowley ha[s] recommended to me as the properest person f[or m]y purpose, has been these 5 weeks past down in [S]urry: several letters have been sent to him and as no answers have been received, we imagin the letters have never been delivered: to morrow [I s]hall set out myself in quest of him, and if I have the good luck to meet with him, I shall fix the [time] for his attending me. The usual & settled price is [h]alf a guinea a day and Mr. Bateman is to find men to carry the staffs & chain & bear their expences: Mr. Cowley thinks Bateman much preferable to any other, as he has an easy & clear manner of expressing himself & communicating his ideas, and will take pains to make the young Practioner well acquainted with the business.

Before this comes to hand, you will have learnt by mine of the 19 april the issue of the intended m[a]tch ti's entirely broke off, the mother could not bea[r] to part with her daughter: I can not say my [disappointment] gives me any great uneasiness; I might perh[aps] have liked the young lady in time & upon a farther [acquaintance] but I knew too little of her to be in love[.]

If I can get a ship about 4 weeks hence bound to Maryland, I shall certainly take my passage [on] her I believe Mr. Buchanan will bear me comp[a]ny: Should there be no vessel ready to sail about [t]hat time I may perhaps sail in the New-York p[ac]ket not withstanding the inconveniences of such a round about Voyage, for I am determined, if possible to be at Annapolis in Septbr.: this may be my last letter to you from London, wishing you yr. health and our happy meeting I am Dr. Papa

Yr. most affection[a]te & dutiful Son

Ch: Ca[r]roll

P:S:

Capt. Lewis has got a little packet for you containing my Journal and the newspapers: Capt. Lewis has been very civil to me, I desire you will return his civilities & if convenient invite him to dine with you.

ALS, Carroll Papers, MS 206, MdHi. Addressed by CC. Endorsed by CCA. Margins damaged.

1. Either John Lewis, master of the ship *Eagle,* or David Lewis, master of the *Patuxent.* *Md. Gaz.,* Aug. 9, 1764; Annapolis Port of Entry Record Books.

CC to CCA

26 July 1764

Dr. Papa,

I have at last pitched upon a ship: she is called the Randolph Capt. Walker & sails for James River in Virginia: the Capt. is not certain as to the time of his sailing but imagins it will be about the middle of September at farthest. I shall leave behind me all my heavy Bagga. to be shiped on board of Hanson and only take with me my Cloaths.

I am much obliged to you for letting me settle at the rate of 8 per Ct. But that affair is entirely broken off nor do I chuse to renew it, tho' I had sometime ago a very fair opening: but the young lady has been bread up with very high notions not at all answerable to her fortune; a domestick wife not so fond of show and parade, who is not above the business of her family, will best suit me: the mother is a vain empty woman who knows but the daughter may take after her? I do not chuse to run the risk.

I sent the letters & papers concerning the neutrals to the Coffee house as directed: but as the Duke of Nivernois[1] had left London sometime before they came to hand and as most of the differences between the two Courts were then compromised & settled, I imagin all application from the poor neutrals will meet with little or no success.

I shall call upon Mr. Sitwell before my departure & press him to do something for Mr. Reresby. Since my last I have been down in Sussex with a Surveyor to survey land. I have surveyed about 150 acres of which I kept a field book & have since protracted my work on Paper. I think I understand the theory perfectly well, & a little more practice will make me quite master of the business. I shall go out once more into the field with the Surveyor.

Mr. Crookshanks has been in town some time past: he was under a necessity of leaving Paris when the last oath was tendered to all Jesuits under the Jurisdiction of the Prosecuting Parliats. All those who refused to take the oath were compelled to leave the kingdom: the oath was of such a nature, that one only excepted, thought he could reconcile it to his conscience: however all men thought it incompatible with his honour & dispise him for his servile compliance: he was a man of some eminence & had a large & extensive acquaintance with the greatest families in Paris, who have since looked so very cooly on him as to discountenance his coming to their houses.

Pompadour's death it was imagined would occasion an alteration of measures: but the same measures are persued & the same men govern.

Mr. Crookshanks does me the pleasure to dine with me now and then: he always enquires after you & expresses a great regard for you, & I am convinced he is sincere in his expressions of esteem & friendship: the arrêts were not published when he left France nor are they yet: I sent you some time ago the most curious Pamplets in vindication of the Jesuites which I hope you have long since received.

As to political news during the recess of Parliament you can not expect much: the minority still dine in Allbamarle Street:[2] I hear some complaints about their expensive dinners, but the deliberations of the Senate do not transpire. I am of opinion they will oust the present ministry dispised and hated as it is by the greatest part of the nation:[3] it requires great abilities in the minister, if unpopular, to stand his ground long in such a country as this.

I have nothing more to add at present but my compliments to my friends whom I soon hope to enjoy: this will be my last from London should nothing particular occur in the interim: wishing that I may find you in perfect health I am Dr. Papa

yr. affectionate & dutifull Son

Ch: Carroll

ALS, Carroll Papers, MS 206, MdHi. Endorsed by CCA.

1. Louis-Jules-Bardon Mancini-Mazarini, duc de Nivernois (1716–1798), was the French negotiator at the proceedings that formulated the treaty of Paris ending the Seven Years' War.

2. Probably the "New Whigs," who met at Wildman's tavern on Albemarle Street in London. Among the group's members was Edmund Burke. Jarrett, *Britain*, 284–285.

3. The unpopularity of the Grenville ministry was initially attributable to the furor over John Wilkes and subsequently to a deepening economic depression for which the public blamed the restraints placed on American trade by the administration's policies. Political infighting at the highest levels worsened the situation. Grenville resented the meddling of the king's favorite, Lord Bute, and pressured the king to curtail Bute's influence. For his part, George III found Grenville arrogant and wearisome and tried on several occasions to persuade other qualified men to replace him. Despite these difficulties, the Grenville ministry endured until July 1765, when the king finally succeeded in convincing the marquis of Rockingham to form a government.

CHAPTER 3

Adjustment and Courtship
Maryland, 1765–1768

. . .
.
.

Shortly after his return to Maryland, Charles Carroll began corresponding with his English friends. Notwithstanding the intensity with which he had longed to be reunited with Charles Carroll of Annapolis, his letters reveal that he felt less at home in America than he had anticipated. Conditioned by his experiences abroad to perceive the world through the value system of a British aristocrat, CC found America's more egalitarian society with its less rigidly defined class structure and behavioral norms disconcerting and offensive. In many ways, he remained an exile, a stranger in his own land, confronted with the necessity of reconciling his English tastes and notions with the realities of American life.

The most pressing challenge that awaited CC upon his arrival in Maryland was to marry appropriately and produce an heir to carry on the Carroll heritage. The letters he wrote to his English friends in 1766 trace his courtship of his cousin Rachel Cooke and the despair he felt when she died unexpectedly, shortly before the wedding. With no marital prospects, at the advanced age of twenty-nine, he professed to have "grown quite indifferent to every thing in this world even to life itself" and declared his intention to pursue eternal rather than temporal happiness, a course requiring that he "patiently submit, I was going to say chearfully (but I have not virtue enough to do that) to the crosses & trials of this life." Convinced that he had "come to the dregges" of his existence, CCC thought it not "surprising that I should wish the bitter potion down."[1] Less than a year after Rachel Cooke's untimely death had induced this paroxysm of despair, CCC again became engaged, this time to Molly (Mary) Darnall, another, much younger cousin, twelve years his junior. The scandalous careers of Molly's father and grandfather had left her and her mother, Rachel Brooke Darnall, destitute, and by 1761 CCA had taken both of them into his household.

Delighted with the match, the elder Carroll confided to CCC's English friend William Graves that, in the seven years Molly had lived in his house, he had never "had Reason to Chide Her," but, he hastened to add, she was CCC's "owne Choice," not his![2] All of CCA's subsequent correspondence with his son reveals the deep and abiding affection and the constant, solicitous concern that characterized his relationship with his daughter-in-law. CCC described his intended to William Graves as follows: "The ladys name is Darnall: of a good family, without any money: in every other respect she is such as you would recommend to yr. friend: chearful, sweet tempered, virtuous & sensible—her person is agreeable & cleanly[.] Cleanliness in a woman Graves with me is a strong recommendation the more so, as it is a quality very often wanting in the fair sex at least I have found it so, perhaps you may have had better luck than yr. hum: Servant—if women who live by a certain profession are so deficient in an essential point of their calling, what are we not to apprehend from wives, who are above those little arts of pleasing: many married men have complained, that prostitutes are neater than their wives: I presume they spoke from experience."[3]

Although impatient for his initiation into what he once called "the misterious rites . . . of Hymen,"[4] CCC had to delay his marriage plans for nearly a year because of a legal technicality. Still a minor at nineteen, the prospective bride could not sign the marriage settlement required by her future in-laws. To assure the legal validity of Molly's assent to this document, whereby she disclaimed any right to the fortune if CCC died, the Carrolls deemed it necessary to have an act passed by the Maryland legislature enabling her to assume adult status. By publicly questioning the need for this routine procedure, Daniel Dulany, scion of a family for whom the Carrolls had a longstanding enmity, caused CCC a measure of personal embarrassment that he never forgave or forgot.[5] The wedding finally took place at CCA's imposing brick house on Duke of Gloucester Street in Annapolis, on June 5, 1768, the day after the passage of the enabling act.

1. CCC to Christopher Chapman Bird, Mar. 8, 1767, below.
2. CCA to William Graves, Dec. 23, 1768, below.
3. CCC to Graves, Aug. 27, 1767, below.
4. CCC to Bird, Sept. 17, 1766, below.
5. Daniel Dulany's efforts to block the passage of the enabling act sought by the Carrolls would be publicly recalled in 1773 during a heated debate in the press between CCC and Dulany, when an anonymous muse published a snide little verse referring to the earlier incident in the *Md. Gaz.* (June 24, 1773, below).

CC to CCA

Hampton 8 Decembr. 1764

Dr. Papa,

I arrived this day at this place in good health after a tedious & stormy passage of a 11 weeks[.] We left Gravesend the 19 Septbr. & had the greatest prospect of making a short passage till we got to Bermudas about the latter end of Octbr: we were driven back by strong north west winds & tossed about the whole month of Novembr. inso much we scarce made 100 leagues in our way in 30 days.

I have brought all my baga. with me, which is pretty considerable: One Mr. Campbell a storekeeper has also a cargo aboard: I shall take the oportunity of shiping my baga. on board the vessel that is to carry his goods: we intend going up the bay in her ourselves: it will require some time to unship, discharge the duties, & reship the goods when we have hired a vessel: it will be, I am affraid, near the end of the month before I shall have the satisfaction & Joy of embracing you[.] A Servant is Just now going off to York & waits for this letter which is the reason of its shortness. I am Dr. Papa

yr. affectionate & dutiful Son
Ch: Carroll

P:S:

I shall go to Norfolk to morrow or the day following.

ALS, Carroll Papers, MS 206, MdHi. Addressed by CC. Endorsed by CCA.

. . .
.

CC to CCA

Norfolk 20 Decembr. 1764

Dr. Papa,

Mr. Hinson[1] is just going up the Bay: I take this oportunity to Inform you I am well and shall sail from this place to morrow or the day following if the wind permits. I arrived at Hampton The 9 instant & wrote to you immediately at my landing. We had a long passage of 11 weeks. I have been detained here by waiting for a vessel to take two or 3 cargoes to Annapolis & other places up the bay: I thought it a good oportunity to convey my baga. home. Mr. Hinson is upon the point of sailing I hope to be with you next thursday at farthest[.] I am

yr. affectionate son
Ch: Carroll

ALS, Carroll Papers, MS 206, MdHi. Addressed by CC. Endorsed by CCA.

1. Probably Capt. Joseph Hynson (variously Hinson). Price, *Johnson's Letterbook*, 66, 130, 160.

CC to CCA

10 Janry. 1765.

Dr. Papa,

I sailed from old point comfort the 26 of last month in the evening: 27 Before day we were opposite to the mouth of Potomack & were driven back by a strong north west wind as far as the southermost of the Tangier Islands, which with difficulty we weathered & came to an anchor that night between those islands & the eastern shore: 28 The wind abating it came to the southard next morning & we proceeded up the sound with an intent of passing thro' Hooper's or Cages streights: a Pilot we took on board undertook to conduct us thro' the latter but being unacquainted with the chanel he run us aground by which unlucky accident we lost near 24 hours of fair wind & I have been deprived the satisfaction of being long since with you[.] 29: The next day, there being a high tide the vessel was got off but the wind shifting to the north west we were detained 3 or 4 days in those streights: Janu: at length we extricated ourselves & anchored last friday morning off point look out at the mouth of the Potowmack[.] Janu: 4: That evening we got underway: at 12 at night it began to snow but the wind continued favourable: about 4 saturday afternoon 5 the weather cleared up & we found ourselves not far from Poplar Island: the wind began to head us & we were o[b]liged to run in between Kent & Poplar Islands where the vessel [still] remains & is likely to remain as long as the frost continues. I landed with some diffi[cu]lty last Monday 7 on Kent Island & rode to Mr. Sadler's[1] where I was very hospitably entertained: I arrived yesterday 9 at Mr. Brownes[2] where I now am, & have met with the most friendly reception: I shall go over to [M]r. Halls[3] to day, who has pressed me to make his house my home while I continue on the eastern shore. I was determined to go round the bay: but Mr. Browne & Mr. Hall have persuaded me to drop that scheme as attended with a good deal of danger & as there is a probability of my getting to Annapolis sooner by waiting for a thaw. Mr. Hall has hired a man to convey this letter: I thought this absolutely necessary as you must be under great apprehensions on my account if you have received my letter by Hinson who sailed from Norfolk 2 days before I left it: I am in very good health but vexed at my being detained so long from you & under great uneasiness from the anxiety I am sensible you must feel for my safety: Pray remember me to my Cousin Rach: Darnall & all my friends I am Dr. Papa

yr. most affectionate Son
Ch: Carroll.

ALS, Carroll Papers, MS 206, MdHi. Endorsed by CCA.
1. Probably a member of the Sudler family, an Eastern Shore clan with roots on Kent

Island. Louis C. Sudler, Jr., comp., "The Sudler Family of Maryland" (Chicago, 1977), un-paged.

2. Possibly John Brown (variously Browne; ?–1793), of Upper District Hundred, Queen Anne's Co. Although Brown, a farmer, had a modest public career that included service as a county justice, in the lower house (1773), in Maryland's provisional government (1774–1775), and in the post-Revolutionary legislature (1778–1780), it was probably his family ties that recommended him to the Carrolls. His father-in-law was the Scots merchant William Carmichael of Chestertown, in Kent Co., and his brother-in-law William Carmichael became an associate and correspondent of CCC during the American Revolution. *Bio. Dic. Md. Legis.,* I, 175.

3. Probably Francis Hall (1732–1798), a Roman Catholic who lived at Bolingly (variously Bowlingly), his wife's home on Queenstown Creek in Queen Anne's Co. Bowie, *Prince George's,* 416–417.

CC to CCA

25 Jany. 1765

I take this oportunity by Mr Tylghman[1] to inform you I am well but out of all patience with the weather: I see no prospect of the frost braking up and am very apprehensive I shall be detained a month longer on this side the Bay:[2] the eastern shore gentlemen have been very kind, I have been kept in continual exercise ever since my arrival in repaying visits: I have visited Colonel Tylghman[3] Mrs. Blake at Wye,[4] & have had an invitation from Colonel Loyd:[5] he wrote me a very polite letter by his eldest son,[6] but there being then a prospect of a thaw; & the bad weather setting in Since I have not as yet waited on the Colonel & am doubtful wether I shall or not as his house is at a considerable distance. I have no cloaths fit to appear in by me.

Mr. Edward Tylghman[7] has sent me an invitation to come & see him: Mr. Richard Tylghman, the colonel's son[8] & Mr. Cook[9] will attend me to his house. The Messenger returned here last sunday night, he saw a man drowned in crossing Susquahanna: he had a pistole[10] a day by agreement, I thought it better to pay the hire high as it was, than let you continue under the uneasiness and doubt of my being safe.

The Vessel I came up the Bay in, lays within Kent point all my books, cloaths, & other baggage are in her. Pray give my compliments to all friends: Mr. & Mrs. Hall[11] desire me to present you with theirs. I am Dr. Papa

yr. affectionate Son
Ch: Carroll

ALS, Carroll Papers, MS 206, MdHi. Addressed by CC. Endorsed by CCA.

1. Tilghman.

2. CC's gloomy prediction that he would be another month trying to cross the bay to Annapolis proved inaccurate. A break in the weather — and in his fortunes — was reported in the Feb. 14, 1765, issue of the *Md. Gaz.*: "We are now so free from ice here, that Boats cross the Bay as usual. Tuesday last arrived at his Father's House in Town, Charles Carroll, junr., Esq: (Lately from London, by way of Virginia) after about Sixteen Years absence from his Native Country at his Studies and on his Travels."

3. Col. Richard Tilghman III (1705-1766) lived at the Hermitage on the Chester River in Queen Anne's Co. His Roman Catholic wife, Susanna Frisby, was a granddaughter of Maj. Nicholas Sewall, CC's maternal great-grandfather (see Appendix I, Chart H). Colonel Tilghman served as justice of the provincial court (1746-1766). Richard Tilghman Earle II, sketch of the Tilghman family, 1839, Vertical File, MdHi.

4. CC's Roman Catholic kinswoman Sarah Darnall Blake (1705-liv. 1780), who lived at Sportsman's Hall on the Wye River in Queen Anne's Co. See Appendix I, Chart F.

5. Col. Edward Lloyd III.

6. Edward Lloyd IV (1744-1796), elder son of Edward Lloyd III and Anne Rousby Lloyd, lived at Wye House in Talbot Co. and after 1772 also kept a house in Annapolis. A planter with mercantile interests and scion of Maryland's wealthiest family, Lloyd occupied the top rung of the province's social ladder. His public career began in 1771 with his election to the lower house. He served in all but two of the conventions that composed the provisional government (1774-1776), on the first Council of Safety (1775), on the Executive Council (1777-1779), and as a delegate to the Continental Congress (1783-1784). Chosen a senator from the Eastern Shore in 1780, he was a member of the Maryland Senate until 1788 and again from 1791 to 1796. He married in 1767 Elizabeth Tayloe, daughter of John Tayloe of Mt. Airy, Richmond Co., Va., and Rebecca Plater Tayloe, and fathered a son, Edward Lloyd V, and six daughters. *Bio. Dic. Md. Legis.*, II, 537-538.

7. Edward Tilghman (1713-1785) of Wye, Queen Anne's Co., was a younger brother of Richard Tilghman III. He served as high sheriff of Queen Anne's Co. (1739-1742), justice of the peace (1743-1749), and in the lower house (1746-1750). Appointed rent roll keeper of the Eastern Shore in 1750, he was dismissed for incompetence in 1756 but was reelected to the lower house in 1754 and continued in that position until 1771. His third wife, whom he married in 1759, was Juliana Carroll, the daughter of CC's second cousin Dominick Carroll (see Appendix I, Charts B and H). *Bio. Dic. Md. Legis.*, II, 820-822; Donnell MacClure Owings, *His Lordship's Patronage: Offices of Profit in Colonial Maryland* (Baltimore, 1953), 89, 177.

8. Richard Tilghman IV (1739-1810), eldest son of Richard Tilghman III and Susanna Frisby Tilghman, served as clerk of Queen Anne's Co. until the American Revolution. He married his first cousin Elizabeth Tilghman, daughter of Edward Tilghman of Wye, and fathered one child, a son, who predeceased him. Earle, sketch of the Tilghman family, Vertical File; Appendix I, Chart H.

9. William Cooke (1746-1817) was kin both to CC and Richard Tilghman IV. The son of John Cooke of Graiden, Prince George's Co., and CC's great aunt Sophia Sewall Cooke, William Cooke began his study of law in Maryland and in 1768 traveled to London, bearing letters of introduction from CCC, to continue his legal education at the Inner Temple.

(See CCC to Edmund Jenings, Apr. 14, 1768, and CCC to William Graves, Apr. 16, 1768, below.) Upon his return to Maryland in 1771, Cooke entered the law practice of Thomas Johnson and subsequently handled a number of legal matters for the Carrolls. He married Richard Tilghman IV's sister Elizabeth, and their son Richard became her brother's principal heir, changing his name to Richard Cooke Tilghman. Earle, sketch of the Tilghman family, Vertical File; E. Alfred Jones, *American Members of the Inns of Court* (London, 1924), 51; Appendix I, Chart H.

10. A Spanish gold coin worth between sixteen and eighteen shillings.

11. Martha Neale Hall (1738–1789), daughter of Edward Neale of Queen Anne's Co. Bowie, *Prince George's*, 416.

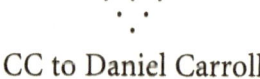

CC to Daniel Carroll

5 Septb. 1765

Dr. Sir,

Where this will find you I am uncertain but at what [ever] time or in what ever place I hope it will find you well. Yours of the 5 ultimo from Capt. Carroll's I red soon after the date thereof with yr. will enclosed. You must be sensible what cogent reasons I have to make me averse to the office of an executor. The striking example before me is sufficiently discouraging — but should there be an occasion for my acting, which I sincerely wish there may not from affection for you & your children[1] I am willing to act, and will endeavour to discharge my trust as much to the advantage of the children and with the same integrity my Father discharged a similar trust reposed in him — But I can not flatter my self my pains & trouble will be so amply rewarded as my Father's have been; for ransack the world and you will find few men of Digges sagacity & unsuspicious temper, or endued with the noble genorosity of a Hill.[2]

Things are pretty much in the same situation as when you left us. The Stamp Act[3] continues to make as much noise as ever — the spirit & discontent of the people rather encreases than diminishes — The Stamp Master of Boston has been obliged to resign his office: the house building there for the reception of the stamps has been levelled with the ground. Our stamp master Zacharia Hood[4] is hated & dispised by every one: he has been whipt pilloried & hung in effigy in this Place, Baltimore town & at the landing — the people seem determined not to buy his goods. His last dying speech has its humour — it contains, as most dying speeches, a succinct acct. of his birth & parentage & education — going from school he was bound apprentice to a Merchant noted for his skill in the exchange of money — some one of the crowd asked when the speech was read from the gallows who the Merchant was — the hangman replied old Nick —

The house hired by Hood for his stamps was pulled to the ground 2 nights ago — I have heared it was insured.

Our [e]vents move on heavily — John[so]n[5] has been very much out of order — he is now mending but is unable to do business: our petition has been over ruled — the adjourned Provincial Court is setting — the court in course sets next week. The small pox is entirely out of town. Yr. daughter Molly has been indisposed with a fever this week past, the fever has intermitted. She is now much better — enclosed you have her letter — I shall take care to make her write often. Give my love to Daniel & remember me to Cousin Jacky — All your relations & friends are well — Yr. humble servant holds it out bravely — I hope to escape the fever & agues this season at least — My father has sold all his Tobo. the Elk ridge[6] to Maverie[7] at 16/8 — the Potomack[8] to Stweart & Campbell[9] at 15/ and 4 per Ct. for Cask —

The little treatise on painting I desired you to get was wrote by Webb[10] — it is a thin duodecimo well known to all the book sellers' — should you meet with any other books (I mean of a late publication) entertaining & instructive you may purchase them for me — But do not put yourself to any trouble or inconvenience — The Philosophe bienfaisant wrote by King Stanislaus[11] is worth yr. reading — should you chance to meet with a correct Paris edition in yr. way, please to buy it for me — Pray do not neglect writing as often as you have an oportunity & let me know what success is likely to attend your principal design[12] — that you may meet with success in that and every other enterprise is the sincere wish — Dr. Daniel

of yr. affectionate Cousin & friend

Ch: Carroll

ALbDrS, CCC Letterbook, 1765–1768, MS 203.1, MdHi. Recipient noted by CC in letterbook.

1. Daniel Carroll III and Mary Carroll (1754–1784). See Appendix I, Chart J.

2. A reference to the involvement of Ignatius Digges and Clement Hill in the disagreement over CCA's administration of the estate of his brother Daniel Carroll of Duddington.

3. The Stamp Act, passed by the House of Commons on Feb. 27, 1765, by the House of Lords on Mar. 8, and scheduled to take effect on Nov. 1, constituted the first direct tax Parliament had ever levied on Great Britain's North American colonies and was intended to raise money for their defense. Initiated by George Grenville, the measure directed that revenue stamps, ranging in cost from a halfpenny to as much as ten pounds, be affixed to all commercial and legal documents, including newspapers, broadsides, almanacs, pamphlets, licenses, ship's papers, and even dice and playing cards. Penalties for noncompliance were to be meted out by British admiralty courts, where there was no trial by jury, and by American common-law courts. To mitigate colonial opposition, Grenville appointed Americans as stamp agents, but the gesture had no effect in stemming the outrage that erupted when the news of the statute's enactment reached the colonies in mid-April. Mobs and groups of men calling themselves Sons of Liberty formed in cities throughout colonial America to threaten stamp agents, attack the property of men in positions of royal authority, and seize

and burn the hated stamps. Merchants in New York, Philadelphia, and Boston stopped all trade with Great Britain, courts closed rather than use the stamps, and the American people in general simply refused to comply. With business virtually at a standstill by the time the Stamp Act took effect, British merchants also brought pressure to bear at home. The combination of American protests and British opposition persuaded Parliament to repeal the Stamp Act in March 1766.

4. Maryland's stamp distributor, Zachariah Hood (?-1789), an Annapolis merchant, was in England at the time of the Stamp Act's passage and received his commission before returning home. Upon his arrival in Annapolis, he became an object of constant abuse by the act's opponents. After the destruction of his warehouse, Hood fled to New York, where he was pursued by New York's Sons of Liberty, and went on to Long Island where he was found by a group of fifty "volunteers" who forced him to resign his post. Hood returned briefly to Maryland and then left for the West Indies, where he began an unsuccessful effort to gain compensation from Parliament for his losses. Ultimately, he received more sympathy from the Maryland assembly, which, in December 1766 at the insistence of Gov. Horatio Sharpe, voted him a reimbursement of one hundred pounds for the damage inflicted by the mob on his warehouse. Ronald Hoffman, *A Spirit of Dissension: Economics, Politics, and the Revolution in Maryland* (Baltimore, 1973), 51.

5. Thomas Johnson (1732-1819). The fifth child and second son of the dozen children born to Thomas Johnson of Calvert Co. and Dorcas Sedgewick Johnson, Thomas Johnson went to Annapolis as a young man to seek employment. Hired by Thomas Jennings, a register of the land office, Johnson also commenced the study of law with Stephen Bordley and rode the circuit with another politically ambitious lawyer, Samuel Chase. Elected in 1762 to represent Anne Arundel Co. in the lower house, Johnson retained his seat until 1774, when he commenced his Revolutionary career, serving as a member of Maryland's Committee of Correspondence, the first Council of Safety (1775), in each of the nine conventions (1774-1776), and as a delegate to the Continental Congress (1774-1776). Chosen the first governor of the state of Maryland (1777-1779), Johnson subsequently represented Frederick Co. in the House of Delegates (1780-1781 and 1786-1787), was chief judge of the general court (1790-1791), sat on the Board of Commissioners for the District of Columbia (1791-1794), and was an associate justice of the U.S. Supreme Court (1791-1793). From 1776 until his death, Johnson and his wife, Anne Jennings Johnson, whom he married in 1767, resided at Rose Hill in Frederick Co. Their family included three sons and four daughters. *Bio. Dic. Md. Legis.*, II, 495-496.

6. The Elk Ridge tobacco was the crop grown on Doohoragen Manor.

7. Maverie was probably a factor.

8. Tobacco produced by Carrollton Manor tenants and transported to the Prince George's Co. inspection station at the head of Rock Creek for inspection and marketing.

9. Merchants John Stewart (?-1771) and Duncan Campbell (?-by 1811) were active in the Maryland and Virginia trade. Price, *Johnson's Letterbook*, 179.

10. Daniel Webb (1719?-1798) was born in County Limerick, studied at Oxford, and was the author of several works on art. His study *An Inquiry into the Beauties of Painting* . . . was published in London in 1761.

11. Stanislaus Leszcynski (1677-1766), king of Poland (1704-1709, 1733-1735) and the father-in-law of Louis XV of France. Following his loss of the throne as a result of the War

of the Polish Succession, he was made duke of Lorraine and Bar, two duchies in eastern France, in 1738. His *OEuvres du philosophe bienfaisant* was published in Paris in 1763.

12. One of Daniel Carroll's objectives may have been the enrollment of his son at Bruges College, where Daniel Carroll III matriculated in 1766. Holt, *St. Omers,* 59.

∴·

CCC to William Graves

15 Sept[br]. 1[76]5

Dr. Graves,

I have at last had the satisfaction of recing a letter from you when I had almost begun to think you would verify the old Proverb out of sight out of mind — I did not finish the remdr of my Journey by land, because I had reasons to believe it would sooner be compleated by water, and with greater ease to myself: tis true I had cause to repent this resolution; but the hardshi[p]s of the Bay expedition now they are over, will as you observe, serve for an amusement hereafter — forsitan et hoc meminisse juvabit.[1] The gentleman who informed you of my Fathers having presented me with £40000 Cy. on my arrival was misinformed, or was willing to impose on you a piece of news of his own coining — not only 40000 pounds but the whole of my Father's estate is at my disposal we are and we like to continue, on the best terms, never Father & Son were on better. Matrimony is at present but little the subject of my thoughts, indeed I am uncertain wether I shall ever marry — unless I meet with a lady of good sense & good nature the sole consideration of getting an heir will not induce me to enter into an union in which the heart is to have but little or no part — such a close & tender tie should result from esteem & mutual love else they are likely to terminate in hatred & contempt; or at least in cool indifference — As to travelling in America besides that there is little worth a travellers notice, there is this disadvantage attending a long Journey — his affairs will suffer greatly in his absence: our estates differ much from yours — the income is never certain it depends upon the casual rise or fall in the price of Tobo. Few with us rent their lands & those who do receive the rents in Tobo.; not withstanding these disadvantages and some others more personal & applicable to myself my views reach not beyond the narrow limits of this province; so little is my ambition, or my bent to retirement so strong, that I am determined leaving all ambitious pursuits to confine my self to the improvement you recomd. of my parental acres: may I not enjoy as much happiness in this humble as in a more exalted station? Who so happy as an independent Man? And who more independent than a private gentleman[?]

[...][2] I agree with you to hoard up wealth by saving is a paultry means of [...] & yet without fear of falling under this censure I will frankly confess I do not intend, as you advise, to spend my annual income: to what purpose? to gain the esteem of men? Is not that esteem oftener forfeited than gained by spending — I am resolved to live as becomes a gentleman: to avoid every appearance of meaness, of prodigality & ostentation. I assure you I would not accept my Fathers estate upon condition of consuming the annual profits, in gaudy equipages, empty pomp & show and in company more empty than these.

Another argument against engaging in such an expensive and consequently dissipated life, is that I have no precedent to plead, & surely this will have its due weight with a lawyer. I should be loth to make the precedent my self: the gentlemen of this Province were never fond of expence & less now than ever; in these times of necessity and oppression it is a duty every man of fortune owes his country to set a example of frugality & industry to the common people: necessity, says the proverb, is the mother of invention, I may add, of industry too: the mistaken policy of England as I observed before will force us to be industrious: our inability while loaded with oppressive taxes to purchase yr. manufactures will oblige us to manufacture for ourselves: the worst of evils this, that can possibly befall England, the loss of liberty excepted: that indeed seems already lost or near expiring — Must we not think so when the guardians of liberty & the subjects' rights are the first to infringe them. That they may have been infringed by the late acts and more particularly by the Stamp Act is the general opinion of these colonies: not all the eloquence of Mansfield can persuade us that Englishmen by leaving their country to settle in these parts thereby lose the privileges of englishmen & the benefit of the Common Law: By that Law the most favourable to liberty we claim the invaluable privilege, that distinguishing Characteristick of the English constitution, of being taxed by our own representatives, to say & this has been said & insisted on [. . .][3] to the oppression the cruel mockery of our [understandings]. The Method you propose of the Parlt's. fixing the sum to be raised and leaving to the different goverts the ascertaining of the ways & means of levying their respective proportions will never be embraced by the Colonies unless they are constituted Judges of the necessity or even of the expediency of such levies. The different & indepdt govts would never agree in settling their quotas — each would endeavour to shift as much of the burthen from itself as possible: where then will you place the supreme & coercive power? In the Parlt of England? But then the same difficulty occurs & that Great constitutional maxim of granting supplies with our own consent would be equally violated: could we be said to grant freely & of our own consent when forced by a superior power? Whatever threats are thrown out or force employed to make the Americans as compliant as the Parlt, They will never depart from the essential right of internal taxation without which our property would be at the mercy of every rapacious minister: England restrains our trade she appoints our Governors, lays duties on our exports & imports & the exertion of this power or right as a necessary consequence of our dependence on the mother country has all along been admitted & acquiesed in by the colonies; t'was in that sense I admitted the propriety of her taxing us; that is disallowing drawbacks & emposing duties on our imports & exports from Grt Britain & Ireland—Nothing more was attempted while I was in England or I believe thought of at that time.

The preamble of the Stamp Act is as allarming as the Act itself; the sole reason given for passing it is because such & such duties had been granted to his Majesty the preceeding Sessions, thus they may go on ad infinitum: allowing this unbounded power in a set of men at so great a distance & so little acquainted with our circumstances & not immediately affected with the taxes laid upon us, what security remains for our property; that fence against arbitrary exactions? Are we to trust to the moderation of a British Parlt? Have we reason to rely solely on that? Men who have been so profuse & lavish of their constituents money will they be sparing of ours & better managers for strangers? The Stamp Act has taken away in part the trial by Juries: has curtailed the liberty of the Press: petitions, atho' the subject has an undoubted right to petition, were rejected with scorn on the frivolous pretence no petitions could be recd when the house had once gone upon a money Bill—do not these proceedins carry with them the strongest marks of despotism[?] You I know from yr. love of liberty detest them as much as we do: The Stamp master at Boston has been obliged to throw up his office: ours I imagin will follow his example or may repent it. The house building at Boston for the stamps, & the house in this place hired for the same use have been levelled with the ground: this spirit of opposition to Stamps, & stamp men, & stamp laws is diffused thro out the colonies from the cape of Florida to the land of Labrador—

I am much obliged to you for the Pamphlets. I am more interested than you imagin in yr. political parties & disputes;[4] at least I am very desirous of knowing what is going on in the Capital of the English empire. There was nothing in the Pamphlets but what I understood: should some passages occur in future Pamphlets so personal or local as to be obscure or unintelligible at this distance, a few marginal notes of yr. own might clear up the difficulty. I therefore beg you will continue to send me the most interesting Pamphlets[.] As I shall take the liberty to trouble you every now & then for books pray set down the prices of them & of the Pamphlets & send the acct. by yr. Servt. to Messrs. Perkins, B:[5] & Browne in Dolphin Court Tower street & it will be immediately discharged. In my last[6] I informed you I should if in my power employ Mr. Taylor: my Father never ships any Tobo. he finds it much more to his advantage to sell it here: I mention this because our factors chief profit is on the sale of the Tobo.[7] I suppose Mr. Taylor would be content with 2½ per Ct. commission on goods bought—for what we import for our own use may amount communibus annis to £500 sterling[.] Would so inconsiderable sum as £12..10 comon. on 500 answer Mr. Taylor's expectations? or be adequate to the trouble of buying the goods? We are fully convinced of being greatly imposed on by Our factors both in the quality & price of our goods: from Mr. Taylors known integrity & assiduity I am lead to think, should he engage in this business, that the goods will be well bot. This will enduce others to employ him: his Comon. will rise in proportion to the number of his Employers: and a Comon. on 1500 or £2000 is not to be overlooked: we shall remit Bills, others may do the Same or consign him their Tobo. As Mr. Tayler will always have ready money of ours in his hands we expect the usual dist. upon prompt payt. for the goods bought[.] But there occurs difficulty wh that gentleman is not perhaps aware of: Our factors are closely combined: tho hating & hated by each other they confederate to oppress us; conscious of their iniquity they will be desirous of concealing it or at least willing & united to oppose any one who attempts to detect or put a stop to their illicit practices: they will refuse to take on board their ships goods bot. by Mr. Tayler: but of this he is the best Judge, you may consult him on this subject & communicate his answer to me.

Yr. Jant to Switzerland I make no doubt has afforded you much pleasure, particularly as you travelled with such agreeable compy. I should have been tempted when so nigh Venice, to have made a visit to that city, but I suppose yr. time would not permit you to extend yr. excursions so far. Mr. Power is certainly an agreeable man, I am sorry on both yr. accts. that you are now deprived of his company & conversation as I am sure the loss of yours is equally felt by him. Pray remember me to my worthy & good friend Mr. Crookshanks: it gives me pain to hear he has been so much out of order, but now he is out of the reach of the Parliat. of Paris & at liberty to range about I hope he will recover his health apace: I desire my complts to the gentlemen of my acquaintance at the Crown & Anchor[8] — I am Dr. Graves

affectionately yours
Ch: Carroll of Carrollton[9]

ALbDrS, CCC Letterbook, 1765–1768, MS 203.1, MdHi. Recipient noted by CCC in letterbook. Top margin of fols. 1–3 damaged.

1. "Forsan et haec olim meminisse iuvabit" — "Perhaps one day it will please us to have remembered even these [trials]." Virgil Aeneid 1.203.

2. A line and three-quarters of the manuscript is missing.

3. One line missing.

4. CCC initially wrote and then struck out "squabbles."

5. Buchanan. Perkins, Buchanan, and Brown was a London mercantile firm.

6. Not found.

7. By the middle of the eighteenth century a large share of the tobacco trade was handled by resident factors who purchased the tobacco in the colonies and shipped it to European markets.

8. The Crown and Anchor in the Strand, a popular tavern where Samuel Johnson and James Boswell sometimes dined. Dorothy M. George, "London and the Life of the Town," in A. S. Turberville, ed., Johnson's England: An Account of the Life and Manners of His Age (London, 1952), I, 182.

9. This is the first surviving letter where CCC used the appellation "of Carrollton." He continued the practice, with only a few early exceptions, for the rest of his life.

CCC to Christopher Chapman Bird

28: Septbr. 1765

Dr. Xtopher,

I wrote to you last July or some time thereabouts & inclosed a letter to my good & worthy friend Mr. Fentham,[1] wh I hope are both come to hand[2] — A month ago I received a Parmesan cheeze, wh I have not yet opened, and the newspapers[3] — I am much obliged to you for both, but desire you will not for the future be at the trouble of taking in the Papers — They should be sent by every opportunity & there are many oportunities wh from the little connection you have with this country, you cannot possibly be informed of in time[.] Papers of a late date afford us entertainment, those of 2 or 3 month's standing are not more entertaining than those of 2 year's past: I have desired Mr Perkins to send us the Magazines & Papers for the future — I was a little disappointed in not receiving a letter with the cheeze; such a neglect in a Merchant I think inexcusable, in a friend almost unpardonable: this accompanies 6 wild turkies for yr. Father & a flying squirrel for yr. Aunt Esther: I hope I shall be able to procure a mocking Bird by next fall —

Our Provincial Court & assembly are setting: before you receive this, you will learn from the papers that a committee of deputies from the different assemblies or Parliaments of the Colonies is to meet at New york the first of Octbr. to draw up a petition agt. the stamp act & to advise & consult, about such measures as they shall think most conducive to the general good & prosperity of their country:[4] Our assembly has appointed three to attend the congress:[5] £500 Cy. has been voted to defray their expences with proviso to receive more if necessary, & to account for the surplus. Most of the Stamp [Stributors?] have resigned their offices; id est[6] have been obliged to throw up their dirty employments: Our Stamp Man from servile instrument of oppression is become an object of pity & contempt: he has withdrawn himself from the just resentment of his fellow citizens & forsook this his native country wh he dared not, though willing, to oppress: I should be more full & circumstantial but I doubt not the London prints will make you acquainted with the minutest transactions: I can only say with Portius, the dawn is overcast, the morning lowers & heavily brings on the day — big with the fate of — Liberty.[7]

In prose should the stamp Act be enforced by a tyrannical soldiery our property, our liberty, our very existence are at an end — and you may be persuaded, nothing but an armed force can execute the worst of Laws. Thus you see how necessary it is at this critical juncture to have cool, dispassionate, condescending men at the helm — It is sometimes with Governments as with private men, they obstinately persevere from resentment & passion in measures, which unbiassed reason would condemn.

By this I hope you are Father and that you still think matrimony the happiest state of life[8] — but tell me, now the honey moon is over, (dont read this to yr. wife) what are yr. real sentiments of that sweet slavery: is the way strewed over with flowers? Are there not some thorns & sharpe ones too? Two hearts united in tender, simpathetick feelings, endearments, mutual compliance, & condescention, are not all these the rant of Poets the language of heated imaginations, or do they exist in real life? I suppose they are exagerated: the sweets of matrimony are blended no doubt with the bitters — nor is any state or condition of life exempted from its share of evil. I am single, have a great fortune, enjoy my health tollerably well, my desires are far from being unbounded & yet there is still something wanting — I have too good a memory or too much sensibility: the love of retirement growes upon me — even melancholy pleases[.]

Remember me in the kindest manner to yr. Father & Aunt & to Mr. Fentham — Assure Mr. Chapman of my esteem & present my compliments to all who have not yet forgot me & Believe me to be Dr. Xtophr

yr. sincere friend
C: Carroll of Carrollton.

s:s:

Be pleased to send me as many of the statutes as are published and get them bound in the same manner as law-books are generally bound — You have my subscription receipt: Perkins will repay you.

ALbDrS, CCC Letterbook, 1765–1768, MS 203.1, MdHi.

1. Possibly the English Jesuit Henry Fentham of Nottinghamshire who studied at St. Omers from 1753 to 1756 and entered the novitiate at Watten. Holt, *St. Omers*, 99; Henry Foley, ed., *Records of the English Province of the Society of Jesus* . . . (London, 1877–1883), VI, 498.

2. Letters not found.

3. Preceding "newspapers," CCC wrote and then struck out "London."

4. The Stamp Act Congress met in New York City in October 1765, with four colonies — North Carolina, Virginia, Georgia, and New Hampshire — declining to send representatives. The consensus of the meeting was embodied in the Declaration of Rights and Grievances, written largely by Pennsylvania delegate John Dickinson, for submission to the king, Lords, and Commons. The document asserted that, since the colonists were not and could not be represented in Parliament, the only constitutional taxes that could be levied on them were those imposed by colonial legislatures. The congress also drafted petitions demanding repeal of the Stamp Act and other objectionable measures passed by Parliament.

5. Maryland's delegates to the Stamp Act Congress were Edward Tilghman, William Murdock (c. 1710–1769), and Thomas Ringgold (1715–1772). Murdock, a Prince George's Co. merchant, served in the lower house from 1749 until his death; Ringgold, a Kent Co. attorney and a merchant, served there from 1761 until 1770. *Arch. of Md.*, LIX, 21; *Bio. Dic. Md. Legis.*, I, 59–63, II, 606–607, 694–695.

6. "That is."

7. CCC adapted these lines from Joseph Addison's popular play *Cato: A Tragedy:*

The dawn is overcast; the morning lowers,
And heavily in clouds brings on the day,
The great, the important day, big with fate
   of Cato, and of Rome. (1.1)

8. Christopher Chapman Bird married Anne Webbe, a distant relation of Sir Thomas Webb. Burke and Burke, *Landed Gentry of Great Britain and Ireland,* II, 876.

· · ·
· ·

A Fragment of a Letter by CCC to Unknown

<u>September</u> 30, 1765.

Nothing can overcome the aversion of the people to the Stamp Act, and their love of liberty, but an armed force; and that, too, not a contemptible one.

To judge from the number of the colonists, and the spirit they have already shown, and which I hope to God will not fail them on the day of trial, twenty thousand men would find it difficult to enforce the law; or, more properly speaking, to ram it down our throats. Can England, surrounded with powerful enemies, distracted with intestine factions, encumbered and almost staggering under the immense load of debt—little short of one hundred and fifty million pounds— send out such a powerful army to deprive a free people, their fellow-subjects, of their rights and liberties? If ministerial influence and parliamentary corruption should not blush at such a detestable scheme; if Parliament, blind to their own interest, and forgetting that they are the guardians of sacred liberty, and of our happy constitution, should have the impudence to avow this open infraction of both, will England, her commerce annihilated by the oppression of America, be able to maintain those troops?

The absurdities of such an attempt are so glaring, the evil consequences so obvious, that unless a general frenzy has seized the whole English nation, I cannot suppose that a measure will be adopted which will inevitably end in the ruin of the English Empire.

At a moderate computation, the inhabitants of these continental colonies amount to two million five hundred thousand; and, in twenty years' time, as propagation increases in proportion to the means of an easy subsistence, the number will be doubled; reflect on the immense ocean that divides this fruitful country from the island whose power, as its territory is circumscribed, has already arrived at its zenith, while the power of this continent is growing daily, and in time will be as unbounded as our dominions are extensive. The rapid increase of manufactures surpasses the expectations of the most sanguine American.

Even the arts and sciences commence to flourish, and in these, as in arms, the day, I hope, will come when America will be superior to all the world. Without prejudice or partiality, I do not believe the universe can show a finer country — so luxuriant in its soil; so happy in a healthy climate; so extensively watered by so many navigable rivers, and producing within itself not only all the necessaries, but even most of the superfluities of life.

A great many gentlemen have already appeared in homespun, and I hope soon to make one of the number.

Many imagine the Stamp Act will be suspended for a time, till some expedient may be hit on to reconcile the exemption we claim from a parliamentary taxation with the right and power asserted of late by the Parliament. If the act be suspended until such an expedient can be found, it will be suspended for all eternity.

PT, J. C. Carpenter, "Historic Houses of America: Doughoregan Manor, and Charles Carroll of Carrollton," *Appletons' Journal,* XII (Sept. 12, 1874), 323. No manuscript version found.

. . .
.

CCC to Perkins, Buchanan, and Brown

5 Octbr. 1765

Gent,

I have wrote to Mr. Gordon[1] a gentleman of my acquaintance to desire him to buy me a couple of brood Mares: he is to apply to you for the money: I have limited a price Mr. Gordon is not to exceed 35 guineas for each: but as he is a gentleman of honour and I can place a thorough confidence in him, pay whatever sum the price of the Mares will amount to. When they are bot. you will have timely notice given to look out for a proper ship: this trouble will entirely fall upon you, and I beg they may be entrusted to some careful Captain: Pray endeavour to procure a groom to take care of them on the passage: such a one will be absolutely necessary & may be had at any of the livery stables in London and engaged to undertake the voya. on very moderate terms; if he understands his business, he need not fear of meeting with good encouragement in this country:

The enclosed paper[2] will serve to direct you in providing all necessaries for the Mares: but double the quantity of oats water hay &c must be laid in, as there will be two mares, and the inclosed calculation is only for one which was sent sometime ago to Mr. Tasker and you will observe was bought for £25. Give the Capt. particular instructions to fill the Butts at the last Port — you must provided against a long Passage by laying in sufficient Provender & water for 12 weeks at least — The Mares should never be put into slings but in very bad weather, they ought to stand in the hold upon fine shingle ballast & have room enough to lay down. Other necessary considerations may occur to you.

This goes with Capt. Heyton;[3] by him I have sent 6 wild turkies & a flying squirrel to Mr. Bird, which I desire you will order to be delivered with the in[c]losed letter for that gentleman: the french letter is to be forwarded to Bourdeaux:

The greatest confusion will ensue from the late impolitical & arbitrary stamp Act: It is the general opinion no business will be done after the first of Novembr. when that act is to take place: the people are so enraged, that they will, ti's thought, proceed to the greatest lengths, even to the burning of the stamps: should the stamps be burnt all law proceedins & indeed every other business will be at stand: trade will suffer most & consequently the Merchants who trade with America: in my opinion they deserve to suffer & to feel the effects of an act which they ought to have petitioned against, nor is it any excuse or extenuation of their neglect to say their petition would have been ineffectual: their own interest if not the interest of their employers, which I am sorry to say, seem to be two very distinct & seperate interests, should have induced them to exert the same vigour, which they shewed on former occasion in opposition to a powerful minister & to an act not half so destructive of liberty as the present & wh would have proved very beneficial to the provinces of Maryland & Virginia:[4] Pray present my complts. to Mr. Jo: Perkins & to Mr. Eure[.] I am gent,

yr. most: obed: hum: Sevant

C:C: of Carrollton

ALbDrS, CCC Letterbook, 1765–1768, MS 203.1, MdHi. Recipient confirmed by subsequent correspondence.

1. Lockhart Gordon (1732–1788), the youngest brother of the earl of Aboyne. *Debrett's Peerage of the United Kingdom of Great Britain and Ireland,* 18th ed. (London, 1829), II, 584–585.

2. Not found.

3. Probably Richard Hayton, master of the *Trotman.* Annapolis Port of Entry Record Books, I, MS 21, MdHi.

4. Probably a reference to the excise bill of 1733, a measure proposed by Robert Walpole to curtail smuggling and streamline the collection of duties on imports to be consumed within Great Britain. Walpole wished to add tobacco and wine — routinely smuggled into England in large quantities — to the list of imports required to enter the country through bonded warehouses under the jurisdiction of salaried excise inspectors. This aroused the ire of London merchants, who condemned the scheme as a tyrannical extension of government and joined with Walpole's political opponents to force him to withdraw the bill. Chesapeake planters might have benefited from passage of the excise bill because a curtailment of smuggling would have raised the price of tobacco. Derek Jarrett, *Britain, 1688–1815* (New York, 1965), 191–195.

. . . .
.

CCC to Thomas Bradshaw[1]

21: Novenbr. 1765

Dr. Bradshaw,

I have taken up my pen more with a view of apologizing for my long silence & the best apology for it is to brake it than induced by the importance or novelty of any thing I have to say: 15 months & more are now elapsed since we parted at St. Albans[2] in wh space of time there has been no thing ocurred that deserves yr. notice or a place in this letter but what you already know: the proceedings of these colonies & their civil officers created by a late arbitrary & unconstitutional Act, their unamity & spirited opposition to measures destructive of all liberty & property are now become a matter of public concern & notoriety: I therefore refer you to the news papers & Pamphlets writen on this subject for full information for it would swell this letter to an extraordinary size, were I to enter upon a topick which now engrosses the fears, the thoughts & the conversation of all men on this continent: if you are any ways curious or desirous to enter into the merits of a cause, the most important & interesting & of the utmost consequence to the British Empire, I must reccommend to you a Pamphlet lately published in this province entitled the Claim of the colonies from an exemption of taxes &c considered[3] — it is wrote with that strength & solidity of argument as must convince the understanding of the unprejudiced; & with that elegance & beauty of style as can not fail pleasing good judges & men of taste.

I have seen Mrs. Lee[4] but twice or thrice since her arrival[.] She has brought with her, her good nature & her oddities: these have not escaped censure; her dress was criticised by the ladies — & I think with reason, it was quite what the french call outré.[5] Yr. acquaintances here are all well: Lee[6] as fat as indolent, & as good natured as ever: Key[7] as fond of company if his business would permit him to indulge his inclination: however the love of money seems at last to ballance the love of mirth & ease: if his health will admit of close application to his business, he will soon have more than any Lawyer in this Province: & I really wish he may meet with no interruption from sickness: We often when a little older have too much reason to repent the irregularities of our youth. As to yr. humble Servant he is much as you left him, as thin, as easy & as sincere & unalterable in his friendship — still a Batchelor & likely to remain so, not from any fixed purpose, or former disappointment, but merely from indifference. At our years the passions grow cooler, & our reason generally operates the stronger in proportion to the abatement of youthfull heat: a man of common sense at 28, is well convinced or ought to be of the emptiness of that passion wh exists nowhere no where but in romance and in chusing a wife he will not chuse a meer mistress; an agreeable, sweet tempered sensible companion would certainly or should be his choice. If he marries he will marry from affection, from esteem, & from a sense of merit in his wife whom he will look upon in a better light than a meer bedfellow—it is indeed a misfortune too common that the generality of women neglect to improve their understandings; their whole time being taken up in emptiness, at best in adorning & setting off to advantage their charms: they do not reflect that those in the eyes of the world have but a few years to last, & in the eyes of a husband but as few months & good nature, & Good sense, improved by reflection, by reading by the conversation of men of sense are the only means to secure the affection of a husband & to perpetuate that empire, wh beauty first established: what more dreadfull, what more irksome than to be linked for life to a dull, insipid companion, whose whole conversation is confined to the colours & fashions of her dress, the empty chit chat of tea table, or to the salting of hogs—Nor would I be understood to insinuate that the domestic cares & charge of a family are beneath the notice & dignity of wife: our attention to such duties as fall to the share of a mistress of a family, far from being derogatory, would do honour to a lady in the highest station:[8] But I have dwelt too long upon this subject, & you may think my observations if not impertinent at least tedious & common: I acknowledge them to be common & from thence I conclude them to be just: if there is nothing new or diverting in the manner, it is purely owing to the inability & dullness not to the inclination of the penner who would not if he could help it tire his friend: however you are under no obligation of reading this thro' & whenever you begin to be weary throw it aside or into the fire.

I had almost forgot to tell that Mrs. Lee is pretty far gone with child[9] it seems she is desirous of making up lost time: she informs me, but I pay little regard to her intelligence, that you have met with a disappointment in love: & that yr. resentment or love was so great that the Lady's refusal forced tears from you—This part of the story is not at all probable & made me discredit the whole—but if there should be any truth in it, I wish you better success in your next attempt. Pray present my compliments to Mr. Russel's family & to the Clerks.[10]

The climate [here][11] is delightful particularly the Autumn: the weather is now as mild & serene as it generally is in England in August & Septbr. Many who have travelled thro' the colonies give the preference to Maryland, both in point of climate & the fertility of its soil & the sociability of its in[h]abitants: As the English Constitution is hastening to its final period of dissolution & the symptoms of a general decay are but too visible, I advise you to sell yr. estate in England, & to purchase lands in this province where liberty will maintain her empire, till a dissoluteness of more luxury & venality shall have prepared the degenerate sons of some future age, to prefer their own mean lucre & the bribes & the smiles of corrupting & arbitrary ministers, to the true patriotismn & to true glory & to the publick weal—no doubt the same causes will produce the same effects & a period is already set to the reign of American freedom—but that fatal term seems to be at a great distance—the present generation at least & I hope many succeeding ones in spight of a corrupt Par-t will enjoy the blessings & the sweets of liberty—but should you not care to follow my advice & become an inhabitant of this country that you may not survive the loss of it in yr. own is the wish of one who has the prosperity of both at heart and desires to be ranked not only in the number of the friends of freedom but of yours—

C: Carroll

P:S:

I shall be much obliged to you for two couple of the slow Kentish beagles: two dogs & two bitches: if you can procure such (& I apply to you as a sportsman) be pleased to send them early in April to Mr. Perkins & Co in Dolphin court Tower street, who will reimburse any c[h]arge or expence you may be put to in executing this important commission.

ALbDrS, CCC Letterbook, 1765–1768, MS 203.1, MdHi.

1. Thomas Bradshaw (1733–1774), of Hampton Court, Middlesex, served as chief clerk at the Treasury (1761–1763), as a Member of Parliament (1768–1774), and at the time of his death was a lord of the Admiralty. Lewis Namier and John Brooke, *The House of Commons, 1754–1790* (New York, 1964), II, 110–111; Gerrit P. Judd, *Members of Parliament, 1734–1832* (New Haven, Conn., 1955), 128.

2. A city located some twenty miles northwest of London.

3. [Daniel Dulany], *Considerations on the Propriety of Imposing Taxes in the British Colonies, for the Purpose of Raising a Revenue, by Act of Parliament,* printed anonymously in October 1765 by Jonas Green. CCC appears to have confused its title with that of a pamphlet by William Knox, *The Claim of the Colonies to an Exemption from Internal Taxes Imposed by Authority of Parliament, Examined . . . ,* published in London earlier in the year and arguing the opposite point of view. "Daniel Dulany's 'Considerations,'" *Md. Hist. Mag.,* VI (1911), 374–375; Lawrence C. Wroth, *A History of Printing in Colonial Maryland, 1686–1776* (Baltimore, 1922), 224.

4. Ann Russell Lee.

5. "Extreme."

6. Philip Thomas Lee.

7. Edmund Key.

8. CCC's first version of this letter to Bradshaw contained these sentiments about women and matrimony: "Love only & esteem should in my opinion be the sole inducements to make a man give up his liberty, wh with all its boasted privileges I would resign if my heart & my reason would jointly point out where the [surrender?] might be made: in plain english reason & love must direct my choice—The American ladies in purity of manners may safely be pronounced equal to the English, in beauty I fear many would be thought as most inferior, they want that delightful bloom wh the Poet compares to the blended whiteness of the lily with the blushing rose, so conspicuously displayed in the complexion of english Virgins—and surpassing all description: the most material obj[ecti]on to matrimony is the danger of being linked for ones life with a dull companion; a man of

sense will soon be satiated with charms, wh free & easy enjoyment renders familiar & less pleasing: then are the arts of a mistress to be laid aside or sparingly used & the charms of conversation be substituted to those of beauty, to prolong its empire wh otherways will be of short duration." CCC Letterbook, 1765–1768, MS 203.1, MdHi.

9. Although the Lees eventually had five children—four daughters born between 1767 and 1772 and a son born in 1776—Mrs. Lee did not carry this pregnancy to term. See CCC to Bradshaw, Aug. 26, 1766, below.

10. The Clerks were merchants from the same area of southwestern Scotland as James Russell. In December 1757 Thomas Clerk (1722–1770), a partner in the London house of Innes and Clerk, married Russell's daughter Sarah. Clerk had established his own firm by 1763. His younger brother, Duncan Clerk (1731–1791), was a merchant in Lisbon and London. Jacob M. Price, "One Family's Empire: The Russell-Lee-Clerk Connection in Maryland, Britain, and India, 1707–1857," *Md. Hist. Mag.*, LXXII (1977), 179–180.

11. Possibly struck out.

. . .

CCC to Edmund Jenings

23 Novr. 1765

Dr. Jenings,

I wish this letter may be as welcome as I think it will be unexpected: if it should be welcome it will excuse its not coming sooner & if unwelcome it comes too soon: the first thing I suppose you will be desirous to know, is how I like the country: the climate is certainly upon the whole much preferable to yours: the heats of the summer are indeed dangerous & disagreeable to persons who are obliged to expose themselves to the sun but a few days excepted are very supportable to one in my situation who can confine himself to his house: As to the people, you know they do not want understanding nor the use of it: the common sort & indeed the better (be it spoken between friends) have not that same opinion of strict justice & integrity & least do not pay that regard to it in their dealings, which I could wish for their honour & for their advantage: there is a mean low dirty envy which creeps thro' all ranks & can not suffer a superiority of fortune, of merit or of understanding in a fellow citizen: either of these are sure to entail a general ill will & dislike upon the owner: my fortune will certainly make me an object of envy, but I do not think myself in any danger from a superiority of merit or of understanding: we have political parties amongst us but they are too trivial & of too little consequence for me to relate or you to hear: I shall only observe, they seem to me to spring from the same source yr. factions have theirs: the want of a sufficient number of lucrative offices to gratify the avarice or the ambition of the Outs.

But indeed our political quarrels are now forgot or lay dormant while the dread of the Stamp Act continues, & the common danger out weighs private concerns. You are too well acquainted with the english constitution & the Interests of America not to see what a fatal blow both have received from that & other late injudicious & arbitrary Acts: I shall not therefore make any comment upon those measures: their dangerous tendency is obvious and the consequences too dreadful of submitting to a Parliamentary taxation — I will not presume to fix bounds & to circumscribe the power of Parliament: but certainly bounds must be fixed & there are certain known fundamental laws essential to & interwoven with the English constitution wh even a Parliament itself can not abrogate: such I take to be that allowed maxim of the constitution that invaluable privilege the birth[right] of englishmen of being taxed with their own consenst: the definition of freedom is the being governed by laws to which we have given our consent, as the definition of slavery is the very reverse: but I am imperceptibly sliding into a subject which will lead me too far & which on that very account I would purposely avoid — If you have a mind to see the claim of the Colonies from an exemption of taxes laid by Authority of Parliament, fairly stated, fully discussed, & asserted with great solidity & strength of argument, I must refer you to a Pamphlet of Dulanys bearing much such a title; & of which many copies have been transmitted to London, & I make no doubt one to you by Mr. Brice:[1]

The Merchants at New York & Philadelphia have come to a resolution not to send for any more goods of the manufacture & growth of Grt. Britain, & to contradict the orders already given, till a repeal of the Stamp Act is obtained:[2] this resolution will in my humble opinion avail us more than petitioning: for as Mr. Dulany well observes should the people of England be so deaf as not hear & be moved with our complaints or so blind as not to see the effects of this industry, they will not be so callous as not to feel them. I had almost forgot to mention that our Stamp [man reported here that, partly thro' your means and solicitation, he obtained his odious office; indeed I never gave credit to the report, and thought he only made use of your name to palliate his crime: for surely a friend to liberty, an American born, would never solicit an office which would destroy the existence of the one and consequently the privileges of the other. Pray present my compliments to Mr. Gray whom I esteem as a man of merit and worth, tho' perhaps no fast friend to this country, as having a large share of property in the Islands for whose interest acts have been passed diametrically opposite to ours. All your acquaintances here are well except Mr. Key: he seems to be in a dangerous way and I understand Doctor Hamilton[3] has been sent for, which he seldom is but in cases of extremity and danger: I have nothing more material to add but to conclude with assuring you that I am Dear Jennings,

Your friend
Charles Carroll of Carrollton

by which appellation, if you favour me with an answer, direct to me your letter.]

ALbDr, CCC Letterbook, 1765–1768, MS 203.1, MdHi. Final page missing and supplied, in brackets, from Field, *Carroll,* 100.

1. John Brice III (1738–1820), son of John Brice II and Edmund Jenings's stepsister, Sarah Frisby. *Bio. Dic. Md. Legis.,* I, 165–166.

2. The New York merchants were the first to adopt nonimportation. On Oct. 31, 1765, they met and agreed to include instructions with orders for British goods directing that if the Stamp Act were not repealed, all orders, both current and previous, would be countermanded. The Philadelphia merchants followed suit on Nov. 7. Merrill Jensen, *The Founding of a Nation: A History of the American Revolution, 1763–1776* (New York, 1968), 129.

3. Possibly John Hamilton (1697–1768), a Calvert Co. physician. Newman, *Early Families,* II, 419; Barnes, *Marriages and Deaths,* 78; Eugene Fauntleroy Cordell, *The Medical Annals of Maryland, 1799–1899* (Baltimore, 1903), 655.

· · ·
·

CCC to Daniel Carroll

17 March, 1766.

Dear Daniel,

Your Letters of the 27 November and 21 December[1] are come to hand, both which I answer in this: nothing but a great regard for you and your children, and a confidence that from the example [?] they would be grateful, could have induced me in compliance with the request to engage to act as your Executor, however remote the possibility might be of my undertaking that so unwelcome and melancholy office.

When you write to your Brother remember me to him in the most affectionate manner: and give my love to Danny.

We are still uncertain of our fate, and as men under such a dreadful uncertainty are generally forming conjectures, as either their fear, or their hopes preponderate, so our conjectures are various on the proceedings of this Session, according to the different disposition of sanguine or desponding men. Hope in general outbalances fear: and most are of opinion that the Act will be repealed—of this I am, I must confess, myself—and if the resolutions of the Parliament are not guided by resentment, or by the heat of party and private, interested views, but should flow from the dictates of cool reasoning and good policy, no thinking man can once doubt what will be the result of their debates.

Many imagine the Act will be suspended for a time, till some expedient may be hit on to reconcile the exemption we claim from a Parliamentary taxation, with that right and power so impolitically asserted of late by the Parliament: if the Act should be suspended till such an expedient can be found out, it will be suspended for all eternity: unless indeed the Parliament should be content with resolving they have such a right and never attempt to carry it into execution; but in that case, it is more probable that immediately on passing this resolve, they will repeal the Stamp Act: since the leaving that odious Law suspended and hanging over our heads, like an immense ruin ready to fall and crush us to atoms by its weight, will only increase the apprehensions and ill humour of the colonists, and confirm in them a habit of industry and manufacturing which nothing but oppression could have lead them into and perhaps nothing but a prospect of the same returning upon them once more, will be able to keep up. What! will the solid advantages of a most profitable, extensive trade, be given up to an empty point of honour? will the very being of Great Britain be hazarded for a thing so unsubstantial? A vote of the House of Commons asserting their right to tax the colonies, without an intention to enforce it, deserves no better appellation: and intention or resolution to enforce it, are much worse. The wisdom of the English Senate hath been much applauded — and times of faction and tumult excepted, equally famed for equity and moderation. These motives joined with a motive still more powerful, their own interest, which they are too clear sighted not to see, will all strongly operate in favour of America.

The clamour of the People out of doors proceeds from their ignorance, prejudice and passion: it is very difficult to get the better of these by reasoning: we have a much more persuasive and shorter argument and better fitted to their capacities than reasons drawn from the principles of government and from our own in particular, an argument rather levelled at their pockets than understandings which may indeed greatly contribute by emptying of those to open these: We have nothing to do but hold our tongues, be frugal, industrious, and cloath ourselves; our linen and woolen drapers, who affect to be our sovereigns, will cool, when the fumes occasioned by too much eating and drinking, have had time to disappear; those haughty manners so unbecoming of fellow subjects and so ungratefully thrown out, they will then own [?] against a people from whom they draw their chief subsistence. Your account of the debates in the House of Commons was very entertaining; the remark of the member who was to gladen his constituents' hearts with the views of no monies to be raised, made us all laugh. Jonas Green [2] has the letter, and intends to inset some extracts he has made out of it in his newspaper.[3] I am not in the least surprised at your being disappointed with the speakers, I am doubtful indeed whether you were really disappointed. You must have been too well acquainted with the Parliament, matters and men, to expect any Ciceros or Demostheneses. Mr. Jordan [4] is not yet arrived, I wish he was, that I might have my books and satisfy my curiosity, for you have raised it not a little by the account you have given me of the man: you say he has a considerable influence with the Proprietary: from whence is his influence derived? the scandalous Chronicle here says from the charms of his wife: it was even hinted that the sending him here was only a scheme to get him out of the way: but his Lady's coming with him seems to destroy that report.

In my last of the 22 December [5] I informed you of the breaking up of our Assembly in an angry and discontented temper, of a scheme which had been formed for emitting Bills of credit to the amount of £50000, the amount of the publick debt, and how that scheme was prevented by the miscarriage of the Journal, by the house insisting that Mr. Ross' claim as clerk of the council be inserted in it.[6] If you have any doubt about the Justice of that claim, when you have read the messages between the houses on that subject, your doubts will be entirely removed. The Messages of the upper house were penned by Daniel Dulany. Their spirit and poignancy must have disgusted our Patriots: that gentleman is growing unpopular; it was given out that he had promised under hand, the Journal would pass. I do not believe it: his conduct in this affair, has been uniform and he seems to have made, for once, a sacrifice of popularity to principle: a Pamphlet of his is now in the press: the intent of it is to undeceive the People who have been too long deluded with false representations maliciously thrown out against the Clerk's claim.[7]

Franklin,[8] I hear, has miscarried in his design of a change of government; his disappointment will check the career and thwart the views of some men in this province, who tho' they have less understanding, have the same disposition to gratify their own private resentment, ambition, or avarice, at the publick expense.

You may probably have heared of the association of the "Sons of Liberty" at New York. Letters said to be written by some of those Sons were sent to Mr. Lund[9] of Baltimore town proposing such an association there. The gentlemen readily come into it: the letters were communicated to Paca[10] and Chase,[11] who were to solicit an coalition of the inhabitants of Annapolis with the Sons of Liberty of Baltimore. The first step was to open the public offices immediately to proceed with business as usual. The letters from New York were produced and publicly shewn on the hill, when the whole town was assembled; the subscribers were men of little note; some expressions were very unguarded, to say no more. The scheme of opening the offices seemed to the most thinking men of the town, improper at that juncture. We had felt the inconvenience from a suspension of public business, and knew them, however grievous, not insupportable. It was but waiting a few weeks longer, when we had reason to expect very favourable accounts from England; it was time to act desperately, when our affairs were desperate; should force be used to carry the act into execution, there was little prospect of its being opposed with any success: these reasons urged by the principal gentlemen of the town had the desired effect. Nothing was concluded on: the Friday following this meeting, which was on the Wednesday, the Sons of Liberty from Baltimore town arrived in this city. They were for opening the offices immediately; the townspeople appointed a committee to confer with them; at last it was concluded that the offices should be opened by the 1st of April, if they were opened sooner to the Northward. A committee of the Sons of Liberty was named to desire the officers to open their offices on that day and to insist on written answers to their request: their answers were printed in Green's paper; I think them very unsatisfactory—however, they satisfied the Sons of Liberty, who were on this occasion more easily satisfied than they usually are: The next day they returned to Baltimore: the officers of whom answers were required, were Daniel Dulany, Brice, and Dr. Stewart.[12]

You have herewith a copy of the genealogy you desired. This, I imagine, will meet you in London on your return from Ireland, unless a prospect of succeeding in your business should detain you in that Island longer than you at first intended. Be pleased to call upon Mr. Bird in White Friars, just behind the Temple: he will be extremely glad to see you as a relation and friend of mine: his sister is a most amiable and deserving woman, for whom I shall ever entertain the sincerest friendship and I desire you will inform her of these my sentiments. I left a subscription ticket for the statutes with Mr. Bird's son: I have wrote to him to send in the volumes which are already published — and I should be obliged to you for bringing with you the remaining volumes.

This letter is already too long, but as I am writing to you, I neither think the time or trouble lost: the most trivial occurences to one at that distance and so generally acquainted with the inhabitants of this Province, must be entertaining. For this reason I am going to communicate the following intelligence, which may properly without any derogation to the persons concerned be ranked on that head. Dr. Thompson [13] has quarrelled with Clt Hill on his divulging a conversation of Thompson's, at his own house: a challenge was given — but the peacemaker of Mallborough, Justice Hepburn,[14] interfered and prevented the consequences of such a duel. Thompson being tied up from avenging himself of his Antagonist, a reflection on the Roman Catholics and a high chained compliment to Daniel Dulany single combat [?] had recourse to his pen. He published longer letters filled with sarcasms on Hill's tatling disposition, his ignorance, and illiterateness, with his own sentiments on the Stamp Act.[15]

This affair is now almost forgot. Thompson and Weldon have lately had a battle: Weldon was drunk, and he has received a gash in his face with a hanger which will ever remind him of his indiscretion: nothing else occurs to me at present; perhaps something may before I have an opportunity of sending this:

PT, Field, *Carroll*, 108–114. The letterbook drafts of the letters that CCC wrote between Nov. 23, 1765, and May 27, 1766, were stolen from the MdHi in the late 1960s. Transcriptions of this correspondence appear in the seriously flawed Field, *Carroll*, edition and include CCC to Thomas Bradshaw, Dec. 8, 1765, CCC to Daniel Carroll (incorrectly identified by Field as Daniel Barrington), Dec. 22, 1765, CCC to Christopher Bird, Dec. [30], 1765, and CCC to Daniel Carroll (again incorrectly identified by Field as Barrington), Mar. 17, 1766. Although textually suspect, CCC's letter of Mar. 17, 1766, as presented in Field's collection, is reproduced here because it suggests CCC's attitudes concerning popular protest and provides information about Maryland politics during the Stamp Act disturbances.

1. Not found.

2. Jonas Green (1712–1767). A member of the third generation of a family of New England printers, Jonas Green served as an apprentice to his father, Timothy Green, the official

printer of the government of Connecticut, before moving in 1735 to Philadelphia, where he worked for both Benjamin Franklin and Andrew Bradford. In May 1738, a month after he wed Anne Catherine Hoof, Green moved to Annapolis to succeed William Parks as printer to the government of Maryland. Although government imprints such as the proceedings of the general assembly and editions of session laws composed his main livelihood, Green also published the *Md. Gaz.* from 1745 until his death. Politically conservative, he reported anti–Stamp Act speeches and the actions taken against Zachariah Hood in the spring of 1765 and produced Daniel Dulany's pamphlet *Considerations of the Propriety of Imposing Taxes in the British Colonies,* but he avoided a decision about printing on stamped or unstamped paper by suspending publication of the *Gazette* between Oct. 10, 1765, and March 1766. Although his status as a craftsman denied him entry into the socially elite ranks to which he aspired, Green joined the Tuesday Club, the literary society founded by Dr. Alexander Hamilton, in 1748, and he was a member of the Annapolis Common Council and a city alderman. His marriage produced fourteen children, eight of whom died young. Barbara J. Little, "Ideology and Media: Historical Archaeology of Printing in Eighteenth-Century Annapolis, Maryland" (Ph.D. diss., State University of New York, Buffalo, 1987), 118–132.

3. The *Md. Gaz.* of Mar. 13, 1766, published extracts from "very warm debates in the House of Commons about the Answer to the King's Speech" derived from a letter dated London, Dec. 21, 1765.

4. Virginian John Morton Jordan (?–1771) emigrated to London to become a tobacco merchant. There he earned the favor of Frederick Calvert, sixth Lord Baltimore, who sent Jordan to Maryland in 1766 as his special agent with orders to sell proprietary manors and reserved lands and, in conjunction with deputy secretary Daniel Dulany and Gov. Horatio Sharpe, to initiate a much needed reform of the proprietary revenue system. Jordan had considerable influence by virtue of his relationship with the proprietor, and he eventually played a significant role in having Sharpe replaced as governor. James Haw, "The Patronage Follies: Bennet Allen, John Morton Jordan, and the Fall of Horatio Sharpe," *Md. Hist. Mag.,* LXXI (1976), 135, 144–146.

5. Printed in Field, *Carroll,* 103–106.

6. Payment of the salary of the clerk of the Council, a position held at this time by John Ross of Annapolis, had been disputed by the two houses of the Maryland legislature for a decade, with the lower house insisting that the remuneration be drawn from the proprietor's revenue rather than public funds because the clerk, like the Council, represented the proprietor's interests. In retaliation, the upper house refused to appropriate funds for the government's budget, known as the Journal of Accounts. As a result of this stalemate, the public debt accumulated for nine years and by the fall of 1765 totaled 3,950,482 pounds of tobacco and £305 7s. sterling. Efforts to resolve the matter by attaching riders to other legislation were unsuccessful. Charles A. Barker, *The Background of the Revolution in Maryland* (New Haven, Conn., 1940), 331–335; *Arch. of Md.,* LIX, xlix–liii.

7. Daniel Dulany's pamphlet, *The Right to the Tonnage, the Duty of Twelve Pence per Hogshead on All Exported Tobacco, and the Fines and Forfeitures in the Province of Maryland, Stated . . .* (Annapolis, 1766), substantiated the proprietor's claim to these traditional sources of revenue but did not mention the dispute over how the clerk of the Council should be paid.

8. Benjamin Franklin (1706–1790). Notwithstanding his multifaceted career as an au-

thor, diplomat, editor, inventor, politician, printer, scholar, scientist, and statesman, Franklin had little formal education. A native of Boston, he was apprenticed at the age of twelve to his brother, a printer. In 1723 he ran away to Philadelphia, where he became a printer, the owner and editor (1729–1748) of the *Pa. Gaz.*, and the publisher (1732–1757) of *Poor Richard's Almanack*. He also founded the debating club (1727) that in 1743 became the American Philosophical Society, a library (1731), the city's first fire company (1736), and the Academy of Philadelphia (1751), from which the University of Pennsylvania developed. His electrical experiments and invention of the Franklin stove (1742) and the bifocal lens established his reputation as a scientist and inventor. He began his public career in 1736 as clerk of the Pennsylvania assembly and later became a member of that body (1751–1764), deputy postmaster of Philadelphia (1737–1753), and joint postmaster general for the colonies (1753–1774). In 1754 he was part of Pennsylvania's delegation to the Albany Congress in New York, where representatives from several colonies adopted a "Plan of Union" that was based on his ideas but was later rejected both in London and America. Appointed Pennsylvania's agent in Great Britain in 1757, he spent five years in London trying to persuade the British government to remove Pennsylvania from the Penn family's control and make it a royal colony. He left Philadelphia for London again late in 1764 and remained there until 1775, defending the Americans' position and working for reconciliation between the colonies and mother country. A delegate to the Second Continental Congress (1775–1776), he served with CCC on the commission sent to secure the support of Canada in the spring of 1776, assisted in drafting and was a signer of the Declaration of Independence, and was appointed first postmaster general (1775–1776). Commissioned by Congress, along with Silas Deane and Arthur Lee, to procure military supplies and assistance from France, Franklin played a major role in achieving the Franco-American Alliance (1778). He ended his diplomatic career as a negotiator of the peace with Great Britain (1783) and his political career as a member of the constitutional convention (1787).

9. Transcribed incorrectly by Field, CCC's reference is to William Lux (c. 1730–1778), a merchant who, in late February 1766, organized Baltimore's Sons of Liberty, a group of merchants and tradesmen committed to radical action in protesting the Stamp Act. Lux began his career in the 1750s as a shopkeeper and steadily expanded his mercantile endeavors to include shipowning, retailing, and the tobacco trade. By the end of the 1760s he was also handling through his stores a large portion of the Maryland business of the Philadelphia firm Willing and Morris and had, by the mid-1770s, become one of Baltimore's most prominent merchants. In partnership with his nephew Daniel Bowley, Lux operated a wharf and a ropewalk, and, during the Revolution, he acted as a Continental purchasing agent. Although elected to the first and fourth Maryland conventions, Lux concentrated his political efforts at the local level, serving on the Baltimore Co. Committee of Correspondence (1774) and Committee of Observation (1774–1776) and on a committee for the defense of Baltimore (1776). He and his wife, Agnes Walker Lux, whom he married in 1762, had two sons, one of whom died before reaching adulthood. Hoffman, *Spirit of Dissension*, 38–40; *Bio. Dic. Md. Legis.*, II, 556–557.

10. William Paca (1740–1799), younger son of John Paca and Elizabeth Smith Paca. Born in what is now Harford Co., Paca spent his adult life in two principal locations—Annapolis, where he constructed a magnificent Georgian mansion and a garden of his own design, and at Wye House, the equally impressive residence he built on Wye Island, Queen Anne's Co.,

in 1791. He studied at the College of Philadelphia (University of Pennsylvania), receiving a bachelor's degree in 1759 and a master's degree in 1762, and in 1759 came to Annapolis to study law with Stephen Bordley. In 1761 Paca spent about six months at the Inner Temple, returning to Maryland in the fall of that year. His marriage in 1763 to Mary Chew, step-daughter of Daniel Dulany, Sr., and an heir of Maryland's wealthiest merchant, Richard Bennett, improved Paca's social standing and brought him a substantial fortune. In 1777, three years after the death of his first wife, Paca married another wealthy woman, Ann Harrison, a daughter of Philadelphia merchant Henry Harrison and Mary Aspden Harrison. Besides the three sons produced by his marriages, Paca fathered two natural daughters, both of whom he acknowledged and supported.

Paca's activities during the Stamp Act crisis launched his political career and positioned him to become one of Maryland's most important Revolutionary leaders. A member of the lower house (1768–1774), he served in six of Maryland's nine conventions, on the first Council of Safety (1775), in the Continental Congress (1774–1778), where he was a signer of the Declaration of Independence, in the Maryland Senate (1776–1780, 1786–1791), and as governor (1782–1785). Believing that a strong central government would infringe upon the rights of states and individuals, he declined to be a delegate to the Constitutional Convention in 1787, and he led the Antifederalists in opposing ratification. He sat on the U.S. district court of Maryland (1789–1799). Gregory A. Stiverson and Phebe R. Jacobsen, *William Paca: A Biography* (Baltimore, 1976); *Bio. Dic. Md. Legis.,* II, 632–635.

11. Samuel Chase (1741–1811), the son of the Reverend Thomas Chase and Matilda Walker Chase, was born in Somerset Co. First educated by his father, who became rector of St. Paul's Parish, Baltimore Co., in 1745, Chase moved on to read law in Annapolis under John Hall. By 1765 he had been admitted to the Annapolis mayor's court, the county courts of Anne Arundel, Baltimore, Frederick, and Prince George's Counties, and the provincial court. He held a seat in the lower house (1765–1774), led the opposition to the Stamp Act, and served on the provincial Committee of Correspondence (1773–1775), in all but one of the conventions (1774–1777), on the first Council of Safety (1775), and as a delegate to the Continental Congress (1774–1778), where he was a signer of the Declaration of Independence. With CCC he was a member of the commission appointed by Congress to seek Canadian support for American independence (1776), and he sat in Maryland's House of Delegates (1777–1783, 1786–1788). An Antifederalist, he was a leader in opposing the ratification of the U.S. Constitution. In 1804, during his tenure as associate justice of the U.S. Supreme Court (1796–1811), Chase was impeached for improper judicial behavior by the House of Representatives, but the Senate acquitted him in March 1805.

Chase was married twice, first, in 1762, to Ann Baldwin, who bore him seven children, four of whom—two sons and two daughters—survived her death in 1776. With his second wife, Hannah Kitty Giles, whom he wed in 1784, he had two daughters. Although Chase and CCC were close allies in the Revolutionary movement until 1779, Chase's political ambition, combined with his chronic shortage of money, led him to involve himself in profit-making ventures that caused Carroll to question his motives and character. Their confrontation in the pages of the *Md. Gaz.* in 1781–1782 marked the end of their formerly cooperative relationship, but by the beginning of the nineteenth century they had reestablished a cordial acquaintance. *Bio. Dic. Md. Legis.,* I, 214–216; Hoffman, *Spirit of Dissension,* 242–268.

12. According to the Mar. 6, 1766, *Md. Gaz.,* John Brice II (1705–1766), a justice of the

provincial court, and Dr. George Steuart (1700–c. 1784), a judge of the land office, initially sent verbal replies to the questions put to them by the Sons of Liberty. When their interrogators rejected these responses as "a great Indignity," Brice and Steuart prepared written answers. Affirming his "Attachment to the Liberty of the Subject here," Brice said he would confer with his fellow justices about opening the court at the time it was due to reconvene, while Steuart asserted that the land office was indeed open for business. Although the Sons paid Dulany a visit, the deputy secretary nevertheless presented them with a written statement explaining that he could not direct the courts to act when they were not in session. Aubrey C. Land, *The Dulanys of Maryland: A Biographical Study of Daniel Dulany, the Elder (1685–1753), and Daniel Dulany, the Younger (1722–1797),* 2d ed. (Baltimore, 1955), 268–270.

13. Probably Dr. Adam Thomson (?–1767), a prominent colonial physician. Educated at the University of Edinburgh, where he was a classmate and friend of Dr. Alexander Hamilton, Thomson developed a method of smallpox inoculation. Barnes, *Marriages and Deaths,* 184; Cordell, *Medical Annals of Maryland,* 650–651.

14. John Hepburn (1710–1775) of Prince George's Co., a justice of the provincial court. Bowie, *Prince George's,* 727 n.

15. Not found.

$$\cdot \; \cdot \; \cdot$$

CCC to Edmund Jenings

27 May — 1766

Dr. Jenings,

I have before me your obliging favour of the 28th. of Febry.[1] in answer to mine of the 28th. of Novemb. last. My long silence from my arrival in this Province to the date of that letter might reasonably enough create a suspicion of having forgot or at least neglected my friend. Distance of time & place & new connections are too apt to make us forgetful of the old — whatever failings I may be subject to, I am exempt from this: no distance either of time or place will ever efface, or even diminish the traces of a former friendship, which I shall always be glad to keep up by a constant intercourse of letters, the only means now left, or probably that will ever be afforded us again.

I have the pleasure to inform you that I have heared your Pamphlet[2] well spoken of by many & those too, good Judges of literary merit: the Revolt, of the united Provinces or rather the just assertion of their liberties, was well introduced, very applicable to the point, & filled with Judicious & well timed observations: Your conduct has evinced your attachment to your native country; which as to my self I never doubted of — indeed no man can be solicitous for the prosperity of G:B: who is not equally solicitous for the interests & wellfare of her colonies — We have just received the news of the repeal of the Stamp Act:[3] this act of Justice & condescention in the Parliat. will I hope greatly contribute to restore peace & tranquillity to these lately distracted provinces, & renew in them their usual confidence in, & affection for their mother country—nothing but a repeal & that too, absolute, & immediate could have had the desired effect—The minds of men were estranged; a spirit of resentment roused by oppression had diffused itself thro' all ranks—you have shewn what despair may do in a people, who deem an abject[4] slavery the worse of evils: an equitable & moderate government only can insure the dependency of these colonies: a constitutional dependance they are proud of—an abject subjection they disdain. Can it be thought possible to keep them under such a subjection: numerous, & encreasing daily, in numbers & in wealth, & disjointed from Britain by an immense Ocean, will they suffer themselves to be oppressed by an enferior force? Would it be prudent to make Acts now, to which half a century hence, no obedience maybe paid—The Parliat. should be cautious how they pass such Acts, or establish such regulations, which maybe hereafter complained of as grieveous oppressions—Acts restraining our trade, & manufactures within ourselves, will certainly a few years hence fall under that denomination—Mr. Pitt's speech[5] which in every other respect was worthy that truly Great Man, in this seemed to be contradictory & to establish a doctrine diametrically opposite to the principles of Liberty which he so nobly asserted: the distinction too between an absolute legislative authority, devested of the power of taxation, appears to me a contradiction in <u>terminis</u>—how can legislation be absolute & supreme when destitute of a power which is it very soul & essence: & without which every legislature must be acknowledged incompleat, & inadequate to the ends of govet. Here then says the great Commoner let us draw the line—Where? I am sure it will [be] a mathematical line existing only in idea: the Commons of G:B. have only a right of taxation by virtue of their representation & if this Principle is admitted as I think it is on all sides they certainly have no right to tax America (I reason logically since the doctrine of a virtual representation[6] is exploded & this is the conclusion I must draw from that <u>datum</u>, whatever resolutions or acts may be passed by the Legislature of G:B—)

Upon what Principle let me ask you did the Americans refuse to submit to the Stamp Act—upon the Principle of not being represented, you will no doubt answer—true: but what did they apprehend from a want of representation? an oppressive & partial & unequal taxation: therefore from a purity of reasoning all Acts hereafter passed by the legislature of G:B: manifestly oppressive, partial & unequal, will probably meet with the same resistance from the same principle: For instance would not an Act prohibiting the Colonists from clothing themselves with their own wool, hemp & flax be every whit as partial & oppressive as the Stamp Act; it certainly would be & infinitely more so: yet if I do not mistake the great Commoner's meaning, such a statute might be enacted by the Parlt. in consequence of its supreme & absolute Legislation—What inconsistency! Quod cunque ostendis mihi sic, incredulus odi.[7] I am aware of an objection you are ready to make & therefore shall endeavour to obviate it: if the colonies are permitted to manufacture within themselves, they will gradually become unserviceable to G:B: & in time utterly independent — to this I can only answer — that where land is cheap, men are generally averse to manufactures, necessity only will compell them to it: if G:B therefore can supply her colonies cheaper & better than they can supply themselves, she need not be apprehensive of their manufacturing for themselves; If not, no restraining acts will be found to answer the end[.] If I could make a coat of my own wool, much cheaper & better than what I could have from England, would it not be the highest injustice to force me to forego such an advantage: would it not be raising a very heavy tax upon my property without my consent, either by myself or by my representative. Another argument occurs to me why such an Act would be not only unjust, but impolitic — the People on this Continent are encreasing fast; it is with difficulty even now they can be supplied from Britain — must those who from their circumstances, situation & numbers can not be cloathed in english manufactures, go naked? Many other reasons must occur to you, why G:B: should not exert such a power, even supposing it lawful, which I think would be denied upon the same principle the Right of taxing was denied: It is expected the Parliament will allow us to emit a paper currency under proper restrictions — men in trade say it can not be carried on without it; I am not conversant in these matters — but I know it is extremely difficult to get in even small sums, from people who are in very good circumstances — & this difficulty can be owing to nothing but a scarcity of circulating Cash — [8]

You desire me to give you every information in my power of these colonies & particularly of this Province — I must refer to others whom you may know [in] England or correspond with here, who from their long connections & acquaintance with these colonies are able to give you much better information than you can possibly expect from me.

I return you many thanks for the valuable present of the three busts:[9] I wish this country could boast such Great Originals, or artists who could execute such exquisite copies. All who have seen them admire them;

I read yr. Letter to Bordly[10] & Brice: they & all others are well convinced you was no ways intentionally accessary in procuring the unhappy Hood the office of Stamp Man: this Retch is now forgotten & still in exile — it is thought he will never return to this Province.

Poor Key died at Marlborough the Beginning of this month of a consumption:[11] with frailties too incident to humanity he possessed several good qualities. If you see Mr. Graves inform him that I have red. his letter with the books & Pamphlets he sent me & [two] lett[ers] from [12][.] I shall write to him by the shipping in the fall — Before you receive this, I shall have entered into the holy state of matrimony: I have made choice of a lady about 23 years of age,[13] handsom enough, genteel, sensible & good natured:

ALbDr, CCC Letterbook, 1765–1768, MS 203.1, MdHi.

1. A draft of this letter may be found in Edmund Jenings (1703–1756) and Edmund Jenings (1731–1819), Letterbook, 1753–1769, fols. 280–285, Manuscripts Division, ViHi. Jenings affirmed his affection for America, his distress at Great Britain's recent actions, and his agreement with Daniel Dulany's Stamp Act pamphlet, and he denied that he was responsible for Zachariah Hood's appointment as stamp master for Maryland.

2. Possibly *The Present State of Holland; or, A Description of the United Provinces; Wherein Is Contained a Particular Account of the Hague, and All the Principal Cities and Towns . . . Manner's and Custom's . . . East-India Company . . . Commerce, in Asia, Africa, and America . . .* , 4th ed. (Leiden, 1765).

3. The House of Commons voted to repeal the Stamp Act on Mar. 4, 1766, and the House of Lords followed suit on Mar. 17. The repeal received the king's assent on Mar. 18 and took effect on May 1. The Apr. 10 *Md. Gaz.* reported the news of the repeal. Land, *Dulanys of Maryland,* 270; Barker, *Background of the Revolution,* 311 n.

4. Possibly struck out.

5. William Pitt urged the House of Commons to repeal the Stamp Act on Jan. 14, 1766.

6. The doctrine advanced as a justification for Parliament's levying of taxes on the American colonies. While conceding that British subjects could not be taxed without representation in Parliament, proponents of virtual representation maintained that all British subjects, whether qualified to vote or not, were in fact represented in that body, "virtually," if not "actually," because of a presumed mutuality of interests that enabled members of Parliament, though elected from specific boroughs and counties, to represent the whole nation. The position of the American colonists was held to be analogous to that of British subjects living in England who did not have the franchise. (Edmund S. Morgan and Helen M. Morgan, *The Stamp Act Crisis: Prologue to Revolution* [Chapel Hill, N.C., 1953], 75–77.) Daniel Dulany successfully challenged this reasoning in his pamphlet *Considerations on the Propriety of Imposing Taxes,* which asserted that, while the idea of virtual representation might be substantiated in the case of resident English nonvoters on the basis of community interests and the opportunity to secure the franchise, the position of American colonists was materially different. First, there existed no mutuality of interests between Americans and English politicians. Second, English boroughs and counties were represented in Parliament, however unequally, but no part of America could make that claim. Finally, American colonists, deprived of representatives to put forth their interests in Parliament, were forced to rely solely on the process of petitioning. Ibid., 79–81; Land, *Dulanys of Maryland,* 263.

7. "Whatever you thus show me, I disbelieve and despise." Horace *Ars poetica* 188.

8. The lack of an adequate supply of currency caused constant problems for all of Great Britain's mainland North American colonies, and Parliament's passage of the Currency Act of 1764, which prohibited the colonies from issuing paper money as legal tender, seriously aggravated the problem. Ultimately the Maryland assembly solved the colony's need for a circulating money supply in 1767 by issuing 173,733 dollars of nonlegal tender at the rate of 4s. 6d. sterling to the dollar. To insure that the nonlegal tender would be negotiable, the assembly backed it with £25,000 sterling that the colony held in Bank of England stock. Hoffman, *Spirit of Dissension,* 56–59.

9. According to Jenings's letter of Feb. 28, he sent CCC an "Actual & Lively Represen-

tation of Pit, Wolfe, & Prat A Patriot & a Genl & a Lawyer to whom America is much indebted." Jenings to CCC, Feb. 28, 1766, Letterbook, 1753-1769, fols. 284-285, ViHi.

10. John Beale Bordley (1726/7-1804), who lived in Baltimore Town in 1766 and later on Wye Island, Queen Anne's Co., was Edmund Jenings's half brother. Bordley's father, Thomas, was Jenings's mother's second husband. *Bio. Dic. Md. Legis.*, I, 145.

11. Edmund Key died at Upper Marlboro, Prince George's Co., on May 4, 1766. " 'News' from the 'Maryland Gazette,' " *Md. Hist. Mag.*, XVIII (1923), 178.

12. Word omitted.

13. CCC intended to marry Rachel Cooke (c. 1743-1766), his first cousin once removed and a sister of the William Cooke he met during his enforced sojourn on the Eastern Shore. See Appendix I, Chart H.

· · ·
·

CCC to Daniel Carroll

29 May 1766

Dr. Daniel,

I wrote to you the 17th. of last March since when We have recd: your very interesting letters of the 4 of that month & 12th. of Febry.[1] — We are particularly obliged to you for the full, distinct, & the best acct. I have met with of the Parliamentary debates on the Stamp Act — a few days ago the news was recd. of its repeal having passed all the branches of the legislature — The Brutum fulmen[2] that preceeded the repeal does not in the least damp our Joy — It will not hurt as much to resolve or pass an Act that the Parlt. has a right to tax America,[3] if they never put [it in] practice — Mr. Pitts speech has been in all our newspapers — there are fine sallies in it mixed with absurdities — I pardon these on acct. of those — the menaces thrown out to restrain our manufactures were ad captandum vulgus:[4] he carried his idea of Parliamentary power in that point beyond the possibility of execution & therefore he did not speak his real sentiments — an argument that proves too much proves no thing.

How does the thick damp air of Ireland agree with you? Are you likely to succeed? If you return by the way of London, pray do not forget to call upon Mr. Bird in white Friars — Our assembly broke up the day before yesterday — the Clerk's claim still remains where it was no talk of another visit from the back woods:[5] Dulanys Pamphlet has set that affair & the other contested points dependent on it, in a clear light — It will not bear annalysing being chiefly an extract from the records & Journals of the assemblies. This last Sessions the lower house sent up the several claims on the Journal, thieir own for attendance omitting the Clerk's in two distinct Bills the upper house to the grt. seeming disappointment of the lower passed the former but rejected the other — I say seeming, because we have reason to think their disappointment was mere pretence, & that they expected the upper house would pass the one & reject the other, since this very expedient of satisfying the clamorous public was proposed to the lower house in a message from the upper in the preceeding Sessions.[6]

The old Assize Law has been revived this last Sessions & passed without opposition by the upper house: a law calculated to encrease fees & to prolong suits at Law—[7]

Jordan & his lady arrived here about 10 days ago; I do not hear he is much taken notice of: almost all the gentlemen have waited on him: entre nous il est un peu Gascon — sa femme est Jolie, et voila peut etre le vrai merit du maris.[8] All the Books & Pamphlets you sent me are come safe to hand; we are much obliged to you for them. My Father is well & desires to be remembered to you — Before you receive this, I shall probably be married to Miss Cooke: Jack Brice will soon follow my example or perhaps set me one: old M'accubbins[9] & Brice have, it is said adjusted all matters[10] — Anderson courts Miss Milly Ogle, & has wrote home to his Father to obtain his consent. It is thought it will be a match.[11]

Yr. mother & sisters[12] were all lately well as also yr. little daughter, who has red the things you sent her: she was in town at the races the 13 instant with her Aunt Digges,[13] whom I then saw for the first time — Hamilton's horse Figure[14] wone the first days Mr. Calverts Regulus[15] the second day's purse. When you write to yr. Brother remember me kindly to him & give my love to Danny — I have now mentioned all the private & public occurences that I can think of at present — & shall therefore conclude with wishing you health & happiness I am Dr. Daniel

affectionate friend & kinsman

C:C:

ALbDrS, CCC Letterbook, 1765–1768, MS 203.1, MdHi.

1. Not found.

2. "A harmless thunderbolt." Pliny *Natural History* 2.43.113.

3. The Declaratory Act, passed the same day the Stamp Act was repealed, asserted Parliament's right to enact laws binding on the American colonists in all matters and the colonists' obligation to obey them.

4. "To sway the crowd."

5. On Dec. 10, 1765, Gov. Horatio Sharpe warned the lower house that some three hundred or four hundred armed men had gathered at Frederick, Md., with the intention of marching on Annapolis to force the assembly to resolve the impasse over the Journal of Accounts. Only a small band eventually came to Annapolis, however, and with the intention of petitioning the assembly rather than intimidating it. Barker, *Background of the Revolution*, 331–335; *Arch. of Md.*, LIX, liii–lvi.

6. The dispute over the payment of the Journal of Accounts and the clerk of the Council's salary remained unresolved during the short seventeen-day legislative session of May 1766. *Arch. of Md.*, LXI, lxiii–lxiv.

7. The assize bill had been another source of friction between the upper and lower houses of assembly for many years, with the lower house maintaining that civil and criminal trials should be held in the counties where they arose rather than in the provincial court in Annapolis. The bill to which CCC refers provided for cases to be heard by two itinerant provincial court justices sitting in the various counties but stipulated that no infringement of the county courts should occur. Ibid., xxiv–xxv.

8. "Between us, he is a bit of a braggart. His wife is pretty, and perhaps that is the real merit of the husband."

9. Nicholas Maccubbin (1709–1787).

10. John Brice III married Mary Clare Maccubbin, a daughter of Nicholas and Mary Clare Carroll Maccubbin, on Oct. 30, 1766. *Bio. Dic. Md. Legis.*, I, 165.

11. Sometime during 1767–1768 Meliora Ogle (1750–c. 1775), a daughter of former Maryland governor Samuel Ogle and Anne Tasker Ogle, married James Anderson (?–1785), son of William Anderson, a former ship captain turned London merchant. James Bordley, *The Hollyday and Related Families of the Eastern Shore of Maryland, Including the Trumun, Vaughan, Covington, Lloyd, Robins, Chamberlaine, Hayward, Carmichael, Murray, Bennett, Earle, Chew, Hemsley, Tilghman, Goldsborough, and Other Families* (Baltimore, 1962), 286–293.

12. Mary and Elizabeth Carroll, who lived with their mother, Eleanor Darnall Carroll, at Rock Creek, Frederick (later Montgomery) Co.

13. Mary Carroll Digges, the wife of Ignatius Digges.

14. Dr. Thomas Hamilton of Prince George's Co. imported Figure, an English thoroughbred stallion, in 1765. Fairfax Harrison, *Early American Turf Stock, 1730–1830* . . . (Richmond, Va., 1934–1936), II, 147; Allen Eustis Begnaud, "Hoofbeats in Colonial Maryland," *Md. Hist. Mag.*, LXV (1970), 215.

15. Regulus belonged to Benedict Calvert. Begnaud, "Hoofbeats in Colonial Maryland," *Md. Hist. Mag.*, LXV (1970), 215.

. . .
.

CCC to William Graves

16 July 1766

Dr. Graves,

This is to acknowledge the receipt of yr. several letters of July 21. 1765 — Decbr. 18 1765 & of the 3d. April 1766[1] — I can not answer them fully by this opportunity[.] I was attacked the 15th. of last month with a sharp fever which continued without any intermission for 12 or 13 days; it has hung upon me ever since but I have had many intermissions, & as I begin to recover my strength & appetite, I hope I shall soon shake it off entirely — I was to have been married the 8th. instant to a well bred, amiable, sweet tempered young lady — (you see what influence yr. advice has on me) but as I am reduced very low by this fit of sickness I fancy I shall postpone my marriage to the first of Novbr. & if I do not recover my health

& strength I shall drop all thoughts of entering into that state — Long before the fever broke out I had been in a declining way but I flatter my self that I shall now enjoy a better state of health, than I have enjoyed for these 3 or 4 years past.

I sent you Mr. Dulany's phamlet by the first opportunity after its publication here — & probably that was the packet the Capt. called upon you to know whether you had received: yr. Letter desiring me to give you all the information I could collect from the writings & conversation of the most sensible men here about the stamp Act, did not come to hand till some time last July — By sending you Mr. Dulany's Phamplet, wh I see Mr. Pitt made great use of in his speech[,] [2] I gave you all the information I possibly could give you on the subject. That you did not receive that Phamplet was no fault of mine. You should never blame too hastily[.] Please to present my thanks to Mr. Hussey for so nobly supporting the rights & liberties of the Americans.[3] I have sent him by this opportunity two Bear hams, I wish they may prove good, the hunter who brought them to me assured me they were excellent — I have directed the Capt. to leave them at the Crown & Anchor for Mr. Hussey.

I have received all the books & Phamplets you mention excepting Voltaires letters, which are not yet come to hand tho' I believe they are on board a ship in Patuxent. Be pleased to forward the enclosed to Mr. Gordon by the first opportunity: I am quite tired of writing. Tho' I have a great deal more to say I must conclude with assuring you that I [am]

Yr. affectionate & sincere friend
Ch: Carroll

P:S:

22d.

to send the enclosed to Mr. Gordon immediately after i'ts receipt: to send me the Antiquities of Ireland:[4] to write a note to Lewis bookseller, to send me the second volum. of Warners & Gahagans Irish histories & the second volum. of Indostan if Published — this is the substance of the postscript to this letter —

ALbDrS, CCC Letterbook, 1765–1768, MS 203.1, MdHi.

1. Letters not found.

2. William Pitt's use of Dulany's pamphlet *Considerations on the Propriety of Imposing Taxes* in the House of Commons debate, Jan. 14, 1766, is discussed in Moses Coit Tyler, *The Literary History of the American Revolution, 1763–1783* (New York, 1897), I, 110–113.

3. Richard Hussey, CC's friend from his London days, advocated the repeal of the Stamp Act before the House of Commons in February 1766.

4. *Cat. Lib.*, no. 1132, lists Sir James Ware, *The History and Antiquities of Ireland . . .* , trans. Walter Harris (Dublin, 1764). Ware, a distinguished antiquarian, originally published his *De Hibernia & Antiquitatibus ejus Disquisitiones* in 1654; the first English translation appeared in 1704.

CCC to Lockhart Gordon

18th. July 1766

Sir,

By the past mismanag[emen]t of Perkin's & Brown & from their th[ou]ghtlesness, I am aff[rai]d they will neglect to give you timely notice of an [op]portun[ity o]f sending the Mares. Vessels sail from London for [this Pro]vince almost in every month. Pray do not depend on Perk. & Brown for information: by sending yr. Servant to the Virga. & Maryland coffee house in Corn-Hill you may always know whether there [are] any ships to sail for this Province & the time of their sailing & whether they are light ships for in such only can the Mares be shipped: when you have pitched upon a proper ship pray let Perkins know it by a line that he may have time to prepare water casks &c &c—I am quite ashamed of the trouble I put you to in this affair, but I would very willingly do as much for you. Should the Mares not be shipt off by the last of next Octbr. pray sell them, for they will be too heavy to be shipped after that time & the weather too stormy, & as the Colts will drop about the beginning of April they would be too tender to support the fatigue of the Voya. & in all probability would die on their passage[.] If you send the Mares, [be] pleased to send with them their's & Blank's [pedigree]s. By Perkins & Brown's letter to us & y[r]: n[ot]e to them, I find you had only 18 [days] n[o]t[ic]e a much shorter warning than they [give] to the[ir] shopkeepers for shipping their g[oods]. I am Sir

yr. most obt. & obliged hum: Sevt.
Ch: Carroll of Carrollton.

P.S

With the purchase money you may buy two other Mares, if you meet with any to yr. liking. I would not have them sent to a horse because it may be the occasion of their not being shipped in time & we have excellent Stallions in this country. If you purchase other Mares pray be attentive to their size & colour: I would have stout strong Mares & bay: our full blooded Mares in this province are all too small.

ALbDrS, CCC Letterbook, 1765-1768, MS 203.1, MdHi. Recipient noted by CCC in letterbook.

·   ·   ·
·

CCC to Christopher Chapman Bird

22 July 1766

Dr. Xtopher,

I have now before me yours of the 2d. Janry. 1766: in which you acknowledge the receipt of my Letters of the first of Augst.[1] & of the 28th. of Septbr. but you take not the least notice of a Postscript to the last letter, wherein I desire you to send me the Statutes that are already published by Bathurst: if you remember I left my subscription ticket with you. I wrote to you the 30th. of Decbr.[2] much to the same purpose, but as you are entirely silent as to that letter, I suppose it had not come to hand, when you wrote yours of the 2d. of Janry.; upon reflextion it was impossible it should.

It gives me great satisfaction to hear you are so happy in yr. present state: from the Character you give me of yr. Lady, & from the knowledge I have of yours, I think yr. friends have the strongest reasons to expect a continuance of yr. happiness. I really Join with you in opinion that every State has i'ts thorns, & that the matrimonial one if entered into with prudence, hath the fewest. At least I was going to try the experiment: I was to have been married the 8th. instant, but a sharp fevear seized me about the 20th of last month; it continued without intermission for 13 days & from that time, tho' with several intermissions, it has hung upon [me] till a few days ago: I hope I have at last shook it off But I am extremely reduced: however I now begin to recover my appetite; strength I hope will follow—yet I am still, not as I should be: if my constitution does not mend this poor puny body cannot possibly endure much longer: I have this to comfort me, that I am not so much attached to this life but that I can part with it without any great regret, or so affraid of death, as to shrink back with fear & trembling at its nearer approach. If I do not deceive myself I could meet it even with composure.

Pray present my compliments of congratulation to Mr. Huddlestone on his marriage.[3] What follows is particularly addressed to yr. Father, for I know old people have more thought than young. I should be much obliged to my old antagonist, whom I long to see & to beat at Chess, to send me some grafts of the large Morello cherry[4] in Mr. Francis' garden at Nightengale Hall:[5] he may send the Grafts to Mr. Webb seedsman in Bridge street Westminster directed to my Father—Webb will take care to forward them to us by the first opportunity, at least desire him to do it. My sincere respects to yr. Aunt whom I shall always esteem as one of the best of women I ever knew: I do not forget Mr. Chapman: remember me to you sister & to her husband[6]—& be perswaded that I am

yr: affectionate friend
C:C: of Carrollton.

P:S:

Pray present my compliments to Mr. Scaen[7] & to his daughters. What I am going to ask, from our friendship I have reason to think you will readily perform: it is to find out Mr. Lockart Gordon brother of the Earl of Aboyne,[8] Mr. Graves can probably tell you where he lodges if Graves should be out of town, you may find him out by a proper enquiry. Mr. Gordon has bought for me two blooded Mares as he is gentleman of pleasure & no ways concerned in trade, he can not be informed of the time when ships sail for this Province, & I have great reason to suspect that Perkins & Brown will take no great pains to inform him: Be pleased therefore whenever you go by the Maryland & Virga. coffee house in Corn Hill to enquire whether there are any ships to sail & when for this Province, & whether they are light, for in such only can the Mares be shipped — Give Mr. Gordon timely notice that is 20 or 30 days at least, because the Mares are in the country & it will take some time to bring them up to town & to provide necessaries for them on the passage — Let Perkins & Browne know that there is such a ship to sail in such a time & that my Mares will embark in her: I should be glad you would person-ally acquaint them when the ship is to sail, as I think it will mortify them not a little: indeed they deserve to be mortified. I hope this will reach you by the 20th. of Septbr. at farthest; I have wrote to Mr. Gordon by this opportunity to sell the Mares if they are not shipt off before the last of Octbr.

I shall endeavour to get more wild turkies eggs & have them hatched by tame turkies: I intend to keep them all the winter & perhaps to the month of June or July, about which time, Capt. Henrick by whom I write this, generally sails for England. Henrick is very careful & obliging: the birds too will be stronger & they will have the advantage of a Summer's passage, & I dare say will arrive safe.

ALbDrS, CCC Letterbook, 1765–1768, MS 203.1, MdHi.

1. Neither letter found.

2. An excerpt of this letter is printed in Field, *Carroll*, 107–108.

3. Ferdinand Huddleston married Mary Lucas in 1766. Geoffrey Holt, *The English Jesuits in the Age of Reason* (Tunbridge Wells, Kent, 1993), 89–92.

4. Morello cherries are cultivated cherries derived from the sour cherry *Prunus cerasus.*

5. Nightingale Hall may have been the Birds' country seat at Reigate, where CC often visited during his student days in London.

6. Hester Bird (1740–1821) married Edward Ferrers (after 1737–1794) of Baddesley Clin-ton, Warwickshire, in 1763. *Obituaries*, Catholic Record Society, XII (London, 1913), 151; Burke and Burke, *Landed Gentry of Great Britain and Ireland*, I, 410.

7. Probably "Scawen." See CCC to Christopher Chapman Bird, Mar. 8, 1767, below.

8. Charles Gordon, earl of Aboyne (1726–1794). *Debrett's Peerage*, 18th ed., II, 584–585.

CCC to Perkins, Buchanan, and Brown

23 July 1766.

Gent:

Be pleased to forward Mr. Gordon's lette[r] to him immediately after it comes to hand. I hope the Mares will be shipt off before this reaches you: should they not be shipped before the last of Octbr, I have ordered them to be sold[.] This will be a great disappointment to me & I shall lay it entirely upon you: many vessels sailed from London much about the time Hayton sailed I shall instance only one Capt. Banning[1] now in this Port & a light ship. You had, I understand by yr. Capt. given him over as missing, you was therefore very uncertain as to the time of his arrival, nay you had begun to despair of his arrival, consequently you could not certainly inform Mr. Gordon, when yr. vessel would sail, & this uncertainty was the cause why you gave him so short notice: Mr. Gordon who is often out of town, should have longer notice given him (especially as you knew the Mares were in the country) than a shopkeeper who is always behind his counter, & has his Bales to send on board from his own shop. I am Gent,

yr. most: hum: Sevt.
C:C: of Carrollton.

ALbDrS, CCC Letterbook, 1765–1768, MS 203.1, MdHi.

1. Jeremiah Banning (1733–c. 1798), master of the ship *Pearle.* Annapolis Port of Entry Record Books, I.

CCC to William Graves

12 August 1766.

Dr. Graves,

I promised in my last to answer at large yr. letters of the 21 July 1765, 18th. Decbr. 1765, & your last of the 3d. April 1766: I am now going to fulfill that promise. I had heared, long before I received your letter of the 21 July of the addition made to the Master's Sallary upon wh I sincerely congratulate you.

You complain of my having neglected to have informed you of the principal objections agt. the Stamp Act & the mode of collecting it: if you peruse attentively my letters you will find that I have mentioned most & the principal objections that were made here to that Partial Law. Viz the taxing a free people without their consent, the Trial by Juries broken in upon, the establishment of the vice admiralty

Courts in subversion of the Common Law the Liberty of the Press curtailed. I sent you Mr. Dulany['s] Pamphlet by the first opportunity after its publication, I sent it for your own information & that you might communicate it to Messrs. Hussey, Champion & Pratt—

Pray tell Mr. Barington that as a Lawyer or Judge I should pay great deference to his opinion, but As a politician, I think his views are not very extensive.

My Father is greatly dissatisfied with his present Correspondents; I Proposed to him to try our acquaintance Taylor, but he says I can not conceive the difficulties of corresponding with one out of the Trade: I must submit to his knowledge & experience in these matters.

The Colonies are far from aiming at independency; if indeed slavery & dependency be convertible terms & if your government should not make the proper distinction, & should treat us not as subjects composing a part of the same society & intiteled to the same privileges with the rest, but should look upon us as slaves & use us as such, I believe every American would disclaim that sort of dependency[.]

Can you doubt of our dependency, since the passing the late famous Act for securing the dependency of America?[1]

No argument should be drawn from cases or contingencies which probably can never happen: such I take to be those extreme cases, those state exigencies you hint at & wh Mr. Hussey well observed could hardly ever really exist[.] A rapacious & unpopular minister, who is driven to his shifts, may indeed be very willing to suppose their existence But I will suppose some such extreme exigency to call upon the Americans for supplies: are the[y] not the best Judges of what they can bear? Have they not a competent Legislature within themselves to raise taxes? Believe me the people will always most chearfully submit to those taxes which are imposed by their own representatives.

Suppose, say you, the Americans should not raise money in case of war on their continent? I will not, I can not suppose any such thing; the case hath never yet happened: their own Intst. would prompt them to open their purses & to act with spirit, if the war was undertaken for their defence. But in the present situation of things it is almost impossible there should be a war on this continent; our enemies the french are subdued & driven out of N: Am: the Spaniards are too inactive, too feeble, & at too great a distance to hurt us: the Indians are now peaceable & overawed by our forts & garrisons in the heart of their Country.

By what title are the Commons of England <u>sovereing</u> [sovereign] Judges over the Commons of America? Except the late ex post facto Law, is there any other statute declaring the Parlt. to have a right of imposing taxes on the Americans for the single purpose of raising a revenue? Your reasons in support of that wild assertion are far from being satisfactory, till you bring better, I must differ from you in opinion. The Americans did petition: these petitions were rejected because the house had gone into the consideration of the Bill. But a reflection did not, it seems, occur to you, which strikes me; a minister may huddle a bill thro' both houses: we are at a great distance, a Bill once past is not easily repealed. You say in many of Our charters, there is an express reservation to the English Parlt. of the power of taxing them: of all the Charters, I remember but one, that of Pensylvania, which hath such a clause. You suppose a great deal more than I shall grant, when you say it can not be supposed that the Legislature of G: B: will wantonly & unnecessarily impose any tax or that if any act of theirs be found inconvenient or oppressive, but what they will alter soften, or repeal it. What more oppressive & unnecessary tax, than that imposed by the Stamp Act. And yet what a struggle in Parlt. did the repeal occasion! The Eloquence of a Pitt, a Camden,[2] or a Hussey could hardly prevail over a faction, that seemed bent on the ruin of England & of her colonies.

I thank you for the Pamphlet on general warrants,[3] particulary for the notes: they cleared up some passages I could only guess at: I am also much obliged to you for Blackstone's book:[4] I cannot see that it is the least infected with the original Tory education of the author: his principles as far as I am able to Judge are quite consistent with the mixed nature of our govt.: would not the Whiggish principles if strictly adhered to & practised by Whiggish ministers when in Place, soon destroy not only the prerogative of the King, but even his very office. The genuine Principles either of Whigism or Toryism are equally dangerous to our constitution! The power of the King & Lords would be annihilated by the former, by the latter the Liberty of the subject would be taken away & despotism established in its stead.

You seem to take great offence at my saying that The King with the Assemblies may raise troops & money in these colonies without the Intervention of Parlt. Whatever you may think, this method upon trial will always be found the least liable to exception & the most pleasing to the people: it was practised with success during the late war: should this doctrine obtain, you are of opinion that a king of England, might make himself absolute by means of Ireland & the Plantations: was you really serious when you wrote this? The absurdities of such a supposition a moments reflection will discover: Troops are to be raised in America, paid by America (for I suppose the Parlt. would not pay them, & I will be hanged if we pay them for such a purpose) to be transported in English bottoms, & protected by english men of war: but, pray where would the King find the money to pay his men of war & transports? Would the Parlt. set still & take no steps to tye such a blundering King's hands, or neglect to make a severe example of his ministers? England can never be enslaved but by a corrupt Parlt. — this and the immense load of the national debt are the only evils she has to apprehend. This last only, as productive only of the first — Your Position that Ireland & America belong to the King Lords & Commons is quite new & I believe not warranted by any authority, nor defencesible upon the principles of reason or equity. Your forcible expression of belonging, if applied to Ireland, is proper enough: (how[ever] see what Swift says on the occasion in his 4th. Drapier's letter Pag: 130: Octo. Dublin Edition)[5] for England has all along treated the innocent & injured Irish, as slaves & beasts of burthen. But America, thank God, is at too great a distance to be treated in that manner; & the Americans have too much spirit to submit to such indignities, & will in a few years have a force sufficient to repel them if offered.

As to declaratory Acts made in consequence of some question lately started, they must be looked upon only as ex post facto laws contrived to meet with the circumstances of a particular case: the Parlt. hath passed an act asserting its right to tax America: our assemblies, not one excepted, have resolved that the <u>Part.</u> hath no such right: the question therefore of right is ad huc sub Judice[6] still undecided: for it can never be determined by the resolves or Acts of the Parlt. or of the Provincial assemblies, since both are Judge & party in their own cause. When an important question of right is moved between two large bodies of fellow subjects, the only equitable or possible method, unless they have recourse to the argumentum baculinum,[7] of settling the dispute is by recurring to the first principles of the Constitution, & from their decision there should lay no appeal — You hint artfully enough that these colonies have been settled by aids & supplies from Parlt.: the fact is not so; for excepting Georgia & Hallifax both ministerial Jobs,[8] the settlement of these colonies have not cost the Govert. one shilling, & what ever sums have been expended in their defence, England hath been amply repaid by the immense profits of her trade to America.

I assure you I read no controversy: the title of the book on miracles raised my Curiosity & hath not satisfied it. By this time Jean Jacques Rousseau, I doubt not is tired of the wilds of Darby shire:[9] that restless fantastical Philospher can not live long in any place. I should not be surprised at his writing a satire upon the govert. on purpose to draw upon himself a prosecution. I am Dr. Graves

yours &c.

ALbDr, CCC Letterbook, 1765–1768, MS 203.1, MdHi.

1. The Declaratory Act.

2. Sir Charles Pratt, who became Baron Camden on July 17, 1765, denounced the Stamp Act in his maiden speech before the House of Lords.

3. Possibly *Considerations on the Legality of General Warrants, and the Propriety of a Parliamentary Regulation of the Same . . .* , a pamphlet published anonymously in 1765. *Cat. Lib.,* no. 831.

4. Probably volume I of Sir William Blackstone's *Commentaries on the Laws of England . . .* (Oxford, 1765–1769).

5. Writing under the pseudonym "M. B., drapier," Jonathan Swift (1667–1745) published four letters in 1724 protesting the sale of a patent to William Wood for the supply of copper coinage to Ireland. Although the coins were badly needed, the Irish were incensed because the contract required numerous kickbacks — including a payment of ten thousand pounds to the king's mistress. In addition, the coins' light weight amounted to a hidden tax of several thousand pounds a year. Because Parliament had passed the legislation without the consent or advice of the Irish, Swift maintained in the fourth letter that "government without the consent of the governed . . . is the 'very definition of slavery' " (*DNB,* s.v. "Swift,

Jonathan"). Partly as a result of Swift's pamphlets, the English were forced to rescind the patent.

6. "Still in litigation."

7. "Argument by use of force."

8. The settlement of Georgia was financed by private subscriptions augmented by a ninety-four-thousand-pound subsidy from Parliament. (Basil Williams, *The Whig Supremacy, 1714–1760*, rev. C. H. Stuart, The Oxford History of England [Oxford, 1962], 309–310). Halifax was established in 1749 by Lord Halifax, president of the Board of Trade, to strengthen Great Britain's hold on Nova Scotia.

9. Jean Jacques Rousseau, seeking to escape arrest after the condemnation of *Emile* by the parlement of Paris, accepted David Hume's offer of sanctuary in England and arrived in London in January 1766. He subsequently retired to Wooten in Derbyshire, where he remained until 1767.

· · ·
· ·
·

CCC to Thomas Bradshaw

Augst. 26 1766

Dr. Bradshaw,

I have received your agreeable favour of the first of May[1] with the beagles: all those who have seen them & pretend to be Judges, praise them much & applaud your choice & good Judgt. The old Bitch pupped on the passage: she had 5 puppies: two are dead: the remaining 3 tho mangy are likely to do well:

I have shewn yr. letter to several, who all think it a very curious one: I must needs own it was somewhat too scientifick & replete with too many terms of art to be understood by one so little a sportsman as myself: the Connoisseurs allow yr. precepts to be admirable, and such as could only be laid down by one thoroughly versed in the theory & practice of hunting.

I am pleased to hear you are provided with two hunters so much to your mind: I wish they may carry their rider safe over hedge & ditch & thro' all the dangers of the chase & long be useful to a master, who I am sure will treat them with proper care, & use them with that lenity which is due to their merit.

Your poor friend Key died sometime last June a martyr to Intemperance: he was really possessed of many good qualities to which you are no stranger, & could he have subdued his passions or restrained within proper bounds, would have been serviceable to his friends & to his country.

Lee is as fat, as easy, & I fear (but this entre nous) as Indolent as ever: I think he has too much modesty, the worst of all qualities in a Lawyer, ever to succeed to in that Profession. His wife Mrs. Lee is Just as you knew her—she miscarried sometime ago in romping with Mr. Anderson.

Do you still live in the Temple? & do you propose following the conveyancing business? I think it a pitty after so much time & mony spent to drop that scheme — If you become eminent, you will be enabled to leave a splendid fortune to your son — I take it for granted you will marry & have one: and what signifies it whether a man is taken up with a fox chase or drawing of deeds: for altho' it would [be] difficult to decide wh is the most rational of the two employments, certainly one is infinitely more profitable than the other.

I hear our friend Jenings is going to be married to a sister of Mrs. Jordan's: if there be any truth in the report I wish him Lucky Joy in the choice [of] a good wife; if like her sister, I should think my friend's choice a good deal influenced by beauty: not but that the lady may be possessed of many other good qualities: but I do not know how it is beauty & other good qualities seldom meet in the same person.

I was to have been married the 8th. of last month to an amiable young lady, but was taken ill with fevers in June wh continued without intermission 10 or 12 days, & hung upon me with various intermissions till the middle of July: they gave a great shock to a frame naturally weak: however I have now shaken them off & have recovered my spirits, appetite & strength — If I continue thus recruiting I hope to be married early in Novr. — besides the power of example there are many other rational enducements to marriage; for I cannot agree with Swift that no wise man ever married from good sense: this reflection however true if applied to most marriages in high life is much too [severe?] & too general: matrimony & good sense are not incompatible: however should you differ from me in opinion & side with so great an authority, as I hate disputing & am now determined I will not enter upon a discussion of this nice subject, or produce reasons in support of my opinion: but do not think that this resolution proceeds from a diffidence of a weak cause: do we ever want reasons to support what we approve, or to condemn what we dislike? Whatever may be yr. opinion of this matter, that you may find the happiness you persue in acting in conformity to it, & in determining yr. future conduct is the wish of your sincere friend

C:C:

ALbDrS, CCC Letterbook, 1765-1768, MS 203.1, MdHi.
1. Not found.

∴

CCC to Christopher Chapman Bird

17 Septbr. 176[6][1]

Dr. Xtopher,

I have been pooring these two or three days past over old Accts of near thirty years standing that are now become the subject of a chancery suit[.] My spirits are quite sunk with the fatigue however my perseverance & application will I trust enable me to expose the folly & malevolence of my advisaries.

My last to you was dated 22d. of July: the principal subject of that letter was to desire to inform Mr. Gordon, who has bought me a couple of brood Mares, of an opportunity to ship them for this country, as I had reason to suspect Messrs. Perkins [&] Browne would give themselves very little trouble about it. My suspicion was well grounded: several ships are arived that sailed from London [the?] latter end of June: as they Mares are not come, I suppose Mr. Gordon was not made acquainted with these opportunities, & consequently I must attribute my disappointment to my Correspondents neglect—I do not imagin they will be shiped this fall: a gentleman of my acquaintance will soon embark for London, as he will arrive time enough to have them sent early next spring I shall desire him to take that trouble upon himself, you need not therefore give yourself any farther concern about them.

I have not been able to procure the wild turkies eggs—I f[org]ot to speak in time: I shall not be so forgetful next spring. Pray do not follow my example & forget to send the statutes that are already published; nor to put yr. Father in mind of the Morello grafts from nightengale Hall. Multiplicity of business & the sudden notice of this opportunity obliges me to be short: about the 10th next Novembr. I shall be initiated in the misterious rites, as Milton calls them of Hymen: a greater commendation I cannot make of the young lady than by pronouncing her no ways inferiour to Louisa and that the sweetness of her temper, and other amiable qualities have contributed to efface an impression which similar qualities had made on a heart too susceptible perhaps of tender feelings & on a mind not sufficiently strengthened by Philosophy to resist those & the united power of good sense & of beauty.

If you see Mr. Graves pray present him with my compliments: Remember me kindly to yr. Father & Aunt: I hope I still retain a place in their affections at least they do in mine, neither have I forgot my good friend Mr. Chapman, when he thinks of me, let him say a prayer for his old acquaintance: I am &c

ALbDr, CCC Letterbook, 1765–1768, MS 203.1, MdHi.
1. Misdated 1765.

CCC to Esther Bird

6 Octbr. 1766

Dr. Madam,

I hope you will excuse the freedom I have taken in requesting the favour of you to chuse the silks and other articles contained in the enclosed Invoice: your known good nature, readiness to oblige, & true taste induced me to make this request: thus you see Madam what it is to have an obliging temper, and pleasing fancy. These amiable endowments altho' they endear you to all who have had the pleasure of yr. acquaintance have, I dare say, in more instances than the present, drawn upon yourself the trouble of executing commissions more disagreeable: indeed I can not but flatter myself from the regard you was so kind to express for me when in London, that you will not think this commission disagreeable or too troublesome: from this persuasion chiefly I have ventured to make the proposal. The Brussel's lace & necklace I leave entirely to [yr.] own choice & fancy, and as I am utterly unacquainted with the prices of such things, I shall not limit you to any price: Every Lady should strive to be, what the Spectator[1] finely expresses, <u>elegantly neat</u>: magnificence & finery in Cloaths is neither mine nor the lady's taste: she would chuse them decent, handsom & genteel:[2] if 10 or 12 guineas more in the price of a necklace or of the Brussel's lace will buy them elegant, do not stick at such a trifle: I do mean that a handsom suit of Lace, or Necklace can be bought for 10 or 12 guineas: but that if a handsome necklace or suit of lace could be bought at twenty guineas for instance, I should not begrudge 10 or 12 guineas more to purchase them handsomer & of a better design & more highly finished: this is the only Rule I shall pretend to lay down to [a] lady of yr. prudence, oeconomy & taste — as to the silks, there are, I see some general directions given, which you will be pleased to follow —

I wrote to yr. nephew the 17 of last month & in that letter acquainted him with my intended marriage which I believe if nothing unforeseen happens will take place the first week in Novenbr. You have no doubt some curiosity to know what sort of choice I have made: were I not afraid of doing injustice to the lady, I would endeavour to present you with her Picture; but I have been so accustomed to draw uggly likenesses, that I fear I shall make but a bad hand at handsom one — This much I will say, & this is her chiefest commendation, she has your good sense, a temper equally sweet as yours, and a modesty that would charm a Rake — for Rakes, they say Madam, are as fond of modesty in a wife, as any other set of men. And Pray why? Is it because the lustre of <u>that</u> virtue shines brighter in their view which they most want, or secures to them a fidelity which their conduct may not deserve. I could propose a question still more difficult to be resolved & tho' I do not expect a solution of it from you, yet I shall propose it. Why are the ladies fonder of Rakes than of other men? Perhaps you will deny the allegation: I could support it by numberless examples drawn from ancient & modern history, I could produce many living witnesses of its truth, but the subject would lead me too far, & you might enterpret the attempt as a satyr upon your sex — I assure you I have been sharing my reflections & [not?] pronouncing Judgt. on that aimiable part of mankind, since the opinion a charitable lady of yr. acquaintance was pleased to form of me behind my back from such little inadvertancies — and that opinion too was delivered seriously & deliberately before a sister whom at that time I would have given the world, to have entertained a better of me. Well then since the subject has some how unaccountably led me to the lady: I may mention her name. How is Louisa: there [was] once more musick in that name than in the sweetest lines of Pope:[3] but now I can pronounce it as indifferently as Nancy, Betsy or any other common name—if I ask a few questions, I hope you will not think that I am not quite so indifferent as I pretend to be—but I protest it is mere curiosity or mere good will that prompts me to enquire after her—is she still single?[4] Does she intend to alter her state, or to remain single—if she thinks of matrimony, my only wish is that she may meet with a man deserving of her—

I shall write to yr. nephew by this opportunity & desire him to call upon Mr. Perkins for what money you may lay out in the purchase of the sundry articles in the Invoice—Pray Rember me to your Brother, for whom as for yourself as I shall ever retain an unfeigned esteem & sincere regard. I am Madam &c—[5]

ALbDr, CCC Letterbook, 1765–1768, MS 203.1, MdHi. CCC Letterbook contains a second version of this letter, dated Oct. 20, 1766, sent "for fear of miscarriage" of the first.

    1. A reference to a series of essays, written largely by Joseph Addison and Richard Steele, first published in the *Spectator* (1711–1712).

    2. In the Oct. 20, 1766, version of this letter, CCC wrote: "If my first letter comes to hand you will see I have not tied you down to any price—but have left the whole to yr. discretion, & good management; confident that you are a much better Judge of a lady's dress than myself & that you will avoid the two extremes of extravagance, & meanness & in chusing apparel for my wife will follow the rule, which you have laid down for yourself & consult rather decency, neatness, & genteelness than finery & magnificence." CCC Letterbook, 1765–1768.

    3. Alexander Pope (1688–1744), English poet.

    4. Martha ("Louisa") Baker married in 1767.

    5. CCC struck out the following postscript: "P:S: I had almost forgot to mention that I would chuse to have the silks made up in London: I have accordingly sent the measure of the lady's stays, & of the skirts of her Robes. I hope you will excuse any impropriety in my expressions, for I confess an utter ignorance in these matters—The silk marked θ is for a young lady who lives with us: the initial letters of her name are wrote on her measure—I desire they may be made in the fashion by some skilful mantua maker for our American ladies are every whit as fond of fashions as the English—women will be women in spight of us Philosophers, husbands, Popes, Bishops, & Priests—They must they will be humourd—& the sooner & the more chearfully we poor retches comply, our compliance has a better grace. Pray do not shew this part to yr. Brother, he will say ah poor Carroll I thought it would come to this." (CCC Letterbook, 1765–1768.) The "young lady" was Molly Darnall.

CCC to Christopher Chapman Bird

Octbr. 13th. 1766

Dr. Xtopher,

In my last of the 17th. of Septr. I informed you of my going to be married: you will see by the Invoice enclosed in yr. Aunt's letter, that I have taken the liberty to desire her to buy for my wife the several things therein mentioned & have wrote to her that I should beg the favour of you to call upon Mr. Perkins for the money & I shall write to Mr. Perkins to let you have what ever money the things bought may amount to: at present I can give no sort of guess what sum may be wanted.

I imagin this letter may reach you about the middle of Janry.: the ships generally sail for this province in April — Yr. Aunt will therefore have full time to get the silks made up & sent with the rest of our goods in Mr. Perkins' ship — Be pleased to see them carefully packed up in a strong tight trunck & let the trunck be covered all over with matting bound fast with good cord — This precaution I think necessary, as for want of it, my Cloaths sufferd much on [the] passage — You need not send the trunk to Mr. Perkin's house, it maybe more conveniently shipped from yours (& I beg you will see it stowed away in some safe place:) but I would have you call upon Mr. Perkins and acquaint him that you have such a trunk or packages marked C:C: & numbered 1: 2: &c — & directed to me, which by his leave you intend to put on board his ship: I should not be so particular in my instructions to one so well acquainted with business as yourself, were I not apprehensive some difficulties might be started by Mr. Perkins & some objections made to taking the package on board: the Tobo. Merchants do not chuse to have the goods shipped in their vessels which they do not buy themselves, & I have heared instances of goods being lodged in their ware houses which the persons for whom bought could never prevail upon the Merchants to ship — I would not have it appear that you mistrust any thing of the sort from Mr: Perkins — see the trunk or trunks if more than one will be necessary, put on board the vessel: take two receipts or bills of lading from the Capt. & inclose one of them in a letter to me by the same ship; the [other] keep by you. Should he be privately instructed not to receive them pray endeavour to get them shipped on some other vessel bound to this Port, Pataspsco, or petunxent rivers. Give my complts to Mr. Brunetti —

Should yr. Aunt be dead (which God forbid) I must entreat of you to prevail upon yr. lady to take the trouble upon herself: you, if I mistake not have a pretty good taste in the nick nack way as well as in other matters & I am sure would very willingly assist with yr. advice should it be wanted.

But I must frankly own I trust chiefly to yr. Aunt, she I know has an excellent taste — Pray send me some of the seed of that blue blossoming tree in the outward walk of yr. garden at Ryegate — if you are curious & desire it, I can send you some seeds, & plants that may be curiosities in England—have you heared any thing of that rascal Harry? He will come in here some time or another a convict if he escapes hanging & if I meet with the Chap I shall put in mind of yr. £1000—

I have nothing more to add at present but to wish you your health & every sort of success which may contribute to yr. happiness here & hereafter. I am &c—

ALbDr, CCC Letterbook, 1765-1768, MS 203.1, MdHi.

. . .
.

CCC to Edmund Jenings

14 Octbr. 1766

Dr. Jenings,

I received this day yours of the 21 July[1] with the history of the late Minority[2] for both of which I am extreamly obliged to you. The history I have not had time to peruse but from the contents it must be Interesting & consequently an agreeable present[.] Such performances are generally entertaining but particularly to People so far remote from the scene of action who have not the opportunity from conversation or connections of being made acquainted with the secret springs & workings of party—The busts of the three great men you sent me last year & this book altho' in themselves very acceptable presents have an additional value from the proof they carry with them of yr. friendship & remembrance. I do not care to be behind hand in such offices; as petits soines[3] (permit me for once to borrow an expression from the french language as one of equal import does not occur to me in the English) at the same time they contribute to keep alive & to nourish friendship, display a generous spirit and a turn of mind truly amiable: but in this respect you have greatly the advantage of me from yr. situation: I really know of nothing this country produces worth yr. aceptance: for as to red birds, squirrels, & mocking birds they may please children or women, but to you as they have not novelty to recommend them, they can be of no value either as an amusement or curiosity. If you have a turn for gardening or exotick Plants & flowers I shall perhaps be able to send you such of these which as uncommon in England may afford you some pleasure as a florist, or matter of thought & speculation as a naturalist, or Philosopher.

We have heared of the late changes in the ministry & the most unexpected one of Mr. Pitt's being created an Earl[4] from its being unexpected I would not have you infer that it is thought unmerited: on the contrary none in my Judgement are deserving of a peerage but such who have been useful to their country & have persued its true Interest & glory: and no doubt the Original Intent of bestowing such honours & creating such distinctions [. . .] our subjects was to reward conspicuous merit how often they have been conferred with this view it does not belong to me to say: in the presence instance the spirit of the Institution has been complied with: whether other motives besides the mere rewarding of merit induced his Majesty to raise the great Commoner to the dignity of an Earl, as the ways of Kings are inscrutable — he is the fittest Judge — Yet perhaps the splendor & eclat of nobility may outshine the Patriot's lustre as lesser luminaries disappear before the sun or shine with diminished light: whatever effect this change may have on that great Man's future conduct & principles, his past & importance services should ever be remembered by a greatful people: his memory will ever be revered by the North Americans, at least who owe to his eloquence & protection the enjoyment of whatever is most sacred dear to them.

By the last Philadelphia paper I find there is a report that the King of Prussia had lost his reason: if what you write me of his demand of 2 millions, his connections with France, & Prince Ferdinand's entering into that Powers pay, are true, this madness has seized him in a lucky time for us: as it will probably prevent a war in which, considering the great abilities of that Monarch, we could scarcely come off with honour. France has lossed so much by the late war, that I am convinced she will when sufficiently prepared seek some opportunity of renewing it: Spain from a Jealousy of our growing power & her connections with France will probably be engaged to take part in the quarrel agt. us: the Armament too filling out under Capt. Wallace will encrease her Jealously & fears: sensible of her weakness in those parts for which it is said that squadron is destined, & of this importance also, she has always endeavoured to strut out every European power from those seas and the present attempt to make discoveries & settlements [in] the Southern Ocean will [be] deemed little less than an actual declaration of war.

It does not clearly appear from the Papers what discoveries Commodore Biron[5] has made or where those discoveries lay: by some accounts it should seem that the Commodore has discovered an Island laying off the Patagonia coast in the Attlantick near Cape Horn: by others that he has found out some Islands in the south sea hitherto unknown & which are said not to be far remote from the Main Land — As to the wonderful stories of giants, little horses, great treasure & little danger of resistance from an unmarmed people they are thrown out ad captandum vulgus or perhaps to engage adventurers by the strong incentitives of curiosity & avarice passions generally the most prevalent in such men, to embark [in] the fleet now preparing to sail in the quest of further discoveries.

Should an authentick account be published of Birons voya. I should be much obliged to you for it: but I insist on yr. sending to Mr. Perkins for the money, or I will by no means suffer yr. willingness to oblige me to be expensive to yourself.

Mr. Brice died on the circuit about the middle of last month:[6] his eldest son is to be married soon to Miss Maccubbin: & yr. humble expects to set him an example or to follow his the 5th. of next month: it happens to be gun powder plot[7] — but no wonder that a blooded minded Papist should chuse for feasting & merriment a day wh had like (if you believe the story) to have proved so fatal to a Protestant King & Parliament — Now I have mentioned Protestants & Papists, I could wish & I believe you wish with me, that the unhappy differences & disputes on speculative points of Theology had been confined to divines; or that the happiness of mankind had been the object of those disputes: the savage wars & cruel Massacres, the deliberate murders committed by law, under the sanction of Religion have not reformed the morals of men they have indeed answered the purposes of ambition, & fury they have glutted the Revenge of an enraged Party & sometimes too they have served the cravings of Lust. In this enlightened age we have no reason to expect a renewal of such horrors: but were men as easily misled, there would not be wanting leaders to encourage & incite them & to act the scene over again — excuse this degression not in favour of its novelty, but its shortness — I wrote to you the 27 of last May wh letter I hope you have received — Nothing occurs to me at present worth yr. notice — but to assure you that I am

Yr. sincere friend:

C:C

ALbDrS, CCC Letterbook, 1765–1768, MS 203.1, MdHi.

1. Not found. There is an undated draft, congratulating CCC on the repeal of the Stamp Act and discussing ministerial changes, in Jenings and Jenings, Letterbook, fols. 296–299.

2. John Almon, *The History of the Late Minority; Exhibiting the Conduct, Principles, and Views of That Party, during the Years 1762, 1763, 1764, and 1765* (London, 1765). *Cat. Lib.,* no. 494.

3. "Little cares."

4. In July 1766 William Pitt, newly created earl of Chatham, agreed to the king's request that he form a ministry to replace that of Lord Rockingham. Taking for himself the office of lord privy seal, Pitt made Augustus Henry Fitzroy, the third duke of Grafton, first lord of the treasury, Lord Shelburne secretary of state for the southern department, Lord Camden lord chancellor, and Charles Townshend chancellor of the exechequer.

5. John Byron (1723–1786) commanded the *Dolphin* on a voyage to the South Seas in 1764–1766.

6. John Brice II died Sept. 24, 1766. Donnell MacClure Owings, "Supplement" to *His Lordship's Patronage,* unpublished typescript, Library, MdHi.

7. The Gunpowder Plot was a conspiracy among a number of zealous Roman Catholics to blow up Parliament on Nov. 5, 1605, when the king and members of the royal family were present for opening ceremonies.

$\cdot \; \cdot \; \cdot$
$\cdot$

A Waiver of Consanguinity

Octr. 14th. 1766

I have granted a Dispensation to Mr Charles Carrol of Carrolton to marry his Cousin Miss Rachel Cook witness my hand

John Lewis S.J.[1]

ADS, Carroll-McTavish Papers, MS 220, MdHi.

1. John Lewis, S.J. (1721–1788), came to Maryland in 1750 and from 1763 until 1773 served at the Jesuit mission at White Marsh in Prince George's Co., west of Annapolis. Weis, *Clergy*, 53.

$\cdot \; \cdot \; \cdot$
$\cdot$

CCC to Perkins, Buchanan, and Brown

15th. Octb. 1766

Gent,

Be pleased to forward the two letters herewith inclosed to the persons to whom directed—I have desired Mr. Bird to buy some things for me, which may amount to a considerable sum, but whatever money he may call for on my acct, let him have it. Should the Mares not be shiped before Mr. Charles Digges arrives in London, you need not give yourselves any further Trouble about them: I am sensible the shiping of Mares is some what out of the usual tract of yr. business & therefore may be attended with some inconvenience & trouble: as I am willing to give you as little trouble as possible, I have desired Mr. Digges as a friend & acquaintance to take the charge of the Mares upon himself: & have also requested the favour of him to buy me a Curricle:[1] you will therefore be pleased to advance the ready money that he may purchase the Curricle at the lowest rate, & ship the Mares at the least Cost. I am Gent:

yr. most obd. humble Servt.

C:C:

ALbDrS, CCC Letterbook, 1765–1768, MS 203.1, MdHi.
1. A two-wheeled chaise drawn by two horses.

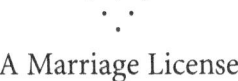

A Marriage License

[Nov. 1, 1766]

By his EXCELLENCY

HORATIO SHARPE, Esq;
GOVERNOR and Commander in Chief in and over
the Province of MARYLAND.

WHEREAS, Application hath been made to me, by Charles Carroll Esquire and Rachel Cooke to be joined in Holy Matrimony: These are therefore to License and Authorize you to solemnize the said Marriage, between the said Persons, according to Law; there appearing no lawful Lett[1] or Impediment, by Reason of any Pre-Contract, Consanguinity, Affinity, or any just Cause whatsoever, to hinder the same.

GIVEN under my Hand and Seal, this 1st: Day of November in the Year of our Lord 1766

Hora. Sharpe

To the Reverend Mr. Brogdon[2] or any other Minister legally Qualified —

DS, Carroll-McTavish Papers, MS 220, MdHi. Printed form; blanks filled in by an unknown hand.

1. "Hindrance or obstruction."

2. William Brogdon (1710–1770) of Calvert Co., an Anglican priest who studied at Trinity College, Dublin, served Queen Anne's Parish in Prince George's Co. from 1751 until 1770. Weis, *Clergy*, 35.

CCC to William Graves

27th. Novr. 1766

Dr. Graves,

The young Lady to whom I was to have been married died the 25th. Instant: she was acknowledged by all her acquaintance, to be a most sweet tempered, amiable & virtuous girl: I loved her most sincerely & had all the reason to believe I was as sincerely loved — Judge of my loss & by it of what I now feel — but I must drop this melancholy subject; my heart is too full & my mind is at present too discomposed, to permit me to be as full & circumstantial as usual — I shall therefore come immediately to the subject of this letter, & be as brief as possible —

You inform me in a postscript to yr. letter of the 18th. Decr. 1765 that Mr. Gordon had told you he had procured two excellent Mares for me: Messrs. Perkins & Compy in their letter of the 13 Janry. 1766[1] write to my Father as follows — We have paid the honourable Lockart Gordon Esqr. £75:0:0 for two Mares wh he has purchased for yr. son with wh we debit yr. acct —

The following is an extract of their letter of the 7th. May 1766[.][2] Mr. Gordon who bought you the two mares has been out of town for a long time past, & tho' we made all possible enquiry, we could not find out where to direct to him, but we left a note at his lodgings in town acquainting of the time the Trotman would sail & desiring him to send for the Mares, that every thing might be got ready for their being ship'd — in answer to wh we have recd a letter from him of wh the inclosed is a copy — Here insert the Copy —[3]

In their letter of 6th. June 1766[4] they say we have red a message from Mr. Gordon acquainting us the Mares are not yet returned from Lincolnshire, but that he expects them in about a fortnight, when he will assign them over to us, as he will be going out of town soon after —

Extract from their letter of 24 June 1766[5] — we have not heared any thing more from Mr. Gordon concerning the Mares —

Extract from their letter of 5th. Septr. 1766[6] — We are much at aloss to account for Mr. Gordon's strange behaviour about yr. Mares, for we have not been able to get any intelligence of them since we wrote to you of 6th. June, tho' we have sent many times to his lodgings, but he has always been out of the way — We are informed he is now at Tunbridge Wells, to wh place we have wrote to him, but have not yet red an answer from him — In June he informed us the Mares would be in town in a fortnights time, when he would assign them over to us — but not hearing from him in that time we sent to his lodgings & found he was gone out of town but to what place was very uncertain, so that we can not say whether they are yet come to London or not —

You have now the whole transaction before you & I leave you to Judge of Mr. Gordon's conduct in this affair — I have hitherto censured my Correspondents imputing the neglect of not shipping the Mares entirely to them: but I now plainly perceive my censures were too precipitate & that the blame rests solely on Mr. Gordon — had that gentleman declined the business at first, I should have no reason to complain: but I think & I dare say you will think so too, that I have reason to complain that when he had promised to buy the Mares, he should neglect doing it, or if bought assigning them over to my Correspondents agreeable to his promise —

It is certain the keeping the Mares in England a twelve month longer than necessary will be a heavy charge & added to the first cost will greatly inhance it: in equity I do not think myself liable to such charge: it will be hard to be saddled with that additional expence as it arises merely from Mr. Gordon's neglect — Indeed were I not acquainted with Mr. Gordon & knew him as a man of honour incapable of falsehood, I should suspect he had not bought the Mares — I beg you will talk to Mr. Gordon about this affair: & if you think proper you may shew him this letter — as it is a nice & delicate subject I leave the management of it entirely to yr. prudence & discretion. I am Dr. Graves

&c

P:S:

By the June Magazine I find there have been lately published 3 volumes of Swift's litterary Correspondence — If they are genuine, I should be glad to have them —

p:s: to be added to Mr. Graves Letter — [7]

If you find, what I surmise, to be true viz that Mr. Gordon has not bought the Mares: I desire you will demand of him the money wh he has recd of Mr. Perkins & yr. receipt shall discharge him from the same — Possibly, he may tell you that he hath not yet bought but will buy the Mares, or perhaps that finding the Mares could not be shipped, he had sold them & bought others —

To take away this subterfuge or to detect i'ts fallacy if made use of, it would not be improper to start the subject as it were accidentally & seemingly to enquire of Mr. Gordon with out any design of whom the Mares were bought. You must be sensible that if Mr. Gordon contrary to what he told you & contrary to what he wrote to Mr. Perkins, has not really bought the Mares, having once deviated from Truth, he merits no further confidence & it would not be prudent in me to trust to him a second time —

I realy wish for Mr. Gordon's sake as much as for my own that my conjectures may be with out foundation — I am unwillingly lead to them by several strong circumstances; & if what I attribute to a worse motive should be the meer effect of thoughtlessness, it is such thoughtlessness as well Justifies me in drawing a conclusion so disadvantageous to the honour of that gentleman & so contrary to the opinion I had conceived of him —

If you can recover the money of Mr. Gordon & I beg you will press him for it, be pleased to pay it to Messr. Perkin & Co.

ALbDr, CCC Letterbook, 1765–1768, MS 203.1, MdHi.

1. Not found.
2. Not found.
3. Not found.
4. Not found.
5. Not found.
6. Not found.
7. CCC added his second postscript on the page of the letterbook following his Nov. 28, 1766, letter to Charles Digges, below.

. . .
.

CCC to Charles Digges

28 Novr. 1766

Dr Sir,

I have had the great misfortune to lose Miss Cooke: she died the 25th. Instant —
you who were well acquainted with her must be sensible how great a loss [I] sustained: I assure you I feel all the weight of it —

As I shall not now want the Curricle I desired you to buy for me, you need not
give yourself any trouble about it — Hayton by whom I send this is gone on board;
& if the wind will permit will sail immediately: the want of time & my distress
obliges me to be short — I am Dr. Sir

yrs. affectionately
C: Carroll

ALbDrS, CCC Letterbook, 1765-1768, MS 203.1, MdHi. Recipient's name noted by CCC
in letterbook.

. . .
.

CCC to Charles Digges

Decr. 2d. 1766

Dr. Sir,

By Mr. Perkins last Letter of the 5th. Septbr. I have strong reason to suspect that
the gentleman whom I commissioned to buy my Mares has not bought them — If
you find this to be the case I must request the favour of you to take that trouble
upon yourself or to imploy some one in whom you can confide as an honest man
& Judge of horses to buy me a couple of 3, 4, or 5 year old fillies — They must have
the following qualities: to be of the best blood, as I intend them for brood Mares:
they should be large beautiful & Bony: Bay I think preferable to any other colour
& Bay Mares are I believe generally reputed the best — their pedigrees to be made
out & properly attested —

I imagine two fillies of the above age & answering the above description may
be had for 30 guineas each — I should not chuse to exceed £75 or guineas for the
two — I particularly recommend their having full blood, beauty, size & strength.

Thus much I think necessary to say to you on the subject — if I have omitted
any thing material yr. Judgt. will supply that defect — [1]

As we have very good Stallions in America, you need not send them to the horse
in England — unless they should be bought time enough to be covered in April &
shipped in May or June about wh time I suppose you will take yr. departure from

London for I should chuse to have them come in the same ship with you or if that Can not be conveniently done, that you should see them shipped in some other vessel before you sail—

If you send them to the horse send them to the very best—& pray take all the precautions in yr. power to have them properly served—

Yr. friends & relations are all well—The Journal will pass & there will be an emittance of Bills of credit to the amount of 65 thousand pounds—in dollars & aliquot parts[2] of Dollars—my Father desires his complits to you—[&] sincerely wish yr. health & safe return & am Dr. Sir

affectionately yours

ALbDr, CCC Letterbook, 1765–1768, MS 203.1, MdHi. Recipient's name noted by CCC in letterbook.

1. Written here and then struck out: "The reason for my not chusing to have Mares exceeding 7 years is this: at that age the mark goes out of their mouth & consequently the purchaser is more liable to imposed upon—but Mares of 9 or 10 years are as good to breed from as any & if you can be assured that those you buy do not exceed 10 years, I would as willingly have them of that age as under."

2. An even part—divided without a remainder.

·   ·   ·
·

CCC to Christopher Chapman Bird

8 March 1767

Dr. Christopher,

Yours by Capt. Craig of the 6th. Novemr. 1766[1] I did not receive till the first of March: Craig's vessel had been in near 6 weeks before he could find or did find an opportunity of conveying the letters & trees, & books to Annapolis: these with the Parmesan Cheese are all safely come to hand: the grafts are alive & likely to do well—I am much obliged to my worthy Friend for them & I wish he may be as lucky in getting the wild turkies I propose sending him this summer—The twenty forth volu: of the Statutes is missing owing I suppose to the neglect of the Publisher, Binders or Packers—Be pleased to apply to Mr. Bathurst about it or to the Binder: the want of this volume makes the set incompleat—

The lady's name to whom I was to have been maried was Cooke a Cousin of mine but not the same I spoke of to yr. Aunt—She possessed every qualification requisite to make me happy—virtue, prudence & consequently good sense, a chearful & even temper an agreeable person—her death was the greater shock to me as it was not apprehended: she had been ill 4 or 5 weeks—but the Doctors either knew not or dissembled her danger—

During her illness I often visited her—her Father's house not being more than

22 or 23 miles from ours — The last visit I paid her was on the twenty fifth of Novr —
on that day she died in about 3 hours after my arrival — she retained her senses
almost to the last: perfectly resigned to her fate she seemed to feel much more for
me than for herself: I make no doubt if Virtue is to be recompensed in a future state
she now enjoys perfect happiness — what must not I have felt during this distresful
scene of wh I was not only an eye witness but the Principal Sharer? Yr. heart is too
tender not to partake even at this distance of yr. friend's grief & to sympathise with
him — All that now remains of my unhappy affection is a pleasing melancholy reflection of having loved & being loved by a most deserving woman. I really know
not how it is but either from lowness of spirits, or from a puny weekly frame perhaps from both as reciprocally the cause & effect — I am grown quite indifferent to
every thing in this world even to life itself — I assure you I speak it without affectation & with due submission to the will of God — I care not how soon a period is
put to this dull sameness of existence here — but I am sensible to merit immortal
happiness we must patiently submit, I was going to say chearfully (but I have not
virtue enough to do that) to the crosses & trials of this life, nay we must drink up
the very dreggs of it — I am come to the dregges of mine — is it then surprising that
I should wish the bitter potion down —

Do not be startled at this morality — I am now virtuous in earnest: at least
ernestly desirous of being so: would to God I had always been of this way of thinking or had acted always in conformity to it — Virtue, believe me, is the only foundation of happiness in this life: there can be no other foundation for happiness in
the other but virtue — reason & revalation both teach this — constant experience
too confirms it to be true — else whence that perpetual anxiety, those endless restless desires in men possessed of all worldly advantages: dignities, power, wealth,
strength, beauty health wisdom, even these favourites of nature are as craving as
uncontented as her most destitute unprovided Children — Why? These men want
virtue! Their desires are insatiable because not fixed on the only object capable of
satisfying Man & intented to satisfy him by rendering him compleatly happy —
Infinitude — & to the enjoyt. of this, virtue only can intitle us.

I am sorry I have put you to the trouble of applying to Mr. Molleson[2] about
shipping the Mares — Mr. Gordon has been strangely neglectful in that affair: I
imputed the whole blame to Perkin's & Brown but I now find it rests solely on
Mr. Gordon — he is a gentleman of honor & veracity or else I should suspect the
Mares had never been bought — All's well, they say, that ends well — I shall chearfully put up with a year's disappointment if I receive this next spring the Mares,
answering the description Mr. Gordon gives me of a Chesnut Mare he had already
bought for me — As there is a perfect understanding between my Father & me so
there are no transactions wh we keep secret from each other: & this accounts for
Mr. Brown's writing to my Father about the Mares: it was the same thing as writing
to myself[.]

I am pleased with the account you give me of yr. little girl as I am with every thing which I think contributes to yr. happiness—for that reason I should be glad to hear you had a boy: altho' you have too much sense to be out of temper at not having one, yet as Such an addition to yr. family would be an encrease of yr. felicity, I can not help sincerely wishing it—from the same motive I could wish were it lawful the reversion of the 200 per An: already vested in you—but this would be wishing my friend's success at the expence of others: & I am sure he has too right a notion of friendship to desire or to expect it from me: besides as most wishes, it would be empty—I am concerned for poor Francis! not for his death for no man is to be pitied on that score! but for his not having made the proper use of life.

Yr. mentioning Ryegate has recalled a thousand pleasing Ideas to my mind: how many happy hours have I past in that pretty spot with an innocent, chearful & contented family—the peace of wh the worst of tempers could not disturb— excuse this reflection on an Aunt who hated the best of sisters. If possible my regard for that amiable woman[3] is increased: my poor dear Miss Cooke often put me in mind of her—there was a striking likeness in their temper & manner, without partiality to the one or flattery to the other I never knew nor do I believe there ever were sweeter & better dispositions.

The Farm leased of Mr. Scawen will be a great addition to what your Aunt holds in her own right—I should be glad to know for what term of years it is taken & at what rent. Mr. Scawens' family I hope is well be pleased to present them with my complts.

I suppose yr. untractable landlord thought the conveniency of the wharf at white Fryers would induce you [to] submit to his extravagant demands[.] I am glad he has been disappointed & that you have found a house in Westminster & a wharf so much to yr. liking: do not forget to let me know yr. directions—

Remember me in the kindest manner to yr. Father & to Mr Chapman, yr. sister, & to Mr. Brunetti: you say, you often talk of me: in return I often think of you, and wish to be with you as sincerely as you wish for me[.]

But I am afraid we shall never meet again in this world: let us retrieve this misfortune as much as lays in our power by a constant intercourse of letters—I promise to be punctual on my part till death shall put an end to all human connections— I heartily wish you well—

P:S:

Pray be more particular in yr. letters: the most trifling circumstances at this distance are interesting—you say nothing of Brunetti: is he alive is he dead? Has he shaken off his unhappy connection with the woman he kept—Has Huddlestone any Children: has yr. sister had another?

ALbDr, CCC Letterbook, 1765–1768, MS 203.1, MdHi.
1. Not found.
2. William Molleson (c. 1732–1804) became James Russell's business partner following

his marriage to Russell's daughter Eleanor in 1762. The business partnership was dissolved in October 1765, and Molleson then entered trade on his own and became Russell's competitor. Price, "One Family's Empire," *Md. Hist. Mag.*, LXXII (1977), 181–186.

3. CCC struck out the words "your Aunt Esther" in favor of the phrase "that amiable woman."

. . . .
. .
.

CCC to Edmund Jenings

9th. March 1767.

Dr. Jenings —

I received a few days ago yr. kind letter of the 18th. of last Novr[1] — Your desire of being ranked in the number of my friends is extremely flattering: I assure you you may depend on holding one of the first places among them, and I hope you will not think me unworthy of being one of the fore most of yours —

Yr. congratulations on my marriage to my Father & to myself are an instance of yr. friendship: we look upon them as the dictates of a heart really interested in our happiness and as such we sincerely thank you for them —

You must have received before this comes to hand the news of Miss Cooke's death: from the sweetness of her temper, virtue & good sense, & from our mutual affection I had the strongest assurances of happiness in the married state. It has pleased God to teach me by this severe visitation that no happiness but what results from virtue, is permanent & secure — Happy is the man who makes a right use of such trials & can draw some consolation from affliction itself —

I must confess Mr. Pitt's Idea of a supreme legislative authority stripped of the power of taxation appears to me to be inconsistent — & nothing that he has yet advanced clears up the inconsistency to my satisfaction —

How can a legislative power be said to be supreme which is limited? And certainly a legislature wh can not extend itself to & embrace every part of govt. must be acknowledged to be so. But taxation is no part it seems of legislation — because all monies are the grant of the commons alone: but is not this very giving & granting an act of legislation? Is not the consent of the lords, who are not the presentives of the People, requisite to such acts by virtue of wh these monies are collected[?] Mr. Pitt indeed, says, that their consent to such grants is only requisite to cloath them with the form of Law — but suppose the lords should refuse their consent — could monies be raised upon the people by order or ordinance of the house of commons only? surely not with out a breach of our constitution —

Had Mr. Pitt said: the house of Commons as the Representative of the People in England give & grant &c: & that from this power lodged in that house in virtue of its representation all grants of money should take their rise, he would have said nothing but the truth — But as the House of Commons of England, is not the Rep-

resentative of the Commons in America, it wants therefore that necessary qualification on wh all grants of money are supposed to be made & consequently the
Jurisdiction or power of Parlt. cannot be said to be so supreme & complete over
America, as it is over England. But this inconsistency in Mr. Pitt's speach is not
what displeases me most—Supposing what he advances to be true that the legislature of G:B: is supreme in all other instances but that of taxation, the Americans
are exposed to an equal[2] danger of slavery & oppression.

If for instance the Parlt. should have the right, & should exert it to restrain us
from manufacturing; this Restraint would be more oppressive than the Stamp Act
itself—as it would force thousands to go naked, & those who are able to purchase
the woolens & other commodities of Britain to pay extravagant prices for them—
If I am to be fleeced, an American might say, if my money is to be taken from
me without my consent, it is immaterial to me in what manner this is effected
whether by a tax upon paper, or by an exorbitant price for goods, which I am ne-
cessitated to take agt. my will—I do not see how you can reconcile this assertion of
Mr. Pitt's with his principles of liberty—unless perhaps he saw that the Assertion
could be attended with no danger: as the impracticability of the measure, would
always defeat the principle & render it useless.

There certainly never was a more awkward & bungling attack than what you
mention made by the Outs on the present administration—if the embargo laid on
wheat was an exertion of the prerogative not strictly legal,[3] yet the measure was
confessedly necessary & done with the approbation of the whole privy council—
no stretch of the Prerogative for the general good will ever endanger our constitution—

I have some confidence from the abilities & integrity of some of the men now
in power, that such measures will be pursued as will tend greatly to the advantage
of Our country—but these measures I am afraid will only afford a temporary relief: they will scarce outlive their authors, unless the principal evils wh threatnen
our constitution are eradicated; Slow & alternative remedies will not restore us to
perfect vigorous health: our wounds are deep: they must be probed to the bottom
many rotten parts must be amputated. The number of great & lucrative posts in
the distribution of the crown should be lessened together with their profits. The
immense debt one of the principal sources of the dearness & badness of our manufactures ought to be at least in part, discharged: the venality, avarice, & profussion
of all orders of men impaired by wholesom laws and the universal depravity of
their manners reformed—these vices in all states have ever been destructive to
publick liberty—they certainly will prove so to ours, unless a speedy & efficacious
remedy is applied—when I reflect on the inveteracy of the disease & the difficulty
of finding out a proper rememdy I almost despair of a cure.

A medium of trade is absolutely necessary to a trading people: such has been
found the want of it in this province, that even the resentment & spirit of party
itself has given way to so useful a measure—the payt. of the Journal, or in other

words of the publick debt has been put off for many years by a contest between the two houses on the subject [of] the Clerk of the councils claim—The publick necessity has at last forced the houses into a compromise & the Journal is at length passed;[4] the provincial debt amounted to fifty odd thousand pounds: to pay this off & to answer other purposes an emission of 65 thousand pounds has been made in dollars and aliquot parts of dollars at 4/6 Sterling each—The Clerk's allowance is to be deposited in the treasurers hands, till the legality of his claim shall be ascertained on appeal to the King & Council—A lottery has been set on foot to raise 1000 pounds towards defraying the expence of an agent at home to be employed in prosecuting the appeal on this & other grievances—

I have not heared what number of tickets have been sold or whether they do sell. I am inclined to think this lottery was only proposed to save appearances: it is certain the dispute was pushed much beyond the importance of the subject— & the lower house might imagin that as the matter had been carried thus far, it could not with propriety be dropt all at once—As a Bill for an Agent would not pass the upper house on the conditions proposed by the lower, this scheme of a lottery was adopted—if it does not fill—why then the people will prudently keep their money in their pockets, no defection from the publick cause can be imputed to the lower house—and their honour is saved—[5]

I am yours sincerely—

ALbDr, CCC Letterbook, 1765–1768, MS 203.1, MdHi.

1. Not found. Edmund Jenings's undated draft of this letter appears in Jenings and Jenings, Letterbook, fols. 310–311. After congratulating CCC on the marriage he assumed had taken place, Jenings attempted to demonstrate to his friend the validity of William Pitt's seemingly contradictory "Idea of a Supreme Legislative Authority divested of the Power of Taxation," argued in favor of the embargo on exporting grain as necessary to prevent starvation, and characterized the duke of Grafton, Lord Chatham, Lord Northington, Lord Camden, and Lord Shelburne as "able & willing Advocates for Truth & the public Welfare."

2. "If not greater" written after "equal" and then struck out.

3. Because of extremely poor harvests in the summer of 1766, the price of wheat and other grain products soared, triggering bread riots throughout England. In an effort to control escalating prices, the ministry prohibited the export of grain from England, although Parliament had enacted legislation limiting the imposition of embargoes until grain reached a specified price. The opposition denounced this suspension of Parliament's ordinance as "arbitrary" and "dangerous," but an effort to overturn Chatham's ministry failed. Jensen, *Founding of a Nation*, 218–219.

4. During the fall 1766 session of the Maryland general assembly, the two houses compromised their long-standing stalemate over the Journal of Accounts and the clerk of the Council's salary by enacting legislation that allowed the clerk's claim to be levied as a tax. The law also provided that the monies be impounded pending a final decision by the king in council upon the legality of the claim on public revenues. With the clerk's claim thus disposed of, the lower house passed the Journal of Accounts.

5. The "Liberty Lobby," as this venture was called, was the method devised by the lower house to finance the expenses of an agent who would present to the king the grievances of the people of Maryland against the proprietor. Despite extensive advertising, however, the high price of tickets—thirty shillings each—evidently dampened public enthusiasm. An insufficient number of chances were sold, and even though the delegates themselves bought up five hundred tickets in May 1768, no drawing was ever held. Barker, *Background of the Revolution,* 337–338.

∴

CCC to Perkins, Buchanan, and Brown

13 March 1767

Gent,

Be pleased to forward the inclosed letters as soon as they come to hand—& to send by the first opportunity a piece of printed Kenting,[1] or linen to make me some handkerchiefs: I leave the choice of it to Mr. Brown[.]

I really ask yr. pardon & hope you will excuse my imputing to you the neglect of not shipping the Mares: I am now convinced that Mr. Gordon was solely blameable: I wish I may not be disappointed a second time—I am Gen:

yr. most &c—

P:S:[2]

ALbDr, CCC Letterbook, 1765–1768, MS 203.1, MdHi.
1. A fine linen cloth.
2. The space following the "P:S:" is blank.

∴

CCC to Edmund Jenings

1767 August—13th

I have received your kind letter of the 3d. of last May[1] with the essay on crimes & punishments & the tracts relating to the Roman Catholicks—for which I am much obliged to you: the author of the essay on crimes & punishments has displayed a great fund of humanity in his little work, interspersed with many Just & Judicious observations—the comment is plainly the production of Voltaire pen:[2] his sacarstical wit & humour are so peculiar & original that [they] easily distinguish his works. The free thinker's letters were wrote I suppose on the Bishop of London's shutting up some of the R:C: Chapels[3]—Seehy tho' condemned to a milder death than Calos, seems to have met with equal malice & injustice in his prosecutors[.][4] It is really surprising that in this age the two most enlightened nations of Europe shoud give such shocking instances of religious fanaticism — I am of opinion, were an unlimited toleration allowed of & men of all sects were to converse freely with each other, their aversion from a difference of religious principles would soon ware away — At the same time, if none but who professed the established religion were admitted to posts of profit & trust & the exclusion of all others made the sole punishment of their dissenting from the established mode of faith, this measure might probably make more proselytes thereto, than even the rigorous execution of penal laws — No persecutions have ever been found effectual in suppressing of any religious Sect, unless such as will totally exterminate it either by banishment or by putting to death men women & children — the nature of man is such that he can not be [lict?] out of his opinions tho' he may be laughed or coaxed out of them: Force of all others is certainly the most improper argument to convince the mind — those against whom it is employed are apt to conclude that their opinions can not be confuted by other arguments —

I did not hear of my friend Col: Ludwell's death[5] till I saw an acct of it in the english papers — I really was much concerned at the news for I had a sincere esteem & regard for that worthy gentleman: his remembrance of me in his last moments as it is a proof of his friendship, can not but be pleasing — I have not as yet heared from the executors: one of them in a letter to a lawyer of this place, first informed me of Co: Ludwells having left me the choice of his books: I have wrote to that glentleman [gentleman] for a copy of the will so far as it relates to me as yet have rced no answer — If Miss Ludwell[6] is still in England please to assure her of my best wishes for her health & happiness —

As to your censures on the want of Patriotism, the venality, profusion, & corruption of the great I am afraid they are too well founded in truth — as Individuals having an Interest in the welfare of our country we can not but wish well to it: but such is our situation in life at least mine, than we can do but little more — Providence has placed us at too great a remove from those stations where the example of disinterestedness & publick spirit because seldom & more conspicuously displayed has a proper influence on the actions of the great — the honesty & uprightness of a private man may gain him the confidence & esteem of those with in his own circle & within the narrow bounds thereof it may per Chance procure him one or two imitators: I am resolved never to give myself the least concern about politicks but to follow the sensible advice given by Candid to improve my own little spot to the utmost & to remain content with the profits a grateful Soil & laborious industry will supply.

This conduct as it will make me independent & I hope virtuous, for virtue & independency are seldom separate, so it will afford me an amusement of all others perhaps the most rational — omne tulit punctum qui miscuit utile dulce[7] — Swift, I think, says some where that a man who by his superior industry & application makes an acre of ground produce two for one in the customary method of cultivation, is of more real utility to his country, than all the politicians that ever existed or will exist in it —

Perhaps before you receive this I shall be married. I have been so successful as to gain the affections of a young lady[8] endowed with every quality to make me happy in the married state: virtue: good sense & good temper: these too receive no small lustre from her person, which the partiality of a lover does not represent to me more agreeable, than what it really is[.] She really is a sweet tempered, charming, neat girl a little to young for me I confess — especially as I am of weak & puny constitution but in hopes of better — hope springs eternal in the human brest — we are always wishing & hoping for one thing or another, amongst others what I now hope & wish for is yr. health & happiness & that you will place me in the number of yr. friends — if you doubt of having two; at least look upon me as one — for I really am so —

C.C.

ALbDrS, CCC Letterbook, 1765–1768, MS 203.1, MdHi. Recipient's name noted by CCC in letterbook.

1. Edmund Jenings's undated draft of this letter, expressing his condolences for CCC's "Loss of Her who you intended to compleat your Happiness," his hopes that "the Merit of some other of your Countrywomen will soon remove your Regret & give You the Happiness you deserve," and reporting the news of Philip Ludwell's death, appears in Jenings and Jenings, Letterbook, fols. 326–327.

2. Caesare Bonesana Beccaria, *An Essay on Crimes and Punishments* . . . (London, 1767). An edition appeared in 1767 with a commentary attributed to Voltaire. Jenings's letter of May 3 characterized the work as reflecting the spirit of Montesquieu.

3. Richard Terrick (1710–1777) became bishop of London in June 1764. His actions against Roman Catholic chapels began in late 1765.

4. Nicholas Sheehy (1728–1766), an Irish Catholic priest, and Jean Calas (1698–1762), a Huguenot merchant from Toulouse, were both convicted on hearsay evidence and executed as a result of religious intolerance. Sheehy, openly hostile to English rule in Ireland, was initially arrested and accused of treason for an attack on English troopers near Clonmel. Acquitted at a trial in Dublin, he was rearrested, tried in Clonmel, and condemned for the death of an informer whose body had never been found. In France, Calas was accused and convicted of murdering his eldest son to prevent his conversion to Catholicism, when, in reality, the boy had committed suicide and the parents had attempted to hide the fact. Calas was broken on the wheel before being strangled and burned. After Calas's widow escaped to Geneva, Voltaire took up her cause, and in 1765 Calas and his family were cleared.

5. Philip Ludwell III died in England on Mar. 25, 1767, at the age of fifty-one. Jenings had written that "our Friend Coll: Ludwell . . . died after a long decay the 25th of March last and I attended His Remains to the Grave. He was ever Mindful of you and has left to you as token of His Esteem the Choice of his books in Virginia." Edmund Jenings to CCC, [May 3, 1767], Jenings and Jenings, Letterbook, fols. 326–327.

6. Ludwell left three unmarried daughters: Hannah Philippa (1737–1784), Lucy (?–1814),

and Frances (1750–1768). This is probably a reference to Frances. Edmund Jennings Lee, *Lee of Virginia, 1642–1892: Biographical and Genealogical Sketches of the Descendants of Colonel Richard Lee* . . . (1895; reprint, Baltimore, 1974), 129–130.

7. "He has carried off everything who has mixed the useful and the pleasant." Horace *Ars poetica* 343.

8. Molly Darnall.

∴

CCC to William Graves

27th. Aug: 1767

I have yours of the 4th. of last Febry.[1] now before me: for I keep all your letters not only because coming from you they are really dear to me, but because without doing this it is almost impossible to be a good correspondent: when we are writing to a friend with his letter upon table, we are reminded of many little circumstances contained in it wh otherwise would have escaped our notice—thus a kind of continued conversation is preserved, & we answer his questions as if present, and are at liberty to propose our own in turn—

I am quite of yr. opinion & I adopt all yr. arguments in favour of the matrimonial state: after such a declaration you will no doubt expect to hear that I entertain fresh thoughts of matrimony—I not only do, but the thing is already concluded on & the ceremony will be performed some time in Septr. or Octbr. next: the ladys name is Darnall: of a good family, without any money: in every other respect she is such as you would recommend to yr. friend: chearful, sweet tempered, virtuous & sensible—her person is agreeable & cleanly[.] Cleanliness in a woman Graves with me is a strong recommendation the more so, as it is a quality very often wanting in the fair sex at least I have found it so, perhaps you may have had better luck than yr. hum: Servant—if women who live by a certain profession are so deficient in an essential point of their calling, what are we not to apprehend from wives, who are above those little arts of pleasing: many married men have complained, that prostitutes are neater[2] than their wives: I presume they spoke from experience—

You say, you believe Gordon will send the mares by & bye & behave himself like a gentleman: the enclosed extracts of two letters received from a friend in London will convince you of the contrary—I have sent a power of Attorney to Mr Perkins to sue him for the money. I am very sorry that I ever commissioned Gordon to buy the mares not merely from the disappointment I have met with & the loss I am likely to sustain, but on account of the indelible stain [on] his character, which all the blood of all the Gordons will never wash away. Gordon, I dare say, had once good principles; there perhaps was a time in his life when the very thought of such an action would have brought a generous glow upon his Cheek—how dangerous is the love of pleasure in all men! particularly in those whose means are so scanty

& whose desires unbounded — poverty and a strong propensity to pleasure in the same person are incompatible with honesty. I have directed Perkins to recover the money of Gordon, because as you are acquainted with him, I thought it would be disagreeable to you to undertake that business.

The addition of Swifts works which I have, is the Dublin octavo of 1735: I mention this because you say you did not chuse to send the 3 volu: of his correspondence without knowing the size of my Addition that you might purchase them of the same size with it —

I have received all the books mentioned in yr. last for wh I am much obliged to you; But I must recommend to you to get all the books you send me bound in London: the binding of them here amounts to more than the prime cost.

I propose writing to Barrington to thank him for his ingenious present: he has displayed a great extent of reading, in his work,[3] perhaps an affected knowledge of the languages, and a turn of thought or humour peculiar to himself, with here & there a specimen of false wit —

I intend to peruse it a second time more attentively — for it is a book that will bear rea[ding] [. . .] named, I should have [. . .] been the Author from several of the ob[servations] [. . .] particularly.

Mehegan's history[4] has not only the merit of [. . .] Style, & a well digested plan, lucidus ordo,[5] to [. . .] contains several judicious & some few striking & ne[w] [. . .] his religious sentiments altho' bold & free, are yet so artful [. . .] not to expose him in the present situation of France [. . .] confinement in the Bastile: but I cannot help thinking that such a[n] apprehension has made him more cautious than otherwise he [would] have been in exploding the prejudices of education: an expression very commonly used by certain authors who were they able to root out those prejudices, that is the Christian Religion, would not I verily believe substitute a better system in its place —

Be pleased to send the inclosed letter by yr. Sert. to Lewis the book seller: it relates to the histories of Ireland by Warner & Gahegan[.][6] I had the first volumes of both from Lewis from whom I expect the second volumes when published — as also that of Indostan: my Clerk is now making out a list of my books, wh if compleated time enough, I intend to send with this[.] My Father does not want any other histories of Ireland: he desires his compliments to you: the old gentleman as he often hears me speak of you, has conceived a regard & liking for you — Be pleased to send me the best edition of Vitruvius Britannicus — I believe there are 3 volumes of that work —

The subject you propose to be discussed by Mr. Dulany, he would not I imagin care to attempt as a matter of meer amusement unless the discussion might answer some publick end — & I much doubt whether a thorough investigation would any ways conduce to the mutual advantage of the colonies & mother country.

[. . .] will not bear a [. . .][7] difficulties too & danger would dissuade [. . .] to the task from attempting it: his friends might [. . .] him periculosam opus aloe tractas

& incedis [. . .] ontos cinen doloso.[8] Tacitus in speaking of [Trajan sa]ys duas res olim dissociabiles conjunxit Imperium & [liber]tatem:[9] let english ministers endeavour to imitate Trajan [let the]m assert & maintain the general superintending & controlling power of England & at the same time studiously avoid such measures as are subversive of American freedom: if this freedom & that power are res dissociabiles, incompatible, I am sorry for it — but let us retain our liberty whatever becomes of the power —

Since I wrote the above, I have seen the resolutions of the house of Commons of last May[10] — the duties intended to be imposed on several commodities therein enumerated are to raise a fund for supporting a board of commissioners of the customs & to render the governors & chief officers of the civil department [very?] independent of the people — how this measure will be relished by the colonists who are clear sighted & Jealous enough of their governors, you will easily guess: without any pretensions to Prophecy I foretell it will give great disgust & such impositions on goods of the manufacure of g:B or exported from thence will certainly lessen the consumption of them: & will have this further bad effect: the increased value of English manufactures will force the colonists to manufacture for themselves — tho' I expect to hear soon of some act to restrain us from manufacturing altogether: there is already an act prohibiting slitting mills in America[11] — why not make an act to prohibit us from making shoes, stockings or corse linens & woollens? In short an act might be so penned as to oblige us to purchase all those articles from England at what price the English shopkeeper chuses to put on them, or in case of our inability to pay for them to go naked — this would be a very wise act and productive of the following salutary affects — first the English shopkeepers, Merchts & tradesmen would reap an exorbitant profit for what goods could be disposed of — tho' this profit might lessen the consumption yet the Bala. would still be the same in yr. favour: it comes to the same thing whether 20 bales of Merchandise sell at £12 each, or 40 at £6. Another advantage would result therefrom to the nation wh you are not perhaps aware of — the good people of England, are remarkably tractable, submissive, orderly, & the least given to riots of any people in the world: particularly the Journey men & handy craft men — to what purpose to confine such tame spirits to close labour 6 days out of 7: now in my scheme their profit would enable those mechanicks to divert themselves 3 days in the week, these they might employ in manly exercises: Jumping, restling, heaving the bar,[12] boxing &c such sports would fit them to fatigue & to the toils of war; & invigorate their bodies, now perhaps somewhat enfeebled by a sedantary life. But the chief Benefit which would accrue to G:B: remains to be told —

If the greatest part of the Americans were constrained to go naked as they certainly would by such an act as above mentioned, it is more than probable the many diseases incident to this climate would soon put a stop to population: the severity of the weather would pinch to death thousands of poor naked americans who had heretofore been used to cloathing — England would then have nothing to fear from our numbers, whatever she might from our resentment of such usage — you know the old proverb nothing so dangerous as to provoke a person able to revenge the provocation. If England forces her colonies to rebellion, she must take the proper steps to make that rebellion ineffectual by reducing their strength & the most effectual way of doing this is by putting a stop to the encrease of our people — but whether this will answer the end of colonization I submit to the wisdom of higher powers.

As the bear hams did not succeed, I have been looking out for some venison hams but hitherto without success: if I can procure any you shall have a taste of American venison at the crown & Anchor — I think our venison when fat preferable to yours. I am Dr. Graves &c —

ALbDr, CCC Letterbook, 1765–1768, MS 203.1, MdHi. Recipient's name noted by CCC in letterbook. Parts of pages three and four missing.

1. Not found.

2. CCC first wrote and then struck out "cleaner."

3. [Daines Barrington], *Observations on the Statutes, Chiefly the More Ancient, from Magna Charta to the Twenty-first of James the First* . . . (London, 1766). *Cat. Lib.,* no. 76.

4. Guillaume Alexandre Méhégan (1721–1766), *Tableau de l'histoire moderne* . . . , 3 vols. (Paris, 1766). *Cat. Lib.,* no. 1357.

5. "Clarity of arrangement." Horace *Ars poetica* 41.

6. CCC's note to Lewis, dated Aug. 29, 1767, follows this letter to William Graves in the letterbook.

7. First half of two lines missing, with the remainder of each line struck through.

8. Possibly "You discuss and advance a dangerous work from the political wing."

9. "He brought together two things that were previously incompatible — imperial rule and liberty." Tacitus *Life of Julius Agricola* 3.1.

10. The Townshend Acts, proposed in May 1767 and assented to by the king on June 29, to take effect Nov. 20, levied duties on colonial imports of tea, paper, glass, and paint. Additional legislation empowered superior court justices to issue writs of assistance, created new admiralty courts, and established an American board of commissioners of the customs, located in Boston and responsible directly to the Treasury board in London.

11. The Iron Act of 1750 prohibited the colonists from building rolling, plating, or slitting mills or steel furnaces in an effort to prevent the manufacture of iron products in America. Charles M. Andrews, *England's Commercial and Colonial Policy,* The Colonial Period of American History, IV (New Haven, Conn., 1938), 349 n.

12. Probably the Highland sport "tossing the caber," which involves throwing a pole or spar.

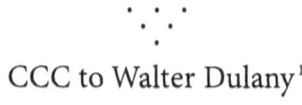

CCC to Walter Dulany[1]

Aug: 29 1767

Sr,

I just received the inclosed from Mr. Brookes.[2] I suppose it will be necessary to apply to Mr. Alexander[3] — or as your brother[4] is at Hunting Ridge[5] Mr. Brooke might advise with him what steps to take — I am informed that negroes sell cheap in Virginia: as they are much wanted at the works would it not be pro[per] to direct Clt. Brooke to attend the Sales? Next Octbr. I am told will be the best time to purchase when it is probable the gentleman says from whom I had my information, young likely country born negroes may be bought at £25 or 30 Sterling — I am Sr.

Yr. most hum: Sert.
Ch: Carroll of Carrollton

p:s:

You may write by the bearer to Mr. Brooke & direct him how to proceed in the affair if you think proper —

I think Mr. Brooke shou'd apply to Mr. Alexander for Directions how to proceed in the above Affair, and also take my Brother's Advice. My Bror. I believe will be down to morrow at this Place, so that Mr. Brooke shou'd go to him to day —

I shou'd be for purchasing Negroes in Virginia, since they are to be had so cheap there as Mr. Carroll mentions — I know of but one Reason against doing it of this Side of Winter, which is that we shall probably have them all to cloath with Goods bought here, for it is very uncertain whether our Goods will come in in time from England; however I am willing to run the Risque — Mr. Carroll had better write a circular Ltr to the Compy on this Subject and have the Opinions of all the Gent, as this I suppose will be sent to Mr. Brooke —[6]

Yrs.
W Dulany

Mr Brooke should apply to Mr. Alexander and follow his advice — as I suppose we shall be Perplexed with a Lawsuit about the Land I think the Clerk should make out a state of the Compas Case and send a Copy to Each of the Compa and Have Copies Ready for such Gentn of the Law as the Compa Chuse to Employ — I shall be Glad to Purchase Such Negroes as the Compa want in Virginia if they Can be Had on The Terms Mr Carroll mentions[.]

My ⅓ of Any fee for Mr Alexander I will send at any Time[.][7]

C Carroll[8]

I concur with Mr Carroll Barr that Mr. Alexander's Advice be taken, & after taken, that it ought to be followed. My Proportion that is to say $\frac{1}{10}$[9] of the fee will always be ready.

D Dulany

ALS, Carroll-Maccubbin Papers, MS 219, MdHi. Addressed by CCC to Walter Dulany. Endorsed by CCC: "B:C 1767 29 Augst."

1. The Baltimore Company partners frequently communicated by means of a "circular" letter to which each man added his remarks and signature in turn. In this case, CCC was the initial author and Walter Dulany the first recipient.

2. For CCC's cousin Clement Brooke (?–by 1809), the clerk of the Baltimore Company, see Appendix I, Chart E. Brooke's letter, dated Aug. 27, 1767, informed his employers of the forcible entry onto a company tract by the property's former owner in an attempt to reassert his claim. Carroll-Maccubbin Papers, MS 219, MdHi.

3. Probably Baltimore lawyer Robert Alexander (1740–1805), whose father-in-law, Alexander Lawson, had worked for the Baltimore Company. *Bio. Dic. Md. Legis.*, I, 103.

4. Daniel Dulany, Jr.

5. Hunting Ridge, a country seat located west of Baltimore Town, was originally owned by Daniel Dulany, Jr.'s father-in-law, Benjamin Tasker, Sr., a founder of the Baltimore Company.

6. In the manuscript, this paragraph follows the writer's signature.

7. In the manuscript, this sentence follows the writer's signature.

8. Charles Carroll, Barrister.

9. Daniel Dulany, Jr., and Walter Dulany, each having inherited half of their father's original one-fifth share in the Baltimore Company, were each responsible for a tenth of the ironworks' expenses.

$\cdot \cdot \cdot$

CCC to Christopher Chapman Bird

Sept 10th. 1767

Dr. Sir,

My last to you was dated the 8th. of last March: the last ship expected from London is arrived and no letters from you: what am I to think of yr. silence or what can I impute it to? I hope no disaster has happened in yr. family or to yourself which occasions this strange, I had almost said, neglect of your old acquaintance: indeed your silence is the more surprising, as I not only expected letters from you, but to receive some things which I took the liberty of troubling your Aunt to buy for my Cousin Miss Molly Darnall & who is greatly disappointed at not receiving them— I never once doubted of getting them by some of the latter ships as Mr. Perkins had informed me in his letter of the 2d. March 1767[1] of having sent to acquaint you with Kiltey's sailing & having received this answer from you that you had some things to ship, but that they could not be shipt by Kilty — I suppose because they were not ready at the time of his sailing —

Mr. Perkins & Co. in his letter of the 7th. Feby 1767[2] Informs my Father that they had recd my letter of the 16th Octbr. desiring them to pay you for some things which I had desired your Aunt to purchase for me; that you had called upon them the 19th. Janry, when they paid you £200:0:0 — they also inform my Father in the same letter, that the letters inclosed to them for you & yr. Aunt, were forwarded immediately on the receipt of them, but that Heyton in his letter from the downs mentioning the melancholy news of Miss Cooke's death, they sent to acquaint you of it, desiring you not to proceed in executing the order, since wh they say they have not heared from you —

Immediately on the death of Miss Cooke my Father wrote to yr. Aunt counter-manding what I had desired her to purchase for that lady: at the same time re-questing the favour of her to buy the few things mentioned in the Invoice, marked M:D — that letter was dated the 26th. of Novr.[3] & I suppose came to hand by Heyton, and I doubt not yr. Aunt received it.

As the things contained in M:D's Invoice could not amount to above 20 or 30 pounds at most, & as the largest & by much the dearest part of the commission was counterorder[d] there must be a considerable balance in your hands, of the £200 paid you by Perkins — I have sent to Mr. Perkins an order upon you for the whole £200: being uncertain whether any part of it has been expended; if any part of the £200 has been laid out in the purchase of the things for Miss Darnall, you are to be allowed what ever those things bought amount to upon yr. delivereing them to Mr. Perkins & Co., & their receipt for the Balance will be a sufficient discharge[.]

In my last of the 8th. of March I informed you that the 24th. volu: of the Stat-utes was missing: it certainly was never sent — as the want of that volume will make the whole set incompleat, I beg you will apply to Mr. Bathurst for it, perhaps the binder may have neglected to bind it & may have it in his shop; Mr. Bathurst is I think accountable for the loss of that volume & obliged to make it good —

I had bespoke some wild turkies & had actually agreed with a poor man for 5 which he had found & was raising for me: I intended to ship them in one of the forward ships, but when I sent for them the poor fellow informed the Messenger, that his landlord had obliged him to part with them, altho' he alledged that they were engaged to me: you will imagin this landlord knows nothing of politeness or the obligation of a promise & was never out of the wilds of America; yet he was educated in England & is now member of our lower house of Assembly & styles himself a gentleman: but there are such natures which no education can alter or reform —

I desire to be kindly remembered to all the family and conclude with hearty wishes for yr. happiness — I am &c —

ALbDr, CCC Letterbook, 1765–1768, MS 203.1, MdHi. Recipient noted by CCC in letter-book as "Mr. Bird Junr."

1. Not found.
2. Not found.
3. Not found.

. . . .

CCC to Perkins, Buchanan, and Brown

10th. Sept: 1767.

Gent,

I have left the inclosed to Mr. Bird open for yr. perusal: be pleased to seal & deliver it together with my order upon him for the £200 which you have herewith: As I had desired his Aunt to purchase a few articles for Miss Darnall, wh were not countermanded, it is probable, she has made that purchase[.] You are therefore to give Mr. Bird a receipt for the Bala. of the £200: after deducting the price of those things when delivered to you care, & I beg the favour of you to send them with our other goods by Kiltey.

The £75 pounds repaid by Gordon to Mr. Digges are lodged with Mr. Philpot, who is to pay it away to Mr. Wildman for two Mares to be shiped in Lewis next spring. I am &c

ALbDr, CCC Letterbook, 1765–1768, MS 203.1, MdHi.

. . . .

CCC to Thomas Philpot

1st. Octbr 1767

Sr.

Mr. Charles Digges informs me that he hath lodged with you £75:0:0 the money he received of Mr. Gordon, and has directed you to pay it to Mr. Wildman when that gentleman delivers into your hands two blooded fillies which are to be shiped in Capt. Lewis—

I understand since that Mr. Wildman breeds his horses of his own: gentlemen Jockies, you know are not very scrupulous in putting off the worst: he has sent in to Mr. Barnes a couple of fillies which turn out but indifferently: these reasons have induced me to caution you agt. too implicit a faith in Mr. Wildmand's words or Judgt. You would oblige me by consulting with some other person a Judge of blooded horses before you strike a bargain with Mr. Wildman—

Unless the fillies he offers, answer nearly the following description, I would not have you buy them: as the expence & risk of importing fillies are considerable, I should chuse to import none but the very best —

1st. then the fillies you are to ship to me must be handsom: secondly large of their age: this qualification I beg you to attend to as essential: 3dly bony — 4th of a bay colour — if fillies having all the other qualities above specified, should happen to be not bay, I would not have you except to them merely on that account: my meaning only is that I should prefer bay fillies equally good in other respects to those of any other colour — I suppose Mr. Digges left with you proper instructions for shipping them: I shall not therefore be at the trouble of repeating those instructions: Capt. Lewis I am convinced will take great care of them on their passage[;] one thing I must recommend to him viz to lay in plenty of water & provisions for them — I had almost forgot to mention a very material point: that is to have their pedigrees made out & well attested — I desire my complts to Mrs. Philpot and am with real & sincere wishes for yr. success in trade Sr

Yr. most hum: Servt.
Ch: Carroll of Carrollton

P:S:

I desired Mr. Philpot to send in a groom to take care of the fillies on their passage, unless there should happen to be a servt. on board, who would take care of em —

ALbDrS, CCC Letterbook, 1765–1768, MS 203.1, MdHi. Recipient noted by CCC in Letterbook.

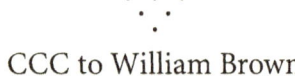

CCC to William Brown

17 Octbr. 1767

Miss Darnall has taken the liberty to request Mrs. Brown to purchase some articles in the inclosed Invoice: and I doubt not but Mrs. Brown will be so good natured as to execute the commission to Miss Darnall's Satisfaction: I compute her invoice will amount to £150 or 160 pounds: perhaps it may amount to £200: on this head I can say no more than this, let the things be bought at the best rate — but at the same handsome & genteel —

Be pleased to forward the inclosed letter to Harrison as soon as it gets to hand: I have directed him to make me a suit of Cloths for an approaching solemnity which I imagin will take place some time next May: I therefore desire that my Suit & Miss Darnalls things may be sent in some early ship: if they can be got ready time enough I should chuse to have them sent by Capt. Hendrick —

From these circumstances you will not be at a loss to guess the nature of the solemnity hinted at above — I wish you success, health & happiness my complts to Mr. Perkins & his brother: I am Sr.

yr. most hum: Servt.

CC

ALbDrS, CCC Letterbook, 1765–1768, MS 203.1, MdHi. Recipient noted by CCC in letterbook.

. . . .
. .

CCC to Mr. Harrison

19 Octbr [1767]

Sr,

The last Clothes you sent me fit me very well except that the breeches are a little too narrow over the knee — As soon as this reaches you I desire you will make me a plain frock suit of superfine white cloth waiscoat & one pair breeches of the same: I should chuse to have the coat & waiscoat lined with white silk: this is to be a marriage suit: let it therefore be made genteel without any lace about it either of gold or sylver — As soon as it is finished send it to Mr. Perkins well packed up. I am &c —

ALbDr, CCC Letterbook, 1765–1768, MS 203.1, MdHi. Recipient noted by CCC in letterbook.

. . . .
. .

CCC to William Graves

7th. Novr. 1767

Dr. Graves,

My last to you was dated the 27th. August; I shall here touch upon the most material parts of that letter least it may not have got safe to hand —

I informed you in the aforesaid letter that I expected to be married this last Octobr. to Miss Darnall but the frequent prorogations of our Assembly wh will be disolved of course next month have hitherto prevented our marriage from taking place: A new assembly will be chosen this winter, wh will meet early in the spring:[1] & then I propose getting a law passed to empower Miss Darnall, who is under age, to consent to a settlement in bar of dower[2] — If I succeed in my application to the house for this purpose, I imagine I shall be married some time next May —

You did not send me the 3 volumes of Swifts correspondence, because you said you did not know the size of my addition of his works — it is the Dublin 8o. 1735 —

I should be glad to have a Pamphlet of Swifts intituled — Reasons humbly offered to the Parliament of Ireland for repealing the sacramental test in favour of the Catholicks[3] — vide Orrery's remarks on the life & writings of Swift — Pag: 181 — Duodecimo — 1752[4] — where an account of this Pamphlet is given — Pray do not omit to send me the remaining volumes of Blackstone's commentaries when they are published — there is a little tract referred to in a note of the second book of his commentaries Pag: 202 wh I am desirous of having: it is intitled an essay on collateral consanguinity[5] — do not forget to send me Vitruvius Britannicus and the best edition of it — as I have the first volume, if you can by accident light upon the second & third volumes you need not buy the first — but rather than be without that curious & entertaining work I would have you purchase the 3 volumes.

Whatever books you send, be pleased to get them bound in London, for the binding here amounts nearly to the first cost —

I wrote to Mr. Barrington by the same opportunity I wrote last to you,[6] to thank him for his ingenious observations on the Statutes: you may inform him that he shall certainly have a taste of some venison hams next spring or summer for I have bespoke some of two or three different people, who I dare say will not disappoint me.

Our Clerk has been sick ever since the middle of Septr. so that he has not been able to compleat the Catalogue of my books; and I have been taken up so much with business of more consequence, that I have not had leisure time to do it myself —

I have not amongst my collection either Addisons works (the spectators & tatlers excepted)[7] nor Drydens: no english gentleman should be without those authors, you will therefore be pleased to send me the best edition of their works —

I do not as yet hear that the late duties imposed by act of Parliament on paper & other articles imported here occasion any great disgust:[8] the Act to suspend the legislation of New-York[9] is most resented, & justly ought to be, as a most open & formidable attack upon the general liberties of Ameria[.] I need not point out to you the dreadful tendency of such measures: they are really the most destructive to the true Interest of England, that can possibly be devised and pursued: as to the impositions on the sundry manufactures or exports from Britain, the most clear sighted Americans look them in their true light, as premiums upon their own manufactures[.]

By the late prints we have learnt the death of Charles Townshend:[10] he was, I believe, esteemed to have great abilities, but bore the Character of a time serving man; yet I am at loss to guess, why that character was so peculiarly applicable to him wh seems to be a general character applicable to and adapted to all your great men, of all parties —

Pray what are your sentiments of the late expulsion of Jesuites from Spain?[11] General accusations agt. a body of men of great crimes & misdemeanors, without particular proof, are to me strong confirmations of the falsity of those accusations — it is my private opinion, that the Rm. Cath: princes are desirous of rooting out the regular Clergy in their dominions, not only with a view of seizing their estates, and enriching with their plunder a few court favourites, but to ease their people of a dead weight and themselves of a political incumbrance — had I more time I should swell this letter to much greater seize [size]: for I take a particular pleasure in writing to you because I have a sincere friendship & esteem for you — wh neither distance of time & place will efface — I am Dr. Graves &c —

ALbDr, CCC Letterbook, 1765–1768, MS 203.1, MdHi.

1. The Maryland assembly was formally dissolved on Dec. 7, 1767, and new elections were ordered. The new legislature convened in May 1768.

2. An agreement by which the bride accepted a fixed lifetime settlement in exchange for relinquishing her dower right to a specified portion of her husband's estate, if he should predecease her. Still a minor at age eighteen, Molly Darnall could not, without legislative action, legally bind herself to such a contract.

3. Probably Jonathan Swift, *The Advantages Proposed by Repealing the Sacramental Test, Impartially Considered; to Which Is Added, Remarks on a Pamphlet Intitled, The Nature and Consequences of the Sacramental Test Consider'd* (Dublin, 1732).

4. John Boyle, fifth earl of Orrery (1707–1762), *Remarks on the Life and Writings of Dr. Jonathan Swift . . .* (London, 1751).

5. William Blackstone, "An Essay on Collateral Consanguinity . . . ," in *Law Tracts . . .* (London, 1762).

6. CCC to Daines Barrington, Aug. 29, 1767, not printed. CCC Letterbook, 1765–1768.

7. Joseph Addison (1672–1719), an English essayist, poet, and statesman, contributed essays to the *Tatler* (1709–1711) and the *Spectator* (1711–1712), which were subsequently reprinted in various editions. *Cat. Lib.* lists his *Works . . . ,* 4 vols. (London, 1721) (no. 13) as well as the *Spectator,* 8 vols., with no date of publication (no. 1025).

8. The populace of Maryland, in contrast to their behavior during the Stamp Act crisis, remained generally indifferent during the years when the Townshend Acts were in effect. The colony's merchants, when called on to adopt a policy of nonimportation, vigorously resisted such suggestions until the spring and summer of 1769, when they agreed to a very partial and lax boycott. When news of the repeal of the Townshend Acts reached the colonies in the fall of 1770, the nonimportation movement ended quickly in Maryland as it did elsewhere. Hoffman, *Spirit of Dissension,* 84–91.

9. In June 1767 Parliament passed the New York Suspending Act, which prohibited the New York legislature from passing any laws until it voted supplies for British troops as required by the Quartering Act.

10. Charles Townshend (1725–1767) died on Sept. 4.

11. During March 1766 violent riots occurred in Madrid and elsewhere in Spain. Caused mainly by high food prices and unpopular royal decrees, the violence forced King Charles III to make certain concessions, most of which he later retracted. By implicating the Jesuits as instigators of the mob activity, the king, who regarded the Jesuits as a threat to his own authority at home and to Spanish authority in South America, was able to expel the order from Spain and all her colonies in April 1767. P. E. Russell, *Spain: A Companion to Span-*

ish Studies (London, 1973), 149; Richard Herr, *The Eighteenth-Century Revolution in Spain* (Princeton, N.J., 1958), 19–22.

· · ·
·

CCC to Richard Corbin[1] and Robert Carter Nicholas[2]

8th. Novr. 1767.

Gentlemen,

I have made choice agreeable to the bequest of my worthy friend Colonel Ludwell, of the books, on the opposite side of this[3] — The presses & shelves are referred to, that you may the more easily discover at one view what books I have chosen —

A very sincere friendship subsisted between us: the legacy he hath bequeathed to me, and particularly the manner in which it is expressed, is a proof of that friendship: and I have accepted of this token of my friend's remembrance, more from this motive, than from any real want of the books I have selected from his collection for my own use — I desire the books may be safely packed up & sent by water to Annapolis directed to Charles Carroll of Carrollton — I hope you will excuse the [trou]ble you are put to on my account, as I would will[ing]ly undertake the same to serve you — I am Gent,

yr. most obdt. hum: Servt.
Ch: Carroll of Carrollton.

P:S

If it should be too troublesome or it should not lay in your way to look out for a proper opportunity of sending the books to Annapolis, you will be pleased to commit them to the care of Sir Peyton Skipwith[4] with whom I am well acquainted & who will take the proper care of them —

ALS, Nathaniel Paine, *Signers of the Declaration of Independence,* II, 76, Paine Family Papers, MWA. Addressed by CCC to "The honourable Richard Corbin Esqr. and Robert Carter Nicholas Esqr. at Williamsburg Virginia." Text damaged at seal, address badly stained.

1. Richard Corbin (1708–1790) of King and Queen Co., Va., an executor of the estate of Philip Ludwell, with whom he had served on the Virginia Council in the 1750s. Prominent and well connected, Corbin was a member of Virginia's House of Burgesses (1748–1749), the Virginia Council (1751–1776), and the Board of Visitors of his alma mater, the College of William and Mary (1776), and was receiver general of the colony's quitrents (1754–1776). A loyalist, Corbin retired from public life when the War for Independence began. He married Betty Tayloe, daughter of John Tayloe of Mt. Airy, Richmond County, Va., and Rebecca Plater Tayloe. Rutland, *Mason,* I, xlv, c; Abbot, *Washington: Colonial Series,* I, 71 n.

2. Robert Carter Nicholas (1728–1780), also an executor of Philip Ludwell's estate, was colonial Virginia's leading attorney. A member of the Virginia House of Burgesses (1756–1775), a delegate to the Virginia conventions (1775, 1776), and treasurer of the colony (1766–

1776), he served on the Virginia Committee of Safety (1775-1776). Although a staunch defender of colonial rights, Nicholas nevertheless opposed radical resistance to the crown's authority and the Declaration of Independence. In 1779 he was appointed a judge on Virginia's High Court of Chancery. His wife was Anne Cary, daughter of Wilson and Sarah Cary. Rutland, *Mason,* I, lxxxiii; Abbot, *Washington: Colonial Series,* I, 260 n, and Abbot, *Washington: Revolutionary War Series,* I, 435 n.

3. The list of books does not appear on the verso of this letter. CCC's copy is printed in Appendix II.

4. Sir Peyton Skipwith (1740-1805) held large tracts of land in Mecklenburg, Surry, and Halifax Counties in Virginia. "Historical News," *WMQ,* 3d Ser., IV (1947), 404; Jackson T. Main, "The One Hundred," *WMQ,* 3d Ser., XI (1954), 382; Burke, *Peerage,* 15th ed., 917.

CCC to William Graves

16 Janry 1768

Dr. Graves.

I hope you have received my last letter of the 7th. of Novr. by that you will learn that my marriage with Miss Darnall was put off till this next spring, in order to obtain an act of Assembly to empower the young lady to consent to a settlement in bar of dower — I am informed that nothing less than an act of the legislature can make a settlement in the case of a minor binding in law: This is the opinion of one of the best lawyers in this province, with whom I have advised upon the occasion: but if a valid settlement notwithstanding the disability of non age[1] can be made without having recourse to the legislature, the legislature will not interpose to give a legal Sanction to what may be legally effected in an ordinary way: nec deus intersit, nisi dignus vindice nodus[2] — nor would I chuse to trouble myself or the Assembly with an application of the sort unless I were convinced of the reasonabless of such application — & of the impossibility of removing the legal impediment by any other method — I have also another motive yet stronger for not applying to the assembly vizt. the uncertainty of its meeting: it now stands prorogued till some time Next May — and I have reason to think from some circumstances it will not meet till the fall, and I doubt whether it will meet even then — for I have been told not to look for that event, till the exigencies of government shall make it absolutely necessary. Thus you see, if the settlement can not be securely made with out an act to give it a legal force, I may wait 2 year's longer: that is till the young lady comes of age: she will be 19 years old the 19 of next March — I leave you to Judge how disagreeable such a delay must be to one in my situation — I wish you would apply to one or two able lawyers for their opinion upon this point: inclosed is an order in blanck upon Messrs. Perkins &c for what money it may be necessary to give to the Lawyers for their advice: and I desire, they may cite the authorities for the opinion they give — pray do not lose any time after the receipt of this in getting their best opinion and transmitting it to me by the first opportunity that offers; & a duplicate of it by some other for fear of a miscarriage of the first — The New York packet sails every month from Falmouth: the time of her sailing, if I am not mistaken, is advertised in some of the publick papers — You may send a copy of the Opinion by that Packet & the original by some vessel bound directly to this province — I hope to receive an answer from you to this some time next July or sooner or as soon as possible.

By the laws or the usage of this Province widows are intituled to one third of the real estate during life, and to one third of the personal estate absolutely; and negroes are accounted as part of the latter —

The bulk of my estate consists of negroes & money — we have near £30,000 Ster at Interest & above 300 negroes worth at least on average £30 Sterling each — In case of my death, a very large proportion of my estate would probably be carried into another family to the prejudice of my own children, or of the heir at Law — The young lady to whom I am to give my hand, and who already has my heart, altho' blessed with every good quality, has not been favoured by fortune in respect to money — and this among many others is a strong instance of partiality & blindness of that goddess or that riches are not always bestowed upon the deserving — I mention not this circumstance as an objection to the lady (I prefer her thus unprovided to all the women I have ever seen, even to Louisa) but only as a reason inducing the necessity of a settlement and strongly justifying it — for I am willing & desirous that all my future actions should stand the test of those two severe Judges Reason & Justice.

It certainly frequently happens that women marry under age in England: and I believe there are few marriages without a previous settlement: now unless those settlements are binding to what purpose are they made? And if binding upon minors upon what principle, or by what means do they acquire their validity and force —

If my estate consisted only of lands, the difficulty might more easily be got over and my widow might be effectually barred of her dower in those lands, by giving me only an estate for life in them, and limitting an estate tail to my issue, with remainders over to such persons, as my Father might think proper to appoint, or by creating trustees to support contingent remainders[3] — I said the difficulty might more easily be got over, for even supposing the monied estate out of the question, that is that my estate consisted solely in lands, yet this measure would lay me under very great hardships — I should not have a dower [power] of selling my lands, in case the confusion of the times or any other cause, should incline me to part with them or make that step ever so necessary: it might ocasion ungratefulness & disobedience in my children knowing their own independence: it would deprive me of the power [of] leaving the greatest part of my estate to the most deserving of my children, of providing by will for my widow & thereby testifying my affection for her, by that substantial & last token of it, and finally it would divest me of the right, in case I should die issueless, of settling my estate in such manner, as prudence, justice, & affection might require it should be settled.

But in what manner can the monied part of [the] estate be protected from the claim of dower? All the money is upon bond at Interest on personal security: the very nature of which security must be ever flux & changeable: the securities must be often changed, bonds renewed, often times sued, the sums recovered by Judgement on such suit, or paid in by choice of the debtors, are to be let out at Interest to others on fresh bonds — Can the monies now on bond, be vested in me as trustee with powers adequate to the above purposes, & with a right of using & applying during my life as I shall thin[k] proper the annual & growing Interest on the principal sums, and of disposing by will of both interest & principal — I say can this be any way effected, so as to prevent the claim of dower, or can all these powers be given to me without giving me at the same time a fee simple in the personal or monied estate? Pray consider the matter well — Could the monies on bond, be thus vested in me as a trustee, with such full powers, would it not be necessary to appoint other Trustees and in that case should I be liable & how far liable to their controll? Might not the personal estate be settled in this manner? Might it not be given to me for life, remainder to my first second or third son, as I should appoint by my will, in tail or in fee simple, and in case I should leave no issue then to trustees now in being to support such future disposition of it, as I may think proper to make —

The late Act imposing duties on Glass & paper and other articles exported to America, occasions a good deal of discontent especially to the northward — Associations are entered into to encourage industry & home manufactures: the spirit of opposition gains ground: these associalitions first set on foot at Boston, have been extended in to most of the neighbouring governments:[4] A political writer in Philadelphia, who styles himself a farmer, has published several letters in the Phil: papers[5] not only against the policy but even the justice & validity of the Act — chiefly upon this principle: that the laying a tax or duty on the enumerated articles exported from G:B: is effectually laying a tax upon the colonies without their consent: since the Parliament has a right [or?] power to oblige us to take those articles from G:B. and a power also of restraining us from manufacturing, the articles on wh the duties are imposed a power not only claimed but exercised, in preventing the use of slittling Mills — I have not time to enter into the merits of this performance, or to give you an abstract of his arguments: & if I had time it would be giving myself unnecessary trouble, as I propose sending the Phil: Papers to you by the first Ship that sails from this Province to London — You have herewith a copy of my last letter: I desire my complts to all my acquaintance at the Crown & Anchor — I am &c —

ALbDr, CCC Letterbook, 1765–1768, MS 203.1, MdHi.

1. The state of being a minor.

2. "Bring in no god, except [to untangle] a knot worthy of a champion." Horace *Ars poetica* 191.

3. CCC is suggesting that in order to keep his estate intact and to secure it from right of dower, he could specifically confine inheritance to children fathered by him, thereby effectively forestalling any claims by offspring from his widow's second marriage.

4. In contrast to their behavior during the Stamp Act crisis, northern merchants were generally reluctant to join nonimportation in 1767, and it was not until the spring of 1768 that Boston, New York, and Philadelphia presented a united front in support of the boycott. Jensen, *Founding of a Nation*, 265, 287.

5. John Dickinson (1732–1808), the son of Samuel Dickinson and Mary Cadwalader Dickinson, was born in Maryland, raised in Delaware, and studied for three years in the Middle Temple before commencing the practice of law in Philadelphia. He served in the Pennsylvania legislature (1762–1765, 1770–1776), where his support for the proprietary party placed him in opposition to Benjamin Franklin. Although he was a skillful lawyer, Dickinson's real interest lay in history and political philosophy, and his writings played a highly significant role in molding public opinion. *Letters from a Farmer in Pennsylvania, to the Inhabitants of the British Colonies* (Philadelphia, 1768), written in opposition to the Townshend Acts, brought him wide acclaim. An erudite defense of the colonies' constitutional privileges, the essays originally appeared in the *Pennsylvania Chronicle* between November 1767 and January 1768 and were then reprinted in pamphlet form and widely distributed in both America and Great Britain. An undated edition is listed in *Cat. Lib.*, no. 809.

Despite his cogent affirmation of colonial rights against Parliamentary taxation, Dickinson was a conservative whig, and as the imperial crisis escalated in the early 1770s, he criticized his more radical counterparts for their willingness to use force in achieving their objectives. Elected to the First Continental Congress on Oct. 15, 1774, he urged moderate responses to British policy; in the Second Continental Congress, he opposed declaring independence but abstained from the final vote. When a peaceful resolution of the conflict became impossible, Dickinson helped draft the Articles of Confederation and served briefly in the Pennsylvania militia, but these activities failed to secure his reelection to Congress. He then retired to his country estate near Dover, Del., returning to Congress in 1779 as a representative of that state. He was governor of Delaware (1781), chairman of the Annapolis convention (1786), a delegate to the Constitutional Convention (1787), and a strong supporter of ratification. He married Mary Norris, daughter of Isaac Norris of Philadelphia. Smith, *Letters*, IV, 364 n, V, 563 n; Jensen, *Founding of a Nation*, 242–243, 700.

· · ·
· ·

CCC to Edmund Jenings

April 14th. 1768

Dr. Jenings,

I embrace this favourable opportunity by Mr. Wm. Cooke a relation & particular friend of mine, of writing a few lines to Introduce him to yr. acquaintance &

to recommend him to yr. friendship, of which I am sure you will experience him deserving: his design of coming to London, & all other particulars relating to himself, he will best explain & in a much shorter time by word of mouth than I can do by a letter — I have only to add to the above recommendation of this young gentleman to yr. regard, that what services you may please to do him in the acquirement of legal knowledge either by yr. own assistance, or of others with whom you may bring him acquainted, I shall esteem as a testimony of yr. friendship for me and as an obligation done to myself.

Among the many other differences between friends & lovers Swift has pointed out one, which I think particularly applicable to you — vizt. the dislike of writing letters to your friend: I can easily conceive why lovers are constantly scribling, but I cannot as easily discover why friends should not write to each other twice or thrice a year — to impute this neglect to laziness would be to suppose a want of friendship: to a multiplicity of more important business would imply a small share of it: for what can be more important than to preserve a solid & disinterested friendship, & what better method of preserving it in the case of absence, than an uninterrupted intercourse of letters?

I think I have got you in a dilemma, & [if] you can find nothing of more consequence, pray make your vindication the subject of our next letter — as a lawyer I doubt not you will have many shifts, & as an ingenious & witty man you will have much to say for yourself — but know that nothing but solid argument will be admitted at the bar, & by the Judge before whom you are to plead; a Judge I must confess very much disposed to acquit you, & who will readily excuse your past conduct, by your avoiding for the future yr. only fault, to which it has hitherto been liable —

Mr. Cooke will deliver you along with this a venison ham, wh is to be eat in the same manner that dutch smoaked beef is eat — I must refer you to him for an acct of the present transact[ions] in America, & of my critical & very uneasy situation: for suspence of all others is the most so, particularly in love, a passion wh, must less than offer suspence, will hardly admit of delay: Mr. Cooke will explain this passage should it want an explanation — but I am determined, as determined as Cæsar when he passed the Rubicon: my scheme indeed of the two is the more laudable, but in some instances such schemes are equally perilous, tho' not in the present: virtue, good sense, sweetness of temper, & the [a]greeable & amiable person of the young lady insure me the happiness which I earnestly wish for — I am &c —

ALbDr, CCC Letterbook, 1765–1768, MS 203.1, MdHi.

CCC to William Graves

1768 — April 16th.

Dr Graves —

This will be delivered to you by Mr. Wm. Cooke, a relation of mine for whom I have a sincere friendship & esteem, and whom upon acquaintance I make do doubt you will find worthy of yours — It was this gentleman's sister I was to have espoused sed dîs aliter visum[1] — Mr. Cooke intends to remain in London two or 3 years in order to perfect himself in the law by a diligent application to that science & a constant attendance on the courts & by such further helps as his residence in the temple[2] or some other Inn of court may afford him: an acquaintance with, & the conversation of some good lawyers will I apprehend be particularly useful to him, not only by their pointing one a proper method & proper books, but by resolving such difficulties as may occur in the course of his reading[.] It is with this view chiefly that I make bold to recommend him to you for advice in the profession wh he has embraced, and in which you have acquired a considerable degree of knowledge — any assistance you may lend him in this way, or any services you may please to confer on him by introducing him to a good acquaintance, he will gratefully acknowledge & I shall deem as conferred upon myself. His finances are too scanty to permit him to keep constantly the same agreeable company with wh you bought me acquainted: however by a well regulated oeconomy at other times, he may now & then afford to spend his half guinea, if that expense should be necessary to procure him the acquaintance & countenance of learned & sensible men — Mr Cooke has for some years past applied himself to the study of the law, & I believe he is pretty well acquainted with the practice of the courts & Judicial proceedings:[3] for any further particulars relating to this gentleman, I must refer you to himself: I have sent by him 3 venison hams wh you will be pleased to accept of for your use & the gentlemen's at the Crown & Anchor to whom, particularly to Barrington & Hussey I desire to be remembered —

I hope you have received my several letters of the 16 & 22d. Jany.[4] & 7th. of Febry[5] & have complied with what I have therein requested of you — not that I think the opinion whatever it may be will be necessary for the regulation of my conduct. An assembly will set the 19th. of May, when I intend to apply for a bill to dispense with the disability of nonage: such applications, I believe, are not uncommon, in the present instance it is Just & reasonable & can be attended with no inconvenience to the public & consequently I have solid grounds to hope for its success[6] — Be pleased to send me the 5th. volume of Bacon's abridgt. I have the other four — you will receive along with this the farmer's letters in a series of Philadelphia news papers — they are since published in Phila. in a separate phamlet. I have wrote for a set expressly for you, but have not yet received it — The venisons hams must not be boiled, they are to be eat like dutch hung beef, sliced very thin & spread on bread & butter—The bear-hams I have not yet got—I long to hear from you & hope to have that satisfaction soon, as several ships from London are daily expected—

ALbDr, CCC Letterbook, 1765–1768, MS 203.1, MdHi.

1. "But the gods decreed otherwise." Virgil *Aeneid* 2.428.

2. William Cooke was admitted to the Inner Temple in 1768. Jones, *American Members of the Inns of Court,* 51–52.

3. It is unclear whether CCC intended to underline portions of this sentence or strike them out.

4. CCC to William Graves, Jan. 22, 1768, not printed. The letter reiterated CCC's concerns about legally securing his estate through a marriage settlement. CCC Letterbook, 1765–1768.

5. CCC to Graves, Feb. 7, 1768, not printed. The letter ordered a number of books. Ibid.

6. The petition, drawn in the names of Henry Darnall, Jr., Rachel Darnall, Robert Darnall, and Mary Darnall (the prospective bride), was first considered by the upper house on May 30, 1768, and, after discussion on June 1 and 2, was passed with the reservation of Daniel Dulany, who maintained that "the general existing Laws" made such a bill unnecessary. Enacted by the lower house on June 2, the bill was assented to by the governor on June 4. *Arch. of Md.,* LXI, 288–289, 291–293.

Thomas Digges[1] to CCC

June 3. 1768.

Sr.,

I trouble you with the following Lines at Mr. Neales[2] Request, who desired me to informe you whether he has Power to dispense with the Impediment of Consanguinity[3] between you & Miss Darnall without applying to Mr. Lewis;[4] to which I answer in the Affirmative. Mr. Neales going off to Baltimore and the Incertainty of Mr. Lewis's returne almost induced me to make a Tender of my Service to you, but I did not know whether it woud not look like intrueding or interfereing in anothers Province in Case Mr. Lewis shoud return to Annapolis by tomorrow. If he calls upon me to day, you may depend upon my hastening him on to Annapolis that you may not be disappointed. I sincerely wish you and Miss Darnall all Happyness in the State you are just entering upon, and that God Allmighty may shewer down his Blessings upon you both. My kindest Respects to Cousin Carroll. I am Dr. Cousin

Your affectionate Kinsman and humble Servant

Thomas Digges

ALS, Carroll Papers, MS 216, MdHi. Addressed by Thomas Digges. Endorsed by CCC.

1. Thomas Digges, S.J. (1711–1805), brother of Ignatius Digges. Bowie, *Prince George's,* 275–276. For his familial ties to the Carrolls, see Appendix I, Chart I.

2. Bennett Neale (1709–1787), the son of Anthony Neale of Charles Co. and his second wife, Elizabeth Digges Neale (Christopher Johnston, "Neale Family of Charles County," in *Md. Gen.,* II, 254–255). He is apparently the priest listed in Weis, *Clergy,* 57, as "Benedict Neale."

3. Consanguinity, the relationship by descent from a common ancestor, posed a problem that required an ecclesiastical dispensation because CCC and Molly Darnall were first cousins once removed through the Brooke line and second cousins once removed through the Darnalls. See Appendix I, Chart G.

4. John Lewis, S.J., had signed the waiver of consanguinity that gave permission for CCC and Rachel Cooke to marry.

· · ·
· ·

The Marriage Settlement between CCC and Mary Darnall

[June 4, 1768]

This Indenture Quinquepartite[1] made the fourth day of June in the year of our Lord one thousand seven hundred and sixty eight between Charles Carroll of Carrollton of the first Part, Henry Darnall Junr. of the second part, Rachel Darnall wife of the said Henry of the third part and Mary Darnall Daughter of the aforesaid Henry and Rachel of the fourth part and Robert Darnall uncle to the said Mary of the fifth Part Whereas a Marriage is intended by the Grace of God to be shortly hereafter had and Solemnized between the said Charles Carroll and Mary Darnall Daughter of the said Henry Darnall Junr. Now therefore this Indenture Witnesseth that for and in Consideration of the said intended Marriage and for the sum of five shillings Lawful money of Great Brittain to him the said Charles Carroll of Carrollton in hand paid by the said Henry Darnall Junr. at and before the ensealing and delivery of these presents the Receipt whereof the said Charles Carroll doth hereby Acknowledge and also for Providing a competent Jointure and livelyhood for the said Mary Darnall in case she shall after the said intended Marriage happen to survive the said Charles Carroll her intended husband and for Divers other Good causes and considerations him thereunto especially moving He the said Charles Carroll Hath given granted and confirmed and by these Presents Doth give grant and confirm unto the said Mary Darnall one Annuity or yearly Rent charge of Three hundred pounds Sterling a year to be issuing out of all that Island lying in Chesapeak Bay commonly called and known by the name of Poplar Island containing one Thousand Acres more or less and out of the Rights members and appurtenances thereof To have hold preserve receive and take the said Annuity or yearly Rent Charge of Three hundred pounds Sterling per Annum to the said Mary Darnall and her Assigns in case the said Marriage between her and the said Charles Carroll shall take Effect and she happen to survive him from and immediately after the Death of him the said Charles Carroll for and during the natural Life of the said Mary Darnall to be paid to her and her Assigns at the ffeast Days of St. Michael the Arch Angel and the Annunciation of the Blessed Virgin Mary by even and equal portions in full bar lieu and satisfaction as well of her Dower and thirds and Right and Title of Dower and thirds which she shall or may have claim and Demand or be entituled unto of in or to all and every the manners Lands and Tenements Rents and Hereditaments whereof or wherein the said Charles Carroll is shall or may be seized during the Coverture between him and the said Mary Darnall as also of all such shares Customary parts portions Rights Interest and Demand which she shall or may or can have claim Demand or be intituled unto out of in or to all or any of the Goods Chattles or Personal Estate of the said Charles Carroll which he shall leave at his Decease by or by Virtue of the Laws Usages or Customs of this Land And the said Charles Carroll for himself his Heirs and assigns doth hereby further grant that if the said Annuity or yearly Rent Charge of three hundred pounds per Annum or any Part thereof shall happen to be behind and unpaid by the space of thirty Days next after the said ffeast Days on which the same ought to be paid that then and so often During the natural Life of the said Mary Darnall it shall and may be Lawfull to and for the said Mary Darnall and her assigns into the said Island and also into any other the Lands Tenements or Hereditaments of which the said Charles Carroll shall die seised to enter and Distrain for the said Annuity or yearly rent Charge of Three hundred pounds Sterling and all arrears thereof and the Distress and Distresses there from Time to Time had and found to take lead drive carry away detain Impound sell and Dispose of for the Paying and satisfying her the said Mary Darnall and her Assigns the said Annuity or yearly Rent Charge of Three hundred pounds sterling and all arrears thereof and all her and their reasonable Charges and Expences And the said Charles Carroll for Himself his Heirs Executors and Administrators doth hereby Covenant and grant to and with the said Henry Darnall Junr. his Executors and Administrators that the Heirs Executors or Assigns of him the said Charles Carroll shall and will in case the said Marriage between him and the said Mary Darnall shall take Effect and she happen to survive him well and truly pay or cause to be paid unto her the said Mary Darnall or her Assigns the said Annuity or yearly Rent Charge of Three hundred pounds Sterling yearly and every year from the Death of the said Charles Carroll during her Natural Life at the said ffeast days appointed for Payment thereof by even and equal portions According to the True Intent and meaning of these Presents and shall make and begin the first payment thereof on such of the said ffeast days as shall next happen after the Death of the said Charles Carroll And it is hereby Covenanted granted Declared and agreed by and between all the said Parties to these Presents and it is their true Intent and meanings and the Intent and meaning of these Presents that the said yearly Rent

Charge of three hundred pounds Sterling is and shall be and the said Mary Darnall doth hereby Declare and agree that she doth and will accept the Same as and for a full plenary compleat and satisfactory Jointure and Provision and in full Bar and satisfaction of her Dower and Thirds and all Right and title of Dower and Thirds of in and to the Real Estate whereof or wherein the said Charles Carroll during the Coverture between them shall or may be seized and of all Right Title parts shares Interest or Demand which she shall or may or should or might have claim or Demand unto of in or to all or any of the Goods Chattles or Personal Estate of the said Charles Carroll which he shall leave at his Decease by or by Virtue of the Laws Usages or Customs of this Land In Witness whereof the Parties to these Presents have hereunto interchangeably set their hands and seals the Day and year first above written

Char: Carroll of Carrollton   Mary Darnall
Henry Darnall Junr
Rachel Darnall   Robert Darnall

Signed sealed and delivered (the words money in the fourth line and accept in the twenty fifth line being first interlined) By Henry Darnall Junior & Robert Darnall
In the presence of us
Willm. Digges Junr.[2]
Joseph Digges[3]
By Charles Carroll of Carrollton, Rachel Darnall and Mary Darnall
In the presence of us
Chas Digges.
Ann Darnall[4]
Mildred Hanson[5]

DS, Carroll-McTavish Papers, MS 220, MdHi.

1. "Five-part."

2. Possibly William Digges, Jr. (by 1721–1805), a son of John Digges of Conewago and a cousin of Ignatius Digges. Bowie, *Prince George's*, 279, 281, 288–289. See also Appendix I, Chart I.

3. Probably Joseph Digges (1747–1780), a physician and a younger brother of Charles Digges. Dr. Digges was a member of the Charles Co. Committee of Observation in 1776, served as surgeon to that county's militia (1777–1778), and was appointed surgeon to the Maryland Marching Militia by the Executive Council in September 1777. In late 1778 he received the Council's permission to go to Bermuda in an effort to improve his failing health; he died at Teneri in the Canary Islands. *Bio. Dic. Md. Legis.*, I, 270; Henry J. Berkley, "Maryland Physicians at the Period of the Revolutionary War, January 1775 to the Cessation of Guns, April 1783," *Md. Hist. Mag.*, XXIV (1929), 6; *Arch. of Md.*, XVI, 362, XXI, 222; Appendix I, Chart I.

4. Molly Darnall's aunt. See Appendix I, Chart F.

5. Mildred Hanson (c. 1746–by 1796) was the daughter of Samuel Hanson and Anne Hawkins Hanson of Green Hill, Port Tobacco Hundred, Charles Co. By 1778 she had married Dr. William Baker, a Frederick Co. physician and land speculator, with whom she had six children. *Bio. Dic. Md. Legis.*, I, 111, 407; Harry Wright Newman, *Charles County Gentry: A Genealogical History of Six Emigrants . . .* (Washington, D.C., 1940), 240, 242.

CCA to William Graves

23 Decr. 1768

Dr. Sr.,

The Friendship you bear my Son (wh is manifested by yr Remembrance of & Correspondence with him) leaves me no rome to doubt a letter from me may be acceptable to you, Especially as it will informe you that His Mariage was entierly to my Satisfaction, & that I think He has a well grounded prospect of as much Happyness as Can be Hoped for in a Conubiall state. My Daughter in Law is very agreable, she has a great share of good sense, a solid Judgement, she is strictly virtuous & perfectly good natured. I speak not what it may be thought I fondly wish my Character of Her is founded on a long & intimate Acquaintance: She has lived with me since she was 12 years old & in the Course of more than Seven years I have not had Reason to Chide Her. Dissimulation is not very Common in youth, few at least at Nineteen years are perfect in it. Have I not then Reason again to tell you I think my Son will be Extreamly Happy with His Lady — You must also know she was entierly His owne Choice, He had not the most distant Hint from me that Miss Darnall would make a good Wife. They Cannot want, If they are tollerable OEconomists, for I have put my Son in Possession of at least £1000 ster: pr Anm: He keeps my Books & takes what Money He Pleases[.] He lives in my House at Annapolis, I am Retierd to a very Pleasant Healthy Seat in the Country where I employ my Self in Farming, Planting Meadow Making &c Amusements very agreable to me, & when I want Money I Call on my Son to supply me. You know my Son, I therefore shall say no more of him than that I am Happy in Him & that He seems to be getting the better of a Puny Constitution. In one of yrs to him I think you advise him not to Hoard, I think He should live so as to make a decent provision for Younger Children & to leave the Estate to His Eldest Son as Entier & in as good Plight as I shall leave it to Him, for althô I see a large & independent Fortune will not make the Possessor if of a mean & Servil temper independant, yet it must make him inexcusable if He be not so. Here is a great deal of Private & Family Affairs, But I flatter myself they will in some Measure be interesting to you on my Sons Account[.]

As I have taken the freedom to write to you, I must say some thing of Poor

America, or rather of Poor England, for I am perswaded if She persues the steps she Has taken She will Have Abundant Cause to Rue Her folly—

By the Considerations the Farmers Letters &c you must see Wee know our Rights & that We want not Pens to Assert them & to Alarm us when they are Attacked[.]

The Stamp Act was A Rash & Inconsiderate Measure & very prudently dropt. But the Act past at the same time declaring[1] insted of dissipating our Fears threatned us with a Renewall of unconstitutionall Attacks on Our Liberties & Properties. Those threats have been immediately Succeeded By Acts Establishing New officers among us & imposing Duties on goods which we are not permitted to import from any other Place But Great Brittain[.]

As to the 1st. The Establishment of a Board of Trade,[2] We all Plainly see that it is done to Encrease a Parliamentary dependance by the Creation of New Officers. To the Same end are a great Number of Troops kept up in America, not to Secure our Conquests, for if that were the intention, why are troops employed elsewhere than among the Conquered.

Is England or America most injured by the Number of Civill & Military Officers & troops among us? The first spend their Sallaries, the other their pay in America, in this America is not injured: But if the Establishment of unnecessary Officers, if the Support of useless troops Creates a Servil & unconstitutionall dependance in the House of Commons in England, is not England the greatest Sufferer by the Measure?

As to the 2d: The imposition of new duties, It may be urged that the Board of Trade at Boston is Appointed to prevent Smugling & to Secure the duties laid by Acts of Parliament. Does the Board of Trade, the Commissioners of the Customs, the numberless tribes of Tidewaiters Land Waiters[3] Searchers A navy of Sloops Cutters & Custom House Boates &c &c Prevent Smugling in England? If not, will a Board of Trade in Boston or in Every Colony prevent Smugling in America. Trade in its Nature is free, it is a Maxim which I will support by the following Tale which I read long Since but in what Author I Cannot recollect. The Dutch when Contending with Spain for Liberty, Prohibited by a Severe Placart the Furnishing the Spaniards with Navall or Military Stores. A Dutchman was Caught Transgressing & Called to an Acct for it: His defence was Trade in its Nature was free & Open to all Mankind & that if He Could see a Prospect of Great gain by a Voyage to Hell He would Venture the Singeing of His Sails—

I will not Sr Attempt to Prove that the Parliament Cannot Consistently with the Constitution, Our Rights & Liberties tax us[,] That I apprehend to be done demonstrably by the Author of the Considerations & the Farmer, I have not seen that their Reasoning has been Attempted to be Answerd, if Attempted, No such answer has Reached me—

I think there are many strong Arguments to be Deduced from Prudence &

Policy which should in my Humble Opinion induce Great Brittain not to Attempt to tax us[.]

By what is generally asserted on Yr side the Water you are beat out of all Trade to all Places Except to Yr Colonies by being undersold in Every forreign Market by yr Rivalls in Trade. If this be so, it is immateriall to me to Enquier whether it be owing to the weight of yr Taxes or the Luxury or high Price of the Labour of yr Poor Manufacturers[.]

But under these Circumstances if Yr Colonies be yr Chief yr only Valuable Customers, is it Prudent is it Politick to drive them from You?

Every duty imposed on the goods you send us Opperates Apparently as a Bounty & Encouragement to us to Manufacture Species of Goods[.]

That we Can Manufacture all goods wh you Manufacture is undoubted, & that you will force us to do so by yr Present Measures is Certain[.] Interest thô a strong is not the strongest motive to incite us to Manufacture; Resentment, a Conviction of the injustice with which we are treated, the not Answering the Slighting our legall Consititutionall applications to the Crowne for Redress, A view of the Chains you have imposed, yr Seeming Determination to Rivet them on us will Compell us to Manufacture[.]

Rage & Resentment Operate beyond all imagination more forceibly than interest, but when United Can they fail of producing the Effect wh: you ought to dread?

Surprising & Astonishing was the progress of Manufacture Here Especially in the Wollen & Linnen Branches upon the passing the Stamp Act: The repeal of that Act gave a great Check to them, But they are reassumed not with a Noisy & ostentatious Parade, But wth a Sullen Resentment & determined Resolution Never more to abandon them. At that time I manufactured a Sute of Cloaths for my self & wore it to incite others to follow my Example: I dropt my Manufacture & laid aside my Cloaths upon the repeal of the Stamp Act. I have this year Built a Commodious House for as Many Manufacturers as will be able to Cloath between three & four hundred Slaves[.]

With Contempt we read the silly & inflammatory Articles in many of yr news Papers giving Accts of the factious state & inclinations of the Americans to Break the Happy Connextion which has Hither to Subsisted between them & their mother Country, & we Pity the Credulity of those who Have sent troops hither to Compell us to Obedience if their fears have been feigned I leave You to find an Epithet which may set their duplicity in the most odious light for I Cannot recollect one — Could they not distinguish between a steady & determined Resolution to Maintain our Rights & Rebellion, Any Measure deviating from a stupid passive Obedience to Unconstitutionall Measures Was by Such Week Heads deemed a Rebellion[.] There is a very wide distance Between Murmuring Complaining Petitioning & Remonstrating & Rebellion. I should think Men who Have been Accustomed to the frequent tumults & insurrections of Tinners Colliers Cole Heavers

Weavers & Sailors should not be frighted out of their Senses at two or three trifling Mobs of the Boys & Rabble of Boston —

America is Sensible it is not yet time for Her Wantonly to have recourse to the Ultima Ratio Regum,[4] However Grieviously Provoked She Has Appealed to Her Sovereign to the Laws to the Constitution, on these she Relys for the Protec[ti]on of Her Rights & Liberties, Should that Relyance be frustrated (which the Suppression of Our Legislatures & Many other Rash & Bold steps on Yr Side seem to indicate) We Have it thank God in our Power to Bring You to Reason By the easy legall means of Manufacturing & taking nothing from you unessentiall to our Existence. Perhaps Many may do more & follow the Dutchmans Example by takeing nothing from you which by any Means may be had Cheaper from a[ny] other Quarter —

We have been informed that the Different applicatio[ns] of Our Colonies to the King have not only been slighted But that they have not been Sufferd to be Presented. Is it possible? Have we not a right to Petition & to be Heared?

Our Legislatures are threatned to be Suppressed That of Boston is Suppressed for not Complying with a Ministeriall Mandate[.][5]

Would any Minister dare to tell an English House of Commons that they should not be Sufferd to meet that they should be dissolved unless they Complyed with Measures dictated by Him? Have we not as undoubted a Right to Legislation in our Severa[ll] Provinces as You have in England? Would a Mi[nis]ter dare to treat us in so imperious a Manner if H[e] was not assured of impunity? Would He not treat y[ou] in the Same Manner Could He do it with the Same Security[?] We Cannot think you are Realy anxious to pres[erve] yr owne Rights while you tamely see those of yr fellow Subjects so flagitiously invaded — Are not Such steps as distant as Heaven & Earth from justice? If they are ought they [not] in prudence & good Policy to be not only dropt & disavowed, But severely Censured by an upright British House of Commons?

Nations as well as individualls are Subject to persist in wrong Measures, it is deemed a Weakness, it is thought dishonorable it Mortifies our pride & self Conceit to retract & Acknowledge an Error, in vain does the injustice of the Action stare us in the face or sober Reason Condem it —

Should the Colonies by Necessity be forced into a Counterband Trade, Considering the vast Extent of our Sea Coast our Numberless Navigable Gulphs Bays Rivers inlets & Creeks will it be possible for Great Brittain to suppress it? What she in Vain Attempts at Home, will she be able to performe at Such a distance? Trade is of a very delicate Nature, it may by imprudent Measures be forced out of its old Channell, But it may prove impossible to bring it back —

Cast yr Eye on a Map of America Consider the immense unpeopled tract, Consider the prodigious Rapidity with which it is setling Will England in time to Come be able to Compell Such an immense Country Peopled by Miriads to Submit to Arbitrary Laws or despotick Ministeriall orders[.]

Cast yr Eye again on the Map of America Contemplate that part of it allready

Peopled with (in my Opinion) 4 Million of Souls, Should they be forced by ill Policy to Resistance & in time to Come that may be the Case & should it be the Case, Will it be easy will it not be almost impracticable to keep Such Numbers and Such an Extent of Country in due Obedience[?]

Look on the inconsiderable Spot which Constitutes the Seven United Provinces. The People of that Spot Bafelled the Power of the House of Austria & shook of[f] the Spanish yoke.[6] It is true France assisted them, England assisted them. Should English America be ever unfortunately forced to take up Arms & be unable of Herself to Vindicate her freedom, Will not France Spain & even the Dutch Lend Her a Helping hand? Should Such an Event bee in the Wombe of Time what A figure will England Make bereaved of so much of Her Power and Trade[.]

The Pretexts on yr side the Water for taxing America, are the Expence incurred in the last War by defending us, the Continued Expence of a standing Army for our Protection, yr Heavy taxes & insupportable Nationall Debt.

It is Certain we wanted no Protection agt: the insignificant Colony of Quebeck, We did agt: France. France Attacked us to Encrease Her Power & withdraw our trade from England. England Supported us to Preserve Her Power & Trade, self interest was Her view & only view. Our present treatment is a proof of Her Tenderness twoards us.

Why are you at the Continued Expence of Maintaining standing forces among us? They are Hatefull in our Eyes & looked upon by us as the Harbingers of Despotism: They Ought to be Hatefull to You as they Increase Ministeriall influence by giving an undue & additionall Power to the Crowne. If Forces in America are necessary they Can be only so in the Conquered Colonies, if it be profitable to England to Secure the Possession of those Colonies England ought to be at the Expence of the troops Necessary to Secure the Possession of them, for Qui sentit Commodum Sentire debet et onus—[7]

As to Yr Taxes & Nationall Debt, that they are not both lessened is due to yr Corruption. The Debt gives a too irresistable Power & influence to the Crowne & Ministers for them to wish it diminished. While it Subsists it is vain to Expect a Diminutian of taxes. America Contributed more than Her share to the Expences of the War Here, She Contributes more than Her share to yr Taxes by the Consumption of Yr Manufactures—

Do you apply to us as Beggars, Shew that you are reall objects of Charity. Supposing a Drunken profligate able Bodied Sturdy Beggar should apply to you for Alms would you bestow it? When we see Princely Estates Suddenly made by Contractors &c When we See Numberless Sine Cure Offices of immense Annuall Value Held, When we See great & unmeritted Pensions with out number bestowed to the 3d: & 4th Generation Can you Expect that we Can be prevailed on to Gratify yr Cravings or Contribute to yr Profusion.

What must be the end of this shameless long Continued Want of Honour publick Spirit & Patriotism Will not yr Profligacy Corruption & Venality Sink you into

Anarchy & destruction. All states labouring under the Same Vices Have met with the fate which will be yr lot: That fate is impending it Cannot be far off; The Same Causes will ever produce Similar Effects.

If I have given a true Picture of yr present state & I think I have without higthning the Coulors or Strengthning the Features (if yr Dayly Papers Periodicall & Occasionall Phamphlets deserve the least Credit) are you not A people devoted to & on the Brink of destruction[.]

I Began to be Acquainted with the World in the year 1720 Memorable by the ruin of not only the unthinking adventurers in the South Sea stock But of numberless widows Helpless Minors & innocent Infants: A year infamous to some very great Personages if it be true that they Profited immensely by the Cheat.[8] Soon after Sr Robt: Walpole[9] was made primier He Reduced Corruption into a Regular Sistem which Since His time to the Present Period has been improved & founded on so Broad & Solid a Basis as to threatten the Constitution with immediate Ruin & allready to have left to the People little more than the Appearance of Liberty — Could the Transactions of the Period I mention be exposed to Publick view would they not Excite Horror & detestation. If no roome is left to the Present Generation to improve in Corruption, they Have in faction, Ætas pejor Avis & I may without pretending to be a prophet venture to say Mox datura Progeniem Vitiosiorem[.][10]

I am Sensible Dr Sr I have said little or nothing but what must have occurred to You or to any Gent: of Reflection, But it is with the deepest Concern I have said it & with this Mortifying Conviction that what I have said & all that more may be said on so Interesting a Subject Wil not be of the least avail. The Evill is so inveterate as not to be Eradicated by Reason Ense recidendum est[11] for the state of Anarchy you seem to be in gives me grounds to fear the Constitution Cannot be Supported By any others Means than the Sword. America has little roome to Hope that A People so regardless of their owne Liberty should be Attentive to Preserve [thirs?] Nor Have I the Vanity to think any thing I have said Can or will Have the least Effect, for Althô you Have the Honour to be in a Publick station Jacta est Alea,[12] Our fate will be decided at least for a time before this will reach you[.]

In yrs of Aprill the 3d: 1766 to my Son you write as follows. The Foreign states that Constitute a part of the British Empire, that is Ireland & America Belong to the British Commonwealth, that is to the King Lords & Commons[.]

Pray Sr pardon me if I Call in Question the Propriety of that Position. I Believe it would be flatly denyed by Ireland & that if you attempted to tax them that you would not find so dutifull an Opposition as has been persued by America. They would Hardly Supplicate, you would Hear the Thunder of the Irish Lords & Commons —

If you Have no more right to tax us than you Have to tax Ireland, Why do you do it? Is it because you think we Cannot resist? That would be acting like a Bully who Swaggers when He is shure of Comeing of[f] with whole Bones —

Yr Sentiment is quite New to me, nor Can I Recollect that I have ever met with anything Similar to it in any of Our Histories or other tracts which have fell into my hands Antecedent to the Present Controversy Between England & its Colonies—

I never understood the Lords & Commons of England Claimed any Dominion. Their Province I have all ways Conceived was to advise the Crowne, Watch over & Guard their owne & Constituents Rights & Liberties, Grant their Money, Bring Great Delinquents to Justice, Enact Laws &c[.]

I look upon our Legislations to be every way Similar to Yours & that the only difference between them Consists in yr Superior Power (understood as force) & Opulence. We are not Certainly the Subjects of Subjects. Our Constitutionall dependance on the Crowne is sufficiently & Effectually Secured by its Appointment of Governors & all other Officers Civill & Military & by a Controul on the Laws passed by our Assemblies—

Yr Mode of Expression in my poor Opinion Could not at any time be made use of with Propriety But under Cromwells Usurpation, or in Case of a Change in the Constitution from A Monarchicall to a Republican forme, then the Majesty of People the Dominion of the People might be properly Asserted[.]

When I sat downe to write to you I little thought my letter would have run into such a length, it is not wrote with a view of Drawing an answer from you, it would be presuming too much, & Considering yr Occupations the task would be unreasonable. If in any Parts of it I have expressed myself with too much Acrimony Pardon it: You see an old Man may be Warmed by a love of Liberty & of His Country, that Love I hope will recommend me to yr Esteem which I sincerely Covet being very truly Dr Sr

Yr Mo: Obedt: & Mo: Hum: Servt
C:C:

ALS, Carroll Papers, MS 206, MdHi. Endorsed by CCA: "1768 Decr: 23 Copy of my Letter to Mr Graves."

1. Between "declaring" and "insted" CCA has left a line and a half of space.

2. A reference to the creation of an American board of commissioners of the customs.

3. Customs officers. A tidewaiter boarded incoming ships to enforce customhouse regulations, and a landwaiter was responsible for recording imports for tax purposes and for seeing that correct procedures were followed.

4. "The final reasoning of kings," the motto that appeared on Louis XIV's cannon.

5. The Massachusetts General Court was suppressed by Gov. Francis Bernard in July 1768 on orders from the secretary of state for the colonies because it refused to rescind and expunge from its journal Samuel Adams's circular letter denouncing the Townshend Acts. The letter asserted that adequate colonial representation in Parliament was impossible, opposed efforts to make colonial judges and governors independent of legislatures, and urged that the assemblies of the other twelve colonies explore the possibilities for united action.

6. The seven northern provinces of the Netherlands joined together in the Union of

Utrecht in 1579 in an effort to rid themselves of Spanish rule. In 1648, after a protracted struggle, Spain recognized the independence of the Republic of the United Provinces by the treaty of Westphalia.

7. "He who realizes the convenience must also pay the charge."

8. The South Sea Company was a joint stock company chartered in 1711 to monopolize trade with Spanish America, convert some nine million pounds of unsecured national debt to a lower interest rate, and provide competition with the Bank of England and the East India Company. The failure of the South Sea Bubble in 1720 ruined thousands of investors and resulted in the return to power of Robert Walpole, who had allegedly profited from the scheme. Jarrett, *Britain,* 144–145, 164–170.

9. Sir Robert Walpole (1676–1745) served as prime minister from 1721 until 1742. His ministry became synonymous with corruption because of his skillful manipulation of patronage, which enabled him to manage the House of Commons, neutralize his political rivals, and extend the power of ministerial government. Ibid., 170–177.

10. "An age worse than their grandfathers' . . . soon to produce a more degenerate offspring." Horace *Odes* 3.6.45.

11. "It must be cut away with the sword." Ovid *Metamorphoses* 1.190–191.

12. "The die is cast."

www.ingramcontent.com/pod-product-compliance
Lightning Source LLC
Chambersburg PA
CBHW020645110726
47901CB00001B/61